D0935220

LEARNING AND INSTINCT
IN ANIMALS

LEARNING
AND INSTINCT
IN ANIMALS

by

W. H. THORPE

Sc.D., F.R.S.

Fellow of Jesus College, Cambridge, and
Professor of Animal Ethology in the University

A new edition, extensively revised and enlarged

HARVARD UNIVERSITY PRESS
CAMBRIDGE · MASSACHUSETTS

First published 1956
Second edition 1963
Reprinted 1966
Printed in Great Britain

TO THE READER

IT is the hope of the author that this book contains material of interest to students approaching the investigation of animal behaviour from many different angles. One of the major objects in writing it has been to point out to psychologists and learning theorists on the one hand and to zoologists and physiologists on the other how dependent each is, or ought to be, on the work and viewpoint of the other. To this end it has been thought necessary to provide a critical discussion of certain crucial parts of both instinct-theory and learning-theory and to give a detailed survey of the learning abilities of the main animal groups considered in relation to their instinctive equipment and the problems which they meet under natural conditions. Again the theoretical and philosophical implications of modern behaviour study have been much in mind and an attempt has been made to deal briefly with certain aspects of such questions in Part I—especially the problems of directiveness and purposiveness, of the nature of drive and the place of this concept in the theory of instinctive behaviour.

But the attempt to cover such a wide field means inevitably that different readers will find different parts of the book of prime interest. Nor will all wish to read the chapters in the same order. The author has attempted to follow the natural and logical order of proceeding from the general to the special. But that is not necessarily the best order for most types of reader. Those who are already familiar with the recent work and outlook of comparative psychology and who have some knowledge of modern instinct-theory may well find it best to start with Part III, which relates the learning abilities of animals to the degree of development and organisation of their instinctive actions and to their behaviour in nature. Such a reader will probably refer at first to Parts I and II only for an understanding of some of the concepts of instinct-theory and for the classification of learning types employed, postponing the reading of them until later. Again, the 'ethologist' who has concerned himself mainly with instinctive behaviour will probably be more familiar with the general range of facts given in Part III, will use that section primarily as a work of reference and will find it best first to read Part II—which deals with the types of learning and their inter-relations, illustrated by typical examples. Lastly those who are primarily interested in the more theoretical and philosophical aspects of behaviour study and who are less familiar with the work of the 'learning psychologists' and 'ethologists' will prefer to read Parts I and II first, followed by certain chapters of Part III as illustrative of the wide diversity of behaviour in the animal kingdom.

PREFACE TO 1963 EDITION

An author does not lightly undertake the revision of a work ranging as widely as this one. Nevertheless when the opportunity arose for the production of a new edition in 1962 I felt that it must be taken. The six years since 1955 when the first edition went to press has been a period of very great research activity—far greater, I would say, than in any comparable earlier period. This activity has been particularly evident in three fields: 1. In the theoretical field important concepts have been subjected to much more precise analysis and clarification than hitherto. 2. Straightforward experiment and observation on behaviour has continued apace but with great refinement of technique, and often a more sophisticated experimental approach. 3. Studies in the neurophysiological field, both in regard to the central nervous system and the sense organs, have progressed enormously: again both on the experimental and the technical side. This rapid development of the subject of ethology has therefore resulted in a mass of new material greater than I for one had expected to accrue in ten years from the date of first publication.

In revising this work I have tried not to make more corrections and emendations than the work seemed really to require and I have endeavoured to retain the original individual approach to the subject. In particular I have tried to keep the reference list from growing inordinately, and in order to do this I have where possible quoted only summary papers and books which themselves have a good and up-to-date reference list and where the details of the latest sources can be found. Nevertheless, in spite of this, the additions to the reference list have crept up by about 300 additional titles.

In preparing this new edition I have been particularly indebted to Dr. B. B. Boycott, who provided me with a very extensive manuscript revision of that section of Chapter X which deals with the Cephalopods. Behavioural and neurophysiological work on this important group during the last six years has been very particularly important and nothing less than an extensive re-writing of the relevant parts would do justice to it. Similarly, Mr. C. J. Pennycuick brought up to date the section on bird orientation. Finally, once again I am indebted to Miss E. M. Barraud for the immense amount of detailed and careful work she has put into typing the new draft, providing the reference list, revising the indexes, etc. Without this careful work of hers the new edition would have taken twice as long to prepare. The acknowledgments to those who helped in the first edition will be found under the appropriate heading at the end of the book.

W. H. THORPE.

Jesus College and
Sub-department of Animal Behaviour,
Department of Zoology, Cambridge.
October 1962.

CONTENTS

L.I.A.—I*

PLATES

PART I

SOME GENERAL CONCEPTS

CHAPTER I

DIRECTIVENESS AND PURPOSIVENESS

A WORK such as this which attempts to relate two modes of development of behaviour, instinctive and learned, apparently so different, is in fact dealing with a particular form of one of the central problems of biology. It follows therefore that whatever particular aspect of the subject of learning and its relation to instinct we are discussing, we are never really very far from problems of philosophy which are common to the whole of biology. At certain points in the account these may seem very remote and academic; at others they are either just underneath the surface or are clearly emerging. So it seems necessary to say something at the outset about the general philosophical approach which underlies the present studies; for without this serious misapprehensions are likely to arise from time to time as a result of the use of words such as 'purpose,' 'expectancy,' 'anticipation,' etc.

From the philosophical point of view, the central problem of ethology is the relation between purposiveness [1] and directiveness, and it looks at times as if this is the same as the relation between learning and instinct. All biologists agree that the behaviour of organisms as a whole is directive, in the sense that in the course of evolution some at least of it has been modified by selection so as to lead with greater or less certainty towards states which favour the survival and reproduction of the individual. All machines are also directive in the sense that their parts have been designed or selected so as to behave in a particular way whenever activated by an external source of power; but not even the most elaborate machine, such as an electronic calculator, is purposive. So for the ethologist the question is, 'How much, if any, of the animal's behaviour is purposive and what is the relation of this behaviour to the rest?'

One key argument advanced in this book is that perception is not simply an automatic response to simple sense-data or, in human terms, not merely cognition, but is, on the contrary, an active organising process, itself possibly including an element of purpose, tending all the time to build up the primary perceptions into more and more complete and unitary systems. If this is so, then perception is obviously a process in time rather than an instantaneous event, and involves three elements—

---

[1] 'Purpose' here has the usual meaning—a striving after a future goal retained as some kind of an image or idea.

conation, memory or comparison, and anticipation. When an object is recognised or remembered, the fact of recognition implies some sort of latent readiness to react appropriately. In human perception, as Price (1932) has shown, the very idea of a material object is dependent upon an element of anticipation. He says 'every perceptual act anticipates its own confirmation by subsequent acts.' Whitehead (1929), whose philosophy of organism is perhaps, among modern philosophies, more sympathetic to an understanding of the biological approach than any other, considers the act of perception as the establishment by the subject of its causal relation with its own external world at a particular moment. Whitehead argues that every vital event, in fact, involves a process of the type which, when we are distinguishing between mental and material, we describe as mental —the act of perception. And there is a very strong case to be made, as Agar (1943) has shown, for the theory that a living organism is essentially something which perceives. Therefore some element of anticipation and memory, in other words *some essential ability to deal with events in time as in space is, by definition, to be expected throughout the world of living things*.[1] Now, of course, it is only too easy for the uncritically minded follower of such a philosophy, where we are starting with our own perceptions as a standard, to fall into the error of assuming memory and anticipation of a far greater degree than can, in fact, possibly be occurring in the lower animals. Such a view certainly does not follow from the conclusions of Whitehead, nor would it have been countenanced by him. There is no ground whatever for supposing any well-defined intellectual or mental content in the elementary anticipations which characterise the behaviour of the lower animals. Agar considers that such may rather be conceived as nothing more than anticipatory feeling after continuing experience. Now there are varying grades of unity in living organisms and varying grades of co-ordination of actions forming their units. A degree of unity may obviously be brought about as a result of a mere aggregation of a multitude of similar biological units, whether it is the cells of a sponge or the worker ants of an ant colony. Elsewhere we see examples of a much closer co-ordination, as in the metazoan body, where the activities are more intimately related —with the result that the organism behaves, in some respects at least, as a unit responding as a whole to the various situations and stimuli which it encounters. Whitehead holds that any unit of life is, in fact, a perceiving subject, and these perceiving subjects are grouped together in regions or nexus of activity so that they act causally as a unit; and to such a causally

[1] Perhaps the most fundamental feature of Whitehead's approach is the conclusion that every enduring object, from electrons to human minds, is a temporal nexus of occasions, each with its characteristic specious present, showing a continuity of character from occasion to occasion. His system leads eventually to a form of pan-psychism in which unconsciousness is taken to be a later development in evolution. The biological significance of Whitehead's system is admirably summarised by Agar.

acting unit Agar has given the name of 'agent.' Now an agent may or may not also be a subject. In the case of the animal as a whole or of the cell, the agent is itself a subject. An agent such as a muscle, being a nexus of cells, is a nexus of subjects, but it does not seem necessary to assume that it is, as a whole, a subject of a higher order, any more than a Termite colony need be so regarded. A cell, though a subject, must probably also be considered a nexus of living sub-agents. This is not the place to follow up such a line of argument. It has merely been briefly outlined in order to stress the ubiquity of the idea of hierarchy—whether we are discussing the instinctive behaviour of animals at a relatively high level or the most elementary responses of the simplest forms of life. Agar, following and building upon the ideas of Whitehead, goes on to consider living agents first as elementary subjects, for instance cells, or if these are considered as nexus of subjects, the sub-agents of a cell; or they may be nexus of subjects whose unity of action is due to similar environment provided by the biological field of which they form a part. The higher grade of living agents is reached when a nexus of subjects in combination gives rise to a subject of a higher order. Agar uses the term 'central agent' for such a subject of a higher order. And so we are brought to the question of the existence of a centrally directing drive or integrative agent which causes the animal to behave as a whole of a higher grade.

Before continuing, it is perhaps as well to make clear that in using words such as 'anticipation' and 'purpose' we need not, *as biologists*, consider ourselves as coming to any definite conclusion as to the relation between mechanism and mental events. If we decide, as a result of experiment, that an animal is behaving purposively as distinct from directively, we mean that its behaviour is such that it cannot be fully or reasonably explained by mechanisms at present known to be operating within the body of that animal; although, if we *can* point to a sufficient mechanism, that does not necessarily mean that true purpose is absent—even though as practising scientists we may decide that for the time being at any rate it is no longer our concern. As far as we know, everything that goes on in the bodies of living organisms, all transformations of energy that result in work being done, are due to arrangements which *in certain respects* are comparable to man-made machines. As Agar says, mechanisms may be on a gross, anatomical scale or they may be of molecular dimensions, and it is one of the tasks of biology to investigate and attempt to understand these mechanisms down to the most minute detail. Thus, it is true to say that in organisms every change from the simplest physiological process to the most complicated behaviour is related to and in a sense dependent upon mechanisms in this sense; but the existence of such mechanisms does not in any way provide a philosophical explanation of living things. So, while the postulation and investigation of mechanism is an essential method of approach for biologists, it is inconceivable as a fundamental explanatory principle in a biological philosophy. On the other hand, as Woodger (1929, quoted Agar, 1943) has pointed out, we may talk of purposes in animals as in human beings, but the causal efficacy of purpose cannot be proved in the sense that all other possible explanations are excluded. 'It is always possible to defend microscopic mechanism in principle, if anyone wishes to do so, by making your mechanism complicated enough and by postulating enough sub-mechanisms to meet all contingencies.[1] It cannot then, be refuted, but neither can it be verified.' Agar adds, 'Anyone who accepts this explanation must of course accept it also for his own consciously purposed acts unless he holds that there are factors in human behaviour which are different not only in degree but in kind from the factors determining the acts of lower organisms.'

Nevertheless, we are entitled to claim that when the words purpose, expectancy and anticipation are used, we are, *as biologists*, for the time being speaking of a mechanism which acts in given circumstances *as if* it were purposive, expectant or anticipatory, as the case may be, and reserving judgment on more fundamental issues. This question of the mechanism of purpose is of course very much to the fore at present, and likely to be so for a long time, because of the development of electronic calculating machines and the astonishing performances which they display. Norbert Wiener and others have demonstrated the similarity between the behaviour of such a machine and that of the human nervous system, and it is not unusual today for communication engineers and neuro-physiologists to speak as if they believe that the key to a complete understanding of the nervous system, and so of the higher organisms in general, lies in the principles developed in such calculators. It is, however, clear—as elsewhere pointed out—that such artifacts really give us no more than an analogy of the regulatory processes which establish control in a living organism. These theoretical models are research tools which represent a method of describing the thinking process in disciplined language. They may be 'brain extensions,' but they are ineluctably non-purposive in that they can never, from the nature of the case, express personal experience or take responsible decisions. (See D. M. McKay, 1953.)

Sommerhoff (1950), bringing together an unusual combination in the same person of mathematician, physicist and biologist, has made a brilliant effort to make biology philosophically respectable by expressing the directiveness and adaptiveness which constitute the essential characteristics of living systems in strictly objective physico-mathematical terms. In claiming success for this effort, he argues that such 'objective purposiveness' can and must be rigidly separated from the subjective or

---

[1] There is a point at which this argument fails. See essays by Humphries-Owen and Dalcq in L. L. Whyte (1951).

'psychological' concepts of conscious purpose with which his system is unable to cope. But here I think he fails; for from his arguments it follows, in fact, that some machines would inevitably be classed by him as living, while some human beings would be regarded solely as machines.[1] His arguments have shown, perhaps more dramatically than ever before, that *both* subjective and objective concepts are necessary in the scientific study of life, and that a biology which succeeds in being purely objective, however powerful it may be in parts of its field, must fail to provide a full biological philosophy—just as surely as a purely subjective biology would be unthinkable. In other words, subjective concepts derived from introspection are among the essential tools for the study of life, and the only hope for a complete biology is to combine subjective and objective in the right proportions, using each approach with due circumspection and adequate safeguards as it is required. All our concepts in whatever field are, of course, in the last resort subjective in that they are the conscious expressions of our own experience; but, above all, we have to beware of falling into the trap, which has so frequently ensnared past students of living matter, of supposing ourselves objective when, in fact, we are being subjective. First and all the time we must know exactly where and to what extent we are using and relying upon subjective concepts. Only so can biology hope to deal adequately with the vast theoretical problems that confront it. Above all, must it avoid the sterile and futile division into opposing vitalist and mechanist camps which the experience of the past hundred years has shown to be philosophically so stultifying. D'Arcy Thompson, in the introduction to his great work *On Growth and Form*, has much to say on this and kindred subjects, which biologists, psychologists and philosophers would do well to read and re-read. We may quote one sentence here: 'Still, all the while like warp and woof, mechanism and teleology are interwoven together, and we must not cleave to the one nor despise the other; for their union is rooted in the very nature of totality.'[2]

Caution is also necessary in making assumptions about the nervous and other mechanisms operating in different animal phyla. Thus it is evident that similarities in the powers of control which we can find between many protozoa and many higher vertebrates must be mediated by entirely different mechanisms, and Pantin (1952) has recently sounded a warning against the danger of assuming that because the same end result is achieved by organisms of a very different anatomical construc-

---

[1] Sinnott (1950) argues persuasively that since "each of us is *inside* a living organism" we have a real introspective knowledge of that directiveness which is objectively characteristic in greater or lesser degree of all organisms, and that directiveness and purposiveness are in fact the objective and subjective aspects of the same fundamental biological quality.

[2] For an original and stimulating discussion on Teleology, see Scheffler (1959).

tion, there must, therefore, be the same physico-chemical mechanism at work in all cases. On the contrary, living beings do the same thing by many different routes and in many different ways, and they may well all be different from the way in which the calculating machine achieves its result. As Sinnott (1950) says: 'After all, we are not made of tubes, wires and gears, but of protein molecules, and our bodies are triumphs of chemical and not mechanical engineering.' So, while we may certainly explore to the full clues which the behaviour of calculating machines may give us, we must be very critical of evidence which suggests that the two are homologous.

Perhaps the real difference of viewpoint among behaviour students is that between the older or hormic psychologists and the behaviourists and other subsequent workers whose activities have led to present-day ethology. The difference between these two groups is very largely a question of the existence of a general or centrally directing drive. The earlier school of psychologists, taking their start from the study of man, assumed the organism as a whole to be purposive in the sense of being directed by a purposive drive which expressed itself in the various specialised faculties and activities. There was assumed to be a central unity which differenti-ated itself in varied subsidiary activities by means of the various systems of organs. But the biologist is not likely to forget that there are a great many organisms in which the evidence of any central co-ordination is extremely slight. Thus in the Echinoderms the tube feet act very largely as reflex systems independent of the whole organism, and the animal appears, superficially at any rate, to be a 'reflex republic.' It has recently been made clear by Smith (1950) and Kerkut (1954) that there is, in fact, more central co-ordination in Echinoderms than was formerly thought; nevertheless, in some species of starfish the lack of co-ordination between the arms occasionally results in the animal actually being pulled in two merely by the antagonistic activity of its own tube feet (Kerkut, *loc. cit.*).

The task of the neuro-physiologist during the first half of the present century has, of course, largely been to study the modes of integration of numerous simple 'units' of behaviour, such as reflexes (which although simple in their way are, nevertheless, directive), into larger, fewer units which show a more comprehensive directiveness. The stage reached by ethology in this particular task is that at which the behaviour is regarded as composed of about six independent 'instincts.' Nutrition, Fighting, Reproduction, Social Relations, Sleep and Care of the Body Surface are those which at present seem an indispensable minimum in studies on birds and mammals. Each of these instincts is, of course, directive. But is there also any truly purposive element in them or in an over-all centre controlling the whole organism? Is the animal an 'instinct republic' or an 'instinct oligarchy,' or is there in any sense a single governing purposive centre or influence? This is the fundamental question.

When we come to consider the higher groups such as birds, the question of the existence of a higher co-ordinating and drive-emitting centre becomes crucial for our understanding of animal behaviour. If the animal is more than an 'instinct republic,' in what sense is it more? The view of the instinct-theorist as to the nature of animal behaviour postulates, as in Tinbergen's system, a top centre for each separate instinct; but nothing is said about the relation between and the co-ordination of the five or six top centres which are postulated. And so it becomes important to consider how far there is evidence of learning motivated by a general drive quite independent of the motivation of particular instincts. The author has previously taken the line (Thorpe, 1950) that one of the most fundamental of all activities is to organise the environment, and that the primitive conative faculty of insight inherent in the very nature of perception must have been part of the very early stages in the development of the living organisms. This idea is further developed in Chapter VII, but it is not, at first sight, always easy to find very clear evidence for motivation for learning independent of any of the main instincts. However, the evidence is, in fact, present in considerable quantity, and Thacker (1950) has stated as a result of experiments with the maze learning of rats that 'motivation for learning is central and neural and that organised and proliferated cognitive structure itself is the goal towards which learning moves.'

First let us look at the evidence provided by studies on the effect of irrelevant drive on performance. Hull has concluded that an alien drive contributes to the elevation of the *general* state or level of excitement in the organism, but Siegel (1946), in studying the effect of alien drive on habit strength and resistance to extinction, was unable to find any clear evidence to support Hull's theory. Nevertheless, both Webb (1949) and Walker (1951) have shown with rats, that again both hunger and thirst can produce a *generalised* drive state, and so have provided what appears to be quite satisfactory confirmation of Hull's thesis, though some more recent results (Miles, 1958a and b, and de Vito and Smith, 1959) indicate that irrelevant motive has only a very small effect on rat behaviour in the maze situation.

Then a good deal of evidence has recently accumulated, particularly as a result of the work of Amsel (1950), that situations which give rise to anxiety (which can be regarded as a differentiated form of the pain reaction) are particularly potent in producing a general drive. A general anxiety produced in this way is thus regarded as a secondary need. Amsel found that if the incentive for a rat was the necessity to avoid or reduce discomfort or pain, and hunger was developed as a primary irrelevant need, no effect was produced in that there was no indication that the two primary needs summated. On the other hand, hunger and the secondary need clearly did summate, and it was also found that anxiety will compete with and so reduce a previously established consummatory response, such as the act of drinking. The conclusion of Amsel and Maltzman (1950) is that the state of emotion following a painful stimulus increases water consumption with rats when the stimulus has preceded the drinking period daily for some days. These conclusions are confirmed by Siegel and Brantley (1951), who found that rats made emotional by slight irritation or constant disturbance, such as that from 'faradic teasing,' eat more when subsequently placed in a familiar situation than do the controls; and Ullman (1951) has also produced evidence for increased eating behaviour during shock, when eating becomes generalised tension-reducing response. (Cf. footnote on p. 94 below.)

When we come to the higher mammals, there is some suggestive evidence that learning can occur solely as a result of motivation by a manipulation or exploration drive. Thus Harlow, Harlow and Meyer (1950) described how their rhesus monkeys would quickly learn a puzzle which involved a manipulation of separate parts and the fitting of these together, even though solving the puzzle brought them no reward. The monkeys were successful at about the 1 per cent. level of significance, the monkeys in the control series being given puzzles which were incapable of solution. Subsequent introduction of food into the puzzle situation tended to disrupt rather than to facilitate the learning response. Harlow and McClearn (1954) also found manipulation a sufficient motive for learning a discrimination. These authors are unable to interpret these results except by postulating a manipulation drive which is not only strong but extremely persistent, and they suggest that a drive of this sort represents a form of motivation which, at any rate in the higher mammals, may be as primary and as important as the homœostatic drives. In fact, these experiments with monkeys agree precisely with those on latent learning in the maze situation; for the manipulative habits of the monkeys and apes can be looked upon merely as a particular form of the general tendency to explore the environment and learn its characteristics, of which the maze running of the white rat is also an instance. Butler (1953) has even demonstrated that in monkeys visual exploration alone (e.g. being allowed to look out of their boxes and so explore the environment visually) is sufficient incentive for learning. Butler and Alexander (1955) have shown that rhesus monkeys will apparently work to attain a relatively fixed amount of daily visual exploratory experience—that is to say, about 40 per cent. of the total testing time. The animals were tested ten hours daily. (See also p. 103 below.) Moon and Lodahl (1956) (ref. in Berlyne, 1960) have shown that change in illumination will enforce lever pressing in rhesus monkeys and indeed in rats and mice also. Miles (1958a) has also shown that in cats manipulatory and exploratory activities are rewarding in their own right and that the postulation of a derived incentive function is unnecessary.

That the latent learning of the rat may be closely linked with spontaneous alternation behaviour in the maze has been shown by Montgomery (1951), who considers that the exploratory tendencies of rats produce a satisfactory theoretical basis for alternation behaviour and (Montgomery, 1954) for learning. In this connection it is interesting that Glanzer (1953) allows for spontaneous alternation and related phenomena in essentially the same way by considering it as an expression of 'stimulus satiation' (see p. 61 below). He thinks thus because he finds the reactive inhibition theory of spontaneous alternation inadequate to explain his results, while the concept of stimulus satiation serves to unify under a single theory such diverse phenomena as inhibition, exploratory behaviour, latent learning, Krechevesky's 'variability' and the phenomena which Karsten described in 1938 as satiation. Crowcroft (1954) finds that in certain strains of mice exploration is the dominant drive—so strong that they will even interrupt aggression in order to explore. Zimbardo and Miller (1958) have advanced the hypothesis that, in rats, the opportunity to explore a novel environment or to effect a stimulus change in the environment is the reinforcing agent.

Subsequent to 1955 experimental work and publication upon the topic of curiosity and exploratory behaviour has increased enormously. Barnett (1958) has reviewed much of the literature. He makes the particularly important point that exploratory learning in rats gives the maximum of information about the environment in the safest possible way, and thus has important survival value. He also points out that the study of exploratory behaviour has thrown new light on motivation since it has shown that exteroceptive stimulation has a necessary arousal function that influences the animal's general level of activity. Berlyne (1960) has given a very full discussion of the topic of curiosity, from both the behavioural and physiological aspect, and in particular has related it to the matter of arousal by means of the reticular system and other neurophysiological mechanisms of attention. He also emphasises the importance of the idea of expectancy as part of the process of anticipatory arousal, a point that has also been emphasised in recent years by the Russian worker Sokolov. Deutsch (1960a), in a widely ranging theoretical work, has devoted a short critical chapter to the topics of curiosity and exploration, stressing that explanations in terms of curiosity may involve many as yet unanalysed components. He has a valuable word of caution when he says 'we simply do not know the rat well enough as an animal to invoke such entities as a curiosity drive with any certainty on most of the occasions where it has allegedly been observed.' I am in full agreement with him when he adds that the factors involved in exploratory and curiosity behaviour of animals are most likely to emerge from studies with these animals in semi-free environments.

Another line of evidence on this and similar problems, especially that of expectancy, comes from the work of Deese (1951). This author first trained rats in a U maze to make a simple discrimination, the maze being so designed that the response could be based on a wide variety of available cues, proprioceptive, intra-maze, etc. Once they had been trained to make the correct choice, this choice could be extinguished simply by placing them in the goal box without the presence of food. Thus extinction of the choice response did not depend upon unreinforced performance of that response. These results and others like them indicate that not all extinction depends on the response introduced, for when the animals which had been given the opportunity to inspect the empty goal box were subsequently given the usual extinction procedure, they made a significantly lower percentage of correct choice than did the controls. Moreover, a response extinction showed a spontaneous recovery after rest, whereas non-response extinction showed no such recovery. These facts suggest that when the animals are forced to make an unreinforced response during extinction, there may be some inhibition introduced by the response; *but this is temporary*. At any rate, it cannot be the essential mechanism responsible for extinction. Such results seem to give a very strong a *priori* case for explanation in terms of 'expectancies.' It would seem on the face of it that the concept of expectancy is so alien to the behaviourist school, even in its latest manifestations, that the inclusion of such a concept in any theory of the Hullian type would be inconceivable. However, one can find amongst recent writings of members of this school suggestions that even this may not be impossible. Thus Denny and Davis (1951), discussing the problem of latent learning and having confirmed some of the latent-learning data, suggest that the difference between Tolmanites and Hullians on this major issue is one of semantics, and Behan (1953) has argued that expectancy can actually be derived from Hull's theory and can be included in the Hullian theory of behaviour. The argument is complex and involved and need not be gone into here, but the fact that it can even be seriously proposed is eloquent comment on the development which has taken place in Hull's system since it was first put forward. (See also MacCorquodale and Meehl, 1954.)

SUMMARY

1. The significance of the concepts of directiveness and purposiveness and their relation to behaviour study is briefly considered.

2. It is suggested that the concept of perception includes an actively

organising, possibly a purposive, element; and that perception is a basic characteristic of the drive of the living animal.

3. The question of the existence of a general as opposed to a specific drive is regarded as of great importance in any theory of the behaviour and nature of the living organism.

4. It is concluded that there is now substantial and precise evidence for a general drive in a number of animals, and that this can be looked upon as an indication of a primary motivation which to some extent, however slight, is superior to the governing centres of any of the instincts or of their combinations, and finds its most characteristic expression in exploratory behaviour in all its various forms. It is closely linked with the ideas of 'expectancy' and 'purpose.'

CHAPTER II

THE NATURE OF DRIVE AND ITS PLACE IN THE THEORY OF INSTINCT

THE adventures through which the idea of instinct has passed during its long history would provide a stimulating, indeed an exciting, theme if properly traced by a biologist with the needful equipment of classical and historical learning. W. M. Wheeler (1939), in his short but brilliant essay on the subject, has given an indication of what might be done by a scholar with the right and rare combination of abilities, and Wilm (1925) has surveyed the field from the point of view of the historian of psychology. In so far as the word denotes a single fundamental idea, one may say that it is perhaps the earliest biological concept relating to animal behaviour that the human race produced. Of course, it is inevitable that a word which has had such a varied history and has become such an important item in our everyday vocabulary should have many variations, overtones and complexities of meaning. And these overtones and subtleties have naturally been the despair of biologists. It is therefore small wonder that as soon as the work of zoologists and physiologists had provided even the semblance of a reflex theory of animal behaviour, i.e. in the early decades of the twentieth century, the concept of instinct tended to be increasingly avoided and, indeed, considered disreputable. In fact, the physiologist, experimental zoologist and comparative psychologist had almost completely abandoned the word by 1920, and it lingered only in the vocabulary of the psychologist concerned with human behaviour and of that of the more naturalistic type of zoologist. This situation, as we see now, was so obviously a false one that it could not last—for rejection of the term meant that an essential idea was being left out of biology and psychology only to enter by a side-door under another name. And so it was merely a matter of time before its loss began to be felt and the way opened for its return.

Now which among the varied meanings of the word is the fundamental one that was being so grievously, if subconsciously, missed? Modern workers on instinct, especially the comparative ethologists who have been mainly responsible for the resuscitation of the term, have tended to concentrate their attention on the fixed-behaviour co-ordinations, the elaborate specific action patterns which had certainly of late been grossly neglected by the general biologist even though they offer splendid material for observation, experiment and phylogenetic comparison. But, important though this aspect is, and profitable though its critical and thorough study has been shown to be by the modern school of comparative ethology, it is not, perhaps, the most fundamental of the concepts involved. The original Latin word, of course, implies 'being driven from within,' and this fundamental part of the concept is the one which, as Wilm has shown, goes back to Thales. It was this idea which was basic to all Western schools of thought, whether theological, psychological or mechanistic-physiological, at least down to the early seventeenth century. There seems to have been nothing corresponding in any degree of detail to the nineteenth- and early twentieth-century concepts of reflex and tropism before Descartes; [1] and such concepts do not appear to have had much influence on biologists studying behaviour until the work of Bethe, Loeb, Thorndike, Watson and finally Pavlov seemed to make the concept of a reflex [2] machine reasonable. As their ideas gained ground, so the original concept of instinct faded farther into the background. But prior to these workers, zoologists and comparative psychologists (e.g. Darwin) were thinking of instinct primarily as some sort of innate urge for activity directed towards ends biologically desirable yet essentially unknowable to the organism concerned—and even the physiologist Bekhterev (1913) considered 'instinct' to be the same as motivation. Indeed, this view continued right through to the present day in the writings of the comparative psychologists McDougall, Bierens de Haan and E. S. Russell. But the vast majority of those who threw over the overt concept of instinct were forced to reintroduce surreptitiously, if not subconsciously, some of its more important features; and the most fundamental of these was covered by the term 'drive,' or more correctly 'internal drive.' [3] It is interesting, therefore, to look at the idea of internal drive as it is found in recent and present-day psychology and ethology. But before we do this a serious source of misunderstanding and confusion must be cleared up. This arises from the double meaning of the word 'innate.' Thus the word 'innate' may imply any or all of the following: (1) inherited or genetically fixed and therefore characteristic of the species; (2) internally co-ordinated; (3) internally motivated. Both instinct and reflex may be innate in senses (1) and (2). Only instinct has an internal drive or motivation in sense (3).

[1] According to Sherrington (1940) it was Thomas Willis (1664) who was the real father of the concept as a scientific rather than a philosophical idea; *not* R. Whytt, as argued by Skinner (1931).

[2] In the present work the term 'reflex' is always used, in the restricted sense, to mean a partial reflex, cf. Thorpe (1950), Agar (1943).

[3] Drive can in its widest sense be defined as 'the complex of internal and external states and stimuli leading to a given behaviour' (Thorpe, 1951). If the word 'external' is omitted we have, of course, the definition of internal drive.

But this approach only serves to distinguish internal from external motivation. It does not distinguish innate habits or behaviour from acquired habits and behaviour. In discussing this problem it is worth considering how in fact we recognise an instinctive action when we see one—that is, to give a purely practical definition. Here the best method of approach is to consider the origin of behavioural complexity (Thorpe, 1961c). Where, then, does the complexity of the behaviour come from? If we can see the necessary complexity in the input from the environment which is being or has previously been experienced, then we are justified in assuming provisionally that it has been learned. If, however, there is complexity in the behaviour pattern which is not seen in the immediate or indeed the whole previous experience of the individual animal, then we have to assume that this complexity comes from somewhere else; and that it can only have come from the inborn organisation of the animal. This is best illustrated by an example: If a bird such as a Whitethroat or a Garden Warbler, hand-reared from the egg in a soundproof room and maintained under a constant and simple regime of physiological stimulation, comes in due course to produce the perfectly characteristic and exceedingly elaborate song of its own species, then we can say quite definitely that there is no system of stimulation in the environment to which it has been exposed which can 'account for' the complexity of this behaviour pattern of singing. Therefore we conclude that the behaviour pattern is innate in the sense that it must be in some way coded genetically and in the central nervous system and that it is not even dependent on auditory feed-back—as has been shown by operatively deafened birds. To take this matter a little further: to say that a behaviour pattern is innate is not simply just to say that it is unlearned.[1] If we say it is innate with good reason we imply that we have some sort of a clue as to the physiological mechanisms or conditions under which the behaviour pattern is produced. If we follow the origin of an innate behaviour pattern right back to the gene mechanism, we have to assume that the instructions to the animal to develop in such a way—that, for instance, the song of a particular kind is produced when the bird is mature—has been coded in the D.N.A. of the gene. Now this D.N.A., complex though it is, has not the kind or degree of complexity which the mature organism shows. In other words, it has a complexity which is potential, which can be expressed by the organism in the course of its development. So this argument is no pre-formationist one. The instructions in the D.N.A. mean that as the organism starts to develop and as it continues to do so, it has within it orders to take certain things from its environment and leave others, to accept certain kinds of stimuli and to leave others, and so to build up its own internal milieu, taking from the

---

[1] Lorenz (1961) has contributed an important discussion on the implications of the deprivation experiment in studies concerning the relation between instinct and learning.

environment at every step the materials and stimulation that it needs. This is what the genetic instructions are doing. This is the programme to which they insist that the animal conform. So at every step in its development the animal is obviously dependent upon its environment but with each step is becoming increasingly more able to make and control its own environment. And, of course, we must remember that the D.N.A., specific though it is in its arrangement, is not the whole of the zygote but that a very specialised environment is provided for the D.N.A. by the ovum in which it first starts to function. So in the case under consideration we are justified in saying that the behaviour pattern is innate in the sense that the complexity which it displays arises primarily from the instructions in the germ cell and not from the instructions which are contributed by the environment. As the internal milieu of the organism itself is also an extremely complicated environment for a developing organ such as the nervous system, and as this internal milieu is itself the outcome of instructions laid down in the germ plasm, and as there has been interaction between these two throughout the life of the developing organism, so we must modify our statement by saying not that 'the complexity is in the germ plasm' but that it is 'within the animal and is the expression of a code within the germ plasm.'

The term 'drive' in its earliest usage in behaviour literature probably meant little if anything more than a state of internal activity or disequilibrium of the central nervous system, or of glands or viscera in their turn stimulating the nervous system. This activity could be conceived as either actual or potential—some sort of state of tension or loading ready to activate the animal—what is termed nowadays 'mood' or, in German, 'Stimmung.' As long as the meaning of drive was thus restricted, it was unobjectionable enough, even to the avowed opponent of 'instinct,' although of little value to anybody. As early as 1911, however, Ladd and Woodworth were using the term to cover the mechanism by which activity was internally governed and directed along certain channels, and so the door was opened for the re-occupation of the comparative psychologists' mansion by those teleological devils which some optimists thought had been so firmly excluded by the behaviourists. Perry's concept of determining tendencies followed, and soon we had a whole host of 'drives' sufficient in variety and number to satisfy any nineteenth-century naturalist. And although there were many attempts to keep the term 'drive' for the undifferentiated activity and use the word 'motivation' for the directed activity, these were swept aside and we soon got hunger drives, thirst drives, homœostatic drives, fear drives, self-preservatory drives, mating drives, excretory drives, sex drives, locomotory drives, nest-building drives, manipulation drives, migratory drives, anxiety drives, exploratory drives, fighting drives, fleeing drives, escape drives, social drives, pain-avoiding drives, respiratory drives. comfort drives. first-order drives and second-order drives, all in glorious confusion. It is, in fact, clear that to classify innate drives into such mixed categories as homœostatic, physiological, mating, maternal, etc., while no doubt sometimes convenient, is a confusion of ideas and is apt to be misleading. All drives are in a sense physiological, and all tend to lead to behaviour which is in the long run of survival value.

Another feature most objectionable to the physiologist was the tendency to conceive of the drive as a form of 'nervous energy,' as something under pressure flowing down pipes and opening valves. Indeed, it was this very postulation of imaginary forces which was the chief reason for the rejection of instinct by behaviouristic psychology. But, undesirable as such a term as 'nervous energy' may be, it is quite clear that, since innate behaviour is in the main directive and not random, one must either have a directiveness within the drive itself and must accept a wholeheartedly psychological [1] (if not teleological) description of instinctive behaviour; or else one must postulate a system of channels, ducts, conduction paths or some other patterned or structural organisation, which could be regarded as self-stimulating within the C.N.S. Once this latter hypothesis is accepted, it is in some respects immaterial whether we conceive of the drive in terms of pressure, potential or what-not. So long as we keep clear in our minds that such similes are only figures of speech, models to aid our thinking, they *need* do no harm.

The attempt to escape from the impasse by regarding all drive as an expression of some primary physiological need achieved little success, for it was soon found that even the hunger drive amounts to something more than the immediate effect of the hunger pangs or hunger contractions. For example, the hunger contractions are rhythmic and intermittent, whereas hunger is continuous. There must therefore be at least some C.N.S. mechanism which carries on the stimulation provided by the intermittent visceral contractions. While all components of the drive can, of course, be directive, it would seem that only the C.N.S. component can have the necessary complexity of structure to enable it to originate or provide true purposiveness. We are now beginning to understand how intimately interlocked are visceral, hormonal and C.N.S. factors in the internal drive. Quite obviously internal drive is something much more complicated than mere visceral stimulation, and so the present picture is one of internal drive in the form of patterns of activity in the C.N.S. which can be either the result of visceral stimulation or the result of hormonal stimulation, or can be truly endogenous in the sense of originating within the nervous system itself (Adrian, 1950); while, of course, combination effects of all three must occur. Bullock (1961) sums up the present situation from the neurophysiological point of view admirably when

[1] Cf. Chapter I, p. 8.

he says, 'One way of stating the function of the nervous system or of any significant part of it is that it formulates appropriately patterned messages in code.' He shows that such a variety of examples of nervous organisation for controlling behaviour are now neurophysiologically established, mainly in the invertebrates, that we have ample factual evidence for the existence of neuronal devices which, singly and in co-operation, can account for all postulated types of organisation of behaviour: from behaviour of the highest degree of complexity on the one hand, to extreme flexibility on the other, and from systems exhibiting complete peripheral initiation and control to those where this is exclusively central. Thus to account for the temporal patterning of nervous discharge we can, according to Bullock, have (a) systems which take their timing cues solely from peripheral causes as in the reflex eye-blink to an approaching object; (b) sensory feed-back from proprioceptors, such that a feed-back loop may (c) exist with a central pace-maker so that the feed-back may start the next cycle of events before the central pace-maker comes into operation. A system of this kind is well suited to give a spontaneous rhythm modulated in frequency by feed-back, i.e. a central automatism, the phasic input of which may alter but not stop the rhythm. Then (d) we may have the feed-back affecting not the pace-maker but the followers, thus altering not the frequency of the rhythm but its form. And finally (e) a central automatism without feed-back is now known in a number of cases. Indeed, the evidence now available for the existence of primary pace-maker cells and groups of cells completely independent of patterned feed-back for their timing control, seems to me to be of fundamental theoretical importance for ethology. Moreover, there is now evidence for the existence of more than one localised pace-maker region within a single cell.

One might enlarge further on the history of the drive concept in psychology and explore many attractive and diverting pathways, but it would be of doubtful advantage; and enough has been said above to suggest that, within the existing system of instinct, the idea of drive appears to have become the source of a good deal of confusion.[1] Few who use the term within this system seem really satisfied with it, and this lack of satisfaction is very likely due, in the main, to an appreciation (perhaps subconscious) of the impasse which it conceals. Thus the 'descriptive behaviourism' of Skinner, which takes up a defeatist attitude towards epistemological problems and 'true' causal analysis, and is in many respects both anti-physiological and anti-psychological, not unexpectedly defines

[1] Although, as will have been apparent from the above discussion, and particularly from the account of Bullock's views, there are undoubtedly unitary drives emerging from the central nervous system, the drive concept has often proved dangerous in that it is, when unqualified (see p. 15 above), a blanket term covering behaviour which is in fact the product of many different motivations both internal and external, Hinde (1959a and 1960) has discussed these and cognate matters acutely.

drive as 'a verbal device with which we account for a state of strength' (Skinner, 1953, p. 144). Let us, therefore, leave the term 'drive' for a while and turn to other characteristics of instinctive behaviour. Perhaps they will supply some gleams of light by which some of these inconsistencies in the idea of drive can be better seen and unravelled.

The other main characteristics of instincts, about which there has long been more or less general agreement, are three. Firstly, instincts are innate in the sense of being inherited and so largely specific. Secondly, they usually involve complex and often highly rigid patterns of behaviour, in which numerous muscles, muscle groups and whole organs and organ systems are beautifully co-ordinated. Thirdly, instinctive actions are characteristically evoked by complex environmental situations, such as elaborate visual or auditory patterns, to which the senses appear to be inherently tuned so that the animal tends to pay attention to particular objects, or objects in a particular setting, and often appears to be seeking such objects with great perseverance and sometimes intelligence.

In the late 'thirties two students of behaviour, K. S. Lashley (1938) and K. Z. Lorenz (1935–9), realised independently that the aspect of instinct which would be most rewarding of close study was not specifically the drive itself, but rather the internal system of co-ordination of special behaviour patterns on the one hand and the special receptive sensory mechanisms on the other. In fact, they concentrated their attention on the whole specific sensori-motor organisation of the behaviour patterns, considering the complex and stereotyped action system to be more fundamental to the subject than any question of drive. They suggested that a study of these mechanisms themselves might throw light on the problems of drive and motivation. Earlier, Woodworth in his system of 'Dynamic Psychology' (1918) had attempted a similar approach, and had pointed out that habit mechanisms, at any rate in human beings, may become drives; implying that, since in his view and that of many earlier writers habit and instinct had much in common, the co-ordinating mechanism of the behaviour pattern itself might be generating the drive. This view was strongly criticised at the time, but, at least as far as habit is concerned, Woodworth did produce some substantial arguments. These were taken up by Lashley (1938), who suggested that *all* cases of motivation might well turn out to be of this nature. That is to say that, physiologically, all drives are no more than expressions of the activity of specific mechanisms, and that a general drive is really nothing more or less than the partial excitation of a very specific sensori-motor mechanism irradiating to affect other systems of reaction.

Lashley's ideas, penetrating though they were, aimed at little more than supplying some general directions for future experiment and theorising. Lorenz's contribution, which contains complete the same basic idea, is vastly more comprehensive and important, since it yields in fact a thorough-going theoretical system of instinctive behaviour—a system which has many ramifications and aspects, and which undoubtedly provided a more comprehensive framework for the description, codification and further investigation of instinctive behaviour than any which had preceded it.

Previous to Lorenz's time, the two groups of workers engaged in the study of instinct were, in fact, very far apart. The psychologists, struck by the undoubted modifiability and adaptability of some examples of instinctive behaviour, and by the almost uncanny appearance of purpose so often displayed, fastened on the psychological aspects of instinctive behaviour as fundamental. The mechanist-physiological school, on the other hand, apart from one or two outstanding investigators of which, as has just been said, Lashley was one, became obsessed by the extreme fixity of much instinctive behaviour. Inhibited by the often frightening complexity of the perceptual side of instinct, they tended to ignore per-ception and the releaser problem and concentrated instead on the appar-ently more tractable problems of the stereotyped fixed-action pattern of instinctive behaviour, and so tried to fit everything into a system of chain reflexes.

Such, then, was the situation at the time at which Lorenz's scheme was elaborated. Lorenz's main argument is that in each example of true instinctive behaviour there is a hard core of absolutely fixed and relatively complex automatism—an inborn movement form. This restricted concept is the essence of the instinct itself. Lorenz originally called it 'Erbkoor-dination,' and we have now come to refer to it usually as the *fixed pattern* or *fixed-action pattern.* Such action patterns are items of behaviour in every way as constant as anatomical structures, and are potentially just as valuable for systematic phylogenetic studies. Every systematist working with such groups as birds or higher insects will be able to recall examples of the value of such fixed behaviour patterns in classification. Where, as is so often the case, such action patterns constitute an end-point or climax of either a major or minor chain of instinctive behaviour, they have come to be known as *consummatory acts*—a term which, as we shall see below, has its counterpart, if not its origin, in much earlier writing, both of physiologists and psychologists.

Lorenz's contribution to the concept of the internal drive, which, as we have shown above, was independently arrived at by Lashley at about the same time, consists primarily of his concept of *reaction specific energy,* now usually included in the concept of *specific action potential* (S. A. P.) (Thorpe, 1951). Lorenz points out (1) that the co-ordination mechanism of each fixed pattern tends to build up a kind of specific tension in the central nervous system, and if the animal does not find itself in the appropriate situation for the action pattern to be released, this specific action potential is, as it were, dammed up. The damming-up process results in (2) a lower-ing of the threshold for the stimuli effective in releasing that particular action pattern. Indeed, if continued long enough, the tension may accumu-late to the point at which the action pattern goes off without any external stimulus at all, as it were forcing its way out and giving rise to what is called (3) vacuum activity ('*Leerlaufreaktion*'), but for which a better term is perhaps *overflow activity* (Armstrong, 1950). Examples of what appear to be this kind of phenomenon will be found in this book.

In considering evidence suggestive of specific action potential, let us first take some examples under exact experimental control: Kohn (1951) found that the perception of and/or acts involved in ingestion and swallow-ing played a large part in the reduction of specific action potential in the rat, and that direct injection of food into the stomach had not the same effect. Similarly, Bellows (1939) and Holmes (see Morgan and Stellar, 1950) found that in dogs provided with an œsophageal fistula so that water swal-lowed when drinking did not enter the stomach, it was the duration of the act of drinking that was the central controlling factor. It made little dif-ference whether the water entered the stomach or merely dripped away through the fistula. However, in all such examples considered as evidence for specific motivation a doubt still remains, for the effects of learning and habit formation are not completely separated from those of innate co-ordinations. What is required is the very difficult experiment of separating nutrition and digestion from the act of swallowing, right from the begin-ning, so that the latter is never reinforced by ingestion of food or water, but is allowed to display its own motivation independent of all else.[1]

Then, turning to observations on the whole animal, we may recall the constant activity of the hunting dog and the pouncing cat, often quite unrelated to the state of hunger of the animal. With hand-reared animals this kind of thing is sometimes particularly in evidence, as, for example, a hand-reared Tawny Owl (*Strix aluco*) (Thorpe, 1948) which, after being fed, would act as if pouncing upon living prey though it had never had the experience of dealing with a living mouse. An entertaining and some-what similar example which was recently brought to my notice concerns the young of the Flying Squirrel (*Glaucomys volans*) in Florida. Hand-reared young of this species, when given nuts, would go through all the motions of burying them in the bottom of the wire cage and then go away contented, even though the nuts were exposed to full view (Dickin-son, personal communication, 1952).

Some of these instances at once suggest what we usually call 'play,' and

---

[1] Observations on the sucking of young puppies, see Chapter XVI (p. 449) below, come nearer to this ideal. Much other recent work both with rats and dogs is discussed by Watson (1961), and Deutsch (1960*a*). The recent Russian work (see Razran, 1961) is also closely relevant.

will be discussed in that connection later. There are various possible explanations for behaviour which can be described as play, and it would be a mistake to think that at present they can all be brought together in one category. But these and many other examples do seem to support the 'common-sense' view based on everyday observation, that the potential behind particular action patterns varies considerably in the same individual from time to time without being by any means always an expression of the general state of activity or degree of fatigue of the animal as a whole. In other words, it looks as if there is some part of the total drive [1] set aside or specialised for a particular set or group of instinctive actions. On the other hand there is as yet no fully satisfactory demonstration that the threshold of release of a given action pattern is indeed correlated exactly with the fluctuations of a specific drive, and bears no relation whatever to the general state of activity and sensitiveness of the animal; although van Iersel (1953), by his work on the parental behaviour of the stickleback, has recently provided further evidence pointing in this direction. He finds that, with increasing motivation, releasing mechanisms tend to become more active in the sense of being less selective. Prechtl (1953) also, studying the begging behaviour of young Passerine birds, finds exactly similar effects with increasing hunger, and general observation suggests that it is widespread. (See also Hinde, 1959.)

Now it will be seen at once that, from the drive point of view, the essential feature which the schemes of Lashley and Lorenz have in common is the idea that ontogenetically the drive originates from the specific pattern—not the pattern from the drive. In other words, we are dealing here with an inverted theory of drive—the tail is wagging the dog. Thus, when it appeared, perhaps the first of the many merits of Lorenz's scheme was this very concept of *action specific energy*. Skinner's (1933 and 1935) formulation of the concept of 'operants' contains much the same idea, and Hull (1943), in his postulates 6 and 11, accepts something very similar; but his insistence on the necessity for need reduction as a form of reinforcement makes his scheme less useful than that of Skinner.

It is interesting to consider what is essentially the same problem as it is met by neurologists and others who are studying the first responses of the embryonic vertebrate, and who are trying to relate the data on neural growth with the progress of development of behaviour in the life of the animal concerned. A recent discussion of this subject (D. Hooker, in Weiss, 1950) has shown that there are two opposing points of view, at present extremely difficult to reconcile, about the initiation of exteroceptive neuro-muscular responses in mammals, and especially in man. Firstly, observers,

---

[1] The evidence for the existence of general drives has been briefly summarised in Chapter I (p. 9 *et seq.*, above), and is also dealt with in Chapter VII.

when studying the 'first' responses to stimulation, find behaviour which, though often simple, is by no means always so, and, indeed, may sometimes be quite complex. All are agreed about that. Disagreement comes over the next step and divides such workers into what may roughly be called the 'isolated reflex group' and the 'total pattern group.' The isolated reflex group regards the simpler types of response as the fundamental reflex from which, or on which, more complicated behaviour forms are built up by the addition of successively added simple reflexes, each of which is subsequently integrated with those which have appeared before. This group is also convinced that such initial simple reflexes can be elicited only during the first few seconds after exposure of the embryo, and while it is still connected by the intact placental circulation. They affirm that all responses elicited, at however early an age, when once the placental connections have been disturbed, are abnormal and are probably caused by the commencement of asphyxia. The total pattern group, on the other hand, think that such early simple responses as occur are not true reflexes at all, but are caused by direct mechanical stimulation of the muscle tissues underlying the extremely delicate embryonic and early fœtal integument. This group believes that the earliest true reflexes involve the entire functional neuro-muscular mechanism then available. In response to light tactile stimulation (usually in a circumscribed area of the facial region), the responses are neither simple nor local. As neuro-muscular connections develop, they extend chiefly caudally, involving more and more of the trunk in a reflex of the same character as that first appearing. This integration of the expanded reflex, as it is called, precedes the development of the added areas involved, and is an essential component of the normal process of development within the nervous system. In other words, integration is primary and all the specialisation secondary. As later growth proceeds, localised *specific* reflexes appear, and these thus modify the total character of the initial behaviour pattern. These specific responses are not in any sense 'simple,' but are made visible by increases in the number of nerve fibres. Workers who take this viewpoint also maintain that the essential character of the first reflex is not, in fact, immediately altered by interference with the placental circulation.[1]

[1] In considering this apparently fundamental disagreement, it is important to realise, as Hooker points out, that there are other considerations which have considerable bearing on the plausibility of the explanations which the two schools advance and about which there is, in fact, little or no dispute. Firstly, it is known that the muscles develop to a stage at which they will respond to an electrical or mechanical stimulus long before any functional nervous mechanism has been elaborated. Secondly, the motor nerves are functional before the sensory nerves, the sensory and intercalated elements of the reflex arc being the last to become functional. Finally, proprioceptive reflex motor nerves very probably become functional before the exteroceptive ones. To the present writer, at any rate, these points, about which there is general agreement, seem to favour the viewpoint of the total pattern group quite strongly,

The bearing of this controversy on the question of the theory of instinct lies in the fact that the consummatory acts or fixed-action patterns are certainly not reflex in any restricted sense of the term. They are whole patterns of co-ordination involving many sets of muscles and many parts of the animal. Spurway and Haldane (1953), in discussing vertebrate breathing, suggest that reflexes may often represent ancestral instincts that have lost the appetitive behaviour and internal drive which had been necessary during earlier stages of evolution. Whatever evidence there is for such patterns of co-ordination generating specific action potential, it seems quite clear that such potential is not normally generated by simple reflex responses, though traces of it may sometimes be found in the form of variations in latency. It is not to be thought that a final verdict for one or other of the groups of genetic neurologists mentioned above would either confirm the Lorenz-Lashley concept or irrevocably destroy it. But if it is true, as the total pattern group contend, that the first actions of the animal occur well before there are sensory and intercalated elements present and functioning in the reflex arc, then it does seem much more likely that it is these co-ordination patterns which could be responsible for the development of the drive behind specific elements of behaviour. If, on the other hand, the isolated reflex group proves to be right, then whatever may be generating the earliest activity is probably not identical with what appears as specific action potential in the mature animal.

It is particularly interesting, from the ethological viewpoint, to consider how the concept of action specific energy has since fared, and how well it has survived the ordeal of fifteen years' consideration and research. The original attractiveness of the concept to the student of animal behaviour was the ready explanation it offered of the kind of behaviour, discussed above, where, with a lowering of the threshold, we get a tendency to vacuum activity or *Leerlauf*; and particularly in those instances in which behaviour goes off in the wrong context yet to the evident 'satisfaction' of the animal. But, impressive though this evidence is to the observer, if for no other reason than because it is so common, it is not the only possible explanation. As we have seen, it has not, in fact, been easy to

and to furnish an *a priori* reason for regarding their system of explanation as more practicable. Further, Barron (1950) has pointed out that all the workers, whatever party they belong to, appear to accept the total pattern principle with regard to the development of activity of the axial musculature, derived from the somite and supplied by the ventral branches of the spinal nerves. He thinks, therefore, that the question might be restated; does the neural control of the appendicular musculature develop in association with, or independently of, the axial system? It may even be as he suggests, that the controversy can ultimately be resolved if one looks at it in terms of differential growth, rates characteristic of organisms at different evolutionary levels. It is certain that neither side can at present produce *decisive* evidence in favour of its particular view, but Barron points out that the evidence on which the 'isolated reflex group' base their conclusions is certainly far from conclusive.

obtain experimental evidence for specific motivation and the best experimental approach to the subject is the indirect one of attempting to demonstrate *action specific exhaustibility*.

Tinbergen and his co-workers (1943), in studying the Grayling Butterfly (*Satyrus semele*), obtained results which at least strongly suggest, if they do not prove, the occurrence of specific exhaustibility, and which, if confirmed, would seem to provide reasonably strong evidence for specific action potential. The male butterfly has a characteristic upward flight from the ground in response to the sight of the female butterfly flying past above it. In a large number of experiments the characteristic female flight was imitated by dummies moved over the experimental ground on the end of fine threads. As will be seen from

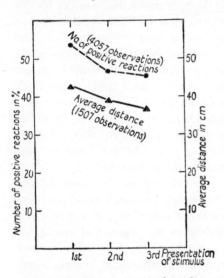

the accompanying graph (Fig. 1), when the same dummy was presented three times in succession, the interval between tests being not more than twenty seconds, a consistent and significant falling off in the percentage response and in the average flight distance was observed. The butterflies can, presumably, fly long distances, and it seems inconceivable that there could, in this particular instance, be any general exhaustion of the flight mechanism. Precht and Freytag (1958) have used this method in their study of the factors controlling the behaviour of Salticid spiders. They were able separately to exhaust a number of different responses and study the independent rates of their recovery. (See also the

Fig. 1—Graph showing waning of response of male Grayling Butterfly to moving model of female as a result of repeated presentation. (After Tinbergen, Meeuse, Boerema and Varossieau, 1942.)

work of Rilling *et al.*, summarised on p. 239 below.) That one can hardly be too careful about the interpretation of such experiments is, however, made clear by the work of Wigglesworth (1949), who has shown that it is possible to exhaust the flight mechanism of *Drosophila* without apparently weakening in any way the ability to walk. At first sight this might seem to be the case of a central nervous exhaustion of the co-ordination mechanism of the flight behaviour. In fact, it is nothing of the sort, but is due apparently to complete utilisation of the readily available carbohydrate reserves which are necessary for the action of the flight muscles but which are not required for the exercise of walking. However, where we are merely con-

cerned, as with the Grayling Butterfly, with two kinds of flight, it does not
seem likely that the nutritional exhaustion theory could possibly hold,
and therefore we seem to have a *prima facie* case for the exhaustion of
a specific nervous co-ordination mechanism or Habituation. However,
even now there remain some difficulties. The fading of the response may
have been due to recognition by the insect that the stimulus was an inadequate one; in this connection we are reminded of the work of Rand (1941)
(see p. 69 below) on the response of the Thrasher (an American bird
of the thrush type) to an artificial snake made of rubber. It was found
that the response to the rubber snake, however realistic its movements may
seem, soon fades, whereas the response to a real snake does not. Also,
there is the evidence produced by Strauss (1938*b*) of the fading of response
on the part of small birds to mounted owls and hawks, which may have
been due to some incompleteness of the stimulus, such as a lack of movement. Similarly with the Grayling Butterfly it is hard to be sure that the
stimulus is fully adequate and we need to know whether the response
is elicited at full intensity, whether there is any response specific decrement, and whether there is any tendency for such decrement to persist.
If restoration is complete after a short period of inactivity, and if the
answers to the other queries are all affirmative, then we may assume
true specific exhaustibility. If not, it is still open to us to regard the
phenomenon as habituation until we can differentiate by studies on duration and stimulus specificity. Hinde (1954*b*) has recently given a comprehensive discussion of varieties of response-waning with special reference
to the innate predator-mobbing response of the chaffinch. From this it is
clear that at least four types of change in responsiveness are involved:
(1) Changes specific to the response but not to the elicitory stimulus. Recovery at least moderately rapid. (Reduction of specific motivation) (See
Hinde, 1954*a*.) (2) Changes specific to the stimulus. Recovery moderately rapid. (Stimulus satiation—releaser satiation.) (See Prechtl, 1953;
Glanzer, 1953 and 1958.) See also Rilling, Mittelstaedt and Roeder (1959)
for the differing effect of optimal and sub-optimal dummies (cf. p. 239
below). (3) Changes specific to the response. Recovery extremely slow or
absent. (Instinctive regression—implying a disintegration of the central
nervous co-ordinating mechanisms.) (Thorpe, 1951*a*.) (4) Changes specific
to the stimulus. Recovery extremely slow or absent. (Habituation.) (See
Thorpe, 1951*a* and *b*).

Thus, strictly speaking, only if we can affirm that habituation is characteristic of appetitive behaviour not consummated and can then show
specific exhaustibility in a consummatory act fully released, shall we have
firm ground for asserting that specific motivation—by which, we may
remind ourselves again, we mean the motivation arising from the activity

of the co-ordination mechanism of a consummatory act—has been demonstrated.

Although van Iersel's (1953) demonstration of the significant lowering of the sex drive of the stickleback as a result of performance of the corresponding appetitive behaviour of courtship seems to be further evidence for the concept of specific action potential, it is, I think, generally true to say that recent studies on this and other animals have not, on the whole, provided the new evidence that might have been expected. For instance,

FIG. 2—Three types of display activity in Mallard differing in pattern but biologically equivalent.
(a) 'Grundspfiff' or 'Grunt-whistle.'
(b) 'Kurzhochwerden' or 'Head-up-tail-up' movement.
(c) 'Ab-auf bewegung' or 'Down-up' movement.
(After Lorenz, 1941.)

Lorenz himself (1941) has shown in ducks of the genus *Anas*, that the three types of display activity (1) 'Grundspfiff,' (2) 'Kurzhochwerden,' (3) 'Ab-auf bewegung' (Fig. 2), while very different in pattern, are biologically all exactly equivalent and must summate in lowering specific action potential. In other words, it seems pure chance which of the three appears. Tinbergen and van Iersel (1947) found no evidence of differences in specific action potential between the types of fighting in the stickleback. Again, Schenkel (1948), in his studies on wolves, has shown that sparking over or displacement as between the different but related behaviour patterns is so frequent that the concept of specific action potential begins to lose its meaning and to have little, if any, utility; and this sparking over is certainly very characteristic of higher mammals. On the other hand, plenty of evidence has accumulated that the internal drive is not by any means equally and uniformly available to all the behaviour patterns of an instinct; in other words, that the energy of the internal drive, while not perhaps action-specific in the degree to which Lorenz originally supposed, is still specific to classes of behaviour patterns rather than to individual patterns themselves.

If we cannot obtain good evidence for reaction specific exhaustibility what other criterion is there? It is clear that 'energy' with *some* degree of specificity, channelled in some way or another, is fundamental to the modern concept of instinct. This is obvious from the stress laid on the fixed patterns of instinct as *consummatory acts*—acts which complete a reaction chain and give very plain evidence of release of appetitive tension. Just as the concept of specific action potential had its counterpart in the 'spinal contrast' and 'rebound' phenomena of an earlier stage of reflex physiology, so the modern scientific distinction between appetitive behaviour and consummatory act did not really begin with Lorenz, nor even with Wallace Craig or Heinroth. Sherrington, in 1906, if not earlier, was using the term *Precurrent Response* for something very like, if not identical with, *Appetitive Behaviour*, and *Consummatory Response* for our *Consummatory Act*.[1]

So there is really a great deal of justification for regarding certain instinctive acts as truly consummatory and relieving 'tension' and 'pressure' in some way; although, as we shall see, perceptions can be goals and reinforcements just as much as acts.[2] But this does not *necessarily* mean that the mechanisms for action co-ordination are actually generating any 'potential'; before release they may merely be blocking a drive coming from elsewhere in the nervous system, or they may, indeed, be producing some antagonistic force—some negative feed-back. But before looking into these possibilities we must consider more recent advances in instinct-theory in relation to the evidence for displacement. Two major concepts on the motor side of instinct-theory have been the displacement or 'sparking over' concept of Kortlandt and the hierarchy system of N. Tinbergen.

Displacement is the performance of a behaviour pattern out of the particular functional context of behaviour to which it is normally related.

---

[1] The same concept is implicitly accepted in Hull's (1943) 'Postulate 3.'

[2] As an experimental example of this we may cite the demonstration that the mere perception of a stimulus, e.g. gastric distension by a bladder in œsophagostomised dogs (Towbin, 1949) acts as an important factor in thirst satiation even though there has been no fluid intake at all. (See also Chapter II, p. 22, above.) In this particular case, as in many others, it is impossible to say whether the consummatory qualities of the stimulus are innate or have been acquired by learning.

(See Armstrong, 1950; Thorpe, 1951b.) Displacement activities are usually recognisable by being jerky, uncontrolled or irregular, often incomplete; sometimes without *specific* releasing stimuli and appearing out of context—that is to say, the reaction is one that fails to reach its normal goal. Originally it was thought that displacement was evidence of the 'charge' attached to one instinct, having been denied opportunity for adequate discharge through its own consummatory act or acts, sparking over to set going the consummatory act or acts of another instinct. This simple interpretation of sparking over does in fact probably apply in certain instances, but its application seems to have been very much reduced by recent critical experimental studies of displacement in birds. The outcome of both the study of the preening behaviour of terns (van Iersel and Bol, 1958) and of displacement grooming in the Chaffinch (Fraser Rowell, 1961) has been to indicate that most if not all displacement results from conflict. In the terns the occurrence of displacement is shown to depend on the relation between the conflicting drives: the strength of these must not diverge too much from a certain ratio which may be called effective equality. Similarly with the Chaffinch, there is no evidence for the hypothesis that displacement is caused by a 'surplus' of drive sparking over from some other instinctive system of organisation. In other cases of careful analysis, namely those of Andrew (1956) and Morris (1956) in birds and of Sevenster (1961) who deals with the mechanism of displacement in the Stickleback, the same general picture emerges. In all carefully studied examples then, displacement can be regarded as a process of disinhibition taking place in a conflict situation.

The concept of nervous hierarchies was first introduced into human psychology by Herbert Spencer in the second edition of his *Principles* (1870–2), but the idea came to life again recently in relation to the innate behaviour of animals when Tinbergen (1951a) published in outline a scheme for symbolic representation of instinctive behaviour in the wide sense, involving the concept of a series of 'centres' (which are regarded as 'functionally characterised systems not necessarily with any precisely limited anatomical location') organised in a hierarchy of different levels superimposed on one another, each level being primarily activated by a drive descending to it from the one above. This scheme has now become well known, and is proving valuable in stimulating and co-ordinating experiments on instinctive behaviour. It suggests, although it does not necessarily demand, structural organisation in the nervous system. This need not be physically localised in centres which will ultimately be revealed by histological methods, but may be fixed and co-ordinated in some way not yet understood. As will be seen from the accompanying diagram (Fig. 3), this hypothetical neurophysiological organisation comprises a series of mechanisms at different levels for the loading and release of

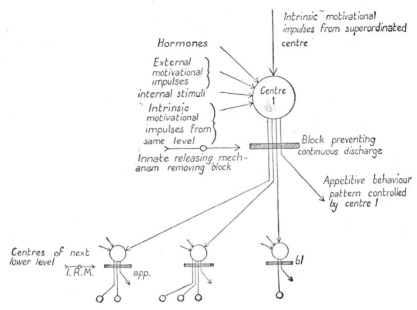

FIG. 3—Hypothetical organisation of an instinctive centre at an intermediate level. (After Tinbergen, 1951a.)

which internal and external factors are necessary, and which respond to these factors by producing co-ordinated movements each apparently directed towards the attainment of a specific goal. Thus, the highest centre of all is supposed to provide motivational impulses which flow down without hindrance into the next centres below, which centres are regarded as being at the level of the major instinct. Besides these motivational impulses from above, whose existence is still unproved, though they seem probable enough, other impulses impinge upon the centres of the major instinct. These can be listed as: (1) hormones, or other chemical stimuli; (2) sensory stimuli coming from the viscera of the animal; (3) impulses which may be intrinsic to the centre itself; and (4) external stimuli loading the centre from outside by means of the external sense organs. In the particular instance with which Tinbergen has been specially concerned, namely the stickleback, this centre at the level of the major instinct would be a territorial centre; this is, the centre which activates the behaviour concerned with taking up a territory in spring.

In all the channels which flow downward from this centre, there is supposed to exist a physiological mechanism which effectively prevents all discharge of activity unless the animal encounters the right environmental situation and stimuli to remove or release this block. Thus there is an *innate releasing mechanism* (I.R.M.), as was postulated by Lorenz, which is in some way attuned to the biologically right stimulus in the environment (in this case it may be the appearance of the sexual partner), and which is, as it were, unlocked by the appropriate releaser, thus allowing behaviour to proceed to the next lowest level. These in their turn incorporate blocks and, so long as these remain, action of these lower centres cannot proceed. The activity will therefore be diverted into the type of action known as *appetitive behaviour* (see Fig. 4).[1]

The question of appetitive behaviour is to be discussed below and need not concern us at the moment, nor need we now stop to deal with the subject of releasers, the whole of the perceptory side of instinct being an aspect which is conveniently discussed apart from the activity side. The point which has been made here is that there is now a good deal of evidence to suggest that the 'energy' is no longer action specific below the third level in the diagram (Fig. 3), but can often activate other centres at the same level. Still less is it specific at the level of the consummatory act. These connections between the centres at the same level seem to be necessary in order to allow for the displacement activities which, as mentioned above, are, in fact, such a feature of behaviour in the higher animals. This, however, means that the 'structure' of the individual centre is not only immensely more complicated than this very diagrammatic representation suggests, and—as the author of the scheme would be the first to admit—it is also of a rather different plan. If we are to allow for displacement between all the main centres, the fan must in many cases become a network, and, indeed, since it is the same muscles which are activated in many different behaviour co-ordinations, and often the same co-ordinations in different instincts, the network must be a very complicated one. Now,

---

[1] Recent developments in the technique of brain stimulation for the study of the innate behaviour of the domestic fowl (von Holst and von St. Paul, 1960) have become something of a landmark for ethology. Only the first preliminary results of this neurophysiological study have so far been published, but it has already been shown that point stimulation by oscillating current at a wide variety of loci in the brain stem elicits a very broad range of both simple and complex movements belonging to many different instincts. These include highly characteristic and ethologically unmistakable actions of care of the body surface, picking and cleaning, orientation in space, directing attack or escape behaviour to a particular direction, behaviour appropriate to attack on or flight from different kinds of enemies, agonistic behaviour, sexual behaviour, and the care of the young. There is no evidence as yet that any of the loci touched by the electrodes are, in a morphological sense, unique centres for the behaviour elicited; on the contrary, it is often clear that the impulses are conducted to distant and, as yet, unlocated systems which themselves control the behaviour. Among the questions upon which light has been thrown already are those of central adaptation, lowering of threshold, the significance of sub-threshold excitation, and the summation of sub-threshold events to rise above the threshold. Since many single acts are contained in more than one complex system and since many such acts may be elicited at a great many different loci, the present overall picture of the organisation of an instinctive centre of the central nervous system is very similar to that envisaged by Tinbergen's well-known system—that is, a network which is also in some degree a hierarchy, or a network with intermediate integration levels.

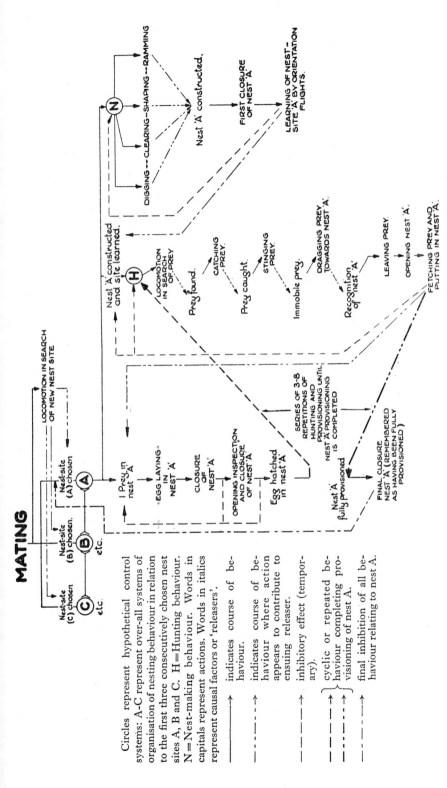

Fig. 4.—Diagram to show complexity of organisation of an appetitive behaviour system within the reproductive instinct of the female of the hunting wasp (*Ammophila campestris*) subsequent to mating. (Original. Based on observations of Baerends, 1941.)

it may be that these inter-connections, as Tinbergen (1951a) himself has suggested,[1] do not in reality run directly from one centre to another, but by way of the super-ordinate centre; and certainly they must provide some resistance since displacements are always characterised by 'loss of energy' (Tinbergen, 1952). Perhaps the inhibition of one centre by another is in reality a sort of competition, the inhibiting centre, by decrease of resistance, draining, impulse flow, at the expense of other centres. This certainly seems reasonable; but it does become apparent that, in adopting this system, we have in fact gone a long way from the original concept of Lashley and Lorenz of the co-ordination mechanism of the consummatory act as, mainly or entirely, providing the drive.

Of course, in so far as the appetitive behaviour incorporates fixed-action patterns, the co-ordination mechanism of these could be thought of as generating drive in the same way. But the more variable the appetitive behaviour, the less feasible this explanation becomes unless there is a culminating action pattern acting as the terminus. Failing this, the only way in which we can conceive of a highly variable system being directively activated is by some directive or purposive influence external to it; i.e. the drive. So we get back to something resembling the drive of the earlier psychologists as some sort of *directive* stimulus, provided from the highest centres and coming down a series of channels to activate particular effectors.

But the question which now arises is, can such a mechanism be looked upon as probable in view of our present knowledge of the flexibility as well as the fixity of instinctive behaviour? Can such a mechanism be feasible without bringing back into the concept of drive something of the original 'psychological' qualities of conation which were originally postulated? The merit of Lorenz's original plan was largely that it seemed to avoid many of the less desirable psychological implications which were attached to the idea of a drive and replaced them by a beautifully clear concept of the specific co-ordination patterns generating, so to speak, the animal's behaviour. But this avoidance of these implications was apparent rather than real. They were, in fact, merely being relegated to and confined within the appetitive behaviour. And so it is not surprising that present-day workers on instinctive behaviour, as for example Tinbergen himself (1952), are using the term 'drive' more and more, and are using it in such a way as to lead inevitably to the term assuming the connotation it bore in the past when used by psychologists. This is one of those challenging situations which makes the subject of instinct at present so attractive and so stimulating, both to the psychologist in the older sense and to the modern comparative ethologist. Psychologists have always been struck by the appearance of intense emotion which animals and humans display

[1] See also Bastock, Morris and Moynihan, 1953.

when suffering from thwarting of 'instinctive' drives. It has indeed been said that emotion is the boiling over of a heated instinct. This, of course, fits in beautifully with the concept of the damming back of specific action potential—if for 'emotion' we substitute some term less saturated with qualities of human mental life.   But the essence of the matter is whether or not present studies of instinct are going back, as in some ways they seem to be, to the idea of a directive drive arising mainly outside the supposed system of channels in which it is 'flowing,' or whether we should still regard the channels as providing most or all of the requirements for a system of explanation. In other words, is there something purposive about the central nervous drive itself, or is the appearance of purposiveness really only a directiveness which arises from there being a large number of alternative preformed channels or pathways for the consummatory act? That such a system would give an appearance of purposiveness is evident when we consider that one of the chief criteria for the attribution of purpose to an active system is whether or not it employs variable means to an invariable end. For, if there is only one course of action open to an organism, and if this action must always be performed without any short-circuiting before the stereotyped consummatory act is discharged, then we can have no data on which to decide for or against purposiveness. Similarly if appetitive action shows extreme variability, it appears random and so again must seem non-purposive. We regard a set of actions as purposive if they are neither completely stereotyped on the one hand nor completely random on the other, but show a large but not unlimited series of alternatives for action—in other words, 'hypothesis.' But, given some alternative for action, a secondary criterion of purpose or directiveness becomes available; that is, of course, the tendency to choose the more expeditious or simpler of two or more courses of action—which, as we shall see below (Chapter III), is one of the criteria for learning; and, indeed, in the forms of conservation of equilibrium, adaptation and the principle of parsimony or least action, is typical of life itself. But before we can discuss this further we must consider in more detail the concept of appetitive behaviour.

The term *appetitive behaviour* is used by present-day writers on ethology to mean the flexible or variable introductory phase of an instinctive behaviour pattern or sequence. As can be seen from an inspection of Tinbergen's hierarchic system of instinctive behaviour, the appetitive behaviour is regarded as a kind of side-channel[1] into which the drive flows when all the outlets from the centres of the next lower level are blocked by their respective I.R.M.s. This, of course, does not imply that the appetitive behaviour is regarded by the author as essentially simple—

---

[1] This is perhaps simply an outcome of the hydraulic metaphors in which the theory was originally conceived.

it may (Fig. 4) be quite as complex as the consummatory act. Rather he seems merely to be suggesting that it is an alternative, more circuitous route which can be entirely cut out if the releaser for the consummatory act appears to be encountered immediately, and so is outside the main course through which the instinctive behaviour itself, in its strict sense, runs. The origin of the term 'appetitive' in behaviour study has already been considered. Wallace Craig (1918) regarded appetite, or appetence as he sometimes called it, as a condition that showed itself externally as a state of agitation which continues for as long as a certain stimulus—for which he coined the ugly word 'appeted' stimulus—is absent. He said, 'When the appeted stimulus is at length received, it stimulates a consummatory reaction, after which the appetitive behaviour ceases and is succeeded by a state of relative rest.' He also employed the concept of aversion in the opposite sense, as a state of agitation which continues as long as a certain stimulus, referred to as the disturbing stimulus, is present, but which ceases, being replaced by a state of relative rest, when that stimulus has ceased to act on the sense organs. He points out that appetitive behaviour is thus, from one point of view, a reaction to the absence of something, and this is exactly what Lashley meant when he spoke of instinct being a reaction to a deficit. It may be convenient here to give one example, although of course many others may be found in the pages that follow, of an appetite for an instinctive or consummatory action pattern. A dove, exhibiting nest-building activity for the first time, continually picks up straws with a characteristic innate movement and shows a tendency to build them into some sort of nest. When an *experienced* bird first finds a straw, he seizes it immediately and toys with it, sometimes making movements resembling those by which he would build the straw into a nest. This *seems* to generate an appetite for building the straw in (although we cannot in this case rule out independent fluctuations in the drive as a cause of the observed behaviour change), and when this appetite is sufficiently aroused he flies to the nest, guided by associative memory, and performs the consummatory act completely. The young female continues toying with the straw an excessively long time, not carrying it at all, even though she may be very near the nest, but at length, when she does go to the nest with her straw, she makes well-ordered, apparently instinctive movements to build it in. The same sort of thing is apparent with an *inexperienced* young male dove locating a nesting-site for the first time. At first the dove, standing on his perch, spontaneously assumes the nest-calling attitude—body thrown forward and head down, as if neck and breast were already touching the hollow of the nest—and while in this attitude the nest-call is sounded; but all the time he shows

---

[1] Complex though Fig. 4 is, comparison with Fig. 65 of Baerends' 1941 paper shows it to be much simpler than the facts really warrant.

dissatisfaction, as if the perch were not a comfortable situation for this behaviour. He shifts about and performs the action, first in one place and then in another, until he finds a corner which more or less fits his body when in this posture. He is seldom satisfied with the first corner found, but tries one after another and then perhaps comes back to the first. If now a suitable nest-box, or ready-made nest, is put into the cage, the inexperienced bird does not recognise it as a nest, but sooner or later he tries it for nest-calling, and in such trial the nest evidently gives him a strong and satisfying stimulation—a stimulation which no other circumstance has supplied. In the nest his attitude becomes enhanced; he turns from side to side, moving the straws with beak, feet, breast and wings as if, to quote Wallace Craig, 'rioting in the wealth of new luxurious stimuli.' He no longer wanders restlessly in search of new nesting situations, but remains satisfied with his present highly stimulating nest.

It seems fairly clear from the latter example that there is no innate visual recognition of the nest as something appropriate; the bird has to get into it and experience its characteristics with other senses besides vision before he, as it were, realises its possibilities. And there is, of course, a great deal of appetitive behaviour in which the locomotory or other activity is largely random, being merely restricted within certain rather ill-defined limits. Obviously the male dove does not search for a nest site outside the territory which it is inhabiting at the moment, probably it does not look for sites on the ground; but presumably if it wanders sufficiently persistently through that restricted region it will find any appropriate stimulus that may be there.

Hinde (1952) has shown that nest-site selection in tits is very similar. The birds 'inspect' a great variety of crannies ranging from obviously impossible places to 'perfect' nesting-holes. It is clear that the tit must possess the I.R.M. for a 'perfect' site, otherwise it would be content with some imperfect one which it happened to encounter at an early stage in its appetitive behaviour. But this cannot be the whole story, for if, on the other hand, the bird responded only to the stimuli indicative of a perfect site, it would fail to nest if such were lacking. Actually we find that the 'best' available site is used—a nest-box seems to be a super-normal releaser, and is preferred to natural holes; but if not even a 'good' hole is available the threshold of acceptance is so much lowered, presumably as a result of the build-up of the reproductive drive, that a quite inferior site may be adapted or 'made do' with. This is a very different situation from that which obtains with much sexual behaviour where, although super-normal releasers are usually effective, sub-normal ones generally fail: and this is of course eugenic, for a sexual response to a sub-normal releaser would in effect be a response to an inappropriate object and would be wasted.

Much of the food-searching behaviour of lower animals consists of unoriented locomotion. The hungry wireworm wanders at random in the soil (Thorpe, Crombie *et al.*, 1947), turning back only when it encounters some definitely unfavourable stimulus, such as soil which is physically wet or, on the other hand, soil in which the air spaces are at less than saturation. In the same way extremes of temperature are avoided, and the wireworm which encounters light will also turn back. But within these wide limits persistent random wandering is likely to be efficacious as a means of finding the required food. Such cases offer no particular difficulty; they can be fitted very easily into a hierarchic scheme of instinct, and do not raise any specially troublesome problems concerning the drive. It is important here, however, to remember how universal is appetitive behaviour, as Sherrington saw, and there are few if any innate actions without at least some appetitive characteristics being discernible.[1] Thus, as Zener (1937) has pointed out, the apparent simplicity of the conditioned salivary response is illusory. It results simply from the experimental restriction of observation to a single component of behaviour. When the conditioned salivary response of dogs is being investigated, the experimental arrangement and design is such as deliberately to rule out all appetitive action; and if the limits are removed at least partially, the salivary response reveals itself, not as a single simple item of behaviour but as an independent component within a complex, widespread, highly organised and apparently directed behavioural act. It is when we come to the more elaborate types of appetitive behaviour, where complex types of directed locomotion are interlaced with specific taxes and subsidiary instincts, as in the typical breeding cycle of birds, or as in the very elaborate nest-making and provisioning behaviour of the hunting wasps, that the problem of its significance for the concept of drive emerges. Here again we should remind ourselves, as Wallace Craig reminded us, that such complex chains within appetitive behaviour are not chain reflexes, although chain reflexes must have their part in the organisation of this as well as of other behaviour; rather they are chain instincts, and the instinctive drive is in some way behind all the separate behaviour elements, linking them together and co-ordinating them.

When we come to the more elaborate types of appetitive behaviour, where mere unoriented locomotion cannot be sufficient for finding the appropriate situation for the consummatory act, but where obviously there has to be some sort of direction, the matter becomes much more complicated. This is briefly indicated in the accompanying table (Table I), which is explained below. Thus, in this situation, the 'goal' is not the consummatory act itself but the experience of having constructed a perfect,

[1] In land mammals the appetitive behaviour of breathing shown by submerged Amphibia is not normally seen, but may be evoked by abnormal conditions (Spurway and Haldane, 1953). (See also Chapter XIII, p. 323.)

TABLE 1

Inventory of Actions, Materials and probable Releasers used by Long-tailed Tit in building nest: eighteen releasers (including the four materials); fourteen distinct movements or combinations of movements. (Based on observations by Tinbergen, 1953.)

Releaser	*Action*	*Object Sought and/or Manipulated*
1a. Territory	Searching	Nest site
1b. Nest site	Collecting	Moss ⎤ 1b and c alternate
1c. Nest site	Placing	Moss ⎦ until:
2a. Tufts of moss in fork	Collecting	Spider's silk ⎤ 2a, b and c
2b. Spider's silk on moss	Rubbing	Spider's silk ⎬ alternate a number of times, then
2c. Spider's silk stuck to moss	Stretching	Spider's silk ⎦ back to 1

[Periodical alternation of actions and object manipulation in $(1b + c)$ and $(2a + b + c)$ until platform built.]

3a. Platform	Collecting	Moss
3b. Platform	Sitting	
3c. Action of sitting	Placing material on rim	Moss
3d. Moss on rim	Sideways movement of bill (sideways weaving)	
3e. Moss on rim	$(2a + b + c)$	
3f. Moss on rim	Vertical movements of bill (vertical weaving)	
3g. Curved nest rim or cup outside bird's body	Steady rotation of body during building	

[Periodical alternation of actions and object manipulation in $(1b + c)$ and $(2a + b + c)$ and $(3a + b–f)$.]

4a. Nest-cup	Breast pressing
4b. Nest-cup	Trampling with feet
4c. Nest-cup	Turning

[Periodical alternation of actions and object manipulation in $(1b + c)$, $(2a + b + c)$, $(3a–f)$ and $(4a + b + c)$.]

TABLE I (*continued*)

Releaser	Action	Object Sought and/or Manipulated
5a. Nest-cup more than about one-third built	Collecting	Lichens
5b. Outside of nest-cup unevenly or incompletely covered with lichen	Weaving from inside	Lichens
5c. Outside of nest-cup unevenly or incompletely covered with lichen	Weaving from out-side	Lichens
5d. ditto	Actions of 2b and 2c from new positions, i.e. outside cup	

[Periodical alternations of all five sets of actions.]

6. Cup about two-thirds built	Change of movements (especially 3g) so as to leave an entrance hole. Special weaving and other movements on the rim of the entrance hole	
7a. Completed dome	Collecting	Feathers
7b. Completed dome	Lining	

or virtually perfect, releaser for the next phase of the appetitive behaviour. It is extremely difficult to suppose that the few innate movement patterns whereby some of the more elaborate types of nest are constructed could possibly themselves be adequate for the production of a complete and perfect nest. If the movements are few and stereotyped, then the I.R.M.s that are to ensure the choice of the right materials and the cessation of activities at the right moment must be all the more elaborate to compensate for the relative simplicity of the actions.[1] Let us follow out an actual example step by step and make an inventory of the actions and releasers involved.

Tinbergen (1953) has described in preliminary outline the system of actions employed by a Long-tailed Tit (*Ægithalos caudatus*) when building its domed nest. He considers it remarkable that such a complex and beautifully organised structure can be built with 'a repertory of relatively few simple movements.' So it is; but he gives an undue impression of simplicity and fixity by concentrating on the movements and passing over the fact that the releaser or perceptual side is extremely complex— for at least eighteen releasers must be involved in the nest-building process alone! Nor, after all, is the effector organisation so very simple, for fourteen movements or distinct combinations of movements seem to be involved. When a nest site has been chosen within the territory, moss is collected and placed on the branch. Most of it falls off, but the action continues until a few pieces have stuck. 'Moss on site' appears then to be the releaser for collecting nest material No. 2—namely spider's silk. This is 'rubbed' on the moss until it sticks, when 'silk on moss' releases the stretching movements by which the silk is used for binding. All these various operations now continue in alternation until a platform is built. The platform releases the action of collecting moss and 'sitting.' Once the bird is sitting on the platform it can place moss around itself and so begin to construct the cup—this is done by a new 'sideways weaving' movement and later by 'vertical weaving.' At about this time the presence of a curved rim outside the bird's body apparently stimulates the steady rotation of the body during building. Now all previous actions are combined in alternation until a distinct nest-cup has been constructed. A well-formed nest-cup must then be the releaser for two new actions—'breast pressing' and 'trampling' with the feet. Thus the process continues with these two new actions incorporated until the cup is about one-third complete. A cup of these dimensions now releases the collection of building material No. 3—lichens. These are added to the nest on the *outside* only, by stretching out over the rim from inside the nest (weaving from inside) and by hanging on the outside in various more or less acrobatic attitudes. Other nest-building actions are now performed in these new attitudes. The releaser for the building in of lichen must presumably be 'outside of nest unevenly or incompletely covered with lichen.' Nest-building now proceeds by means of five alternating sets of actions until the cup is about two-thirds built. When this stage is reached the size of the bird begins to determine the fact that a dome is constructed, the bird reaching up and over as far

---

[1] Thus many releasers must have inhibitory as well as releasing functions, and indeed there must be innate inhibitory mechanisms as well as I.R.M.s (cf. Hinde 1954*b*).

as it can. But now the co-ordination of movements is changed again in such a manner that a neat entrance hole is left at one point—presumably a convenient point for entry from the direction from which the nest is usually approached. Now special weaving and other movements are made whereby the rim of the entrance hole is strengthened. Finally, the domed nest, properly lichened and with a perfected entrance, is a final releaser for fetching innumerable feathers and for lining. Thus, as will be seen from the accompanying table (Table I), four different materials must be innately recognised and must serve as releasers for picking up, while at least fourteen other releasers must enter into the whole chain of events. The inventory of actions includes 'searching,' 'collecting,' 'rubbing,' 'weaving,' 'sitting,' 'pressing,' 'trampling,' 'turning' and 'lining' with at least four other combinations of actions—making thirteen in all. So much for simplicity! But perhaps the most significant point of all is the evidence provided that the bird must have some 'conception' of what the completed nest should look like, and some sort of 'conception' that the addition of a piece of moss or lichen here and here will be a step towards the 'ideal' pattern, and that other pieces there and there would detract from it. The bird does not, in fact, go on building up the top of the nest indefinitely; it does not build downwards along adjacent twigs or cover *them* with lichen; it does not close up the entrance hole from outside. Its actions are directional and it 'knows when to stop' in that the fully-fashioned nest is the releaser for the next stage in the breeding cycle.[1]

Precise experimental study of nest-building including investigation of the role of hormones in the regulation of nest-building behaviour has been carried out by Hinde *et al.* (1958–60) on canaries and by Lehrman (1959) on doves. A summary of this work will be found on p. 350 below. See also the work of Boesiger and Lecomte (1959) on nest repair by Blue and Great Tits (p. 350 below).

What may be called working towards an 'ideal releaser' is shown in many cases with animals far lower in the zoological scale than birds. Hingston (1926–7) has described experiments with Eumenid wasps, which can be induced to break off the routine task of constructing and provisioning their mud-pot nests and to repair artificial injuries by a series of actions apparently quite different from those normally employed in the routine of nest-making. He described how *Eumenes conica*—an Indian potter wasp or mason wasp—builds clusters of clay cells and afterwards deposits an egg in each, fills it with caterpillars and seals it with a lid; eventually the whole cluster is covered with a layer of clay. If a rent is made in the side

---

[1] Great adaptability in regard both to site selection and materials used is of course far from uncommon, particularly in species which construct elaborate nests. The Wren (Armstrong, 1955) provides a good example.

of a cell, it may be some time before the wasp shows any signs of having perceived the damage. One of the caterpillars may fall out through the hole unnoticed, perhaps a second will stick in the hole but with part of its body hanging out, blocking the aperture enough to prevent those brought later from falling through. When the wasp has put the caterpillars in, she seems to notice the hole for the first time and examines it carefully, and then, with great and prolonged effort, she manages to stuff the larvæ back, after which she goes away and collects a pellet of clay with which to mend the hole.

Another striking instance concerns *Rhynchium nitidulum*, which builds pots not unlike those of *Eumenes*. The pot is of clay covered with resin and sealed with a lid after having been filled with caterpillars, and when one pot is finished others are built alongside until a cluster is formed. Here again a hole is made, which the wasp sooner or later notices. She first makes a long but ineffectual attempt to mend the hole with bits of resin pulled from the wall of the pot. This is unsuccessful and, in the particular case described by Hingston (1927), two hours of effort were brought to an end by the coming of night. On her first return visit next morning, she carefully investigates the hole again, goes off a second time and brings back a pellet of mud and, entering the cell through the hole, sets about repairing the damage. First she works on the edge of the hole, filling in irregularities until the ragged opening is converted into a regular circle, then the hole is closed with a flake of clay which is dexterously curved into the natural rotundity of the pot. Finally, resin is fetched and smeared all over the pot until it blends with the whole. As Hingston points out, in this case the wasp appears to repair the hole by a method, different from that employed in closing the mouth of the pot, for she does the repair by a different set of actions. Hingston adds, 'When closing the pot she sits outside and from there introduces clay. When repairing the hole she examines it from both sides and then, having made a choice, elects to do the repair from within.'

Darchen has published over a number of years the result of many interesting experiments on the technique of construction of the comb in the honeybee. The reference quoted (1959) summarises most of this work. The author stresses that cell construction in the honeybee must be regarded as a specifically social phenomenon, not to be fully understood in terms of the behaviour of a single bee isolated from the society. That this attitude is largely justified is shown by the discovery by Butler (1954) of the queen substance. It is now known (Butler *et al.*, 1962) that this substance is 9-oxodec-*trans*-2-enoic acid, that it is produced by the mandibular glands of the queen and spreads throughout the colony by the regurgitation of food from worker to worker. The presence of this substance in the colony inhibits queen-cell building and other activities appropriate to control of reproduction and to swarming. Besides the queen substance which acts through ingestion only, there is an inhibitory scent found on all parts of the body surface of the queen which can exert a small effect without actual ingestion. The exact source and constitution of this is not yet known. Some observations of Chauvin (1958) suggest that the method of communication between members of a colony of the ant *Formica rufa* when building its nest is in some respects similar to that of bees. Thus if wooden boards are stuck into the dome of the nest so as to divide it into quadrants the ants will carry out repair work to one or at most two of the quadrants, neglecting the others. But if the boards are perforated below the surface so that the ants can pass through, nest construction continues normally. These observations suggest that there is a net of communications beneath the surface.

Perhaps an even more remarkable example of such flexibility in repair is shown by the work of Dembowski (1933) on the tube-building of the caddis larva of the genus *Molanna* (Fig. 5), quoted by Russell (1945). If deprived of its case, the insect will build a new one of the same pattern, and this it does by burying itself in the sand, backing downwards, and pushing a mound of sand grains towards its head, at the same time binding them into a loose bundle with silk from the labial glands. This forms an anchor to which the insect then attaches its anal hooks. Having done this, it makes a ring or section of tube round its body, carefully selecting suitable pieces to fit into the growing mosaic by adding material from the anterior edge. The ring is gradually extended into a tube which, when long enough, is cut free from the holdfast. Wings are built by stretching at full length out of the tube, but as the insect always keeps its anal hooks within the tube, it cannot reach back far enough to complete the hinder part of the wings, and it usually achieves the normal and typical shape by lengthening the tube in front and cutting it off behind. Cutting away an unwanted part may also occur as follows: if a number of larvæ are ejected from their cases but allowed to return, they fail to get back to the right ones, and some of course get cases which are too large and others too small. The larva which gets into too large a case first cuts off a piece of the front of the tube and then a piece of the overhanging roof, as shown in the accompanying illustration (Fig. 5), thus getting once more a tube of the right size. But the power of adaptation to accidental injury of the case does not end here. If the roof is damaged, the missing part may be simply replaced. If the hinder part or up to 15 per cent. of the case is removed, an extra piece will be built on in front and the posterior part of the case is cut away. The insect may then extend it in front as before, or alternatively it may turn round and restore the missing part and then turn back again. Thirdly, it may turn round, build wings and roof at the hind end, making them effectually the front end for the rest of its life. If more than the posterior half of the case is cut away—if, say, two-thirds is removed —then the variety of response is very great. Dembowski described six main ones: Firstly, a new case may be built, a piece of the old one merely being used as a holdfast which is later cut away. Secondly, the case may be repaired by building on its front. Thirdly, repair may be accomplished by building on at the back and then turning and cutting off the roof and front part of the tube, then rebuilding the former. Fourthly, there is the possibility of building a new front end on to the hinder part and inhabiting it, but leaving the original front intact so that we now have a tube with two fronts. Fifthly, a new front end may be built and the rest trimmed off so as to create a permanently reversed tube.

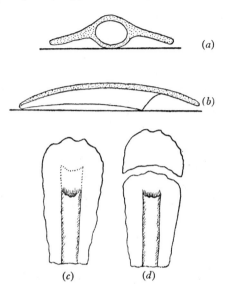

Lastly, the insect may build first in front and then cut off the new roof, reverse and build the hind end. In all these examples we get the impression that the goal is not a sequence of actions, or not that alone,

FIG. 5—The case of the caddis larva *Molanna*.
  (*a*) Section.
  (*b*) Side view.
  (*c*) & (*d*) Alterations made when a small larva acquires too large a case.
    (*c*) A section of the front end of the tube removed.
    (*d*) A large part of the overhanging roof removed (following day).
(After Dembowski, 1933.)

but the construction of a case, or nest, of a particular pattern. It is true that these observations are in one sense unsatisfactory, in that the experiments should really have been performed only with animals which were constructing their cases for the first time. For otherwise it is always possible to argue that the previous experience of building a completed nest or tube by an innate chain-reflex series of actions may have *resulted in* a learning of the details of the goal object. Indeed, Dembowski has shown that there is improvement in case-building with repetition of experience, for when four consecutive cases are built by the same individual, the fourth is better in a number of respects than is the first. But, whether previous experience does or does not lead to the learning of details of the final stimulus, this work does very strongly suggest the existence of an extremely short-term purpose guiding the actions towards a goal.

Further observations on the process by which *Molanna* selects the material for its case are provided by Szlep (1958*b*).

Fankhauser and Reik (1935) in America have published accounts of the nest-building of the caddis-fly larva, *Neuronia postica*, when supplied with abnormal materials for making the cases and when the first and second pairs of larval legs are lacking. Even in these conditions, the larva showed remarkable adaptability in achieving the construction of cases which were surprisingly near normality. Dudziak (1950) has carried out a similar study on the caddis *Phryganea* and Miklaszewska (1948) on the aquatic caterpillar of *Nymphula*. Brickenstein (1955) finds however that the snare construction of the caddis *Neureclipsis* is very dependent on water-current and other conditions. See also the work of Szlep (1958*a*) on the effect of external factors on the structural properties of the web of the Garden Spider. Lecomte (1957, in press) has described the remarkable variety of apparently adaptive methods by which spiders of the genus *Nephila* deal with foreign bodies placed in their webs and the damage to the webs caused by them.

Perhaps we should mention one final example, in some ways the most remarkable of all. Lindauer (1952) in his studies of the division of labour among workers of the hive bee has shown that the programme of work carried out by the individual is not determined by the physiological state of the insect, but is dictated by the needs of the colony as a whole. It seems clear that regulation by the colony's needs must be through an elaborate series of releasers, mostly proprioceptive, since in the darkness of the hive vision is impossible. Thus the individual cell-building worker seldom or never herself carries out in complete, correct and uninterrupted sequence the whole process of cell construction. Yet she does every action in this sequence innumerable times as and where required. She may start a cell with the wax plates from her own glands which she has manipulated, she may then put the finishing touches to another cell using wax supplied by another bee or perhaps a bit of old capping taken and moulded up from a cell temporarily out of use. Then, again, sometimes using wax from another worker, sometimes her own, she will perform the laborious and delicate tasks of planing and polishing to produce the thin cell walls—all this in the intervals of performing duties of entirely different kinds, such as feeding larvæ, storing nectar or attending the queen. The same problem has been studied by Free (1955) in relation to the colonies of bumble bees.[1]

[1] The logical and statistical pitfalls involved in attempting to interpret observations on sequences of behaviour are only just coming to be realised. Thus Wenner (1961) has shown that the behavioural sequences observed in a honey-bee colony might, if the system is in fact controlled by a Markov process, be explicable on three assumptions: (i) that transition from one activity to another takes place at random; (ii) that the probabilities of transitions to different activities differ, depending upon the nature of the two

To recapitulate: It seems, then, that in much of appetitive behaviour the animal's own activities, provided they are proceeding in a co-ordinated manner and in the *right direction*, must be self-rewarding and self-stimulating until the full releaser for the next stage of the appetitive behaviour has been achieved. Thus it often appears as if the releasers which are active during the progress of the appetitive behaviour act not merely as releasers of specific action potential which has already accumulated, but also as a stimulant enabling the behaviour concerned to maintain or increase more action potential. In other words, much appetitive behaviour is also in a sense the consummatory act.

This is already becoming apparent in work on imprinting in relation with the following reaction of young Moorhens and Coots (Hinde, Thorpe and Vince, 1956), and the fact has also been commented upon by Hinde (1952) with special reference to the Great Tit. Hinde concludes that appetitive behaviour and consummatory act differ only in degree, and that no absolute distinction can be made between them. Both are to some extent 'spontaneous' in that they show evidence of internal activation, and both are stereotyped to some degree and show some rigidity. Thus the classic examples of appetitive behaviour and consummatory act can be regarded as the two ends of a series ranging from extreme variability and plasticity on the one hand to almost complete fixity on the other.

It is of course in oriented, as distinct from unoriented, appetitive behaviour that the system can be self-reinforcing and re-exciting; and in such a process learning plays an essential part. Psychologically it appears as if the animal is both self-re-exciting and is also responding to dimly perceived goals which are striven for. In other words, it exhibits the appearance of conation. There is no doubt, as will be made clear in later chapters, that one of the functions of learning, or conditioning, within the appetitive behaviour is to sharpen and adapt and modify the I.R.M., and that the releasing situation for the consummatory act is achieved by the activities of the animal itself coming progressively nearer to the full or 'ideal' pattern. In at least the more variable types of appetitive behaviour, the animal must often be working out its own releasers, and the details of its actions are being moulded in part by the environment, until by one of perhaps a large number of alternative routes—routes which vary greatly in detail—the final releasing pattern is achieved. This 'working out' of a releaser may be a literal building up as in nest-building, or it may be a correct orientation to an external object. Thus a correct orientation to a nest site which leads to the first stages of nest-building

activities involved; (iii) that the probability of the same transition changes with the age of the individual or under environmental change. This and other aspects of the problems raised by the observation of random and non-random sequences of behaviour and their relation to Markov chains have been discussed by Cane (1961).

or a correct orientation to the opposite sex so that the display is fully stimulative will help in each case to build up the releasers necessary to unlock the I.R.M. blocking the next phase of the main line of the instinctive behaviour. In appetitive behaviour, learning must also enter to develop the I.R.M.[1] which releases the next element. This implies that the releaser for appetitive behaviour must include, or incorporate, some kind of one-way gradient, such that the more generalised or less specific elements only act as releasers for the appetitive behaviour until a more detailed form is learnt. Such learning proceeds by a process such that the stages nearer to the full specific pattern are more effective as reinforcing activities than are the stages farther removed therefrom.[2] Thus, perhaps by a kind of trial-and-error learning process, an *extremely limited* insight that the animal seems to have into the immediate nature of its goals is developed and increased by an insight *arising out of* experience.

The theoretical implication of such flexible appetitive behaviour is fundamental for the idea of drive. The concept of a drive coming from above, through predetermined channels or along prearranged paths, and so taking the animal inexorably towards a particular consummatory act, could provide a theory that would work well enough for much of the simple and more stereotyped kinds of instinctive behaviour. But how can a superimposed drive, coming from a higher centre, account for the types of behaviour we have just been considering, unless in fact there are already, preformed within the nervous system, a series of alternative paths of great elaboration, in some cases almost unlimited elaboration, each leading to the same final goal? That such could be the complete explanation of the nest-repair abilities of some of the higher Hymenoptera, or indeed of the nest-closing and nest-approach behaviour of insects such as *Ammophila*, seems highly improbable.

---

[1] It is envisaged that the innate releasive mechanism is modified as a result of experience of particular situations in which the response did or did not lead to a closer approximation to the goal situation.

[2] The concept of heterogeneous summation (Seitz, 1940), whereby different elements which go to make up a total inherited releasing pattern can act separately, but can also summate to give steadily increasing stimulation as more and more elements are added, can no doubt help here. But it is scarcely credible that every conceivable component of a complex releaser is separately and independently inherited as a distinct unit acting autonomously. It is far more in line with our present understanding of perceptual processes to suppose that the recognition of the over-all pattern is the fundamental innate unit, and that the animal is also endowed with a faculty of learning or perception whereby the details of the pattern later come to be perceived in relation to the whole. This secondary learning of the individual components of a total pattern is such a general feature of examples of animal behaviour as different as the locality learning of Hymenoptera and the recognition of individual members of the species by birds (see pp. 427 *et seq.* below) that it is reasonable to assume that it is also involved in the process of responding to details of the releasers. The matter should be tested critically by comparing the innate response of 'naïve' animals to the parts, *followed* by the whole, with that to the parts *after* experience of the whole.

It seems, therefore, that the facts of variable and highly oriented appetitive behaviour are incompatible with any theory postulating *solely* a drive imposed from above, discharging down particular paths or channels—though this seems a necessary part of any comprehensive theory. Clearly we also need the concept of action specific energy, as originating from the, as yet unrealised, consummatory act. Moreover we must suppose that the very process of sharpening and developing the I.R.M. by learning and of building up a complex releasing situation, in which the specific movements of the animal and the products of these movements are combined to form a releaser, is itself producing and accumulating more specific action potential. In other words, the appetitive behaviour actions are not by themselves fully consummatory. They are, however, self-stimulating and consummatory when they are proceeding towards the proper goal. There is a one-way character about them. If they are, in fact, to perform the necessary function in the life of the animal, we must suppose that there is a self-reinforcing and stimulating tendency when they are proceeding in the biologically correct or appropriate direction, and perhaps a self-inhibiting tendency when they are misdirected.

The fact that the I.R.M. is, within limits, modifiable and adjustable and capable of building itself up in this manner should, of course, occasion no surprise. Modern views, actually dating from Woodworth (1915), which regard perception as a reaction, suggest that it is possible to treat perception in many respects like a response (Berlyne, 1951), and that the building up of complex perception may resemble in a number of ways the build-up of a motor habit. It is interesting, in this connection, to note that Prechtl (1952) has shown that fatigue may occur in the centre of the I.R.M. as well as in the nervous mechanism controlling the response, and the work of Glanzer, Deese and others on stimulus satiation quoted in Chapter I (p. 11) is very relevant here.

In conclusion, it seems that we have first to get back to the idea of action specific 'energy' being generated, through some feed-back or other mechanism, by the later or lower elements in the hierarchy of behaviour, as originally postulated by Lorenz. Also we have to assume (as did the hormic psychologists) that there is within the drive itself some inherent directiveness, some extremely restricted purposive influence, perhaps, identical within the expectancy and insight discussed below, which is in some degree independent of any pre-existing channels. In fact, both conclusions seem to be an essential part of a complete theory. What cannot possibly provide an adequate account of all animal behaviour is the conclusion that all is the expression of some non-directive force rigidly confined within a previously co-ordinated system of conduits.

Up to this point we have been using the term 'appetitive behaviour' in a fairly restricted sense, for behaviour where fixed-action patterns or random locomotion are a conspicuous feature. But ethologists tend now to include more and more of learning within appetitive behaviour, since appetitive behaviour is by definition a variable part of instinct. So we must now look at the drive in learning and in perception, consider what it implies and what its scope is, for it seems unlikely to be fundamentally different in the two contexts.

SUMMARY

1. The history of the idea of instinct is briefly traced. It is suggested that the most essential and fundamental part of the concept is that of 'internal drive,' and that this drive cannot be considered solely as the expression of some primary physiological need in the ordinary sense of that term.

2. Other important characteristics of instinct are three: (a) It is an inherited system of co-ordination; (b) it involves more or less rigid inherited action patterns; and (c) more or less rigid inherited releasing mechanisms. Largely because of the complexity of the perceptual side, the workers who provided the impetus for modern ethology, especially Lorenz, concentrated attention on the 'fixed-action pattern' or consummatory act. Such fixed-action patterns are often as specifically constant as are anatomical structures, and are potentially of equal value for phylogenetic studies.

3. Lorenz's chief contribution to the concept of drive was that of action specific 'energy'; according to which the fixed-action pattern is supposed to provide the chief source of the drive and not *vice versa*. This has the great advantage that it accounts for the consummatory act being the effective goal of the behaviour, and so, in many instances, obviates the clearly impossible alternative necessity of supposing that the animal is aware of the biological final cause of its activities. It also provides a convenient system accounting for the phenomena of vacuum activities and displacement.

4. The distinction between appetitive behaviour and consummatory act, although relative rather than absolute, was another methodologically very important advance, due primarily to a physiologist (Sherrington), but developed later by ethologists.

5. Embryological studies now suggest that, ontogenetically, complex muscle co-ordinations resembling fixed-action patterns precede responses of the simple reflex type in mammals.

6. The types of evidence for the reduction in motivation specific to a group of activities are briefly considered.

7. The hierarchy system of Tinbergen is discussed with special reference to the problem of the nature of drive. The difficulties in the way of

visualising the hierarchy mechanism as a system of completely preformed and discrete channels are regarded as insuperable. Nevertheless some substantial new support from the neurophysiological side has recently been produced.

8. The concepts of releaser and innate releasive mechanism are briefly outlined.

9. The concept of appetitive behaviour is regarded as crucial for the problem of drive. Where appetitive behaviour is relatively stereotyped and consists of random or unoriented locomotion, as in klinokinesis, it raises few questions. But where it is more variable and has to be precisely directed or oriented, some important problems arise. In order to account for the flexible directiveness of appetitive behaviour, that is for the overall appearance of purpose displayed, there are two possible alternatives. It is necessary either to postulate a very great variety and complexity of preformed pathways which serve as alternatives, some of which come to be preferred by a trial-and-error process as a result of reinforcement by the attainment of a releasing situation and the ensuing consummatory act. Or, failing this, one must assume a directiveness in the sense that progressive approximations to the 'ideal' releasers are perceived and so reinforced, with the result that the animal, by means of an extremely short-term purposiveness and anticipation, succeeds in steadily sharpening the configuration of the I.R.M. Thus by gradually building up its own releasers, the appetitive behaviour becomes directional. It is concluded that the I.R.M. must have inhibitory as well as releasing functions and that there may, indeed, be special 'Innate Inhibitory Mechanisms.'

10. It is thus suggested that, to account adequately for all varieties of appetitive behaviour, it is necessary to assume that the fixed action pattern, by a feed-back mechanism or some other device, is effectively generating some specific action potential, and that apart from mere directiveness some extremely short-term purpose in the drive itself must also be postulated. The concept of appetitive behaviour as the expression of nothing more than a completely non-directive force, or drive, rigidly confined within a previously co-ordinated system of conduits, seems inadequate.

PART II

LEARNING

CHAPTER III

HABITUATION

It will be seen from what has been said already that a very large part of learning in animals is to be considered as the process of adjusting more or less fixed automatisms or patterns of behaviour and more or less rigid releasing mechanisms to the changes and chances of life in the world. The extent of the possible adjustment is always limited though it may vary greatly, being in some circumstances very large and in others almost infinitesimal. But whether large or small, it is the object of this chapter, and of some of those that follow, to consider learning from this point of view, and see how far it can be fitted into the current concepts of instinct; and in particular how far its comprehension is furthered when it is regarded as characteristic of appetitive behaviour.

Since the term 'learning' itself, as used in everyday speech, is certainly not an absolutely precise one and will be found on reflection to contain many overtones of meaning, it is hardly to be expected that complete agreement can be reached about its definition. We can define learning as that process which manifests itself by adaptive changes in individual behaviour as a result of experience; or, to put it another way, the organisation of behaviour as a result of individual experience. This is certainly not a definition which will appeal to all, but perhaps it has fewer objectionable features than other comprehensive definitions of learning, unless these are made so general and imprecise as to lose almost all exact meaning.

Hilgard and Marquis (1940) define learning as a change in the strength of an act through training procedures (whether in the laboratory or in the natural environment) as distinguished from changes in the strength of the act by factors not attributable to training. But to rule out new acts and new combinations of acts in this way seems unjustifiable and in fact contrary to the authors' own implicit usage. Skinner (1953, p. 65) introduces an equally arbitrary restriction of another kind. He reserves the term for 'the reassortment of responses in a complex situation'—a definition which surely begs almost all questions. However, it is apparently designed to *exclude* rewarded learning, for which he reserves the term 'conditioning.' In the definition proposed for use in this book, the terms which are most likely to give rise to criticism are the words 'adaptive' and 'experience.' The very term 'learning,' in fact, implies 'adapted,' and the definition

here adopted, like all others, must be regarded as in some respects a com-
promise. An organism which is learning is certainly not a completely
passive entity entirely at the mercy of the external forces impinging upon
it; and if we agree to keep the word 'experience' in our definition—a
word which, by the way, itself conceals something of the concept of learning—we are thereby recognising, and are indeed to some extent taking
up, the position of Agar (1943), who regards the idea of experience as
a fundamental one in theoretical biology. 'Experience', then, must stand;
but perhaps we can get over some of the objection to the word 'adaptive'
by making it clear that by 'adaptive change' we mean a change which is
'economical' over a considerable stretch of the animal's life.

In the Hilgard and Marquis definition it is the word 'training' which
is the chief source of ambiguity. It may seem at first sight that both
'adaptive' and 'training' could be left out in each case; and that learning
can be defined merely as change in individual behaviour as a result of
stimulation. Such a definition, however, opens the door more widely to
many kinds of change in which behaviour tends to disorganisation. Such
changes commonly result from fatigue, from injury and from sensory
accommodation. Also there are those changes due to 'inertia'; as where an
organism continues for a while to perform a set of actions into which it
was originally forced by the environment, even though such action has
become useless or deleterious to the organism. If this difficulty is to be
evaded, therefore, it is necessary to rule out, so far as possible, the effects
of violence, surgical or otherwise, and of all stimulation so excessive as
normally to be injurious to and avoided by the organism. So we come back
to the necessity of trying to define learning solely in terms of conservation
of the whole organic system concerned, and once we do that the idea of
adaptation again comes in. And certainly the expression 'training procedures' itself contains this concept. So it seems best to make it clear that in
the present state of knowledge we are bound to consider the animal not
merely as a physico-chemical mechanism, however elaborate, but as an
organic or vital system in the usual present meaning of the term. And in
the individual, self-preservation by means of adaptation to a changing and
unstable environment is one of the most reliable criteria for distinguishing
living from non-living.

Many workers have considered that the more or less frequent repetition of a stimulus or of a changed situation is necessary for learning; but,
while it is true that most learning comes about as a result of repeated application of a stimulus or combination of stimuli, such repetition can be no
necessary part of the concept because we all know that learning can, on
occasion, result from one experience only.

It is of course important, in any study of animal behaviour, to be on
our guard against confusing change of behaviour due to learning with

change of behaviour due to growth and maturation. It is easy enough to distinguish between these in a verbal definition: it is sometimes far from easy to separate them in practice. If, for instance, we follow the development of a young bird, we see almost daily changes in its behaviour and capabilities. Yet it does not follow that these represent learning. Ahlquist (1937) has provided some interesting facts on the time of appearance of the maturation of various instinctive behaviour patterns of the young of various species of *Sterna, Larus* and *Stercorarius*. At first sight these might appear to be due to differences in individual learning ability. In fact, they are nothing of the kind; although, as we shall see later, learning often has an important part to play in perfecting the skill with which an animal develops such actions. Such examples show how dangerous it is to dogmatise upon the subject without determining by actual experiment how far learning enters into the story. Tinbergen (1951*a*) has pointed out that maturation of behaviour in the young bird differs from its annual development in the adult bird in an important respect. The annual growth of behaviour patterns in the adult is due to changing hormone concentration, and with growing hormone concentration it is appetitive behaviour which is manifested first, the full consummatory act not appearing until the appetitive behaviour is complete. The reaction is thus completed by an extension from the generalised behaviour towards the more specialised behaviour until the instinctive consummatory act is reached. In the growth of instinct in the young bird the stereotyped components at or near the end of the chain come first; while the introductory elements, which constitute the appetitive behaviour, are added afterwards—a complete reversal of the order found in annual maturation.[1] Thus a young bird may go through the motions of drinking water but have to learn from experience that water is the stuff to drink; and similarly with bathing. Again, the young bird will display the pecking response almost perfectly co-ordinated from the first, but in many cases it has to learn entirely by experience what is good for food. That is, it has to learn the appropriate objects of its inborn automatisms. Of course, as the frequent references to the innate releasive mechanism in this book show, many animals also have inborn perceptual filters or recognition mechanisms which tend to restrict their first efforts to the most appropriate objects. Thus young chicks (Rheingold and Hess, 1957) tend to peck at objects which show a combination of bright, reflecting surfaces and movement, and this of course has the effect of attracting them to drops of water, and to wet places. Similarly, as has been shown on p. 141 below, the initial preference for round three-

[1] Tinbergen originally based this statement upon what was apparently a misinterpretation of the work of Kortlandt (1940). Nevertheless there seems to be considerable evidence for it.

dimensional objects will also help young chicks to peck at water drops, as well as food grains.

There is no doubt that in some instances birds learn to improve the actions themselves as a result of practice, but it is extraordinary how small a part practice appears to play in many cases. To give one example only, Grohmann (1938) reared young pigeons in narrow tubes which prevented them from moving their wings. Thus they could not carry out the incipient flights which would naturally be regarded as in the nature of practice. When Grohmann's control birds, which were allowed free 'practice flights' every day, had progressed to a certain point, both groups were tested for flying ability, but no difference was found between them. In other words, the instinctive behaviour pattern of flight had been maturing at a steady rate, quite irrespective of the birds' opportunity of exercising it. Those that had been kept in the tubes had reached just the same stage of development as those that had had what appeared to be the 'advantage' of practice. There is little reasonable doubt that at a later stage further skill in the fine adjustment of flight is acquired as a result of practice (the whole subject is discussed more fully below, where examples will be found from many other groups), but this work of Grohmann's suffices as yet another warning to show how cautious one must be in interpreting what appears to be the learning behaviour of young birds.

A very similar story emerges from studies of the first flights of insects, although here the learning component is reduced almost if not quite to vanishing point. Thus Peterson, Lundgren and Wilson (1956–57) found that with the butterfly *Pieris napi* the fundamental motor patterns of flight are already fully developed in the emerging butterfly and the effects neither of maturation nor of practice could be detected. It is true that over the first few days there is an increase of flight capacity, and this more persistent flight habit may possibly be due to a development of motor ability as a result of maturation. However, it is significant that the rate of hardening of the wing cuticula is rather similar to that of the increase of flight capacity, and is perhaps the only factor increasing flight capacity during the first days after emergence.

Viewed from one standpoint, learning ability appears to show an essential uniformity throughout the animal kingdom, displaying a smooth and gradual course of development from the simplest a-cellular animals right up to man himself. Seen from another angle, discontinuities appear. There are phases and periods of development in every science where it is profitable or convenient to emphasise the similarities, and other phases where understanding is better reached through distinguishing differences and attempting to formulate them as exactly as possible. From the theoretical or philosophical standpoint, it is sometimes revealing, even though from a physiological point of view it must almost certainly be erroneous, to consider all learning throughout the animal kingdom as a single type of process. But although it is sometimes profitable to look for differences and at others to concentrate on similarities, the field of learning is so vast and the manifestations of learning ability so numerous, that it is not in practice possible, either on the descriptive level or for many purposes of analysis, to consider learning as a simple coherent and indivisible phenomenon. If only to grasp and co-ordinate the available facts, we have to produce some sort of classification. It cannot really be a physiological classification—knowledge is as yet far too fragmentary for that. It has to be, therefore, a behavioural classification.

At first sight a convenient way to divide up the subject might seem to be into effector learning on the one hand and receptor learning on the other. According to this plan, effector learning would be change in the degree and organisation of the muscle contractions, and receptor learning would be change in the organisation of perceptions and in the responsiveness to stimuli (cf. Chapter IV). Such division, however, while most attractive at first sight, quickly runs into difficulties. While it is undoubted that with the production of a new action pattern or 'habit' we do get a simple change in the organisation of muscle contractions, yet we must not forget that such a change is bound up in the most intimate manner with the change in the organisation of the proprioceptive stimuli which are being received as a result of those very muscle contractions. If our physiological techniques and knowledge were vastly greater than they are, it might be possible to make such a distinction. As it is, it appears to be quite impossible to do so and that what we would call effector learning becomes merely another name for proprioceptive learning. This, in fact, might not be a bad line of demarcation. We might consider learning as being conveniently divisible into two types: (a) that which is involved with the organisation of and response to proprioceptive stimuli, and (b) that which is concerned with the organisation of all other stimuli. But whether that is convenient or not, it does not make the fundamental distinction between two types which a true division into effector and receptor learning would make. It is merely just another way of separating or cataloguing sensory stimuli. Moreover, the facts of re-afference, as seen particularly in optomotor responses and taxes (Mittelstaedt, see Dijkgraaf, 1953), speak against it.

This attempt to divide learning into effector and receptor learning has been made the basis for a rather different classification by Pringle (1951). He considers together two types of conditioning, members of the first sharing the feature that the release of the response has no influence on the learning process. In this category come classical conditioned reflexes, or conditioned reflect Type I, and the phenomenon known as latent learning which, from this point of view, can be defined as the association of indifferent stimuli or situations without patent reward. All other types of learning, as he points out, are different, in that the release of the response or at least the direction of the process, i.e. whether the result is positive learning or negative learning, depends on the nature of subsequent events. In this category come habituation, conditioned reflexes Type II, trial-and-error learning and insight learning. But while such a division shows up this one important relation, there are others which it obscures, and it has some of the drawbacks shown by the system discussed above and due to the fact, there referred to, that our knowledge of the organisation of proprioceptive stimuli is still so rudimentary. From the behavioural, evolutionary and phylogenetic point of view it is much simpler, therefore, to consider habituation first, in that only one exteroceptive sensory field is necessarily involved; it is non-associative, and is in that respect simpler than the rest. Moreover, habituation, as will be seen, in so far as it can be considered as the dropping out of the response when that response does not lead to a consummatory act, can be more closely and directly related to the system of instinctive behaviour than can associative conditioning. Let us, then, take habituation first.

To Humphrey (1933) must be given the credit for the first clear and comprehensive discussion of habituation and the first full exposition of its fundamental importance. Used in its widest sense, habituation is a simple learning not to respond to stimuli which tend to be without significance in the life of the animal; and stimuli which are without significance obviously cannot serve to release consummatory acts. Habituation thus implies a tendency merely to drop out responses, not to incorporate new ones or complicate those already present. In this respect it is certainly the simplest kind of learning and something like it is universal in animals. Perhaps, indeed, in one or other of its forms it may be said to be one of the fundamental properties of living matter. Phenomena resembling habituation in at least some respects have been known and studied in human beings for some thirty years. Thus Dodge (1923) recorded the after-nystagmus of the eyes following cessation of rotation, and found habituation occurring both during a number of trials spaced out at intervals of some minutes and also from day to day during a series of trials lasting a week. Because of its importance for airplane pilots, the psychology and physiology of nystagmus habituation has been the subject of a considerable volume of subsequent work, much of which is summarised by Wendt (1951). There appear to be two forms of the phenomenon, present both in men and monkeys, one type being preventable by keeping the human subject attentive to the external surroundings. This fact probably accounts for the very conflicting accounts that have been published as to the ability of airplane pilots and others to accommodate themselves to repeated rotation. Dodge (1927) also investigated habituation of patellar and eye-blink reflexes as a result of repeated series of stimulations extending over nearly two years. It was found that while knee-jerks became slower but changed little in amplitude, the eye-blink changed little, if at all, in timing but decreased in extent.

But perhaps the first precise account of habituation in animals as distinct from humans is that given by Humphrey, using the snail *Helix albolabris*. When the sub-stratum on which the animal is walking is subjected to a mechanical shock, the tentacles are at once withdrawn for a short time. If the mechanical shock is repeated at regular intervals and the intensity of the stimulus maintained exactly constant, the extent and duration of the tentacle withdrawal steadily decreases until finally the animal has become absolutely indifferent to the stimulus. If, during the course of the experiment, the intensity of the stimulus is increased, then the response reappears for a while, only to wane again on repetition.[1] As Humphrey pointed out, habituation, or something very like it, is found in organisms of all evolutionary grades, and many examples will be given later in this book. Habituation can, therefore, be defined as the relatively permanent waning of a response as a result of repeated stimulation which is not followed by any kind of reinforcement. It is specific to the stimulus.[2] and relatively enduring, and so it is natural to regard it, provisionally at any rate, as distinct from fatigue and sensory adaptation. Such a distinction is particularly necessary with habituation because it is a waning of a response; but it is, of course, also necessary, as with other types of learning, to attempt to distinguish it from maturation and injury.

The distinction from fatigue may in some respects be artificial, for it is to be noted that muscle physiologists are placing much less reliance than formerly on the idea that fatigue is the result of accumulation of waste products. Firstly, apparent fatigue may, as in the flight muscle of *Drosophila* (Wigglesworth, 1949), be due as much to overstrain of the mechanism for mobilisation of the glycogen reserves as to undue concentration of metabolites. Then there are likely to be fatigue phenomena at the motor end-plate and the synapse, and so we see that muscular fatigue is more plausibly regarded as a state of disequilibrium involving a number of factors, including perhaps interference between two or more nervous processes, rather than a simple matter of waste-product accumulation. (See also Berlyne, 1951.) However hard it may be to make a distinction between fatigue and habituation in vertebrates and the higher invertebrates, it becomes far more difficult, if not impossible, to do so in the

---

[1] A more detailed account of this work appears in Chapter X, below.

[2] A more or less temporary decrease in responsiveness which is also specific to the stimulus, is probably best regarded as 'stimulus satiation' or 'releaser satiation' (see Chapter II, above). But so few examples have yet been analysed that the term 'habituation' will certainly continue in use for a long time to come as a provisional general expression for various types of stimulus-specific response-fading.

lower organisms where there is no clearly defined nervous system. But for the present we must consider it only as it is manifest in organisms at or above the annelid-arthropod level.

The practical reasons for distinguishing between habituation and sensory accommodation are obvious; for a fairly rapid recovery from stimulation to be ready to respond again is a *sine qua non* for efficient sense-organ function. An eye or a nose which is insensitive to stimulation on Tuesday because it was exposed to it on Monday is either an exceedingly inefficient organ or else it has been over-stimulated to such an extent that we can say it has been injured. And so we take it for granted, as a general rule, that the long-maintained waning of response as a result of a stimulation must be a kind of learning, and we assume that it is correlated with a change in the central nervous system and not merely with one in the sense organ. Here again there is, of course, no absolute certainty, and indeed we have no grounds whatever for assuming that because the waning of a response is a brief matter it cannot be due to a central nervous change and must be peripheral. There is the temporary 'stimulus satiation' mentioned above. Some recent work by Dethier (1952) has illustrated this. Dethier studied the response of the tarsal receptors of the Blowfly when stimulated by solutions of certain sugars, the degree of the response being evaluated by recording the tendency of the animal to extend its proboscis and to drink. It was found that what had previously appeared to be a simple sense-organ accommodation could be secured by exposing the sense organs in one front leg only and then testing the response by stimulating the unexposed contralateral leg just as well as by exposing the same leg again. The effect was of extremely short duration: for sucrose it varied from 1 to 13 seconds. But while it is very likely that the tarsal chemical sense organs had become accommodated to some extent, these experiments seem to show quite clearly that the process which was being measured was not sensory accommodation but a state which had been brought about at some level in the central nervous system. So, while an effect of long duration must certainly—one would think—be central, an effect of short duration may be either peripheral or central or both. Further details of these important experiments will be found below in the chapter dealing with arthropod and insect learning.

Observations of this kind raise again the whole problem of fading of responses and their relation to habituation. Sherrington (1906, p. 222) pointed out that the waning of the scratch reflex under fatigue gives a slower rhythm and a sluggishness for the later beats which is not found in waning due to inhibition, and Konorski (1948, pp. 78–9) has no doubt whatever that the mechanism by which habituation takes place, while it may be analogous to the extinction of the conditioned reflex, has no relation at all to the gradual fading of spinal reflexes through their too frequent repetition, or to the decrease of reaction of a neuro-muscular prep-aration kept in an unstable physiological state, etc. He points out that in these latter cases the disappearance of the function is explained by a period of sub-normal excitability following fatigue or poisoning or other lesion, or by some cyclic change. Habituation, by contrast, cannot be referable to any of these categories. He adduces many proofs. First there is the clear evidence that habituation takes place even when the intervals between the stimuli are very long—24 hours or even longer—so that neither a functional exhaustion nor a sub-normal period can possibly account for the process. Again, habituation (as shown in Pavlov's experi-ments) occurs more rapidly the better the functional condition of the ner-vous system, and it certainly seems to be more marked in animals higher in phylogenetic development and of a more elaborate grade of nervous organisation. Thirdly, it is known that in animals in which the cerebral cortex has been removed, habituation usually takes place incomparably more slowly than in normal animals and often cannot be demonstrated at all—although Lebidinskiaia and Rosenthal (1935) report what appears to have been true habituation of the orientation response to sound in a decorticate dog. So he concludes that in a normal animal the kind of stimulus which provokes an orientation reaction leads to changes of two kinds in the nervous system. Firstly there are cycles of comparatively short duration consisting of transient changes in the excitato-inhibitory organisation of the nervous system resulting from the given stimulation. This is the property by virtue of which the nerve cells react to the incom-ing impulses with the given pattern of excitability changes, and is simply the expression, in what we might call neo-Pavlovian language, of the concept of specific motivation. Secondly there are certain more promi-nent changes or transformations which arise in particular systems of neurones. They are generally called plastic changes and are evidence of plasticity in the nervous system. These are, in fact, all the changes which we shall consider as conditioning and learning, whereas the changes of the first type include, besides changes in threshold and level of specific motivation, such things as changes of excitability due to reflex antagon-ism. It is axiomatic that excitability is a universal feature of the nervous system, and so we must expect excitability changes to be characteristic of all studies of nervous-system behaviour. Plasticity, on the other hand, is in general a characteristic only of the highest division of the nervous system, and in the higher vertebrates especially of the cerebral cortex.

The Pavlov school have, of course, studied what is essentially habitua-tion under the term 'extinction of the orientation reflex,' a term which, while once useful to the physiologist, is clumsy and inadequate when we are considering the biology of the animal as a whole. Certainly the process of extinction of a conditioned reflex under internal inhibition shows many of the characteristics which we seem to see in habituation, and Konorski thinks of the two as analogous. He assumes, for instance, that habituation upon the repetition of a stimulus is due to a formation of inhibitory connections between certain intervening centres in just the same manner as he explains the extinction of conditioned reflexes. He points out that this would explain the striking qualitative similarity of the properties of the two processes: for instance, when the application of a stimulus is suspended for some time, the response which has been habituated tends to recover spontaneously in much the same way as does the extinguished conditioned reflex. Similarly the habituated response can even (according to Konorski, p. 145) be dis-inhibited by another extraneous stimulus, and so forth. He suggests the only important difference between the two processes is that, whereas the extinguished conditioned reflex and the superimposed inhibitory conditioned reflex are both acquired and are dependent mainly on the cerebral cortex, the response which is subject to habituation is itself inborn or presumed to be so. With mammals this is of sub-cortical origin, unlike its inhibition which, being formed 'on the basis of the animal's individual experience, originates chiefly in the cerebral cortex' (p. 146). But though, up to a point, extinction of conditioned reflex and habituation can be compared in this way, we must remember that an explanation of the normal C.R. extinction in terms of 'counter conditioning' is possible, and, indeed, in the typical process of extinction there is strong evidence that something more than habituation is involved, and that the effects of sheer repetition are complicated by the fact that this repetition is taking place in connection with a conditioned response which is in some degree incompatible with it. In other words, there is a competing response which acts as an inhibitor. The question is—can we conceive of habituation as being the expression of any such inhibiting competitor? But before we can answer this question we must inquire how far the interference theory really covers the facts of the extinction of the normal conditioned reflex. In fact, we find that it runs into great difficulties, for in the first place there are so many examples of such extinction where the stimulus is merely withheld and there seems to be nothing in the nature of a competing stimulus to provide the supposed interference (although, of course, it is easy to miss the new stimulus if the experimenter is not particularly looking for it). Then, as Razran's (1939) review shows (see also Spence, 1951), conditioning tends to be faster under spaced trials, whereas extinction is superior when the trials are massed; and there are many other examples in which the two processes are affected differently by identical treatment. So we are forced to the conclusion that interference, though a factor real enough in certain situations, cannot provide a full explanation of the classical reflex inhibition, and therefore, *a fortiori*, cannot serve as a theoretical basis for habituation. In fact, it looks as if the 'decrement by repetition' which is the core of habituation is also present in examples of classical C.R. extinction, but that in many such cases there is something else, namely competition, also present.

We are therefore thrown back on some concept such as that of the Internal Inhibition of Pavlov or the very similar Reactive Inhibition (I_R) of Hull. Let us now consider these.

Pavlov (1927) in developing his theory of Internal Inhibition always assumed from the outset that inhibition is an active, independent, inhibitory state which counteracts the excitatory effect of conditioning. As Spence (1951) shows, he first thought of this as dependent upon the lack of the unconditioned stimulus, or—as we should say—the failure to encounter the releaser for the consummatory act appropriate for the appetitive behaviour in question. However, mainly because of the puzzling effects of 'massed' as compared with 'spaced' trials referred to above, he later modified this concept slightly and assumed the existence of an inhibitory state developing *pari passu* with the series of presentations of the conditioned stimulus, and that this 'state' or 'centre' is weaker and less stable than is the excitatory condition. Thus when trials are spaced, the inhibitory influence has time to drain away and so excitatory conditioning is dominant; where, however, trials are massed the inhibitory 'influence' accumulates more fully, and so slows up or even prevents normal positive conditioning. The disinhibiting effect of an extraneous stimulus was, however, a crucial difficulty for Pavlov's theory, and he had to fall back on the concept of 'irradiation' from the centre of the extraneous stimulus. Such language is now somewhat 'dated' and later authors (e.g. Humphrey, Konorski) stress the inhibitory and facilitatory effect respectively of antagonistic and allied reflexes. Konorski in particular has shown that if an indifferent stimulus precedes the termination of an unconditioned stimulus, it becomes a 'signal' for its termination, and so establishes an inhibitory conditioned reflex by a process of interference. But though this is true, there still seems to be room for Pavlov's concept in a more psychological form—namely, that the new stimulus acts as a 'distraction' in the sense that it interrupts or decreases whatever plastic process is proceeding at the same time, whether it be acquisition or diminution, by 'diluting' some of the action potential. Thus it seems as if many examples of 'Experimental Extinction' must include something in the nature of competition or interference, together with two other processes—one temporary, the other relatively permanent. The first of these two is specific to the response, and is probably synonymous with the reduction of specific action potential; while the second is specific to the stimulus and is essentially what we call Habituation.[1]

Hull (1943) has produced a system which is very close to that of Pavlov but shows some advances on it. Pavlov's original 'inhibitory tate' is represented in Hull's formulation by Reactive Inhibition or I_R. This is regarded as building up, as in Pavlov's later view, by the activity of a response system, so that when it becomes linked to a new stimulus it gives rise to Conditioned Inhibition I_R. Thus in general Pavlov's 'Inhibitory State' is equivalent to $I_R + {}_sI_R$. Beyond this point Hull assumes that this inhibitory state can be the source of a drive—a drive for rest (just as we now know the drive for sleep to be positive and active). In other words, ${}_sI_R$ can be regarded from the motivational point of view as dynamically identical with ${}_sE_R$ or, if we are speaking of secondarily acquired drives, $f({}_sH_R \times D)$.[2] Thus we can assume that inhibition, being now regarded as an active state, can be thought of as in competition with the original positive response, and so the theory of interference can be applied. The concept of habituation and that of ${}_sI_R$ in Hull's formulation can be considered as similar in effect, but differing primarily in the fact that Hull thinks of ${}_sI_R$ as being generated at every performance of the response, rewarded or unrewarded—whereas habituation occurs only with non-rewarded response.

It is somewhat remarkable how readily the Hull formulation, incomplete though it is in its lack of inclusion of the concept of instinctive drive,[3] resembles some sections of the Lorenz hypothesis and how readily a translation can be made. Let us now look at the problem in the light of Lorenz's views, and we shall see that the Lorenzian ideas can be used to bring closer to one another several of the apparently conflicting hypotheses we have been considering. In particular I think we can now see that there are a number of different phenomena which have been included under the terms extinction, inhibition and habituation, and that, in fact, each of the theories discussed may have useful application to certain examples and yet all may fail to cover certain cases.

Taking innate responses to start with, there is firstly a short-term central exhaustion of an innate response which it seems reasonable and adequate to consider simply as the reduction of specific action potential by repetition. Such waning cannot be re-established or 'disinhibited'

---

[1] Other types of change less likely to have a part in ordinary experimental extinction but nevertheless doubtless important in much general behaviour are mentioned in Chapter II (p. 27, above).

[2] In these formulæ D=Drive strength, H=Habit strength, I=Inhibition, S= Stimulus, R=Response, E_R=Conditioned Excitation or Excitatory State.

[3] Hull has a term, ${}_sU_R$=unlearned receptor-effector connection, but he makes little use of it and it fails to help him very much because he has no separate component, U_R and does not really consider U as if it were concerned in drive production.

by an extraneous stimulus, and so there seems no need to assume the activation of any separate inhibitory centre or the building up of any positive inhibitory state. Examples of this kind of change will be found on p. 336, below; although it may be hard to find instances which have been established as consisting solely and purely of this 'action specific exhaustion,' yet there seems little doubt that it is a primary element in, at any rate, some examples of that 'decrement by repetition' which so many workers have noted.

Secondly there is little doubt that Pavlov was on the right track in the early part of his book (1927) when he thought of internal inhibition as in some way dependent on the lack of the unconditioned stimulus. Thus the appetitive behaviour (to use the term in its original literal meaning) is evoked by the total drive situation; but the behaviour can never run to its complete innately determined conclusion, as the consummatory act, because the appropriate releaser is never encountered and the 'block' in (Tinbergen's sense) never removed.[1] This can of course lead ultimately to alternative lines of appetitive behaviour or to displacement activities merely on the original principles of Lorenz. But it seems more probable that the 'block' component of the innate releasive mechanism is something more than a block. It is an inhibitory centre preventing the performance of the consummatory act, so that its removal acts not merely to reduce the specific action potential but serves as a specific reinforcement; of course, exhausting the specific appetitive behaviour at the time, but also more permanently lowering the threshold for release of that particular line of behaviour in the future by more or less permanently reducing the inhibitory potential. And so a situation which is not associated with the removal of the block contributes to the building up of inhibition, and, conversely, 'reinforcement' is looked upon in some respects as a process of disinhibition—although differing from it in being more lasting. Thus if we regard the 'centre' of the I.R.M. as an innate piece of organisation but one which behaves like the I_R of Hull, we can regard the typical process of habituation as the primary (in the sense of being innately determined rather than acquired) example of Inhibition $_sI_R$.

---

[1] An interesting example where the absence of something which was formerly present can act as a releaser is supplied by Barrass (1960). In studying the courtship of the parasitic hymenopteran *Mormoniella vitripennis* he finds that a mounting male moves over the female's body until she is still. Only then can he perform courtship movements, and only then will these be performed in the correct position. As long as there is contact between the male's head and the female's antenna, the male remains in the courtship position and does not proceed to move back and attempt copulation. The depression of the antenna by a female assuming the receptive position results in an absence of contact and this absence releases the copulation behaviour. It can be said that in many insects the releaser is 'the inhibition of an inhibition' (Roeder, personal communication) and this can be equivalent to the removal of one of Tinbergen's blocks. For a valuable discussion of neural mechanisms in insect behaviour, see Vowles (1961).

The more restricted the appetitive behaviour is and the more specific the I.R.M., the easier it is to regard it simply as a block; and in these cases the concepts of S.A.P., action specific exhaustion and threshold changes can carry us most if not all of the way. But on the contrary, the less specific it becomes and, as in many mammals, the less restricted are the consummatory acts, the more necessary it is to postulate separate inhibitory centres in some way linked with the various expectancies so that the finding of the 'reward' reduces the inhibition. In such animals, therefore, the ideas of conditioned inhibition $_sI_R$, reaction potential $_sE_R$ and acquired drives ($_sH_R \times D$), with the related concepts of disinhibition and interference, become useful, and there is no doubt a whole series of situations within elaborate appetitive behaviour ranging in varying degrees from pure habituation to the most complex type of interference. But for the time being it is best to use 'habituation' primarily to mean the *long-term stimulus-specific waning of a response* due to failure to release the consummatory act.

But there remains to mention, as a type of change specific to the response, true instinctive regression and its parallel in learning. There is a certain amount of evidence (see Chapters XIV-XVI below) on birds and mammals that instinctive behaviour patterns not only build up to full functional activity by a process of maturation during the individual life; they may also eventually regress if completely unused. Now, this could, of course, be an actual disruption of a pattern of neurone organisation, a true atrophy of the structure we call instinct. We have no adequate data to go upon at present. But it does at least seem plausible to assume that if our view of habituation is correct, it could be merely an extreme instance of development of inhibitory potential by the I.R.M.[1]

When we come to permanently 'forgetting' a learned task, we can say little more, at any rate as far as animals are concerned. But the general trend of such evidence as there is seems to point to forgetting as being not a failure of central motivation but an effect of retroactive inhibition, such that competing responses, learned subsequently, interfere with the process of recall. But whatever the truth it seems clear that the slow but

[1] Sauer (1955), describing the changes in behaviour of the Whitethroat during its lifetime, has pointed out that of course with maturity the distinctive behaviour patterns and call notes of the juvenile are no longer used. But their central nervous mechanisms are not destroyed; they are, under natural circumstances, only blocked. After accidents owing to illness, or in the natural course of ageing, they can reappear in a sort of *regressive* behaviour. The more the bird declines from health, the more its behaviour and call notes regress to the juvenile and finally to the earliest nestling state, exactly in the reverse way from that in which the development has proceeded in the first place. Sauer finds that the song of a sickening male also shows signs of regression; it becomes rough, broken up into short unmelodious fragments and more and more adulterated with alarm notes or fragments of them. (See also Kruijt's observation on the Burmese Red Jungle Fowl mentioned below, p. 465.)

irrevocable loss of behaviour patterns, whether instinctive or learned, should be a very rewarding subject for study.

Habituation is most evident in nature in relation to those more generalised and elementary stimuli which serve to put the animal in the mood for flight, and is, as we have seen, manifested when these stimuli are not followed by full release of the appropriate consummatory act nor by any other appropriate form of reinforcement. When this is realised it will be seen why this simple form of learning is so universal in relation to mild shock and warning stimuli of a generalised nature. Some animals have precise instinctive responses to the appearance of that particular species or kind of predator which is most dangerous to them. Thus, Lorenz showed that grey geese gave the warning call and took avoiding action instinctively when a model resembling a bird of prey was drawn on wires over the enclosure in which they were kept. He pointed out that the maximum response was produced by a model which, in size and proportions, resembled as nearly as possible the Sea Eagle (*Haliætus albicilla*). There has been much work by Nice and ter Pelkwyk, Rand and others on the instinctive recognition of enemies by birds. The only object to which Nice and ter Pelkwyk's hand-reared Song Sparrows showed alarm was a model of an owl or a stuffed owl specimen. There seems little doubt from this work that the Song Sparrows recognise owls instinctively, but that the appropriate response to other enemies, such as cats and snakes, must be learnt. That this is not by any means a general rule is shown by Rand's (1941*a*) work on the Curve-billed Thrasher (*Toxostoma curvirostra*). Here the response to most enemies has apparently to be learnt, but there does seem to be an inborn response to a snake, dependent upon recognition of a pattern of stimuli, the core of which is the gentle, undulatory movement of a long flexible body. But this instinctive response to a particular species or type of predator is probably rather rare. As I have argued elsewhere (Thorpe, 1944), most animals, particularly small or defenceless animals, are subject to a great variety of dangers from many different kinds of predators and from other causes, and for them a specific instinctive response to each kind of predator and to any and every danger is out of the question. Therefore, instead of, or in addition to, any specific response, they have an instinctive equipment whereby they tend to take avoiding or self-protective action to a wide range of stimuli which are likely to be signals for danger, especially (1) any moving object; (2) any stimulus or situation which is strange; (3) any stimulus which is sudden; or (4) of an unusually high intensity. This mechanism with its wide scope ensures that they are on guard against most of the usual risks of life. But, obviously, sensitiveness to such a wide range of stimuli would, if the response were completely automatic and unvarying in intensity, make life impossible. Hence the need for some form of learning which saves the animal from wasting its energies in responses to stimuli which experience shows to be harmless or of no significance. Habituation exactly meets this need and is well-nigh universal. To quote, almost at random, an example from a paper by Crane (1941) on the crabs of the genus *Uca*, on the west coast of Central America: these Fiddler Crabs, as they are popularly called, have a great variety of enemies yet they are adept at escaping them all, while wasting as little time as possible in their burrows. 'Noises ranging from the cries of their bird enemies to the shouts of human beings, whistles, cannon fire and dynamite have no meaning for them. Neither did the passing of butterflies or wind-blown leaves within an inch or two of their eyes, but a bird flying over them within 25 feet, or a plane within, say, 200 feet, was the alert which sent all crabs scurrying to the mouths of their holes, where they froze, poised for instant flight within.' The 'take cover' signal was the approach of a bird either on foot or wing within 10 to 20 feet (depending on both bird and crab), and the approach of a human being within, on the average, 30 feet.

In those cases in which there is an inborn response to the specific pattern of a predator, the effect of repeated stimulation without any injury following, still provides something of a puzzle; though much light has been thrown on the matter by the work of Hinde (1954a) discussed below (Chapter XIV). One would have expected that the usual situation would have been that shown by mice (Zippelius and Schmidt, 1956) where the releaser for the retrieving response of the parent is the supersonic calling of the isolated young. This releaser has such an imperative effect on the parent that the retrieving response to it is practically inexhaustible. However, Hinde has shown that the repeated display of the model of an owl to young Chaffinches may cause a drop in number and frequency of alarm notes over a period of fifteen minutes, and this looks very like habituation. On the other hand, this fading of the response of the Song Sparrow to predators did not last, and when they were tested again a day or two later, it was back at its original intensity. Thus, though there may be short-term fading, Nice and ter Pelkwyk say that 'memory has been shown to be of great importance in enemy recognition,' and that even the memory of circumstances connected with a *single* occasion when an owl model was presented will cause alarm which persists after several months. Thus one young Song Sparrow, which had been brought into a room in which a stuffed owl was placed on the corner of a piano, showed strong alarm even months afterwards when brought into the same room, even though the owl was not there, the alarm evidently being associated with the particular spot where the owl model had once been. Similarly, Lorenz's (1939) account of his experiment with the response of geese to hawk models suggests that the reaction, far from showing habituation, is highly persistent. So much so that, even though never reinforced by any harmful result, the response remained so intense that the experiments were eventually brought to an end by the birds taking avoiding action as soon as they saw Lorenz or his assistant climbing the tree ladders prior to the commencement of an experiment. The geese had come to associate this act with the subsequent appearance of the hawk models in the sky. Strauss (1938b), on the other hand, reports fading of responses to mounted owls and hawks, but in these cases it does not appear certain whether the response was inborn or acquired by learning.

It seems nevertheless that, as we should expect, habituation is almost universal in connection with responses to mild and generalised warning stimuli. It is much less in evidence, though by no means always absent, in those exceptional cases where avoidance of danger is based on inborn response to the pattern of a *specific* predator.

Recently further results have been obtained by Hinde (1954a, 1961b), working with the response of Chaffinches to owl models and by Prechtl (1953) analysing the gaping response of young passerine birds, which suggest that in considering habituation the distinction between specialised and generalised stimuli is not altogether sound, and that something like habituation to the pattern of predator attack may take place under conditions in which one would think it would be extremely dysgenic. Hinde (1961b) shows that many of his results can be understood in terms of an interaction between long-term incremental and decremental effects, and concludes that concepts like habituation, extinction, adaptation and fatigue, while valuable in a descriptive sense, do not necessarily imply unitary underlying processes, and need much further analysis than they have as yet been given. The matter is also discussed by Broadbent (1961) and Vince (1961a). The discussion of the latter author in particular shows how careful we have to be before deciding what precise variables in a situation may really be responsible for observed changes in a given response. A fuller account of this matter will be found on p. 379 below. The inborn nature of some of these responses to predators, and the possibility that they are so deeply ingrained as to be resistant to long periods of geographical isolation, has been indicated by the observation of Orr (1945) that some of the Geospizidae ('Darwin's Finches') in the Galapagos Islands still retain the innate response to the pattern of the flying hawk even though the single species of hawk now occurring in the Galapagos (*Buteo galapagœnsis*) almost certainly does not attack them (Lack, 1947), and even though there can have been no other comparable predators in the islands for many centuries. Yet how can we square such observations with the tolerance which some chaffinches rapidly acquire even though they are exposed not merely to stimulation but also to reinforcement in the form of attack by the living predator? One's first reaction to such anomalies is to conclude that the animals' perception of the over-all situation is much more complete and subtle than one had suspected, and that automatic though the response to such live stimuli is, yet over and above it in a higher governing 'centre' is a very elaborate and nicely adjusted perception of the whole environmental situation. In other words, the bird habituates to an owl attack in a particular aviary or experimental cage, provided it survives at all, but still remains on the alert to the same pattern of stimulation of attack when it is experienced outside, in at least a slightly different environment and circumstances—as of course it will be in the wild. But attractive though this hypothesis is, the available evidence (Hinde, 1954a) suggests that it does not, in fact, apply and that there is another similar alternative which should be considered. It is per- haps a more likely possibility (Verplanck, verbal communication) that an occasional flight of the predator acts, in nature, as an intermittent and irregular reinforcement, and thus prevents the habituation effect which is observed under experimental conditions. Some of the various anomalies in habituation are perhaps less puzzling when it is realised that every experience involves tendencies for both an increase and a decrease in the response on a later presentation, and that which is to be the stronger will depend on particular circumstances.

The role of habituation has been emphasised in relation to 'negative reactions,' i.e. avoiding and fright response, because it is in this connec- tion that it first appears in phylogeny, and it is here that its importance is greatest and is most clearly seen. But similar considerations presumably apply (Thorpe, 1944) to positive reactions, i.e. those which have as their goal the satisfaction of some need, such as the getting of food. In those monophagous or oligophagous animals of specialised feeding habits in which the food-getting behaviour is released by some complex or highly specific situation or set of stimuli, it is inconceivable that habituation could operate unrestrainedly without disastrous results to the animals. An animal that ceased its food-taking reactions because, for a while, its at- tempts proved unsuccessful would indeed be in a poor way. In order to live it must persevere. Extensive habituation in such a case would seem to be biological nonsense. With polyphagous animals of generalised feeding habits, on the other hand, the environmental situations which release feeding behaviour are probably very general and non-specific (e.g. the pecking behaviour of a young chick). The animal has to learn, from among a great variety of objects, which are edible. This process is prob- ably not only a matter of associative learning on the trial-and-error principle, as is usually assumed; on the contrary, there is little doubt that here, in addition to positive association, habituation also plays its negative part, causing objects and situations which fail to give any satisfactory sensation, or any advantage, to be more and more neglected. Harris (1943) has considered the role played by habituation and other non-associative factors in the normal laboratory process of positive conditioning in rats, and Karn and Porter (1946) and Yerkes (1934) have done the same respectively for maze performance in rats and the solution of multiple choice problems by Chimpanzees.

The concept of habituation also plays an important part in Berlyne's (1950) theory of the nature of exploratory behaviour. Thus if it is assumed that a stimulus which involves novelty will arouse a drive-stimulus response [(R$\sim$SD) in Hull's formulation], then exploratory behaviour, by making the stimulus more familiar, will induce habituation— in other words, it will tend to reduce the drive dependent on novelty. And, as Broadbent (1952, unpublished) suggests, the process of habituation resulting from the frequent presentation of stimuli while still indifferent may be at the bottom of the difficulty of demonstrating sensory preconditioning.

There is clearly great scope in the study of the relations between fatigue, reduction in specific motivation, sensory adaptation, extinction (external and internal inhibition) and habituation for profound and interesting physiological work. All that has been done so far seems to carry us a very little way towards providing answers to the kind of question which the ethologist is most concerned to ask. While we may have to wait a long time for such answers, there is no doubt whatever that, biologically speaking, habituation plays a part of immense importance in the lives of animals, and that it is one of those phenomena of learning which are not only important in themselves but which have their place in almost every example of more complex learning performance. No experimenter on maze running or problem solving, no worker who is using puzzle-boxes or carrying out detour experiments, no person who is concerned with the tending or training of animals in any form, can afford to neglect the problems of habituation. They are well-nigh universal.

Summary

1. Learning is manifested particularly within appetitive behaviour, and is regarded biologically as the process of adjusting more or less fixed automatisms and releasing mechanisms to a perpetually changing environment. It is considered that the concept of learning necessarily involves the idea of adaptation, as indeed does the concept of life itself, and accordingly it is defined as *that process which manifests itself by adaptive change in individual behaviour as the result of experience.*

2. The importance of distinguishing learning from the growth and maturation of innate behaviour patterns during the life of the individual is emphasised, and criteria for doing this are suggested.

3. While certain broad similarities are found common to all types of learning, from the simplest to the most complex, it is probably physiologically erroneous to assume that all learning is the expression of a single fundamental process. Accordingly a classification into categories or types of learning is essential both from the theoretical and the practical points of view.

4. Examples of Habituation are given. This is in many respects the simplest type of learning. It is specific to the stimulus and may be defined broadly as *the relatively persistent waning of a response as a result of repeated stimulation which is not followed by any kind of reinforcement.* 'Stimulus satiation' is superficially similar, but is of very brief duration; in at least some cases it is evidence of sensory accommodation as distinct from a central phenomenon.

5. Criteria are given for distinguishing habituation from the effects of fatigue, maturation and injury. It is also distinguished from other central nervous phenomena, such as the transient waning of reflex and other responses which are response specific and are due to reduction of specific motivation.

6. The relation between habituation on the one hand and the Experimental Extinction and Internal Inhibition of Pavlov, and the Reactive Inhibition and Conditioned Inhibition of Hull on the other, is discussed in detail. It is concluded that all these concepts serve a useful function, but that habituation is to be distinguished from them, and that a particularly significant form of it can then be defined as the *relatively permanent waning of a response due to the failure to release the appropriate consummatory act.* But it is concluded that there are to be found, within elaborate appetitive behaviour, a series of situations, all involving waning of responses through lack of reinforcement, but ranging from pure habituation on the one hand to the most complex types of interference on the other. Thus it seems as if many examples of 'Experimental Extinction' must include something in the nature of competition or interference, together with two other processes—one temporary, the other relatively permanent. The first of these two is specific to the response, and can be described as a decrease in specific motivation, while the second is specific to the stimulus and is essentially what we call habituation.

7. Consideration of the relation between the release of the consummatory act and reactive inhibition suggests that the so-called 'block' incorporated (in Tinbergen's scheme) in the structure of the Innate Releasing Mechanism is, in fact, something more than a block; it is often an inhibitory centre actively counteracting the appetitive drive, and it follows from this that reinforcement can be looked upon to some extent as a disinhibitor.

8. The problem of slow and permanent atrophy or regression of

instinct as a result of complete lack of expression is discussed. It is compared with the true 'forgetting' of a learned task, and it is suggested that both may perhaps be regarded as instances of extreme development of inhibitory potential and so covered by a type of interference theory.

9. Some examples of the very wide biological significance of habituation are given.

CHAPTER IV

ASSOCIATIVE LEARNING: CONDITIONING AND TRIAL-AND-ERROR

FROM the most remote times people have believed that animals learn in the sense of being purposive and intelligent and able to produce actions appropriate to a new problem—as the fables of Æsop testify. In particular, animism and metempsychosis are expressions of this, and are vastly more ancient than anything we can call science. In contrast, the scientific study of animal behaviour can, with some truth, be said to have commenced with Darwin and to date from the publication in 1872 of his *Expression of the Emotions in Man and Animals*; although information on the learning process as distinct from the study of instinct was very largely anecdotal for a further twenty-five years until the first experimenters, influenced by the associationist ideas of philosophers such as Hobbes (1588–1679), Hume (1711–76), David Hartley (1705–57) and James Mill (1773–1836) began their work. Hobbes can be said to represent the beginning of philosophical associationism; while Hume developed it and Mill brought it to its theoretical climax as a principle of the mechanical compounding of stimuli. Thus the modern experimental study of animal learning really commenced when Thorndike (1898) started systematically to apply these associationist ideas to problems of animal learning more or less independently from human psychologists such as Ebbinghaus (1885), who had been working along the same lines.

So it was that the study of association commenced well before any systematic attack was made on the simpler problem of habituation which we have been considering in the last chapter. The type of theory which Thorndike evolved came to be known as connectionism, and was based on his famous experiments in which cats and dogs learned to escape from puzzle-boxes. These boxes were so constructed that the animal could not possibly see, even if it were capable of understanding, the way in which the latch worked. The cats were kept before the experiment without food until they were in a state of great hunger, and they scratched about *more or less* at random until by accident the lever was depressed and the door opened. Once an animal had accomplished its escape in this way, there was an increasing tendency to repeat the successful action, and so in a fairly brief time the task of opening the box was learnt to perfection. This of course is, in fact, an example of what we now call trial-and-error learning (or, alternatively, instrumental conditioning, or conditioned reflex Type II). But it was experiments of this kind which historically prepared the way for the acceptance of the classical conditioned reflex theory with which historically it overlapped and which, because it seems a more elementary conception, is not infrequently thought of as having priority in every respect. It was the Russian school which, initiated by I. M. Sechenov (1829–1905), followed by Pavlov (1849–1936) and V. M. Bekhterev (1857–1927), first provided some sort of physiological explanation as to how a fixed inherited behaviour pattern might be modified and adapted by the individual to suit particular conditions and problems.

The essential ideas of connectionism which were inherent in Thorndike's work, and which, if not actually elaborated by him, were made precise by the work of his immediate followers, were four in number. First it was assumed that there are 'bonds' present in the higher centres which are capable of linking together discrete stimuli and units of behaviour, and that the more of these potential bonds are present the greater the potential intelligence of the animal. Associative learning thus consists in establishing or making functional the appropriate bonds. Secondly, the bonds are, according to the so-called *Law of Effect*, strengthened by reward. Thirdly, the bonds tend to link more easily those stimuli and responses which are more nearly adjacent in time or space—this being the principle of contiguity which was more especially the contribution of Guthrie (1933, 1935), and which was developed much later. Fourthly, the principle of similarity assumed that the bonds would tend to link more readily, presumably by some process of conceptual generalisation, those stimuli which are similar.

The next important development of associationist theory was the behaviourism of Watson (1907). Perhaps it did not contain anything very new; indeed, one might say that all its essentials were contained in the writings of Thorndike, and that the influence it had on the comparative psychology of the time was due primarily to the conditions which existed when it was put forward. This new theory was concerned essentially with habits. Not only was it fundamentally associationist or connectionist in outlook, it also prided itself on being purely objective—with the implication perhaps that it was thereby more nearly a physiological rather than a psychological system. Perhaps we should not have heard so much of Watsonian behaviourism had it not been that, within a few years of its publication, the work of Pavlov and of Bekhterev began to be known outside Russia. Pavlov's ideas fitted admirably into the Thorndike-Watson scheme, as they had done in Russia into Sechenov's (1863) concept of 'reflexes of the brain,' and seemed to stress and reinforce the objective and superficially physiological ideas of Watson. They seemed, in fact, to give them physiological respectability. Indeed, as Konorski (1948) has pointed out, Pavlov resolutely turned his back on all attempts at the psychological understanding of the facts which he had discovered and which served as the foundation for his theory, was contemptuous of introspection and deliberately rejected it. But there was another reason for the liaison. Perhaps an even greater merit for the behaviourists, although less openly emphasised by them, was that it seemed to offer a way of eliminating that troublesome and ambiguous concept, instinct. Be this as it may, a mechanistic stimulus-response psychology soon became dominant, against which, amongst the then well-known investigators in the United States, practically only Yerkes stood out. It is perhaps significant that this one prominent dissentient should be a man who has devoted himself mainly to investigations of anthropoid behaviour. In its modern form this trend of associationism is represented by the vast system of Hull, the core of which is the identification of reward or reinforcement with need reduction. If one attempts to summarise in a few words the essence of this system, one might say it is that 'learning only proceeds when it leads to a reduction of need.' Need in this context is not usually defined, but one is often led to assume that it is physiological need which is implied.[1]

About the same time that the work of Pavlov and his associates was becoming widely known, another school was developing in Germany based on the pioneer work of Wertheimer (1912) on the visual perception of movement. This work, together with that of Wertheimer's disciples, Wolfgang Köhler and Koffka, was destined to have a profound influence on both theory and experiment. But the First World War delayed this effect, and it was not until after 1918 that the fundamental concepts of the Gestalt school, as it had then become known, namely insight, *pragnänz*, etc., began to have their full influence.

The implications of the Gestalt and other field theories for the study of animal learning and perception and its relation to instinct will be considered more fully below, but a brief summary here will perhaps help us to place ideas of conditioning and learning in a clearer relation to one another and to animal behaviour as a whole. According to the Gestalt school, insight involves the perception of relations, and it is implied that the organism acts as intelligently as it can, so that the *insight* solution is the natural solution, and that only if the problem is too difficult or is presented in too difficult a way is trial-and-error learning resorted to. Moreover, according to this view, the tries in trial-and-error are real tries and

---

[1] It is perhaps worth pointing out that if this theory is followed strictly, it implies that learning by punishment means that—except in so far as punishment focuses attention—escape from punishment is the reward or reinforcement; a complication to the theory of considerable importance, and one which does not seem to have been adequately accounted for in the systems of either Hull or his followers. This matter will be referred to again later in connection with the concept of reinforcement.

not merely random movements. How fundamental is the difference between the classical associationist position and that of the Gestalt school is
realised when we consider that the latter, in fact, completely reverses the
main associationist assumption of the law of effect and consequently
reasoning becomes essentially mental trial-and-error. Other important
consequences of this outlook are that perception and learning are brought
closer together and that psychological organisation is assumed to move in
a given direction, i.e. towards the state of *pragnänz*, which can perhaps be
roughly translated as 'compact and significant,' in other words, towards
the state of a good gestalt. This cuts the ground from under the concept
that learning always involves reduction of need, since organisation of the
environment, the perceptual world, into a good gestalt may itself be an
adequate reward. This is not the place to follow up the implications of
such a conclusion. Suffice it to say that a controversy was thus started
which still continues; although as Hebb (1949) has shown, both sides have
by now moved very far from their original positions, and indeed Koch
(in Estes, Koch *et al.*, 1954) finds in the 1949–51 developments of Hull's
system an attenuation of the reinforcement principle so extensive that
'its consequences are, *in effect*, indistinguishable from an association by
contiguity assumption' (p. 155). Nevertheless, there has been, and indeed
still is, even among those who yielded most readily to the gestalt arguments, a tendency to assume that they apply only to man and higher
animals, and that, when dealing with invertebrate behaviour, and indeed
with that of most of the vertebrate groups, associationist and conditioned-
reflex theories can be expanded to satisfy all requirements.

The Conditioned Reflex

Under the term 'associative learning' a number of different phenomena
which it is not always easy to define sharply are, in fact, grouped together. These phenomena may vary from the simplest conditioning to
the more elaborate forms of trial-and-error learning and the learning of
simple mazes, and, indeed, four of the seven classes of learning proposed
by Tolman (1937) in connection with his studies of string-pulling by rats
could be considered as 'associative.'

Thus it is important, both theoretically and for the sake of orderly
description and discussion of learning abilities, to make as clear a distinction as we can between the various types and degrees of associative learning. Konorski, who has perhaps as wide and profound a knowledge of
conditioned-reflex experiments as any modern investigator, includes under
the heading 'C.R.' both the classical C.R. of the Pavlov school and trial-
and-error learning, which he calls respectively Type I and Type II. Here
we shall use the term C.R. for Type I only. And by it we mean the classical
C.R. of Pavlov. Konorski himself points out that the great merit of Pavlov

is that from the immense chaos and complexity of the acquired activity of the organism he separated out an apparently simple and elementary phenomenon, reproduced it in a pure form under laboratory conditions and proceeded to make it the basis for all his studies. As Konorski says, 'If Pavlov's idea was really sound and his C.R. *is* actually an elementary phenomenon of acquired behaviour, then his method should be accepted as a most valuable instrument for the analysis of animal behaviour. But if it is not so, and if the principle of reflex [conditioning] does not show the proper way to the understanding of cortical activity . . . then the science of C.R. will lose much of its value and significance.' Taking into consideration the immense amount of experimental evidence accumulated by students of learning in physiological laboratories all over the world, particularly in Russia and America, Konorski formulates the general principle of the C.R. in the following words: '*If two stimuli s1 and s2 are applied in overlapping sequence, the stimulus s1 being antecedent, then, with repetition of such a combination, a plastic change in the nervous system is formed, consisting in the stimulus s1 acquiring the ability to elicit the response of the same kind as the stimulus s2.*'

It will be seen from this that the classical C.R. consists essentially of the passive establishment of a connection between a normal reward and a new stimulus. This new stimulus is usually indifferent in the sense that it does not innately release any specific responses, and thus does not normally have any 'meaning' for the animals. Thus by the conditioning process a response which was originally an inborn or habitual response to the reward or reinforcement is released by the new stimulus. The term 'overlapping sequence' implies the association of the stimulus and the reward in time in such a manner that the stimulus terminates either immediately before the commencement of the reward or, if they overlap, well before the latter's termination. This is made clear by the accompanying diagram (Fig. 6), which shows under what conditions we may expect a C.R. to become established.[1] After considering what appeared to have to be the essential elements of conditioning, the 1949 Round Table Conference on nomenclature in animal behaviour, of which Professor Konorski was a member, arrived (Thorpe, 1951*b*) at a somewhat simpler definition, which is as follows:

'*Conditioning = the process of acquisition by an animal of the capacity to respond to a given stimulus with the reflex reaction proper to another*

[1] Backward conditioning has often been regarded as impossible and alleged examples discredited. It seems now, however, that certain instances of it are definitely established. Razran (1956) summarises the subject. He regards it as a genuine conditioned reflex associative manifestation explained by his theory of 'dominance contiguity' and says that stable backward conditioned reflexes can be obtained and maintained 'under favourable experimental conditions.'

stimulus (the reinforcement) when the two stimuli are applied concurrently for a number of times.'

It seems clear that the C.R. itself does not appear ever to constitute the whole learning process, at any rate in animals of sufficiently high grade of organisation to be capable of directed movements. Rather it represents an artificially isolated part thereof, and as such its study is of interest and importance so long as its artificial limitations are kept in mind. How far it can be considered as the fundamental unit out of which the most complex learned responses of the whole animal are constructed

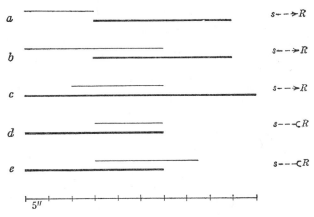

FIG. 6—The effect of the sequence of stimuli upon the formation of the conditioned reflex.
Thin lines denote the duration of the initial stimulus, thick lines denote the duration of the reinforcing stimulus.
s – – → R, excitatory conditioned reflex;
s – – –⊂ R, inhibitory conditioned reflex.
(Time, 5-second intervals.)
(After Konorski, 1948.)

is a further question. In this connection it is important to emphasise three points. The first is that the concept of the local or partial reflex as the 'automatic response of a single organ system to a simple stimulus' is an idealised concept which in fact is seldom or never realised in experimental investigation. As Sherrington (1906) made abundantly clear, the organism's response is always multiple, involving a large number of receptors and that, far from being independent of one another, the responses show a great deal of mutual excitation and inhibition. Secondly, few of the stimuli which evoke even the simplest reflexes are in fact simple; for, however simple the salient feature of the stimulus situation may appear at first sight to be (e.g. the odour of food or a sudden sound), the animal is reacting not to this element alone but to a more or less complex stimulus situation consisting of the element itself differentiated against a complex and changing background. Of course, in a simple animal the stimulus perceived is vastly simpler than that experienced by, say, a dog or a human being. If we take the case of the simplest of all orienting reactions, for example photokinesis in an animal such as a Planarian with a low grade of receptor organisation, the organism is responding to change in intensity of stimulus—the accommodation of the sense organ itself being such that its response varies according to its past experience. It has, in fact, been suggested that there is a slowly changing photochemical equilibrium in the eye which provides the animal with the rudimentary form of memory required for the reaction. But even in such an extreme case it is safer to omit the word 'simple' from our definition. Thirdly, there seems to be no escaping the fact that the conditioned reflex is essentially 'anticipatory' in nature (cf. Zener, 1937), or is at least an artificially isolated part of a whole pattern of behaviour which must be characterised as expectant. That is, the animal is behaving *as if* expecting, as a result of its past experience, a definite event at a given time.

The importance of the classical conditioned reflex in the physiology of behaviour has been that for a long while it provided by far the best technique for enabling a part at least of a learning process to be investigated quantitatively and to be subjected to an exact analysis. It is not, however, always realised how artificial and isolated the classical conditioned reflex is, and how completely passive and otherwise unresponsive the animal must usually be before it can be demonstrated. Thus the physiologist, investigating the conditioned reflex, studies an artificial and isolated part of the learning process; the appetitive motor-behaviour normally associated with the unconditioned stimulus (e.g. the food-seeking response and the alimentary response) being purposely eliminated by the experimental conditions. Yet even under the conditions of the physiological laboratory this ideal state is seldom realised. Under natural conditions, on the other hand, the animal is always actively up and doing, continually receiving stimulation from a large number of sense organs which interact on one another.

Nevertheless, conditioning, even in the strictest sense, is a form of learning; a method by which the innate releasing mechanism is elaborated or modified to fit the environmental situation more exactly. Moreover, it is interesting to note that conditioning often tends to be more rapid when two consecutive stimuli belong to different sense modalities than when they are from the same—as was shown by the work of Winslow *et al.* (1938) with cats. The systematic and quantitative study of reflex conditioning has, of course, given rise to an immense body of knowledge. R. S. Woodworth (1938), in his *Experimental Psychology*, says: 'It is perhaps no more remarkable than other types of learned response, and we cannot regard it as an element out of which behaviour is built. But it does open a window into the dynamics of behaviour, and it furnishes a tool for the investigation of the senses of animals. . . .'

Humphrey (1933) regards the classical conditioned reflex as being 'an incompletely recorded case of habit.' Habit as we know it outside the laboratory is certainly a much more stable affair than the evanescent and delicate phenomenon of Pavlov's sound-proofed laboratories; and although Youtz (1938) considers that classical conditioned responses are characteristically *well* retained and are extremely resistant to forgetting, it is important to remember (e.g. Gagné, 1941) that in both classical and 'instrumental' or 'Type II' conditioning the degree of retention is closely related to the conditions of training, so that it is hardly possible to compare the various 'classical' and 'instrumental' studies at present available, since these conditions vary so greatly. Youtz's conclusion that classical and instrumental conditioning are *essentially* alike seems at present to go beyond the evidence. The conditioned reflex is, then, best regarded as a minute and artificially isolated piece of the learning process of the animal, and in the isolating procedure it seems that something important is lost. But the conditioned reflex is the basic element of that part of learning which consists in adjusting the innate releasive mechanism to the complexities of the external world. In this way it obviously plays an important part in adapting the receptor side of instinct as a result of experience.

But it is necessary to emphasise again that we must not expect to find that the simplest learned responses of the whole animal under natural conditions can ever be equated with a simple conditioned reflex and nothing more. The claim which made the conditioning theory so attractive to the psychologists of the 'twenties was that upon the conditioned reflex could be founded a scientifically determinate psychology parallel to an exact physiology. This is now obviously an illusion; though we must not thereby be led into the opposite error of assuming that a full physiological description based on newer theories and the better understanding of nervous mechanisms is thereby impossible.

Another assumption which has proved to be erroneous is that made by many workers, including, for instance, Konorski and Miller (1937), that in the classical conditioned reflex the action pattern always remains unchanged irrespective of the unconditioned reflex which serves for reinforcement. It is now recognised that conditioned and unconditioned responses are probably never identical, and that the one is not simply a duplicate of the other. Because Pavlov measured only the salivary secretion and neglected any precise measurement of motor behaviour—in fact, because he did his best to eliminate it altogether—this essential fact was obscured. When we look at the differences as well as the similarities between conditioned and unconditioned behaviour, it at once becomes evident how complex is the conditioned response, Hilgard and Marquis

(1940) describe four different kinds of response which they include in classical conditioning; but, as we shall see, it is doubtful whether numbers 3 or 4 really belong there at all. However, it is of interest to consider them *seriatim*. First come those exceptional instances in which the conditioned response does appear to be an *almost* exact replica of the unconditioned; thus, as they point out, in the earliest stages of conditioned leg-withdrawal, dogs act in the presence of the conditioned stimulus as though they were being shocked. More commonly we get (2) Fractional Component Responses, where in many experiments it is found that the conditioned response is merely a component of the unconditioned. Thus, by a series of processes of habituation, conditioned salivation may be elicited without chewing, conditioned chewing without swallowing or conditioned leg-withdrawal without the barking which was part of the initial reaction to shock. In other words, 'the conditioned response resembles but does not completely duplicate the unconditioned.'

More significant are those examples (3) where the conditioned reflex appears to be a preparation for the unconditioned stimulus but does not resemble the unconditioned response at all. Thus Zener, referred to above (Chapter II), in describing certain classical conditioning experiments with dogs, in which care was taken to record by cinematograph the complete behaviour of the animal, reports how, when looked at minutely, the conditioned reflex is found to differ in posture and in completeness from the unconditioned. It also differs in that it includes many behaviour patterns, such as stamping, yawning and panting, which are presumably to be interpreted as displacement activities and which do not appear as part of the unconditioned response to food at all. The dog, in fact, appears to be looking for and expecting the fall of food, and shows it in a readiness to perform the eating behaviour which will occur when the food falls. Moreover, the less the restraint that is applied in such experiments, the greater becomes the activity of the animal and the more evident is its anticipatory nature. In other words, if allowed to do so the appetitive behaviour enters more and more into the picture, and adds complication upon complication to the actions which are finally elicited. Thus the behaviour is best regarded not as a new form of conditioning but as conditioning in a more natural and less completely isolated state than is customary in physiological laboratories.

Finally (4), Hilgard and Marquis consider it necessary to distinguish 'pseudo-conditioning,' which can be described as a heightened state of excitement such that the animal is sensitised to stimuli not normally arousing response, and they point out the confusion which can result from assuming that all such modifications are, in fact, part of the conditioning process. This again is merely a state of expectancy, the behavioural expression of which cannot be entirely suppressed and which seems to be essentially part of the process we have just been considering. There seems to be no sufficient reason for giving it a new name.

During the decade 1950 to 1960 a volume of work has been published in the U.S.S.R. dealing with interoceptive conditioning and its relation to conscious and unconscious processes. The whole subject has been summarised by Razran (1961). Interoceptive conditioning is classical conditioning in which either the conditioned stimulus or the unconditioned stimulus or both are delivered directly to the mucosa of some internal organ. When both stimuli are interoceptive the conditioning can be called inter-interoceptive. When only the conditioned stimulus is interoceptive but the unconditioned one exteroceptive, the name might be intero-exteroceptive conditioning. Thirdly, the designation of extero-interoceptive conditioning can be reserved for situations in which only the unconditioned stimulus is interoceptive. The results show that interoceptive conditioning, whether involving conditioned or unconditioned interoceptive stimuli, is readily obtainable and, as one would expect, very largely unconscious in character. Interoceptive stimulations are, of course, by their very nature, much more recurrent and regular and more immediately bound up with the life of the organism, so that interoceptive conditioning is, as Razran says, 'an almost built-in function that is constantly generated and regenerated in the very process of living and acting'. Interoceptive conditioning is somewhat slower in formation than is exteroceptive, but, once conditioned, it is more firmly fixed—that is to say, less readily extinguished. Razran stresses that this body of work, showing as it does the ubiquity, largely unconscious character and ready all-round conditionability of interoceptive stimulations, provides a wholly new approach to our thoughts about conscious and unconscious reactions. Indeed, it brings up fundamental questions as to the idea of the conscious and the unconscious. Extensive though the work is, it is still in a somewhat preliminary phase and no doubt the results and implications of it are likely to become much clearer in the years ahead.

Instrumental Conditioning (Conditioning Type II), and Trial-and-Error

Trial-and-error learning, of which instrumental conditioning is the core, is a different matter from the classical conditioned reflex in a number of important respects. These differences are, in fact, so marked that there is much to be said for Konorski's view that these reflexes represent a separate kind of plasticity and do not come within the scheme of the Pavlovian conditioned reflexes at all. Firstly, Type II differs from Type I chiefly in that the response is an independent 'voluntary' somatic action of an animal showing active appetitive behaviour, is not originally necessarily connected with the reward, and both stimulus and reponse precede the reward in time. Thus in this type of conditioning the stimulus becomes connected to the response as the result of a kind of retroactive influence exerted by the reward. Then in trial-and-error learning, much more conspicuously than in classical conditioning, the pattern of the reflex depends on whether the reinforcement is positive or negative, i.e. a 'reward' or a 'punishment.' In the former, the response is the movement (e.g. leg withdrawal or pecking) provoked; in the latter the animal not only neglects objects resembling the noxious stimulus situation, it is the corresponding antagonistic movement which is evoked, or else some avoiding action such as shaking the head which will get rid of the unpleasant object.

There is now plenty of evidence for subcortical conditioning, and Girden and Culler (1937) found that even under complete curare paralysis, which is assumed to inhibit cortical functions completely, reflex twitches of skeletal muscle can still be conditioned. It is also very significant that Culler and Mettler (1934) have shown with decorticate dogs that while classical conditioned-reflex formation can be achieved, the formation of Type II conditioned reflex is impossible. Moreover (Konorski, 1948), in dogs the pyramidal system seems to be a necessity for the formation of Type II reflexes, and it is supposed that it is this feature which gives to the motor activity of the process its characteristic of 'voluntary activity.' Finally, there is the extraordinary efficiency of 'partial reinforcement' in the case of Type II. There are many studies (Humphries, 1939, 1940, 1943, with human subjects and with rats, and Finger, 1942, Mowrer and Jones, 1945, etc., with rats and Longo and Bitterman, 1960, with fish *Tilapia macrocephala*) which indicate that 50 per cent. reinforcement may be as effective in conditioning, and provide as much or more resistance to experimental extinction, as does unfailing reward on every performance. Skinner, indeed (1938, p. 288) has succeeded in establishing a Type II conditioned reflex in the rat when only one in every 192 responses was reinforced (1953, p. 70) and Ferster and Skinner (1957) report that in experiments with the pecking behaviour of pigeons two birds were able to respond in a sustained fashion when only one in every 875 responses was reinforced by obtaining food. Similarly with pigeons under schedules of intermittent reinforcement, they state that as many as 10,000 responses may appear before extinction is substantially complete—a phenomenon utterly without parallel in classical conditioning, but recalling at once the persistence and relative fixity[1] of what we ordinarily call habit formation. Hull (1940–1 unpublished, quoted by Spence, 1951) has a possible explanation of the *greater* resistance to extinction in human subjects under partial reinforcement, the design of the extinction experiments being such that

---

[1] Thus one of Mostler's (1937) Pied Flycatchers refused a warningly coloured bait as a result of a single unpleasant experience fourteen and a half months previously. See also the criticism of Youtz on p. 83, above.

there is less change in the patterning of the stimulus for the 50 per cent. than for the 100 per cent. group. It is doubtful, however, whether this could account for all the observed effects, at any rate in animal experiments. Denny (1946) has pointed out that with rats learning a T maze, secondary reinforcement may be contributory to the effect, and that when secondary reinforcement is entirely eliminated the 50 per cent. group require twice as many trials as the 100 per cent. group. It seems probable that such secondary reinforcement (see Miller, 1951, for a valuable summary of the subject) is an important component of the sum total of reinforcing elements active in a typical partial reinforcement experiment; and it does go some way to explain the animals' persistence and success in the complex situation of a trial-and-error experiment as compared with the difficulty of conditioning in the excessively simplified circumstances of a classical C.R. experiment. But the explanation must not be pushed too far, and it seems most unlikely that all the characteristic and significant results of partial reinforcement experiments can be accounted for on this basis. Indeed, there seems little doubt that most of the results of such experiments are an expression of the fact that the appetitive behaviour is allowed scope to play its part more fully, and so some of the extreme artificiality of the classical C.R. situation is avoided. The fundamental nature of the differences has been emphasised by Hilgard and Marquis (1940, p. 152), who show that partial reinforcement illustrates very strikingly the distinctions between the two types of conditioning and the difficulty involved in bridging the gap between them. When we turn over all these differences in our minds, we see at once that what we are speaking of as conditioned reflex Type II is none other than our very old friend 'trial-and-error learning' in its simplest form, as demonstrated in the well-known experiments of Grindley (1932) on guinea-pigs.

The stability and resistance to extinction of many examples of conditioned reflex Type II or trial-and-error learning may perhaps be ascribed to the feed-back from avoidance movements acting as a conditioned inhibitor. This argument has been developed by Soltysik and Zielinski (1962). The authors emphasise, however, that the explanation, although fitting many observations admirably, is so far conjectural and in need of much more experimental verification than has as yet been provided. In this connection the work of Gorska and Jankowska (1961) on the effect of differentiation is important. It provides results which are at present difficult to harmonise with those of Soltysik and Zielinski in that they show that, in dogs, the proprioceptive feed-back enhances only the skill and precision of instrumental reactions but is not necessary for the execution of a simple motor response. It seems from their results that afferent influx plays only a supplementary part in simple voluntary movement, moderating its character and increasing its precision, but that the simple movement itself requires no afferent information since this feed-back is not involved in the reflex arc of Type II conditioned reflexes. The further outcome of these studies will be awaited with great interest. For a general penetrating study of these problems, see Seward (1958).

The essence of trial-and-error learning is *the development of an association, as the result of reinforcement during appetitive behaviour, between a stimulus or situation and an independent motor action as an item in that behaviour when both stimulus and motor action precede the reinforcement and the motor action is not the inevitable inherited response to the reinforcement* (Thorpe, 1951).

The term was first employed in animal psychology by C. Lloyd Morgan in 1894, and was brought into general use by Thorndike in 1898. Although at that time its meaning was somewhat vague, it is now as fully precise as any of the other terms which are in common use in describing learning. Although classical conditioning is thus historically, and also in many instances experimentally, the artificially isolated perceptual part of the natural process of trial-and-error learning, a number of authors have, by a curious inversion, considered trial-and-error learning as merely a form of conditioning—as the term 'Conditioned Reflex Type II' itself implies. The term 'instrumental conditioning' (Hilgard and Marquis, 1940) has also been much used, and has great convenience as signifying the motor conditioning which is the basic element of trial-and-error. Quite apart, however, from the fact that trial-and-error was first in the field, there seems good reason for retaining the term for the whole learning process. Thus, trial-and-error is *essentially* instrumental conditioning, but apart perhaps from some exceptional cases of the acquisition of skill, it always contains a subsidiary element of Pavlovian conditioning as well. The term trial-and-error has the great merit that it is simple and expressive, and draws attention to a fundamental distinction from classical conditioning which other terms obscure. Trial-and-error learning has sometimes been described merely as 'habit formation,' but this phrase is unsatisfactory since it is vague and, in common usage, includes all methods of acquiring automatisms (Thorpe, 1950).

As an example to contrast with classical conditioning, let us consider a young chick which, pecking at random on the floor of its box, accidentally strikes some object which is edible. As soon as this is in the bill the inborn response of swallowing takes place. Thereupon the reward of having secured food exerts a retroactive effect upon the pecking behaviour, so that in future there is a greater tendency to peck at objects which have the same appearance as the first satisfactory mouthful. Thus with increased experience and aided by the process of habituation more and more objects unsuitable for food tend to be ignored and the attention concentrated more and more upon grains of corn and other things likely to be edible.

The chief difference between the classical conditioned reflex and instrumental conditioning, and the way they interlock in trial-and-error learning, is shown in the accompanying table (Table II). In Grindley's experiments, which were among the earliest to show trial-and-error in a fully controlled laboratory situation, a guinea-pig was placed in a comfortable harness. The commencement of the experiment was signalled by the sounding of a buzzer which continued until the animal made accidentally a turning movement of the head, say, to the right, when automatically the buzzer immediately stopped and a portion of food, e.g. carrot, was delivered on the food receptacle in front of the animal. Thus the external stimulus (St.$_e$) in this case was the buzzer, the reward or reinforcement (Rwd.) was of course the food and the voluntary 'response' (Rsp.$_v$) was the turning of the head. In this situation the reward never comes before the response, and the stimulus, the response and the reward are all initially independent and are not linked by any innate proclivity. So the reward exercises a retroactive influence, causing a stimulus to become connected and remain connected to a response when both the stimulus and the response precede the reward in time and when the response is not originally a response to the reward.

In these experiments the buzzer (St.$_e$) is in some ways a complicating factor masking both some of the similarities and some of the differences between instrumental and classical conditioning. Presumably the chief function of the buzzer is not as a stimulus to be conditioned but as a stimulus which will provoke restlessness and some degree of appetitive behaviour. We may regard the consummatory act of eating carrot as the basis of the learning process, and the voluntary response (Rsp.$_v$) of turning the head with its reafferent stimulus (St.$_p$) as corresponding to the 'stimulus' of the classical conditioned reflex.

Thus the animal learns to associate not an external stimulus with the ensuing reward but the proprioceptive and other stimuli proceeding from a voluntary act with the coming of a reward, and it performs this particular action as an appetitive action *in anticipation* of an ensuing reward. But I know of no case, whether of guinea-pig in a Grindley apparatus or, from Skinner's very extensive later work, of a rat in a 'Skinner box,' in which the animal habitually chews (i.e. executes the voluntary element in the consummatory act) if its head turning or its lever pressing fails to secure food. Perhaps this is the clearest of all pieces of evidence that trial-and-error is expectant and anticipatory.

Another feature of much if not all trial-and-error learning is that the trials are indeed genuine trials in the sense of being real attempts to cope with the problem situation. This may be little evident in lower animals,

TABLE II—*Diagram to illustrate the Two Types of Conditioning as components of Trial-and-error Learning.*

	Initial State	Training Process	Result
Classical Conditioning	$[($Rwd. $\longrightarrow$ C.A.$_i)$	St.$_e \longrightarrow ($Rwd. $\longrightarrow$ C.A.$_i)$	$[$St.$_e \longrightarrow$ C.A.$_i]$
Instrumental Conditioning	$\left($Rwd. $\longrightarrow \begin{pmatrix} \text{C.A.}_i \\ \text{C.A.}_v \end{pmatrix}\right)$	$\left(\begin{matrix} \text{Rsp.}_v \\ + \\ \text{St.}_p \\ + \\ \text{St.}_e \end{matrix}\right) \longrightarrow ($Rwd. $\longrightarrow$ C.A.$_v)$	$[$St.$_e \longrightarrow$ Rsp.$_v]$ anticipates $- - - \rightarrow$ Rwd.
Trial-and-error	$\left($Rwd. $\begin{matrix} \longrightarrow \text{C.A.}_i \\ \searrow \text{C.A.}_v \end{matrix}\right)$	St.$_e \longrightarrow \left(\begin{matrix} \text{Rsp.}_v \\ + \\ \text{St.}_p \end{matrix}\right) \longrightarrow ($Rwd. $\begin{matrix} \nearrow \text{C.A.}_i \\ \searrow \text{C.A.}_v \end{matrix})$	$\left[\text{St.}_e \begin{matrix} \nearrow \text{C.A.}_i \\ \searrow \text{Rsp.}_v \end{matrix}\right]$ anticipates $- - - \rightarrow$ Rwd.

Rwd. = Reward[1] (e.g. food).
C.A.$_i$ = Involuntary element in consummatory act (e.g. salivation).
C.A.$_v$ = Voluntary element in consummatory act (e.g. mastication).
Rsp.$_v$ = Voluntary act as part of appetitive behaviour giving st.$_p$.
St.$_e$ = External stimulus (e.g. buzzer).
St.$_p$ = Proprioceptive or reafferent stimulus.

([1] For a discussion of the nature of reward and the place of perception of consummatory acts therein, see pp. 116, 145.)

where the sensory equipment is such that only the most elementary degree of problem-solving behaviour can be expected; for it is almost impossible to set a problem in the ordinary sense of the term to an animal which has the projicient senses poorly developed. But as we go higher in the scale it becomes more and more evident that the trials are very far from being random. Work with rats using many different types of mazes has shown that just as a rat can adjust itself the better to partial reinforcement when it comes in some regular order rather than when it is random (Tyler *et al.*, 1953), so it does not attempt to deal with the maze situation in a random manner. On the contrary, it shows signs of having a definite system—a set of 'hypotheses' as Krechevsky calls them—and it can be predicted with a reasonable reliability what turns will be attempted and in what order they will be taken. Some blind alleys, for instance, will be entered infrequently, others significantly more often. Krechevsky in his first experiment showed that different rats tend to use different sets of hypotheses when learning a maze. When he analysed the pattern of turns made by a given animal on each trial in the maze, he found that some reacted consistently to spatial cues, using their vision relatively little; the response of others was primarily visual, while yet others would show both types of behaviour. Thus in practice the animal often appears to select one type of cue, and if he succeeds on this basis will not use the others at all. If, however, he is unsuccessful, the less preferred responses are brought into use, and so we get the appearance of a systematic variability in behaviour. Cole (1951), in his work on discrimination reversal learning in monkeys, finds evidence for both Krechevsky's hypothesis theory and Spence's continuity theory[1] and that they are, in fact, complementary. Thus if the problem presented to the animal is just within the range of its capacity to form 'hypotheses,' it does so; but if the problem is just too difficult, the more primitive form of continuity behaviour is resorted to.

Krechevsky and others have used this hypothesis behaviour as an indicator for the effect on learning of various brain lesions, and have shown that normal animals will, in many types of experiment (Krechevsky, 1937), show a greater resource and variability in the number of alternative paths they will try than will animals which have less of the cortex functional. Here it seems that the number of hypotheses is roughly proportional to the *total amount* of cortex available, but not to the particular parts of the cortex which have been removed. In further experiments (Krechevsky, 1938), in which the animals were given a detour problem,

[1] The theory that discrimination learning involves a gradual and continuous process of building up the excitatory strength of the positive cue as against the competing strength of the negative cue. The continuity-discontinuity controversy is well discussed by Osgood (1953, pp. 446–55) and a valuable recent critical summary is contributed by Broadbent (1961).

the apparatus was so constructed that at the first choice-point the rat had to discriminate between lights of two intensities, choosing the path towards the brighter. It could choose between a long spiral path along which the food and light were visible all the time and the short path through a tunnel directly to the food. This short path was, however, psychologically the 'longer' detour, because the animal had to leave the field where the light and the food were visible. It was found that a high proportion of the animals with impaired cortex chose the spiral, longer path, even though it was shown in another experiment that their intensity-discrimination powers were quite unimpaired; and so we see that, while they could make the comparison between the intensities perfectly well, in fact as well as the controls, they tended to depend much more on the light cue than did the normal animals. In other words, once again the variability of their behaviour was reduced.

If we look at animals given a different kind of problem—one in which they have to manipulate something rather than take a particular direction or route, the same result emerges. In such problem-box experiments a variety of actions may be attempted, and these again are not random. The animal with the complete cortex can vary its behaviour and, above all, combine the individual behaviour items in its repertoire more readily into a successful and rapid solution of the problem than can the others.

In the maze experiments there has been much discussion as to how far some of these preferences or 'hypotheses' may be due to some quite simple tendencies characteristic of the individual animal. For instance, a forward-going tendency or a tendency to centrifugal swing which is held to account for some of the preferences shown by an animal when it approaches a turn in the maze. But, although such suggestions have clarified some features of maze learning and have shown that some of the rats' maze performance is attributable not to learning itself but to factors inherent in the maze pattern, yet these do not render unnecessary a 'hypothesis' theory or something similar.

To sum up, then, we see that classical conditioning is the establishment of an association between a normal reward or reinforcement (which can usually be regarded as involving a consummatory act) and a new external or exteroceptive stimulus, which is initially indifferent in the sense that it does not innately release any specific responses and so does not originally have any 'meaning' for the animal. Instrumental conditioning, on the other hand, is the establishment of an association between a voluntary motor act as part of appetitive behaviour primarily as perceived by the animal's proprioceptive organs, and the normal reward or reinforcement—which again involves a consummatory act. Thus both combine to make up the full normal process of trial-and-error learning; the first by conditioning the external situation to the *innate releasing mechanism*, the second by conditioning a voluntary motor act of the appetitive behaviour to the *innate motor mechanism* of the consummatory act. Thus Exteroceptive stimulus + I.R.M. = reflex conditioning. Proprioceptive stimulus + I.M.M. = instrumental conditioning. And reflex conditioning + instrumental conditioning = trial-and-error learning. Both components of learning are regarded as essentially anticipatory in the sense of having prospective reference to an ensuing reinforcement in the form of a reward or a consummatory act, but whereas the first component is essentially passive, the second involves active trial or appetitive behaviour.

While we have, for the sake of simplicity, so far spoken of the reinforcement or consummatory act as innate, we must remember that second-order conditioning, in which learned or habitual actions and rewards take the place of innate ones, is also extremely common in higher animals. Thus it is, in fact, often very difficult to determine whether a response is learned or instinctive. One would have thought that the response of a dog to the smell of meat would surely be inborn, yet the experiments of Cytovich (1911) (see Konorski, 1948, p. 123) suggest that the dog's response to meat odour is probably not an inborn unconditioned reflex but is the result of trial-and-error learning. In order to demonstrate this the dogs were fed exclusively on milk for a long time after birth.[1] When the animals were shown meat for the first time, no salivation was evoked either by its sight or its smell, and only when meat had been fed to them once or twice did the conditioning process commence which led eventually to the misleading appearance of an unconditioned reflex.

For trial-and-error learning, then, one must have appetitive motivation (e.g. the drive of the pecking response), often appearing as if governed by 'curiosity' relating to the external world; and so we see that trial-and-error learning is especially characteristic of the unrestrained animal in something like its normal environment actively performing one of its normal activities. It is, taking the animal kingdom as a whole, infinitely the most important learning process involved in adjusting the 'voluntary' actions to the environment. It enters into every positive example of individual adaptation of motor behaviour, and there is no instance of adaptive modification of actions, however 'insightful' and 'intelligent' it may appear, that does not comprise trial-and-error learning in at least some degree. All training of animals—whether for locomotion or other utilisation of muscle power, whether of sheep-dog, circus elephant or human baby (Skinner, 1951)—depends upon it at some stage if not at every stage; and there is nothing that can be called a habit which lacks it altogether.

---

[1] The experiments are not fully convincing in that the possibility of instinctive regression was not apparently allowed for. Nevertheless, it seems unlikely that this would have accounted for the results.

Play as Practice and its Further Significance

Finally, if trial-and-error learning is a means of acquisition of skill—if, indeed, practice does make perfect—we should expect play to have an important part in the development of motor habits in the young animal. This is probably true; but play is also much more. Groos (1898) regarded all incomplete reactions as play, and described the biological value of them as practice. But the evidence for this is still very weak (Beach, 1945), and the practice theory obviously neglects some very important considerations, which have become much more evident in the light of the modern reformulations of instinct theory. Firstly, behaviour having the superficial appearance of play may merely be an essential step in the maturation or seasonal development of a more or less rigid consummatory act or other inborn behaviour pattern. As we have seen above (p. 57), it is characteristic of initial maturation that the more stereotyped components or consummatory acts at or near the end of a chain of instinctive behaviour elements tend to appear before the introductory elements which constitute the appetitive behaviour. This often results in the said consummatory acts being unrelated to the normal stimulus and so appearing to be *in vacuo* as *vacuum activities (Leerlaufreaktionen)*.[1] Similarly in the annual or seasonal development of behaviour, where a rising hormone concentration can be assumed as the immediately efficient cause, the appetitive behaviour may be incomplete in itself, or if complete may appear disoriented because the consummatory act cannot yet be performed.

Now, both these situations may be found to be favourable for learning and for the acquisition of skills. In other words, both *may* provide opportunities for 'practice.' Yet obviously neither implies the occurrence of 'play' in quite the normal colloquial sense of the word. From our point of view the most important of the many strands of meaning inherent in the ordinary usage of the word is that of 'freedom.' Applying this idea to ethology, we should expect to find play in those situations where behaviour has become temporarily or permanently freed from restriction. We should

---

[1] Examples of this are not infrequently seen in animals in zoos. Dr. Belle Benchley has described to me one experience she had of at least two fatal panics of captive Zebras and of Prong-horned Antelopes at the San Diego Zoo; thus supporting the well-known statements of Antonius and Lorenz on this point. Perhaps such instances can be related to the well-known shock disease which besets wild mammals when first taken captive. Christian and Ratcliffe (1952) quote fourteen examples in four families of carnivora, all of which were species adapted to lives of sustained and violent activity, yet all of which died after relatively minor stress—such as being transferred to new quarters or disturbed by repairs to adjacent cages. Ten of them were known to have died of convulsive seizure. It is suggested that they died of hypoglycaemia resulting from inability to respond to sustained stimulation because the adrenal cortices, and in some cases the pituitary bodies, had undergone partial atrophy through inactivity.

not anticipate it where the appetitive behaviour, even though flexible, is primarily tied to and motivated by the drive arising from the co-ordination mechanism of an unreleased consummatory act or a consummatory situation not yet attained. Thus we should hardly expect to find much evidence of play in invertebrates because not only is the behaviour simpler and more rigid in such groups but also because, as all the evidence goes to show, the link between appetitive behaviour and consummatory act is much stronger there than it is in the 'higher' animals. True play may be expected wherever the circumstances of environment or life history are such that appetitive behaviour can become emancipated from the restriction imposed by the necessity of attaining a specific goal; in other words, in the young of animals with prolonged post-embryonic development and where the primary needs are satisfied by the care of the parents (i.e. in nidicolous birds and in mammals) and, above all, under conditions of domestication. This is not, of course, to be taken to imply that learning in the appetitive phase of behaviour only occurs as and when that appetitive behaviour becomes detached from the organisation for the consummatory act. To do so would be contrary to the whole central argument of the present book. It is rather the scope of the learning which differs in the two instances. In the normally activated appetitive behaviour a new obstacle or hindrance will, of course, draw the attention of the animal to that obstacle, and as a result it will learn something about it and about ways of circumventing or avoiding it. This is the process by which the world of an instinctively motivated animal becomes delimited, and by which appetitive behaviour becomes oriented and perfected through the types of learning we have been considering. But the instinctive drive is not thereby lessened; on the contrary, it is usually heightened and the threshold lowered, and if the behaviour is sufficiently variable or flexible we get the subjective impression of purposiveness or foresight. If, however, the goal of the instinctive drive is satisfied either by the abnormally easy conditions of life, or by attentions of the parents, or by the care of a human master or keeper, then, provided the appetitive behaviour is not too strictly tied to the consummatory act but has, or has appropriated, some motivation of its own, we get the beginnings of a general exploration of the environment. This may often take the form of 'play', and is particularly likely so to do in species where the bodily organisation is such as to allow the manipulation of discrete objects or 'things' in the environment. This process of play obviously may lead to a relatively enormous widening of the animals' horizons, for there is evidence both from field observation of birds (e.g. Bower Birds) and from experimental work on mammals (e.g. Montgomery, 1954, on rats, Harlow and McClearn, 1954, on monkeys) that learning ability can be based solely on an exploratory drive and that (certainly for rats and probably also for monkeys) a novel stimulus can function as a reinforcing agent and itself *increase* the exploratory drive.

Provided, then, that the conditions of life are easy, play, however great its practical value may be as a means of learning about and so mastering the external world, is always in danger of becoming the main outlet for the animals' energies, and so dysgenic.

In such a situation the animal (as Bally, 1945, says) now gives the impression not of foresight but of 'back sight' (*Rücksicht* in a naïve or literal sense); also, indeed, of insight and perhaps even of reflection and consideration. Hindrances and obstacles are no longer simply objects to be avoided or surmounted in the course of a sequence of oriented instinctive behaviour; they have become objects of investigation in themselves. The instinctive limitations are now in a measure transcended and new worlds are opened up; new freedoms have been achieved.

But when we come to birds and mammals with a family or social life, yet another aspect of play becomes evident. Lorenz (1935) makes the point that an important difference between play and mere vacuum activity is that, while the majority of vacuum activities are probably identical with the autochthonous or true ones as far as the central nervous processes are concerned, in the true play of social animals all the social inhibitions are maintained even when the playing is violent and passionate. Thus there is no doubt that the playful combat between two young dogs is fundamentally different from serious fighting.[1] However fierce they may appear they do not bite one another seriously, and we seem justified in saying that they are obviously 'not in earnest.' In other words, we are now bringing in the 'higher' or more psychological concept of 'pretence.'

Meyer-Holzapfel (1956*a* and *b*) has made a careful study of the characteristics and implications of the play of mammals. She shows that this may include innate patterns, acquired patterns and combinations of the two. It is not directed towards a specific consummatory situation (that is to say, it is not 'in earnest'), it is performed for its own sake, or, in other words, it is *its own* consummatory act. It has its own appetitive behaviour and may be correlated to an object, including the animal's body as a whole or its parts. Play has often a social component, as in play with a partner or partners used as an intermediate object, and play is often repeated a very large number of times in succession. It will be seen from this that play is very close to exploratory behaviour. In no case is a major instinctive drive involved, though play is probably often an expression of a general drive which is largely suppressed as soon as the specific drive is activated. It may be said that when we have a general drive we can recognise it by lack

[1] It is significant that as soon as play activities become social, freedom immediately necessitates the 'conventions' of animal play resembling the voluntarily accepted rules of human play. (E. A. Armstrong.)

of preference for any instinctive actions over learned ones (cf. p. 10 above). Rensch and Dücker (1959) have made a detailed study of the play of *Mungo* and *Ichneumon*; of particular interest is their description of the way in which play with real prey usually changes into 'serious' behaviour and then leads to killing and eating. Similarly, playful defence may change into serious defence, but play-fighting rarely leads to a serious fight. Rensch and Dücker give references to other important studies of Meyer-Holzapfel, Tembrock and others (see also Matthews, 1952, and Adamson, 1960).

This consideration of animal play and its function in acquiring skill, in mastering the external world and in extending the perceptual horizons, inevitably raises the problem of human play. What light, if any, does the study of animal play throw upon the play and freedom of human beings? To follow up this fascinating matter would be far outside the scope of this book, but a few words may be said about Bally's stimulating study of this subject in his book *Vom Ursprung und von der Grenzen der Freiheit* (1945). He opens with a quotation from Schiller: 'Der Mensch spielt nur, wo er in voller Bedeutung des Wortes Mensch ist, und er ist nur da ganz Mensch, wo er spielt.' But his study shows in effect how basically similar in many respects is play in animals and humans. There is, indeed, good reason for thinking that the prolonged childhood of the human species, coupled with the extreme infantile sexuality (occurring as it does so long before there is any possibility of consummatory sexual behaviour), have been of prime importance in the process of freeing appetitive behaviour from the primary needs. This and man's growing mastery of his environment have been the essential first steps not only for play but for all those activities which transcend mere maintenance and which underlie the mental and spiritual development of man; activities which, though originating in 'play,' have produced real advances in knowledge and comprehension of the scheme of things, and which may, for all we know, offer vistas of advance in the millennia to come, compared to which our present understanding will seem exceedingly puny and childish.

Summary

1. The origin of connectionist or associationist psychology is briefly traced, and the work of Thorndike, with its concepts of 'bonds' strengthened according to the 'law of effect,' is placed in its contemporary setting. The relation of Pavlov's work and the Behaviourism of Watson to early associationism is considered, together with its present-day descendant in the form of Hull's great system. The effect on learning theory of the rise of Gestalt psychology is briefly described.

2. The classical conditioned reflex is discussed in relation to behaviour

theory. It typically results in linking the innate response proper to one stimulus to another stimulus when the two stimuli are applied in overlapping sequence. It is thus looked upon as an artificially isolated part of the natural 'anticipatory' learning process; the appetitive motor behaviour normally associated with the unconditioned stimulus having been suppressed. Its chief function under natural conditions seems to be that of adjusting the innate releasive mechanism (I.R.M.) to the complexities of experience which the external world provides.

3. The various so-called sub-types of conditioned reflex are considered as resulting from the incomplete elimination of the normal appetitive behaviour.

4. Trial-and-error learning is the name for the kind of total learning process in which the phenomenon known as 'Instrumental Conditioning' or 'Conditioned Reflex Type II' is fundamental. In contrast to the conditioned reflex, it concerns the adjustment of the appetitive motor behaviour —the 'voluntary' muscular movements—to the changing environment. It is also 'anticipatory,' and the trials are to be thought of as in some degree genuine trials in the sense of being real attempts, however simple and elementary, to cope with the problem situation. Thus appetitive motivation is necessary before the process of trial-and-error learning can begin.

5. No absolutely precise distinction can be made between trial-and-error learning and instrumental conditioning, which primarily involves proprioceptive stimulation, in contrast to the classical Pavlonian conditioned reflex which primarily involves exteroceptive stimulation. But it is suggested that instrumental (or perhaps better motor) conditioning is the essential basis of trial-and-error. Certain examples of skill-acquisition can be regarded as pure instrumental conditioning, but in nearly all natural examples the full learning process is made up of both motor conditioning and classical conditioning combined. This combined process is what we call trial-and-error learning. Just as classical conditioning is an artificially isolated part of a whole natural learning process, so the attempts to isolate instrumental or motor conditioning often turn out to be artificial too. But since instrumental conditioning carries with it and implies the presence of the motivational drive of the appetitive behaviour, it comes very much nearer to constituting the whole associational learning process than classical conditioning ever does by itself.

6. The phenomena included under the term 'play' are critically considered, since it is often taken for granted that play is exclusively the expression of incomplete consummatory acts the biological function of which is to acquire skill by a process of trial-and-error learning. It is pointed out that while this is undoubtedly true and play does provide important opportunities for practice, the idea of 'freedom' inherent in the colloquial use of the word also has important implications for ethology.

Thus true play is to be expected where appetitive behaviour becomes emancipated from the restriction imposed by the necessity of attaining a specific goal. Such play can lead (and in evolution appears to have led in birds and mammals) to an enormous widening of perceptual horizons and thus to the development of exploratory drive. Thus the process of freeing appetitive behaviour from the primary needs increases perception of and mastery over the environment, and must have been one of the first and perhaps the most important of the behaviour changes which made possible the development of social life in the vertebrates, and indeed ultimately the mental and spiritual life of man himself.

CHAPTER V

LATENT LEARNING AND INSIGHT LEARNING AND THEIR RELATION TO TRIAL-AND-ERROR

(a) Latent Learning

A MAZE can be defined as a detour problem in which the goal is not visible from the start, and which therefore, however simple it may be, cannot be fully and immediately mastered by insight. Since a fully insightful solution is then ruled out, this solution must be, in part at least, by trial-and-error. The first question then is—how far can the traditional type of trial-and-error theory account for maze learning?

It can of course be supposed that the animal learns, on the earliest runs, that part of the maze nearest to the food-box; and then on consecutive later runs slowly adds to that section a 'knowledge' of the previous bit of the maze; so building up by a series of conditioned responses a complete learning of the maze from the food-box backwards. But, in fact, there is strong evidence that something more than a theory of *traditional* or 'random' trial-and-error learning is required to account for a good deal of maze behaviour; for, as Dennis and Heineman (1932) showed, the rats' behaviour in the maze is, in fact, non-random from the start. The more elaborate types of maze differ from the simpler ones chiefly in their complexity and the length of time taken over the trial runs. In the learning of complex mazes, the obvious reinforcement of the conditioning process comes only at the end of a particular combination of trial acts. The very simplest types of maze, such as the dual-compartment maze and 'Y' and 'T' mazes, having only one choice-point, may for a higher animal be little more difficult to learn than is a simple food discrimination habit. But one of the drawbacks of the maze technique in animal behaviour studies is that it is difficult, if not impossible, to vary only one factor at a time. The addition of an extra turn or an extra blind alley to a maze makes it more difficult in several respects: firstly—considered as a series of right and left turns— there are increased chances of error; secondly, the path is more complicated and so more difficult to learn as a whole; and, thirdly, it is longer, with the result that the time which elapses between the trial act and the reinforcement is also increased. This delayed reinforcement is probably for many animals the critical factor in the situation, but it is often extremely difficult, if not impossible, to disentangle these various effects; the whole response of running a labyrinth is extremely complex, and its complete analysis correspondingly difficult. Nevertheless, the maze technique has one substantial advantage, which is that for many animals the problem set is a very natural one. Many animals have to find their way about in the wild, and to ask them to learn a maze is to put them a problem in the solving of which they are likely to be able to show their abilities to the full. Warren (1957) has compared the maze learning abilities of animals of various phyla. He finds it possible to range his examples in two progressive series with respect to increasing rates and limits of complexity: (a) an invertebrate series from annelida to insects and (b) a vertebrate series from fish to mammal.

As the study of maze learning in rodents has progressed, more and more results have come to hand which to make the simple trial-and-error hypothesis seem increasingly inadequate as a complete explanation of performance. Lashley (1918) and Simmons (1924) were among the first to produce evidence for non-rewarded maze learning; but perhaps the first set of experiments which really brought this problem into full relief were those of Blodgett, who coined the term 'latent learning' to denote learning without patent reward or, to define it more precisely, the *association of indifferent stimuli or situations without patent reward* (Konorski in Thorpe, 1950).

Blodgett (1929), Elliott (1930) and Tolman and Honzik (1930b) showed that rats which had experienced daily unrewarded runs through a maze on ten successive days, when presented with food in the food-box displayed a very striking decrease, both in errors and times of running, as compared with a control group (see also Haney, 1931). What the technique does, then, is to turn the maze into a special kind of detour problem in which the goal has been shown to the animal before it has been 'labelled' as a goal. Maier (1932) showed that a very simple maze may be entirely mastered through random exploration; the introduction of a reward, therefore, merely causes the animal to demonstrate its learning. Further confirmation of this was provided by Daub (1933), Herb (1940), C. E. Buxton (1946) and Karn and Porter (1946). The fully 'trained' animal, once it has found food in one part of the maze, can then go direct to that point from any other part of the maze in which it is placed. Oakes (1956) has demonstrated latent learning with rats in Maier's three-table apparatus (Fig. 14).

In the above experiments it is the incentive that is withheld or manipulated. Another method of approach to the latent-learning problem has been via differential motivation experiments where the drives are manipulated. Leeper (1935) found that when rats were given runs in a 'T' maze with hunger and thirst motivation on alternate days, they learned almost as much from their incorrect responses as they did from their correct ones. Thus when, satiated with food, they mistakenly entered the food-box where they did not eat, they nevertheless learned something about the food-place which was of use to them on the next day when they were hungry—and *vice versa*. Spence and Lippitt (1940) followed this up by training food-satiated rats under thirst motivation and then testing under a hunger drive, but failed to find evidence of latent learning. Kendler (1946, 1947), Kendler and Mencher (1948), Grice (1948) and Walker (1948), all similarly obtained negative results in spite of special precautions to ensure that the goal objects were fully obvious to the rats. These results have been held by some to be destructive of the latent-learning hypothesis; but it now seems fairly clear that, in fact, they are not so. They merely seem to show that under conditions of strong motivation by a primary hunger or thirst drive, *generalised* exploratory learning characteristic of appetitive behaviour may be inhibited—as, indeed, one would expect from general principles concerning the incompatibility of drives. That this is probably the true explanation is indicated not merely by the success of the straight latent-learning experiments referred to above (Blodgett, Elliott, Haney, Daub, Herb, etc.), but also by some earlier experiments of Spence and Lippitt (1940) in which rats were trained under *satiation for both food and water*. Under these conditions, as in the later experiments of Meehl and MacCorquodale (1948), we seem justified in assuming that the satiation of the primary needs allows the general exploratory appetitive behaviour or drive to assert itself, and the animal is once again free to collect general information about the topography of its environment.

An excellent summary and evaluation of the whole body of latent-learning experiment and theory as far as it concerns the maze learning of rats has recently been contributed by Thistlethwaite (1951). The latent-learning and differential motivation experiments are, as we have seen, not always consistent in their results. This, however, should cause no surprise since there are still many improvements to be made in the control and design of such experiments. The results of latent-learning research are already so crucial that we may be sure that new developments in this field will quickly take place and that the already voluminous latent-learning literature on the rat will continue to increase. Yet, even with the rat, the strength of the latent-learning results as evidence not only for an exploratory drive but also for some form of expectancy theory is already most striking. It is noteworthy that MacCorquodale and Meehl (1954), although starting out with a highly critical attitude, found themselves, after a very detailed study, 'somewhat more impressed by the over-all trend of evidence than we had expected to be'; and when we consider the strong support now available from other and lower animal groups, we seem safe in taking latent learning as remarkably well established.

But how far is latent learning entitled to the distinction of a separate category, and what are its essentials? And if it is a distinct type, how is it to be related to the other categories of learning? It seems that latent learning involves the following three separate elements which are characteristic, in that they are not necessarily found in the simpler types of learning. It is often learning without specific motivation by any of the primary needs; it results in a kind of 'transfer of training,' whereby the animal can use its learned behaviour in response to changed motivation; and it denotes a faculty enabling the animal, without any trial-and-error process, to 'select' or attend to certain parts of the previously learned whole as a signal for the whole or in relation to certain specific needs (Thorpe, 1938, 1943–4).

With regard to the question of motivation, it might be objected that there can be no action or learning without it, and that the animal in the maze, if neither seeking food nor motivated by one of the other primary needs, is trying to get out; in other words, is activated by the 'need' to escape. To use Russell's (1935, 1938) terminology, the whole environment has escape valence. Now, this may well be true in part—the animal may be, in effect, exploring its environment as *a result of* its need for food or escape. But this, of course, does not mean that the process can be regarded as an example of simple trial-and-error learning; for the rat, by its efforts, does not get food nor does it escape (see Haney, 1931; Daub, 1933; Herb, 1940); therefore, on the pure trial-and-error principle there is no adequate basis for such learning as is manifested. Actually what we have here amounts to much the same thing as exploration for its own sake—generalised exploratory appetitive behaviour (Thorpe, 1944). We may say that 'the animal tends to explore its surroundings: that it has a tendency to investigate its environment.' Indeed, it has recently been shown not only that pure manipulation of a mechanical puzzle is an adequate motivation for the learning of new discriminations and the acquisition of new responses in rhesus monkeys, but that *visual exploration* alone will also serve as a reward (Harlow, in Brown *et al.*, 1953; Butler, 1953; Harlow, Blazek and McClearn, 1956).

Berlyne (1960) shows that other experiments achieve a more stringent demonstration of the reward value of sights and sounds by making stimulus consequences independent of manipulatory behaviour once they have been introduced. The power of the stimuli in question to *reinforce* an investigatory response is also separated from any power they may have to *evoke* such a response, by withholding them until the response has been executed. Thus Moon and Lodahl (1956) have shown that a change in illumination will reinforce lever pressing in the rhesus monkey as it will in the rat and the mouse.

Monkeys will also learn to open a door with the possibility of looking out of the box in which they are confined as the sole incentive, and they will form a discrimination between colours characterising a door that can be opened and another door that will not yield to pressure.

Experiments in which monkeys are free to push and hold open a door *ad libitum* for long periods have shown how astonishingly resistant this behaviour is to extinction or satiation. Butler and Harlow (1954) found that three normal animals continued to repeat the response for nine, eleven and nineteen hours respectively before giving it up. Six animals tested for ten hours on each of six consecutive days spent about 40 per cent. of the time looking out. Frequency of door-opening responses was lowest when the door gave out on to the empty room, higher when it exposed a display of fruit and other food, higher still for the sight of a toy train in motion and highest of all for the sight of another monkey. (Butler, 1953, etc.)

The conclusion that the exploration part of the behaviour is learned, not innate, has been expressed by Berlyne (1950) in an elaborate Hullian manner by postulating that a stimulus which involves novelty (or certain forms of novelty where the animal's attention is innately restricted) will arouse a *drive-stimulus-producing response* $(R \leadsto S_D)$ which he calls *curiosity.* He assumes that as a curiosity-arousing stimulus continues to affect the receptors, curiosity will diminish in that the novelty of the stimulus is diminishing. From this it follows on Hullian principles that any activity such as 'exploration' which increases stimulation by the curiosity-arousing stimulus will therefore be reinforced by the usual process of reduction of S_D, and so will be *learned.* Thus Berlyne first makes the big initial assumption that novel patterns of an often very high degree of articulation and differentiation can be differentiated by an initial learning process from familiar ones—that is, he assumes unrewarded learning to start with. He then supposes that novelty gives rise to an internal $R \leadsto S_D$ process called curiosity and with these two assumptions he can account for appetitive exploratory behaviour as learned rather than innate. But he has, in fact, by so doing merely transferred all the complexity of concept from the instinctive act (consummatory act) to the hypothetical internal drive state and the learning ability involved in perception. It is these phenomena of response to novelty by curiosity to which Pavlov refers as the 'investigatory reflex'; a highly inappropriate term, in that if this complex behaviour is described as a 'reflex,' the term 'reflex' loses all precise meaning and becomes a synonym for response. Latent learning may also be a clumsy and in some ways misleading term, but we shall make a great mistake if, having classified the phenomenon as 'exploration' or 'investigation,' we are satisfied with that and assume that all is fully understood and the observations of little significance. On the contrary, they are of the greatest significance; for, in describing a piece of behaviour as 'exploratory' or in speaking of 'an exploratory instinct,' we are at once placing the organism on a relatively high behavioural level. Indeed, we must expect to find that animals which are capable of any *complex* homing behaviour are, *mutatis mutandis*, psychologically in advance of those which are not.

The difficulties of interpreting such a performance in terms of association theory have been mentioned above, and Maier and Schneirla (1935, pp. 404–6) equate latent learning with insight learning. At one time I argued (Thorpe, 1943–4) that latent learning does not *necessarily* involve insight learning in that the situation provided by the provision of a reward is not essentially a new one, but later (1950) concluded that this was a mistake, and so am in agreement with Maier and Schneirla that since the performance does undoubtedly involve simultaneous integration and reorganisation of previous experience, the distinction is not valid. The term 'latent learning' is to some extent an unsatisfactory one in that it stresses a particular aspect of the performance which is peculiarly dependent on the artificial conditions of the experiment, and in many respects the term 'exploratory learning' is to be preferred (Thorpe, 1944). For the latent-learning experiments have not only provided something of a transition between the concepts of trial-and-error learning and insight learning; they have also drawn attention to important capabilities of animals in the field.

Observations and experiments on the homing of animals in the field cannot, of course, be expected to yield readily the precise evidence of this 'latent' or 'exploratory' learning, which, when applied to suitable cases, laboratory methods can provide. But where, as for instance in some species of Sphegid wasps, we find a homing response to a complex environmental pattern very rapidly learnt by the individual as a result of specific orientation excursions—yet, at the same time, a response which is to some extent flexible and adaptable as the situation requires—we have reasonable grounds for the assumption that powers essentially equivalent to those concerned in latent learning must be involved.

The matter of the perception of and response to novelty mentioned above raises further interesting theoretical problems. These are put, to some extent, by the facts of habituation, but much more acutely by these exploring animals. It is not merely that *anything strange* within very wide limits will elicit exploration. Even more effective is a *familiar object in a new context*. Some strange variation of something familiar is particularly potent, as Hebb (1946) found in his studies of fear in Chimpanzees, and is often responded to at first by an avoiding reaction which *rapidly* reduces stimulation. This 'fear,' which is of course equally characteristic as a response to familiar stimuli of unusually high intensity, is obviously the best way of responding to situations which may be acutely dangerous. It may be more or less slowly extinguished by habituation if no dire results occur, and cautious investigation may then follow. On the other hand, if the novelty of the stimulus situation is less intense, the gentler method of cautious investigation which *slowly* decreases the intensity of stimulation from the unfamiliar object by allowing it to become gradually familiar may be best from the start. And so we see that the difference between curiosity and fear may, in the first place (Berlyne, 1950), be one of intensity only. But whether the object is mainly strange or only partially so, whether there is exploration or flight, there is implied a highly organised background of the familiar against which something new stands out requiring investigation. The investigation completed, this new object is 'built in' to the perceptual world as something which is now familiar and which can henceforth be ignored or which can be utilised later, by 'transfer of training,' in a different context. This inclination to attend and respond to stimuli which, owing to a relatively *recent* change, stand out from a familiar environmental background is very evident in Berlyne's (1951) experiments with humans, where the effect of novelty was found to be particularly strong if the changed stimulus continued to undergo changes. A very noteworthy result here was that the effect of change is not directly proportional to the amount of change; in fact, a smaller change may be more stimulative than a large one. For it was found that the effect is not so apparent when there are several changed stimuli and only one remained unchanged. Such facts serve well to illustrate the great complexity of response to novelty, at any rate in the higher mammals. Although, as Berlyne shows, the interpretation of such data on Hull's system is not impossible, they do seem to give a strong *prima facie* case for some kind of field theory.

In the 'lower' vertebrates and 'higher' invertebrates, the perceptual world is preponderatingly instinctively determined, and latent learning, if it occurs, probably plays only a relatively small part. As has been pointed out before (Thorpe, 1944), the world of these animals in the main consists of (*a*) fairly exactly defined favourable stimuli or situations which release positive and specific responses concerned with food-getting, mating, etc., modifiable to a slight extent by associative learning, and (*b*) rather vaguely defined warning stimuli and situations which release avoiding reactions on which *habituation* (and, to a lesser degree, associative learning) works to produce modifications advantageous for the life of the animal. In addition (*c*) there may be, in exceptional cases, specific enemy recognition of the stereotyped kind described elsewhere (p. 69).

In the 'higher' vertebrates, on the other hand, the perceptual world is, to a lesser extent, determined by instinctive dispositions. Although habituation to generalised warning stimuli may still play a large part—e.g. Kuhlmann (1909) on young birds—their complex behaviour patterns are to a greater extent built up by a process of 'taking notice of' or 'investigating' a large variety of environmental factors and combinations of factors which have not any specific valence for the animal to start with. This building up, no doubt, proceeds by all types of learning, but probably much of it is due to something very like that which, when seen in a rat in a maze, we call latent learning and which is based on a tendency to 'explore the environment.'

While it surprises no one that something like latent learning should be displayed by mammals and by birds with their proverbial powers of orientation, it may come as something of a shock to comparative psychologists who work primarily with mammals to find learning of this kind displayed at a high level among invertebrates. It is true that, with the confirmation of the work of von Frisch in the orientation of the hive-bee, we are now prepared to believe almost anything of bees, but there are certainly many insects other than bees, and many invertebrates other than insects, in which latent learning and similar performances can be discerned. A number of examples of it will be found in chapters that follow. Suffice it to say here that it is highly probable that exploratory learning of this kind is involved in the topographical orientation of the Orthoptera, the Lepidoptera and perhaps also in that of the dragon-flies (Odonata) such as *Calopteryx virgo*, with their highly developed compound eyes[1] and dependence on vision; while something very similar to it has been shown experimentally to occur in a parasitic Ichneumonid, *Nemeritis canescens* (Thorpe, 1938, 1943–4). That it occurs among many of those higher Hymenoptera (Sphegidæ, Pompilidæ, Vespidæ, Apidæ, etc.), which forage in a more or less well-defined area and return at regular intervals to a particular nest, can now hardly be doubted. The beautiful experimental work of Baerends (1941) has shown the behaviour of the hunting wasp *Ammophila pubescens* to be of extraordinary complexity. The female, which digs and provisions a burrow in three stages lasting over several days with intervals in between, may have as many as three different nests under construction at one and the same time (Fig. 7), each in a different stage of completion. Besides provisioning visits, on which she brings a paralysed caterpillar to add to the store of food for her offspring, she pays occasional visits during which no prey is brought. The function of these visits is to determine whether or not the egg has yet hatched. The further provisioning of the nest depends on what the wasp finds on this 'inspection visit'; and thus this single experience may regulate the behaviour of the wasp, in regard to that particular nest and that nest only, for the following twenty-four hours or more (Fig. 7). Baerends' work has also shown the extraordinary ability these insects possess of learning the detailed topography of their territories, and I have been able (Thorpe, 1950) in this

---

[1] It is worth noting that compound eyes are not essential to form-sight in Arthropods, but that rudimentary form-sight may be achieved by means of groups of a few simple stemmata (as in lepidopterous larvæ), provided that the animal performs appropriate rotary and to-and-fro movements of the head (Dethier, 1942, 1943).

same species to demonstrate the ability to make a smooth 'planned' detour around a new obstacle (Fig. 46, p. 232) comparable to that detour behaviour which is taken as evidence of insight in the classical experiments on the subject. Thus no one who has experimented with Sphegids (e.g. the

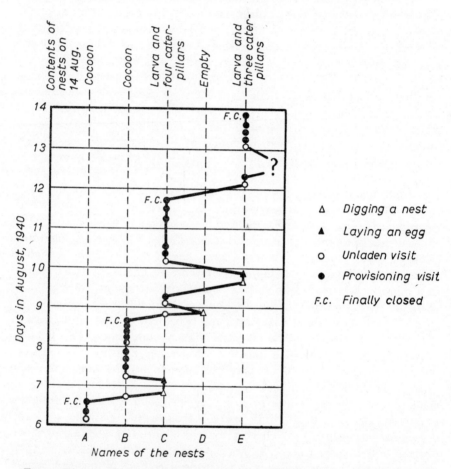

FIG. 7—Diagram of the nesting activities of an individual ♀ *Ammophila* wasp (GO) from August 6–14. (See also Fig. 4, p. 33.)

All evidence about one nest is given in a vertical column at the top of which the condition of the brood on August 14 is given. (After Baerends, 1941.)

females of *Ammophila pubescens*) when dragging their prey towards the nest can fail to be astonished at the appearance which they present of possessing a highly detailed knowledge of the general surrounding area. When in possession of prey they can easily be picked up and transferred in a dark box to another place, 100 feet or more away. (Another example

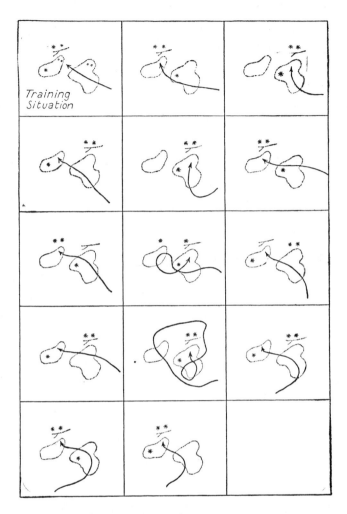

Fig. 8—Homing flights of the wasp *Philanthus triangulum* in experiments in which landmarks (three pine cones, indicated by stars, and a forked twig) are displaced. The two irregular areas indicate bare patches of ground on which nest entrances were situated (each marked by two dots in the first picture). Note that when the landmarks were moved separately or in partial combination the wasp did not orient by one particular object but by the whole group of landmarks. The highly variable flight lines of the wasp showed that it was not dependent on a constant succession of discrete stimulations in order to reach its goal but was relying on its memory of the situation as a whole. (After Tinbergen, 1942.)

of the inhibition caused by conflicting drives!) Yet when released they seldom show any signs of disorientation, but will immediately set out on and maintain a new course irrespective of the innumerable obstacles on the stony heaths on which they live, and arrive without hesitation at a closed nest (Figs. 47–8, pp. 232–5), the entrance to which is so well camouflaged that the human eye finds it impossible to detect un-aided—or even to remember when shown, unless deliberate note of the position has been taken by means of in-tersecting sight lines on conspicuous landmarks. The use of such landmarks for direction finding has been the sub-ject of detailed study in the wasp *Phil-anthus triangulum* by Tinbergen and Kruyt (1938) and van Beusekom (1948). It seems difficult to avoid the conclu-sion from such work that there is a *fundamental* similarity between such behaviour in insects and our own use of landmarks for finding our way about (Figs. 8–10). When we consider the in-feriority of even the best compound eyes of Arthropods to the eyes of mam-mals and birds, it is difficult to regard such insects as inferior to those groups in their ability to correlate and co-or-dinate their visual and other impressions for purposes of orientation. That such a performance is possible does, indeed,

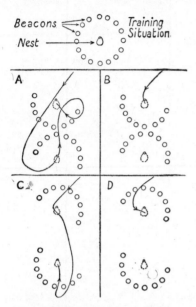

FIG. 9—Homing flights of *Philan-thus triangulum* in four experiments, A–D, in which parts of the total land-mark situation (circle of pine cones) are changed. (After Tinbergen and Kruyt, 1938.)

provide a problem for the neurologist, for the insect brain has, of course, nothing closely corresponding to the highly convoluted cortex of mammals.

(b) *Insight and Insight Learning*

In considering the categories and classification of learning, the next problem that arises is that of insight. Here it is important to make a clear distinction between insight itself and insight-learning. As a practical and convenient definition, I consider insight to be primarily a matter of the organisation of perceptions and to mean *the apprehension of relations*. Insight learning, on the other hand, includes as an essential element the appropriate organisation of effector response, and can, I suggest, be de-fined as *the sudden production of a new adaptive response not arrived at by trial behaviour* or as *the solution of a problem by the sudden adaptive reorganisation of experience*. Thus insight-learning seems to be a kind of action by hypothesis, and has often been held to be evidence of ideational processes. The concept of insight has been the subject of experiment and debate among psychologists ever since the term was brought into use by Köhler (1921), and there seems as yet no prospect of a generally agreed conclusion, though substantial progress has undoubtedly been made. Much of this discussion has centred round the question whether trial-and-error learning and insight-learning are two fundamentally different phenomena, and, if not, which of the two reveals more clearly the fundamental nature of the learning process. Here, it seems to me, the discussion has suffered from two defects. First, it has not been sufficiently recognised among psychologists how closely bound up with form vision and spatial

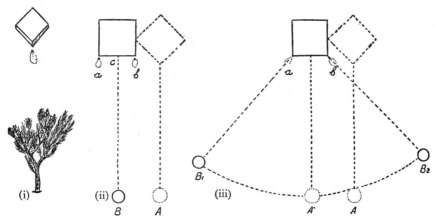

FIG. 10—Diagram showing training of homing *Philanthus triangulum* to a pair of 'landmarks' (pine branch and square block).
    (i) Initial training.
   (ii) Both landmarks displaced and block rotated through 45°. (A=training situation, B=experiment.) The wasp chose point c.
  (iii) Displacement and rotation of both landmarks. (A: place of the branch in training. B_1 and B_2: places of the branch in test after displacing (A^1) and rotating.) The wasp chose corner a when the branch was in position B_1 and b when it was in position B_2.
(After van Beusekom, 1948.)

representation is the *traditional* concept of insight. Second, the neglect of the study of invertebrate behaviour has given the impression that insight-learning is a characteristically human faculty hardly to be expected in a subprimate mammal and, of course, out of the question in an Arthropod (see Yerkes, 1943, p. 169). We now see what an astonishing misconception this is.

The question of the relation between trial-and-error and insight-learning has been profoundly influenced by the development of ideas as to the nature of reinforcement and their bearing on the Law of Effect.

The concept of reinforcement in the classical conditioned reflex hardly bears on the fundamental issue. Pavlov and his followers assumed as given that there exists an initial innate physiological construction whereby the giving of food 'satisfies' and so assuages a physiological need or drive. The mechanism of this was not inquired into and so all that was needful to 'account for' the conditioning process was a 'principle of substitution' or 'signalisation' according to which 'a conditioned stimulus acting at the time of an unconditioned response tends on its recurrence to evoke that response and hence may be said to substitute for the unconditioned stimulus' (Hilgard and Marquis, 1940). While such a formulation is adequate to the Pavlovian experiment in those exceptional instances where the conditioned response is either an exact replica of the unconditioned or is one of its components, it is clearly insufficient (Skinner, 1938, p. 111) where the conditioned response is obviously different from the unconditioned. To cope with such difficulties, which of course are inescapable with trial-and-error, the Principle of Effect has been evoked. The concept of a reward as in some way automatically stamping in a random action which happened to have been successful, had a tremendous attractiveness for the Behaviourists of the first decades of the present century, and this was what the principle supplied; but unfortunately it did not give any guidance as to the mechanism by which such a stamping in could be effected, and it thus raised the problem of the nature of reinforcement in an acute form. In its first presentation Thorndike (1911) emphasised that the hypothetical bonds were strengthened by stimuli which were followed by satisfaction for the animal, and weakened by those which preceded discomfort. It was assumed that assuagement of all the primary needs, such as hunger, thirst, sex, etc., would, for animals in the appropriate physiological state, give satisfaction; as also would escape from painful and uncomfortable circumstances. It was soon seen that owing to the difficulty of obtaining any measure of the satisfaction of a stimulus apart from its efficiency in reinforcement, the argument was really a circular one: stimuli reinforce because they satisfy, and they are assumed to satisfy because they reinforce. Skinner's use of the term 'reinforcement' is also deliberately circular, for he says (1953, p. 72), 'the only defining character of a reinforcing stimulus is that it reinforces.' Thorndike (1911, p. 245) tried to get over the difficulty inherent in assuming that conscious affective states were controlling animal behaviour by restating his law in a different form. He said, 'By a satisfying state of affairs is meant one which the animal does nothing to avoid, often doing such things as attain and preserve it. By a discomforting or annoying state of affairs is meant one which the animal commonly avoids.' This statement is, of course, just as circular as the other, although it has the merit of drawing attention to the point later emphasised by Muenzinger and Dove (1937) that while reward leads to uniformity of behaviour, punishment gives rise to variability.

The law of effect is as has often been pointed out (e.g. Hilgard and Marquis, 1940, p. 85, who give an admirably clear account) a modification of the law of contiguity. The response to be stamped in must be near in time to the reinforcement, and the last response which occurs prior to the reward is the one most strongly reinforced. But, as has been shown above, the temporal relations are different; for whereas with the principle of substitution the strength of the conditioned response depends upon the occurrence or degree of the unconditioned response, according to the principle of effect it depends upon the occurrence and intensity of the reward, which, of course, is subsequent to it and so is 'retroactive' (see p. 86, above, and also Boguslavski, 1957).

It has often been assumed that the conditioning of a 'trace' (the terms 'memory' or 'memory trace' are usually avoided) by the substitution principle might allow for the facts of trial-and-error learning; but there are so many different examples of the latter which cannot be thus accounted for that it cannot possibly be regarded as a satisfactory general explanation. An extremely elaborate system has been built up by Hull (1931) and Guthrie (1935) in which fractional anticipatory conditioned responses play a central part and are supposed to take the place of 'memories' and 'ideas'; but in the view of many critics, among which the present author numbers himself (Thorpe, 1950), the vast extension of this system resulting from its attempts to meet the increasing difficulties or complexities, has involved the virtual abandonment of all those characteristic tenets which constituted its primary virtues. In many respects the Hull theory appears to have become merely a field theory in uncouth dress.

The whole principle of effect runs into difficulties over avoidance training and secondary-reward training as, for example, where with conditioned response to shock the omission of the shock stimulus strengthens the response. The lack of shock can only be regarded as a reward on the assumption that the animal has developed an expectancy of shock. Moreover, while a positive reinforcement can theoretically be accounted for on the basis of trace conditioning, the 'stamping out' by a negative reinforcement cannot be so explained since, as pointed out above, it leads to variety rather than uniformity of action. An animal in an experimental situation which has previously led to a noxious stimulus may show a variety of new responses—cowering, backing down, escape by a new route, etc.—the only possible interpretation of which appears to be that an 'anticipation' of the noxious stimulus has been acquired. May (1948) has attempted to overcome such difficulties in certain types of experiment by postulating 'fear' as a drive. Such a stratagem is entirely superficial for, unless we accept the James-Lange theory, the term fear by definition connotes anticipation.

Especially is the principle of effect inadequate where the 'reward' is something other than the satisfaction of a primary physiological need, and this is why the latent-learning experiments are so crucial (see pp. 116, 145, below). All these and many other difficulties eventually led Thorndike and others (see Postman, 1947) to abandon the law in its original form. We may quote a paragraph from a more recent critic. Hebb (1949, p. 178) says of Hull's system:

'Its weakest point, and clearest departure from the facts, is in the treatment of motivation as biological need.

'In the first place, the apparently clear and precise definition of a need will not hold water. A need occurs "when any of the commodities or conditions for individual or species survival are missing." One of these needs is "the occasional presence and specialised reciprocal behaviour of a mate." But the absence of a mate cannot excite sensory receptors. The injection of male hormone would not affect the needs of the animal, as defined, since he is still incapable of fertilising a female and contributing to survival of the species. Yet his behaviour sexually is that of a normal animal once the injection has been made.

'The preciseness with which "need" has been defined is illusory. It is a biological statement that does not coincide with the psychological conception Hull had in mind when he wrote. First, then, it must appear that Hull's reformulation of the law of effect is not the precise postulate that it was meant to be. A system of deductions that makes repeated use of it may have a fundamental flaw.'

The latest and perhaps the most thorough critic of the system, Sigmund Koch (1954), says that attenuation of the reinforcement principle in Hullian theory has recently proceeded so far that its consequences are now in effect indistinguishable from a contiguity assumption. Speaking of the latest (1950-1) changes in postulates, he says, 'these changes impose so great a restriction upon the theory as virtually to legislate it out of existence' as a tool for the prediction of behaviour. He concludes that the only thing that it is now qualified to predict is the form of a standard learning curve!

And so we come to the Principle of Expectancy. Let us consider how far this can help us over some of those acute difficulties encountered by substitution and effect theories.

The principle of expectancy in its essence assumes that a reinforcement must be such as to confirm an expectancy and that all animal motivation which results in learning by the trial-and-error process must involve some element of reference to, some apprehension of, a time dimension. Sherrington (1906) saw this clearly when he referred to 'instinct with its germ of anticipation however slight,' and many psychologists and behaviour students have invoked it under the terms 'foresight' (McDougall), 'prospective reference' (Hobhouse), etc. In fact, it seems safe to say that perception of a time dimension including an element of expectancy is as fundamental to organisms as is perception of space.[1] Expectancy is a commonplace to those working regularly with the higher mammals. A classic example is provided by the work of Tinklepaugh (1928) who studied the behaviour of monkeys in delayed response tests. The monkeys were shown food of various kinds such as banana, carrot, lettuce, etc., hidden under inverted cups. Before they were allowed access to the cups some of the preferred foods might be replaced by less favoured ones, without, of course, the monkey being allowed to see this being done. As soon as they were allowed access, the monkeys went at once to the cup under which they had seen the preferred food, such as banana, being hidden and were visibly disappointed when they found lettuce. Though reasonably fond of lettuce under normal circumstances, they refused to accept it in place of the anticipated banana. The quantitative demonstration of expectancy in lower mammals is far from easy (Seward, 1956). Goodson, Scarborough and Lewis (1957) have shown that expectancy can be demonstrated in rats in an appropriately arranged T-maze but that it extinguishes rapidly. The way in which the expectancy principle plays an essential part in wider views of the action of proprioceptive organs in the control of taxes is both interesting and, I believe, highly significant. Thus the 'reafferentation' principle of E. von Holst and H. Mittelstaedt (1950; see also von Holst, 1954) postulates a taxis mechanism such that an *expected* reafferentation prevents abnormal or inappropriate reaction, while an *unexpected* deviation from the normal will produce either abnormally strong reaction or abnormal cessation of reaction according to the design of the experiment. This has been analysed in great detail in the Mantis by Rilling *et al.* (1959) (see p. 239 below; also Dijkgraaf, 1953). Thus the organism is enabled to distinguish between real and apparent movement, and is prevented from confusing stimuli resulting from its own movement with those resulting from movement of the environment.

The orienting reflex has been a major subject of research in the U.S.S.R. during the fifties. It is through this door that the Russian researchers approach the problems of cognition and perception, problems which have come to possess an intense interest for them in recent years, as is evinced by the work of Sokolov (1958), discussed by Razran (1961) and also by Berlyne (1960).

This study of the orientation reflex by the conditioning method ties up,

---

[1] Physiologically, expectancy must be thought of as a pattern of transient facilitation and inhibition arising out of high-level central nervous (in mammals cerebral), activity. (Sperry, 1955). Sokolov's (1960) scheme of the orienting reflex involves the concept of a neuronal model corresponding to 'expectation,' the model being postulated as a chain of neural cells which preserve information about the intensity, the quality, the duration and the order of presentation of stimuli. If the stimulus does not coincide with this neuronal model—that is to say, if the stimulus has novel properties—then an orienting reflex results.

of course, very closely with the modern interest in curiosity and arousal systems and the relation of the reticular formation to these. Razran (1961) stresses that one of the main points of interest of the orienting reflex for modern Russian workers is the fact that although no one would claim that cognition is a *sine qua non* of orienting reflex action, nevertheless fully developed orienting reflexes are cognitive or, to put it another way, cognition may be said to emerge from the orienting reflex, as the material basis. This kind of approach leads Sokolov to the view that at least some kinds of orienting response involve something in the nature of expectancy.

But to return to the question of expectancy principles in learning theory. Let us first take the reinforcement resulting from the satisfaction of primary physiological needs—hunger, thirst, sex, parenthood, etc. It is possible to imagine an animal (though difficult to find one, apart perhaps from the most degenerate internal parasites) in which the conditions of life are so simple and the possible behaviour patterns so few that learning is completely unnecessary. With such an animal continuous performance of the innate repertoire of movements has such a high probability of achieving the goal that learning ability would be quite superfluous. Here the expectancy principle has no necessary place. But suppose, as is the case with the vast majority of animals, that the appetitive behaviour is in some degree variable and that it is advantageous to select a particular form or combination of appetitive behaviour acts as appropriate to a particular environmental situation. Then for reinforcement to be effective we have to assume some kind of anticipation [1] during the appetitive behaviour to account for the retroaction of the reward. It does not matter for present purposes whether the reinforcement, consummating, for instance, the hunger drive, is one of the consummatory acts of predation, mastication and swallowing, or whether it is the visceral stimulation resulting from an adequately filled stomach by which the hunger pangs are allayed, or whether it is the more stable or complete nutritional state which results from the digestion or absorption of food (Harris *et al.*, 1933). Whichever it is, we have to assume that some action specific potential has been dispersed and 'tension' accordingly reduced.

The point is that in order for learning to occur, the reinforcement must in some sense confirm an expectancy. Now, of course, we must not for a moment assume that on its first performance of an appetitive action the animal necessarily 'knows' what its behaviour should lead to. It is abundantly clear that, in many cases at least, it cannot possibly do so. But there is also good evidence that on first performing an innate consummatory act, organisms (see, for example, Wallace Craig quoted p. 37,

---

[1] An expectancy which need not be assumed in the case of the pure habituation mechanism but which seems to be essential both for *preventing* habituation by reinforcement and for the working of a trial-and-error mechanism.

above) will show some evidence of surprise—a form of the ' "ah-ha" erlebnis' of Bühler. The behaviour is such as to suggest that the animal is expecting 'something' *but does not know what*, having perhaps an extremely generalised or elementary innate releasive mechanism. By trial-and-error it acquires, perhaps extremely slowly, perhaps very imperfectly, an insight into, a perception of, temporal relations; to quote Tolman's vivid but awkward phrase—a 'what-leads-to-what' expectancy. And this *'understanding'* is the essential basis of reinforcement in a trial-and-error learning situation.

Berlyne (1960) refers to expectancy as a device which cuts down the cost of adjustment. If the event that calls for action is part of a regularly recurring sequence of events, its predecessors can serve as warning signals. Expectations open the way to preparatory and avoidance responses or to prior selection of response by reasoning; all of which will raise the chances of success when the heralded event arrives. Expectations may diminish stress by making adjustment less abrupt. They will usually be accompanied by high arousal as well as by responses that identify the particular event that is expected. But there will be times when the precise nature of an impending occurrence cannot be anticipated; either because the appropriate cues are lacking or because their significance has not been learned. In such cases an executive response cannot be pre-selected. But those component processes of the orientation reaction that come into play in coping with any urgent situation, and do not depend on the specific properties of the situation, can, perhaps, be mobilised in advance. This is a third mechanism, that of *anticipatory arousal*. It requires the presence of a pattern of cues indicating how arousing, novel, 'conflictful,' important, etc., the experiences of the next few moments are going to be, without telling exactly what they will contain. The benefits of anticipatory arousal are that, without affording all the advantages of a specific expectation, it will permit speedier and more energetic action when the anticipated event has been detected as a result of the heightened sensitivity of receptor organs, etc. If the anticipated event has unpleasant aspects that nothing can mitigate—if it is, for example, a piece of irrevocable bad news—anticipatory arousal will make it easier to withstand the shock perhaps by producing some anticipatory habituation.

Another important conclusion follows from the expectancy principle. Not only may the appetitive behaviour which constitutes the 'trial' part of trial-and-error be largely non-random in the sense of being innately restricted, it is or becomes non-random in at least some degree as a result of being expectant. Thus trials are in a great many cases real trials, and may be based upon real hypotheses however elementary and feeble. They are often part of 'cognised behaviour routes leading to the satisfaction of expectancies.' Thus in one of Guthrie and Horton's experiments quoted by Hilgard a cat in a puzzle box, in an interval of trying to escape, accidentally backs into the trigger-post when it is in the process of backing up for another try. By this accident it opens the door. 'Its behavioural try next time may be quite inappropriate because it was simply backing up [not trying] when the door opened. Some of the cats apparently never got it cognitively clear that responding to the post had anything to do with opening the door.'

Finally, we come again to exploratory learning or latent learning, and see that merely getting to know the environment, that is having insight, is the adequate reward. Then we cannot escape the conviction, as I hope the following chapters will make clear, that for animals with a homing or exploratory drive merely getting to know the environment is tension-reducing: in other words, the fuller organisation of sense data or primary perceptions into a good gestalt can be an adequate reward. Now, of course, it is always open to those who try to express all learning in terms of reduction of need to say that the satisfaction of an exploratory drive is need reduction. But while this may be true enough, it is, in fact, a verbal quibble, for, as we shall see below, the very perception of the gestalt, which is the reinforcement, itself involves a process basically identical with insight. Followers of Hull who take this line here, in fact, throw out the baby with the bath-water. (See also Hilgard, 1945, pp. 344-5.)

It seems to the writer that the reluctance of connectionist schools of behaviour study to face the real problem of reinforcement and its relation to the drive in learning has been at the basis of the real ineffectiveness for comparative studies of the so-called 'laws of learning' which they have as yet produced. Only if it is based on a really thorough study of the innate effectory and perceptory systems of the animal and the bearing of the innate system on the internal drive will any system of learning form a reliable guide for further investigation and prediction of animal behaviour. Both Hull (1943), with his 'reactive inhibition' I_R and his 'unlearned receptor-effector connection' S_UR, and Skinner (1938) have made some of the necessary basic postulates. But it is to be doubted whether any systems will have much success in this direction unless they are prepared to utilise and incorporate every relevant fact of physiology and ethology. Systems which are by definition 'molar' are foredoomed to failure in at least some parts of their task.

So it is that in my view the work of recent years has, on the whole, confirmed many of the conclusions of Adams (1931) that all learning is in some degree the manifestation of a process basically identical with insight. According to him, trial-and-error is merely a means whereby the experimenter measures the rate of the learning process; if learning is slow, we call it trial-and-error; if rapid, we call it insight. In the latter case the rate is sufficiently rapid to enable us to see the true nature of the learning process of which it is an extreme instance.

Perhaps the arguments as to whether certain performances of rats in mazes represent insight or trial-and-error learning would have been somewhat less prolonged if the abilities of some of the 'lower animals,' such as insects, had been known. For in some of these creatures we find examples of different types of learning often less complicated and overlain by irrelevant complexities of response than in the mammals. One of the great difficulties encountered in the separation and classification of different types of learning is the fact that we can hardly ever find in nature an example of a learned response which can be regarded as belonging to one type and one only. Thus trial-and-error, in fact, includes both types of conditioning and often some habituation as well; what seems to be imprinting may turn out to be habituation plus insight-learning: and what seems to be insight-learning may on investigation be found to be latent learning plus trial-and-error. The truth is that, according to the simplicity or complexity of the problem which an animal faces, it will vary the combination of the components of its repertoire of learning abilities. If the task is not too difficult insight may provide the clue at once, but if the task is very involved, the simplest kind of trial-and-error, together with habituation, may be the only possible method of procedure.

SUMMARY

1. The learning of simple mazes by a 'pure' Trial-and-Error process is considered. The extension of the simplest kind of 'Y' or 'T' maze by the addition of one or more extra 'blinds' or sections at once makes the maze more difficult in at least four respects, of which the delay in reinforcement is considered to be the most important.

2. The story of the Latent-learning controversy is briefly summarised, and it is concluded that the existence of 'unrewarded' learning has been established by these experiments.

3. Latent Learning is defined as *the association of indifferent stimuli or situations without patent reward*. It is thus distinct from classical Trial-and-Error. Apart from this lack of what is normally regarded as essential reinforcement, there may also be lack of *specific* motivation or transfer of training to a different motivation context. On the perceptual side it involves simultaneous integration and reorganisation of previous experience, and so is inseparable from insight-learning. It is regarded as the laboratory version of that learning as a result of exploratory behaviour which so many homing animals, both vertebrate and invertebrate, display under natural conditions of life. It appears to occur at least as low in the zoological scale as the higher Arthropoda.

4. Latent Learning, in so far as it is exploratory, raises some problems concerning 'novelty' similar to those posed by habituation. It presupposes a background of the familiar against which some new stimulus stands out, and in higher animals a novel variation of something familiar may be more potent in producing response than a stimulus situation which is entirely new. In general, a new stimulus that is very intense provokes flight, whereas a similar stimulus of lesser intensity releases cautious investigation which slowly decreases the intensity and unfamiliarity of the stimulus and so leads to habituation. Thus fear reactions and exploratory reactions are evoked by the same stimulus at different intensities.

5. *Insight* is concerned with the organisation of perception and is defined as *the apprehension of relations*. Insight-learning involves *the production of a new adaptive response as a result of insight* or as *the solution of a problem by the sudden adaptive reorganisation of experience*. Insight and Insight-Learning are then discussed in relation both to Trial-and-Error and to Latent Learning. It is considered that the concept of Reinforcement is crucial here. Theories of Reinforcement based on Substitution, Law of Effect and the Principle of Expectancy are considered in turn.

6. The Principle of Substitution is considered as only adequate to the Classical Pavlovian Conditioned Reflex. The Law of Effect is found to encounter fatal difficulties in avoidance and secondary reward training and consequently the Principle of Expectancy is required.

7. The Principle of Expectancy is considered as an inevitable outcome of the fact that some perception of time or duration is as fundamental to the animal organism as is perception of space. It must find a place in any comprehensive physiological theory of learning. It is no more possible to take an animal completely out of time than it is to take it completely out of space.

CHAPTER VI

THE EVIDENCE FOR INSIGHT LEARNING
AND INSIGHT

FROM what has been said above it can be seen that latent learning, which for various reasons it has been convenient to deal with first, can easily and correctly be regarded as a form of insight-learning, and, indeed, there are examples of latent learning which are almost purely perceptual and which can be regarded as practically pure insight. Moreover, whether we regard the solution displayed by the maze-running rats in the typical latent-learning experiment as a new adaptive response or not, it is certainly an adaptive reorganisation of experience, and such trials as there have been are merely the result of the normal exploratory drive. There are, however, several other types of experiment which have been traditionally regarded as evidence for insight which it is convenient to mention here. It has, for instance, often been assumed, and with much reason, that the ability to use a tool, provided it is not merely the result of trial-and-error learning, is evidence of a real comprehension of spatial and mechanical relations and therefore of insight; and so in the chapters that follow we shall consider the evidence for tool using by animals under the heading of 'Insight.' In fact, tool using is not an easy concept to define and, while we may readily agree that the use of a stick by an ape to reach an otherwise inaccessible banana is tool using, there are innumerable instances in wild nature where definition is far more difficult. There is perhaps little doubt that when the Californian Sea Otter (*Enhydra lutris nereis*) brings a boulder up from the sea bottom and cracks the shells of 'Abalone' and other molluscs against it (Fisher, 1939), true tool using is displayed. But when a Song Thrush uses a stone on which to break the shell of a snail, or when the Bearded Vulture (*Gypætus barbatus*) drops bones from a great height on to a rock with the result that it can then extract the marrow, are we concerned with tool using in the ordinary sense of the word? The general conclusion would, I think, be negative, since these objects are not manipulated and are never in any sense an extension of the bodily mechanism.

While a well-designed experiment in which the ability to use a stick as a probe or a rake seems about as good an example of true insight as one could expect to get, recent work has shown very clearly how cautious we must be in describing even this as a *new* response; for the danger of any definition of insight which attempts to exclude the adaptive reorganisation of previous experience has become very obvious. Birch in 1945 studied the influence of previous experience in insightful problem solving, the animals used being nursery-reared Chimpanzees whose previous experience of sticks was fully known. They were required to use a hoe to get food which was otherwise out of reach. Only two out of six succeeded in a 30-minute test, and of these two only one used the stick as a functional extension of its arms. This was the one animal which had, in fact, had an extensive opportunity to use sticks and had played with them on a number of occasions. After these first tests, all the animals were given similar experience of playing with sticks and were then all re-tested. All six thereupon used the sticks as a functional extension of their arms within 20 seconds of the beginning of the experiment. With such a result it is obviously quite impossible to distinguish between latent learning and insight-learning, and here certainly the previous experience provides results out of which an adequate pattern of response can be produced. Here again, there is no overt trial-and-error shown in the actual experiments, but trial-and-error has been taking place as a result of the play which has been going on in earlier situations.

String-pulling tests are really a form of tool using, and are particularly interesting in the study of bird behaviour, where the ability to reach food by pulling up and holding a string is well known in a number of groups. The significance of this behaviour is discussed in Chapter XIV, below. The same method has been used with mammals, e.g. Tolman's work (1937) on the acquisition of string-pulling by rats, and Finch's (1941) experiments with Chimpanzees. Tolman regards his results as clear evidence of the two most advanced of his seven classes or types of learning—inferential and inventive learning—which may be said roughly to correspond to the present definition of insight learning, inferential learning being the approximate equivalent of latent learning and inventive learning the production of a new response. More recently Nissen, Chow and Semmes (1951) have made a fuller study of the effects on learned and other behaviour of restricting the opportunity for tactile, kinesthetic and manipulative experience in Chimpanzees. They found that, while restriction of the use of the hands and arms had no noticeable effect on the development of visual discrimination ability, including perception of size, form and depth, it did hinder the development of tactual motor co-ordinations, and, indeed, seemed to have effectually inhibited some of the behaviour, such as climbing and grooming, which is normally regarded as part of the instinctive pattern. (Cf. Chapter XVI, p. 461, below.)

Detour Behaviour

The ability of an animal to make a detour round an obstacle without preliminary random trial-and-error behaviour has long been regarded as evidence for insight learning, and there has been much work on this subject using various mammals for experiment. But, as has been shown above (p. 100), not only does the difficulty of a detour problem depend upon the length and complexity of the detour, but also upon whether or not the goal can be seen by the animal throughout the course of the detour route. A detour during which the goal is out of sight even for a very short space of time is often much more difficult [1] to accomplish than is one where it is in full view throughout. Moreover, with work of this kind it is always risky to put much reliance on detour performance unless the first responses of the previously untrained individual are studied under controlled conditions, and unless the previous experience of that individual is adequately known. It is practically only with rats that these conditions have been fulfilled, but here the detour method of studying insight has been very profitable, although the results have been by no means consistent. Figs. 11–13 show some special types of 'maze' which have been used to study insight in rats, and a further discussion of the subject will be

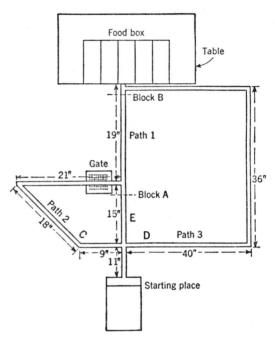

FIG. 11—Tolman and Honzik's apparatus to test for learning by insight in the rat.

The pathway is elevated. Preliminary training taught the rat that, after finding path 1 blocked at A, he could reach the food-box via either paths 2 or 3. Evidence of 'insight' occurs when, finding path 1 blocked at B, the animal selected path 3 (which was not preferred under ordinary circumstances) instead of path 2, which was now as inadequate as path 1 to take him to the food-box. (After Tolman and Honzik, 1930a.)

found in Chapter XVI, below. Those who found what appeared to be satisfactory evidence of a sudden insightful solution were Higginson (1926), Hsiao (1929), Tolman and Honzik (1930), while insightful behaviour in rats in the standard detour experiments has been described

[1] There are striking exceptions—as in certain cephalopods when a glass screen is interposed (see Chapter X, below). No doubt the relative development of visual and tactile senses is a determining factor here.

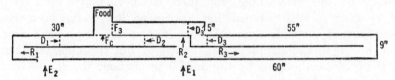

FIG. 12—Maze used by Hsiao *to* study insight in the rat. E_1 and E_2 represent alternative entrances. When the starting-box was placed at E_1, E_2 was closed, and when it was placed at E_2, E_1 was closed. D_1, D_2, D_3, D'_3, F_3 and F_C are doors made of wire mesh. They hang from the top and swing only in the directions indicated by small arrows. They are manipulated by the rat itself. The maze presents three alternative routes to food (irrespective of whether the entrance is at E_1 or E_2). The first route, R_1, starts from the entrance (either E_1 or E_2) and thence goes via D_1 and F to food.

The second route, R_2, starts from the entrance and thence goes via D_2 and F to food. The third route, R_3, starts from the entrance and thence goes via D_3, D'_3 and F_C to food. It will be noted that routes R_1 and R_2 converge into a final common path, viz. as part of the section between D_1 and D_2 and the common door F_C, leading from this section into the food-compartment. (After Hsiao, 1929.)

by Helson (1927) and Hamilton and Ballachey (1934). On the other hand, Valentine (1928), Gilhousen (1931) and Keller and Hill (1936) obtained negative results in this type of experiment (see also Dove and

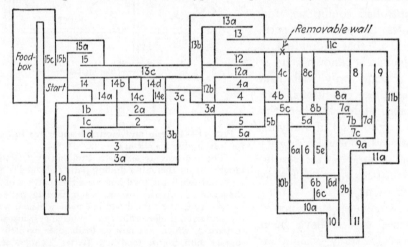

FIG. 13—Shepard's test of 'reasoning'.
The odd numbers indicate the true path; the even, blind alleys. After rats have learned the maze, the section indicated by 'X' is removed, thereby causing a previous blind alley to become a short-cut through the maze. On discovering the change, rats immediately use the short-cut. (After Maier and Sheneirla, 1935.)

Thompson, 1943, and Heron, Oxman and Singley, 1946). Grabowski (1957) describes what appears to be insight in the Chow dog but Wyrwicka (1959), as a result of an extensive study of detour behaviour in young puppies, comes to the conclusion that the detour reaction is a locomotor

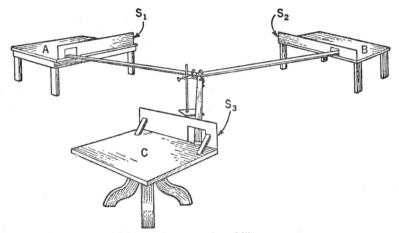

FIG. 14—Apparatus used for testing reasoning ability.

The pathways are 8 feet long and the small tables vary in size, shape and character. S_1, S_2 and S_3 are wooden screens placed on the tables to obstruct vision from one to the other. After exploring the three tables and runways (experience I) the rat is fed, let us say, on Table A (experience II). It is then, let us also assume, placed on table C. After reaching the joint origin of the three paths, the animal now has a choice between A and B. If it chooses A, it is credited with a correct response. Exploration precedes each test. The rat is started from different tables from test to test. In a group of such tests, a score of 50 per cent. would occur by chance. The difference between the number of correct and incorrect runs divided by the number of tests would yield a chance score of zero. In some rats this score has reached 90 per cent. (From the original of Fig. 1, N. R. F. Maier, *J. Comp, Neur.* **56**, 181.)

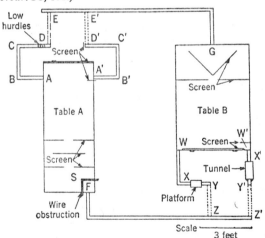

FIG. 15—Diagram of apparatus used for testing the ability of rats to integrate four separate experiences.

The tables and pathways form a continuous indirect route from the starting-point, S, to the food-place, F. The two pairs of broken lines, DE, D'E', and YZ, Y'Z', indicate sections of interchangeable pathways. Since but one member of each pair of the interchangeable paths was in place on each test, the route to food could be varied from day to day. Screens obstruct the vision so the pathway could not be seen until after a choice had been made. The route to food on each day could be determined only from the specific part experiences given immediately before the test. Characteristic landmarks making for visual, tactual and kinæsthetic sensory differences are present to reduce confusion. (After Maier, 1932.)

conditioned reflex which is acquired by an animal usually early in its life. This reflex is later widely generalised—that is to say, it may appear in all conditions similar to those to which it was primarily established. Very similar to the experiments with 'mazes' just mentioned are those of Maier with devices (Figs. 14 and 15) designed to test what he calls reasoning ability; that is, the ability to manipulate the effects of previous experience to provide a novel solution. It is generally agreed, in spite of the criticism of Wolfe and Spragg, that rats do show insightful behaviour in such circumstances, but there does not seem any adequate reason for separating success in such tests from the other tests of insight, as do some others, e.g. Munn (1950).

Apart from special detour experiments, the ordinary standard type of experiment on rats has produced a great deal of evidence of 'intelligent hypothesis,' and it must be emphasised that this 'hypothesis' is not, as some have tried to argue, just a kind of behaviour—it is something *inferred from* behaviour (Prentice, 1946). As Harlow (1949) has shown in experiments with monkeys, the process of acquiring a 'learning set,' that is, the process of learning to learn, often transforms an animal from one whose attempts seem nearly if not quite random into one which appears to proceed by true hypothesis and insight; and such hypotheses can reasonably be regarded, at least in many of the experiments with higher mammals, as involving ideation. Harlow's work gives point to the suggestion of Cole (1951) that where a problem is just within the range of the higher capacities of an animal to form hypotheses, we find true 'insight learning' or 'hypothesis learning.' But where the problem is just too difficult for the animal to form any 'hypotheses' about it, then we find regression to a more random and primitive procedure, and we get the kind of behaviour reported by Spence (1937) when working with highly complex problems. No doubt, also, the conflicting results obtained in the course of all types of these experiments is due to the fact that this higher type of learning ability varies very greatly from one individual to another, and that quite a large sample has to be taken before one can be reasonably certain of getting one or more individuals of high ability.

Individual variation in learning ability is evident throughout the animal kingdom, and it is, of course, at the higher levels that this variation is most noticeable. Other methods which have been used in the attempt to investigate insight are the delayed-response method, multiple-choice tests and the double-alternation problem. The idea behind all these methods was that they would, if successful, give evidence of ideas, images and symbolic processes in the animal's mind. This seems reasonable in the case of delayed response. But there does not, in fact, seem to be any reason for thinking that the other two methods do necessarily provide evidence for ideation as distinct from generalisation and the perception of relations. A great many animals can, indeed, show varying degrees of delayed response—some, such as the insects *Ammophila* and *Nemeritis*, of several days; while birds may remember landmarks and, under experimental conditions, other patterned stimuli of great complexity for years. Apes can remember the details of tasks and problems involving the use of tools for very long periods without practice, and Klüver (1937) has demonstrated such memory in Cebus monkeys lasting for three years. But such memory feats of birds and mammals, while of great interest, are not, of course, on the same footing as true delayed response, and do not in themselves tell us very much about any mental processes which may be going on. There is, however, evidence that mammals (e.g. Chimpanzees) find delayed response immensely more difficult if spatial cues are lacking (Yerkes and Nissen, 1939); and Nissen, Riesen and Nowlis (1938) did not succeed in obtaining non-spatial delay of more than 40 seconds. This conclusion that spatial situations can be more easily symbolised and so remembered probably applies to birds also (see also Finch, 1942).

It has often been noted in mammals that an effective delayed response performance is only possible if the bodily orientation has been maintained during the delay period. An example of this is given by French (1959) for Squirrel Monkeys. The same state of affairs is very noticeable in dogs and cats subjected to pre-frontal lesions. These animals may perform excellently in delayed response tests prior to operation but after operation success depends on the maintenance of postural orientation. At first this was thought (Konorski, 1961) to be indicative of a loss of recent memory following the pre-frontal lesion but subsequently (Lawicka and Konorski, 1961) it has been found that the tendency to choose the wrong food tray was not the result of impaired memory traces but because of a post-operational tendency to repeat the last reinforced run. In other words, the operated animal has a stronger perseverative tendency.

The multiple-choice method, by which the animal is required to select from a set of boxes which vary in number and position the box which always bears a certain relation to the others, has been solved by both birds and mammals. Such a performance seems to be good evidence of generalisation and certainly of the perception of relations, and is thus evidence of insight, although not of insight learning as here defined. Then there is the double-alternation problem, which tests an animal's ability to respond to temporal relations in the same way that the multiple-choice method tests response to spatial relations. Thus an animal may be required to turn twice to the right or twice to the left in finding its way through a maze so arranged that no aid is obtained from differential sensory cues. Here, again, success has been recorded a number of times, and is evidence for insight rather than for insight learning. Nevertheless, it may be that, as the work of Lukaszewska (1961) suggests, some animals have an ability to make a correct return along a path which they have previously traversed on their outward journey for food. Lukaszewska found that her rats were capable of 90 per cent. correct return on four different mazes independent of special experience in those mazes. It seems as if the ability to find the proper way back is either inborn or is acquired early in life as a result of general exploratory activity. Ants (see Schneirla, 1933, *a* & *b*, p. 245, below) give some evidence of similar powers. There are also the results of Otto Koehler and his pupils with mice, not yet fully published, showing that mice trained in one maze immediately run the same maze pattern in mirror image or with all angles modified by a constant percentage.

All these methods, then, are bringing us up against this question of perception of relations, and this, of course, goes right to the very basis of the problem of visual organisation and form sense, and it is probably artificial, though it may be convenient, to attempt to separate the two. It is in this connection that the use of visual illusions in experiments on animal behaviour is of interest. As we shall see below, some of the well-known illusions to which human visual perception is subject can also be demonstrated with no great difficulty in birds. But if we want the best possible evidence of ideational abilities, it is better to look at the number-concept experiments and at the evidence for true imitation, for these seem to provide evidence for abstraction and for self-consciousness in a way that the other type of experiment we have just been describing does not.

Imprinting

Before, however, we come to the consideration of perception and the relation of insight to it, and before we consider the number concept and imitation, there is one other example of learning to deal with. This, while perhaps not justifiably regarded as a separate type, is of rather exceptional theoretical interest: it is known as Imprinting. The first systematic observations on this subject were those of Heinroth (1910), who found that young geese reared from the egg in isolation react to their human keepers (or to the first relatively large moving object that they see) by following them as they would their parents. This need happen for only a few hours (possibly only for a few minutes in some cases (Lorenz)) for the young bird to accept a human as its proper associate and to retain for the rest of its life a tendency to take to human beings as both parent companion and fellow-member of the species to which later the sexual behaviour will become attached. At this early stage the attachment is not to an individual human (though that will often come with longer association) but to 'humans.' Geese probably show this behaviour in its most extreme form, and it appeared from the work of Heinroth, Lorenz and others that with these birds, imprinting is peculiar in the following respects:

(1) The process is confined to a very definite and very brief period of

the individual life, and possibly also to a particular set of environmental circumstances. (2) Once accomplished it is often very stable—in some cases perhaps totally irreversible. (3) It is often completed long before the various specific reactions to which the imprinted pattern will ultimately become linked are established. (4) It is supra-individual learning—a learning of the broad characteristics of the *species*—for if this were not so and the bird at this stage learnt (as it can easily do later) the individual characteristics of its companion, the biological effect would be frustrated.

Imprinting, in fact, resembles the development of human visual perception in that it seems to proceed from the seeing of gross differences to the seeing of fine differences (Spitz and Wolfe, 1946; Gibson, 1950). The first smile of the human baby seems to be released by the sight of the eyes alone (Ahrens, 1954). Certainly the baby can early see human faces as different from other things but not as different from one another. It is thus a process similar to the 'gestalt' theorist's sharpening of the configuration and is the opposite of generalisation. Ahrens (1954) considers the smiling response of the human infant an instinctive behaviour pattern appearing first spontaneously as a vacuum activity. After an initial stage in which only isolated stimuli are effective, there is the second stage referred to above in which configuration of the eyes becomes the releaser. In the third stage the ability to differentiate increases and gradually the lower half of the face is taken into account. In the fourth stage widening of the mouth into a smile appears as a releaser. The fifth and final stage is reached at six months or thereabouts when the differentiation of the face as a whole is complete. The child can now recognise the person who cares for it and masks are no longer effective.

Imprinting of various degrees of intensity is now known to occur in many birds (Portielje, 1921; Bierens de Haan, 1926; Goodwin, 1948; Hess, 1959, and other references discussed in Chapter XV below), in fishes (Seitz, 1940–2), and something similar is apparent in insects (see Thorpe, 1944). Perhaps the process of acquiring the song by example from the parents, which the Heinroths (1924–33) and others have shown to take place in so many birds, and which may be brought about (as in Nightingale and Blackcap song) by an exposure for one week only six or eight months before is, on its perceptual side, also of this nature. (See Chapter XV below.) Baerends and Baerends–Van Roon (1950), confirming the earlier work of Noble and Curtis, have shown that the parent Cichlid fish may become imprinted to the young as well as the young to the parent, and Lorenz notes that a young Jackdaw may become imprinted to a human if kept away from its own kind, but not if in a flock of more than two or three. If it is permissible, as I have suggested elsewhere (Thorpe, 1944), to extend the concept to cover the possibility of attachment, not to a fellow-member of the species but to the type of immediate environment first perceived by a newly emerged organism so that this becomes the future breeding quarters of the individual, then there are also obvious affinities with exploratory learning.

But the extreme interest of imprinting lies above all in the fact that its study seems to be more promising than that of any other kind of learning for the understanding of the nature of the perceptual side of instinct and its relationship to plastic processes in general. Indeed, the special significance of this process lies, perhaps, in the fact that releasing patterns, the recognition of which is inborn and which thus provide the keys which open the lock of instinctive behaviour, while they must be striking and 'improbable,' are, nevertheless, usually as simple as possible. While the innate releasive mechanism, which is the inborn counterpart of the releaser, will control efficiently surprisingly complex patterns of instinctive behaviour, it obviously has its limits, and where the instinctive releasing mechanism fails the learning ability must come in to complete the reaction. But time is short, and what the animal has to learn is extremely urgent and important for its whole future. It has, in fact, to learn one particular kind of thing and learn it quickly; and so we can see why imprinting should have the tendencies which we do, in fact, often find, of restriction to a rather brief critical period and restriction within more or less wide limits to a particular kind of pattern as an object. Further, neither of these limitations is exact or precise, and neither of them will give a complete separation from other types of learning. Nearly all organisms show some restriction of learning ability to a certain part of the life. There are very few species indeed, the individuals of which can learn as well when old as when young,[1] and so the restriction to a certain period is only an extreme form of what all will agree is a general characteristic of learning. The restriction of learning to a particular kind of object is, of course, to be expected by all students of behaviour who are prepared to admit that there are, in fact, innate perceptual co-ordinations. Only if the animal's perceptions were completely undirected and unorganised, and completely dependent upon learning ability, would we expect complete absence of direction in learning. So here again the restriction characteristic of imprinting is merely an extreme case of something which we find very widely in the animal kingdom. If we are right in considering instinctive recognition of patterned stimuli as representing a special stereotyped form of the more fundamental organising activity at the base of all perception, tending to build up and respond to more and more complex 'gestalts'—then in imprinting we seem to see in ontogeny just that process of complex form recognition and organisation which has taken place in

---

[1] Except, of course, where there is gradual development or metamorphosis such that the younger form lives a more restricted and less mobile life and perhaps has less highly developed sense organs and nervous system.

phylogeny. Thus, where the innate powers of recognition can only carry the animal a part of the way towards its goal, the process is completed and adjusted by a proclivity to attend to certain aspects of a situation and learn in certain restricted times and directions (as in the tendency of a bird to learn and copy the song of its own species in preference to the song of another) so that experience completes for the individual the process initiated by its inherited constitution. A brief outline of the very numerous recent papers on imprinting in birds will be found in Ch. XV.

Ideation [1]

A phenomenon technically described as *reminiscence* has long been familiar to students of human learning. It is observed that when a task has been incompletely learned, the memory for the performance is worse immediately after the last trial than it is some two or three hours later. This improvement is itself followed a few hours later still by further forgetting. In other words, memory improves during the hour or two without practice immediately following a trial, only to be lost again later as forgetting once more gets the upper hand. One of the most strongly supported explanations of this phenomenon has been that mental practice continues for a while subconsciously after overt practice has ceased; and so if the same characteristics of the memory curve could be found in animals, it would give a strong presumptive evidence for ideational processes. Bunch and Magdsick (1933) investigated the matter, using rats in a multiple-T maze, and secured satisfactory and consistent positive results without difficulty. Thus they found the best performance was shown six hours after the last trial, but achievement was still significantly above the zero-hour score at the forty-eighth hour. Magdsick (1936) performed the same type of experiment with animals grouped according to age. All age-groups showed best retention after the one-hour interval, but there was still some trace of improvement the whole of the first week. A. C. Anderson (1937, 1940) obtained similar results, finding improved scores as late as ten days after the test. Partly because of this long-period effect, during which it is difficult to suppose that active mental practice can have been effectively maintained, and partly for other reasons which seem less cogent, he prefers an explanation based on the elimination of errors rather than persistence in the mental task. While such a possibility certainly exists and so throws some doubt on the method as evidence for ideation, it might be plausibly argued that even the preferential discard of errors involves mental reminiscence whereby errors and correct responses are contrasted and dealt with differently.

[1] Ideation may be defined as the occurrence of perceptions, in the absence of the corresponding external stimulation, in the form of images which are in some degree abstract or generalised and which can be the subject of further comparison and reorganisation by learning processes. (Based on G. F. Stout, 1899.)

The ability to deal with number and to abstract a numerical quality from a given number of specific objects provides probably the best evidence available for 'ideational processes.' At present the only satisfactory evidence for such performance comes from experiments with birds and with one mammal, the Squirrel. The detailed account of this work will be found in Chapter XIV, but the general conclusions may be summarised here.

It has been shown that birds (Jackdaw, Raven, Parrot and Budgerigars) and Squirrels (Hassmann, 1952) have a 'pre-linguistic' 'number' sense [1] rising, in outstanding individuals, to include the number seven. They are thus able to abstract the 'concept' of numerical identity from groups of up to seven objects of totally different and unfamiliar appearance. When presented with a number of marks or objects on a cue card, they can learn to 'act upon' that number simultaneously, by selecting a box bearing the same number of spots as the cue card bears objects. In special cases, as trained, but not as a general solution, they can also learn to do this 'consecutively' by taking the same number of grains from a heap or pecking the same number of times at a series of objects presented at randomised intervals—thus combining successive and simultaneous number training. There is some evidence that the 'internal counting' involved is based upon memory of a series of previous actions; for in at least one case a Jackdaw has been seen to externalise its counting by 'intention' bowing (see p. 391, below). This astonishing work of O. Koehler (1951) and his pupils seems finally to have proved beyond question the existence of ideation in animals; for, in contrast to much previous work, it is marked by control so rigorous as to place it in the highest class of animal-behaviour studies. It suggests that man and animals may have a pre-linguistic 'counting' ability of about the same degree, but that man's superiority in dealing with numbers lies in his ability to use, as symbols for numbers, words and figures which have not the same, or indeed any, numerical attributes. It is interesting that Hayes and Hayes (1951) suggest that man's superior ability to use word symbols as language may be his most important *genetic* advantage over the apes.

There remains the whole question of imitation as evidence of ideation. Much so-called imitation amongst animals is either social facilitation or local enhancement, and probably need not involve any high form of insight learning. There is obviously (Thorpe, 1951) an enormous amount of what appears at first sight to be some kind of imitation occurring amongst birds and a small amount among mammals; but although this is clear enough, it is by no means so clear what this behaviour involves psychologically, nor how far, if at all, it implies that kind of self-consciousness

[1] A capacity to recognise as similar, groups of diverse objects which resemble one another solely in being composed of the same number of elements.

which we ourselves experience when we intentionally imitate the acts or the voice of another person. In order to attempt to clear the ground in this matter, it is necessary first to consider what has been called *social facilitation*. Birds are, on the whole, social creatures, and it is to be expected that the behaviour of one individual should be influenced by that of others without necessarily involving imitation in the true sense. Imitation as a whole, then, might be described as 'social learning,' and social facilitation can be described as 'contagious behaviour,' where the performance of a more or less instinctive pattern of behaviour by one will tend to act as a releaser for the same behaviour in another or in others, and so initiate the same lines of action in the whole group. A short account of this kind of behaviour in birds will be found in Armstrong (1947), and the same author (1951) has recently provided a critical discussion of the whole subject of 'mimesis.'[1] Yawning provides a commonplace example of social facilitation in humans—everyone knows how contagious this is and how entirely different it is from imitation; a yawn by one person being sufficient to release the behaviour subconsciously in others.

It is obvious that in considering such an action as being a releaser, we are dealing with something a little different from the releasers normally occurring in social behaviour as between parents and young or as between the sexes, where one instinctive act of one bird brings about another instinctive act in another bird. In social facilitation, on the other hand, the releaser and the act released are the same, and for this reason we get the superficial impression of a transference of mood, as if the appearance of a member of the species in a certain mood creates a similar mood in another individual. First it may be pointed out, as was suggested by the work of Popov (1930), quoted by Razran (1933, pp. 286–7), that social facilitation can be based merely on a type of conditioned reflex or trial-and-error learning. Thus if pigeons are fed in flocks the feeding behaviour of any given bird will be accompanied, and often preceded, by the sight of other birds feeding. Therefore an ordinary conditioning process will give rise to social facilitation. We have little or no evidence to go upon as to how far conditioning of that kind gives rise to social facilitation in nature. On the other hand, this transference of mood mentioned above has been tested in social species. Thus Katz and Révész (1921) showed that chickens that were fed in isolation until they were satiated and would no longer accept food, would immediately begin to eat again as soon as they saw other birds eating. Akhmeteli (1941) found that feeding behaviour can be formed in an untrained pigeon merely through watch-

[1] Armstrong (1951) has proposed the term *'mimesis'* to replace *'social facilitation.'* While this is convenient in some respects, it has the drawback that *'mimetic'* suggests both 'imitation,' from which it must be sharply distinguished, and 'mimicry,' which has an entirely different meaning in zoology. For these reasons the older term is retained in spite of its clumsiness.

ing the behaviour of a trained pigeon in response to a food-box. Here again habit seems to be solely the expression of the social character of the pecking behaviour.

The same kind of effect appears in the work of Rouse (1906) and of Howells and Vine (1940). The latter, when studying the learning ability of chicks, found that, with social species such as this, the ordinary discrimination-box experiments, in fact, involve more than mere discrimination unless very great precautions are taken. Thus a chick learns more readily to go to a chick of its own breed than to one of another breed.[1] That a great deal of behaviour may be based on social mood-transference of this kind is shown clearly by the work of Nice (1943) on the Song Sparrow. Moreover, the recognition of certain enemies—e.g. cat, snake and Cowbird in species where, in contrast to the Song Sparrow, it is not based on an instinctive mechanism—is probably handed on from generation to generation, not so much by the experience of the dire results of attack but by the alarm displayed by the parent birds or by members of other species when they see one of these enemies.

Not only will satiated chicks be stimulated to feed by the sight of other individuals feeding: the reverse effect has been recorded. Thus Katz (1937) showed that chickens that are in a restive and excitable state due to hunger, when placed with satiated chickens will for a time quieten down, apparently satiated, even though they are not fed, and Lorenz (1935) has recorded similar behaviour among Night Herons. Some instances of this kind suggest that mood may (under certain conditions) be transferred not only from members of a certain species but even between different species and quite different groups of animals. (See Thorpe, 1951.) Some striking examples will be found under 'Bird-insect Nesting Associations,' Chapter XV, below.

A special form of social facilitation, still possible where only a very slight degree of social behaviour exists, is that known as local enhancement. This may be defined as an apparent imitation resulting from directing the animal's attention to a particular object or to a particular part of the environment. Thus Lorenz (1935) found that when a flock of ducks was confined in a pen, at one place in the fence of which there was a small gap, the successful escape of one bird did not lead to any general improvement in performance by the others. If, however, one duck happened to be near to or following close behind another at the time of its escape, this had the effect of attracting the bird's attention to that particular region of the fence and so indirectly helped it to solve the problem.

[1] It is rather remarkable that such a difference should be manifested as between different breeds of the same species. It seems very doubtful in this case whether the preference of a chick for its own 'kind' is instinctive; it may well be that it is the result of early conditioning.

Morley (1942) has some interesting observations on Marsh Tits finding their way to bait in a trap. Once one tit had found the way others were observed to solve the problem very quickly, and although some of these instances looked at first sight like true imitation, there seems no clear evidence for this, and it is much more probable that the success of one bird resulted in the attention of the others being directed to the relevant part of the apparatus. On the other hand, Allee and Masure (1936) found that the presence of a second Shell Parakeet (whether forming a hetero-sexual or a homosexual pair) in the maze during training resulted in a decreased rate of learning, presumably because of distraction; but with Goldfish the opposite effect has been recorded (Welty, 1934). The habit of piercing the covers of milk bottles recorded of several species of tits in England (see Hinde and Fisher, 1952) may be learnt from one individual by others. It seems that trial-and-error learning is adequate to account for the achievement of the pioneers, and that local enhancement accounts for the spread of this and other similar (Buxton, 1948) feeding habits of tits.

From this brief account it is clear that imitation must be defined very carefully if the term is to have a useful meaning. *By true imitation is meant the copying of a novel or otherwise improbable act or utterance, or some act for which there is clearly no instinctive tendency.* Defined in these terms, we see that true visual imitation becomes something which apparently involves self-consciousness and something of intent to profit by another's experience; and it becomes doubtful whether (except pos-sibly in cats) we can find any certain examples of such behaviour any-where in the animal kingdom below the Primates. But since song and call-notes play such an important part in the social organisation of birds, one must be particularly careful about the subject of vocal imitation, since this may in many cases be a kind of trial-and-error phenomenon. This is because 'the action of uttering a sound is unique amongst all actions in one very important respect; namely, whereas action of any other kind cannot be perceived by the actor in the same way in which it is per-ceived by his fellow creatures, and in which he perceives their bodily movement, the *sounds* he and they utter are [presumably] perceived by him and by them in much the same way. Suppose then a creature, a child or animal, endowed by nature with a number of vocal motor mechanisms which enable it to utter a variety of sounds expressing various emotions or impulses. Whenever any one of these is set in action the creature hears its own voice uttering a corresponding sound; in consequence, this sense impression becomes associated with that motor mechanism, so that the hearing of a sound tends to innervate that mechanism. Now, suppose the creature to hear the same sounds uttered by another. The sound will have the same effect; namely, in so far as the creature responds by vocal utter-ance, it will tend, in virtue of the preformed association, to utter the same sounds that it hears' (McDougall, 1936, pp. 174–5). Thus we see that apparently very complex and elaborate imitation of sounds by birds may, in fact, be explicable essentially on the basis of trial-and-error learning. This vocal imitation is characteristically a phenomenon of bird life and is accordingly dealt with in Chapter XV, below.

Herbert and Harsh (1944) found that cats will be helped in learning manual skills *within their normal range of ability* as a result of observing the learning processes of another cat, and Kuo (1938) provides some fairly good examples of cats 'learning' rat-killing methods by imitation; but, of course, in neither of these instances can the involvement of an instinctive behaviour pattern be completely ruled out. Chimpanzee studies have provided much *prima facie* evidence for true visual imitation [1] (Yerkes, 1934). But until quite recently strict experimental proof had been sought in vain or at most with uncertain results, and it seemed as if not even apes were able to 'ape'. However, the studies of Mr and Mrs Hayes on the hand-reared chimpanzee, Vicki (see below, p. 461), seem now to have provided clear evidence for true imitation. It does not now seem possible to deny that here at least we have evidence of true self-consciousness and the ability to regard the self as a being in some respects similar to that which is being imitated.

SUMMARY

1. It is doubtful, in view of the effects on tool-using ability of restriction of early manipulative experience, whether any experimentally controlled examples of tool using at present available provide evidence for the sudden production of a completely new response. Nevertheless, they can be regarded as giving satisfactory evidence for insight learning as here defined. The ability of certain species of birds to secure food tied to the perch by a string or thread seems at least to provide good *prima facie* evidence for insight learning.

2. Detour experiments and certain types of maze experiment provide good evidence for insight learning in a number of instances.

3. Delayed-reaction, multiple-choice and double-alternation experiments do not appear to provide unequivocal evidence for insight learning, though they do at least strongly suggest the existence of insight and ideational processes which may have been arrived at in the course of other learning methods.

4. Some examples of the kind of learning characteristic of certain groups of birds and known as 'Imprinting' are briefly described. Imprinting, although probably not to be thought of as a distinct type of learning,

---

[1] The experiments of Loh Seng Tsai on team work with white rats (see O. Koehler, 1953, *Orion*, 8, Parts 19 and 20) are probably explicable on ordinary trial-and-error learning principles.

is of exceptional interest in that it is a very rapid, unrewarded learning strictly limited both in time and direction. Its function seems to be to build rapidly upon and so complete the adjustment of the innate releasive mechanisms of certain innate social behaviour patterns which are of crucial importance in the life history of the organism.

5. Further evidence for ideation is then considered. Reminiscence studies are held to have provided considerable evidence for ideation in rats, and ideation has been proved for birds by the experiments on pre-linguistic number sense.

6. The types of evidence for imitation, as involving self-consciousness and thus ideation, are considered. Social facilitation, resulting in trans-ference of mood and local enhancement, directing attention of associates to a particular object or environmental situation, are regarded as distinct from true imitation. True imitation of improbable acts for which there is no learned or instinctive predilection now seems well established in Chim-panzees. It is still doubtful whether it has been successfully demonstrated elsewhere in the animal kingdom, except possibly in cats.

CHAPTER VII

INSIGHT AND PERCEPTION

IT was, of course, no accident that the first champions of the concept of insight were the gestalt psychologists whose whole position and outlook are based upon the work of Wertheimer (1912) on visual perception of movement. We have only to consider what is the equivalent of insight among the non-visual and non-projicient senses to see at once how primarily 'visual' the idea is. What, for instance, becomes of the concept if it is applied to olfactory sensations? At first sight, because of the traditional and natural restrictions of the word to visual situations, the mere suggestion that it might be applied to olfaction seems ridiculous, and it is significant that of the 700 pages of Koffka's *Principles of Gestalt Psychology* barely more than one page is devoted to non-visual senses. Yet is not insight merely the counterpart in form vision of that power of comparison and generalisation which seems to be characteristic, in some degree at least, of all perceptions?

In this connection it cannot be too strongly emphasised that what 'gets into' the sense organ is not a small replica of the object sensed. With the chemical senses, of course, the object, or an infinitesimally minute sample of what may be considered as the object, gets 'on to' the sensory surface, and there sets up, by chemical or radiant energy, a complex temporal pattern of electro-chemical excitation in the sensory fibres. With the mechanical senses of pain, touch and hearing it is kinetic energy in vastly varying complexities of temporal pattern which does the same. So with radio-receptors such as organs of temperature and light sense, from the simplest photo receptors of a flagellate up to the human eye, it is the same—nothing 'gets in' but radiant energy. True, there is a geometrical correspondence between the projection of the shapes and surfaces viewed and the focused pattern of light points on the retina, and the image is regarded for the sake of discussion as a geometrical arrangement of light points. But as Gibson (1950) has so clearly stated, while the excitation is a corresponding arrangement of discharging nervous elements, the individual points of the image, together with the rays of light which explain the correspondence to the world, are pure geometrical fictions introduced for purposes of analysis, while the individual spots of the excitation pattern are anatomical facts. But this momentary anatomical relation is not transmitted to the brain as such. All that the transmission amounts to is again a series of nervous electro-chemical events in a purely ordinal relationship to one another. Every time the eye moves, the anatomical pattern is completely changed—yet the ordinal pattern is preserved, perhaps by a rapid learning process of some kind, an 'immediate memory,' which unites and maintains as a unitary perception a series of rapidly succeeding patterns of retinal excitation. To quote Gibson (p. 56): 'The *identity* of a given point-stimulus in the eye depends not at all on the anatomical point of the retina stimulated but entirely on the position of that point relative to other points of stimulation. *A given spot of light in a given retinal image is the same spot at different instants of time when its position relative to the order of spots is determined, not when its position relative to the retina is determined.*' Thus the fundamental fact is that 'a spot of light is a stimulus for perception by virtue of its ordinal location not by virtue of its anatomical location.'

If, then, we assume provisionally that insight is perception of relations, it may be possible to link it up much more closely than has hitherto been done with perception as a whole. If it is correct that even the simplest external stimulus is, in fact, a relational one (whether it be the recognition of an odour, a simple sound pattern, a colour or a brightness constancy phenomenon or a figure-background relation), and if the perception of such a stimulus is, in fact, the perception of temporal and spatial relations, then there is in insight something which is also of the very essence of form perception and has its counterpart in all other sensory fields. Thus an element of comparison, which is itself essentially a learning process, enters at the very base of all processes of recognition.

Now, this, it appears, is where the gestalt psychologists have missed an important point. While rightly stressing the wholeness of certain figures as systems of universal interaction, where every part influences every other part, they seem to have no evidence for the assertion that pattern perception is of an *immediate* whole with no element of comparison between its parts entering into recognition. On the contrary, the distinctiveness of the whole seems to derive from the perception of the relationship of its parts. Thus the parts are first perceived only as relations—these are the primary perceptions. With experience these primary perceptions can be combined and built up into more and more complex perceptions or gestalts. These

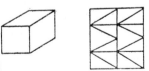

FIG. 16—Figures to show the effect of inclusiveness. For explanation see text. (After Vernon, 1952.)

more complex perceptions may be so different from the simpler ones that the latter become completely submerged and lost in them (Fig. 16), and the total figure may be such a completely new entity that it is hardly possible, except as the outcome of long practice, to see the original parts as

separate structures. But this does not mean that the new whole is independent of the parts; it merely means that the parts have taken on a new
relationship as part of a 'better' configuration. Thus the study of such
figures emphasises the conclusion (cf. Vernon, 1952) that 'the parts must
always be studied in relationship to their membership of the whole which
conditions then' (italics mine). Complex perceptions can, of course, be
still further analysed and broken down into more elementary components
which resemble the 'sensations' of traditional psychology. But no matter
how intensive the analysis, the data are still percepts in that they are relational, not absolute. Thus, strictly speaking, the sensation has disappeared, and we are left merely with perceptions of varying degrees of complexity. This is very much the thesis of Gibson's recent study (1950),
which can be largely summed up (see p. 138) in the sentence '. . . the perceptual impression is the primary one, immediate and independent, the
sensory impression the secondary one, obtainable only by analysing the
perception.' It follows from this general approach that we regard as 'instinctive' those animals which have complex innate perceptions or patterns
of the innate releasive mechanism, while those which have only relatively
simple innate perceptions are thought of as being, on the perceptual side,
without 'instincts.' These latter therefore require a much longer period for
the initial build-up, by various learning processes, of the mature fully
organised ability to respond to the significant patterns presented by the
environment. But the difference between those animals which have and
those which lack 'instincts' is, on the perceptual side at least, one of degree
only; all have percepts of varying degrees of complexity, and that is all
they have.

Hebb (1937, 1949), basing his views on his experiments on rats reared
in darkness, concludes that the gestalt psychologists are right in so far as
figural unity is concerned; that is to say, that there is an innate tendency
to see units, but that shapes have to be recognised by a learning process.
In humans, according to von Senden's observations on the first vision of
patients cured of congenital cataract, even this seems doubtful; though
the data given by von Senden (1932, 1960) are difficult of evaluation. It is
obvious that in evaluating the responses of patients of greatly varying age,
interests, education and intellectual level, it is an extremely difficult matter
to interpret and harmonise the accounts of what, to them, are entirely
new and most puzzling experiences. Moreover, the questions which one
would ask such patients would depend very largely on one's own particular interests and outlook. Thus one interrogator might quite unconsciously extract one type of answer in line with his own predilections,
while another, in all sincerity, comes to quite a different conclusion. But
while it is thus unwise to base very much on the work of von Senden, there
does seem to be in animals and men a primary, if not an inherent, tend-

ency to organise perception into wholes or units and also to distinguish inherently between up and down and to perceive 'space'—'so that line and angle come to dominate perception' (Hebb). But there are still difficulties; perhaps these 'inherent tendencies' may all merely be due to the fact that the proprioceptive and other sense organs which mediate such perceptions come into operation earlier in ontogeny than do visual organs, and so may give an opportunity to learn earlier. The relatively rapid visual recognition of such things, then, may merely be due to rapid sensory transfer. Colour recognition also turns out to be a complex activity. There seems to be little doubt, from von Senden's work, that there was immediate perception of colour by his patients. But may not this have been due to the fact that some colour differences may be perceived through the cataract, and that so, even here, some traces of learning had entered?

Studies of the objects preferred for pecking by young chicks hatched in the dark, when first given an opportunity to use their eyes (Fantz, 1957), have shown that round objects are preferred to angular ones and that both two- and three-dimensional aspects of visual form are important, even at the first attempts. It is possible that with these newly hatched chicks the preference for round objects is merely an expression of the fact that these are at first more easily distinguished from the background than objects of any other kind. Once the powers of vision have been developed by a little practice, different results may be obtained and indeed in many groups of animals there are some indications, very hard to evaluate, of the existence of an 'innate' preference for patterns with more outlines rather than with less. This seems to apply to both octopus and rat and at least one or two examples in both the insects and the fish. The whole subject needs much more careful study but it would be remarkable if the same story applies widely through the animal kingdom irrespective of eye structure.

It seems fairly well established, however, that recognition of a circle is easier [1] than that of a square or other cornered figure, and it has been suggested, partly for this reason, that in the higher mammals repeated eye movements along the field boundaries are the means by which the learning is accomplished. It is doubtful whether this can be true in general, even in mammals, and it cannot possibly be true of the form vision of many animals such as insects, where eye movements are lacking, and in birds [2] where they are greatly restricted. As Mr R. L. Gregory has sug-

[1] The frequent occurrence of ocular patterns (especially on the wings of butterflies and the feathers of birds) as warning signals and as releasers for social behaviour is probably significant in this connection (Tinbergen, 1952; Baerends, 1950). Moreover, the great difficulty in camouflaging the eye in species with concealing coloration is shown quite dramatically by the elaborate disruptive patterns that have so frequently been evolved by animals for this purpose. (See Cott, 1940.)

[2] In birds nearly all the retinal surface lies in the image plane, so that all distant objects are sharply focused. Moreover, the cones are more evenly distributed over the

gested to me, more probably it is form which is first perceived, and that necessity for unceasing and delicately controlled eye movements develops slowly *pari passu* with the development of specialised foveal vision. With such specialised vision, fixation gives 'fine grain' vision over a small angle, while eye movements with memory confer the power of an extensive scanning of the environment. Thus the same eye can function both as a wide-angle lens and as a telescope. Where there is acute foveal vision, eye movements are of course quite essential. But where these eye movements occur it will be necessary to compensate for them by constant and rapid adaptation, and therefore learning must proceed by constructing a perception out of these very eye movements. That this kind of process must indeed be taking place to a considerable extent, even in immobile eyes, seems certain from both new and old studies of the simple eyes of Arthropods such as insects and crustacea.

Exner (1891), in his classic researches into the action of the eyes of Arthropods, suggested that the copepod crustacean *Copilia* was, in effect, scanning its environment with its very simple eye apparatus, and in a famous passage (an extensive translation is given by Wilkie, 1953) visualises the animal as 'fingering over' its visual field just as we do with our fovea. *'Wir tasten mit unserem Blick des Seefeld ab.'* Dethier (1943) has shown that the caterpillars of Lepidoptera can react to form even though they have visual organs consisting only of a small group (six or seven) of stemmata or 'simple eyes' on either side of the head. These stemmata, whether singly or a group, are structurally quite insufficient to mediate form-sight, considered merely as an optical apparatus. But, in fact, form can be perceived provided the head is moved about in relation to the object, and this is almost certainly the function of the 'waving' movements of the anterior part of the body which Lepidopterous larvæ are so often seen to exhibit; the insect is actually scanning the object with its simple eyes, and thus, by co-ordination with the proprioceptive stimuli which inform it of its motions, is able to build up, by a scanning process of temporal summation, an impression of form.

This process is, however, not confined to contexts of form vision only; a moment's thought will show that such temporal summation is a fundamental principle in a very large part of orientation behaviour in the lower animals. Thus in the process of orientation known as 'klinokinesis' (e.g. Ullyott, 1936, on the Flatworm *Dendrocœlum*) and in 'klinotaxis' the operation would be impossible were the animal unable to 'compare,' perhaps by means of the adaptation of its sense organ, present intensities of stimulation with those immediately past. In klinokinesis the field is

retina, instead of being especially concentrated in the fovea as they are in the human eye, so that a bird will be far less dependent on focusing and scanning movements for the recognition of shape and movement. (See Pumphrey, 1948.)

scanned in this way by the animal taking a convoluted path of a relatively constant rate of change of direction, while in klinotaxis the animal instead swings the front end of its body to and fro, thus comparing successively intensities of stimulation to right and left of its axis of progression. It is only later in the evolutionary series when paired intensity receptors appear, mounted an appreciable distance apart (as in the olfactory organs on the antennæ of insects), that *simultaneous* comparison of intensities can be effective in orientation (tropotaxis). But the temporal scanning method is far more ancient and more fundamental. Thus we see that an element of learning or of comparison is entering into orientation and into form perception at an extremely early evolutionary stage, and we are driven to the conclusion that some cases of I.R.M. recognition may be learning which is predisposed by heredity to occur in certain directions, as in imprinting—which, like all perceptive processes, proceeds from the seeing of gross differences to the seeing of fine differences. Thus much instinctive pattern-recognition may be 'learning' which takes only a few seconds. To be sure, such learning could not be 'rewarded' learning in the usual sense of the learning theorists; could not be learning reinforced by the satisfaction of a physiological need. Rather it would have to be something of the nature of latent learning, as it occurs in normal appetitive behaviour where the reward is the finding of the right releaser. But if, as I believe, we can assume in groups such as birds and insects an inherent tendency to learn to recognise certain types of pattern rather than others, then it would seem only natural to suppose that this learning could take place more rapidly than the typical learning of higher mammals. It is certainly true, as a rough generalisation, that first learning is slower in higher than in lower species, but that, though slower in the former, it can ultimately get much farther. These considerations, then, seem to offer some hope of bridging the gap between instinct and learning, and they suggest that examples of learning which is localised in direction and time, as in imprinting, are of great theoretical interest.

But if the very act of recognition itself involves something of the nature of insight which is essentially the perception of relations (for the external stimuli to which higher metazoan sense organs react are all in some degree patterned), it seems to follow that the distinction between inborn and acquired responses has now become one of degree rather than kind. As I have tried to suggest in the last chapter, we must, in view of present knowledge of the mechanism of nerve action, regard all animals as having in some perhaps infinitesimal measure two elementary inborn faculties inherent in the very nature of behaviour—perception of temporal and spatial relations—at the base of all receptor activity and all responses. As we shall see in the following chapter, it may be possible to express both of these in terms of one fundamental activity of nervous tissue, whether central or peripheral, namely temporal adaptation, and Adrian (1947), following up an idea of Craik (1943), has suggested that spatial patterns are in effect translated by the brain into a system of temporal patterns. These theories involve scanning after the manner of a television apparatus. But Gibson (1950) develops this idea further in a rather different form with reference to human form vision. He concludes that the retina is an organ of the body which responds essentially to gradations in intensity of light, not to 'points of light'; and it responds equally readily to an abrupt change of change as to an abrupt change. As a result of these powers it can respond to a differential intensity in adjacent order over its surface. Thus pattern vision is the outcome of an *inhomogeneity* of a set of hypothetical rays, not of the rays themselves.

This will perhaps be best understood by briefly summarising the particular example given by Gibson. If the stimulation is homogeneous, the perception will be of pure areal colour or shade only, e.g. *llll* or *dddd* (l = light and d = dark). If the heterogeneity results from an order containing a single step or jump such as *llllddddd* or *ddddlllll* along one or both dimensions of an array, lines or discontinuous areas will appear; thus it provides the necessary correlates for delimiting the margins or outlines which are necessary for seeing figures or shapes. A third type of order incorporating a cyclical or alternating change such as *llddllddl* when found in both dimensions of an array constitutes, according to his theory, the stimulus correlate of the visual quality of texture, which is equivalent to saying the stimulus correlate of a visual *surface*. Thus these three kinds of order can theoretically account for the perception of pure visual extent, of outline and of surface. Finally a fourth type of order, consisting of a serial change in the length of repetitive cycles of stimulation, as in *dddlllllddddlllddlldl*, would constitute *a gradient of density of texture* which, it can be shown, is an adequate stimulus for the impression of continuous distance or depth. Thus this theory gives us a plausible basis for the *innate* perception of extent, form, surface and depth in both the vertebrate and arthropod eye without the *necessity* of postulating eye movements or binocular vision. But be this as it may, when we look at the matter in this light, seeing all perception as a comparison of relations, the difference between inborn and acquired behaviour becomes chiefly one of degree of rigidity and plasticity, both in perception and response. Gibson, indeed (p. 213), suggests that it is conceivable that every psychophysical relation is partly innate and partly acquired. The implications of this and similar views are that certain general characteristics of visual perception and performance—the response to line, angle and texture—are innate. The first two confer the ability to respond to elementary form, and the last —the response to texture—probably conveys an innate ability to perceive surface and depth. There is also evidence that perception of colour and brightness constancy may be innate. These five abilities can perhaps be regarded as the primary visual 'instincts' found in the majority of animals with highly developed eyes. Similar abilities in other sensory fields could account for innate recognition of elementary chemical and mechanical stimuli.

In addition to the evidence for the innate perception of units referred to above, Hebb (1937) suggests that for at least some animals with binocular vision, depth perception and figure-background relation are also immediate; and the animal can, as soon as its organs are functional and on its very first experience of visual sensations, cope effectively with spatial phenomena.[1] Rats without pattern-vision experience can avoid a 'visual cliff' on first encounter with it (Walk, Gibson, Pick and Tighe, 1958, and Nealey and Edwards, 1960). Moreover, such faculties persist in the rat (Hebb, 1938) after total destruction of the striate cortex, from which it seems that they must be as primitive as discrimination itself. Similarly with colour and brightness constancy in birds and mammals, the work of both Köhler and Katz (see Katz, 1937, p. 75) indicates that the ability is inborn. But individual learning alone, coupled with such inborn faculties as depth perception and constancy relation, will not, for an animal of very limited brain size, be a very efficient means of ordering life in the complex world in which it must survive. Accordingly, the more responses to oft-recurring stimuli and situations can be stereotyped the more the limited neural equipment for plasticity can be reserved for situations where it is indispensable. This is done by specialising the innate perceptory mechanism so as to provide inborn mechanisms for immediate recognition of more specialised stimuli which are unlikely to be encountered except in the appropriate biological situation, namely sign stimuli and releasers (specific odours or sounds, forms or colour patterns, or movements characteristic of the species partner or predator or prey). Concomitantly we have the development of increasingly specialised moods and behaviour patterns associated therewith to form kineses, taxes and instincts.

Following this line of argument a little further, it is hard to avoid the conclusion that this elemental form of insight inherent in all perception, this primary learning ability, is also in some way the core of the primary general *drive* of the animal itself. Indeed, a very similar view, namely that an animal is *primarily* something which perceives, has been developed by Agar (1943), backed by a wide zoological and philosophical knowledge. Woodworth also takes a very similar view: 'Perception is always driven by a direct inherent motive which might be called "the will to perceive"' (quoted by Nissen, 1951, p. 347). In other words, perception is a *first-*

---

[1] Woodworth (1938, pp. 674, 680) comes to the conclusion, after detailed discussion of experiments, that perception of distance is primarily a matter of visual, not oculokinæsthetic, cues, and Gibson's discussion leads to a similar result.

order drive. To quote Thacker once again, 'Motivation for learning is central and neural. An organised and proliferated cognitive structure itself is the goal towards which learning moves' (Thacker, 1950). This involves the view that the primitive conative faculty of insight inherent in the very nature of perception of pattern has developed (Thorpe, 1950) in two directions. On the one hand, in the less specialised conative form of mood and drive it has developed its learning powers to be capable, on both the receptor and effector sides, of coping with an increasingly wide variety of situations expressing itself in the well-known categories of learning that we have been discussing. On the other hand, it has become, so to speak, canalised and specialised on both the receptor and effector sides to produce stereotyped instinctive behaviour where little is left of the original learning element except that which is involved in the recognition of a few particular patterns of environmental stimulation and in the perfection of certain specialised combinations of movement. In doing so it appears to have travelled as far in the direction of innate recognition of complex visual patterns as it has been possible for the hereditary mechanism to transmit, the animal showing an hereditary bias to recognise one kind of pattern rather than another.

SUMMARY

1. It is provisionally assumed that the essence of insight is the perception of relations, and that the concept cannot logically be restricted to visual perception but must be extended to cover all sensory fields.

2. It is pointed out that in form vision it is neither the retinal image nor a geometrical relationship that 'gets into' the brain. All that 'gets in' is an ordinal series of electro-chemical events.

3. It is suggested that although a 'whole' is truly a system of universal interaction, yet it is incorrect to suppose that perception is of an immediate whole without any element of comparison between the parts. Rather the parts are perceived only as relations; this is the primary insight giving rise to the primary perceptions. With experience the primary perceptions can be combined and built up into more complex 'gestalts.' On the other hand, analysis can yield impressions of the parts. Thus, in a sense, perception is primary, while sensation is the result of secondary analysis.

4. It follows that with organisms possessing complex eyes, form vision is primary, ontogenetically, to eye movements. Eye movements become more and more necessary as acute foveal vision develops.

5. Nevertheless, the importance of relative movement, a kind of scanning process, in enabling form vision by means of relatively simple eyes (stemmata), can hardly be over-emphasised and is of great evolutionary significance.

6. Since comparison involves learning, an element of learning enters into all orientation and all perception. Accordingly it is suggested that the difference between inborn and acquired behaviour is of degree rather than kind; it becomes, in fact, a difference chiefly of degree of rigidity and plasticity.

7. The importance of scanning is further emphasised in connection with theories according to which the two-dimensional patterns of retinal stimulation are translated to temporal patterns of excitation.

8. Subject to conclusion 6 above, it is suggested that certain general characteristics of visual perception and performance—the response to line, angle and texture—are innate. The first two in their turn confer the ability to respond to elementary form, and the last—the response to texture—probably mediates an innate ability to perceive surface and depth. There is also evidence that colour and brightness constancy may be innate. These five abilities can perhaps be regarded as the primary visual 'instincts' found in the majority of animals with highly developed eyes. Similar abilities in other sensory fields could account for innate recognition of elementary chemical and mechanical stimuli.

9. Over and above these primary or basic instincts, it has been biologically advantageous for many animals, which have to live in and deal with a relatively restricted environment, to develop their innate powers of recognition to respond to much more complex and specialised patterns of stimulation. This involves the structure known as the innate releasive mechanism.

10. Since the learning involved in the primary perception cannot be altogether of the 'rewarded' type, but is rather the satisfaction of an inherent tendency to achieve a particular type of mental organisation or to develop organisation in that *direction*, it has some general affinity with latent learning. It is suggested that this kind of 'learning' is in some way the behavioural 'core' or primary drive of the animal itself. The animal is thus essentially something which *perceives*.

11. It is thus suggested that the urge to perceive is a first-order drive, and that a plausible argument can be made out for its having developed in the course of evolution in two opposite directions to produce both the many elaborate instincts and the higher learning ability that we find in the higher animals.

CHAPTER VIII

THE MECHANISMS OF LEARNING

THEORIES of learning and retention have in the past been based on the assumption that the originally excited neurones remain active, giving, by a kind of persistent after-discharge, the basis for memory (Edgell, 1924). Some such theory could conceivably be the basis for short-term memory, although even here it falls so far short of present-day requirements that it is hardly profitable to give much space to consideration of it; but it is long-term memory that constitutes the major problem. Theories of the kind advanced by Edgell were tied up with the assumptions that every human brain has far more cells, among its ten thousand million, than it is ever likely to require, and that learning ability is dependent upon having a large number of readily available and hitherto unoccupied 'bonds.' A view somewhat similar to this has again been advanced by Hebb (1961) who suggests that the possession of a large brain capable of learning a great many different things, inevitably means that there are far more neurons present than is necessary for learning some one specific task. He argues that learning will be fast or slow according to the success of the learning organism in establishing environmental control of the excess neural activity in order to prevent or to minimise interference.

It is hardly too much to say that the background of all modern work on cortical function is provided by Lashley's theory of mass action, which was based on prolonged ablation studies with rats and monkeys. Lashley found (what Flourens had suggested a century or so before, on incomparably less satisfactory evidence) that the impairment of performance as a result of injuries to the brain cortex is closely correlated with the extent of the lesion but shows extremely little correlation with its location. As a result of these observations, he put forward the view that what has come to be known as the principle of mass action governs, in a general way, the integration of behaviour. Zangwill (1961), in a recent critical discussion of Lashley's views, has shown that Lashley himself did not support his own theory in anything like the consistent and rigid manner that his followers have sometimes suggested. In fact, he largely abandoned it in relation to visual discrimination habits, and Zangwill shows that its application to the results of maze experiments is, to say the least, equivocal. 'In particular, the claim that the sensory areas of the cortex possess non-sensory functions which contribute to the efficiency of maze performance to an extent proportional to their relative mass cannot be regarded as established.' Zangwill points out that the whole trend of recent work on primate behaviour may be said to favour the differential localisation of specific behaviour patterns, and as a result of this and much other work the mass action hypothesis does not look as plausible and attractive today as it did in 1938. Nevertheless, severe as some of the criticisms of Lashley's position have been, it still appears to hold good for large fields of investigation and, with its converse hypothesis of equipotentiality, still remains the theoretical basis for programmes of research on brain functions. It is against this background that what follows must be considered.

It is a remarkable fact that the same absence of localisation appears to exist in the mechanism for motor organisation. Weiss (1950, p. 107) has drawn attention to the analogy between the innate 'fore-limb field' in the spinal cord of the newt as revealed by his own researches and the 'learned' 'cortical visual field' as demonstrated by experiments such as those of Lashley and his co-workers. In both cases the organisation mechanism for a pattern of activity is, of course, limited to a particular mass of nervous tissue but seems to be universally represented throughout that mass. We can hardly escape the conclusion, therefore, that there are no special cells reserved for particular memories. On the other hand, we cannot get away from the implication that the transmission of nervous impulse from cell to cell does form the basis of integration. Pavlov's theory of irradiation was, at least in its original form, an anti-neurone theory, and Konorski (1948) has given a critical summary and appraisal of Pavlov's views. He points out the extent to which the whole style of Pavlov's theory of brain action is foreign to present-day neurophysiological concepts. And for that reason, if for no other, detailed dismantling of the structure is hardly necessary. He does, however, point out that, because of the complexity and difficulty of the physiology of higher nervous activity and because of the multitude of possible theoretical interpretations of observed facts, any theory, however far removed it appeared to be from current neurophysiology, would be worth careful consideration provided it accorded completely with the facts available and was not internally contradictory. But there are internal contradictions in the Pavlovian system which make it now unacceptable quite apart from its neurophysiological assumptions.

Konorski shows that the fundamental feature of Pavlov's theory is the assumption that both excitatory and inhibitory processes evoked by competing or conflicting groups of stimuli are localised in the cortical centre for these stimuli at the point on the cerebral cortex to which they are 'addressed.' Thus for him the 'original sin' of Pavlov's theory is that it places all fundamental plastic processes at the very beginning of the cortical part of supposed reflex arcs. It is primarily from this assumption that the contradictions which arise have their origin, and thus many of the difficulties which the theory encounters are inherent in its very fundamentals.

Konorski, reacting from the Pavlovian system, suggests that it is the excitation of the unconditioned centre which is the chief feature of the mechanism for plasticity, and so he attempts to bring back the whole theory into terms of the reflex arc and the synapse. He also points out, truly enough, that the Pavlovian assumption that the same stimulus gives rise to cortical irradiation of excitation when reinforced and of inhibition when not reinforced is a gratuitous hypothesis and one which seems to have no particular advantages for the interpretation of learning experiments. Konorski then develops a morphological conception of plasticity which is merely the latest in a long chain of such theories which started with Ramon y Cajal (1904) and proceeded through Kappers (1917), Child (1921), Coghill (1929) and no doubt many others down to the present day. Konorski's particular version of it invokes the assumption that the complete coupling of two neurones is effected by the growth of multiple synaptic contacts,[1] and that there is a maximal possible density or *saturation point* of synaptic contacts between any two neurones. If this maximum density is reached before birth or before maturity, then we have the structures which mediate the innate or unconditioned reflexes. If this maximal density has not been reached, then we have the possibility of completion by means of repetition of associations and so get a conditioning of the reflex. In this manner, since the synaptic connections only have to grow for a distance of about 0·01 of a millimetre (probably less), we have a theoretically possible morphological basis for maturation and conditioning. A synaptic growth theory of this type has obviously many difficulties to overcome and can hardly at present be maintained in its original form, but, as we shall see when discussing the work of Eccles below, the synaptic growth concept has certainly not been exhausted, and in a newer form may prove to be of very great value in a context which no longer necessitates the association of discrete groups of cells with particular memory traces nor the idea that particular individual synapses are reserved for particular associative reactions. It is this particular form of the theory that seems to have been disposed of by Lashley's experiments. As mentioned above, the encephalogram studies point to all the cells of the brain being in almost constant activity, either firing or actively inhibited, and any neurones which retain any kind of special memory trace of an experience must certainly also participate in countless other activities.

There have accordingly been many other hypotheses: W. Köhler (1940) elaborated a theory of brain action which is one of a group of field or vector theories. This theory involves 'fields of forces,' perhaps electro-

---

[1] It has been estimated that there are 1,300 synaptic knobs on a single anterior horn cell (Forbes, 1939).

chemical in nature, which are supposed to 'represent' in some way the pattern of sensory excitation so that the perimeter of the figure forms a boundary separating areas of different potentials. This perhaps helps us to understand certain phenomena such as the dominance of figure over background and also some problems of visual illusion and apparent movement (see Lashley). But I find it hard to get a clear idea of what it really means, and it runs into what seem insuperable difficulties over matters such as figural after-effects (Hebb, 1949, p. 54ff.) and stimulus equivalence. In this, and indeed in some other respects, it resembles Pavlov's irradiation theory. Moreover, it assumes a brain field corresponding in its spatial characteristics to those of the sensory surface and so—at least as far as the storage of memory traces is concerned—seems equally put out of court by Lashley's work.

Lashley himself had previously (1924) developed an electro-chemical theory of a different type which he had hoped would surmount such difficulties, but was subsequently forced to abandon it as of little value. He then developed a theory of interference patterns mediated by constant reverberatory excitation in the system of cortical cross connections described by Lorente de Nó (1934). He suggests that the total action is analogous to the transmission of waves on a fluid surface. Interference in such a system produces a pattern of crests and troughs which is characteristic for each spatial distribution of the sources of wave motion, and which is roughly reduplicated over the surface. He thus, with much ingenuity, gets over the localisation difficulty, supposing that in the cortex a stable resonance pattern (tuned resonating circuits), a sort of standing wave form not unlike the interference pattern of simple wave motion, would be established. And he points out that vast as are the problems yet left unsolved (e.g. the retention of temporal patterns), the recognition and remembering of visual patterns may be simpler than at first appears, for primitive visual memory is a matter of fixation of a direction—or combination of a few directions—in visual space. J. Z. Young (1939) has advanced a similar self-re-exciting circuit theory of memory as a result of his work on *Octopus*.

Perhaps the chief difficulty of these concepts is that of imagining how interference between the different patterns is to be avoided—for it would seem that later memories would distort earlier ones to an extent which simply does not happen. Indeed, as Hebb (1961) has said, the problem of serial order is the crux of the problem of behaviour in the higher animal. In any event, the electro-chemical form of the theory seems to have been rendered even more improbable, if not untenable, by the experiments of Lashley, Chow and Semmes (1951), in which conducting plates were inserted in the brains of monkeys without the anticipated disruptive effect (or indeed any effect) being observed. Hebb (1949, p. 62) has tried to combine the two theories by supposing that a reverberatory circuit might be responsible for short-term memory, as in the memory of numbers which may last a few seconds only, and that such a reverberating memory trace could co-operate with a structural change—such as the growth of synaptic knobs—and carry the memory until a growth change is made. He thus makes an important distinction between short-term and long-term memory. This certainly surmounts some difficulties but not, it seems, the really fundamental ones. Hebb tries to get over the lack of localisation of memory traces by assuming that the functional cell assemblies which are integrated by the morphological changes are not *concentrated* but *diffuse*. And in this way he hopes to lengthen the time during which it is reasonable to suppose a circuit reverberates from the $\frac{1}{100}$ second assumed by Lorente de Nó to a period sufficient for the structural change to proceed. But even if this is satisfactory, which is extremely doubtful, there remains Lashley's fundamental difficulty over cell numbers and the multiplicity of activities of the brain cells. Perhaps some of these difficulties are lessened or overcome by Eccles (1953).

Investigations by mammalian neurophysiologists centre round both the question of localisation and the nature and mechanism of the memory trace and of its fixation—although, of course, the two aspects are inter-dependent and it is not possible to keep them entirely separate. In mammals it is true that most learning involves the cortex, and this is the region where, until very recently, almost all the efforts of neurophysiologists interested in the subject have been concentrated. However, such work as that of Franzisket (1961) on habituation and conditioning in the reflexes of spinal frogs and latterly the extraordinary development of neuro-physiological study of the reticular or limbic system of the brain stem, has shown how far removed from the truth is the idea that cortical mechanisms provide the *sole* medium for the production of learned responses.

Studies of the physiology of nerve conduction are now advancing so rapidly that any theory of brain action is apt to find itself, if not stillborn, at least entering early decline because the primary physiological assump-tions on which it is based are already out of date at the time of its con-ception. For this reason, and because of the enormous complexity of neural processes, there has been a tendency among psychologists to dismiss 'neurologising' as a waste of time, and attempt to rely solely on observa-tions of behaviour without any theorising—as in the 'Descriptive Be-haviourism' of Skinner. It is true enough that there are difficulties in pointing to advances in behaviour study which were clearly dependent on neurophysiology, and the behaviour student must not save himself trouble and responsibility by turning to the neurophysiologist as some sort of high priest of science who can produce for him, when strongly enough urged, *ex cathedra* theories which will guide him on the straight and narrow path. But there is this to be said, and Hebb (1951) has said it very well, that whether physiology should or should not be the guide in the choice of psychological principles, it has always, in fact, been so, and that some at least of the failures of psychologists in the past have been due not to the fact that they have turned to neurophysiology for guidance but rather to the fact that they have turned to a neurophysiology already ten or twenty years out of date. The student of behaviour, if he is to see his problems whole and in true perspective, has to look at them from many different angles and in many different lights, which means that he has to have some acquaintance with a number of different branches of science. With everything developing so fast, it is increasingly difficult for him to keep abreast of advances in all the relevant subjects, and however hard he tries he will no doubt fall behind somewhere and make some mistakes. Nevertheless, this is not an adequate reason for not trying; for it is better to be a little bit behind than right out of the race, and for this reason it seems justifiable to say something about the excellent and stimulating attempts of Eccles (1953) to produce a neurophysiology based on the latest advance in knowledge of excitatory processes and at the same time one far enough advanced to be able to make statements relevant for the student of behaviour. After giving an account of the ionic hypothesis and its significance for the understanding of the membrane both in the resting and active state, he proceeds to consider the transmission of nerve impulses across synapses in sympathetic ganglia. From many studies it appears that, in the function of the central nervous system, inhibition is as fundamental a process as is synaptic excitation, and that while excitation can be conceived as essentially a depolarisation, so inhibition must be regarded as a hyperpolarisation process. Now, just as the depolarisation process seems to involve, whether peripherally or centrally, a chemical transmitter of the acetyl-choline type, so he produces weighty evidence for concluding that a purely electrical explanation of inhibitory synaptic transmission is equally improbable. We are therefore justified in assuming for the present that inhibition is mediated by a specific transmitter substance that is liberated from the inhibitory synaptic knobs and causes an active hyperpolarisation process in the sub-adjacent membrane. If this is so, then it is possible to formulate a relatively simple mechanism for mono-synaptic excitatory and inhibitory action. There are three simple ways in which such a system could be conceived as operating, and they are illustrated in the accompanying figure (Fig. 17). The first possibility is that afferent fibres of, for instance, flexor muscles liberate a substance 'y' which depolarises flexor and hyperpolarises extensor neurones, while another group of fibres liberates a different substance, 'x,' having the opposite action. While this theory explains nicely some of the problems which Eccles considers and which it is not within the scope of this book to discuss, it nevertheless encounters some seemingly insurmountable difficulties and contradictions. The second and third ways are both more satisfactory. The second scheme assumes that each group of fibres liberates two substances, 'x' and 'y,' and that there is, in addition, a specialisation of the sub-synaptic areas such that the appropriate neurones react only to the excitatory or inhibitory transmitter. The third form of the hypothesis postulates only a single substance but assumes a specialisation of the sub-synaptic membrane, such that the substance hyperpolarises one group of neurones and depolarises the other group.

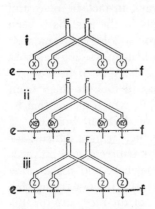

FIG. 17 — Diagrammatic representation of possible modes of mono-synaptic excitatory and inhibitory action, i, ii and iii corresponding to the three situations described in the text. E and F are respectively grouped Ia afferent fibres from extensor and flexor muscles, and e and f respectively the surfaces of the extensor and flexor motoneurones. The synaptic knobs are shown containing the respective transmitter substances which they secrete, those ringed in ii being assumed to be inactive on the adjacent sub-synaptic membrane. The striated and dotted borders on the sub-synaptic membrane signify patches with specific sensitivity. The arrows indicate current flow due to the net cationic-anionic flux across the sub-synaptic membrane. Hence an inward arrow gives depolarisation and excitation; an outward, hyperpolarisation and inhibition. (After Eccles, 1953.)

So we come back to a new form of the kind of morphological explanation which, as we have seen above, was put forward by Konorski. The details of the theory of chemical excitation and inhibition do not really concern us, for it makes no immediate difference whether one or two chemical substances are involved. The point is that both theories involve the development or specialisation of synaptic knobs, and both involve the assumption that the membrane against which the knobs are in contact is itself specialised to respond in a particular way; and Eccles shows (p. 173) that this is by no means an outrageous assumption.

The next step in applying such ideas to the problems of plasticity is to show how repeated excitation of certain synapses can produce a relatively enduring enhancement of reflex function and to show why it is that repeated stimulation is necessary for its maintenance. The most probable postulate is that the pre-synaptic impulse 'becomes a more effective synaptic excitor (or inhibitor) because repetitive stimulation temporarily alters the spatial relationship of the synaptic knobs to the post-synaptic membrane; for example, the knobs may become larger and/or in closer opposition thereto.'

Volume changes (Hill *et al.*, 1950) have been observed in giant axons which have suffered repeated stimulation, and Eccles considers it reasonable to assume that the same thing is happening in non-medullated pre-synaptic fibres also; for the uptake of water is largely determined by the ionic flux that is associated with the nerve impulse. The relatively large surface-to-volume ratio in conjunction with the very small diameter of the fibres could lead to a very great and rapid swelling and a similarly rapid recovery. Moreover, it is the larger radius of curvature which the synaptic knob possesses relative to its attached fibre that would ensure a more ready swelling of the former in response to an increase in turgor of the system—given uniform elastic properties of the membrane. Thus, with a water uptake of the same order as that found in the giant fibre, a 0·3 micron-diameter fibre would more than double its volume to 0·46, and a spherical knob of 1 micron would swell to 1·2. 'If there is a further knob swelling due to fluid flowing from fibre into knob, a very plausible explanation is available of the great increase that occurs in synaptic efficiency during the post-tetanic potentiation' (Eccles, 1953). It is quite possible, for instance, for a doubling of the surface area of the knob to occur. Thus the swelling hypothesis based on the effects demonstrated in peripheral axons seems to offer an adequate explanation for the basic facts of synaptic transmission as far as they are at present known to be occurring in the central nervous system and to provide the beginnings of a modern theory of nervous plasticity.

But, still, such a mechanism could hardly be invoked for anything more than short-term memory. However, Eccles goes on to show that it might be highly significant in initiating other processes of still longer duration. Thus comes the concept that activity enhances 'the functional effectiveness of disused synapses over a much longer period than the several minutes of ordinary post-tetanic potentiation' (p. 209), and that such disused synapses are capable of 'learning' to operate more effectively as a result of intensive stimulation. Thus the plasticity which has been postulated for higher nerve centres in explanation of the conditioned reflex may merely be an expression of the same essential process which is an attribute of the simplest spinal reflex pathway.

Gerard (1961) has pointed out that ignorant as we at present are of the mechanism of fixation, two sets of data give strong clues concerning its nature. First, there is the group of well-known changes that attend continued activity of the neurons: thresholds go through increased and decreased phases, after-potentials are increased greatly in magnitude, and post-tetanic potentiation is associated with greatly increased reflex responses. Secondly, the facts of short-term and long-term memory seem to show that a considerable period—maybe minutes, maybe hours—may elapse between having an experience and fixing it. If neural activity is interfered with during this fixation period by electro-shock, cold-shock, heat-block and the like, fixation is interfered with also and permanent memories are feeble or abolished (Duncan, Ransmeier and Gerard, ref.

in Gerard, 1961). In experiments with hamsters when training in a learning situation, if convulsive electric shock follows the experience by an hour, there is some deterioration; at 15 minutes loss is very considerable, and at 5 minutes, more or less, learning is in effect prevented. If the hamster is promptly cooled after a learning experiment, a shock given an hour later can be as deleterious as one given a few minutes later at body temperature (Ransmeier and Gerard, 1954). Similar results accrue from the study of the effect of a number of drugs on the learning process. Gerard concludes that such facts fit well with a theory of continued activity of the nervous system following the arrival of sensory impulses as a result of which a dynamic memory is fixed sooner or later as a structural one. He suggests that repeated activity of the same neurons with progressively greater and greater residual changes from the continued activity would provide an effective mechanism. At fifty reverberations per second, 100,000 actions could easily occur during the fixation time—presumably sufficient to leave an indelible trace. What this trace can be at the neuronal level is another matter. Geiger has shown a change in microsome number and locus around the nucleus accompanying changes in activity of neurons, and Hill (1950) indicated that the apical dendrite of the pyramidal neurons becomes thicker and more twisted with continuing activity. Gerard (1961) points out that nerve fibres swell when active, throw out additional branches and presumably increase the size and numbers of their terminal knobs. But he adds that the neuron also has an unusually high rate of metabolism and, judging from its behaviour in tissue culture, it may renew its entire mass of protoplasm three times daily. He says 'it is hard to see, therefore, how an enduring modification can be left at the cellular level'. Experience must presumably alter some macro-molecule, D.N.A. or R.N.A. or protein, which can continue to reproduce itself in the altered form as does a mutated gene.

Morell (1961) has put forward evidence that structural changes are in fact produced by continuous neuronal bombardment and shows that there is evidence that changes in the distribution of R.N.A. (perhaps linked with protein or phospho-lipids) form the chemical correlates of this alteration. Taking this as a reasonable working hypothesis, he regards it as perhaps not too far-fetched to consider that the complex of ribonucleic acid and protein represents an essential element in the molecular basis of memory. A concept of this kind ties up admirably with modern views of the protein biosynthesis. (Perry, 1960, personal communication.) It is argued that the information required to control the manufacture of the thousands of proteins which are among the essentials which characterise any given cell is stored in proteins each containing polypeptid chains several hundred molecules long, i.e. the D.N.A. has to spell out thousands of 'words' each several hundred 'letters' long, using an 'alphabet' of twenty letters. It may be supposed that excessive exercise will increase the proportion of myoglobin in muscle; that is to say, the activity of a cell can adaptively influence its mechanisms for protein synthesis. It is suggested that this can happen in brain and that the frequency of activity of neurons could similarly influence protein synthesis and that this might be a means of storing information. If so, the same biochemical process which produces evolutionary mutations might also be producing new states in the brain which play an important part in its activity and its responses. A surprising further piece of evidence for the importance of R.N.A. in the process of learning has recently come from work on the planarian *Dugesia dorotocephala* by Corning and John (1961). These workers permitted the halves of conditioned light-shock worms to regenerate in a weak solution of ribonuclease (R.N.A.–A.S.E.), a compound which is destructive of R.N.A. They argue as follows: 'Conditioned tails, regenerating in the presence of R.N.A.–A.S.E., might be expected to produce anterior portions with a depleted or altered R.N.A. structure, perhaps due to influences exerted at the regenerating interface. Such an organism must then have a naïve dominant head. Conversely, since trained heads only have a non-dominant tail to re-grow, they should demonstrate a greater degree of retention.' The hypothesis appeared to be supported by the results, for the heads regenerated in R.N.A.–A.S.E. exhibited retention as great as that of control heads and tails regenerated in plain water, whereas the tails regenerated in R.N.A.–A.S.E. showed essentially no effect. Whatever may be the outcome of the work on the learning of planarians which is discussed in Chapter X below, it seems clear that there is evidence of regenerative transmission of conditioned responses and that the problem is essentially a physiological one; for however these animals learn, they seem to be able to learn with many if not all tissues of the body, and the basis of memory in this animal is a molecular one.

To return from the sub-cellular to the cellular level: the concept of facilitation, based on a current neurophysiological model of high probability, fits in admirably with the theory so freely advanced in recent years (see J. Z. Young, 1938; Hebb, 1949; etc.) which attributes learning to the establishment of changes in specific patterns of activity created by impulses circulating continuously in the closed self-re-exciting chains of neurones. The anatomical discoveries of Lorente de Nó regarding the arrangements of the neurones in the cortex at first made the postulation of such circuits seem plausible enough. J. Z. Young (1951) has summed up his evidence that some such device for the maintenance of closed circuits operates in the learning performance of *Octopus*, and Burns (1951) has actually found that circulating activity may continue for a matter of seconds in an isolated slab of mammalian cerebral cortex. Such a mechanism can then be thought of as surviving long enough to produce the synaptic plastic changes, and Eccles advances a scheme, shown diagrammatically in the accompanying figure (Fig. 18), which could reasonably serve as a basis for explaining the conditioned reflex by plastic changes

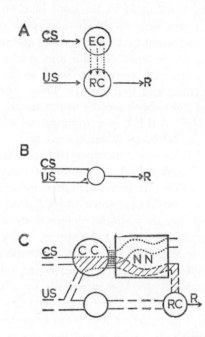

FIG. 18—Diagrams illustrating attempts to explain conditioned reflexes by plastic changes in synaptic connections. CS and US show input into central nervous system of conditioned and unconditioned stimuli respectively. In A the arrows indicate nervous pathways, while B is a redrawing of a highly simplified model in which Shimbel (1950) shows converging synaptic connections of the CS and US lines. In C nervous pathways are drawn as broad bands along which conduction occurs, particularly in the neuronal network, NN. The interruptions in the bands indicate synaptic relays. Nerve centres containing large populations of neurones are indicated by circles, while the neuronal network, NN, would be an extremely complex neuronal system; for example, an area or areas of the cerebral cortex. (After Eccles, 1953.)

in synaptic connections. The reality of spinal conditioning has heretofore been much questioned (Kellogg, Pronko and Deese, 1946) but there now seems no doubt that it is a fact (Hernández-Peón and Brust-Carmona, 1961; also Anokhin, 1961). But whatever the evidence for conditioning in chronic spinal mammals, there is certainly good evidence for it occurring in other groups of animals, e.g. the amphibia (Franzisket, 1955; see also Chapter IV above, and Chapter XIII below).

It has, of course, never been supposed that neo-cortical tissue contains some unique mechanism for learning. All that has been assumed in the classical view is that in the mammals the learning mechanisms are concentrated there. To put it another way (Hernández-Peón and Brust-Carmona, 1961) all levels of the central nervous system seem to be endowed with plastic properties which cannot be ascribed exclusively to any particular locus of the brain. Eccles faces the difficulty inherent in the fact that the experimental demonstrations of changing synaptic efficacy require thousands of impulses or relatively long periods of disuse (Eccles and McIntyre, 1951, 1952), whereas a conditioned reflex can be acquired after very few repetitions, and, of course, unique events can be remembered for a whole lifetime. In this connection the explanation is put forward that with prolonged reverberatory activity in the neuronal network a single event may, in fact, activate each link in a spatio-temporal pattern thousands of times within a few seconds. Thus we arrive at a view strikingly similar to that of Hebb when he assumed that a reverberatory trace co-operating with a structural change can carry a memory until an actual growth change is made, but the suggestion is now enormously strengthened by the newer knowledge on which it is based. A structural basis is thus provided for the storage of information, and so we can think of an engram as not a localised group of neurones but a non-localised patterned association of neurones with many alternative paths and relays which is called into existence and is maintained by increased synaptic junctions and by usage. But storage of information is not everything and, as Sperry (1955) has pointed out, most physiological theories have tended to neglect a factor which psychological and behavioural studies have long shown to be essential, namely the high-level patterns of cerebral activity associated with 'anticipatory set' or 'expectancy.' He looks upon these non-localised cerebral patterns as 'dynamic readjustments in the background of central facilitation.'

It is a main object of this chapter to consider the general principles involved in the study of learning mechanisms rather than the specific features of the neurophysiology of learning in particular groups. Nevertheless, it is inevitable that in the present state of our knowledge it should deal particularly, however simply and inadequately, with the neurophysiology of learning in mammals, since investigations into this group have been incomparably more extended than with any other. In the mammals there are two important discoveries of recent years which bear very closely indeed upon the problem. They are, first, the results of Olds and his co-workers on the primary reinforcement centres which exist in the mammalian brain, especially the brain of the rat, and secondly the enormous development of understanding of the ascending reticular system and other subcortical structures which has arisen from the application of many techniques, but particularly that of the electro-encephalograph. Olds (1955) showed by electrical stimulation that 'the limbic system' (which includes primarily the septal area in its relation to the amygdala, the hippocampus, the cingulate cortex and possibly the hypothalamus and anterior nucleus of the thalamus—an area largely synonymous with the rhinencephalon) constitutes in the main a primary reward centre. When rats are enabled, by pressing a bar, to give themselves electrical stimulation in this area, they press the bar with immense persistence for many hours at a stretch and apparently irrespective of all other needs and stimuli. Here, then, is a primary reward and reinforcement centre within the brain, capable of providing an internal, and in that sense non-sensory, reinforcement sufficient of itself to function as the key to the learning mechanism. Olds and Olds (1961) suggest that the hypothalamus, with its projections to the paleo-cortex and related structures, has some special relation to the mechanisms of instrumental learning and perhaps to associated mechanisms in general. They list a series of learning tasks for which self-stimulation in the median forebrain bundle regions of the hypothalamus is a satisfactory incentive. Operant conditioning of single unit responses, when these were in the subcortex, gave results which suggested that the basic mechanism of instrumental conditioning itself was being observed. Stimulation in the hippocampal pyramidal dentate gyrus region can often cause seizures. There is some evidence that it is also the region of the execution of planned behaviour. It is interesting that hyperstimulation of points for positive reinforcement interferes with learning. Perhaps this is because it merely ensures repetition of the behaviour which has just been performed and this, of course, may be the antithesis of learning. But stimulation of negative reinforcement points seems not to interfere with learning. Galambos (1961) points out that there are now three different studies which suggest the conclusion that the role of reinforcment is to produce a widespread generalisation of afferent signals in the central nervous system together with an increase in amplitude. Magoun, discussing this conclusion (Galambos, 1961, p. 239), says, 'discovery of the role of reinforcement, in generalising and increasing the amplitude of the responses of the central nervous system to afferent signals, represents an outstanding achievement of recent electrophysiological investigation of the processes of learning in the brain.'

Modern work on the neurophysiology and neurology of the reticular or limbic system is already alarming in its proportions and rate of growth. A full summary, even if practicable, would be out of place in a book such as this. Nevertheless an attempt may be made to emphasise those parts of the subject which are particularly significant for the student of animal behaviour. The paragraphs that follow represent the conclusions of a recent summary of my own. (Thorpe, 1961c.)

Myers (1961) has produced evidence for the independent existence of complex memory traces in different parts of the nervous system which may be mentioned first in that it provides a convenient introduction to the problems posed by the study of the reticular system. Myers, working with cats, showed that when habits involving visual discrimination are acquired, some essential event occurs in the cerebral hemispheres. All the cats in Myer's experiments had undergone mid-sagittal transection of the crossing retinal fibres of the optic chiasma before any training was commenced. They were then taught visual pattern discrimination with either the right or the left eye only, whereupon subsequent tests showed that the visual learning had been transmitted to the other hemisphere in spite of the transection of the optic chiasma. It was later found that the communication between the two hemispheres was via the corpus callosum, this structure being able to convey the complex signals which must presumably be necessary to transmit the results of learning of a new visual pattern. Thus this work on the chiasma-sectioned cats has shown that a stable and lasting change is induced in the 'trained' hemisphere receiving the direct afferent stimulation. This change can be called the memory trace. It was then shown that the training hemisphere could induce lasting memory traces in the opposite hemisphere, traces that subsequently may have an existence of their own apart from the influences of the first hemisphere. Perhaps the most interesting outcome of these investigations from the present point of view is that it was shown that transection of broad expanses of corpus callosum anteriorly did not halt transfer, while relatively much smaller lesions posteriorly did so, indicating a clear-cut posterior localisation of the visual 'gnostic' exchange activity. It was then found that the degree of success or failure obtained in contralateral trace establishment through the corpus callosum seemed to depend in large part on the difficulty of the discrimination handled. A corollary is that *the more difficult the discrimination, the greater the number of cells required*. This suggestion receives interesting confirmation from another source. Thus Garcia-Ausst, Bogacz and Vanzulli (1961), during their study by the electro-encephalograph of the evoked responses in man, showed that during the state of attention these responses are of greater amplitude and also that a much larger area of the brain receives the information. It would seem therefore that attention, fine discrimination and employment of a large number of cells go together. Diamond and Neff (for references see Neff and Diamond, 1958) also found that different amounts of neo-cortex seemed to be required according to the degree of complexity of the learning problem. If a two-tone pitch discrimination and a three-tone pattern discrimination are taught to a cat, removal of its auditory cortex abolishes both, and only the simple pitch-discrimination can be relearned—that is, some neural events correlated with the complex 'tone-pattern conditioned reflex' have been removed by partial decortication but the mechanism for a 'simple' conditioned reflex remains. The current spate of work on the functions of the limbic or reticular system of the brain stem has provided further evidence for the mechanism involved in such cases. Thus Hernández-Peón and Brust-Carmona (1961) have found that whereas extensive cortical removals did not prevent conditioning in cats, a small lesion in the mesencephalic reticular formation eliminated visual and acoustic conditioned responses completely, impairing various sensory discriminations to differing degrees. In these experiments it was vision that suffered the greatest impairment, whereas olfaction was least affected. The authors suggest that, among other effects, lesions in this region affect the final integration of the photic impulses which result in conscious vision. They sum up an extremely important and active phase of neurophysiological investigation by saying that whereas the cortex is involved in *complex* learning processes, the simplest types of learning require only subcortical structures, but these also play a more basic part in more complex types of learning for which the neo-cortex is essential. From such results it becomes obvious that for all except the very simplest kinds of learning, and perhaps for those too, the changes which are taking place, far from being instantaneous and confined to a single region of the brain structure, occur over a considerable period of time and in many different loci. Such a conclusion seems at first sight to open the way for a return to the reverberatory circuit theory but in fact the evidence does not really support such a formulation. There is now much evidence from electro-encephalogram investigations to show that the changes recorded by this method occur when the animal is learning, but when the task is accomplished the electro-encephalogram returns to a normal state indistinguishable from that shown before the experiment was started. Thus Yoshi and others (see Magoun, 1958), recording electrical activities direct from the subcortical structures during conditioning, found evidence of this. They used a flickering light as the unconditioned stimulus —taking a response of the same frequency during associated auditory stimulation (which was the conditioned stimulus) as an index of successful conditioned reflex formation. They found that evidences of conditioning in subcortical structures, especially the mid-brain reticular formation, are larger, earlier and of longer duration than in the cortex. From this they suppose that the conditioned stimulus generates impulses which spread, via the brain stem activating system, throughout the brain. After the thalmic reticular system begins to filter the widespread impulses they do not reach regions other than the localised ones where the specific effect of the unconditioned stimulus occurs. It is well known that an animal confronted with a learning task may at first show activity indicating emotional disturbance. Later, as the learning progresses, this hyper-emotional state decreases, to be replaced by an alert or attentive attitude. Finally, the fully trained animal performs his task without showing any particular signs of attention or even of interest—sometimes displaying the appearance of almost deliberate unconcern. It seems likely, as Galambos (1961) points out, that it is these preliminary emotional, attentive and orientation states which are being recorded in the electro-encephalograph; and they are the precursors of the learning process, not the learning process itself. The more difficult and complex the task, the more widespread, prolonged and intense these preliminary activities may be, and they will be found widespread in cortical and subcortical regions. He alludes to the fact that reinforcement of the original signals by various stimuli increases the probability that the response to the conditioned stimulus will be large in amplitude and prolonged in duration at *all sites* where it is recordable. He points out, however, that if the conditioned stimulus is a signal that a response (such as pressing a lever) will avoid shock or procure food, the brain activity evoked by the conditioned stimulus tends to become reduced as the learning proceeds and may, as we have seen, disappear in the fully trained animal. This evoked activity returns, however, when the behavioural response is prevented, as, for instance, by moving the lever out of reach of the animal. It seems clear from this that *the conditioned stimulus can evoke a large or a small response from the brain of a conditioned animal according to the kind of training it has received.* Galambos suggests that this fact may well explain some of the variations in results obtained by workers using this technique for the study of learning.

Another point to bear in mind is that if learning a complex task is accomplished by means of an ordered series of processes in the nervous system, then there may well have to be specific mechanisms for bringing one series to an end before the next starts. Thus there is evidence in mammals that the hippocampus inhibits or limits the orientation response which, if too greatly prolonged, interferes with learning. A number of recent neurophysiological experiments throw light on this inhibitory facet of attention. They demonstrate the existence of efferent fibres that can convey inhibitory influences from the central nervous system to the sense organs and sensory nerve centres. When the central nervous system is strongly alerted by a stimulus from one sensory mode, it can use these fibres to block the transmission of other sensory processes, so that the organism can devote itself more fully to events of over-riding significance. As an example of this one may refer to the inhibitory fibres found by Galambos in the auditory nerve of the cat. Their artificial excitation depresses the electrical activity that auditory stimuli produce in the cochlear nucleus, the first substation on the way from the ear to the cortex. A number of experiments by Hernández-Peón and others show that stimulation of points in the reticular formation of the cat will block activity in sensory pathways whose receptors are simultaneously stimulated. Vision, hearing, smell and cutaneous sensitivity have all been shown to be susceptible to this effect.

Reference has been made above to the individual differences shown by electro-encephalographic records of a number of animals learning the same or similar tasks. Some new results which have recently been published throw striking new light on this matter and also on the vexed question of equipotentiality and mass action. It has been found, as the result of the work of at least three different investigators—Landsell (1953), J. C. Smith (1959) and Pinto-Hamuy (1961)—that the previous behavioural experience of an animal may have a most profound effect upon the degree to which the cortex is equipotential. Thus it has been shown that rats reared in small cages showed (as Lashley found) equipotentiality, whereas rats reared in larger cages with 'furniture' did not. Moreover, rats in a small cage will no longer show equipotentiality if the cage is moved about from place to place in the room, this having the same effect as giving them a larger cage. Again the work of Vince (1961) is relevant, showing in tits the effect on internal inhibition of restriction *versus* richness of early experience. It would be hard to find a more striking demonstration of the fact that ethology has an essential contribution to make to neurophysiology just as the latter has to ethology. Much neurophysiological data accumulated in the past has been greatly reduced in value if not rendered altogether valueless, by neglect of the simplest and most elementary ethological facts. To suppose that a monkey (which is a highly social animal) is 'normal,' either ethologically or neurophysiologically, when isolated in a small cage with its experience and manipulative opportunities restricted in almost every way, is a gross error; and one which may result in misinterpretations and waste of effort in many different directions. It looks, then, as if, as suggested by Segundo (see discussion Hernández-Peón and Brust-Carmona, pp. 411–12), the same lesion may affect different responses under different circumstances, and it may even be that an animal has a 'choice' as to the neural structure it will utilise in a particular learning process. Perhaps we may conclude this summary section by once again quoting Hebb (1961): 'The study of learning without regard to the past history of the animal is totally unrealistic.'

There is a recent and stimulating theory which stresses the parallel between learning and evolution and which, while as yet employing concepts and language somewhat different from those we have just been using, could be fitted in with them and may serve to bring us another step forward. Pringle (1951) points out that learning is an increase in complexity, and that complexity has also been increased in the course of evolution, where the method has been that of selection of improbable states. This evolutionary complexity is primarily an increase in spatial or structural complexity. It is, in other words, an adaptation of form. But all adaptation of behaviour, including all learning, involves an increasing complexity in time, and Pringle suggests that the adaptive modification of present behaviour by past events is called learning when the events have occurred during the lifetime of the individual and instinct when they have occurred previously. Thus we can arrive at a new definition of learning as a temporal increase in complexity, a new temporal relationship between two or more events which arises from the process of adaptation to a changing situation. To justify the application of this hypothesis to the phenomenon of learning, Pringle suggests a type of mechanism which, while at present only an analogy, is consistent with what is known about the neurology of the central nervous system, and which is capable of performing the necessary selective process. Such a process can be found acting in a system of coupled oscillators, and from such a system a model

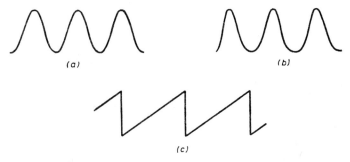

FIG. 19—Types of oscillator wave forms. (After Pringle, 1951.)

can be constructed which has the 'property of evolution.' A characteristic of such a system of coupled oscillators which is particularly relevant to concepts of selection is the phenomenon of 'locking' or 'synchronisation.' In the artificial case of the electronic coupled oscillators, when the natural frequencies of two such oscillators are not too far apart and there is coupling between them in the form of 'non-reactive energy transfer' from one to the other, the two systems oscillate as a single unit at an intermediate frequency, but with a phase difference which is dependent on the strength of the coupling and on the difference between the natural frequencies which each of the two oscillators showed when in isolation. Fig. 19 shows types of oscillator wave forms: (a) being linear or sinusoidal, (b) non-linear or non-sinusoidal and (c) that of the relaxation oscillation. In the case of linear oscillation, if the natural frequency of one oscillator, O_1, is varied, while that of the second, O_2, is maintained constant, the relationship between the natural frequency of O_1 and the observed frequencies of O_1 and O_2 is shown in Fig. 20 (*a*). Synchronisation occurs over a range of frequencies which depends upon the closeness of coupling, and the mutual effect of one upon the other is symmetrical.

Where the natural oscillations are non-sinusoidal, the response of such a coupled pair becomes asymmetrical. Thus, for a non-sinusoidal oscillation as Type B, we find that, as is shown in Fig. 20 (*b*), the frequency of oscillation of the pair, within the range of synchronisation, is now shifted, so that it is always greater than the mean of the two natural frequencies. The result of this is that the faster of the pair appears less liable to be shifted from its natural frequency as a result of coupling than does the slower; in other words, the faster of the pair appears to be able to take charge of the slower and over a given range draw it some way towards itself. When the oscillator wave form is of the relaxation type (Figs. 20 (*c*) and (*d*)), in other words when it is extremely non-linear, the frequency of the two over the synchronisation range is very nearly that of the natural frequency of the faster. When the natural frequency of one oscillator is altered so as to bring it into the synchronisation range, the synchronisation is not always effected immediately. Thus, if the oscillators are only just oscillating and if the oscillations are non-linear, it may take a considerable time for synchronisation to develop, and during this time the actual frequencies approach one another. In the same way, at the other end of the range the break-up of the locking also takes time to occur. So, if the natural frequency of one oscillator is continuously varied, a hysteresis phenomenon is produced—since the range of locking depends on the rate and the direction from which the natural frequency of oscillator 1 approaches that of oscillator 2. If the frequency increases—that is to say, if O_1 approaches O_2 from below, as is shown in Figs. 20 (*b*) and (*d*) —the synchronisation persists beyond the point at which it appears when the frequency is decreasing; that is, when O_1 approaches O_2 from above (Figs. 20 (*c*) and (*d*)). As we see from the figures, with increasing frequencies of O_1 the frequency of O_2 is, as it were, dragged much farther away from the normal than is the case when the frequency O_1 is decreasing.

This asymmetry in the relationship of a pair of such oscillators is the essential feature upon which Pringle's concept of the activity of the population of nerve cells comprising the brain is based. Thus, in his model the process of synchronisation in a population of oscillators corresponds to the reproduction of an individual in a natural population. Once the steady distribution of frequencies of oscillation has become established in a population of coupled oscillators, the asymmetry of the mutual interconnection ensures that the increase in frequency of a single oscillator will have a greater effect on the state of the population than will the decrease.

This at once reminds us of the so-called 'magnet' effect described by

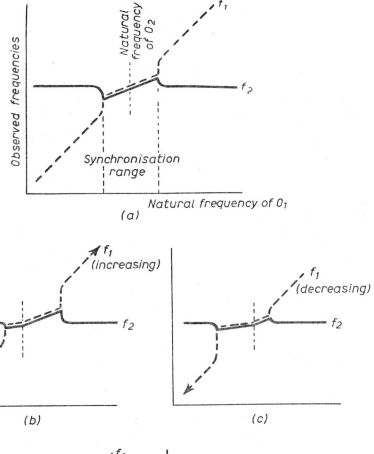

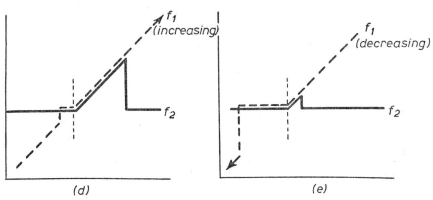

FIG. 20—Diagrams, based on experiments with electronic oscillators, to illustrate the phenomenon of synchronisation. The graphs show the observed frequencies, f_1 and f_2, of two coupled oscillators, O_1 and O_2, as the natural frequency of O_1 is varied.

(a) Linear oscillation.
(b) Non-linear oscillation: frequency of O_1 increasing.
(c) Non-linear oscillation: frequency of O_1 decreasing.
(d) Relaxation oscillation: frequency of O_1 increasing.
(e) Relaxation oscillation: frequency of O_1 decreasing.
(After Pringle, 1951.)

von Holst, according to which one set of organs moving with a given rhythm will synchronise with themselves the rhythm of another set—another pair of fins of a fish, for instance—which is moving at a different and slower rhythm.

Pringle points out that a similar effect is found in the beats of the chambers of the vertebrate heart which also behave like relaxation oscillators in that, the coupling being so strong, the whole heart normally beats as a single unit at a frequency determined by that of the fastest component.

Pringle shows that the first great advantage in assuming a model for learning based on complexity in time rather than one involving complexity of form is the rapidity of the process. Even adopting Eccles's theory, there are difficulties in seeing how a process which involves essentially a structural replication could ever be fast enough to account for the extremely rapid change characteristic of the initial stages of some types of learning, and Pringle puts forward the hypothesis 'that the learning capacity of the central nervous system of animals is a property of populations of nerve cells behaving as loosely coupled oscillators.' He suggests that a probable form of this model 'is one in which the oscillators are not single cells but closed loops or reverberatory arcs of neurones which act as oscillators as a whole.' It is not meant by this that an impulse travels round the arc in the way the concept of the reverberatory arc is usually understood, but that the whole chain of neurones is coupled so that it acts as a single oscillator, each cell influencing the next with a certain lead or lag in oscillation 'so that the whole generates a nearly sinusoidal oscillation when the phase change round the loop equals a multiple of 360 degrees.' In this connection Pringle uses the term 'excitation' to mean the state of the cell which causes the rise in impulse frequency, and not the process giving rise to a single impulse.

If two coupled closed loops of neurones share a cell or chain of cells, we shall get competition in space as well as in time, and so there will be a pattern of oscillations moving over the population of cells as a wave achieving a rapid replication of functional form, while a more rapidly replicating pattern will displace it by competing for the cells which are shared. 'If form is represented as simultaneity of action instead of as the form of an organism or a molecule, its rate of creation from component parts is limited only by the speed of the coupling process which may be very high,' and so the author of the theory escapes from the difficulty of the form-replicating machine as a model for learning. He suggests with a good deal of plausibility that this pattern of simultaneity is the essential feature in the operation of releaser mechanisms, or 'key trigger' mechanisms as he calls them.

With this model as a basis, Pringle proceeds to consider the different types of learning, and shows with surprising ease how they could be considered as brought about by a not unduly complex system of mechanisms of this type. It is not proposed to go into the detail of this here, but it is hoped that the main features of the explanation for each type of learning will be evident from the accompanying Figs. 21–23.

It seems as if some such theory as this should help us to get over some of the fundamental difficulties raised by the morphological conception of plasticity, and the next task would seem to be to integrate it with the more recent theoretical developments in the field of nervous action developed by Eccles which we have been discussing above. There seems no *a priori* difficulty in knitting the two together provided we remember that the term 'excitation' as used by Pringle refers to a maintained state in the cell measurable as some function of the frequency of impulse traversing the axon. It is suggested that it may be equivalent to the slow electrical changes occurring at the ends of peripheral nerve fibres, but it is presumed also to involve internal changes of equilibrium of a chemical kind. The strength of this theory is shown in the way in which it avoids the difficulties which Konorski and others encounter when trying to produce a model for the first rapid steps of short-term learning. It can do this because, in contrast to previous theories, it attributes plasticity to changes occurring within the cells themselves and not primarily to connections between them which, in the first place at any rate, can remain morphologically and physiologically constant.

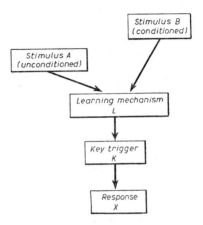

FIG. 21—Schematic block diagram for a conditioned reflex of Type I.

Normally the presentation of unconditioned response A leads to the growth in learning mechanism L of certain rhythmic patterns specific for the release when they reach a certain intensity of instinctive response X through the key trigger K. If the conditioned stimulus B is presented before the presentation of stimulus A, the cells of L are in a modified state when A is presented and the growth of the specific pattern starts. Since the frequencies of the oscillators in L are rising due to the presentation of A, they will 'collect' into their own rhythm C oscillators composed of cells still showing excitation due to B, and beating at frequencies through which the oscillations due to A rise. The extent of the pattern of simultaneity of action therefore grows. When the pattern is established over a sufficiently large part of the population the response X occurs. (After Pringle, 1951.)

Pringle has two corollaries to his system which are applicable to instances of long-term accuracy in memory for which his theory as described so far is probably inadequate. These corollaries do not necessarily follow from the first, and it does not mean that if we find the first useful we have necessarily to supersede the concepts which Eccles and others have produced for long-term retention. Nevertheless, they are of interest not only because of their originality but also because they do show some hope of getting over certain serious difficulties which yet remain. Pringle considers that long-term accuracy in memory might have two possible explanations: the first is the improvement which is achieved by the use of a large number of cells, so that the effect, so far as the animal as a whole is concerned, is the result of an averaging process—the 'statistical stability of the memory process,' as he terms it. The second possibility is perhaps an even more suggestive one, though one cannot at present see how it could be verified directly. It is that the levels of excitation in each cell may react back on its internal chemical state so that memory is effectively transferred to a molecular level. He suggests that it would be possible in this way to stabilise the inherent level of excitation in each cell so that the plastic changes become smaller and smaller in magnitude as the animal ages and the behaviour becomes correspondingly more fixed. With this model it appears that no localised changes such as are conceived of in a changing synaptic resistance need be expected since the memory trace may take the form of a slight change in a large number of cells rather than a large change in any one, and this, of course, would be consistent with the observations of Lashley and others on the absence of localisation of the memory trace. If, then, physical events accompanying association are occurring within the cells of the central nervous system rather than between them, we have the possibility of a transfer of events involved in the mechanism of learning from the level of the neurone down to the level of molecular changes in the substance of the

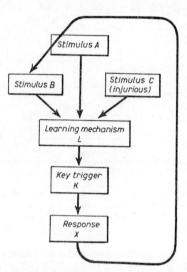

FIG. 22—Schematic block diagram for habituation.

When response occurs it produces a change in the sensory stimuli from A to B, due to the movement of the response. The new stimulus, during the frequency-increasing part of the oscillations which it induces in L, reduces the magnitude of the specific pattern for release of K. As a result, plastic changes occur which make the specific pattern for the release of K grow less strongly on a subsequent application of A. If the orientation reaction is followed by the 'expected' injurious stimulus C, the combined sensory stimulus becomes B+C instead of B alone. But C is a powerful inducer of the specific pattern for release of K, and in this case the pattern grows still further and the plastic changes are such as to encourage its growth on subsequent presentation of A. Thus, the nature of the plastic changes in L comes to depend on the result produced by the development of the pattern. (After Pringle, 1951.)

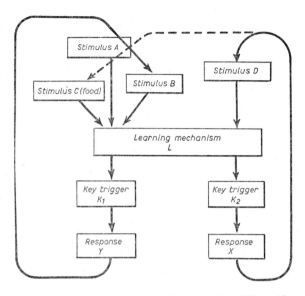

FIG. 23—Schematic block diagram for a conditioned reflex of Type II.

Initially sensory stimulus A releases response X followed (since stimulus B is reinforced by the presentation of food stimulus C) by a further encouragement of the growth of the specific pattern. The procedure may now vary. Sensory stimulus D in this type of conditioned reflex affects proprioceptive sense organs and is only produced by response Y. But sensory stimulus A, or A+B, does not cause the learning mechanism L to develop the specific patterns needed to operate K_2 and release response Y. For selection to take place in L in the presence of stimulus A+D, response Y must be caused to occur. If the movement necessary to produce sensory stimulus D is produced by the operator moving the limbs of the animal passively, then the conditions are not significantly different from those in conditioned reflex Type I, D being then the unconditioned, and A the conditioned stimulus. If, however, there is an element of variability in the learning mechanism L, the specific pattern needed to operate K_2 and release response Y may be developed in the presence of sensory stimulus A, and, if it is developed, adaptation to A+B+D will occur; owing to the plastic changes in L which result, this particular pattern will then be more likely to develop in subsequent experiments. A new response Y can thus become associated with a sensory stimulus A by virtue either of variation in the environment (e.g. by the experimenter) simulating sensory stimulus D (CR, Type I), or by variation in L chancing to operate the key-trigger for the release of the response (T and E).

The interrupted line indicates the more usual form of the occurrence of this system in nature. Stimulus B+C, reinforcing the specific pattern of the release of K_1, is not produced unless the environmental changes produced by responses X and Y both occur; i.e. in other words, food is only obtained by the performance of both responses. The successive presentation of sensory stimulus A will now initially release a series of responses X. The response repetition will continue (unless suppressed by habituation) until either the environmental variation or the inherent variation in L results in the operation of key-trigger K_2. When this happens, the complete sensory stimulus A+B+C+D is produced, allowing selection to occur in L and increasing the chance of sensory stimulus A alone operating K_2. (After Pringle, 1951.)

living protoplasm. In other words, we have now a molecular differentiation rather than a cellular differentiation,[1] and we must remember that if this is indeed happening we still have the possibility that synapse factors are also being changed; and this will give us still further scope for accounting for the facts of long-term memory. This, of course, brings us once again to the question of the functions of D.N.A. discussed above.

Cragg and Temperley (1954) have recently put forward a theory of cortical action which likens the organisation of neurones to co-operative processes such as are known to physicists in connection with ferro-magnetism and similar phenomena. Thus in ferro-magnetism arising from the interaction of atoms which would not otherwise be ferro-magnetic, raising the temperature above the Curie point raises the thermal agitation to the level at which the interaction between the atomic magnets can no longer prevail—with the result that the material ceases abruptly to be ferro-magnetic although the properties of the individual atoms have hardly been affected by the change in temperature. It is suggested that masses of neurones have their cell bodies packed so closely and that the random intermingling of these processes is so complete that co-operative processes are bound to occur. They argue that such co-operative organisation could (by bringing about changes in, for instance, membrane potential) be the basis of memory processes in the cortex *provided* that *no* prearrangement of circuits exists which would prevent indiscriminate synapsing. That such prearrangement is not, in fact, present is suggested by the work of Sholl and Uttley (1953) providing statistical evidence that dendrites in the visual cortex of the cat ramify according to mechanical principles of growth rather than according to any specific circuit arrangement, which—in spite of some of Lorente de Nó's conclusions—seems not, in fact, to exist.

This theory, obviously still in a highly provisional and tentative form, has obvious affinities with that of Pringle and appears compatible with it. The authors claim that by it a number of results can be predicted which are qualitatively verified, or at least capable of being tested, by the electroencephalographic technique. It does certainly seem to offer further possibilities for the explanation in neurophysiological terms of the establishment of short-term memories. Whether it has anything to offer towards the understanding of long-term memory remains to be seen.

Some such theory as Pringle's seems particularly attractive to those who are concerned primarily with the insect brain. Such brains at the

---

[1] Cf. the at present equally unverifiable suggestion of L. L. Whyte (1954) that in certain regions of the cortex 'cytoplasmic transmission supplements neurone-surface transmission and that the memory modification consists in the ordering through many cells of previously disordered or less ordered cytoplasmic protein chains or fibrils. . . .'

height of their evolution are—as we all know from the work of von Frisch on honey-bees and of Baerends on the hunting wasp *Ammophila* —capable of some astonishing performances in the matter of learning. In the insect brain it is very doubtful if there exist the necessary multiple circuits available for any form of reverberatory trace theory to serve. In the insect brains, too, the cell number difficulty seems even more acute. What are we to make of the bee's brain of 2·5 milligrammes in view of its astounding performance? Although it has often seemed apparent that the Hymenoptera must be utilising some cellular or intracellular property perhaps not available to the vertebrates—some property which would allow for increase in the number of fundamental units involved—such a conclusion is perhaps premature. Vowles (1961) suggests that the functional organisation of insect behaviour is often far simpler than is supposed and it is this that is the key to the matter, and not that the insect central nervous system is more complex than histological studies suggest. In fact, the very properties of the insect neuron and the small size of the insect nervous system render necessary the simple organisation of behaviour. To quote Vowles, 'What should arouse our wonder is the success with which simplicity has been crowned.' The matter is discussed more fully on p. 231 below.

It has been pointed out above that since it is temporal and spatial relations that are ultimately dominant in perception, perception itself is essentially a learning process—for obviously the perception of relations must involve comparison and comparison in its turn involves memory and expectation, and so is clearly a form of learning. So it was suggested that perception is itself one of the fundamental motivating entities of animals, and as such could provide one of the bases of the internal drive. Perception and response were presumably originally inseparable in the primitive animal, and obviously response is still the only means that we have of testing animal perception. If, then, perception and response were originally inseparable, we can consider evolution as having been the process of extending and specialising both; perception by the development of sense organs, response by the elaboration of effective mechanisms, the two integrated by the central nervous system. And, as experiments demonstrating the principle of 'reafferentation' show, in proprioception and in the mechanism of orientation by taxis (and as we see right through the studies on 'habituation'), a major step in the organisation of animal behaviour has been the development of methods whereby the individual or the species selectively ignores certain stimuli, or stimuli in certain contexts, and comes to attend to the relatively few that concern it. Thus, in so far as the original faculty of perception retains or increases plasticity during evolutionary development, it becomes the various learning processes that we know. In so far as it becomes canalised and stereotyped in phylogeny, it becomes instinctive behaviour. Is it, indeed, too fanciful to suggest that when a learned pattern becomes stereotyped in instinctive behaviour it 'carries with it', so to speak, some of its original drive; with the result that a fixed-action pattern provides its own motivation and we get the appearance of specific action potential? On this view we can see that instinct can be regarded as a side-shoot from the main stem of the development of learning ability.

Shimbel (1950) has recently developed a learning theory, mathematical in form, which, although outlined in terms of neuronal connections, could perhaps be modified to integrate with theories of another type. It is based on the lowered threshold of neurones in certain conditions and is applied to two 'random-net' models. The first, a so-called ganglionic brain, is assumed to have completely random connection of all afferent tracts, except those which form the pathways for unconditioned responses. Expressions are then derived which measure the learning potentiality of the ganglion —in particular with respect to the number of responses which can be learned (conditioning potential) and the amount of interference between learned responses (redundance potential). Specific learning abilities are then supposed to be due to a tendency to non-randomness in certain regions—regions where axons will *tend* to grow in a given direction, and so a bias for the probability of a given response would be created. He suggests that this would explain Tryon's (1931) work on rats which, having been selected for success in a maze of one pattern, failed to give evidence of intelligence with another pattern. See also the model for synchronous activity in a sheet of neurones randomly connected, developed by Beurle (1956).

We can follow up this suggestion about a tendency to non-randomness as providing a basis for the evolution of instinctive behaviour. Assuming a population with various hereditary biases, then the ability to make certain simple associations would increase the likelihood of survival. Any mutants which would enhance such growth tendencies without significantly changing the other features of the species would be selected. Such a selection would lead to specific neural orientation specially adapted to the enhancement of the 'available' associations. And so eventually the population would have such a great density of 'right' connections that the learning might simply be a matter of a few trials. '*At this point slight hereditary changes in the neural thresholds will make the response instinctive*' (Shimbel). Thus instinctive behaviour is derived from more and more easily learned patterns, and so a primitive organism which evolves a simple innate behaviour pattern sacrifices a portion of its random neural tissue. From this we might expect that in the course of evolution the species will attempt to compensate for loss of its valuable random tissue, which can be the site for the selective processes and which, according to

Pringle's theory, mediates learning, by increasing the size of the ganglion brain and so replenishing it. Thus older, more highly channelled, circuits become more and more deeply embedded in less specialised tissue, and so we see, at any rate in outline, how some of the characteristic features of the mammalian brain might have been produced.

Another important feature of Shimbel's work is its concept of learning as a selective narrowing down to optimal patterns of response, a concept which can also easily be fitted into Pringle's theory. This is not the place to follow up that particular suggestion, but this whole approach to the neurophysiology of instinct and learning seems to make more plausible than ever the theory that, at any rate over big stretches of the evolutionary process, stretches subsequent to the point at which perception and response became separated, instinct can be regarded as a derivation from primitive learning ability—yielding, for an animal in which particular pieces of behaviour are of prime importance, an economic return for its specialisation of nervous tissue.

The theories so far considered have either been directly derived from a knowledge of neurology or have else been readily relatable to some reasonably plausible hypothesis of neural function. Others, while plausible and perhaps on the right track, are at present so far from neurology or so difficult to test experimentally that they must be regarded as outside the scope of this book. But the development of calculating machines, 'servo mechanisms,' and the concomitant science of 'cybernetics,' has given rise to a great deal of intriguing speculation as to the way in which the human brain may function. Much of this speculation is also outside the scope of this book to discuss, as it is beyond the competence of this author to evaluate. But there are a few general considerations which are perhaps relevant.

It is not now difficult to construct machines which display many features of animal behaviour. Thus we can have, or at least see how to design, machines capable of displaying superficial appearances of instinct, of taxes and kineses, of memory, habituation, associative learning 'hypothesis' and trial-and-error—that is, they gain and store 'information.' We can have machines which are self-correcting and self-adjusting. In short, we can have machines which *behave* as do many living animals over important periods of their lives, and which accordingly might seem at first sight to warrant the attribution to them of 'mental' states and even of consciousness. But we must be careful to remember that such an assumption has not as yet the slightest justification. Firstly, most of us assume that the conscious states of our minds are accompanied by the activation of certain brain mechanisms, and it is tempting to argue that the two must *inevitably* go together and that the activation of the mechanisms would inevitably produce the conscious experiences. But from epistemological considerations it seems impossible that this can be so, and we have, in any case, no right to assume that the activation of the mechanisms necessarily produces the sensations—in fact, in the case of the human cortex (Penfield and Rasmussen, 1950) we know that it often does not—though there is still the possibility that conscious experiences are specifically associated with the diencephalon. And then we must remember what calculating machines are not and what they cannot do. They are closed physical systems—not 'open' ones feeding on negative entropy like living organisms. It follows, as von Bertalanffy (1952) has shown, that in general, calculating machines cannot show true 'purposiveness,' or 'equi-finality,' since in a closed system the final state depends on the initial conditions. An open system, on the other hand, which is continually exchanging materials with its environment can, in so far as it attains a steady state, show this state *independently* of initial conditions. And directiveness which can be shown to be a necessary characteristic of open systems does not therefore necessarily imply any 'vitalistic' concept. Calculating machines thus cannot repair and reproduce themselves, although they can conceivably perform deductive inference. To gain knowledge inductive generalisation is necessary, and this they cannot do; nor can they select their own information and so adapt themselves to changing circumstances. As Gregory (1954) says, 'Practical calculating machines must be fed with the relevant, and only the relevant information. This is done by the human operator ... without him the [analogue] machine will not even begin to produce the right answer. We must imagine a machine capable of selecting its own information and devising its own operating rules; it must generalise and develop criteria of relevance.'

Summary

1. Physiological theories of learning and retention are considered in approximately chronological sequence. Those consisting primarily of variations on a theme of neuronal after-discharge are considered as inadequate for anything but extremely short-term memory, and the same applies to the 'self-re-exciting circuit' theories in general.

2. Morphological conceptions of plasticity are then considered and found to be equally inadequate by themselves.

3. Theories of the 'field,' 'vector' and 'irradiation' types are also discussed and criticised.

4. Attempts to combine 'after-discharge' or 'circuit' theories with morphological concepts of plasticity are found to give more promise. In well as the latest of these. The possible relation of developments in the knowledge of protein biosynthesis (particularly the function of D.N.A.

and R.N.A.) to theories of neuronal action and retention in the C.N.S. is stressed.

5. A brief summary is given of the present state of knowledge (based on the use of (*a*) implanted electrodes, (*b*) the electro-encephalograph and (*c*) ablation techniques) concerning the mechanism of learning occurring in the mammalian brain. The particular function of the ascending reticular system is stressed.

6. The concepts of Pringle based on a process of selection within systems of coupled oscillators are discussed, and an attempt is made to link them up with neurophysiological data and with the theories previously outlined. The advantages of such a system for coping with the neurophysiological and behavioural problems presented by a group such as the Arthropoda are stressed.

7. Shimbel's selection theory of the learning possibilities of a 'random net' neuronal model is considered, and it is shown how it can be integrated with Pringle's scheme and with the idea that learning and its associated drive may be phylogenetically primary. It is pointed out how slight hereditary changes in neural thresholds could be effective in making learned responses instinctive.

8. Some of the implications of cybernetic theories for ethology and psychology are discussed.

PART III

THE LEARNING ABILITIES
OF THE MAIN ANIMAL GROUPS

INTRODUCTION

To attempt a survey of the learning abilities of the fifteen or so great groups of the animal kingdom is a somewhat daunting task. To aim at the inclusion of every fact or observation bearing on the subject would obviously be setting oneself a hopelessly remote objective, and one which, even if attained, would merely yield an overwhelming and intractable mass of detail. So the aim must be to select for discussion and appraisal only those observations and experiments which help to elucidate some general principle, which bring out the essential ethological and biological characteristics of the group concerned or which, even though they seem trivial or anecdotal, inspire sufficient confidence to suggest promising lines for further observation and experiment.

The first question asked in selecting facts and experiments for discussion in this section of the book will therefore be—How closely can the work be related to the natural history and biology of the group concerned? Laboratory investigations which seem to have no bearing on the problems and circumstances which the animal encounters in the wild will, in general, be passed over lightly; whereas those which help to illuminate the problem of the adjustment of the innate behaviour patterns to the normal conditions of life will be more fully discussed. We assume that, in general, the extent of the learning ability displayed by any animal group depends firstly on the degree and elaboration of its sense organs, and secondly on the degree of development and concentration of its nervous system. These in their turn are closely related to the degree of locomotor activity which itself affects such things as the variety of prey with which it has to deal. Then again, the more mobile the animal the more elaborate must its orientation mechanism be, and where a particular environment has to be recognised and 'sought' as home, very high powers of landmark recognition may be required. With the lengthening of the individual life-span and the overlapping of generations which usually accompany it, we get more favourable conditions for the development of social life, and with it may come the necessity to recognise not only individual environments as home but other individuals of the same species as mates, offspring or parents. Finally the higher types of learning ability are more especially displayed in the development of powers of manipulation of materials to make nests, shelters, etc. Thus the three factors which are perhaps most important for the evolution of high learning ability are the necessity for precise orientation, for individual recognition and for manipulation of material, and it is with these three aspects particularly in mind that the learning ability of each group will be approached.

CHAPTER IX

PROTOZOA AND LOWER METAZOA

PROTOZOA

SINCE it is quite impossible with present knowledge of the structure and physiology of the Protozoa to say whether the separation of behavioural change into peripheral and central is either possible or justifiable, such a short account as can be given here of the behaviour of the group must of necessity be on a very different basis from those chapters which deal with the higher Metazoa. But whether or not special sense organs are involved, it has long been known that not only the more highly differentiated Protozoa but also the amœboid types respond to all classes of stimuli to which the higher animals respond, with the exception of 'sound' (as usually distinguished from other mechanical stimuli). Again, since in such small and delicate organisms it is often impossible to separate the external and internal effects of environmental conditions influencing behaviour in the way we can in other animals, it becomes correspondingly difficult to make a valid distinction between inborn and learned behaviour. Nevertheless, the Protozoa do undoubtedly show (Jennings, 1906) a number of relatively fixed reaction types which are constant under the usual conditions of existence—e.g. responses to gravity, light, temperature change, contact with solids, etc.—and it was this kind of behaviour which was usually referred to under the term 'tropism' in the earlier literature. There are many examples of behaviour in the Protozoa which appear *superficially* to be instinctive in that they are under the influence of an internal drive and appear only with difficulty to be relatable to external changes. Verworn (1889) was the first of the special students of Protozoan behaviour to emphasise the spontaneity of many of their actions, and he contrasted these spontaneous movements with those others which seemed fairly clearly to be the result of external stimuli. Such spontaneous movements include many of the rhythmic actions of cilia and pseudopodia; but more especially referable to this class are the regular intermittent contractions of stalked or sessile forms, such as *Vorticella, Epistylis* and *Stentor*. Jennings (1906) came to much the same conclusion. But, of course, spontaneous activity need not be occasional or intermittent, and continued activity is the normal state of affairs in *Paramecium* and many other Ciliates. The same is true of activities other than the stalked contraction of *Vorticella*, and Hodge and Aikins (1895) were among the first to study the regular daily activities of the Protozoa. They showed that *Vorticella* is always active in some respects, and that there is much reason for regarding these activities as spontaneous. As Jennings points out, the spontaneous activity is in the end dependent on external conditions in the same sense that the very existence of the organism is so dependent, and in no instance has the *genetic* determination of a twenty-four-hour rhythm been conclusively demonstrated (Calhoun, 1944). But the point of importance is that the activity which is the expression of the energies derived from metabolism often depends more on the external conditions of the past than of the present, so that the organism moves without the present action of any apparent specific external stimulus. However, it is well known that with such an organism as *Paramecium*, when the action of a stimulus actually changes the direction of movement, persistence in this new direction continues even though the stimulus which initiated it may have ceased. Jennings concludes that while careful analysis is usually necessary to determine whether movement is due to present stimulation or not, the evidence in most cases suggests that it is not and that the efficient cause is 'the outflow of the stored-up energy of the organism through the channels provided by its structure.' The work of Holmes (1907) on the rhythmic activity of *Stentor* and *Loxophyllum* lends further support to these conclusions, although Loeb and his co-workers were strong opponents of the theory of spontaneity in Protozoa. Verworn had earlier suggested that there might be levels of spontaneity, the creeping and sessile forms showing a greater variety of activity than do the free-swimming ones.

Subject to the qualifications made at the beginning of this chapter about the impossibility of separating completely peripheral and central phenomena in the Protozoa, we may give a number of examples of behaviour which, if found in higher animals, would be, provisionally at least, regarded as habituation. There are, of course, a great many studies on the acclimatisation of Protozoa to new or changing environmental conditions, but in many of these cases the results apply to the population or race only, and it is quite uncertain whether any similar change is manifest in the individual. This uncertainty is only natural when we consider the very great difficulty of following the behaviour and action of individual Protozoa. In this respect those who work with larger animals, which can be marked and observed from day to day, are at a great advantage. Nevertheless, even in the early work there are a number of instances of individual change in behaviour as a result of stimulation. Verworn (1889), quoted by Jennings, found that amœbæ, which at first react to a weak electric current, may after a time resume their usual movements, disregarding the current entirely, and Harrington and Leaming (1900) show that exposure to white or blue light will cause cessation of movement in an amœba, but that if the light is continued the movements begin again. Folger (1926), in studying the effects of mechanical shock on locomotion in *Amœba proteus*, studied the results that follow a sequence of shocks. He found that a certain period of time must elapse after a response to a certain stimulus before the same stimulus will elicit it again. If the animal receives a second shock before the critical period has elapsed, the reaction time is longer and the following inactive period is shorter than after complete recovery, and Penard (1948) has brief notes on similar behaviour in the Ciliate *Metacystis lagenula* and the Heliozoan *Heterophrys glabrescens*. Jennings also observed that *Stentor, Epistylis* and *Carchesium* will respond to a weak stimulus such as a capillary jet of water, but will fail to react to an immediate repetition of that stimulus. If the stimulation is stronger, as for instance a touch with a glass spicule, the Ciliate may contract several times before reaction ceases, and if sufficiently intense, contraction may continue at each successive application for an hour or more. Danisch (1921) investigated this kind of behaviour more precisely in *Vorticella nebulifera*, administering a mechanical shock of controlled energy to the vessel containing the organism. He found that a shock involving expenditure of 500 ergs required 9 strokes to produce habituation, that of 1,000 ergs 15 strokes, 1,500 ergs over 40 strokes and 2,000 ergs more than 420 strokes over two hours. From this he concluded that fatigue cannot be held responsible for habituation to a less intense stimulus. Jenkins (in Warden, Jenkins and Warner, 1936), summarising the results of these and a number of other similar studies on Protozoa, points out that they gave fairly consistent evidence for three distinct processes, habituation (negative habituation), summation and fatigue.

It is obvious that sensory accommodation and habituation, or something akin to these phenomena, is essential for the mechanism of klinokinesis which is a well-known behaviour mechanism in *Paramecium* and presumably in innumerable other Protozoa. There has been some discussion as to whether the terms 'klinokinesis' [1] and 'avoiding reaction' refer to the same phenomena in Protozoa, and if so which is the most appropriate term (Gunn and Walshe, 1941; Gunn, 1942). In klinokinesis sensory adaptation or habituation is an essential feature of successful aggregation of the individuals of a *Paramecium* suspension in a smooth gradient on the assumption that a random turning mechanism is used; but it is apparently not so important where behaviour such as the avoiding reaction to a sharp boundary is involved. There is, however, good reason to consider the latter as really a special case of the former, for the concept of klinokinesis was introduced for the generalised reactions characteristic of

[1] Locomotory behaviour not involving any steering component but in which there is random turning related in amount to the intensity of stimulation. (Thorpe, 1951.)

organisms in a smooth gradient, the reaction at the boundary being a special case.

Associative Learning

There have been a larger number of experiments claiming to have established the existence of associative learning in the Protozoa and some vigorous discussion has centred around them. Mast and Pusch (1924), in studying the avoiding responses of *Amœba*, described the gradual elimination, as a result of experience, of the ineffective movements comprised in such responses. The organism is allowed to come into contact with the boundary of an illuminated region, and upon doing so it retracts the advancing pseudopod. Other pseudopods are similarly advanced and retracted until finally the organism is moving in another direction. Tabulation of the succession of contacts made in such a situation gives results which recall those of a typical trial-and-error experiment. Mast later (1932) suggested that what appears to be learning in *Amœba* may merely be the local cumulative effect of repeated stimulation, but as Jenkins (*loc cit.*) points out, this hardly explains the fact that the interruptions of from 24 to 48 hours failed appreciably to disturb the continuity of the series. Reynolds (1924) has produced some rather puzzling evidence that in the Protozoan *Arcella polypera* artificially severed masses of protoplasm readily fuse with individuals raised in the same environment but shatter when they come into contact with those raised in another environment. He suggests that this astonishing fact is the expression not of genetic differences but depends upon acquired reactions resulting from the environment, the dominant factor therein being most probably the bacterial flora upon which *Arcella* feeds. It is, however, uncertain whether a genuine behaviour effect is involved here.

Apart from the work above described on the Rhizopoda, practically all investigations on supposed learning processes in the group have been carried out with *Paramecium*, and Wichterman (1953) has recently given a valuable critical discussion of this work. Metalnikov (1907, 1912, 1914 and 1917) claimed to have established that *Paramecium* can learn to recognise indigestible substances and so avoid them, and a number of others, including Bozler (1924*b*), Bragg (1936, 1939) and Mast (1947), have confirmed his conclusion that while these organisms do, in fact, ingest a great variety of particles, more of those taken into the body are digestible than indigestible, indicating the existence of some mechanism or faculty of choice. But Metalnikov went further and, as a result of studies of the content of the food vacuoles of *Paramecium caudatum* placed in suspensions of carmine and other substances for standard periods, concluded that the animal not only selects certain types of particles and rejects others, but can learn to be more efficient in its selection. Wladimirsky

(1916) gave an alternative and not altogether convincing explanation which relied on the assumption that periodic states of depression in the physiological state of the animal could account for the results. On the other hand, Losina-Losinsky (1937) failed to secure satisfactory evidence of this alleged state of depression. Metalnikov had stated that the negative conditioning of *Paramecium* to indigestible grains of carmine was shown by the organism brushing them aside with its cilia although other assimilable substances were taken in as before. He later attempted to establish phenomena more precisely comparable to associative conditioning. *Paramecium* were fed on carmine in a red light until no further ingestion was observed, and when this culture was transferred to a yeast suspension they continued to ingest less in red light than they did in daylight. Similar results were claimed with alcohol as a conditioning stimulus. Many of these results have been adversely criticised, but here again the work of Losina-Losinsky supports Metalnikov, and it is difficult to reconcile the conclusions of these two authors with the opposing ones of Wladimirsky (1916) and Bozler (1924). Certainly, the latter author seems to have demonstrated a number of errors in Metalnikov's conclusions. He observed that the size of the particles had a marked influence on the result, and that if sufficiently small grains of substances such as carmine, sulphur or chalk (about the same size as bacteria) were offered to the Protozoa, they were all driven indiscriminately in the food vacuole. Larger granules were swept immediately away, and intermediate ones were moved about in the oral structures for a considerable while before their fate was finally determined. It is, however, clear that size is not the only factor, for if *Paramecium* is placed in a starch or yeast suspension after having been removed from a carmine-containing medium it will be seen to contain yeast and starch grains up to 6 and 11 microns in length respectively but only the smallest carmine grains, 1–2 microns. Gelber (1952) seems to have provided satisfactory evidence of learning in food presentation tests with *Paramecium aurelia*. She (1958) has followed this up by showing a three-hour retention in the same organism. She suggests that there are extra-nuclear factors in the cytoplasm which may be in control of behaviour. At any rate, whatever these factors are they are apparently not exclusively in the nucleus. Katz and Deterline (1958), however, consider that Gelber's results, as well as those of other authors, do not provide convincing evidence of learning, but are probably due to unlearned changes in intensity of response to the food material used as reinforcement.

Smith (1908) and Day and Bentley (1911) studied the behaviour of *Paramecium* in capillary tubes so small that ordinary movement was restricted; the time taken to find an effective method of turning round in the restricted space was then recorded. These authors found that the average time and the number of unsuccessful attempts was reduced with practice. It has been suggested that such change in behaviour could be accounted for by the accumulation of carbon dioxide in the tube, but this objection seems to have been overcome in at least some of the experiments. Day and Bentley claimed that the results of practice were retained by the organisms even after they had been permitted to swim for twenty minutes in an open dish, when presumably the effects of any carbon-dioxide accumulation would have disappeared. Buytendijk (1919) also suggested that a direct physiological change might be the cause of the results, a change comparable to that shown by organisms treated with chloroform, which causes them to become more flexible so that they can turn more easily in the tube; but this explanation seems to raise almost as many difficulties as the work it is alleged to dispose of.

Bramstedt (1935) claims to have produced evidence that response to heat can be associatively conditioned to the stimuli of light or mechanical shock, and the fact of the association of light with heat has also been confirmed by Alverdes (1937). But here again Grabowski (1939) has argued that chemical change in the liquid arising from heat action might have been responsible for the apparent learning shown, and Soest (1937) was unsuccessful in forming an association between illumination intensity and low temperature. On the other hand, electric shocks, although they could not be associated with darkness, did tend to produce an avoidance of light. Dembowski (1950) has, however, argued that the 'conditioning' of a *Paramecium* to turn at a light-dark boundary by means of an electric shock is spurious. He claims that the animal tends to turn, irrespective of the position of the boundary, at that point where it stays longest during the experiment, and he suggests that an explanation of this can be found in a metabolic trace left in the water. But he does not appear to have carried out the experiments necessary to clinch his conclusions. Again it seems rather unlikely that the results described by Tschakotine (1938), according to which *Paramecium* will not only avoid a beam of ultra-violet light but will continue to avoid the same region for half an hour after the beam has been removed, could be due to a persistent chemical change in the liquid. Bramstedt had also described how *Paramecium* will adapt themselves to the shape of a container and will continue after removal from it to maintain a course similar to its outline, but the evidence for this conclusion does not seem to be conclusive. Alverdes (1939) has attempted to answer the objections raised by a number of the critics of learning experiments in the Protozoa, and the years 1939 and 1940 saw the publication of a number of claims and counter-claims by the workers concerned as well as by O. Koehler and Diebschlag. As a result of this discussion, one receives the impression that although an *a priori* case has been made out for true associative learning in *Paramecium*, the really critical proof has yet to be provided. Certainly some of the results purporting to show learning have been due to incomplete knowledge of the environmental situation, and with such organisms it may be a considerable time before sufficient knowledge as to the influence of the environment has been accumulated to allow full confidence in the results of the above described learning experiments.[1] French (1940a), however, carried out what was in effect a maze experiment by studying the ability of *Paramecium* to escape from a tube which was large enough to allow free swimming and turning. He seems to have established beyond reasonable doubt that the average time for escape decreased on successive trials, and he seems to have also shown that the result was not an expression of a change in general activity. This being so, it seems a fairly safe conclusion that true learning has been demonstrated. French (1940b) also reported individual variations in the rate of learning by 'trial-and-error.' Dabrowska's (1956) attempt to obtain associative learning in *Stentor cœruleus*, using an electric current paired with the response to light, was unsuccessful.

Froud (1949) describes the exploratory behaviour of the hypotrichous ciliate *Stichotricha*. This is a species inhabiting a 'cell' in a *Lemna* leaf, and the two individuals, produced as a result of binary fission, may remain together within the same cell provided there is sufficient room for both to protrude and feed. After fission, the anterior one extends its 'neck' and begins to feed, whereas the other—the 'swarmer'—spends a preliminary period within the enclosing cell engaged in what looks like exploratory activity. After this it partially emerges and sometimes commences feeding. More usually the swarmer leaves the cell without feeding, but before doing so it makes excursions to the aperture, pushing its sister ciliate back, and these exchange movements continue for some time with the swarmer gradually becoming bolder and emerging tentatively through the cell opening. When it has finally squeezed out, its behaviour depends upon local conditions. If there is plenty of the duckweed *Lemna* about and it comes into contact with this, it will crawl over the plant in a persistent and 'exploratory' manner, apparently searching for a possible settling-place. The crawling is the result of the activity of the membranelles and the few body cilia. The front end of the animal is poked into crevices and empty cells, some of which are entered and explored as if to test thoroughly the possible new abode. The creature may remain or it may

[1] Various Protista (e.g. *Euglena limosa*, *Chromulina psammobia*, *Strombidium oculatum* and *Hantzschia amphioxys*) exhibit physiological rhythms (Fauré-Fremiet, 1948–51), such as reversal of phototropic sign, agglutinative capacity, etc., which, while not directly determined by the periodicity of the tide, appear to be synchronised with it. But the available evidence goes to show that this rhythm is maintained in the population by a selective elimination at each flood tide of all nonconformist individuals. So it does not seem necessary to postulate individual learning.

leave and begin the process of trial again; but during this period no feed-ing is done and the free-swimming phase may vary from one to many hours. If, however, there is not much *Lemna* and the swarmer swims straight out into open water after binary fission, the behaviour is dif-ferent. Now there is a rapid forward movement as a result of which a much larger volume of water is explored. The movement is usually for-ward though reversals are not uncommon, and sooner or later, when contact is made with some solid surface, crawling and exploring move-ments begin as described above. It is, of course, impossible to show how far this behaviour is true exploration and how far anything like trial-and-error learning is actually taking place—for instance, possible maturation effects have not been controlled or eliminated; but the behaviour seems significant, not only in that it is suggestive of exploration but that it does illustrate very strikingly relatively elaborate behaviour in a free-living ciliate—behaviour which is apparently initiated by the presence or absence of abundant duckweed, and which continues, even though with much immediate variation, until apparently a virtually perfect situation is encountered for a final settling.

CŒLENTERATA

Spontaneous Behaviour

Jennings (1906) gives many examples of apparently spontaneous be-haviour in Cœlenterates. He found that if a green *Hydra* is left for long periods undisturbed, it does not remain attached at the same spot but moves about from place to place, the direction of movement being appar-ently random. The movement is accomplished by a number of different actions, looping, using the tentacles as legs and, in some manner not yet fully understood, gliding along on the base of the column as do the sea anemones. It appears from the work of Haug (1933) that the orientation of *Hydra* is klinokinetic, but that the stepping movement is of a more complex nature, resembling in many respects an instinctive movement pattern. Thus during stepping the animal is no longer oriented, the step-ping behaviour (which is of an all-or-none character) being in complete control. Ewer (1947) found that the mechanism of orientation to light is so rigid that it remained unchanged even after two generations in abnormal lighting conditions. Jennings (1906) suggests the spontaneous contraction and change of position which constitute a rather subsidiary part of the behaviour of sessile forms has become the rule in Medusæ, which are commonly found swimming by means of rhythmic contrac-tions. In this latter case, since there are certainly no corresponding changes in external conditions, these contractions must be due to internal changes. Recently Batham and Pantin (1950) have shown that with sea anemones, particularly *Metridium*, there is a great deal of spontaneous activity which, because of its extreme slowness, can only be appreciated when the action is speeded up by kymographic recording or lapse-rate cinematography so that it falls within the frequency range of our sensory spectrum. In other words, it is just as likely that important items of behaviour may remain unperceived in the Cœlenterates because they are too slow, as it is that the details of wing movements of flies may be unappreciated because they are too fast for us to see. In each case they have to be brought within the right speed-range to be understood. When a *Metridium* is studied in this way and its behaviour photographically speeded up sixty-fold, elaborate patterns of apparently purposive activity become evident. This activity may consist of unco-ordinated contraction

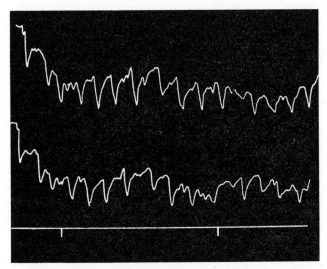

FIG. 24—Inherent activity in *Metridium*. Partially rhythmic contractions (downwards) and extensions of two opposite points on the body wall. Isotonic recording levers. Time interval 1 hour. Record runs from left. (After Pantin, 1950.)

of different parts, but more usually takes the form of a periodical contraction commencing with the longitudinal musculature and followed by peristaltic waves running down the column and resulting in elongation. Though such movements vary greatly in pattern, the activity is often more or less rhythmic, and may continue unchanged under a variety of external conditions and even if the environment is made as constant as possible. Thus it appears to arise spontaneously out of the animal and not merely as a random sequence of accidental responses. There seems little doubt that in the very slow responses of *Metridium* a complex and probably inherent neuro-muscular pattern is involved and that this includes inhibition and the successive activation of two antagonistic muscular systems (Fig. 24). This activity clearly shows some parallel to the internally driven patterns of behaviour found in the central nervous system of more highly developed organisms, and the whole cycle of events observed in, say, the feeding behaviour of an anemone suggests parallels to the instinctive behaviour in higher animals. In both we see directiveness or apparent 'purposiveness,' drive and a selection of varied activities appropriate to attain the immediate goal; though as Pantin is careful to point out, his observations do indicate how some of these behaviour patterns can now be analysed sufficiently for one to conceive of a mechanical model which would do all that we at present know of what the animal is able to do—at least in certain restricted sections of its behaviour. The extent to which elaborate internally driven behaviour patterns may be occurring in the Cœlenterates is also indicated by the work of Yerkes (1902, 1903, 1904) and Perkins (1903) on the medusa of *Gonionemus*. The young *Gonionemus* is often found attached to the bottom by means of adhesive pads on its tentacles. Sooner or later it leaves the attachment and swims upwards with the tentacles contracted and the convex surface of the bell uppermost. On attaining the surface it inverts itself and sinks with the bell relaxed and the tentacles widely stretched in a horizontal plane ready to paralyse any small organisms they may touch. Having reached the bottom, it returns once more to the top, and thus goes through the cycle repeatedly, 'fishing' for its food.

As with the Protozoa, so with the lower Metazoa, the interpretation of experiments on learning is often rendered difficult through lack of knowledge of the releaser system employed by the animals in question. It is therefore worth while to refer to some interesting recent results throwing light on the way in which Cœlenterates recognise their prey. Loomis (1955) has shown with *Hydra littoralis* that glutathione is the chemical releaser for feeding. This substance must diffuse from the body of the prey before a *Hydra* can feed. Starvation lowers the threshold of response to glutathione and if it is put in the water of an aquarium containing hydras they will become cannibalistic. It is evidently a convenient releaser for living prey for it soon disintegrates on death and so does not exude from dead prey. Such a releaser would, of course, be extremely non-specific since glutathione is a common constituent of animal tissues; but then *Hydra* is an omnivorous predator. Passano (1957) has provided a valuable summary of a subject of fundamental importance to the ethologist concerned with the lower Metazoa.

Habituation

Having thus briefly outlined a few salient features of the spontaneous behaviour of the group, we can consider how much evidence of learned behaviour there is. Nagel (1897) described how a ball of filter paper soaked in fish juice will be accepted by tentacles of the anemone *Adamsia* as if it were meat, but if the offer is repeated several times the ball will be rejected. Similar results were later obtained by G. H. Parker (1896) and Allabach (1905) with *Metridium* and by Gee (1913) with *Cribrina*. Jennings (1905) showed that *Aiptasia* similarly could be habituated to repeated food stimulation in circumstances in which the waning was not due to loss of 'hunger.' These and other results therefore certainly do not support the conclusion of some writers that the actinian uses 'practical judgment.' Sensory accommodation or habituation—in so far as they can be usefully distinguished in such a group—is all that is necessarily involved. Indeed, as Allabach and Gee show, the decrease in response could merely be due to the accumulation of mucus on the stimulated tentacles. However, this simple explanation could not be adduced to explain the failure of *Actinia* to respond to repeated mechanical disturbances or *Aiptasia* to the repeated stimulus of dropping water, and there seems no reason to doubt that something like habituation must be general, if not universal, in the group. Although there are, as has been shown, more or less regular changes in behaviour which appear to be so fully motivated internally as to warrant the provisional assumption that they are innate, there are also periodicities which seem to be acquired or imprinted as a result of repeated environmental stimulation. These include most, if not all, of the alleged twenty-four-hour rhythms. Thus Piéron (1909) describes tidal periodicity in anemones which is presumably the outcome of repeated experience of tidal changes and which may also be induced in various ways by laboratory control and Jores (1937) quotes Horstmann (1934) as having established the persistence under constant conditions of the daily periodic change in frequency of swimming movements in *Aurelia*. The literature on periodic behaviour of many invertebrate animals, especially *Actinia aquina*, has been summarised by Hoffmann (1926). Mori (1943–9, 1960) divides the daily rhythms displayed by Cœlenterates and Echinoderms into exogenous and endogenous, and his work indicates that there exist some examples which illustrate these two categories in a pure form, while others are instances of combinations of the two in varying proportions. Thus he finds that the rhythm of the anemone *Cymbactis actinostroides* is easily disturbed, that of *Holothuria vitiens* may persist for a week, while that of *Cavernularia obesa* may continue unchanged in the absence of rhythmic stimulation for 100 days or more; but whether even here the rhythm is *truly* innate is, of course, not known.

The existence of associative learning in Cœlenterates is not very well established, although Bohn (1908) has confirmed the observations of van der Ghinst (1906) that associative memory can be demonstrated in actinians. He describes how if specimens of *Actinia* are taken, some from the under-side of rocks and others from the upper surface, and are placed in an aquarium between two plates of glass, the animals will take up roughly the positions that they had when in their natural surroundings. Thus, those from the under-side of the rocks will attach themselves to the upper glass with the disc directed downwards and the others to the lower glass with the disc pointing upwards. He describes how such behaviour may be modified by forcing the organisms to assume unaccustomed positions, and in this way the original position habits may be eradicated after a period of from twenty-four to forty-eight hours' training and new ones established in their place.

Orientation of sea anemones for feeding purposes is sometimes achieved as a result of the exploratory activities of one or more of the inner tentacles which are for the time being enormously elongated and which 'finger over' the whole environment within reach. Portielje (1933) describes this behaviour in *Diadumene cincta* and gives references to earlier observations of it. He states that eventually the movements of the whole organism appear to become co-ordinated as a result of the 'exploring' activity of one or more of these temporarily specialised tentacles. The conclusion arrived at above that the rejection by the tentacles of *Actinia* and *Tealia* of filter paper impregnated by food substances is due to a simple accommodation or habituation only is rendered somewhat uncertain by the experiments of Fleure and Walton (1907) also using *Actinia* and *Tealia*. Pieces of filter paper were placed every twenty-four hours upon a given set of tentacles. As was to be expected from previous observations, the filter paper was at first carried to the mouth and ingested and later rejected, and after two to five days the paper would no longer be ingested. Finally, after a lapse of a few more days, the tentacles would refuse the paper altogether. When this stage had been reached other tentacles which had not been used during the practice tests were now used for experiments. They, too, would accept the filter paper at first, but would learn to refuse the paper much sooner than did the tentacles first exercised. These authors found that *Tealia* acquired such habits more readily than *Actinia*, but in both genera the effect might disappear within from six to ten days. It is rather surprising that such interesting conclusions have not been further followed up. Among other uncorroborated observations suggestive of highly adaptive and directive behaviour may be mentioned those of Brunelli (1910) on the apparent 'intelligence' of the anemone *Antholoba reticulata* when climbing on to the back of its crab associate. This author finds himself forced to assume an elaborate instinctive organisation, together with an ability for true associative memory. The matter should well repay critical study and experiment in the light of more recent knowledge.

ECHINODERMATA

Von Uexküll was a pioneer in the study of the behaviour of Echinoderms, and in a well-known paper of 1897 he described the sea-urchin as a republic of reflexes. It was his opinion that the characteristic behaviour of such an organism could be fully expressed on the basis of the very rigid character of their reflexes and the relations between them. He considered every reflex to be of the same rank, and could find no evidence of a central controlling unity. Accordingly he argued that just as the action of a colony of ants may appear highly controlled and adaptive even though the actions of the group are merely the sum of the independent actions of a large number of individuals, so the seemingly unified action of a starfish is merely the expression of a summation of the independent actions of the tube feet and other organs. He expressed this by saying that when a dog runs the animal moves its legs, when the sea-urchin runs the legs (spines) move the animal. Yet even von Uexküll showed that there were certain laws governing the change of action of the spines, and further evidence of this integration was supplied by Jennings and later workers. The point of interest here is whether or not Echinoderms exhibit anything corresponding to the instincts of higher animals in the sense that internal co-ordination and drive can be detected.

J. E. Smith (1950) has shown that the patterns of response which follow localised stimulations of the starfish reflect the irradiation of excitation into nervous pathways of progressively increasing extension. Such stimulation leads first to the superficial plexus of the integument, then to the segmental arcs and the extra-segmental arcs, and finally to the central pathways of the radial cord and the nerve ring. He provides considerable evidence that the responses which are elicited through the four systems of nerve tracts, even when they concern the activities of only one kind of organ, do indicate that the excitatory state is modified as a result of transference from one set of neurones to another and, in fact, the behaviour of the starfish displays two aspects of nervous control, one peripheral and reflex and the other central and generalised. So we see that the description of Echinoderms as a reflex republic is only one aspect of the truth. This subject has been further studied by Kerkut (1954, 1955), who found that the tube feet of starfish, although they can point in any direction, are most stable when in the direction of the main radii. Here again it seems that the pointing can be effected either through the central nervous system or directly by the mechanical body tensions acting upon the tube feet. Kerkut found that the excitatory states responsible for effecting co-operation can pass around the nerve ring in both directions and also along the radial nerve cords, and that cutting the tracks of the radial nerve prevents the tube feet apical to the cut from taking part in the orientation changes that are occurring over the rest of the animal. There is, in fact, good evidence that there is a centre that controls pointing in the direction of a given arm, this centre being located at the junction of the radial nerve cord and the circumoral ring. These five circumoral or circumœsophageal centres thus play a role similar to that of the brain in the other inverte-brates. A single cut made in the circumoral ring does not, however, pre-vent the arms on either side of the cut from showing co-ordinated point-ing, and this fact implies that the picture as provided by Smith (1945) of the nerve paths from each centre passing round the nerve ring must be modified to allow for excitation passing in both directions instead of in one only. It therefore seems highly probable that both the central nervous system (consisting of the five centres linked and co-ordinated by the nerve ring) and the various body tensions together influence the orienta-tion of the tube feet during locomotion. The neurophysiology of the star-fish *Asterias* has now reached the point at which some of the simpler behaviour patterns can be described in physiological terms. It can be provisionally concluded that the asteroid nervous system behaves more like a series of nerve tracts than like a simple nerve net (Kerkut, 1955). These conclusions help considerably in accounting for the work of Preyer (1887), who was impressed by the variety of ways in which the starfish *Asterias glacialis* succeeded in righting itself after being turned on its back. He found that no species of starfish rights itself in only one way, and that no *Astropecten*, which is another genus he studied, rights itself twice in succession in exactly the same way. Here is certainly some evi-dence of central control; but there is also an extraordinary degree of variability which could be the mass expression of the individual actions of the tube feet. But in *Astropecten aurantiacus* the tube feet are not necessarily used in turning at all. Instead this may be achieved by the animal resting on the tips of three or four arms and lifting the central disc high, whereupon it turns two of the arms under, at the same time lifting the others upward. It thus falls with the ventral side down. That there is centrally co-ordinated activity in Echinoderms seems, then, vir-tually certain. How far this group also displays centrally *motivated* activity is more difficult to say. According to Pearse (1908) the feeding responses of the sea-cucumber, *Thyone briareus*, are mostly determined by internal factors such as hunger, and only appear after the animal has been left undisturbed for a while. It was found difficult or impossible to induce *Thyone* to feed by external stimuli alone, and in 1885 Romanes (p. 321) had found evidence of the same phenomenon with starfish. Further factors supporting the same conclusions have been provided by Jennings (1907). He found evidence of persistence of impulse, and records cases where *Asterias forreri* will display an obstinate tendency to follow the lead of a certain one of their five rays, the tendency being so strong that sharp differences of exposure to light and shade will have no imme-diate effect in influencing the behaviour. Cowles (1911) also provided plenty of evidence that *Astropecten duplicatus* and *Echinaster crassispina* will move in a previously determined direction when transferred to a slope instead of immediately reorientating themselves with respect to gravity, as might have been anticipated. It is difficult to avoid the general conclusion that some examples of persistence of impulse noted by Jennings are, in fact, leading to a consummatory response in much the same way as occurs in the instinctive behaviour of many higher animals, and of course in the starfish there are patterns of behaviour which are even more elaborate than any here discussed. There is the well-known example of the starfishes *Echinaster* and *Asterias* seizing and devouring quite large prey. Members of both genera when tackling bivalves clutch them with the arms bent in an umbrella-like fashion around the prey, and by a long and steady pull force the shells apart. Such a specialised method of dealing with Lamellibranch prey can hardly be learned individually as the result of experience, and suggests the presence of a well co-ordinated behaviour pattern characteristic of this particular feeding situation.

Stier (1933) has described a daily periodicity expressed both in muscular activity and in alterations of geotropism in the Holothurian *Thyone briareus*. He found that both could be observed by red light to continue after the animals had been transferred to conditions of otherwise continuous darkness. The existence of persistent activity rhythms in *Holothuria* and *Cavernularia* (Mori, 1943–9), has been referred to in the section on Cœlenterata (p. 193) above.

The next question is how far can the responses of starfish be adaptively modified as a result of experience? Preyer describes a number of experiments where the brittle-stars *Ophiomixa* and *Ophioderma* were required to escape from the restriction imposed by five pegs inserted in the angles between the rays, or required to remove a rubber tube which had been placed on one of the arms. Both these 'problems' were solved in a variety of ways, but it is not clear that in escaping from the rubber tube any specially effective method came to be preferred, and Preyer and a number of other workers who repeated his observations have concluded that there was no evidence of improvement with practice. Escaping from the pegs was, however, rather more suggestive of learning ability. Preyer states that with experience the organism escaped in a shorter time and succeeded in reducing the number of useless movements, although he does not give satisfactory quantitative data to support his conclusions. Jennings repeated this on the starfish *Asterias forreri*, and failed to find evidence of improvement with practice. But Ven (1921) in a slight variation of the test, also with *Asterias*, seems to have provided conclusive evidence of a typical learning curve as shown both by the changing ratio between effective and ineffective movements and the time required for escape. In his experiments transverse rods were attached so as to link up the pegs restraining the two most active arms, thus completely preventing escape in that direction. Nevertheless, upon removing

the rods the animal showed definite evidence of directing its efforts towards release in the other direction, suggesting that it had at least acquired the habit of neglecting movements in the direction in which the
previous experience had shown them to be ineffective.

The ability of inverted brittle-stars to right themselves with speed and
precision has also been studied critically. Bohn (1908) concluded that
young starfish are better both at orientation and at righting movements
than are the older ones, and from this it was concluded that there is no
ability to profit by experience. Glaser (1907 studied the righting reaction
of *Ophiura brevispina,* and Kjerschow-Agersborg (1918) did the same
with *Pycnopodia helianthoides.* Neither investigator found any evidence
of improvement with practice. Although these conclusions were in line
with Jennings's own work, he himself suggests that the answers that such
experiments give are not really final since only two of the three necessary
conditions have been fulfilled. He points out (1907) that, in order to show
habit, (1) the problem must be such as to cause the organism to continue
to react until the problem is solved, (2) the situation must be such as to
lead to an attempted solution in a number of different ways, and (3) the
animal must solve the problem in only one or at least in only a limited
number of these ways. It is this last condition which is not satisfied, and
the experiments have failed because of the extraordinary versatility of the
starfish. The animal has so many different possible series of movements
within its repertoire, all of which are likely in due course to have the
necessary effect, that there may be little occasion to prefer any one series
of co-ordinations of them over any other. In order to meet such difficulties
Jennings trained starfish to right themselves only on a certain pair of rays.
He did this by preventing the other three rays from attaching themselves
to the floor by stimulating their tube feet with a glass rod. He found first
that the animals generally tended to turn over on the rays closest to the
madreporic plate, and that some animals could only right themselves
through the principal use of the arm directly opposite to this plate. Jennings' starfish were always trained to use those rays which they had not
previously relied upon for initiating the righting reaction. After a large
number of tests of this kind the animal was given five to ten trials without any interference or assistance, and the results seem to show without
any doubt whatever that the behaviour pattern had been changed by the
period of training and that this change would persist over periods varying
from twenty-four hours to five days. A. R. Moore (1910) tried to explain
away this conclusion with the argument that the training method must have
caused actual injury to the tube feet, but this seems exceedingly improbable and is hardly worthy of serious consideration. It seems, then, that
there is at least real habituation and also some slight associative learning
ability displayed by the group, and that many of the studies which lead

to a contrary conclusion are of doubtful value owing to their lack of understanding of the normal behaviour of their subjects. But obviously much more work is desirable, and the studies of Jennings have given a lead as to the kind of experiment which may be expected to provide conclusive answers and which if followed up would, even at this late date, doubtless provide many further results of value.

CHAPTER X

WORMS AND MOLLUSCS

VERMES

ALTHOUGH the group Vermes is a zoological anachronism, it is still convenient from a behavioural point of view to group together with the Annelida some of the other 'worm-like' creatures. This is chiefly because critical behaviour work on worms other than the Annelids is so slight as to make treatment under a separate heading hardly worth while. Since from henceforth we shall be discussing animals definitely in possession of a central nervous system and in general showing behaviour of a relatively high degree of elaboration, it will be assumed that they also show evidences of what may be called instinctive behaviour, and this side of their repertoire will not be discussed except in so far as is necessary in order to appraise the significance of their learning abilities.

Among the flat worms, the only groups on which there have been any significant studies are the Turbellaria. The tidal rhythm of *Convoluta roscoffensis* has been known for nearly a hundred years as one of the most remarkable examples of mass rhythmic behaviour in the invertebrates, outshone only by the extraordinary reproductive rhythms of a few species of Polychæta such as the Pacific palolo worm *Palolo viridis* with its annual swarming date closely related to one particular new moon of the year. *Convoluta* lives in the sands of the north-west shores of continental Europe. It is green owing to the presence of zoochlorellæ and occurs on the surface in numbers so vast as to colour the sand green at low tide, but rapidly disappears in the lower levels of sand as the tide rises. This movement has been shown to be associated with a negative geotaxis when undisturbed and a positive response to gravity when turbulence commences (Fraenkel, 1929). Nevertheless, rhythmic behaviour which appears at first to be the direct effect of tidal stimulation is retained for about a week in the laboratory even though no mechanical disturbance is given, and it is clear from the account of Gamble and Keeble (1904) that there must be some internal 'clock' which drives the behaviour irrespective of all external stimulation.

PLATYHELMINTHES [1]

Habituation

The few studies that have been carried out on habituation in flatworms have suggested that it is widespread with regard to mechanical stimuli

[1] References in this section will be found in Jacobsen, A. L. (1962).

and changes in light intensity but that it is usually of brief duration, a matter of seconds or minutes. Thus Walter (1908) studying *Dugesia gonocephala* and *D. maculata* reported waning of the response to slight rotation of the aquarium (the response consisting of a momentary halt in the gliding of the animals along the glass). If rotation was repeated at one-second intervals the response faded completely in about twelve trials but was fully re-established after a minute's rest. Somewhat similar figures were obtained for responses both to directional and non-directional illumination. Dilk (1937) obtained further results with *D. gonocephala* showing that habituation to mechanical vibration occurred when the disturbances were of one or two seconds' duration and with an inter-stimulus interval of not more than ten to fifteen seconds. If the inter-stimulus intervals were longer than this and the duration of the stimuli shorter, then no habituation was found.

Habituation has also been studied in one trematode 'Cercaria hamata,' by Miller and Mahaffy (1930). Here an habituation was shown to a shadow stimulus repeated at intervals of less than two seconds. Complete recovery took place within about a minute. Attempts with this animal to show habituation to mechanical stimuli were unsuccessful.

Associative Learning

Van Oye (1920) was the first person to undertake conditioning experiments with flatworms. His technique resulted rather in trial-and-error learning than in classical conditioning and consequently will be referred to again below. Hovey (1929) demonstrated what he called associative hysteresis. This in fact amounted to the reversal of an innate taxis. He used *Leptoplana*, a Polyclad found under rocks on the Pacific shores of North America. When the rocks are overturned the worms begin to move and continue until they reach a shaded area; similarly, when placed in a dish of sea water they tend to move as long as they are illuminated, but are, as a rule, quiescent in the dark. Through simultaneously exposing the worm to light and preventing it from creeping forward when the light was turned on, inhibition of photokinesis was effected. Just as with Protozoa, so with flatworms. There have been many papers published during the last twenty years arguing whether or not true associative learning has been established in the group. The upshot of these seems to be that in the case of spaced trial experiments true classical conditioning has been established in the Planarian *Dugesia dorotocephala* and *D. tigrina*. There is, however, some doubt about the results of experiments in which massed trials were used (Jacobsen, 1962).

Trial-and-error learning has been demonstrated as mentioned above by van Oye (1920) who succeeded in training planaria to approach and obtain food by a new route. This learned response was maintained in a series of tests at two-day intervals but disappeared after a lapse of two months. Since van Oye's results were published there have been—after a lapse of nearly twenty years—a number of other demonstrations of similar accomplishments. Recent workers have taken to teaching planaria to run simple mazes. Best and Rubenstein (1961) employed a number of two-choice mazes, using the flatworms *Cura foremani* and *D. tigrina*. There seems little doubt that here again true trial-and-error learning was demonstrated.

In recent years various attempts to show that the results of training flatworms persisted in individuals regenerated from small pieces of the trained animal have been described, and sometimes embroidered, in the popular scientific press and also the unscientific press. The flatworms are indeed admirable material for the study of the locus of learning just because of their extraordinary regenerative abilities. McConnell, Jacobson and Kimbell (1959a) found that pairing light with shock and using spaced training (50 trials a day) a thoroughly satisfactory criterion of conditioning could be established in *D. dorotocephala*. Once a worm had reached the criterion, it was cut in half transversely and the halves isolated and allowed to regenerate. When regeneration was complete all the animals were retrained to the original criterion. The figures appear highly significant and to show that a specific adaptive change for this particular kind of task must have taken place in various parts of, if not the whole, of the animal's body. In a further study the same workers (McConnell *et al.* 1959b), as yet published only in abstract, cut planaria in half posterior to the pharynx, conditioned the head end, then cut off the regenerated tissue up to the pharynx and isolated the head end. After this had regenerated a new tail they again cut the worm posterior to the pharynx and allowed both halves to regenerate. Thus one group will contain the head half of the original worm, whereas the other group contains animals consisting only of tissues regenerated subsequent to conditioning. Nevertheless, both appear to show a satisfactory positive effect. If these intriguing results are satisfactorily confirmed, they will open a wide field to the study of the chemical basis of memory; for whatever physiological changes are involved in conditioning in flatworms, they appear to be so widespread in the tissues that only a chemical explanation would suffice. It has indeed been suggested that ribonucleic acid (R.N.A.) may be involved in some specific manner (Corning and John, 1961).

ANNELIDA

As has been said above, it is not the purpose when dealing with animals of higher grades to discuss the details of innate or instinctive behaviour. In the Annelids, however, there is an exception which seems justifiable because it concerns a type of behaviour which would naturally be assumed to be reflex had not ample evidence been recently provided (Wells, 1949, etc.) that it is very largely independent of external stimulation. This behaviour covers a number of the rhythmic activities of the lugworm *Arenicola marina*, which lives in estuarine mud in a U-shaped burrow kept open by the respiratory and locomotory movements of the inhabitant. Both the irrigation movements and the actions whereby the sand is ejected from the hind end of the burrow are rhythmic. Feeding is achieved by extrusion and withdrawal of the proboscis, which in their turn create an integrated action of the proboscis itself, the head and the first three trunk segments. The irrigation cycle consists of a regular burst of irrigation movements about every forty minutes. These are largely independent of oxygen lack or of carbon-dioxide accumulation, although asphyxia will result in their temporary acceleration. The hæmoglobin in the blood and muscles provides for a considerable oxygen store, so that the animal can forego respiratory movements for nearly the whole period of low tide. If the worm is attached to a sheet of cork in a dish of continuously circulated and aerated sea water, it will display forty-minute bursts of activity for many hours. The same bursts of activity are shown by longitudinal body-wall strips which contain the ventral nerve cord, in that these trace a complicated pattern which contains conspicuous and vigorous outbursts of activity at the same frequency. From these and a number of other experiments it seems clear that there is a spontaneously cyclic pace-maker in the ventral nerve cord, the brain itself not being necessary. Even though the respiratory cycle is independent of the accumulation or lack of respiratory gases, the feeding cycle might be associated with the state of nutrition or the quantity of material contained in the gut. On the contrary, however, experiments have established that the isolated extrovert of a proboscis with some of the œsophagus gives the characteristic intermittent rhythm of the feeding cycle.

It is clear that in this case the œsophagus drives the proboscis and that the pace-maker is probably a diffuse nerve plexus in the œsophageal wall. Here again, then, we have to deal with a spontaneously active cyclic pace-maker, and there is no evidence at all that anything comparable to a reflex chain is involved. With the defæcation cycle, even more than with the other behaviour cycles, one would have expected a simple reflex mechanism to have been adequate for the purpose; experiments show, however, that defæcation is not dependent on a full rectum, but is, in fact, one more instance of the activity of a spontaneously cyclic pacemaker. So we arrive at the conclusion that all the integrated behaviour patterns which presumably *could* have been achieved by means of a hierarchy of reflexes are, in fact, controlled by spontaneously active 'clocks' —perhaps of the nature of relaxation oscillators—either in the œsophagus or the nerve cord; the œsophagus controlling the rhythm and the nerve cord the respiration and defæcation cycle, both cycles consisting of the periodic evocation—or perhaps suppression—of processes which are in themselves rhythmic. Wells and his co-workers (Wells and Dales, 1951; Wells and Albrecht, 1951a and b) have studied the rhythmic activities of the allied species *Arenicola ecaudata* and of other nearly related worms. This species shows a similar organisation of outbursts but in a more variable and fluctuating pattern. Here the œsophageal rhythm seems to be under the control of the central nervous system rather than of an œsophageal pace-maker. The fact that other worms, such as the Poly- chætes *Chætopterus variopedatus* and *Nereis diversicolor* and also the Sabellids, *S. spallanzani* and *S. pavonina,* also show similar activity pat- terns gives strong support to the suggestion that the mechanism of control is similar in all of them. Wells (1949) suggests that in spite of its apparent improbability, the method of control of these rhythms may, in fact, have survival value. At high tide the worm has a plentiful supply of oxygenated water at its disposal, and at low tide if the sand surface dries it can breathe air. If, however, the burrow were covered with surface water at low tide, circumstances might arise in which respiratory movements initiated by oxygen want, such as are known to occur, for instance, in the larva of the caddis *Phryganea*, might be injurious or even fatal, while behaviour of the 'Arenicola type' would save it. Again, hard frost or heavy rain might perhaps make surface water dangerous at low tide, and so again the method of control exhibited by *Arenicola* might have its ad- vantages. It does not, however, seem so easy to understand why the defæcation cycle should be similarly controlled except in so far as all the actions of a burrow-dwelling animal of this kind are apt to involve some degree of irrigation. Although the evidence for the internal control of these movements seems overwhelming, there is as yet, of course, no final evidence that they are inborn. It is quite possible that the internal mechanism might have been timed and primed as a result of early experi- ence. Further studies on this point should be of great interest. Wells (1961) says of *Arenicola* 'a range of alternative activity patterns is latent in its organisation, and it achieves a respectable diversity of performance by changing the combinations and the sequences in which its muscles contract and relax. . . . The results of experiments suggest that not only in the detailed integration of such acts as proboscis extrusion but also in the patterning of its whole life, the lugworm relies very largely on mechanisms which resemble in spontaneity though they exceed in intricacy the beat of a vertebrate heart.'

Habituation

A great many examples of simple habituation or of changes in some respects resembling habituation have been placed on record for the Annelids. Hargitt (1906, 1909) and A. W. Yerkes (1906) have described a gradual cessation of response to shadows and similar stimuli in *Hydroides dianthus*. Similar habituation has been shown in the sedentary Polychæte *Bispira voluticornis* by Bohn (1902), in the leech *Dina microstoma* by Gee (1913), and in none of these cases does the explanation that the effect is due to fatigue seem to apply. Málek (1927) describes the slow habituation of earthworms to a vivarium in which when fully acclimatised they appear to behave quite normally. The same author investigated the well-known reaction whereby earthworms, in this case *Lumbricus herculeus*, drag leaves into their burrows—showing that an attempt to draw in leaves which are too large or stiff is abandoned after ten or twelve trials. He points out that this elementary type of learning is much more likely to be of significance in the life of the earthworm under natural conditions than is the much slower associative conditioning investigated by Heck (see p. 207, below) by the highly artificial technique of the 'T' maze. Nevertheless, associative learning must also be playing an important part in the development of some aspects of the worms' behaviour. Kuenzer (1958) has made an extensive study of the habituation process in earthworms. He finds that habituation via stimulation of one spot on a segment, extends to the other parts of that segment as well, and to adjacent segments in decreasing strength according to the distance from the original point of stimulation. Even within one segment, however, habituation to mechanical, thermal and electrical stimuli are all independent of one another. Hargitt (1909) found that specimens of *Hydroides* collected in shallow water would respond readily to shadows, whereas specimens taken from a depth of ten fathoms or more seldom reacted. This difference in behaviour seemed to result, as one would expect, from the previous light conditions to which the animal had been exposed and not to depth of water as such, and specimens kept in the laboratory in dim illumination soon ceased to respond.

There are a number of other studies on the habituation of other sedentary polychaetes to sudden diminution in illumination, such animals being from the very nature of their structure and habitat particularly good experimental material. Species studied include *Serpula vermicularis, Mercierella enigmatica* and *Branchiomma vesiculosum* (references in Jacobsen, 1962). But although sedentary polychaetes would seem to offer the most promising material, perhaps the most important work on this aspect of the behaviour of the group has been accomplished with an 'errant' species *Nereis pelagica*. This worm habituates readily to mechanical shock, moving shadow, and decrease and increase in light intensity. Duration of the effect was directly related to the inter-stimulus interval and to the number of stimulations given. Habituation to a moving shadow is independent to that of mechanical shock but habituation to the shadow and to a decrease in illumination were found to be linked in a complex manner.

The phenomenon called 'latent habituation' was also described: if an animal is exposed to repeated presentation of light increments too small to evoke a detectable reaction, the cumulative effect is nevertheless evinced in more rapid habituation when large increments of light are presented. Particularly interesting is the conclusion that *Nereis pelagica* does not recognise the approach of a predator by a simple token stimulus as some sedentary polychaetes may do. The worm is thought to be in a state of partial or total habituation to the simple stimuli which are almost constantly represented in its normal environment, and a predator's approach is recognised by a complex of stimuli.

Associative Learning

There are also a considerable number of observations on the associative learning of the Annelids. That the response to shadows by different species of tubiculous Annelids may be, in fact, due to associative learning has been indicated by Bohn (1902), who claims that *Hermella alscolata* learns to react to shadows primarily as a result of contact with an enemy. The contact with a predator, the turbulence caused by its approach and the corresponding decrease in light intensity all affect the situation, with the result that the worm eventually comes to react to a shadow as if the other two components were also present. A. W. Yerkes (1906) obtained very similar results with *Hydroides* in which the worms were conditioned to react negatively to shadows. Copeland (1930) established that with *Nereis virens* a sudden decrease *or* increase of illumination, if paired regularly at intervals of from 15 to 20 seconds with food presentation, would result, in about six trials, in the animal leaving its tube in response to the light change alone. Thus the worm could be conditioned to respond positively to a change of intensity in illumination irrespective of whether this was positive or negative, and Copeland and Brown (1934) were able to show that negative responses to light and touch which were presumably innate could, by food presentation training, be made positive. Similar results are reported with *Lumbricus terrestris* by Wherry and Sanders (1941). Raabe (1939) found that the worm *Lumbriculus variegatus* could be taught to avoid light or dark as a result of association with a large variety of stimulus combinations, and he found that the behaviour modifications were not taking place exclusively in the brain, for they could still be obtained even after amputation of twelve or more of the anterior segments.

A more elaborate trial-and-error learning, where the animal has to make an active choice in some kind of simple maze, has been demonstrated in a number of Oligochætes. R. M. Yerkes (1912) tested the worm *Allolobophora fœtida* in a simple 'T' maze one arm of which led to a dark, moist chamber and the other to a region lined with sand-paper beyond which contact was made either with a salt solution or an electric shock or both. The worm was initially activated by a touch or by strong illumination on the hind region of the body, and it was found that the habit of turning to one side could be firmly established as a result of something between twenty and a hundred tests. Spaced trials were found more satisfactory than massed trials, and there was a good deal of fluctuation in the day-to-day performance of individuals, depending apparently upon their general physiological condition. Yerkes was able to observe a number of effects of experience all of which contributed towards the total learning process. These included (1) increased readiness to enter the apparatus and to desert it for the exit tube, (2) apparent 'recognition' of the exit tube and increasing avoidance of the sand-paper and the electrodes, and (3) the disappearance of the tendency to retrace the course through the stem of the 'T' and to turn back after passing the choice point. These, combined with a clear increase in the number of correct or shortest trips, give an indication of what might be called a characteristic or normal 'T'-maze performance. Yerkes found that once the habit was thoroughly ingrained the correct performance was not dependent upon the brain, since even a few hours after its removal, the worm would react appropriately. But brain regeneration increased the worm's 'initiative' and also rendered its behaviour less automatic and more variable. Only two individuals were used for this particular work, but the results in general have been confirmed by Swartz (1929) on *Helodrilus caliginosus*. There seems no doubt that in this case, too, a habit to turn to one side was fairly readily produced, but the data are not presented in such a manner that the results may be critically assessed. Heck (1920) carried out similar investigations with the worms *Eisenia fœtida*, *Lumbricus castaneus* and three species of *Allolobophora*. All the species tested showed a learned behaviour which was virtually constant after about 200 trials. Heck carried the investigations further by a reversed training experiment, using individuals which had already been taught to turn to one side only. It was found that they learned the reversed turn, the side which was originally the incorrect one now being the correct, in significantly fewer trials than had been required to learn the original problem; a result which could be taken to mean that the learned change was certainly not merely a position habit or a response which involved a certain group of muscles only but involved the co-ordination of many different factors as a unified whole. Heck also confirmed Yerkes's results on the effect of the elimination of the 'brain.' He showed that worms that had been fully trained retained their abilities unimpaired after removal of the supra-œsophageal ganglion, and also that worms that had previously had this ganglion removed could be trained as easily as could intact animals. Since most Oligochætes are burrowing and soil-dwelling forms, they might be expected to be efficient in learning a tubular 'T' or 'Y' maze. For the free-living Polychætes, on the other hand, such an apparatus seems less appropriate. Nevertheless, Fischel (1933) showed that *Nereis virens* could be easily taught to perform reliably in a 'Y' maze so that the animal always turns to a given side. He suggests that failure in such experiments is most probably due to lack of suitable cues at the choice point, such that the animal is unable to distinguish between them. Copeland (1930) and Copeland and Brown (1934) have also demonstrated what is essentially trial-and-error learning in worms of the same species which were taught to advance along a tube for food which was obtained at the end. They could also be taught to associate touch and changes in intensity of illumination with reward. Arbit (1957) has shown that diurnal cycles of behaviour play an important role in maze learning in earthworms. The ability of the worms to learn varies greatly according to the phase of the worm's diurnal cycle in which the test is carried out. Results such as this raise the whole problem of the design of experiments and the criteria employed in work with such animals. Certainly many of the studies on annelid learning are open to some degree of criticism and it is often difficult to compare the results of one study with another owing to differences of technique. It seems that technical problems of this kind have been more effectively solved in regard to the problem of associative learning in flatworms than they have in the case of the annelids.

Ratner and Miller (1959a) having given a satisfactory demonstration of true classical conditioning in the earthworm, proceeded to show (1959b) that after removal of the pharyngeal ganglion conditioning could be established only with massed trials whereas previously spaced trials were also effective.

The ability of the tube-worm *Spirographis spallanzani* to combine and co-ordinate the tactile stimuli received by its tentacles into an elementary space perception seems to have been satisfactorily demonstrated by Teyrovsky (1922). He found by a series of simple experiments that the animal tests the available space around its anterior end with its tentacles, and as a result controls the curvature and position of its body so as to occupy the space available for food collecting in the most convenient manner without touching the enclosing walls and solid objects in the aquarium. Bharucha-Reid (1956) claims to have established latent learning of earthworms in a T-maze. There seems some doubt, however, whether the control techniques were entirely satisfactory and judgment should perhaps be reserved until the work has been repeated.

MOLLUSCA

The class Mollusca contains organisms of such widely varying degrees of development of sense organs and central nervous system that they can hardly be discussed as a single group. It is, in fact, essential to consider the Cephalopods separately since they display abilities which quite transcend those found elsewhere in the group. The first part of this section therefore deals only with Mollusca other than Cephalopods.

(A) MOLLUSCA EXCEPT CEPHALOPODS

Habituation

It would be expected that the Mollusca would provide numerous examples of habituation, and, indeed, snails were the organisms used in the first careful studies on the subject. Dawson (1911) pointed out the striking difference in response between the pond snails, *Physa,* collected from quiet environments and those from a running stream. E. L. Thompson (1916) carried out an elaborate study of the learning processes in *Physa gyrina,* which provided remarkable evidence for habituation as distinct from fatigue. But it was Humphrey (1930), working with the snail *Helix albolabris* common in the St Lawrence Valley, Canada, who was the first to attempt the quantitative study of habituation. In his experiments snails were placed on a wooden platform which by means of an electrical attachment could at regular intervals be jerked on its ball-bearings. On being first placed on the apparatus they were left undisturbed; during this period they emerged from the shell and began to crawl over the board. When this happened, the regular jerking started, usually at two-second intervals. The first result was a whole or partial withdrawal of the horns or antennæ at each jerk of the platform on which they rested. As a general rule (there were exceptions), the extent of the response gradually decreased with repeated stimulation, until eventually the jerks were followed by no apparent reaction. Occasional late responses might occur, but they became fewer and fewer until, when full habituation had set in, a series of 50 to 60 stimulations might pass without visible response. The animals had by this time become so accustomed to mechanical vibration that it was now difficult to cause complete withdrawal even as a result of a quite violent blow. In this particular investigation there is ample evidence that the results are not to be accounted for by fatigue in any ordinary sense of the term, since a more intense stimulus would tend to restore the response to the original stimulus and a 'fatigue' that is diminished by more intense stimulation of the same kind [1] is a contradiction in terms—although, as the author points out, it is possible that some instances of habituation involve in a highly localised form the same mechanism as that responsible for certain phenomena to which physiologists give the general name 'fatigue.' The implications of this subject are discussed fully in Chapter III and need not be gone into

[1] Prof. Pantin has pointed out to me that even relatively simple systems can show what seems to be habituation—as when an isolated heart that has failed to re-excite itself can often resume activity after a stronger shock than usual.

further here, but it is worth while pointing out that when in certain experiments half-minute intervals were allowed during which the animals received no stimulation, after which period the jerking began again, the responses recommenced. But if the process is continued, a half-minute rest no longer suffices to restore the response, showing that there are different degrees of habituation which could doubtless be graded according to the length of time necessary to restore response. If habituation is carried to the point at which a one-minute rest no longer restores the response, and if now during such a period of rest a steel ball is dropped on the platform, movement of the antennæ will again be observed when the standard stimulation series begins again. So it is clear that habituation, in its short-term aspect, may be removed by rest or extraneous stimulation and re-evoked by further stimulation of the kind originally used. Buytendijk (1921b) in experiments with the pond snail Limnæa found the habituation was an important factor in decreasing the time required to execute the righting reaction. When Limnæa is removed from the substratum, it normally contracts for a while and then extends from the shell again. Buytendijk noticed that the time spent within the shell steadily decreased with repetition provided the animal was handled gently during the test.

Association

The development of associations has often been demonstrated in Gastropods; although Fischel (1931) failed to train Limnæa to make a simple right turn on encountering a row of small stones. Thompson (1917) showed with the watersnail Physa gyrina that a touch on the foot would cause foot contraction but would not affect the movements of the mouth parts. If, however, a touch on the foot was given immediately prior to presentation of lettuce to the mouth parts as the snail was crawling along the surface film of a dish of water, the foot contact would eventually elicit chewing movements although at first it had effectively inhibited the response of the mouth parts to the lettuce. These results are interpreted as showing that the buccal ganglia controlling mouth movement were slowly freed from the initial domination of the pedal ganglia. The acquired response was retained for four days from the completion of the training. If after a successful period of training the snails were given a test series in which foot contact was given without the mouth stimulus, the acquired mouth responses disappeared again after twelve trials; but that the effect had not been completely removed was shown by the fact that the animal could be retrained in fewer trials than were required in the first case. Thompson also studied the behaviour of the same species in 'U' and 'Y' mazes; the rough surface in one arm of the latter being used as a warning stimulus and electric shock as a punishment. Definite evidence of learning could not be obtained in any of these experiments—perhaps because the shock was too long delayed after the warning stimulus had been received. But if a touch on the tentacles preceded the shock, it was found that an association could be established. That Thompson's failure was perhaps due to faulty design of apparatus is suggested by the work of Fischel (1931), who showed that the snail *Ampullaria gigas* can master a 'Y' maze in about ten trials. The habit was, however, very transient and the snails required daily retraining. In spite of this success Fischel failed in his attempts to train his snails in a true 'T' maze, and when he tested them in a run-way ending in three arms in which entry into the middle arm was punished by an electric shock, so that a turn *either* to right or left was the solution, the performance was very doubtful and inconsistent. Under these circumstances success was apparently achieved only when

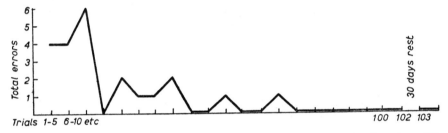

Fig. 25—Error curve for one individual of land-snail, *Rumina decollata*, in a 'T' maze derived by summing errors for each successive five trials. (After Garth and Mitchell, 1926.)

the animals accidentally developed a particular motor tendency which took them consistently into either the right or the left arm. Fischel and also Brandt (1935) regard this as evidence that 'T'-maze experiments with these and other invertebrates merely provide evidence of a 'behavioural inertia' or 'motoric perseveration tendency,' and not of true associative learning; but the work of Garth and Mitchell (1926) and of many other students of invertebrate maze-running renders this explanation unconvincing. These latter authors secured an excellent performance by a land-snail, *Rumina decollata*, in a 'T' maze. The design of the apparatus was essentially the same as that employed by earlier workers, and it was found that the maze could be learned perfectly in about 60 trials and the habit retained through a 30-day period. Fig. 25 shows the learning curves of one individual and Fig. 26 the actual paths followed by a given snail on different trials of the series.

Latent Learning

A type of Molluscan behaviour which has attracted attention since the end of the last century is the homing ability shown by limpets of the

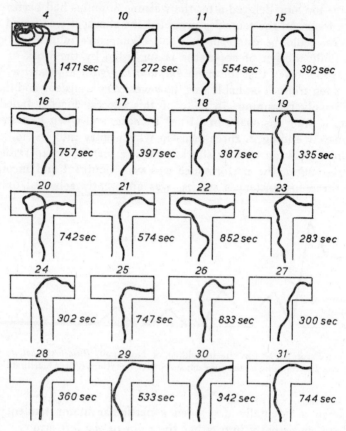

FIG. 26—Actual paths followed by a single individual of land-snail, *Rumina decollata*, in a series of trials (Nos. 4, 10, 11, 15, etc.) in a 'T' maze. (After Garth and Mitchell, 1926.)

genus *Patella* and also the slug-like form *Onchidium*. Many naturalists have observed that individual limpets are normally found in a depression in the rock face which exactly fits the margin of the shell, and that although they make feeding excursions from this position (during which time they browse on the Algæ on the rock surface), they usually return to exactly the same spot. Piéron (1909) showed that this behaviour could not be explained on the basis of an ability to follow a trail or to recognise the site by chemical sense, and he concluded that it was necessary to suppose that co-ordination of at least three different types of sensory impression must be involved.

I myself (1954 unpublished) have observed the return of an individual of *Patella* (*intermedia* or *depressa*) from an excursion of about 20 centimetres. In this case the interest lay in the fact that although returning in a virtually straight line towards its 'home,' the direction of march of the animal brought it in at about 120° to the long axis of the home site. On reaching the edge of this it immediately commenced a right turn without any trial-and-error behaviour, and continuing to turn steadily (at a rate of about 6° per second) through the required 120° as if revolving on a central pivot, settled exactly into its niche. It appeared quite evident that the mollusc was properly oriented throughout; it showed some appreciation, however elementary, of the topography of the environment, and was not dependent on a single simple guiding stimulus. Arey and Crozier (1918) came to conclusions very similar to those of Piéron in their studies of *Onchidium*. The demonstration of such a remarkable achievement is of considerable importance, since if confirmed it implies a sensory co-ordination far in advance of the minimum necessary for the learning of a simple maze, but the records, although providing good evidence of homing, show that the distance from which homing can be accomplished varies very greatly from one individual to another. Thus Davis (1885, 1895, 1903) refers to limpets returning to their sites from a distance of up to three feet, and Morgan (1894), who performed various removal experiments, stated that the number of returns bore an inverse ratio to the distance—only five out of thirty-six of his limpets made successful returns from a distance of more than 6 inches. Piéron obtained similar results in that five out of six returned from 4 centimetres or less, two out of five from 5 to 10 centimetres and only two out of nine from 10 to 20 centimetres. Pelseneer (1935) found that *Chiton tuberculatus* and *Chiton cinereus* would return to their sites fairly readily from a distance of 1½ metres, and H. Fischer (1898) showed a return by *Patella vulgata* to the home site by a route entirely different from that taken on the outward journey.

Although such experiments are, in any case, not easy to interpret, and are often not such as to carry conviction as to detail, taken together they do, at any rate, show that occasional individuals of *Chiton, Onchidium* and *Patella vulgata* can return by a strange route to a known home. But the subject would be worth reinvestigation in the light of modern knowledge about the senses used in orientation and the various sensory possibilities open to invertebrate animals. There have been corresponding and more recent studies on the American limpets of the genus *Acmæa* with very conflicting results. Wilcox (1905) failed to find any evidence of a homing sense in *Acmæa testudinalis*, a New England species, and Wells (1917) obtained no very definite results in a number of studies of other species of the same genus and on *Lottia gigantea* on the Pacific coast of California. Although he does claim that one individual of the latter species proved a very consistent 'homer' and concluded that some of the other marked limpets also displayed a homing instinct, his records give no very satisfactory support to these conclusions.

Richardson (1934) also failed to find evidence of homing in *Lottia gigantea* and *Acmæa persona,* and Villee and Groody (1940) similarly failed during their very careful study of over 200 individuals of five species of *Acmæa.* Nevertheless, against this must be set the positive evidence of Hewatt (1940) that three of his marked individuals did in fact return to the original 'home' in circumstances which made the chance finding of the spot extremely unlikely. Moreover, he carried out some experiments in which the edge of the shell was filed down so that there was no longer the exact fit into the depression which had existed previously; nevertheless, two of the limpets managed to return. From this he concludes that the orientation on to the homing spot is not by the trial-and-error method of fitting the shell into the surrounding rock surface. In another experiment he brought a granite boulder to which four specimens were attached, into the laboratory and placed it in an aquarium into which sea water was allowed to run very slowly. The animals moved upwards shortly after they became submerged and remained near the water surface for $2\frac{1}{2}$ hours. The position of the rock was now reversed so that the limpets were near the bottom and the water was then drained off. A slow stream of water was then sprayed over the organisms, and it was found that three of the specimens returned to their original places on the rock after three hours, even in spite of the complete reversal of position of the latter. These and many similar observations clearly indicated that there was an interesting and important problem still to be investigated.

The matter was carried a great deal further by the late Prof. T. A. Stephenson, to whom I am much indebted for allowing me to quote from an extensive unpublished study by himself, Margaret Wood *et al.* on a number of species of South African limpets. They find that *Patella granularis* in particular is an active species, going for as much as 5 feet from home when on feeding excursions. Individuals living high up on the shore commonly stay on their scars in the daytime, and feed on the damp rocks during low water at night; but those living lower down, where the rocks rarely dry off, may feed actively in the daytime also. Each individual recognises its own scar with great accuracy, even when this is sited among a group of others, and returns to it unerringly after excursions. On one occasion only was a specimen seen to return to the wrong scar. Two marked individuals, A and B, had scars situated side by side on the rock, almost in contact. One night when both limpets were out feeding, A returned first, and sat on B's scar; but almost immediately B came up and pushed A firmly off it. Although, however, the great majority of individuals have a definite scar and return to it habitually, there is some individual variation. A few specimens return, not to a visible scar, but an unmarked area about 6 inches in diameter, and their home is anywhere within this area. One marked individual apparently had no home at all, and although its movements were followed for several months, it wandered at random about the rocks.

The distance to which these limpets wander from their scars, during a given low-water period, also appears to be affected, at least in some cases, by the amplitude of the tide during that period. Some marked limpets moved only short distances during the low-water period at neap tides (at night), but tended to move farther during low water of spring tides.

By following the actual tracks made during feeding excursions by individual limpets, it was possible to show that although they often *do* follow the outward track back home, they are not *dependent* on this

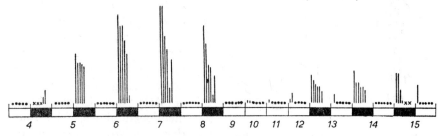

FIG. 27—Observations on a group of 5–6 specimens of *Patella granularis*, near Cape Town, over the period March 4–15, 1935. The numerals represent the dates; black rectangles along the base of the figure indicate records made at night, white ones records made in daylight. A dot means that a particular limpet was on its scar in the daytime, a small cross that it was on its scar in the dark. The vertical lines indicate approximately the distances of limpets from their scars at the times of observation. The diagram shows that these individuals were usually 'at home' when visited in the daytime, usually away from their scars when visited at night. The distances travelled tended to be greater on the nights of March 5–8 (spring tides) than those of March 13–15 (neap tides). (No night records were made on March 9–12.) (Original, courtesy T. A. Stephenson.)

method. Sometimes a limpet returns to the scar by a route different (or partly different) from that along which it went out; and if limpets are removed carefully from their scars (in such a way as to avoid injuring them) and put down on the rock a little way from their scars, they will—at least in some cases—find their scars again, so long as they are not put down too far away from them.

Figs. 27 and 28 show some examples of excursions of this species. Among other species studied, *Patella cochlear* proved particularly interesting in that it is quite usual for small individuals to have their scars on the shells of larger ones, and in an extreme case as many as forty small ones were found on one large one. As some at least of these small ones seem to leave their scars to feed, it is difficult to see how they all get back to their original positions. Ohgushi (1955) finds that the limpets *Siphonaria japonica* and *Patelloida saccharina lanx* can return home after being moved up to 15 cm. from their homes either by following the tracks previously made or by general topographical memory. The longer the animal has inhabited a particular site, the more effective the topographical memory appears to be.

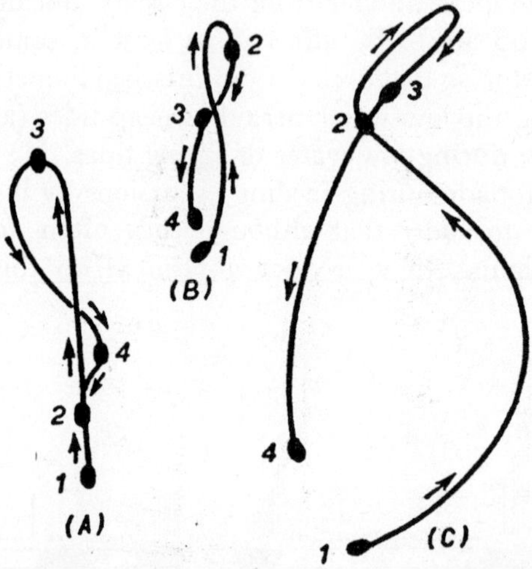

FIG. 28—Records of the tracks followed by three individuals of *Patella granularis* during feeding excursions on intertidal rocks near Cape Town. A = positions occupied by a specimen between about 4.30 p.m. and 9.30 p.m. on April 18, 1936. B and C = positions occupied by two specimens between 5.30 p.m. and 10.30 p.m. on May 1, 1935. In all cases 1 indicates the situation of the animal's scar, the starting-point of its journey; and 4 indicates its position just before its return to the scar after its feeding excursion; the journey in each case was completed by return from position 4 to position 1. In the case of A, this last section of the journey was along the outward track (from 2 to 1). The tracks were made visible by sprinkling fine sand over the damp rock, so that the limpet's foot cleared away the sand along its route. (Original, courtesy T. A. Stephenson.)

Apparent place memory has been observed in a number of other marine and inter-tidal gastropods, but the basis of it has not been properly investigated. Among the forms on which observations have been published are the Prosobranchs *Helcion, Fissurella* and *Calyptræa,* and the Pulmonates *Siphonaria* and *Oncidiella.* That organs of touch are, in most cases, particularly important is, however, suggested by the work of Arey and Crozier (1921) mentioned above, who found that *Oncidiella floridana* was not able to return to its site after removal of the buccal region. Abe (1939), in describing the homing of a 'limpet-like pulmonate' *Siphonaria atra,* says that on the return journey it creeps within a narrow area in which the mantle margins touch the previous path. The length and direction of the feeding excursions vary from day to day, but the range never exceeds about fourteen times the length of the shell. It has often been claimed that terrestrial Gastropods are able to return to a spot from which they have been removed, and P-H. Fischer (1939a) states that *Succinea putris* can return from a radius of 1 to 2 metres. He considers also that the edible snail (*Helix pomatia*) displays evidence of a knowledge of the neighbourhood of its resting-place. P-H. Fischer has summarised these and some other earlier observations on the homing of Mollusca in his text-book *Vie et Mœurs des Mollusques* (1950).

(B) Cephalopods

As with the other molluscs, it is difficult to make any certain statement about the part which instinctive behaviour plays in this group. Immediately they hatch, cuttlefish (*Sepia*) can swim backwards and forwards by means of their funnel and fins, squirt ink, and bury themselves in the sand. Their behaviour in these respects appears to be very like that of adult cuttlefish (Wells, 1958). Observation on the sea shore confirms this and indicates that within seconds of being extracted from their opaque egg they can show a dymantic response (see below), match very closely the colours of a sandy bottom and show attention movements (Boycott, unpublished). The common octopus, however, is less mature at birth and appears to have only limited powers (Vevers, 1961). It has a larval life of some months as a planktonic creature (Rees, 1950) whose behaviour is little known but certainly very different from that of the animal which eventually walks and swims near the bottom, feeding on crabs, lamellibranchs and fish, and having a fairly definite home. Other octopods, however, are—like *Sepia* —more mature and apparently assume many adult habits at birth. Since there is now abundant evidence that cephalopods can learn, though this was once denied (Bierens de Haan, 1926b; Russell, 1934), and since there are such ample opportunities in the normal circumstances of individual life for even the most characteristic locomotory patterns to be learned, it is possible that learned behaviour patterns and responses are far more important in this group than are inborn ones. Nevertheless, apart from the above observations, there are some clues which suggest that not everything is learned. Thus it seems unlikely that the mating behaviour could be entirely learned (L. Tinbergen, 1939) and Boycott and Young (1955a) have described a fright-response posture of *Octopus* which they term 'dymantic', which, while individually variable, is sufficiently constant to be easily recognisable, and is perhaps the outcome of a conflict between the drives of attack and escape. The dymantic posture includes a characteristic colour pattern, produced by chromatophore contraction (the 'startling' pattern). This posture can be elicited in adult octopuses by electrical stimulation of a tract of fibres going from the optic lobe to the magnocellular lobe, and if the supra-œsophageal parts of the brain are removed it releases this response so that the preparation remains fixed permanently in a dymantic posture (Boycott, unpublished). A part of the response can, however, be extinguished.

The 'natural' food of *Octopus vulgaris* appears to be crabs, although they will also feed on a variety of animals, including Lamellibranch and other molluscs, as well as on various species of fish small and slow enough for them to catch. The preference for crabs may, of course, be learned; but Boycott and Young found that the memory for the 'crab pattern' is far more deply ingrained than are other memories and can only be temporarily inhibited. There are indications in the data that the neural processes associating a particular artificial figure with food differ in that they can be reversed by a few experiences involving electric shock, and do not spontaneously return. The only other 'recognitions' which appear of comparable strength and persistence are those which release the movements of attack —small moving objects and sudden but not too great turbulence in the water. Such basic responses to visual movement and disturbance could be the foundation for subsequent learning to discriminate between various objects whether potential food or potential enemies.

Experimental work on the sense organs of the Cephalopods is beginning to help in the study of the behaviour of these animals. The eyes are generally the most highly developed sense organs, and after vision, touch is in all probability the most important of the senses; and as we shall see, it is now clear that the eyes are reasonably efficient for 'form' sight as well as for movement discrimination. For untrained octopuses crabs are more attractive than other objects; white figures more attractive than black; vertical figures more attractive than horizontal when moved vertically—the reverse being true if they are moved horizontally. White circles, diamonds and stars are especially likely to release attack (Young, 1961). We lack any satisfactory evidence about the ability to discriminate colour. The papers of Goldsmith (1917a, b and c), Kühn (1950), Bierens de Haan (1926b) and Mikhailoff (1920) are open to serious objections in this respect. The statocysts are the chief organs of orientation (Boycott, 1960). Wells (1960) has shown that visual discriminations with the statocysts removed are possible; errors occur when the retina comes out of the orientation in which it is normally kept by static information. Preliminary experiments by Hubbard (1960) showed no evidence for the statocysts being used in hearing, but a negative is, of course, difficult to prove. Parriss and Moody (1961) have brought forward evidence that *Octopus* can detect polarised light. And Young (1960c) has related the structure of the retina and optic lobes to the kinds of objects most easily discriminated by *Octopus*.

Habituation

Habituation in *Octopus* was first demonstrated by Buytendijk (1933), who showed that the vigorous investigatory response caused by the movement of a 10-centimetre-square white card in front of the animal rapidly decreased with repetition until it disappeared altogether. Buytendijk's results have been confirmed by Boycott (1954). Thus it has been shown that this extinction of avoidance responses occurs in animals from which the whole of the supra-œsophageal part of the brain has been removed. 'Since the only remaining central connection of the optic lobes is now with the magnocellular lobe, retention of this change in behaviour must be a property of the optic lobes and their subœsophageal connections' (Boycott, 1954). This substantiates and carries further some observations by Buytendijk in which only parts of the supra-œsophageal lobes had been removed. Goldsmith (1917) showed habituation to mechanical stimuli resulting from turbulence. Both Buytendijk and Boycott emphasise the rapidity with which *Octopus* becomes 'tame' when kept in an aquarium, and there seems no reasonable doubt that habituation plays a major part; but since the process of taming has not been analysed, one cannot at present separate associative and other types of learning from habituation.

Some recent results of Wells (1958) with *Sepia*, while bearing some relation to habituation, also illustrate other processes which are much more elaborate. Newly-hatched cuttlefish when given the opportunity will always attack and eat prawns of the genus *Mysis*. The movements for attacking *Mysis* are highly stereotyped from the beginning, but the delay between the presentation of the *Mysis* and the reactions of the *Sepia* decreases with experience, and it is found that this decrease depends upon the number of attacks already made regardless of the age of the animal and regardless of whether it has been allowed to feed after having attacked or not. It appears that there is a kind of facilitation occurring somewhere between the retina and the motor centres, a process which leads both to a reduced delay in attack and a higher probability of attack in a given visual situation. Along with this there is also an increase in the range of patterns of stimulation which can evoke attack. Thus, to start with, attacking is self-facilitating and results in a widening of the adequate stimulus situation. At a later stage the animal appears to learn once again to restrict its attacks, this time not to *Mysis* only but to certain other types of prey as well. Further studies of such early changes in the individual behaviour of cephalopods will surely yield information of much interest.

Associative Learning

It was shown in 1920 by Mikhailoff that *Eledone moschata* was a satisfactory subject for conditioned reflex experiments. The normal animal shows no change in response to a sudden bright light, but darkens and shows the 'eye spots' on its back in response to a gentle touch. Mikhailoff's conditioning consisted in associating tactile stimuli with the switching on of the light and so conditioning the animal to darken when the light is switched on but in the absence of the tactile stimulus.

That *Octopus vulgaris* can quickly establish associations has long been known. Kühn (1930) performed experiments very similar to those of Mikhailoff on *Eledone,* and J. Z. Young and his collaborators have carried out extensive work on trial-and-error learning in this species. This work has been summarised by Young (1961). The general procedure is to keep *Octopus* alone in a rectangular tank with two or three rocks at one end among which the animal settles down and which it appears to treat as its 'home.' Crabs are placed at the opposite end of the tank, attached to a black thread, and are kept gently moving. As soon as the moving crab appears, the *Octopus* swims or walks swiftly down the tank, throws itself over the crab and returns home with it, usually within less than 10 seconds. If the *Octopus* is thoroughly at home in the aquarium, a 500 g. animal will take as much as 10–15 g. of food a day and as many as forty training trials a day can be given (Young, 1961). Training consists in presenting behind the crab an object connected with an electric circuit so that a properly graded shock can be administered directly the *Octopus* grasps the crab. The training procedure is to expose the animal to the unpleasant situation three times a day and to allow it to feed unhindered an equal number of times. The order of trials is systematically varied, so that only once in seven days is the animal exposed to the same combination. This experimental design is, of course, a trial-and-error learning situation, since the *Octopus* starts out to attack and is actively so engaged at the time when it receives the reward or the shock, as the case may be. These negative food presentation experiments have been used mainly for a study of visual perception and brain function, and in this connection will be discussed in more detail below. They have confirmed and extended the work of earlier investigators, especially von Uexküll (1905), Polimanti (1910) and Goldsmith (1917*a*, *b* and *c*).

It was found as a result of these experiments that while the attack of *Octopus* on its prey could quickly be inhibited as a result of experiencing an electric shock, it was impossible to do this merely by placing a transparent glass plate in front of the crab. When this is done the *Octopus* swims straight into the glass partition and persists in attacking again and again in an attempt to get the crab. If some of the arms succeed in reaching it around the edge of the partition, then the *Octopus*, if restrained from withdrawing the crab with its arms, will follow round and secure it. The object of this experiment is to test the ability of the animal to learn to make the detour around the partition without actually touching the crab with its tentacles, and none of the three *Octopus* tested in this way was completely successful (Boycott, 1954). Two of these animals never got round the partition unless they had touched the crab with their arms first, and never learned to do so—even though a black line was painted down the open side of the partition. Occasionally when pushing against the glass wall they would fall through to the other side; but they never profited by this experience even if a trial were given only 30 minutes afterwards. The third animal did show some improvement in that there was a slight decrease in the time taken to come round the edge of the partition, but even this animal after 44 trials never went straight to the edge of the partition, nor did it cease to attack. It appears that *Octopus* cannot normally make detours as a result of visual stimulation alone, but that if tactile stimulation is present this can dominate the situation and provide the basis for making a detour. That *Octopus* would probably be adept at learning a simple maze is now fairly obvious in spite of the early negative experiments of Bierens de Haan (1926). Von Schiller (1949*b*) has shown that certain types of simple detour device can be memorised. This author also found that *Octopus* is capable of a delayed response detour choice of about 1 minute. If the time taken to circumvent a partition was under 40 seconds success was almost invariable. The achievement of delayed response was markedly correlated with the maintenance of the correct bodily orientation, it being essential for the beak and most of the suction cups to be turned in the direction of the bait. It was also necessary that there should be a persistent steady crawling along the continuous wall. If these postural and orientation factors were upset, then the performance scores fell to the chance level. Once the behaviour had been learned, the animals could retain it over a period of some weeks.

Sanders and Young (1940) have demonstrated an interesting difference between *Octopus vulgaris* and the cuttlefish *Sepia officinalis* in this matter of the inhibiting effect of a transparent glass partition upon the attack on prey. The cuttlefish, after training over a period of 20 to 30 hours, would make no further attack on bait (a prawn) placed behind a glass partition, whereas *Octopus* continued to do so indefinitely. This difference may be due to the fact that the force with which cuttlefish hit the glass partition with their tentacles is greater and therefore more 'painful' than for *Octopus*. Both *Sepia* and *Octopus* will hunt round opaque partitions, but the latter must be able to explore the detour with its tentacles first, whereas a normal *Sepia* is able to hunt and follow a prawn which passes out of sight around a corner without this preliminary (Fig. 31). This suggests that *Sepia* and *Octopus* are essentially different in the degree of their dependence on vision for hunting. Piéron attempted to train *Octopus* to remove crabs from an opaque vessel, but the account he gives of his experiments is so imperfect that it is difficult to know what, if anything, is really demonstrated. However, it appears that as a result of exploring the interior of the apparatus with the tentacles, a complex series of associations was built up so that the prey could readily be extracted without futile attacks against the side. Hempelmann (1926), misquoting Piéron, claimed that *Octopus* can be trained to pull a bung out of a bottle in order to get at a crab, but although *Octopus* are able to move quite large and heavy objects with their suckers, and can even work loose and move tightly fitting bungs which offer practically no purchase, Boycott (1954) has not been able to establish that the animal will deliberately remove a stopper in order to reach the bait. Since sooner or later they will, in any case, move almost every movable object within reach, to secure proof is not easy.

Pliny in his *Natural History* describes how *Octopus* will use a stone as a tool, inserting it between the open shells of large bivalves, thus preventing them from closing while the occupant is devoured. Power (1857) claims to have seen an *Octopus* do this with the Lamellibranch *Pinna nobilis,* but there seems to have been no satisfactory confirmation of the story, and Grimpe (1928) and other modern writers (Boycott, 1954) usually regard it as a fairy-tale. However, in view of the building activities of *Octopus* described below, the story still sounds plausible. Dr. S. Stillman Berry, the distinguished malacologist, tells me that *Octopus disgusti* on the coast of Sonora, Mexico, lives in big gastropod shells—especially *Muricanthus negritus.* It finds an oval clam shell which exactly fits the opening of the gastropod shell it is inhabiting and holds the clam shell in tightly as if it were an operculum.

The detour observations quoted above show that given the right kind of sensory cues quite good space perception can be achieved by *Octopus,* and from the accounts of many workers it is clear that there is a good deal of exploration of the immediate locality in which the animal is living. *Octopus* stay for long periods each in its own lair, from which they emerge from time to time to attack their prey, and to which they return; so they must certainly be able to find their way back from short distances without any difficulty. How far long excursions may be made and whether there is any homing from considerable distances has not yet been established, but Cowdrey (1911) instances 50 metres. It would certainly be of interest to investigate such things by systematically marking a large number of individuals. With the development of diving by means of the 'aqualung,' observations of this kind under natural or semi-natural conditions should be relatively easy, and a new field for the study of behaviour of these and other marine animals is opening up. It is, for instance, fairly clear (T. H. Waterman, personal communication) that squids form organised schools just as do fish. As a further example we may quote Cousteau (1953), who describes a 'city' of *Octopus* 'villas'[1] situated in the sea to the north-east of the Porquerolles in the Mediterranean. He says, 'These strange villas are indisputably erected by the *Octopi* themselves. A typical home was one-roofed, with a flat stone 2 feet long and weighing perhaps 20 lb. One side of the stone had been raised 8 inches and propped by two lintels, a stone and a red building-brick. The mud floor inside had been excavated 5 inches. In front of the lean-to was a wall of accumulated debris.' [Crab and oyster shells, shards, etc.] 'When I went closer the tentacle contracted, sweeping the debris up against the door and conceal-

---

[1] The 'building' activities of *Octopus* have been investigated by Frisch (1938) and their territorial behaviour by P–H. Fischer (1939*b*).

ing the inhabitant.' The alternative behaviour patterns available to some cephalopods are very remarkable. Professor T. H. Waterman tells me that some species of squids have alternative ways of using their ink cloud: for instance, some will discharge the cloud and shoot off to hide elsewhere. Alternatively, the cloud may be discharged and the squid float beside it, themselves taking the colour and approximate shape of a cloud, thus apparently confusing predators. Yet again, some will discharge the cloud and hide in or under it.

Insight and Perception

The experiments quoted above on the organisation of spatial perceptions have suggested the existence of abilities corresponding to latent learning, although they have not provided any satisfactory evidence for 'insight-learning.' The recent studies of J. Z. Young and his collaborators on the visual perception of *Octopus* have, however, far surpassed previous work on the sensory abilities of the group and have given us a new understanding of the visual capacities and limitations of this animal. By the technique of electric shock described above, Boycott and Young (1950, 1955a, 1956, 1957) have followed up and made more precise the kind of experiment previously carried out by Goldsmith (1917c) and ten Cate and ten Cate-Kazejewa (1938). An account of the more recent work of Young and his colleagues and of Wells is to be found in Young (1961) which contains detailed references. The training procedure is described (p. 220).

TABLE III—*Responses of Octopus, during first 120 trials of training to react to various pairs of figures* (from Young, 1961).

	figures		errors (actual)			
octopus	positive (food reward)	negative (shock)	positive (60 trials)	negative (60 trials)	total (120 trials)	errors (%)
1	(vertical bar)	(horizontal bar)	14	3	17	14·2
2	(horizontal bar)	(vertical bar)	1	13	14	11·6
3	(horizontal bar)	(vertical bar)	1	11	12	10·0
4	●	○	1	11	12	10·0
5	●	○	11	6	17	14·2
6	○	○	9	19	28	23·3
7	L	L	23	9	32	26·6
8	L	L	5	30	35	29·2
9	L	L	7	27	34	28·3
10	□	◇	34	13	47	39·2
11	○○	○ ○	37	15	52	43·3
12	●●	● ●	49	10	59	49·1

Table III shows some of the pairs of figures to which *Octopus* can be trained to react differentially. Fig. 29 shows the course of learning to dis-

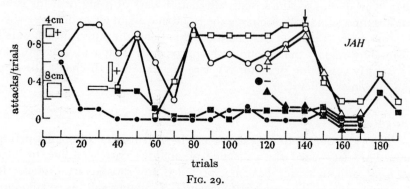

FIG. 29.

From Young 1961. For explanation see text.

criminate between squares of side 4 cm. and of side 8 cm. It also shows that vertical and horizontal rectangles and black and white discs can be discriminated at the same time but that when these figures are first introduced there is some interference with the behaviour of the animal to the first learned pair. Using this training method, it has been shown that the discrimination systems depend largely upon the estimation of vertical and horizontal extent; differences in area, distribution of outline, amount of reflected light and number of angles are also important as attributes in the discrimination of figures.

With these results as a basis, Sutherland (1957a and b) has proposed that the attributes used by octopuses in the analysis of shapes are their vertical and horizontal extents. Thus an animal trained to discriminate a horizontal rectangle from a square will treat a vertical rectangle like a square, therefore not reacting to the rectangle as such. Sutherland suggests shapes with identical projections will not be discriminated (e.g. oblique rectangles), and this appears to be so. As Young (1961) summarises it, 'Sutherland supposes that there might be rows and columns of nerve cells serving to detect the extent of horizontal and vertical contours respectively. Analysers could then extract such parameters as the total amount and direction of change in each projection, or its maximal height. . . .' Alternative mechanisms have been put forward by Dodwell (1957) and Deutsch (1960b) and discussed by Sutherland (1960). Whatever the merits of this argument, Young (1960c) has found anatomical and histological evidence that gives it circumstantial support. He has shown that elements of the retina and the branching of some of the dendrite systems in the optic lobes can be seen to be organised into vertically and horizontally distributed units.

In the process of testing his theory Sutherland (1950) showed that

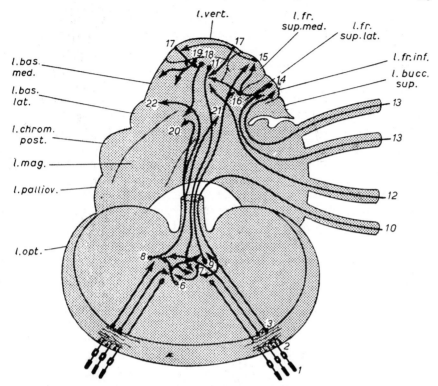

FIG. 30—Diagrammatic lateral view of the brain of Octopus to show the main connections of the vertical lobe system. The optic lobe is displaced downwards. *l. bas lat.*, lateral basal lobe; *l. bas. med.*, medial basal lobe (these two together comprise the posterior basal lobe); *l. bucc. sup.*, superior buccal lobe; *l. chrom. post.*, posterior chromatophore lobe; *l. fr. inf.*, inferior frontal lobe; *l. fr. sup. med.*, medial superior frontal lobe; *l. fr. sup. lat.*, lateral superior frontal lobe; *l. mag.*, magnocellular lobe; *l. opt.*, optic lobe; *l. palliov.*, palliovisceral lobe; *l. vert.*, vertical lobe. (After Boycott and Young, 1955.)

circles and squares can be distinguished by octopuses with about 70 per cent. accuracy, a result somewhat better than that obtained by Boycott and Young (1956*a*) and about as good as an octopus's performance with squares and triangles. This level of discrimination is less good than for other figures (see Table III) and is perhaps surprising in view of the ability of birds and other vertebrates to distinguish between circular and rectangular patterns of similar area, colour and luminosity. Indeed, circles seem to be particularly stimulative to many land animals, very probably because the eye, whether of predator or prey, is such a striking and distinctive recognition mark—as the wonderful devices by which it is camouflaged in so many animals show so clearly (Cott, 1940). There is certainly every reason to suppose that the circular pattern should in general have just as much special significance as a warning of danger in a marine environment as it has on land; but it may be that *Octopus* is not exposed to attack from any predator in which the eyes are particularly conspicuous, although as we have seen *Eledone* itself displays eye-spots on its back when irritated.

As a result of a series of studies by Wells and Wells, listed and discussed by Young (1961), a great deal of information on tactile learning in *Octopus* has been obtained. Although the arms contain numerous ganglia and when isolated from the brain can show many reflexes such as carrying food to the mouth, they are incapable of learning unless the pathways to the brain are intact. Blinded octopuses can recognise food objects with their arms, crabs are transferred to the mouth even when legless, lamellibranchs and pieces of fish are examined by the suckers for 10–15 seconds when touched for the first time and then transferred to the mouth. This time decreases with repeated testing. So that although we do not know to what extent these responses are innate or learned, they can certainly be improved with practice. An octopus will nearly always examine a 'new' object that it can move by drawing it to its mouth. The period of examination of inedible objects varies from one minute to half an hour, but is generally less rather than longer. Repeated testing at two-minute intervals with the same object results in a rapid decrease in examination time and soon the object is not even taken to the mouth but dropped after a cursory examination by the tips of the arms.

Using the technique of giving a shock when one object is touched and a food reward with another, Wells and Wells have shown that octopuses can learn a tactile discrimination. Octopuses learn, for example, to discriminate with their arms between smooth-shelled lamellibranchs and the same species cleaned and filled with wax—a tactile and chemical discrimination.

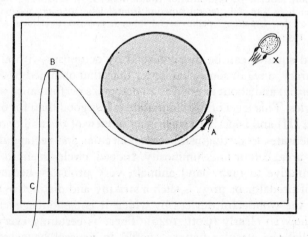

FIG. 31—Detour experiment with *Sepia*. Arrangements of tank to show capacity to hunt when the prey passes out of sight. (After Sanders and Young, 1940.)

Most attention has been paid to their tactile abilities using perspex cylinders with differently incised grooves. Such tests have shown that objects of different roughness are distinguished with an accuracy proportional to the differences in percentage of the grooved surface, but that the pattern or direction of the irregularities is not detected. Octopuses are not, however, able to discriminate between similar objects differing only in weight (Wells, 1961). Proprioceptive information from the arms or from the statocysts (Wells, 1960) 'is evidently not available for integration with other sensory information in learned processes' (Wells, 1961). Wells and Wells have also shown that the inferior frontal (Fig. 30) and subfrontal lobes are essential for the learning of a tactile discrimination. The vertical lobe system is, however, also involved.

The Vertical Lobe System

A major part of work on cephalopods has been directed towards attempts to discover neural mechanisms of learning. A physiological analysis of the brain recognises a variety of levels of motor control of which the sub-œsophageal lobes are lower and intermediate motor centres having only a limited 'reflex' control over behaviour. The supra-œsophageal lobes contain basal lobes (Fig. 30) which are higher motor systems working through the sub-œsophageal lobes to produce patterns of colour change locomotion, attack, retreat and so on. The medulla of the optic lobes forms a very important part of this motor system (for details, see Boycott, 1961). Also in the supra-œsophageal lobes are electrically unexcitable areas which include the vertical, subvertical, superior frontal and inferior frontal lobes. It is these lobes, together with the optic lobes, which are an essential part of the neurology of the visual and tactile learning systems (Fig. 30).

Early works by von Uexküll, Polimanti, Bert and others (see Boycott, 1961) considered that these regions were 'le siège du processus psychiques,' although von Uexküll (1895) was rather more precise when he suggested that they were inhibitory centres. The first anatomically accurate work on the vertical lobe system was by Sanders and Young (1940) who showed that even when extensively damaged, no defects in behaviour appeared unless the animals were tested in some more complex situation. This has been confirmed many times for *Octopus*. Sanders and Young showed that cuttlefish without the vertical lobe complex are unable to hunt prey when it passes out of sight (*c.f.* Fig. 31). They also did the only published work on learning in a decapod cephalopod when they showed that if a normal *Sepia* is repeatedly presented with a prawn behind a sheet of glass, it will shoot its tentacles at the glass but with a steadily diminishing frequency (Fig. 32). Removal of the vertical lobe complex disturbed this state of learned inhibition, but traces of it remained and relearning was as rapid as the initial learning. The accuracy of performance in a learning situation is much greater in a cuttlefish after vertical lobe removal than in octopus (see below). But this is perhaps related to the degree to which the vertical lobe system has evolved in the two groups. That of octopus is notably more elaborate than in cuttlefish. And it may be that the differences are an expression of differences in the degree to which the different levels of the possibly dual memory mechanism have evolved.

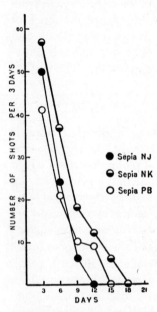

FIG. 32—Graph of course of learning by *Sepia* not to shoot at prawns behind a glass plate on which there is a white circle. The ordinate shows the number of shots made at the glass (i.e. 'mistakes') during successive periods of 3 days. (After Sanders and Young, 1940.)

As far as the vertical lobe system of octopus is concerned, Boycott and Young showed that in visual situations animals discriminating between two different figures each shown with a crab, or between a crab and a fish, are unable to perform the discriminations without the vertical lobe or the superior frontal lobe. However, since the main afferent input to the vertical lobe is from the superior frontal lobe, it still remains unclear what the relative roles of these two lobes are in the memory system. Following up these experiments, it has now been shown that there is a relationship between the amount of the vertical lobe removed and the accuracy of performance of octopuses in a learning situation. However, the vertical lobe is not simply 'the memory store.' Later experiments have shown that there is some retention after removal of the vertical lobe. This is particularly easily seen when examining the learned responses after operation when the training has been done without showing the food stimulus until a decision has been made by the animal. Thus in the experiment in which the octopus appeared to lose the ability to discriminate crab and black circle from crab and white circle when 80 per cent. of the vertical lobe

was removed, subsequent tests with the figures showed that some discrimination in fact remained. It is as if the memory system required to prevent attacks on the crab and figure has to be more strongly represented in the brain since it is a more strongly learned, or strongly innate, stimulus than the figures alone. It also means that there is a learned representation of the figures which is retained by the brain in the absence of the vertical lobes, for without training the octopus would not have shown a differential response to these two. In a series of papers summarised in Young (1961) it has been shown that memories are not completely abolished by removal of the vertical lobe in either kind of situation, although its effects are always greater when the situation is strongly positive. The memory required for less recently learned situations is of a different order of magnitude.

Aside from the neurological mechanisms of discrimination suggested by Sutherland's hypothesis and discovered in the retina and optic lobes by Young as discussed above, studies on the mode of working of the vertical lobe system have reached the stage in which there is a good deal of indirect evidence for postulating a dual mechanism for the establishment of learned responses. In animals trained to discriminate between a crab alone and a crab presented with a square, removal of the vertical lobes abolishes the discrimination if the intervals between the trials are of the order of an hour or more. However, if the animal is tested at a higher frequency, say every five minutes, a discriminating response can be built up. This short-term or transitory memory persists in the absence of reinforcement for periods of only half an hour or so (a much shorter period than the days or weeks of memory in a normal animal). This result led to the suggestion that there are circuits of neurones capable, in the absence of the vertical lobes, of discriminating and retaining a learned response but dependent on the vertical lobes for making the trace more permanent. Young placed them provisionally in the optic lobes. It was supposed that this system was rather like the self-re-exciting system of neurones proposed by Forbes to explain after-discharge in the spinal cord of mammals. The detention of such a system behaviourally in octopus was possibly because of the high frequency of trials that they will undergo without 'fatigue.' Presumably in the normal animal the self-re-exciting system would persist long enough to enable some more permanent change—most plausibly a structural one—to be brought about by the vertical lobe system. There is some circumstantial evidence from other animals to support this kind of conclusion. Stellar (1957) was the first to point out the resemblance between these results of Boycott and Young and those of Milner and Penfield in human patients with lesions to the hippocampus. Such patients showed no impairment of pre-operative memory, no change in I.Q. and no loss of ability to learn. Their defect was one of retention, in that any new material could not be retained for periods of more than half an hour or so.

CHAPTER XI

ARTHROPODS

THE group Arthropoda includes more species than all the other animal phyla put together. Its members inhabit at least as great a variety of environments as do those of any other phylum, and they almost certainly exceed all others in the variety of their life-histories. In behaviour they are equally diverse. The tiniest of them, such as the Tardigrades and some of the Acarina, are smaller than some Protozoa, and have a simplicity of life cycle, sensory equipment and behaviour which makes them seem little more advanced ethologically than the members of that group. At the other extreme the Hymenoptera rival the higher mammals in their powers of orientation and in their ability to learn and to remember elaborate visual patterns. It is, of course, the insects which make by far the greatest contribution to the phylum; both in numbers of species and elaboration of behaviour—a million living species is a conservative guess, for over half a million had been described by 1925 (Schröder), and Imms (1934), indeed, estimated two and a half million to be nearer the world total.

The insects are of particular interest to the student of behaviour, primarily because by developing wings they have mastered another element, and this conquest has in its turn opened up immense possibilities for new ways of life and the colonisation of new environments. It is chiefly this single step which has enabled them to become the dominant group they are. Another outcome of the development of flight has been the necessity for concomitant advances and improvements in the sense organs—since the speed and distance of travel can be so much greater in the air. Thus a premium is set on organs which give perception at a distance, upon organs which give a quick response, and also upon a variety of senses—so that if one sense fails to provide data for orientation to the nest or territory, the animal can fall back on another. So we find that in the insects the senses of vision and olfaction are highly developed, since both are particularly effective for orientation at a distance. The organs of vision are typically compound or faceted eyes, and the olfactory organs are most usually situated in the antennæ. The dependence of so many insects upon flowering plants for their food has also been a major factor in their sense-organ development. Here again not only are specialised olfactory powers well-nigh essential, but form sense and colour vision are also of particular value. Indeed, there is overwhelming evidence that the colours and shapes of flowers have been evolved in response to, and in association with, the evolution of the insects as flower feeders (Baerends, 1950).

It has long been known that among the important characters which serve to attract Hymenoptera to flowers are certain colours, size, disruptiveness, three-dimensionality, velvety surfaces, marking-contrasts and scents (Baerends, 1959). There is no doubt that many of these can be interpreted in terms of flicker. This is well shown by the work of Magnus (1954, 1958) on the stimuli evoking the first courtship approach of the males of the butterfly *Argynnis paphia*. In this case the effect both of rapid movement and larger size seems to be moderately well accounted for. The argument also seems to work well with the visual responses of male houseflies and blowflies. Nevertheless, there seems to be a residue of visual preferences, at least in the honey-bee, which cannot at present be satisfactorily interpreted along these lines. Discussion of this particular problem originated with the work of Herz who interpreted the form vision of honey-bees on gestalt principles. This work has been subjected to much criticism but Sakagami (1956) (ref. in Baerends, 1959) has re-opened the matter by training bees to choose between homogeneous figures in a disruptive background, attempting to form an idea of how the disruptive pattern is received by the eye of a flying insect. He shows the inadequacy of some of the criticisms of Herz's work that had been advanced, in particular the difficulties of explaining how characters which play a role in one reaction are of no effect in another. Nor do the original criticisms seem to account for the fact that relations between parts of the releasing object are of very great importance in some instances. Again, the effects of three-dimensionality and velvety surfaces seem difficult or impossible to explain at present on any flicker theory (Baerends, 1950). The fixity of insect reproductive behaviour is also well summarised by Baerends (1959, see pp. 209–10). The behaviour of both insects and spiders, the building of cases by caddis larvae in the first group and of orb webs in the second, provides beautiful examples of stereotyped motor patterns on which taxis components are superimposed (see Baerends, pp. 212 and 214). An outstanding example of the analysis of the taxis component in an insect is provided by the work of Mittelstaedt (1957, 1962).

Much of the recent work on insects and other arthropods seems to fit in very well with the hierarchy concept of instinctive behaviour of Tinbergen. Perhaps this fact, to which reference is made in Chapter II above (see p. 35 and Fig. 4), receives some further elucidation from recent researches on the mode of action of the insect nervous system. Thus Vowles (1961) points out that the properties of the insect neurone, which are very different from that of the vertebrates, and the small size of the insect nervous system, render necessary a functional organisation of behaviour far simpler than is often supposed. Innumerable students of insect behaviour have been, and still are, astonished that such small animals possess such a big repertoire of actions which cope so efficiently with an extremely complex series of stimulus situations. This complexity still appears marvellous, but at least some examples of it seem to be based on surprisingly simple neural mechanisms. For instance, the understanding of the co-ordination of arthropod movements has been greatly advanced by the work of Hughes on insects and of Manton on the Onychophora and a wide range of myriapods (see Pringle, 1961). Manton (1961) suggests that the nervous system of arthropods is infinitely more plastic and flexible than the hard parts and its actions are not restricted by mechanical factors. Although in many maintenance and sexual responses insects show behaviour patterns of extreme rigidity, when we come to locomotion 'wide ranges of rhythms can be transmitted both forwards and backwards in the same animal, and new timing can be put out when limbs are broken accidentally or experimentally amputated' (Manton, 1961). It follows that some at least of the fixity or apparent fixity of arthropod behaviour is due to the rigidity of the exoskeletal structure rather than to the nervous system.

The study of endogenous nerve activity in insects has been further advanced by Roeder *et al.* (1960) who demonstrate a widespread system of spontaneously active efferent neurones in the male *Mantis religiosa* controlled by inhibitory systems. They conclude that in insects inhibitory control of local endogenous efferent activity by other nerve centres is the rule rather than the exception.

There is hardly any precise knowledge about the relationship between brain structure and learning ability in the Arthropods. A vague correlation can be shown between the degree of development of the *corpora pedunculata,* or 'mushroom bodies,' of the brain and the degree of elaboration of instinctive behaviour, in a series of Hymenoptera (Armbruster, 1919); the worker *Apis* and the queens of *Bombus* (three species) and *Vespa* being at the top of the list in both respects. These mushroom bodies have a dense neuropile made up of a great number of very small cells, and Young (1951) has compared them to the *lobus verticalis* of *Octopus* as the probable centres for learning ability. However, the fact that similar bodies are found very highly developed in *Limulus* and in many Annelida—creatures which show only relatively simple behaviour—renders this doubtful.

Habituation

It goes almost without saying that habituation is a common characteristic of Arthropod behaviour. Doflein (1910) studied it in the prawn *Leander* and noted that it was abolished on transference to a new aquarium and had to be re-acquired. Among the Arachnids the habituation of the spider, *Cyclosa conica*, to the sound of a tuning-fork was established by the Peckhams as long ago as 1887. They found that the spider would drop to the ground at the first presentation of the stimulus, but gradually decreased its response to vibration and after some days ceased to respond at all. Once habituated in this way, the effect would last, in some cases at least, for many days. Habituation to mechanical vibration has also been demonstrated in the aquatic larva of *Corethra* (Diptera) by Harper (1907), and auditory habituation is known in the cricket, *Lyogrillus campestris* (Baier, 1930). A particularly interesting example of rapid and enduring habituation to mechanical stimuli is provided by the work of Faure (1932) on the phases of South African locusts. Hoppers belonging to the phase *gregaria* of *Locusta migratoria*, when taken from a crowd and kept in isolation, soon became quiescent. For the purposes of experiment on the factors which induce the development of the migratory phase, it was necessary to devise a means for keeping isolated hoppers at the pitch of activity normal for life when in the swarm. A great variety of methods was tried, including mechanical stimulation of various kinds, heat, electric shock and visual stimulation by mirrors; but all of them failed to a greater or lesser degree owing to habituation occurring after, at most, two days. A mechanical jarring apparatus was found to give the best result but, violent though this was, it did not completely solve the problem. This work incidentally raises the puzzling problem: How is it that under natural conditions the individuals of the swarm do not become habituated to the stimulation provided by other members of the swarm, with the result that after a while the whole quietens down? No innate visual releaser seems to be involved, since the insects readily become used to the reflection of their own movements in a mirror. The most plausible explanation is that any locusts in a swarm that fail to keep as active as the rest fail to get food, and so a simple food reinforcement would tend to maintain swarm activity at the maximum. The work of Ellis (see p. 239, below) suggests that visual recognition of the companion may be learnt—which would enhance co-ordination still further.

Many small insects are known to be highly sensitive to the texture of the surface on which they move, and the work of Wigglesworth (1941) on the human louse provides some excellent instances of habituation to the tactile stimuli provided by differences in texture.

Well-developed visual organs need considerable powers of accommodation to change in intensity of stimulus if they are to be effective, and while the process of 'getting used to' change of light intensity is almost universal in Arthropods, it is not easy to point to clear cases of habituation. Piéron (1920) claimed that barnacles (*Cirripedia*) may become more or less permanently habituated to photic stimuli, and there is no doubt that many of the instances of retention by Arthropods of responses to rhythmic changes in light intensity must involve habituation among other central plastic processes.

When we come to the chemical senses we find that the place and importance of habituation (in the wide sense) are more clearly established than with almost any other sense. Kunze (1933) showed that in honey-bees sensitivity to sugars such as saccharose and glucose is greatest in the outgoing workers and least in those returning with nectar. Similarly von Frisch (1927, 1934) found that the threshold of bees' taste for sugars was dependent on the availability of nectar and on its sugar concentration, for in seasons when nectar with a high concentration of sugar is easily obtainable the bees will refuse syrup in dilutions which are readily accepted when natural sources are less rich. This response has not been fully analysed, but it seems likely that habituation is the chief process concerned. Even in the *Collembola* with their very simple biology, Strebel (1928) has reported waning of response to certain normally stimulating odours, and also to substances of which the taste is usually repellent. He records gradual adaptation to and increasing acceptance of food which has been made salty, sour or bitter. It has been shown with both *Nemeritis canescens* and *Drosophila melanogaster* (Thorpe, 1938 and 1939) that the natural aversion to the odour of cedar-wood oil can be transformed into a high degree of tolerance, amounting almost to indifference, simply by exposing the adults, shortly after emergence, to an air-stream bearing the odour of the oil. It is clear that in describing such a result one need not assume any type of learning higher than habituation. With *Drosophila* not only could the repellent effect of an odour be reduced by habituation, but in the case of peppermint it could be entirely eliminated. Indeed, in some experiments the aversion was changed in the olfactometer to a significant attraction. Probably the explanation here is that the peppermint used contained small quantities of ester as well as of menthol. The menthol is a repellent and is probably alone responsible for the repellent effect on first exposure. The ester, on the other hand, is attractive, but its attractive effect is at first completely masked by the presence of the menthol. Habituation to the repellent component ultimately allows the attractive component to manifest its effect, and we thus get the appearance of a complete reversal from repulsion to attraction. Similar results were obtained in *Calliphora* by Crombie (1944), and Cushing (1944) found that the natural preference of *Drosophila guttifera* for laying its eggs in a medium which contains fungal growth may be reduced if the larvæ have been reared in a medium free of fungi. This leads on to the subject of pre-imaginal conditioning, to be dealt with later (p. 253).

The ability to distinguish between different odours in a mixture must be of great importance for many insects and is a subject which deserves special research. The work of Ribbands, Kalmus and Nixon (1952) suggests that honey-bees possess a much more delicate capacity for distinguishing between odours in a mixture than has hitherto been realised (von Frisch, 1919).

In the Arthropods the usual method of distinguishing sensory accommodation on the basis of the duration of the effect is less reliable than in higher groups, since there are indications that insect sense organs adapt less readily to chemical stimulations than do those of many vertebrates. This is perhaps to be expected in forms in which odour plays such an overwhelmingly important role in direction finding, but it indicates that a short-term decrease in response is not necessarily evidence for a change in peripheral sensitivity (see the work of Dethier, described p. 62, above).

Habituation in Ants and other Social Hymenoptera

Habituation, particularly to odours, plays such an important part in the organisation of ant colonies that it is convenient to devote a special section to it.

There is much apparently complex behaviour among ants that may involve no more than habituation. It is well known that (as recorded by Fielde and numerous other observers) many species exhibit antagonism to ants of other species and even of other colonies of their own species. It is clear from the work of Bethe (1898), Fielde (1904) and others that this antagonism is mainly, if not entirely, due to distinctive odours. According to Fielde (1901) the antagonism of workers of an ant such as *Stenamma fulvum piceum* is aroused by any ant odour which a given worker has not previously encountered individually. But it is also well known that under various conditions artificial mixed colonies made up of ants of two or more species can be established, and that once the individuals of the respective species or races or nests, as the case may be, have become thoroughly accustomed to one another, the new composite nest is often a stable and permanent entity.[1] Brun (1912) has shown that the circumstances under which there is a good chance of an artificially mixed population of ants becoming rapidly 'allied' are as follows: (1) when both parties are brought into an equally 'difficult' or unusual situation; (2) when both groups are in approximately the same numerical strength and when one group at least is in possession of numerous brood; (3) in the presence of fertile queens; and (4) in the presence of a 'powerful common enemy.' Now, it is clear from Brun's experiments that these results cannot be solely due to associative olfactory conditioning between the individuals of the two groups. Miss Fielde's explanation involves unwarrantably

---

[1] The technique of mixing stocks of bees by distracting them with dust so that the cleaning reflexes for a time dominate all else is a practical utilisation of the same principle.

elaborate psychological concepts yet does not cover the facts. She says:
'Any distinctive odour to which an ant is accustomed and with which it
associates security and satisfaction is attractive to it, while ant odours to
which it is unaccustomed excite alarm and hostility in proportion to their
strangeness.' But in the four situations instanced by Brun (above) the
ants are certainly not all experiencing 'security and satisfaction.' On the
contrary, there is in every case some stimulus situation which by its high
intensity releases a response which temporarily inhibits or overrides the
normal nest defence drive. During this period the process of habituation
dulls the strangeness of the new odour so that it becomes accepted as the
normal background of the new environment, and it is noteworthy that
Fielde (1901) comments upon the increasing 'tameness' of ants which
are frequently handled.

Headley (1941) has some interesting observations on varying antagonisms between the different nests of *Lasius niger alienus var. Americana.*
These ants have more or less well-defined foraging territories, and when
individuals from different colonies meet at a boundary they may either
both turn back or may fight. The ant which is nearest to the centre of
its own territory, i.e. nearest to its own nest crater, is usually victorious.
But there are many variations in antagonisms which must be the result
of habituation. If conditions of terrain chance to be such that encounters
between members of two nests more often lead to retreat than to fighting,
then the two colonies have a better chance of becoming habituated to one
another. Donisthorpe (1927, p. 260) gives a number of records of variations
in antagonisms between queens of *Acanthomyops flavus.* It seems highly
probable that 'habituation' will also account for the instances of acquired
tolerance in other hymenopterous groups. Rau (1928) records much the
same phenomena as between rival queen *Polistes* wasps, and Stöckhert
(1923) says that rival sister queens of *Halictus* 'may compose their differences' and establish a colony on the basis of dual monarchy. Chisholm
(1952) gives evidence that wasps and ants nesting in colonial association
with birds learn to recognise the swaying of the branches caused by the
birds and differentiate it from the similar motion caused by a man with a
stick.

The importance of habituation in feeding behaviour of honey-bees has
been mentioned above, but it must play an even bigger part in their social
organisation. Ribbands and his co-workers (1952) have produced good
evidence that each colony of bees has a characteristic odour which is likely
to differ from that of most other colonies. They have shown that this colony
odour is not mainly, or even primarily, that of the odour of the queen, but
is determined by the food obtained by the colony and is dependent more
or less directly upon differences in the crops harvested. It was found by
means of tracer elements that food exchange between workers is such a

constant feature of bee life that in a very short time a change in the food
being collected has a corresponding effect on the odour of almost all individuals in a hive. Butler and Free (1952) and Ribbands (1953), studying
the behaviour of guard bees at the hive entrance, found that discrimination
between strange and familiar odours plays a part in the recognition of intruders. If intruders once gain entry they often succeed in remaining in a
strange colony for two or three hours, after which—unless food supplies
are scarce and foraging unproductive (Ribbands, 1953)—they stand a good
chance of being completely accepted. This acceptance is no doubt due
partly to mutual habituation and partly to the intruders acquiring the
colony odour of the hive they have invaded.

ASSOCIATIVE LEARNING

Conditioning

Perhaps the simplest examples of associative learning in Arthropods
are those described in moths of the genera *Saturnia* and *Catocala* by
Turner (1914), who conditioned shock reactions to sound stimuli; in
mayfly nymphs, *Heptagenia interpunctata*, by Wodsedalek (1912), who
similarly conditioned the animals to a shadow stimulus; and in cockroaches
by Szymanski (1912). Very similar experimental results have been reported
by Mikhailoff (1922, 1923) and Cate-Kazejewa (1934) working with
hermit crabs of the genus *Pagurus*. Classical conditioning has also been
established in the Horseshoe Crab *Limulus polyphemus* (Smith and Baker,
1960). Rapid habit reversal has been demonstrated in the crab *Geocarcinus
lateralis* but there was no evidence for progressive improvement in reversal
performance over a series of tests, although the pioneer work of Yerkes
and Huggins had provided some evidence for it in the crayfish. It seems
to be lacking in the one species of isopod tested (refs. in Datta, Milstein and
Bitterman, 1960). Shima (1940) describes how a Gyrinid beetle, *Dineutus
orientalis,* can without much difficulty be trained to develop an association between the presentation of food and the presence on the water
surface where it is swimming of waves originating from a tuning-fork.
Frings (1941) has studied conditioning processes in the blowfly *Cynomyia*,
using as the unconditioned response the motions of extension of the
mouth parts. This extension takes place innately as a result of stimulating
the tarsal sense organs with a sugar solution. The training process
consisted of exposing the insect to the odour of coumarin while the
tarsi were in contact with sugar. It was found that normal flies, after
three conditioning periods of six training exposures each, spaced at 12-
hourly intervals, reached a level of about 90 per cent. response to the
odour of coumarin, whereas untrained normal flies showed only a very
low percentage of response. Nearly all the individuals tested seemed to
be capable of learning to associate the odour of coumarin with the re-

sponse, but there were great individual differences in the rate of learning.

Schrammer (1941) has made some observations on the behaviour of newly emerged individuals of the Silver Y Moth, *Plusia gamma*. This moth is known to seek flowers both by scent and by sight. It was found that newly emerged individuals seek by scent only, this apparently being the innate food-finding method. However, after the first few experiences of feeding, vision comes into play—the insects learning to associate the appearance of the type of flower which has yielded nectar with the odour of that flower.

Trial-and-Error

The simplest type of trial-and-error learning is that involved in straightforward food-presentation tests. A good example of this is provided by the experiments of Mayer and Soule (1906) with the caterpillars of *Danais plexippus*, which were able to develop an associative memory of a distasteful leaf (e.g. *Ampelopsis*) lasting for $1\frac{1}{2}$ minutes. In such an experiment the most likely explanation seems to be that the larva, on being presented with the strange leaf, perceives it— probably by its olfactory sense—as something to be eaten. It takes a bite and finds it unpalatable. After a number of trials it comes to associate some specific odour or other quality of that particular kind of leaf with the unpleasant effects experienced subsequently upon eating it, and is thus enabled for a short time to avoid it. Thus the 'reward' or 'reinforcement' here is the unpleasant taste and, as distinct from the course of events in a classical conditioned-reflex experiment, the reinforcement exerts a retroactive influence linking the new stimulus (specific odour) with the 'response,' namely mastication. Exactly similar experiments have been performed upon *Dytiscus* by Schaller (1926), the beetles being trained to avoid meat made bitter by quinine, and O. Koehler (1924) on dragon-fly larvæ (*Æschna cyanea*). Drees (1952) reports that jumping spiders (*Salticidæ*) show a simple negative conditioning to unpalatable prey, and also, rather surprisingly, that their form vision is good enough to make possible the establishment of a simple negative conditioning to triangles and crosses as a result of electric shock.

All these are evidences of negative food-presentation training, i.e. training in which the incentive is the avoidance of 'punishment,' and serve to illustrate the simpler types of trial-and-error learning in insects and their relatives. The more complex types of trial-and-error learning differ from the above chiefly in the degree of complexity of, and the length of time taken over, the trial acts. Rau (1943) has provided evidence for associative learning by the cockroach when depositing its egg-case, and some of his observations suggest the existence of insight learning.

Although Koehler was unsuccessful in conditioning dragon-fly larvæ to respond to a given colour without punishment, the simple hunger drive (positive food presentation training) being quite ineffective, this conclusion certainly does not apply generally to adult insects even of the supposedly lower exopterygote groups such as Orthoptera. Thus Rilling *et al.* (1959) have shown that the strike releasers for food-catching behaviour in the mantis are chiefly (i) prey within reach and (ii) rapid jerky movement of appendages. They found interesting evidence of habituation. This continuous presentation of a strike releaser resulted in more or less rapid response waning. Optimal dummies became refractory only after several hours stimulation. Sub-optimal dummies showed complete refractoriness within minutes. Students of the higher insects have described many examples of such training.

That there is, in fact, a great deal more elementary trial-and-error learning in the appetitive behaviour of even those Arthropods which show no development of social life in the usual sense, is indicated by a number of recent studies. In particular the methods of sex recognition offer a big field for interesting work. Thus Hellwig and Ludwig (1951), investigating the first mating attempts of some Heteroptera and Coleoptera, found that while in the former there was evidence of innate recognition of species and sex by olfactory cues and by a response to simple shapes, some of the latter were much less precisely attuned to the species partner. The Colorado Beetle (*Leptinotarsa decemlineata*), for instance, was at first ready to pair with members of other genera. Moreover, it showed initial appreciation of the long axis of the partner's body but nothing more, and had to learn by trial-and-error between front and hind end. Swiecimski (1957) has shown that Tiger beetles (*Cicindela hybrida*) discern their food by means of vision only and that they have a well-developed memory for visual stimuli, being able to remember places in which bait was once present and able also to recognise the shapes of their prey. Barrass (1960) found when studying the courtship behaviour of the calcid *Mormoniella vitripennis* that the male, after mounting, moves over the female's body until she is still. He performs courtship movements only when she is still and the result of these two facts is that the courtship behaviour is always in the correct position. Consideration of such examples leads on to the discussion of social facilitation in semi-social and social Anthropods. Grassé (1949, Vol. 6, pp. 675–9) states that there is much social co-operation in young spiders of the species *Stegodyphus lineatus* in such activities as hauling in the prey, which is presumably the result of trial-and-error learning, and Chauvin's (1950) account of the efficiency and persistence of the workers of *Formica rufa* when dragging large prey to the nest, seems to leave no room for doubt that much simple trial-and-error learning is involved.[1] Then Ellis (1953) has found that individuals comprising the

[1] See also Sudd (1960a).

swarms of *Locusta* in the young 'hopper' stage often become conditioned after a few days to the typical appearance of their companions in the swarm, so that a fairly uniform swarm behaviour is developed. In maze-learning problems, however, Gates and Allee (1933) found that cockroaches grouped in twos and threes were less active than single ones, and so were less successful. The experiments of von Frisch (1914, 1927, 1937) and others on the honey-bee provide some of the earliest instances of positive food-presentation training in Arthropods, though Schaller's (1926) success in training the water-beetle *Dytiscus* to leave the water to feed on a particular platform of projecting rock parallels von Frisch's work very closely. As will be clear from the account of the direction-finding of the honey-bee given below, the orientation of the workers to the food place (just as to the hive) is, in fact, a highly complex matter. Nevertheless isolated phases of the training process provide such good examples of trial-and-error learning that they are appropriately recalled here. In these experiments the bees are enticed to food (syrup) in glass dishes on a table, and eventually come to feed regularly. Syrup is then provided only on squares of a certain colour, and this colour then becomes associated with the feeding orientation and all the other squares are ignored. Here, it is true, the retroactive action is not at first sight clearly apparent since the colour is presumably visible not merely during the period of orientation but also during the whole time of feeding. Nevertheless, Opfinger (1931, 1949) has shown that it is a true retroactive action. She found that during the period of feeding the bee is uninfluenced by stimuli other than those coming from the food itself—learning to respond to the colour of the feeding-place being only possible during the approach flight. This is especially interesting in view of the fact that this flight lasts on an average only 3 seconds, while the feeding takes about 70 seconds and the departure flight 10 seconds or more. On this approach flight the bee appears to pay attention only to the properties of the food source and its immediate surroundings (colour, form, odour) and landmarks. On the departure flight she learns the relation of more distant landmarks to the feeding-place. Thus, while feeding and foraging the attention of the bee appears to be concentrated exclusively on matters appropriate to the business of the moment. Heran (1952) has shown also that bees trained to take sugar solution from a series of dishes kept at different temperatures could associate the temperature with the food in a particular dish and so learn to forage only at a particular temperature—an interesting instance of powers of temperature perception put to what must it seems be a quite unnatural purpose.

That even a dual-compartment maze is more difficult to learn than a food-discrimination habit is suggested by the work of Mayer and Soule on the larva of *Danais plexippus* mentioned above. These authors found that the larvæ failed to learn the direct path to food in a dual-chamber maze, one chamber being barren while the other contained a growing food plant. Blees (1919) claims that daphnids (Crustacea) can be trained to approach a light source by travelling part of the way through a glass tube in such a manner that the number of collisions with the walls is steadily reduced with experience. Agar (1927), on the other hand, reports that water mites (Hydrachnids), *Eylais* spp. and the Crustacea-Entomostraca, *Daphnia carinata* and *Simocephalus* sp., are unable to master the simplest 'Y' maze even though varied sensory cues were supplied. These Arthropods seem thus to be inferior in learning ability to earthworms which (see p. 205 above) can learn a maze containing a single choice point. Holzapfel (1943) has shown that the spider *Agelena labrynthica* can learn to make detours both when seeking prey and when making for its shelter. Bock (1942), working with isopod crustacea, found that *Asellus aquaticus* could learn a right or left turn in a 'T' maze, and also could be taught to turn one way or the other according to differences in the texture of the floor of the maze. Reinforcement in these experiments was negative and consisted in a light touch with a fine brush. *Porcellio scaber* was also studied. Besides showing success in the same kind of experiment as did *Asellus*, it could learn to take either the upper or lower of two pathways; that is to say, it could learn a 'vertical' 'T' maze; a performance which for some reason seemed beyond the capacity of *Asellus*. The Malacostraca, on the other hand, can master simple mazes easily, and can, with perseverance, be taught relatively complex mazes. (See Gilhousen, 1929, *Astacus*; Agar, 1927, *Parachœraps*; Cate-Kazejewa, 1934; and a number of earlier workers especially Cowles (1908), on learning and habit formation in the crab *Ocypoda arenaria*.) Among the Myriapoda, Scharmer (1935) has shown that *Lithobius* can learn a 'T' maze provided that the two walls differ in texture. Borell du Vernay (1942) found that both larvæ and adults of the Mealworm beetle (*Tenebrio molitor*), when trained in a 'T' maze with electric shock reinforcement, could learn to avoid either the rough or smooth surfaces as required, but that the adults learned better than the larvæ possibly because, owing to the structure of the tarsi, their ability to perceive surface difference was greater. This result should serve as a warning against accepting at their face value experiments which merely report failure of Arthropods to learn mazes. It may often be that the experimenters have failed to provide the animal with the type of cue which it is able to use, or have not provided the right motivation. The question of appropriate motivation requires much more careful consideration on the part of workers on Arthropod behaviour than it has hitherto received. Thus the failure of Mayer and Soule (above, p. 238) to train the larvæ of *Danais plexippus* to take the direct path to food may have been exactly parallel to Koehler's failure in positive food-presentation tests with *Æschna* larvæ.

However, in many higher insects positive training has been found easier than negative as, for instance, with the water-beetle *Dytiscus* (Schaller, 1926), the honey-bee (Hannes, 1930) and with ants (Schneirla, 1929); but it may be that with the less highly organised Arthropods a negative reinforcement is more effective than is a positive one.

Maze Learning and the Orientation of Ants

It has already been shown (p. 235 above) that habituation will go a long way towards explaining many of the learned responses of ant colonies, but this is not to deny that trial-and-error learning must play a large part in ant life just as it does among other social Hymenoptera. Indeed, the existence and maintenance of social life of any complex kind could hardly be envisaged without postulating some capacity for associative learning in addition to habituation; and the ubiquitous phenomenon of trophallaxis provides almost unlimited opportunity for the establishment of association through simple trial-and-error learning. Vowles (1955) suggests that the antennal caressing movements by which ants 'milk' aphides may be learned. Jander (1957) has shown with *Formica rufa* that the ant starts out on its first run with the built-in abilities to follow odour trails and to relate visual angle to kinæsthetic senses. Like the honey-bee, it has a twenty-four-hour clock. The individual then learns on its first run in the spring to include the movements of the sun in its terms of reference. It is able to form associations between the memory of the angles and turns formed during the run and the reports coming from its clock and the sun. To learn this takes from one half to three hours, but the ability is lost by the individual during the hibernation period so must be relearned afresh each spring. It is still questionable to what extent the behaviour of the more highly developed types of ant colonies involves other forms of learning, but there are some indications that 'latent learning' may well play its part in the organisation of such societies. As yet, however, there seem no valid grounds for accepting Verlaine's (1932–4) conclusion that the organisation of aculeate societies is maintained by transmission to 'descendants by example and imitation.' Nor of course is there any sufficient evidence for adopting the strongly anthropomorphic position of Lafleur (1940a, 1940b, 1941a, 1941b) who uses such terms as 'helpfulness' when speaking of ant behaviour. But there is clearly an immense field waiting to be exploited by ethological research and experiment. The surface of the field has as yet hardly been scratched, and we are far more ignorant still about the closely comparable societies of the Termites.

(a) The Army Ants (Dorylinæ)

It is of course a commonplace that anyone who studies the behaviour of ants will see and read of much which superficially suggests insight-

learning of a high order; for instance, the nesting and foraging activities
of the Army Ants (*Dorylinæ*). Yet most workers on the taxonomy of ants
place the Dorylines near the bottom of the family tree, and it is a fact
that, considered from the point of view of general anatomy and the structure of the sense organs, the individuals of the Doryline colonies are of a
very low grade; even though, as a result of their instinctive equipment,
so highly co-operative socially. Readers of that naturalists' classic *The
Naturalist in Nicaragua* (1874) may recall the passage where Thomas
Belt so graphically describes experiments on the deliberate rescue of
trapped workers, the rapid and apparently purposive transmission of information and the extraordinary appearance of ingenuity with which the
army ant, *Eciton hamatum*, will construct living bridges, made up of the
stretched and interlocked bodies of the workers themselves, across obstacles such as streams. That some at least of the seemingly marvellous
powers of concerted action in overcoming obstacles can be described without recourse to the concept of insight-learning has, however, been demonstrated by Schneirla (1933*b*, 1934*a*, 1938, 1940, 1949, 1950), and by Lutz
(1929), and their conclusions seem applicable with little difficulty to many
other examples of elaborate ant behaviour (e.g. Turner, 1907*b*). Thus it
is shown that the alternation of nomadic and sedentary behaviour in
Eciton hamatum depends on the state of the brood, and so ultimately
upon the physiological condition of the queen (Schneirla, 1938). The
raiding of *E. burchelli* (Schneirla, 1940) is initiated through photokinesis,
and its form and type are governed primarily by the inherited behaviour
pattern (the 'rebound pattern') of the individual.

Individual learning (habituation and association) makes a minor though
essential contribution. The concepts of 'pressure' and 'drainage' as applied
to the ant population, coupled with the transmission, based on topo-
chemical sensitivity, of a generalised excitement through the colony (see
also Eidmann, 1927, and Goetsch, 1934) account for a great deal, and it
seems fairly certain that there are no individuals specialised or trained
for leadership nor any highly articulate 'language' such as that of the bee.
Thus raiding columns may set out at random in various directions. The
foragers of those columns which are successful in finding prey cause
excitement among their nest mates as a result of their own excited actions
and because of the booty they are carrying; and this excitement means
that more recruits attach themselves to the successful columns, while the
unsuccessful ones come to be more and more neglected and so dwindle
away. In the army-ant world nothing succeeds like success and nothing
fails like failure. In the advancing swarm the 'lead' arises through the
function of the entire group, all individuals making essentially similar
contributions to 'leadership' under equivalent conditions.

Vowles (unpublished) describes how the *Eciton hamatum*, when foraging, normally proceeds by a series of alternate left and right swings, the path between each swing being more or less straight. This behaviour seems to be innate, but the insect has to adapt it in relation to its own odour trail and when meeting the trail has to learn to cease its normal rhythmic change of direction. It appears also that *Eciton* can learn to recognise the polarisation of its odour trails, possibly through a recognition of the greater concentration of odour nearer the bivouac (Schneirla, *loc. cit.*).

(b) *The Higher Ants (Myrmicinæ and Formicinæ), the Wasps (Vespidæ) and the Bees (Apidæ)*

That learning capacity of a fairly high order must be involved in the orientation of some species of the higher ants has long been evident from the observations of many workers who have studied the insects foraging under natural conditions. Probably in the Amazon Ants (the obligatory slave-makers) the raiding organisation resembles that of the Dorylines. Dobrzanski and Dobrzanska (1960) have shown that in *Polyergus rufescens* if what appear to be exploring individuals are removed from the ground near the nest before noon, it has no effect on the raids of the Amazons. However, other individuals come out of the nest about an hour before the beginning of the raid and by their excitation provoke others to emerge in a mass and commence their aggression. This mass of ants immediately goes forward to the attack in the direction where most of the activators are concentrated; but if most of the individual activators are withdrawn before the mass comes out, then the raid will not take place. Once, however, the attack is well under way it progresses without the guidance of any particular ants, and at this stage removal of the head of the column has no influence on the course of the raid; indeed, just as in the Army Ants, there are no individuals consistently leading the columns. Sudd (1960b), working on Pharaoh's Ant, *Monomorium pharaonis*, found that foraging workers oriented to scent marks on the ground laid by other workers when they were returning to the nest after finding food. When a successful forager arrived in the nest, it activated a small group of workers which, being thus recruited, followed the trail of scent laid by the scout, themselves reinforcing the new scent on their return. However, recruits were not informed by the scout of the nature of the food to which they were recruited, nor of its distance from the nest. When they were running on a system of branch trails, the branches they took appeared to be decided by chance, although abandoned trails which no longer led to food tended to be ignored, apparently owing to the fading scent in the absence of successful foragers to reinforce it. All scouts leave the nest along a route so that the distribution of scouts is related to the finds of food in the past. Dobrzanska (1958) concludes that in species of ants which have a definite division of the foraging grounds, no information is conveyed concerning the nature of the prey discovered. On the other hand, species without partition of foraging grounds possess a precise system of information. On this basis it is assumed that there are at least two forms of adaptation to social foraging. In some species this adaptation consists of a definite partition of foraging grounds, in other species which have no permanent partition the individual which discovers prey notifies other workers of the fact.

The well-established ability of the individual worker to straighten her path with experience, to avoid long detours in favour of a more efficient path from one point to another, and to eliminate excess back tracking, all point to the conclusion that ants should prove quick and capable at learning mazes, and the pioneer investigations of Turner (1907a) and of Schneirla (1929, 1933a, 1933b) have shown that this is so. The extreme of maze complexity which can be mastered by exceptionally capable individuals of *Formica incerta* is shown in Fig. 33. The

Food-place

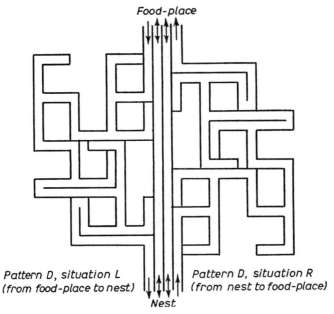

Pattern D, situation L
(from food-place to nest)

Pattern D, situation R
(from nest to food-place)

Nest

FIG. 33—Maze used by Schneirla (1933) in the investigation of ant learning.

performance of a 'fairly successful' individual of *F. incerta* in this maze is shown by the learning curve in Fig. 34. That the light-compass method of orientation is of prime importance in the direction-finding of ants, as well as other homing Hymenoptera, has been clear since the experiments of Brun (1914), and the fact that the ants follow 'odour trails' has been known since the work of Bonnet (1779–83). But the great merit of Turner's and Schneirla's experiments was that they first made clear the relation between visual, olfactory and other clues in ant learning. Thus the direction of the light rays is effective for orientation whenever the differential aspect is marked enough; but when this is not the case, or when visual control is made unstable, other factors become more important. Thus the more often the direction of illumination is changed the less reliable it

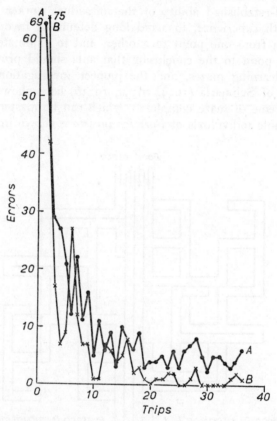

FIG. 34—Learning curve for a fairly successful performance of *Formica incerta* in a complex maze. (Schneirla, 1933.)
A = outward trip to food place.
B = return trip to nest.

becomes as an orienting factor, and the more the unchanged features are relied upon, and other senses, e.g. olfactory, tactile and kinæsthetic, are brought into play. There is prompt recovery when original conditions of illumination are restored.

The maze shown in Fig. 33 is so designed as to provide both direct and alternative routes on both the outward and return journeys of foraging ants, and the right-hand half of the maze is a replica of the left. The ant can thus be set an identical maze problem either (1) on the outward or on the return journey alone (separate situation learning), or (2) on both together (combination problem), or (3) one after the other (successive presentation problem). It is found that the ant learns the pattern much more readily when returning to the nest carrying food than it does

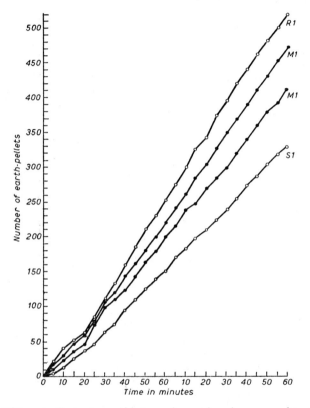

FIG. 35—Different effect of a rapid co-worker and a slow co-worker on the nest-building activity (carrying of food pellets) of the ant *Camponotus japonicus v. aterrinus*.
R 1 = a rapid worker.
S 1 = a slow worker.
M 1 = a medium worker.
(After Chen, 1938.)

if faced with it on the outward journey. The complete combination problem (DR + DL, Fig. 33) proved too difficult for the ants to solve fully, though one individual ant made very remarkable progress in it. In this relatively complex situation there is no evidence for transfer of training, for the problem of the return route is attacked essentially as though it were a new one. (Cf. Free (1958) for work on honey-bees and Free and Butler (1959) for a summary of the situation in bumble bees.) As will be seen later, this evidence of the independence of orientation on the outward and on the return journey receives some support from the work of Opfinger (1931) and Hannes (1930) on the foraging flights of bees, and is best considered in connection with the problem of homing.

The direction-finding of the 'higher' ants has been the subject of a good deal of precise study in recent years by techniques other than that of the maze, and much of this work links up very closely with the earlier work on the maze learning of ants just described. In particular, much new information on the nature and use of odour trails has come to light.

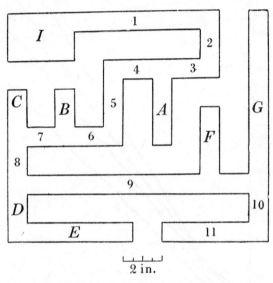

FIG. 36—Maze used by Turner (1913) in training cockroaches.
I = platform on which the animal is placed.
C = goal (i.e. point of entry of home cage).
The numerals 1–7 indicate the direct passageway to C.
Other letters and numerals denote blind alleys.

As Carthy (1950) has shown, workers of *Acanthomyops fuliginosus* which have foraged successfully produce an odour trail consisting of a series of spots of anal secretion caused by the lowering of the abdomen on to the ground at regular intervals during the return journey. In some species the trails are individual, each ant responding only to its own deposits (*Formica*), while in the genera *Lasius, Tapinoma, Pheidole* and *Solenopsis* the trail is specific to the colony (see Vowles, 1955). These various trails are also polarised, for each spot is drawn out, by the locomotion of the ant, to form a greatly extended triangle; but although *M. ruginodis* can recognise the directional properties of a single odour spot (MacGregor, 1948), there seems no good evidence in support of the earlier statements that ants are able to recognise the polarisation of the trail as a whole (Vowles, 1955). When using the sun for direction-finding it is clear that many insects and particularly ants (in that they are relatively slow moving) must steadily change their conditioning to the sun's position during the course of a prolonged run. Since it is probable that the nest odour is identical with trail odour and, as with *Apis* (being presumably dependent on food supply), is changing slowly, we have good grounds for assuming that an associative learning process is also concerned in the development of the power of following an odour trail; but exactly how this learning takes place is not known. Eidmann (1927) found that the return of a successful forager of *Myrmica rubra lævinodis* released generalised excitement in other workers, presumably by chemical stimulation, but that the newly excited workers were ready to follow odour trails to any kind of food which was available. Once they have started to forage, however, they become conditioned to the particular kind of food they have found and cannot for the time being be deflected. Both Heyde (1924) and Schneirla (1934) have shown that in the Formicinæ both soliciting for and regurgitation of nectar involve a strong element of associative learning, the basal releasers being extremely simple tactile stimuli.

While there is no good evidence that any individuals in an ant colony are regular or permanent leaders, it is known from the work of Chen (1938a and b) that a form of social facilitation or social motivation occurs in the ant *Camponotus japonicus*, so that those ants which are for the time being more active are temporary leaders. It was found that all the workers can build nests in isolation, but the work varies with individuals, and that ants that were working in association were quicker in starting work after commencement of an experiment and performed a greater amount of work than they did singly. Ants which were in association worked more uniformly and a rapid co-worker has an accelerating effect (Fig. 35), but this is modified by the fact that the accelerating effect of association is greater for the slow worker than for the rapid ones, so that the average effect of association is to increase speed. It is particularly interesting that the effect is not simply a mass one, as is shown by the fact that the company of one fast-working ant is as effective as the company of a group. Thus the leaders at any one time tend to be the more active and quicker workers, though they are at the same time less cohesive just because they are more 'enterprising,' as is shown by the fact that they work in a greater variety of sites where nest building is required. (Note also the work of Dobrzanska (1958) referred to on p. 244 above.)

The fact that ants can use, alternatively or in combination, a number of senses during orientation has been commented on by both MacGregor (1948) and Carthy (1951). The latter shows that not only is vision employed as in the light compass orientation but also the plane of polarisation may be perceived and utilised, and Vowles (1950) had previously shown ants to be sensitive to polarised light. The ability to master complex mazes indicates that ants have the powers to co-ordinate a series of

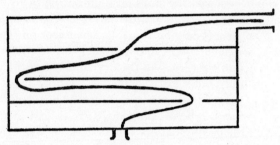

FIG. 37—Simple maze used by Eldering (1919) for training *Periplaneta*.

directional perceptions into a whole; but no critical latent-learning experiments appear to have been done with such ants, and there is as yet no clear evidence that the ant is building up its varied sense impressions into a unitary perception for orientation to the degree and in the manner

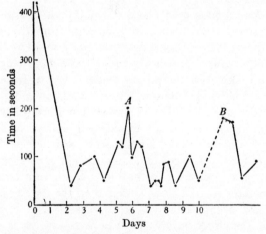

FIG. 38—Learning curve of *Periplaneta*. (After Eldering, 1919.)
(Mean of 5 animals):
A = box turned through 90°.
B = after lapse of one month without training.

which is so well established for the higher aculeates. Schneirla, after having shown (1941) the significance of habituation in the maze learning of ants, followed this by pointing out (1943) the importance of associative processes at each choice point; but he has not so far published the promised study of the integration of maze learning.

Bees and wasps have also been taught to master mazes with from eight to eleven choice points. Colour differences were found to provide valuable cues (Weiss, 1953.)

The only insects other than Hymenoptera which have been taught to run complex mazes are cockroaches, *Periplaneta orientalis* L. (Turner, 1913) and *P. americana* (Eldering, 1919). The maze used by Turner in his training of *Periplaneta orientalis* is shown in Fig. 36. Eldering's results are indicated by Figs. 37 and 38. Both Turner and Eldering comment on the great individual variation in learning ability displayed, a variation that seems to have no relation to age; and similar variation in ant learning ability is described by Schneirla. While various senses may be used, the sense of touch seems by far the most important in the maze learning of the cockroach. Eldering shows that the maze-running habit is not destroyed by narcosis. Two examples of Turner's learning curve for the cockroach are shown in Fig. 39.

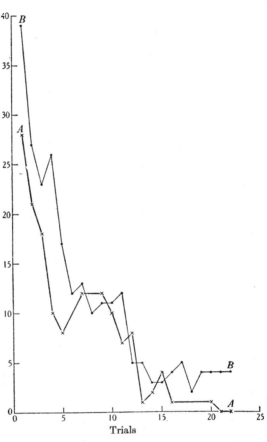

FIG. 39—Learning curve of cockroach. (After Turner, 1913.)
A = total errors.
B = time in minutes required to run maze.
Each curve represents average of 10 cockroaches.

LATENT OR EXPLORATORY LEARNING

As has been argued in Chapter V, it is convenient provisionally to consider those aspects of orientation involving the perceptual organisation of landmarks and other stimuli which the animal achieves in becoming familiar with a territory under the heading 'latent learning.' But before coming to field studies and experiments on such orientation in Arthropods, it will be helpful to consider a simple laboratory version of what seems to be essentially the same process.

The Ichneumonid *Nemeritis canescens* has been mentioned above in connection with studies in habituation. It is parasitic on the larva of *Ephestia kühniella* (Zella) (Lepidoptera). When seeking out these larvæ for oviposition, the parasite is apparently guided entirely by its sense of smell. Although these insects are not naturally responsive to the odour of other related lepidopterous larvæ, experiments using an olfactometer of the McIndoo type (Thorpe and Jones, 1937; Thorpe, 1938) have shown that the females of *Nemeritis canescens* can be rendered positively responsive to the odour of the host larva of strange species (e.g. *Meliphora grisella*; Lepidoptera) either by rearing them artificially upon it or by exposing them, shortly after emergence as adults, to an air stream bearing the odour of the larva, without actual contact being allowed.

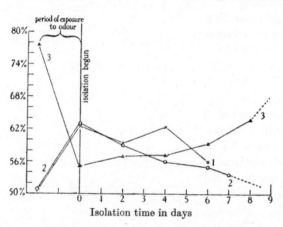

Fig. 40—Curves showing habituation and latent learning in *Nemeritis*. Curves 1 and 2 show latent learning by *Nemeritis* resulting from exposure to the odour of *Meliphora* larvæ; results expressed as percentage attraction to the odour, before and after exposure:
(1) period of preliminary exposure, 48 hours;
(2) period of preliminary exposure, 6 days.
Curve 3 shows habituation of *Nemeritis* to odour of cedar-wood oil expressed as percentage repelled before and after exposure. (After Thorpe, 1938.)

Fig. 40 shows that when tested in a 'Y tube' olfactometer, the odour of *Ephestia* larvæ being carried down one arm and an uncontaminated air stream down the other, the positive response of approximately 85 per cent. is shown to the *Ephestia* odour. In a similar test in which instead of *Ephestia* the larvæ of *Meliphora grisella*, the small wax moth, are used the distribution is random and there is no significant difference between the numbers in each arm. If we now rear on the *Meliphora* and repeat the above test with the odour of that insect in one air stream and the other uncontaminated, we find a significant majority of approximately 66 per cent. goes to the baited side. Yet if these same insects are given the alternative *Meliphora* in one arm and *Ephestia* in the other, approximately 65–66 per cent. will go to the *Ephestia* side in preference to the host on which they have been reared. Nevertheless, if these same insects, either before or after their first testing to *Meliphora*, are given the alternative between an *Ephestia*-baited and an uncontaminated air stream, 85 per cent. will again go to *Ephestia*. It is thus clear that there is an innate positive response to the odour of *Ephestia*, which seems to be maintained irrespective of the host on which the larvæ have developed; but rearing them on a strange host, in this case *Meliphora*, while it does not affect the attractiveness of *Ephestia* when there is no alternative, significantly reduces, but does not completely counterbalance, the innate attraction of that insect when the *Meliphora* is applied as a counter-attraction.

At first sight some might be inclined to the view that this is merely another example of habituation; the insect having become 'used to' the presence of an odour responds by an increased rate of change of direction on its removal, and so appears in the olfactometer to 'choose' the odour. But a moment's reflection will show that such an explanation has an apparent simplicity which is in fact specious. The theory in reality involves an extension of the concept of habituation to cover complex phenomena of a very different nature, and thus entirely robs the term of its original meaning. The essence of habituation is the waning of an inherited or pre-existing response. In this experiment, however, we start out with no response, *Nemeritis* being totally indifferent to the odour of *Meliphora*. What requires explanation here is the building up, by some process other than simple association, of a new response from zero, not the waning of a pre-existing response, and clearly habituation cannot apply in such a case. Nor does it appear possible to hold a mixed-odour hypothesis, in the sense outlined above for the *Drosophila*-peppermint experiments, since it appears extremely improbable that *Meliphora* larvæ would give off an odour that is actually repellent or irritant. Still more improbable is it that the attractant and irritant odours should be so exactly balanced as to give consistently neutral effects over a very large number of experiments (see Thorpe and Jones, 1937, Tables III, IV and XII; and Thorpe, 1938, Tables I, VIIId and XII). How, then, can this result be accounted for?

Experiments of this kind with insects undergoing complete metamorphosis raise two quite different problems. Firstly, the question of the nature of the conditioning or learning process, whether it is truly latent or exploratory learning or whether it is in some way rewarded; and secondly they raise the problem of what we may call pre-imaginal conditioning: that is, a conditioning effect carried over from the parasitic larval stage to the free-living adult stage. If adult *Nemeritis* reared from the host *Ephestia* are confined immediately on emergence in an apparatus through which is pumped a stream of air which has passed over a number of living *Meliphora* larvæ, we find (Fig. 40) that there is still a significant positive effect when the animals are tested in the olfactometer with the alternative *Meliphora* odour. It will be seen that six days' exposure to the odour in this way results in a positive response of 62 per cent., slightly but significantly lower than that from the insects which have been actu-ally reared on the new host. In this case the conditions have been such that all possibility of direct association between the odour of the host and the insect have been ruled out. There has been simply no opportunity for the establishment of a conditioned response of the ordinary classical type, and there can hardly be any reward other than that of a more complete per-ceptual organisation of the stimuli coming from the environment. These experiments, then, suggest that there is a post-imaginal latent learning which makes by far the biggest contribution to the effect, and also a pre-imaginal conditioning or learning of lesser significance. Fig. 41 shows the results of the same kind of experiment using the fly *Drosophila*. This has the advantage that it can be reared in an artificial medium, and so any pre-imaginal conditioning effect is much more amenable to control than with an endoparasite. In a series of experiments insects were reared from a medium containing 0·5 per cent. peppermint. Control insects which have not encountered peppermint in the medium show, when tested fresh from culture, a distaste for the odour such that only 35 per cent. invade the arm of the olfactometer in a standard test with the alternative air stream uncontaminated. In contrast, those which have had previous experience of the odour show a well-marked positive response of approximately 70 per cent. (column IIa). This conditioning effect, which again can be considered as latent learning or at least transference of training (since the adults in the olfactometer experiment are under food satiation) varied with the lapse of time in the same manner as was found with the previous experiments (columns IIb–d). If we now rear the insects on the peppermint-containing medium but wash the pupa in distilled water and isolate them and then test the adult on emergence, we find a slight positive attraction for the peppermint (column III). If we wash them when larvæ instead of pupæ the proportion is slightly but not significantly higher still (column IV), and if we rear the insects on the normal medium without peppermint but expose them in the same manner as described above for the *Nemeritis* for two to five days upon emergence, we get a response of 66 per cent. (column V), which is significantly higher than column III. Similar effects can be obtained (Crombie, 1944) with the blow-flies *Lucilia* and *Calliphora*. With these insects we have the additional assurance that conditioning is not due to some flaw in the experimental procedure such that there is some accidental association between the stimulus and the food reinforcement, since they are in a post-feeding or non-feeding phase; yet even during that time it is possible to condition them. It seems, then, that these results as a whole provide strong evidence for a latent learning of olfactory stimuli which can take place

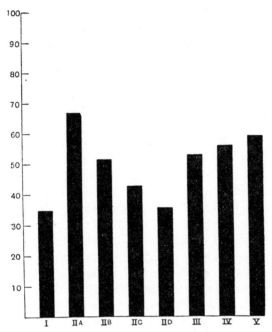

FIG. 41—A diagram to summarise result of experiments with *Drosophila melanogaster* Mg (Wild type 'Oregon R') when tested in an olfactometer with the odour of peppermint as bait. Height of columns indicates percentage of *Drosophila* attracted to the odour of:

I: Insects reared from normal medium and tested fresh from culture.

II: Insects reared from medium containing 0·5 per cent. peppermint. A, tested fresh from culture. B, tested after 1–2 days' isolation. C, tested after 3–4 days' isolation. D, tested after 6 days' isolation.

III: Insects reared from medium containing 0·5 per cent. peppermint. Pupæ are washed in distilled water and isolated, tested upon emergence.

IV: Same as III except that insects washed as fully-fledged larvæ.

V: Insects reared on normal medium but adults exposed to vapour of peppermint for 2–5 days immediately upon emergence.

(After Thorpe, 1939.)

both in the larval and adult stage and which can be transferred to a very slight extent from the larval stage through the adult; in other words, a pre-imaginal learning. It is certainly remarkable that a learning process can be carried through from one stage to another in this way and can survive the intervening pupal period of tissue reorganisation and growth. It must, however, be remembered that the nervous system is, of all the systems of the insect's body, least subject to sudden histolysis and rapid pupal reorganisation, and that, in fact, the nervous system changes from the larval type to the adult type by a series of relatively slight steps. There is no reason for thinking, therefore, that the training effect has to survive a period of *complete* nervous disintegration and reorganisation. That such pre-imaginal conditioning is not confined to olfactory stimulation and is not peculiar to latent learning has been shown by the remarkable results of Borell du Vernay (1942). This author found that it was possible to train both larvæ and adults of the Mealworm beetle, *Tenebrio molitor*, to take a right or left turn in a 'T' maze using a slight shock as reinforcement. In a number of her experiments several trained larvæ were used later as adults, and it was found that these gave better results than the average. There seemed little doubt that there was some carry-over of the learning of this simple habit from the larva to the adult. It is, however, not at all clear what element or elements in the learning process were in fact transmitted. The learning of even the simplest of mazes involves, as we have seen, sensitisation to the experimental conditions, learning to perceive cues such as texture which may perhaps be significant, as well as learning a correct response—in fact, quite an elaborate instrumental or trial-and-error conditioning. It would be a considerable undertaking, though one likely to yield interesting results, to determine, with an insect such as this, all the factors in such a complex learning task which are in fact involved in the retention of the traces of the larval habit by the adult. It is perhaps interesting to recall that there are cases on record (e.g. the Colorado Beetle, *L. decemlineata*) where a behaviour rhythm impressed in the larval stage by a periodic exposure to light and darkness or by a particular feeding rhythm can be to some extent retained in the adult phase (Grison, 1943). For a fuller discussion of this and many other aspects of behaviour co-ordination in this species, see Grison (1957).

Coming now to field observations and experiments on latent learning in orientation: We find that in insects, as in many other invertebrate animals, there are exhibited traces of ability to return to a particular 'home' locality or territory, and this is most often associated with the care of the offspring. In some instances it is possible that the homing faculty depends on no more elaborate sensory mechanism than that involved in simple taxes or light-compass reactions. Nevertheless, it is certain that in a large number of examples this is inadequate and that we have a true place memory. This ability to remain in and to return to a territory certainly occurs in the higher crustacea, e.g. the Fiddler Crabs, *Uca* sp. (Verwey, 1930), and probably also in the Rock Lobster, *Palinurus*. It is also shown in varying degrees by insects of many different grades of organisation, and is by no means confined to those which have elaborate nesting habits or a highly developed social life. Thus the Burying Beetles

(*Necrophorus*) are truly territorial (Pukowski, 1933), and the (at times) gregarious but non-social butterfly *Heliconius charithonia* returns nightly to a roosting-place which appears to be apprehended by a series of landmarks and not found merely by a simple direct orientation to some obvious feature of the landscape (Jones, 1930, 1931). There are various other examples among insects of gregarious sleeping habits (see Rau, 1916) which may well be found to involve orientation responses of a similar type. It seems that exploratory learning of this kind is also involved in the orientation of dragon-flies (*Odonata*), with their highly developed compound eyes and extremely acute vision; although recent work suggests (Moore, 1952) that dragon-flies are, contrary to what has often been thought, not truly territorial insects, and that the observed restriction of individuals to certain hunting 'beats' is a result of a learning to avoid the sites of previous encounters with rival males which they cannot innately distinguish from females. By a series of simple but elegant experiments, Darchen (1952, 1957, 1959) has investigated and quantified the response to novelty of the cockroach *Blatella germanica* during its exploratory learning of an arena.

It is when we come to the higher Hymenoptera, *Sphegidæ*, or digger wasps, the *Psammocharidæ*, or spider hunters, and the truly social bees, wasps and ants, that orientation behaviour is seen at its highest pitch. So much has been written summarising the earlier work on the direction-finding of these insects, and summaries are so easily accessible in standard text-books, that it will suffice to say that it seems generally established that under natural conditions the return journey to the nest falls into three fairly well demarcated sections. Firstly, there is the departure from the food place in the correct direction; secondly, the location of the nest-site or environment of the nest as a whole; and thirdly, the recognition of the nest itself. As many observers have pointed out, the first part of the journey may be different from the rest in that at the start the nest is often out of sight and, in fact, cannot be perceived at all. It is now evident that the preliminary orientation at the commencement of the return is not due to any mysterious 'direction sense,' but (Cornetz, 1911) depends on stimulation received on the outward journey. The light-compass reaction or more complex visual cues are in certain instances essential for the right start of the return trip just as they are for its completion, even though the goal may be well out of sight; and kinæsthetic sense also undoubtedly plays a large part. As an example of the flight orientation of the Hymenoptera, the work of Tinbergen and Kruyt (1938) and of van Beusekom (1948) on the Digger wasp, *Philanthus*, may be cited. This is a wasp which catches honey-bees, which are paralysed and then brought to a previously constructed burrow, made in sandy soil, for storage as food for the larvæ. It is easy to carry out experiments on the orientation of such insects by altering the immediate landscape—moving stones, fir cones, twigs, etc.—while the wasp is away on a foraging flight or, alternatively, while it is inside its burrow. As a result of a long series of experiments, it was found that in establishing its orientation to the hole, *Philanthus* prefers to use flat, segmented objects rather than flat, unsegmented objects of the same size. It prefers three-dimensional to flat objects and nearer rather than farther objects of the same size. It was, moreover, noticed that there was a tendency to orientate by more distant rather than nearer objects which subtend the same visual angle, and also that objects which were present on the first flight after, for example, a period of quiescence due to rainy weather, were more readily used for guidance than objects placed in position later; although the position of these can be quickly learnt and their bearing readily used for later direction-finding. These results on the preferences for distant rather than nearer objects of the same apparent size confirms the general conclusions arrived at from the study of a great variety of lower animals that the visual activity of such forms is dominated by cues from remote objects rather than by cues from near ones, and is explicable on the ground that the more remote objects provide the most stable and constant stimuli which come from the environment. The same principle is found to hold even with the mammals—as Hebb (1949, p. 92) points out. The work of Tinbergen *et al.* was significant in other respects also. Thus it was found that the qualities of a single element of the landmark complex are used to a greater degree after longer training than after shorter. That is to say, the first learning of the environment seems to involve a response in some way to a whole, and that with longer experience an increasing segmentation or articulation of the perceptual field is brought about. This is in line with many earlier studies on the orientation of such insects, and the observations of Adlerz (1900–9), Bouvier (1901), Buttel-Reepen (1907), Friedländer (1931), Rabaud (1924, 1926), Turner (1908) and Wolf (1926–7, 1930) all emphasise the first importance of the general pattern of the site as a whole. The nature of the gestalt perception involved in the orientation of a digger wasp has been investigated particularly thoroughly by van Beusekom (1948) also working with *Philanthus*. He found that the wasp orientates in the first place to a 'nest-hole + a particular configuration of landmarks.' He contrived the situation so that the immediate landmarks were objects, such as fir cones, which were arranged in simple configurations and could easily be moved and exchanged for other objects of similar size. It then became clear that the configuration was the dominant factor, and that the wasp would tolerate great variation in the nature and number of the elements of which the configuration was composed, provided the configuration itself was not altered in any essential manner and provided the number of elements was not so greatly reduced as to result in the actual break-up of the pattern (Fig. 42).

Tinbergen has also found that when the training marks are moved so that the *Philanthus* might be expected to show complete disorientation, it will suddenly utilise new landmarks completely unrelated to the previous orientation marks on which it had apparently been trained—a result which has interesting and suggestive similarity to Krechevsky's work on hypothesis in maze learning. Another feature of the visual orientation of the Hymenoptera which strikes almost all observers who have studied hunting wasps or a hive of honey-bees is the extreme rapidity with which a new arrangement of landmarks near the nest can be learnt. Tinbergen found that if the arrangement of training marks was altered drastically while the insect was down its hole, a single orientation flight of 9 seconds was sufficient to impress all the essential details of the new situation on the animal, and that the learning resulting from this single brief experience of flying in gradually widening curves and circles round the spot would be retained for many hours without further practice and even in exceptional cases for two or three days.

The problem encountered by some of the spider- and caterpillar-hunting wasps is even greater than that which *Philanthus* has to face. *Philanthus* can carry its prey in flight directly to its previously constructed hole, but some other insects have to drag the prey some distance. Some of them, such as *Pompilius plumbeus* cited by Adlerz (1906), quickly dig a small pit in the general neighbourhood of their burrow in which they put the spider prey and, after scratching some sand over it, leave it while they search for the hole and prepare it to receive the victim. Many such examples lead us imperceptibly to what we may consider as insight learning. *Ammophila* hunts caterpillars which are too heavy to be brought back on the wing, and which may thus have to be dragged for a hundred yards or more across and through every imaginable natural obstacle. When doing this the insects are extremely intent upon their work and pay little or no attention to the experimenter. Here the original learning of the territory has probably been in the main effected by observation from the air, and yet the return has to be made on foot. Although the insect may from time to time leave her prey and take short survey flights, this is by no means invariable (Thorpe, 1950), and quite often the wasp seems able to maintain orientation while on the ground as a result of earlier aerial reconnaissance. It is, of course, not easy to be certain that the terrain has never been previously explored on foot as well as from the air, and it is true that a great deal of apparently random exploratory wandering is shown by members of this genus (Thorpe, 1943). But in so far as the insect has appreciated the lay-out of the area as a result of aerial observation and can then utilise this 'plan' while on the ground, we seem to have an orientation ability of extra-

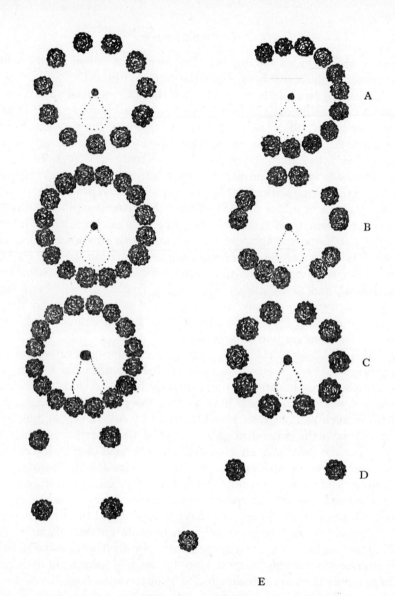

FIG. 42—Experiments on the pattern perception of the wasp *Philanthus triangulum*. The wasp is first trained to locate its nest by a 'landmark' consisting of a circle of 16 fir cones.

A: A tenuous ring of 11 cones is preferred to an incomplete ring of 11.

B and C: A tenuous ring is as good as a full ring provided the gaps are not too big.

D: A ring of 4 is preferred to a 'ring' of 2, or

E: A 'ring' of 3.

Although less than 4 fir cones does not count as a ring, the insect is responding to the configuration in preference to the elements which compose it. (After van Beusekom, 1948.)

ordinarily high type. In such a situation the light-compass orientation is no doubt largely responsible for maintaining direction on the ground, while the air surveys may serve the purpose of relating the direction of the sun's rays to the main landmarks. Molitor (1937) rather surprisingly concludes, however, that light-compass orientation plays little or no part in the direction-finding of *Sphegidæ*.

For a long time after the work of W. Köhler (1921) it was customary, particularly among those who considered themselves as members of the gestalt school, to regard the ability of an animal to make an immediate detour round an obstacle freshly placed in its path without any overt trial-and-error behaviour, as clear evidence of insight in the original sense in which Köhler himself used the term. It is no longer possible to regard detour behaviour, however perfect, as a conclusive criterion of insight. In fact, the performance of making a detour and the power of controlled aiming at moving targets, by means of a process of continuous optic feedback, have much in common. The latter ability has been beautifully analysed by Mittelstaedt (1957) in the case of Mantids. Nevertheless, it is

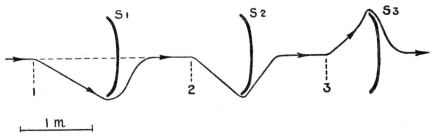

FIG. 43—Diagram to show course taken by an individual of *A. pubescens*, engaged in dragging its prey towards its nest, when confronted on three successive occasions with an obstacle in the form of a metal screen. The numbers 1, 2 and 3 indicate the position of the insect at the moment at which the screen is put into position and S_1, S_2 and S_3 the successive positions of the screen on these three occasions. (After Thorpe, 1950b.)

interesting to see that detour behaviour by the higher Hymenoptera [1] in response to experimentally inserted obstacles has been observed by Adlerz (1900–9) in *Anoplius fuscus* (Psammocharidæ), Turner (1912) in 'Sphex sp.' and by Thorpe (1950) in *Ammophila pubescens*. In this last instance a curved metal screen approximately 50 by 120 centimetres was placed 2 or 3 feet in front of an insect engaged in dragging its prey back towards the nest (Fig. 43). Without a moment's pause to investigate and without displaying the slightest disorientation, the insect diverged just enough to carry it round the obstacle on a perfectly smooth, even course of maximum economy of effort. On one particular occasion the ex-

[1] Heil (1936. *Z. vergl. Physiol.*, 23) has described spontaneous detour behaviour in jumping spiders such as *Evarcha blancardi*, etc.

periment was immediately repeated twice with the same results, but the third time the insect walked straight at the screen, climbed with perfect ease to the top and, without ever letting go of its caterpillar, flew down to the ground on the other side and continued its journey. On subsequent occasions this insect would adopt now one type of behaviour, now another, but in no instance did she ever show trial-and-error. The solution to the problem was always smooth, unhesitating and economical.

This and other individuals which behaved in the same way were then caught and transported in a dark box to a new site, a process taking less than a minute. On release the insect might have been expected to be at least momentarily disorientated. On the contrary, it appeared quite unperturbed, and without any orientation flight set out at once on its new course (Fig. 44). It was again given the detour test three times on its new course, but it reacted as efficiently as before and within a few minutes had arrived exactly on its nest—which was quite invisible to the human eye—opened it and dragged in its caterpillar. Similar experiments with another insect gave identical results (Fig. 45). Although the insects do, on occasion, show some evidence of disorientation, nevertheless the overwhelming impression given (as also recorded by Baerends (1941) and other workers) was one of almost uncanny knowledge of the details of the terrain.

The only other clear instances of homing behaviour in insects which need mention are those of certain aquatic Hemiptera and Coleoptera. Thus the aquatic surface-living Gyrinid beetles, even though describing their whirling courses apparently at random on the flowing water, maintain a constant general position by means—it seems—of visual perception of the pattern of objects on adjacent banks. Since the pattern of visual stimulation is constantly changing with the movement of the beetles, this seems to be essentially a homing reaction. It has been shown that the same 'flotilla' of beetles may occupy an identical location for the whole of a season or even from one year to the next. How far the orientation is to a pattern of objects apprehended as a whole is, however, not quite clear. Brown and Hatch (1929) state that the beetles are completely disorientated if a sudden change in landmarks is made. A simpler instance is provided by *Notonecta* (Schulz, 1931) which, in a flowing stream, can keep its head to the current and remain stationary by swimming in such a manner that its visual impressions are kept constant. In so far as such behaviour is merely the compensation for change in stimulation of the ommatidia, it can be correctly regarded as an example of light-compass orientation (menotaxis). However, there seems little doubt that in some cases more complex orientation is involved.

Much new evidence as to the latent-learning abilities of these homing insects has been provided by the work of Baerends (1941) on *Ammophila*

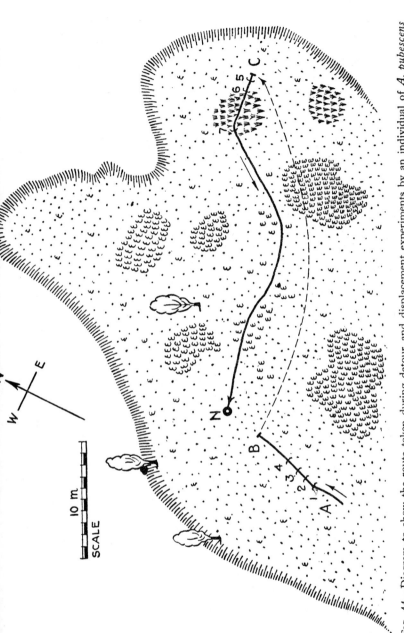

Fig. 44—Diagram to show the route taken during detour and displacement experiments by an individual of *A. pubescens* engaged in dragging its prey towards the nest. Heavy line indicates course of insect. A = point at which first observed. Numbers 1–4 indicate points at which metal screen placed in its path for detour tests. B = point at which insect captured. Broken line indicates transfer of insect in box to release point C. Numbers 5–7 indicate further detour experiments. N = nest. The shading indicates a slight depression in an area of gravelly heath land with small patches and scattered plants of *Erica* and *Calluna* indicated by the symbol 'ε' and with small birch trees (*Betula*) about 4–6 feet high indicated by the conventional tree symbol. The remaining symbol indicates tussocks of *Juncus*, etc. Conditions: Bright sunshine. Noon. July 27, 1947. Eversley Heath, Berkshire. Time taken by insect approximately 15 minutes. (After Thorpe, 1950b.)

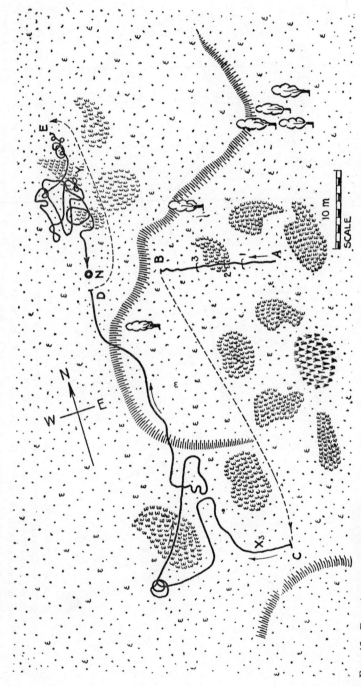

FIG. 45—Experiments similar to those shown in Fig. 44 with another individual. Legend and symbols as Fig. 44. Capture points, B and D. Release points, C and E. Numbers 1–3 indicate points of detour tests. X_3 = site of a group of three short survey flights. Y_1 = site of a single survey flight. Conditions: Bright sunshine. Time 13.30. July 27, 1947. Eversley Heath, Berkshire. Time taken by insect on its routes—A to D, 20 minutes; E to N, 15 minutes. (After Thorpe, 1950b.)

adriaanse (*campestris*) (already partly described in Chapter V above) and by that of Lindauer (1952) on the honey-bee. The new advances made by these workers depended on the working out of a technique for marking individual insects and observing their behaviour as individuals over a long period of time. Long before this technique was developed, Adlerz (1900–9) had suggested, as a result of his thorough field observations in Sweden, that each female of *Ammophila* might be able to look after two or more nests at the same time, and he was impressed by the interest which such females showed in the activity of neighbouring members of the species. Baerends found that the process of making and provisioning each nest falls into three well-defined stages. The nest burrow itself, which consists of a vertical shaft about 2½ centimetres long with an ovoid cell at the bottom, is first made. This task having been completed, the shaft is temporarily closed by loosely filling in the entrance with small stones or pieces of earth. After an absence of perhaps a few hours the wasp returns, carrying the paralysed caterpillar. She deposits it near the entrance, opens the nest, carries the larva down and lays an egg. She then closes the nest with much more care than before; so expert is this closure that when completed it is virtually impossible for the human eye to distinguish the entrance from the surroundings. This second closure completes the first phase of what we may call nest (*a*). Soon afterwards she begins to dig a new nest (*b*). After completing the first phase of this nest, which may take her one or more days according to the amount of sunshine, she returns to nest (*a*) and, before fetching a caterpillar, opens the nest. After a brief visit she may close it again and fly off over the neighbouring heather without apparently having 'done' anything. This type of visit Baerends calls an unladen visit in contrast to a provisioning visit during which a new caterpillar is brought. As a rule, the wasp, after an unladen visit, brings one or more fresh caterpillars, and then leaves the nest alone for a second period of perhaps two or more days. This second phase thus consists of an unladen visit followed by the storing of from one to three caterpillars. After having finished the second phase in nest (*a*), nest (*b*) is reopened and the same second phase performed there also; then perhaps there will be an unladen visit to nest (*a*) again, this initiating the third and last phase, which consists of one or more unladen visits and the storage of from three to seven more caterpillars. This third phase is concluded by closing the nest in an especially careful manner. The wasp now goes to nest (*b*) to accomplish the third phase there and, after having finally closed this, she begins to dig a new nest (*c*). Thus in each nest provisioning occurs in three phases and during every phase the wasp is occupied with one particular nest exclusively although she may interrupt work at that nest for foraging for herself, for hunting caterpillars or for sleeping, but not for working on another nest. Having finished one phase she goes to another nest and works through an entire phase there, and if there is no other nest to provide for, she may start yet another new nest, and so, when weather conditions are extremely favourable, she may get to the point of starting nest (c) before the third phase of nest (a) is completed. Thus she may on occasion have three nests under her care at one time, each in a different stage of construction (Fig. 7). It will be noticed that the second and third phases always begin with an unladen visit, and sometimes a phase comprises nothing but a single unladen visit. This is liable to happen when the nest has been disturbed shortly before the visit or, as Baerends was able to show (as a result of a technique by which nests can be opened without disturbing the surface), when the egg has not yet hatched. This suggests that the unladen visit is in fact a visit of inspection [1]; in other words, that the wasp during this visit experiences releasers which originate from the contents of the cell and which somehow determine whether she will leave the nest alone or go and fetch fresh caterpillars. By a long series of experiments Baerends showed conclusively that the unladen visit determines the behaviour of the wasp during the following hours or even days. Another very remarkable feature is that although the external stimulating situation may be exactly the same during an unladen visit as during a provisioning visit, the wasp's behaviour is greatly influenced by it on the former occasion, whereas on the latter no influence can be traced at all. Experiments suggested a possible explanation of this. If certain objects are put into the cell just before the wasp is due to pay her very first visit—that is, on the visit when she should normally be laying an egg—she did show a response. If the strange object was a caterpillar with an *Ammophila* egg already on it, or if it was a cocoon, the wasp pulled it out of the cell and threw it away. If the object was an *Ammophila* larva, she immediately brought in her caterpillar but omitted to lay an egg. She would often in this situation capture some more caterpillars and store them, still postponing the laying of the egg. So it seems that the presence of a young larva is the releaser which stimulates the fetching of from one to three caterpillars (i.e. the second phase of provisioning), and the presence of an older larva stimulates the bringing of between three and seven caterpillars corresponding to the third phase. Thus, while it is in part at least the amount of food present during the unladen inspection visit which determines the wasp's behaviour in the second and third phase, the wasp is stimulated at her first visit by the state of the larva and perhaps by the presence or absence of an egg. And it seems probable that it is the age of

---

[1] It is true that the behaviour of *Ammophila* is simpler than the classical latent-learning performance of rats in a maze in that the recognition of the stimuli which are perceived on an unladen visit is probably in considerable measure innately determined. But since the outstanding feature about them is the extraordinary latency of their effect, it seems best to discuss them here.

the larva which the wasp happens to find in her nest at her first visit which determines whether she will be brought into the second or into the third phase of provisioning. It is probable also that the age of the larva has the same influence during the unladen visits. An example of this can be seen in Fig. 7 (p. 108).

So we see that these unladen visits are often true visits of inspection in that the quantity of food present determines the subsequent provisioning behaviour, while absence of the larva causes the nest to be abandoned, but that during all provisioning visits except the first the wasp shows no appreciation of the contents of the nest. Another striking outcome of these investigations is the clear evidence that they afford of excellent memory for different nest sites and the ability to respond to releasers received during an inspection visit which has, nevertheless, taken place several hours or perhaps even more than a day before. The work of Lindauer (1952) on the division of labour among the workers of the honey-bee (Chapter II, p. 46, above) yielded striking evidence that the selection of duties to be performed has very little to do with the physiological state of the insect but is dictated primarily by the needs of the colony as a whole. Lindauer in the course of his work followed individual bees for long periods, observing the sequence of actions and duties, and he and his co-workers actually succeeded in maintaining one individual under continuous observation throughout the whole of its life in the hive until it was lost on a foraging flight. Through this very remarkable achievement, which was made possible by an observation hive so designed that it was possible to see into every part, it was found that contrary to previous beliefs by no means the whole life of a worker bee is occupied in work; in fact, in some instances less than half the time was so spent. When there were no jobs to be done the worker might be feeding, resting in an empty cell in an out-of-the-way part of the hive or, as was repeatedly observed, walking all over the hive apparently investigating the state of affairs in different parts of it and, to quote Lindauer in translation, 'quite obviously interested in all that was going on in the hive, constantly poking her head into cells, inspecting some hurriedly, others much more thoroughly.' There seems reason to believe that just as with the exploratory excursions and inspections of the *Ammophila*, this wandering round the hive results in a general learning of the conditions which obtain. It would explain how it is that members of the 'pool' of workers which are unoccupied at any particular time are able, when required, to apply themselves easily and expeditiously to the performance of any particular task. Much work on comparable behaviour in wasps of the genus *Bembix* has been produced by Evans (1957) and Tsuneki (1956, 1957).

*The Behaviour of the Honey-bee as Evidence for Latent Learning and
    Imprinting*

During recent years the study of the orientation methods of the
honey-bee has developed so rapidly and led to conclusions of such far-
reaching importance for ethology that the only way to do justice to it is
to make it the subject of a special section. An insect with such a high
degree of organisation of labour, and having only a limited period of the
year in which to forage, needs some means of communication by which a
scout which has discovered a rich source of food can quickly recruit a
body of workers large enough to fetch the available booty but not so great
as to waste the worker strength of the hive in unprofitable foraging. Besides the necessity for communicating the distance, direction and type of
food available, there also arises during swarming the problem of how the
scout bees searching for new quarters are to transmit to the swarm the
information they have acquired. While innate responses to stimuli and
releasers will go very far to account for the organisation of other complex
insect societies and, indeed, as we have seen, do play a very big part in
the organisation of the hive, the honey-bee type of community life requires a more flexible means of communication. In other words, bees need
a language; and von Frisch, to whom we are indebted for almost all the
essential facts concerning the orientation and methods of communication
of honey-bees, did not hesitate in his earlier papers to speak of 'the
language of bees.' The account of the bee behaviour which follows in the
next few pages is based on the earlier papers of von Frisch and his collaborators over approximately the ten years 1946–56. The main conclusions
of this work have been amply substantiated and need no revision, but some
obscure points have been elaborated in further studies by von Frisch and
his pupils and the work has been greatly extended on the comparative side
by studies on other members of the Apoidæa. All this is summarised by
Lindauer (1961) in a book which is necessary reading for all those particularly interested in the subject.

When a worker bee discovers a rich (natural or artificial) source of
nectar or pollen, she informs the other inmates of the hive of her find by
performing a dance on the comb after her return. Bees which are near
by follow her in the dance,[1] become excited and then apparently fly
out to search for the food indicated. Quite early von Frisch noticed that
there were two types of dance, the 'round dance' and the 'waggle
dance.'

If the food source is not more than 50–100 metres from the hive, the
round dance is performed. This is merely a signal to the other bees to go
out and search around the hive for a food source of the same odour as

[1] First described by Aristotle, *Hist. Animal*, 18, 624 b. 8 (Haldane, 1954c).

that adhering to the body of the dancer. With increasing distance of the food source there is a gradual modification of the type of dance performed until, at more than 100 metres, it becomes the characteristic waggle dance. This is a dance in the form of a very broad figure-of-eight in which the relatively straight transverse path across the middle is known as the waggle run because of the fact that the bee waggles her abdomen from side to side as she traverses it. The number of complete waggle dances in a unit of time decreases with increasing distance of the food source. This inverse relationship is so constant that, by timing the dance with the aid of a stop-watch, one can estimate accurately the distance of the food source from which the dancer brings her burden, and it is clear that this dance gives an effective and reliable indication to the other bees of distances between 100 and 1,500 metres; at 100 metres there being an average of 10 waggle runs per 15 seconds, which drops steadily to an average of 4·5 at 1,500 metres. Later observations have shown that the waggle dance continues to give an accurate indication of the distance of food source up to 11 kilometres from the hive, the rates at this extreme distance still fitting the asymptotic curve obtained for shorter distances. The dance, however, is not effective for *recruitment* of new bees to a food source beyond about 5½ kilometres.

The dancing bee also indicates the horizontal *direction* of the food source by means of the waggle dance.[2] It must be borne in mind that these dances are normally performed on the vertical surface of the combs inside the hive. Under these conditions, the direction of the waggle run of the dance indicates the direction of the food source in relation to the position of the sun, which is represented by the vertical on the comb. Thus a waggle run upwards indicates that the food source lies in the direction of the sun. A waggle run downwards shows that the feeding place is in the opposite direction. A waggle run to the right means that the food source is to be found at the right of the sun and at such an angle to the sun by which the waggle run deviates from the vertical; similarly, a waggle run to the left indicates a feeding-place at a corresponding angle to the left of the sun.

Thus the complete waggle dance indicates both direction and distance of a food source, and constitutes for the colony of bees an extraordinarily efficient method of harvesting as rapidly as possible a new and abundant source of food. The dance is only performed when a worker has dis-

---

[2] Bees cannot indicate a vertical component; they have no word for 'up' in their language. Von Frisch *et al.* (1953) fed bees at a feeding table 50 metres directly *above* the hive at the top of a radio beacon, but the workers gave only round dances and no new foragers found the table. But though they cannot indicate *direction* up or down they can indicate *distance* up or down a vertical surface. Thus if hive and food-place are so arranged that the bees flying from one to the other are forced to traverse a cliff-face then the distance indicated by the dance will include that up the vertical face.

covered, or is foraging at, a particularly rich source of supply. Each performance of the dance on the comb results in a number of other bees setting out and finding that particular food source. If the supply is still rich when the newcomers reach it, they also dance on the combs on their return, and so a numerous band of foraging workers is quickly recruited for work at a rich source of supply. As soon as the source begins to fail the returning workers cease to dance although they themselves continue exploiting that source as long as an appreciable yield is obtained. The result is that any new source of food is rapidly and fully utilised by the colony without any undue waste of time and energy.

The performance of the waggle dance on the vertical comb is so remarkable that we are forced to ask ourselves whether, apart from human faculties, there is anything comparable known in the animal kingdom; for it appears to involve an elementary form of map-making and map-reading, an activity in which the direction of action of gravity serves as a model of the direction of incidence of the sun's rays. We can assume that the main orienting stimulus when the bee is on the vertical comb inside the dark hive is the pull of gravity on the body, presumably perceived by the proprioceptive sense organs at the limb and abdominal articulations. It is astonishing enough to find that there is an inherent instinctive association of the two stimuli so that one replaces the other according to whether the bee is inside or outside the hive. But this alone does not carry us very far, and we seem forced to the conclusion that there must be an inherent recognition of the characteristic movement pattern of the waggle run as equivalent inside the hive to the activity of the foraging flight outside it. This is a big assumption, but it seems to be the minimum for any understanding of the problem, for the opportunities which the individual bee can have for perfecting this astonishing behaviour appear quite insufficient.

Von Frisch has now shown that the direction-giving is, under good conditions, accurate to about 3°, whereas the distance indication is on the average accurate to about 100 metres. The accuracy with which the angle between the axis of the waggle run and the vertical is measured by the bee is an astonishing feature of the results, and from our present knowledge of insect proprioceptors it is not easy to imagine how it is achieved. Indeed, the mere *visual* perception of angles to such accuracy when on foraging flights is very remarkable, for Baumgartner has shown that the minimum angular separation of adjacent ommatidia in the bee's eye is 0·9°. With regard to distance estimation, it appears, as a result of a large number of experiments on efficiency under varying wind conditions, that this is the result of some sensitiveness to the amount of energy expended on the outward flight. Thus the suggestion of Ribbands (1953) that the very slow or incomplete accommodation of a proprioceptive organ on the antennæ, or on some other structure which is bent in flight, might serve the same purpose does not seem necessary at present. The advantage in estimating the distance on the outward flight is probably that the bee is then unladen and her weight and flight conditions constant. On the return flight, the load carried will vary according to whether she is foraging for pollen or nectar, and probably with other conditions also; moreover, it is the correct estimate of distance under the wind conditions of the outward flight that matters. The visual estimation of direction, while theoretically simple enough for an animal with good light-compass orientation such as the bee when foraging in open country without serious obstacles, may nevertheless be a very complex problem under natural conditions—particularly in the broken and mountainous country in which von Frisch's experiments were performed. Bees are somewhat reluctant to fly high, and tend at first to go round rather than over obstacles such as high cliffs and mountain-sides; although later, if the detour is excessive, they may quickly learn to straighten the path. Von Frisch, as a result of some preliminary detour experiments, concludes that bees indicate the actual distance flown on the detour but give approximately the true direction of the food source in relation to the sun—not the direction in which they set out. A moment's thought will show that, in fact, this is the simplest way in which direction-finding could be made effective in country where obstacles have to be negotiated.

From the theoretical point of view it will be seen that the problems of perception and reproduction of the dances are the really crucial issues. Although correct observation and interpretation of the dance are rapidly rewarded by finding food, correct performance of the dance can scarcely be rewarded at all. Here the work of Lindauer has once again cleared up some at least of these difficulties. He finds that very few of the young bees leave the hive on independent excursions; nearly all gain their first outdoor foraging experience as a result of following a dance, and they are unable to emerge and forage successfully until they have attained near perfection in dance-following within the hive. Thus it comes about that a young bee which is already physiologically and socially motivated for foraging may take some days before she is finally and fully alerted and oriented. At first she may have difficulty in turning sufficiently rapidly to follow the dance, and so she appears clumsy and is often confused at the sudden sharp turns of the leader. Then, since her efforts are still somewhat spasmodic as well as inefficient, she is rather easily interrupted by the other workers crowding around, and so may have to wait until she has the luck to follow a dancer in a part where there is not too great a crowd before she herself can perform successfully. In other experiments in which a colony was artificially built up so that only young bees were available to forage, it became clear that the young foragers are, under the circumstances, able to dance correctly even if they have never before come into contact with a dancer (cf. Jander (1957) on *Formica rufa*, referred to on p. 242, above). Therefore we must assume that the pattern of actions and the orientation to perform a circle or figure-of-eight must be completely innate. We also have to assume that the correct interpretation is possible without learning and without any reinforcement provided only that the individual bee has, as we have seen, first learned to follow exactly. It is this following which needs special practice. When young bees are first initiated to dance they tend to follow either type of dance and any dancer with which they come into contact. Later they become specialised, at any rate for a period, and forage only for nectar of a particular type or engage only in pollen gathering. How quickly this process of learning specialised dances comes about apparently depends simply on the frequency of contact between the young bees and the various dance groups. They will tend to specialise in and become attached to whatever type of dance they meet with most frequently in the hive. If no one type of dance preponderates, then this initial period of specialisation may take a long time; on the other hand, if 70 or 80 per cent. of the dances they encounter belong to one type, then that is the type they will learn first, and when this learning is completed they will, for the time being at any rate, ignore all dances except those of their own group.

The waggle dance is occasionally performed on the horizontal surface of the alighting board in front of the hive, and the waggle run then serves as a pointer indicating the *actual* direction of the feeding-place, not its direction in relation to the sun; for obviously, on a horizontal surface the type of dance involving reference to gravity is impossible. The dance on this horizontal plane provides a clue to the real nature of the performance as a whole. It is, in fact, a highly ritualised intention movement in which the speed gives information as to distance and in which the 'waggle run' points directly or 'symbolically' towards the food source.

A bee performing the vertical form of waggle dance on the comb in its normal position can immediately be induced to perform the horizontal form by moving the hinged vertical comb of the observation hive to the horizontal position—provided only that a good deal of daylight is being admitted to the hive (in actual fact so long as some blue sky is visible to the bees). In the dark, bees (as observed by a red light to which they are insensitive) are always disorientated when on a horizontal surface or when daylight is too diffuse or reduced below a certain intensity.

The primitive evolutionary function of this horizontal dance is completely obscure, but its study led von Frisch to another remarkable discovery concerning bee orientation—namely the responsiveness of bees to polarised light. It is evident that bees cannot remember the turns which they have taken on the horizontal plane after they have entered the dark hive, and so can no longer indicate the absolute direction unless they are subject to some stimulus received from the daylight—sight of the sun itself not being necessary. If they are given a strong *beam* of light from an electric lamp inside the hive, the straight run of the waggle dance is found to make the same angle with the lamp as the actual path from the hive to the food source makes with the sun, the lamp being reacted to as if it were the sun. But of course this is a highly artificial situation. As a result of a long series of experiments, von Frisch found that the sight of a very small area (10°) of the blue sky is often sufficient, independent of its direction, to maintain correct orientation of the dance on the horizontal surface. If, however, when the aperture is to the north, light from, say, the western side is reflected down the tube into the hive by a mirror, the bees now dance incorrectly, behaving as if west were north. We are thus forced to the conclusion that daylight in itself, without sight of the sun, has some orienting capacity independent of its direction. A confirmation of this astonishing conclusion was obtained from an entirely different set of observations and experiments, 3,600 in number, planned and carried out in previous years for another purpose.

It is now evident that the only possible explanation of all these similar experiments is that the bees are sensitive to the polarisation of the light reflected from the blue sky, and by this means are able to tell the direction of the sun even though they can see only a small area of the sky far removed from the sun. The light from the blue sky is partly polarised, and this polarisation shows a two-fold relation to the position of the sun; first, the degree of polarisation increases as one passes across the sky away from the sun, to reach a maximum of 60–70 per cent. at about 90°, declining again towards a point opposite the sun. In a considerable circle around the sun and also around its opposite point, the degree of polarisation is very slight. Secondly, the plane of polarisation of the light from different parts of the sky bears a regular relation to the sun's position.

The polarisation pattern presented by the sky when the sun is on the horizon is shown in Fig. 46, and the fact that bees can obtain orientation from the sight of such a small area of sky[1] independent of its direction suggests that they must have an extremely good 'memory' for the details of the polarisation pattern, and must be able to associate this by means of their time sense with the position of the sun in such a manner that they can behave as if they knew where the sun was. In considering the problem of how bees remain orientated when the sky becomes covered with cloud so that presumably neither the sun position nor the polarisation are any

[1] It now appears that the sensitivity of the bees' eyes to the ultra-violet region of the spectrum (3,000–4,000 A) may provide them with a polarisation clue even through considerable cloud cover (von Frisch and Lindauer, 1954). See also Lindauer (1961).

longer available as guides, von Frisch showed that they remain orientated only so long as the light has a high percentage of polarisation. Thus, if he opened up a hive in cloudy weather so that 10° or more of the sky was visible, the dancer could not orientate herself. If, however, a polaroid sheet was interposed between the sky and the hive, the bees' dance indicated that they were adopting the same angle to the pattern presented which, under a blue sky, they would have taken to the locus of this pattern at

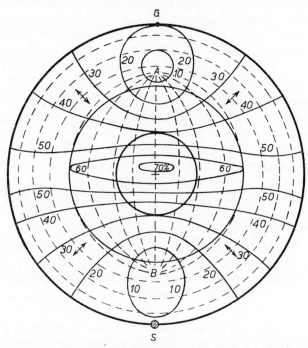

FIG. 46—Diagram to show the quality and intensity of polarisation of light from the blue sky with the sun at the horizon. The cross at the centre marks the position of the observer, S the position of the sun and G the opposite point of the horizon. The figures indicate percentage polarisation, the lines joining points which are equal in this respect. Double arrows show direction of polarisation, plain and dashed lines run at right angles to the direction of polarisation. B = neutral point without polarisation above the sun and A = neutral point also without polarisation in the opposite direction from the sun. (After von Frisch, 1950.)

the time given. Von Frisch took this to mean that they were able to retain the pattern in memory for days and were able to check the amount of the alteration of its position with the time of day. When the polaroid was turned to such an angle that the pattern presented could have been nowhere present in a blue sky at that particular time of day, von Frisch found that the bees' dance was disorientated.

These results seem to imply that the bees' memory for the polarisation pattern and its changes is as good as their memory for the regular daily and hourly changes in the sun's position and also for the identity and relative position of the various terrestrial landmarks which they use in orientation outside the hive. It may be, however, that the perception and memory for details of the polarisation pattern need not be as perfect as this to account for the results so far obtained. Bailey (1953) has emphasised that if we imagine an observer looking at the sky with the sun, for example, in the position indicated in Fig. 47, any part of the imaginary arc which constitutes the equator of the globe of the sky would appear

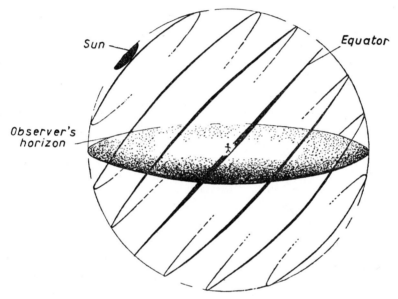

Fig. 47—Perception of polarised light. The relation between the sun and plane of polarisation, as it would appear if this property could be perceived. The earth is represented by a flat disc (shaded) which is pivoted at the centre of a transparent globe, representing the sky. (After Bailey, from Ribbands, 1953.)

to the observer as a straight line in the sky. When looking at this line he could immediately indicate the bearing of the sun which would be at right angles to this line and to his line of sight. Bailey has re-examined the data on which von Frisch bases his conclusion that bees orientate accurately when shown a small portion of blue sky. He found that in von Frisch's experiments they were, in fact, always allowed to see a portion on or very near to this equatorial region or with some artificial equivalent of it. He points out that it would be much more difficult to orientate accurately in relation to a portion of sky from any other region, and he considers that there is as yet no evidence to show that bees do possess this ability. For the time being, at any rate, it seems that these considerations would relieve us of the necessity for accrediting bees with the power of retaining the extremely detailed memory of the whole polarisation pattern which von Frisch assumed.

Further study of the sun orientation in bees has, however, revealed some discrepancies. Kalmus has concluded that bees are innately able to calculate the sun's course in relation to their own orientation either clockwise or anticlockwise, but Lindauer (1959) finds evidence that every bee must learn the apparent course of the sun for the appropriate season and locality. It has been abundantly established now that a wide variety of terrestrial and aquatic arthropods can utilise the polarised light of the blue sky for determining geographical direction, but a surprising doubt has recently arisen as to the mechanism by which the compound eye is able to perceive the plane of polarisation, and it has even been questioned whether the observed responses could not be entirely explained by apparent brightness difference caused by differential scattering or reflection (Waterman, 1959). However, what looks like a final answer to the question has now been provided as a result of varied types of investigation, including electron microscope studies. It seems now clear that there is an optical analyser in the compound eye of insects and other arthropods which confers on the animal the ability to steer by polarised light; and in at least some instances this analyser is used just for this purpose. It is also true, however, that in many circumstances the intensity of reflection from objects in the environment and, in aquatic forms, scattering by suspended particles, can provide cues even where an optical analyser is lacking. The subject is usefully summarised by Carthy (1961).[1]

As a result of his studies of ant orientation, Vowles (1954) has made some suggestions which may give some help in understanding the language of bees. He suggests that a valid distinction can be made between compass orientation to distant and therefore relatively unchanging sources of directional stimulation—namely the sun, the plane of polarisation and gravity—on the one hand, and orientation to nearer objects, such as trees, cliffs, buildings and other such landmarks, on the other. The orientation to the landmarks must obviously be learned, whereas it is not difficult to suppose that an automatic correlation between the sight of the sun's position, the plane of polarisation and the direction of the pull of gravity might be supplied by inheritance; indeed, the work of Lindauer referred to above seems to make such an assumption almost inescapable. It is thus implied that there are two taxis mechanisms, the first common to the three primary stimuli for orientation and the second used for the other more

---

[1] This account of advances in understanding the orientation methods of the honeybee should not be taken to imply that all the problems of insect orientation on migration and homing flights are now solved. As a corrective to such a suggestion, and as an indication of the problems which still require long and critical investigation, the reader is referred to the book of C. B. Williams (1958), especially Chapter VIII.

variable perceptual elements coming from the nearer environment. Obviously the two systems must be very closely interlocked, for since bees can fly to a food source in a remembered position the 'settings' of the primary taxis mechanism must continually be determined and adjusted by experience both present and remembered. Nevertheless, there are, as Vowles points out, cogent reasons for regarding the first taxis mechanism as the primary one, since von Frisch has shown that bees after returning from foraging in overcast conditions do not dance in the hive—'a fact which might be interpreted as showing that although bees learn to associate a particular direction with a particular succession of landmarks, they are unable to perform the reverse process and associate a route flown entirely by landmarks with a particular direction, either in the flight or in the dance.' Such a scheme is of course an over-simplification if only because the dance itself is such a highly elaborate pattern of actions; nevertheless, it has the merit of considering the dance as in part a device for the preliminary setting of the primary taxis mechanism of new foragers.[1]

Although visual stimuli are obviously by far the most important in bee orientation and although ability to learn and memorise them is one of the most remarkable learning achievements which the bees possess, other senses do play their part in maintaining orientation. The odour of the species of flower from which nectar is being collected must, of course, be memorised by the foragers, and probably is of some assistance in the final step of finding the food source. Moreover, the scent of the bees' abdominal glands, which is deposited on the spot where the scout bees find rich food supply, is no doubt helpful in 'pin-pointing' the food sources which are to be worked. Memory for colony odour also plays its part. This, as we have seen, changes with the changing food supply of the colony, and memory of the colony odour must be constantly adapted and adjusted as the season progresses. Ribbands and Speirs (1953) have shown that colony odour is a help to foraging bees in finding a hive which has been moved a short distance. Bee-keepers know that when a hive is moved a little way from its accustomed place a temporary congestion of bees occurs at the original position of the hive entrance. Wolf (1926–27) showed that this is due to the bees using landmarks at a distance from the colony

---

[1] Birukow (1953), experimenting on the Dung Beetle *Geotrupes sylvaticus*, finds evidence for a very similar transposition mechanism. Perhaps such a common setting device for the primary taxis mechanism is commoner than we at present imagine. Sun orientation, together with perception of light polarisation, is also found in 'lower' Arthropods, e.g. wolf-spiders (F. Papi (1955), *Z. vergl. Physiol.* **37**: 230–33) and Amphipods (L. Pardi and M. Grassi (1955), *Experientia*, **11**: 202).

The relative importance of landmarks and 'skymarks' in bee orientation has been investigated by von Frisch and Lindauer (1954). It was found that 'linear' landmarks (e.g. straight roads, canal banks and the edges of long coniferous plantations) in otherwise featureless country may be more powerful as orienting stimuli than clues connected with the sun.

for their orientation rather than looking for the hive itself.[2] He found that colouring the front of the hive reduced the disturbing effect, and that when blotting-paper impregnated with flower scent was pinned inside the hive and thus out of sight, the hive in its new position was found more quickly. This conclusion has been supported and extended by the work of Kalmus and Ribbands (1952), who find that colony odour is at first important in orientation although it is supplemented and later supplanted by visual clues. It is, however, noteworthy that in such experiments some bees, after many correct returns to a new entrance position, if confused by being presented with a dummy entrance, revert to the old entrance. Thus one bee made a series of twelve correct returns on four consecutive days, and then went back to land at the original point on her third trip of the fourth day. Apparently when confronted by novel environmental conditions the previous memory image became dominant. As a particularly interesting example of a modification of the releasing mechanism by learning processes, the work of Manning (1956) on the bumble bee may be mentioned. He found that bumble bees visiting Houndstongue learn the general form of the plant, while those frequenting Foxglove become conditioned to the colour of the flowers.

Tool Using

Some striking examples of tool using among Arthropods must now be considered. Firstly there is the well-known example of the crab *Melia tesselata* (Duerden, 1905) which uses sea anemones of the genera *Sagartia* or *Bunodeopsis* as weapons. The crab holds the anemone firmly in its chelæ, grasping the base in such a manner that the living tool is correctly orientated. It apparently never uses its chelæ for dealing with food, but abstracts much of the food, captured by the anemone, by means of its first pair of walking legs. Then there is the famous instance of the tropical ants *Polyrachis* and *Oecophylla* (Jacobson, 1905, 1908; Dodd, 1901) which make nests and shelters of leaves spun together by means of silken threads. This silk is secreted only by the larvæ, which are held in the jaws of the workers and used as tools for this purpose. The older psychologists regarded tool using as clear evidence of the highest form of 'intelligence,' but I think we need not, in fact, assume any insight learning to be involved, although the full analysis of the behaviour is far from having been achieved (Chauvin, 1952). Rather, the whole series of actions in all probability constitutes a piece of instinctive behaviour of great antiquity and a high degree of fixity—as witness the fact that although the larvæ pupate naked, spinning no cocoon, yet their silk glands actually show a structural modification, being strongly hypertrophied (Ridley, 1890; Doflein, 1905).

By far the most famous instance of tool using among insects is that

[2] The same appears to be true of Bumble Bees. (Free, 1955.)

shown by the sphegid wasps of the genus *Ammophila*. The Peckhams (1898), who were the first to study the habits of these insects in detail, showed that *A. urnaria* fills in the mouth of the completed and provisioned burrow with earth carefully pressed down. An individual wasp which they observed, contrary to what appeared to be the normal behaviour of the species, picked up a tiny pebble in her jaws and proceeded to use this as a hammer, ramming down the soil with swift repeated strokes till the entrance to the burrow was no longer distinguishable from the surrounding earth. Very similar observations had, in fact, been noted earlier by Williston (1892) on *A. yarrowi*, on another unidentified species by Hungerford and Williams (1912) and by P. and N. Rau (1918) on *Sphex* (*Ammophila*) *pictipennis*; in this latter species it is apparently the normal method of burrow closure. Hartmann (1905) records that when *Ammophila procera* is closing its nest it sometimes happens 'that a piece of wood is pressed down tightly, then pulled out and pressed down again, and this is repeated several times so that one might suspect that the wasp were here improvising a tool with which to tamp down the sand.' Armbruster (1921) and Minckiewicz (1933) both record a similar habit for the European *A. sabulosa*, and according to Berland (1935) all individuals of *A. heydeni* use a stone exactly after the manner of *A. urnaria*. Molitor (1931, 1937), however, disagrees; he says that *A. heydeni* only occasionally uses a stone.

From the original observations of the Peckhams (1898, 1900) many biologists and psychologists (e.g. Morgan, 1900; Bouvier, 1922; McDougall, 1936) did not hesitate to describe the exceptional individual as 'a genius leading its species onward to the use of tools' (McDougall). But it is now clear that the act is one which borders very closely on the normal instinctive behaviour of the insect; in fact, in some species it *is* the normal instinctive behaviour. In all species the seizure of pebbles, clods of earth, bits of wood, etc., in the mandibles and the packing of dirt into the hole are part of the instinctive act of filling and closing. Those species and individuals which use a pebble as a hammer therefore appear merely to be combining two features of the instinctive hole-filling process in a rather unusual way. Since the animal is constantly manipulating clods and stones, it has every opportunity to learn by trial-and-error, from the chances of its normal experience, the results of handling hard objects of various kinds. But such behaviour does not necessarily involve insight learning.

Nest Repair among the Eumenidæ as Evidence of Insight Learning

There are on record a number of experiments in which Eumenidæ (Mason Wasps) and Megachilidæ (Mason Bees) have been induced to break off the routine of making their mud nests and to repair artificial injuries to their cells. The authors of these experiments, Hingston (1926–7) and K. D. and W. McDougall (1931), have regarded their observations as undoubtedly indicating insight learning. Hingston's observations are of the greatest interest, but his use of psychological terms is so loose as to invalidate much of his discussion. This defect unfortunately detracts particularly from his book (1928) in which, nevertheless, he has performed a valuable service in gathering together a large number of interesting cases of adaptive behaviour among insects, mainly drawn from his own experience and most vividly described. Two of Hingston's experiments are of particular interest. From among all the examples collected in his work these are the only ones which, I feel, after careful examination, give a *prima facie* case for postulating insight learning. They are fully discussed in another connection above (p. 42) and need not be recounted here.

The example recorded by K. D. and W. McDougall (1931) is so similar to that of Hingston's *Rhynchium* that a detailed account is unnecessary. The account deals with an unidentified 'Mason Wasp' said to be common in North Carolina. In this instance, too, a hole is made in the bottom or side of the pot and the provisions, namely spiders, removed. Here again a repair is carried out, the authors stressing the fact that the exact method and movements of repair are different from those observed during any part of the normal routine of pot-building and provisioning. In this case the repair is performed from the outside, whereas normal construction proceeds from inside. When the repair has been completed there is a good deal of rather aimless patching up with pellets of clay, after which the cell is restocked with spiders and another egg is laid. Again, Rau (1928) describes the reconstruction by *Polistes* wasps of their destroyed nests.

Certainly such observations do at first sight strongly suggest insight learning. The animal *appears* to give a new and adaptive response to a new situation without apparently any process of trial-and-error. But before we can regard such examples as providing positive proof, we must know for certain: (1) that the experimental situation is not one that the insect can ever meet as part of its normal experience; (2) that the behaviour that results is really new. It is clear that we need to know a very great deal about the normal environment and behaviour of the animal under observation, and it is doubtful whether in any of these three cases we really have this knowledge. For instance, with regard to the making of a hole in the pot, are we quite sure that there is no bird or other predatory animal which breaks the cells open in this way and extracts the contents and to which the insect may be adapted?

Nevertheless, the examples of plasticity shown by caddis larvæ in the repair of their damaged cases (see pp. 44 *et seq.*, above), and instances such as those given by Szlep (1952) on the ability of the Garden Spider (*Aranea diadema*) to continue more or less normal web construction even after amputation of certain of the legs and claws, suggests that there cannot possibly exist pre-formed alternative pathways and mechanisms ready for such eventualities. But even here a final judgment must be reserved until such amputation and other experiments have been carried out on individuals which have had no previous experience of constructing their webs, for until this is done it is impossible to evaluate the learning element involved.

Imprinting

While there are no longer any good grounds for regarding imprinting as a clearly distinct type of learning, it is, nevertheless, interesting to consider how far the Arthropods show any performance of this type. As has been shown above, in the pre-imaginal olfactory conditioning of insects we find that influences operating merely through the larval life can have an effect on the behaviour of the adult. Among ants, the existence of the slave-making forms at once suggests the possibility of something like imprinting, although there appear to be no experiments on record enabling one to distinguish between such a process and the effect of repeated and regular associative conditioning. Again, among ants Fielde (1904) described changes in behaviour of such constancy and duration as to recall imprinting.

But besides these cases of olfactory learning there are one or two other examples among insects which, in that they concern responses of projicient senses to complex stimuli, seem to have a closer affinity to the typical imprinting of birds. Regen (1926), investigating the discriminative ability in regard to sounds of the grasshopper *Thamnotrizon apterus*, found that males which had just entered on adult life and had never heard the normal chirping of the species could be induced to sing in rhythmic response with artificially generated sounds over a great range of frequencies. Those adults which had, however, already learnt to sing in concert with others immediately detected any attempt at imposture and were reduced to silence no matter how closely (by human criteria) the artificial sounds approximated to the natural song. Unfortunately the account of these extraordinarily interesting observations does not give us the necessary data to decide whether we have here a true case of imprinting or whether the effect was merely due to the gradual development or maturation of an instinct during the life of an individual. What we need to know is whether males not exposed to the chirps of other males retain their generalised response or not.

It is possible that the concept of imprinting, regarded particularly as a tendency to learn in certain directions and situations only, can help a little in accounting for the development in the individual of the technique of communicating direction and distance by means of the dances as described above (p. 239) for the honey-bee. We have assumed above that there is a common taxis mechanism, instinctive association or inter-sensorial transposition between perception of the sun and gravity so that one replaces the other according to whether the bee is inside or outside the hive; and as we have seen, Lindauer (1952) has established that the young foragers can perform the dance pattern correctly even if they have never previously come into contact with a dancer. This first following of a dancing bee by a young worker does not, of course, lead to any immediate food or other reward, but is self-rewarding in the sense in which we find so much appetitive behaviour to be and presents obvious resemblances to imprinting.

Time Sense

A discussion of the subject of imprinting leads naturally to considerations of impressed rhythms and the nature of a time sense; and that in turn leads to questions of retention and memory.

Perhaps the most remarkable piece of evidence for such imprinting of rhythms comes from the work of Harker (1953) on the nymphs of the Mayfly *Ecdyonurus*. Here there is a twenty-four-hour rhythm of ascent and descent which is so firmly established that it remains unchanged even after five months in continuous light. Although naïve nymphs which have never had any experience of illumination changes show no rhythm whatever, nevertheless, *a single experience* of a light-dark alternation during one twenty-four-hour period is sufficient to set up a rhythm to all appearance as firmly established as that of the normal wild population. Similar rhythms in cockroaches are apparently mediated by a secretion carried in the blood (Harker, 1954). Elsewhere in the Arthropods learned rhythms have been described in woodlice (Isopods), millipedes (Diplopods) (Cloudesley-Thompson, 1951, 1952a) and in a number of Orthoptera and certain species of beetles (Coleoptera), but most of the evidence for a precise time sense in Arthropods[1] comes from experiments on the Hymenoptera.

Beling (1929) was the first to establish that bees have an accurate time sense, and that they will tend to go to a particular feeding-place for food at the precise time of day at which they have been fed previously. Wahl (1933) showed that they are able not merely to remember the time of feeding, but if a concentration of sugar is different at different times of the day, they are able to remember the hour at which it is greatest and will restrict their foraging to that time. As Kleber (1935) has pointed out, such an ability to associate quality and quantity of food supply with the time of day is a great practical advantage, since many flowers tend to produce their nectar at particular times of the day only. If bees were unable

---

[1] A precise time sense is now known to occur in Amphipods (F. Papi, 1955 *Experientia* **11**: 201).

to make such distinctions, a very great waste of forager hours would result. Grabensberger (1933) has established a time sense for ants. This author succeeded in conditioning ants to 3-, 5-, 21-, 22-, 26- and 27-hour feeding rhythms, and he also found it possible to condition termites to a 21-hour rhythm. From experiments with both ants and bees (1934), he concluded that time perception in insects is based on extremely regular metabolic changes in the body which are unaffected by anæsthesia but which are affected by severe chilling and also by narcosis produced by carbon dioxide (Kalmus, 1934). With bees it was found that globulin accelerates food metabolism as does salicyclic acid with ants, and experiments with these substances and with a number of pharmacological poisons again pointed to the rate of food metabolism as being the key factor in the memory. There is some evidence that for bees, but not necessarily for other insects, time-memory is bound up with the 24-hour rhythm, for both Beling and von Fisch noted that if bees are fed at a 48-hour period they also come for food at the 24-hour intervals, and the former author was unable to condition her hive-bees to a 19-hour feeding rhythm. There may be an innate 24-hour rhythm in these insects, for Beling claimed that her bees were still able to recognise the hour of day even though illumination had been kept artificially constant over a long period, but Harker's results show the need for caution in drawing conclusions. Changes in behaviour rhythm tend in some insects to be more easily learnt if they fit in with the 24-hour cycle than if they cut across it. But as with the ant and termite experiments mentioned above, the 24-hour rhythm is by no means completely overriding. It is particularly interesting that Scott (1936) showed that cultures of the moth *Ephestia kühniella* can be induced to establish an emergence rhythm at periods of 16, 20 and 24 hours, but not greater periods than 24 hours, suggesting that there is something fundamental about the 24-hour periodicity. He found that the diurnal rhythm is the external factor which induces the emergence rhythm, but that it reinforces an inherited tendency to a 24-hour periodicity, and he established that the innate character of this 24-hour rhythm is inherited by rearing the moths under constant conditions for three generations without its being disrupted. Apart from this rather special case of an emergence rhythm, there seems no absolutely satisfactory evidence for inherited rhythms in Arthropods but abundant evidence for learned ones. Nevertheless, the evidence points to the existence in many species of a fundamental endogenous rhythm which is geared to the environment by rhythmic external stimuli. The whole matter of innate and 'imprinted' behaviour rhythms and the mechanisms by which they are made possible and controlled has been enormously advanced in recent years, largely by the study of insects. Pittendrigh and Bruce (1959) have described the characteristics of many of these rhythms as (i) temperature-compensated—in contra-distinction to temperature-independent, (ii) governed by an oscillator which is (iii) innate and (iv) self-sustaining; (v) light is the principal time-giver, (vi) there is a common response pattern to single perturbations of the oscillator and (vii) the system is basically a cellular system. Other important references are those by Harker (1958), Aschoff (1958) and Pittendrigh and Bruce (1957).

Apart from the effect of conditions which accelerate or retard metabolism, determining rhythms and time sense, there are a few other studies which provide a little information about the effect of temporary changes on memory and learning ability. Hoagland (1931), again working with ants, found that maze learning could be accelerated up to 100 per cent. by raising the temperature to a point within the range 25°–29·4° C. It was, however, found that above 28° some harmful effects were manifest, and the ants exposed to this temperature very quickly forgot what they had learnt and found it difficult to relearn the maze. Hunter (1932), working with cockroaches, found that cold retarded learning and decreased retention. How far such effects are the direct expression of the change in activity produced it is hard to say. It is easy to understand how cold might retard learning, but not easy to see why it should decrease retention. Ribbands (1950) found that neither anæsthesia by chloroform, carbon dioxide nor nitrogen produced any impairment of memory in bees. Minami and Dallenbach (1946) report that with the cockroach relearning is very poor after a period of forced activity. It is significantly better under conditions in which the amount of rest has been normal, and better still after long periods of inactivity.

Locality Imprinting

But to return to imprinting and to viewing it from another aspect. It may perhaps be permissible to extend the original definition of the term to cover the possibility of attachment not to a living object but to the immediate locality first perceived by the newly emerged organism, so that this particular area becomes by a similar process the future breeding-quarters of the individual. Here, it is true, we are on ground far less secure; yet such a possibility is particularly suggested by a number of observations on the behaviour of solitary bees and wasps—all insects with very remarkably developed powers of vision and homing orientation.

Thus P. and N. Rau (1918) and P. Rau (1934), writing on the localisation of colonies of Bembecine wasps, say: 'The persistence with which *Bembix* adhere to the one location which we have watched year after year is astonishing. Truly their dissemination seems to be nil. Here the wasps of our particular colony have had at their disposal a pasture equal in size to six city blocks in which to choose their nesting-site, yet year after year they limit themselves strictly to two distinct corners of a "base-

ball diamond," in the middle of this field. The fact that each successive
generation should show the same choice and the same persistence (in spite
of interference from disturbance by baseball players) is all the more
astonishing.[1] In another vacant lot a mile away was another colony which,
to our knowledge, persisted in like manner on a small area for three years
(until their extermination by the erection of a building)—although just
across the road was a large tract of land thoroughly suitable to their needs.'

From the account of the Raus, Peckhams and many others there
seems to be no evidence whatever that the limited distribution of *Bembix*
has any ecological basis; it seems extremely probable that other parts of
the field where the colony was situated would have served as well. This
extraordinary restriction suggests, therefore, that the result of the first
locality study of the newly emerged *Bembix* becomes imprinted with
great force, with the result that the spot is 'home' for the individual for
all purposes for the rest of its life. Before, however, we can accept this
hypothesis we must bear in mind the gregarious instinct of this genus,
which may possibly itself be the basis for their topographical conservatism.

Another point, which emerges from the work of Parker (1917), is the
possibility that, in apparent contradistinction to the condition obtaining
in the majority of solitary wasps, odour plays an important part in the
Bembecine's finding of its own skilfully concealed burrow. If this is so, it
is at least conceivable that odour might also be responsible for colony
localisation year after year.

But although the Bembecines provide the most striking example of
this topographical conservatism, there are many other solitary bees and
wasps, and perhaps some social wasps (e.g. *Polistes*), which seem more or
less strongly attached to the place where their mother nested and where
their first locality study was made. Thus Perkins (1919), writing of very
dense colonies of the solitary bee *Andrena cineraria*, says: 'I suspect the
colonising is due sometimes to a natural sociability of the species *or a
reluctance to depart from their immediate birthplace*' (italics mine). He
records a colony probably originally started by a single female, which
steadily increased in size and became a permanently large one. Some of
these colonies persist for many years. Thus one colony at Wotton-under-
Edge, Gloucestershire, was kept under observation for nearly forty years
(1876–1914). It may, indeed, have existed for centuries, for no other
colony of the bee has ever been observed in the district. However, it seems
to have died out some years ago, for I failed to locate it during a careful
search in 1946.

The *Polistes* wasps are insects which form small hanging carton nests
in the tropical, subtropical and south temperate regions of the Old and

[1] It implies, moreover, a stability of population which is extremely difficult to account
for.

New Worlds. *Polistes annularis* and *P. pallipes* are two species found in temperate North America, the young queens hibernating in suitable shelter often some distance from the locality in which they were 'born,' but returning in the spring to the immediate vicinity of the old nests to found new colonies. Of these P. Rau (1929) writes: 'Certain spots are their favourite sites and year after year they nest in certain buildings while other sites which seem just as good are ignored by them.' In some cases they may be attracted to the stumps left after the old nests have been removed, but this cannot be the explanation in all cases; and in certain instances at least it seems that 'the queens remember and return to the region of the old nest site when the time comes for establishing a new home.' On the other hand, it must not be thought that this behaviour is invariable, even with *Polistes*, for the observations of Molitor (1939) on an unnamed European species of *Polistes* have shown that this is certainly not so under all circumstances. Baerends (personal communication) states that *Ammophila* is also apparently very conservative. They seem immediately to adopt as their territory the area in which they emerge, and tend to remain attached to this for the rest of their lives, though they probably do not get to know the details of it until they come to catch and drag prey at a later stage.

Before leaving this subject a final word of caution is necessary. While the circumstantial evidence for locality imprinting among a great many of these aculeate Hymenoptera is very remarkable, we must remember that other insects sometimes show striking locality restrictions under conditions which preclude imprinting. Thus the cluster-fly, *Pollenia rudis*, may occur in a particular room or under one particular eave of a house year after year (D. Keilin, personal communication), but the possibility of imprinting seems ruled out by the fact that the insect is in its early stages parasitic in earthworms of the genus *Allolobophora*. Similarly, the annual swarms of *Danais plexippus* on the famous 'butterfly trees' of California are composed of an entirely new migratory influx every year, so that none of the insects has had any previous experience of the locality. While the locality restrictions of the Hymenoptera, then, are very suggestive of imprinting, in no case has all other basis for the phenomenon been ruled out. We must therefore regard these examples as indicative of the need for further research rather than as satisfactory evidence for the phenomenon.

That habitat imprinting which is really 'homing' to a type of environment rather than to an exact locality, as induced experimentally in *Nemeritis*, may be a widespread and important phenomenon of learning among insects has been discussed by Thorpe (1938, 1940). Thus there may well be 'biological races,' based on conditioning to particular food plants, which are entirely phenotypic in character. Since such food-plant conditioning will tend to isolate those members of the species which possess it from other members associated with other food plants, it will, *ipso facto*, tend to bring about a non-genetic mating restriction or preference.

But obviously only careful investigation can enable us to determine for certain whether a given instance of seeking a special environment is phenotypic, and in very few cases has the necessary information been obtained. Thus the attraction of parasitic Hymenoptera to the food plants of their hosts (Thorpe and Caudle, 1938) may prove to be either innate or acquired or something of both. The method by which such a learnt response to a particular type of habitat, rather than to a unique locality, may be of importance as a factor in the evolution of new races, has been discussed by a number of writers, populations of animals being supposed to be held to a particular habitat by learnt preferences until this preference is reinforced under the influence of selection, so becoming hereditary. The fixation of such a habitat preference by selection is usually known as the Baldwin effect, although it was, in fact, proposed almost simultaneously in the year 1896 by Lloyd Morgan, H. F. Osborne and J. M. Baldwin. Baldwin himself called the effect 'organic selection,' and defined it as 'the process of individual accommodation considered as keeping organisms alive, and so, by also securing accumulation of variations, determining evolution in subsequent generations.' As Simpson (1953) has pointed out, Baldwin used the word 'accommodation' to mean an acquired character and 'variation' to imply a genetic change. The idea put forward by Baldwin proved an attractive one to a large number of writers on evolutionary subjects, but it was not easy to see exactly what the mechanism could be by which the acquired change became inherited. Thorpe (1945b) suggested that recent developments in genetics and in the study of animal learning make the Baldwin concept at once more probable and easier to understand. The argument depends on the fact, which Mather (1943) has pointed out, that the kinds of character which are likely to distinguish races and species are polygenic, and that any small decrease in mating freedom between two populations, whether brought about by natural obstacles or by any other cause, will be sufficient to lessen the intensity of selection for good 'relational balance' (i.e. the balance existing in an outbreeding organism between pairs of different homologous combinations). The result of this will be that when members of two such populations or strains cross, the offspring will be heterotic. Mather further brings forward evidence to show that heterotic individuals are less fit than the parental types, and that the avoidance of heterosis is probably the most widespread stimulant of isolating devices. According to Mather, such a system, once started, is self-propagating and irreversible.

Now suppose for the sake of argument that the initial basis of separation is a host-plant preference, an olfactory conditioning, or a 'locality imprinting' holding the animal to a restricted locality or environment, renewed afresh in each generation; and that this is strong enough and has continued long enough significantly to reduce the intensity of selection for relational balance. There will thus be a definite selective advantage for such new variants as favour more complete isolation. Now among germinal variants of equal magnitude, those which are of the same nature and direction as the phenotypic learned response already operating will be more effective in furthering isolation, and will therefore be most strongly favoured by natural selection. Thus the learned or conditioned response will give momentum to and set the direction for selective processes tending to bring about genotypic isolation. These selective processes will thus bring about the reinforcement and perhaps the eventual replacement of non-heritable modifications by genetic modifications, and will thus closely simulate a Lamarckian effect. It seems probable, therefore, that habitat preference may have an influence at a very early stage, perhaps preceding topographical separation and thus helping to originate it or, at any rate, proceeding hand in hand with it. As Muller (1942) has shown, for spatial or topographical isolation to be an effective splitting agent *alone*, it might have to be very strong, and perhaps in birds such a situation would be very unlikely to occur. 'But the topographical isolation need not be as absolute where it is combined with either acquired or genetic-ecological adaptation to different ecological conditions, as where it constitutes the only isolating factor.'

We still have no examples which we can cite as certain evidence for the efficacy of the Baldwin concept, but there are a large number of cases which offer at least *prima facie* support for the theory, and it may well turn out to be an important agent in sympatric speciation in some groups. Examples from various animal groups will be found in the paper by Thorpe (1944), and the whole subject has been reconsidered by Simpson (1953) and by Dethier (1954).

There have, of course, been numerous studies on the inheritance of specific behaviour traits in mammals where behaviour is exceedingly complex and inheritance, as far as present evidence goes, mainly polygenic. The situation in insects being in some respects simpler, offers better prospects for fundamental analysis. There are now many studies in this field, using insect material, and examples of both polygenic and unifactorial control of behaviour are coming to light. Papers of particular interest are Haskins and Haskins (1958), Manning (1959, 1961), von Hörman-Heck (1957). Haskins and Haskins (1958), studying food habits and cocoon-spinning behaviour of moths of the genus *Callosamia*, found that certain F_1 hybrids resembled the male parent in food habits but, in contrast, in cocoon-spinning behaviour there was clear evidence that the inheritance was polygenic. Manning (1959) concluded that changes in the specific courtship behaviour of certain *Drosophila* species could most readily be produced by the selection of mutations affecting reaction thresholds, and that these would be a first step in behavioural divergence. He also found (1961) that artificial selection for speed of mating in *melanogaster* will change the threshold of the various more purely sexual responses. Spieth (1949 and 1951—ref. in Haskins and Haskins) found only quantitative differences in fourteen strains of the *Drosophila viridis* group. But a different picture seems to emerge from work on the Orthoptera. Von Hörman-Heck (1957) crossed *Gryllus campestris* and *bimaculatus*. In aggressive movements, trembling movements of the antennæ, movements involving the courtship song and sound production, back-crosses indicated monofactorial transmission.

CHAPTER XII

FISH

Introduction

FISH are the dominant class among the vertebrates in the world today, both in numbers of individuals and also in numbers of species. Well over 90 per cent. of the 18,000 species (Mayr, 1946) belong to the Teleost or bony fishes, and it is to this section of the class that the present account is of necessity mainly restricted, for there is at present an almost complete absence of critical behaviour study of the rest.

Uniformity of water as a medium for locomotion and the consequent restriction of ways in which it is practicable for an animal of vertebrate type of organisation to make effective progress through it has tended to produce a remarkable uniformity of bodily structure. The extreme examples of bodily organisation in fishes are, it is true, bizarre and abnormal enough, but they are almost all concerned with a reduction in powers of swimming, and one has only to consider the group as a whole to see what a small minority such forms actually constitute. The vast majority display little more than rather minor and commonplace variations on the basic pattern, and the extreme forms seem merely to emphasise the prevailing uniformity.

From the behavioural point of view there are three characteristics of the group which appear to be particularly significant. Firstly, the elementary social behaviour, which expresses itself in the formation of schools or shoals. Secondly, the lack of prehensile organs and the small part which manipulation plays in the lives of most fishes—which might be expected to limit their powers of space perception. Thirdly, a fact which should tend to counteract this, namely, that most fishes are effectively and actively in a three-dimensional world for the greater part or the whole of their lives. Where no obstacles are present, as in the open sea, this circumstance may not be particularly significant, but where, as in lake and littoral forms, there is vegetation and other obstacles to be negotiated, it must, one would think, aid substantially in the development of competence in spatial orientation and control.

Modern ethology has a particular interest in the fishes, for this group has provided material for some basic and highly critical studies on locomotory movements, on the hierarchical organisation of instinctive behaviour, and on its analysis in terms not of chain reflexes but of reaction chains. Fundamental to this subject is the work of Harris and Whiting (1954) who have recently confirmed the conclusions of Wintrebert (1920) that the earliest contractions of the skeletal musculature of the embryo dogfish are of almost constant rhythm and entirely myogenic in origin and control. At this stage the active myotomes on the right and left sides behave as two entirely different units. Presently, although the two sides are still independent in frequency and phasing, each side may show sudden changes in frequency; this apparently being evidence of the first participation of the nervous system. Later still, co-ordination of the two sides appears, suggesting the first development of central nervous excitation and inhibition. From the work of von Holst (1935–7), Lissmann (1946) and others it appears that the locomotory movements of the mature fish are not necessarily to be interpreted as pure instincts in the sense that the 'locomotory centres' are completely independent of proprioceptive and other peripheral stimulation. Thus any 'locomotory drive' which may exist must be the expression of the activity of the sensory-motor co-ordination system as a whole, not exclusively of the central nervous system. Moreover, the co-ordination of the various movements into an economical and effective locomotory pattern may well be learned as a result of mechanical necessity, and the drive itself thus be acquired. But leaving aside locomotion, we may ask if there is any behaviour more completely inborn.

A very thorough analysis of instinctive behaviour has been provided by the work of N. Tinbergen and his associates on the mating behaviour of the Three-spined Stickleback (*Gasterosteus aculeatus*) (Fig. 48). The male must first receive the appropriate internal and external stimuli for setting up a territory, among which stimuli the sight of green vegetation is necessary. He next constructs a nest,[1] in choosing material for which green is again the preferred colour (Wunder, 1930), and is then ready to receive and conduct a female thither for the purpose of egg-laying. The male's first reaction, the zigzag dance, is dependent on the sight of a female having the swollen abdomen which shows that she is ready to lay eggs. At this stage the special swimming movements made by the female also play a part. She in her turn reacts to the red colour of the male and to his zigzag dance by swimming directly towards him. This action enables him to 'lead,' which simply consists of swimming rapidly towards the nest. This in turn induces the female to follow and again stimulates the male to the next action, which is to show her the nest entrance by pointing his head at it. And so the chain of behaviour patterns of the two individuals proceeds, each one dependent on sign-stimuli, mostly visual, which are different for each of the links, and the function of which is to enable the behaviour to proceed to the next action in the series.

Such an example suggests that it is perhaps not the basic locomotory

[1] Nest making is of course an entirely exceptional behaviour pattern among fishes.

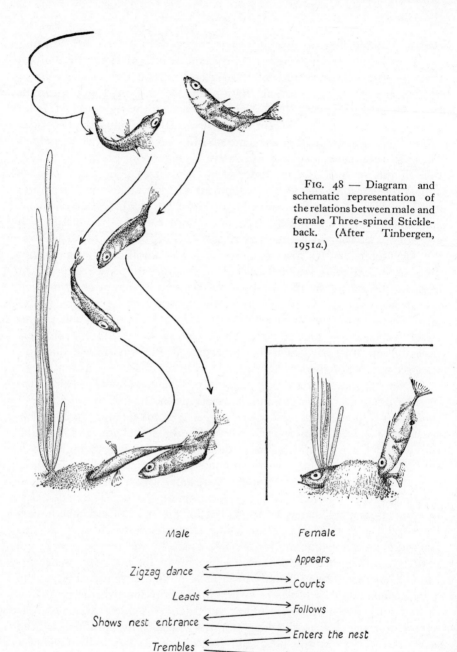

FIG. 48 — Diagram and schematic representation of the relations between male and female Three-spined Stickleback. (After Tinbergen, 1951a.)

Male		Female
		Appears
Zigzag dance		
		Courts
Leads		
		Follows
Shows nest entrance		
		Enters the nest
Trembles		
		Spawns
Fertilizes		

movements themselves, but the ground plan of the over-all *co-ordination* and *orientation* of such locomotory movements which must be inborn. Some of these movements which are less specifically locomotory can probably also be regarded as inborn; for while they may have been ritualised from locomotory components, they cannot themselves be necessitated by stimuli explicable in terms of the hydrodynamical characteristics of the environment. On the contrary, they seem to demonstrate much more clearly the concept of the pure instinct or 'Erbkoordination.' Thus in the case of the Three-spined Stickleback the characteristic expression of the territorial phase of the reproductive instinct consists of the particular orientation of movements in patrolling and fighting activities. In the next phases it similarly consists largely of correct co-ordination and orientation of the movements we have just been describing. But since the orientation or taxis component is shown to be such an important part of the instinctive organisation, we must inquire how much of the releaser system which mediates it is inborn. It now seems fairly clear from the work of Baerends, Seitz, Tinbergen, van Iersel, Morris and many others that in these fishes the inborn releasers are very simple sign-stimuli. These may be chemical, as von Frisch (1941) has shown, for the broken cuticle of an injured Minnow (*Phoxinus lævis*) may release a chemical substance which causes the school to congregate and immediately go into hiding. The releasers may also include a particular movement— such as the trembling of the courting Stickleback or the typical slow, jerky, swimming movement characteristic of the Cichlid parent leading away its young (Baerends and Baerends-van Roon, 1950). Baerends again has shown that relative size may be an inborn releaser, for in the same Cichlids the distance at which the young have to see the parent when following is fixed for a given age.

A very comprehensive analysis of the reproductive behaviour of some other species along similar lines has been made by Forselius (1957). Although the picture that results from this immensely thorough work on the Anabantid fishes is similar to that provided by Tinbergen's classic account of *Gasterosteus*, yet there are some important differences, particularly concerning the extent to which items of the behaviour are entirely inborn. Indeed, it is very easy to over-simplify the consistency and specificity of many of the responses and of the innate recognitions involved. Thus Tavolga (1956) shows that the courtship response of a male Goby to a specific visual stimulus is governed in part by previous experiences, and he quotes Noble to the effect that sex discrimination in *Lebistes* males is a learned response. For a further discussion of this matter, see Aronson (1957). Some of the variations in behaviour of the Three-spined Stickleback itself have been discussed by Guiton (1960). The conclusion is that the behaviour of a fish at different stages does not seem to depend solely on the immediate external situation but is in some degree influenced by previous experience. Indeed, quite large modifications of the normal instinctive orientation of the nest-building movements may be made. For a general review, see Baerends (in Brown, 1957).

Besides movement and size, visual releasers display two other features which are often less easy to evaluate precisely, namely configuration and colour. As an example of configuration alone providing a stimulus, we may mention the outline of the breeding female Stickleback and the threatening attitude adopted by a male at the boundary of his territory and directed towards an intruder of the same sex. This consists of posing in a vertical position, head pointing downwards; and it is by no means the configuration only which supplies the stimulus here, but probably to an even greater extent the displacement 'picking' movements which the male continually makes on the floor of the aquarium. In a great many cases configuration is also linked with colour. Much of the earlier work on colour vision in fishes is suspect owing to lack of understanding of the difficulties of designing critical experiments; but that colour vision does exist in many fishes is now well enough established. An excellent summary of the earlier work will be found in the paper by Warner (1931). Noble and Curtis (1939), in their studies of the Jewel Fish (*Hemichromis bimaculatus*), found that the young were attracted to red, and suggested that this attraction was related to the breeding colours of the adults. The females were found to recognise their own males as individuals by means of the colour pattern on the head; for if the whole body of the male except the head were covered, the female still recognised her mate. If, however, the faces were painted and the rest of the body left its natural colour, recognition was no longer shown. The parent fish were found to distinguish their own young from those of other species by the colour of the face, for if the young fish were stained an abnormal colour they were rejected by their parents. These authors succeeded in inducing *Hemichromis* to rear the young of *Cichlasoma bimaculatum*, and produced evidence that the colour preference of these young was very largely learned. That conditioning in early life can affect the response to colours of several species of Cichlids appears to be fairly clear both from the work of Noble and Curtis and from Baerends and Baerends–van Roon. But there seems little doubt, from the work of the latter authors, that in some species there is a strong inborn preference for a particular colour, and that this preference can be affected only very slightly by experience. Seitz (1940), studying the genus *Tilapia* (mouth-breeders in which there is a marked difference between the reproductive colour patterns of male and female), has shown that simple models do not release courting in the male—which apparently has a very detailed and presumably conditioned knowledge of female characters. It is assumed that this learning process takes place in the schools of immature fishes which show marking very similar to the colour pattern of the ripe female. With the male pattern, however, it is different, for the *Tilapia* male apparently has no opportunity to learn the reproductive markings of a male of its species; nor, indeed, has the female, for a male that assumes this colour immediately isolates itself in a territory. Seitz found that in *Astatotilapia* also, fighting could be released by quite simple models, and that both male and female in this genus must possess an inborn knowledge of the form and probably the colour pattern of the male. But although, as such studies show, learning abilities may play an important part even in such closely organised instinctive behaviour chains as these, nevertheless extraordinarily few cases have as yet been investigated. There is an immense field of work now open to the student.

Having thus briefly outlined the general state of knowledge of the instinct-learning problem in the group, we will next consider those circumstances of the life-cycle in which knowledge of this subject appears to be particularly crucial for understanding the biology of fishes. These circumstances can be regarded as arising mainly in the course of the appetitive behaviour of the feeding, social and reproductive instincts. After they have been discussed, laboratory experiments on fish learning will be briefly surveyed.

Feeding

There seems to be little precise knowledge on record as to the importance of learning in the choice of food by fishes. It appears a reasonable assumption that the snap-response of fish, like the pecking of chicks, is innate, but that a great deal else must be learned. Schreiner (1941) has produced evidence that this response is a true instinct in that it is dependent on an internal level of 'reaction-specific-energy.' The releasing situation, on the other hand, is an entirely acquired one; that is to say, there is no innate releasive mechanism for the object of the snap-reaction. The stimulus situation results from or is dependent upon the complex of a great many external and internal circumstances, though optic stimuli are certainly the most important in this context.

Social Behaviour

The schooling behaviour of fishes is certainly one of the most characteristic features of the life of the group, and a study of its course naturally leads on to the investigation of visual releasers; for it is clear that vision is the main sense governing the behaviour in this group. Parr (1937) showed that this schooling habit in certain pelagic fish is in the first place dependent upon the fact that one specimen moves towards another of its own size class. This response, continually repeated, results in the familiar phenomenon of vast aggregations of oceanic fishes all moving in the same direction. Parr showed that such schools break up at night and are re-formed at dawn, except that with certain species and in certain stages of growth luminescence probably makes the fish visible to one another at night. Morrow (1948), who gives a valuable summary of schooling behaviour of fishes, and Keenleyside (1955), provide evidence that in many species the initial attraction cannot be a learned one since newly hatched individuals will school immediately and that two individuals are sufficient to form a 'school.' The formation of a school thus depends upon the innate attraction which each fish exerts upon the other. Besides the response to the simple scheme provided by a fellow fish, there is probably an innate relative size preference such as Baerends found with the Cichlids. This will lead to the maintenance of an individual distance, and if we assume that the optimum situation for a fish in a school is that it should perceive companions with equal intensity on either side, the fish in the inner parts of the school which have their visual stimuli balanced in this way are likely to be 'content,' while those on the outside, which will be in a state of visual unbalance, would be expected to push vigorously towards the centre. That the sign-stimulus releasing primary schooling response is extremely generalised has been shown by the work of Baerends on *Hemichromis* and *Cichlasoma*.

But there is plenty of evidence that, by an imprinting-like process, this stimulus is soon improved upon and completed by experience. Besides form and size, there is no doubt that here, too, movement is one of the important primary elements in the behaviour. Schlaifer (1942) found that the Chub Mackerel (*Pneumatophorus grex*) would not school with one of the same species which happened to be blind. Although this individual was normal in form and colour, it had a slow, unusual swimming action quite unlike the normal. Breder and Gresser (1941) found that Eyed Cave Fish (*Anoptichthys-Astynax*) would attempt to school with blind individuals but were unable to adapt themselves to the abnormal movements of the latter, and this eventually led to a kind of resentment which resulted in attack. It is evident, both from experiment and from observations in nature, that social responses are rapidly developed by learning in schools. Thus Baerends and Baerends-van Roon, working with Cichlids, were able —by the use of models—to build up schools of a characteristic colour which behaved in some degree as an entity; and there is a good deal of evidence from tagging experiments, such as those of Merriman (1941) on the Striped Bass (*Roccus saxatilis*), which showed that natural schools of fish may be highly stable and be restricted to the same group of individuals over a long period. (That response to quite unnatural forms such as squares and triangles can be learned by fish has been established by the experimental work of Herter (1953)). Although this schooling behaviour is so widely shown among fishes, there are, of course, great differences in the degree of its development as we pass from species to species and genus to genus. Breder and Halpern (1946) found that in *Brachydanio rerio*, which is not a species in which schooling is highly developed, fright induced by a large variety of stimuli will induce *temporary* schooling. These authors attempted to bring about more permanent aggregation by a training process, such that whenever the temporary school started to break up a mild electric shock was given. This, however, had the unexpected result that the shock merely led to fighting behaviour in an otherwise peaceful species, and the authors suggest that the fish refer this unpleasant experience to their immediate companions and so attack them. This rather elaborate explanation is perhaps hardly warranted. It appears likely that in such a fish of no-schooling type the inborn individual-distance response normally tends to keep the fish well separated. This is overcome temporarily by the frightening situation, but the abnormal experience of an electric shock is not frightening in the ordinary sense of the word, for it has no directional component; perhaps it is merely stimulating and so allows or induces the redevelopment of the individual-distance phenomenon. These workers also found that individual fish of this species, reared in isolation from the egg, would join an aggregation at once, but those removed from a group to isolation and then later returned were hesitant. Here, again, it appears that the I.R.M. for schooling is extremely generalised, and that the innate response to aggregation may be modified by experience after it has once been exercised, but may later be abandoned because of enforced isolation. Breder and Halpern obtained similar results with goldfish. Individuals isolated for six months no longer aggregated normally and appeared 'nervous' and unusually sensitive to stimuli outside the tank.

To summarise this section of the subject, we may say that while there is abundant evidence for the development of the schooling response by a learning process, it is in most cases extremely difficult to distinguish between the effects of this and the possibility that an inborn recognition of the species pattern is slowly maturing. Most young fish school heterogeneously and very strongly; a laboratory life of a few months as an adult is often sufficient to inhibit this, and it would seem fairly clear that the concepts both of learning and of maturation would be necessary to account for the many variations of behaviour which have been described.[1]

Schooling is of interest in that it seems to be such a distinct behaviour pattern, and one which is not necessarily linked with any of the main instinctive urges. It seems that one must at present regard it as evidence

---

[1] In considering the response of mature fish to the visual stimulus of other members of the species, one must always remember the possibility that aquarium fish may have become conditioned to the sight of themselves reflected in the walls of the aquarium—perhaps only likely where the illumination is very strong. That fish respond readily to mirror images of themselves has been shown by the work of Spooner (1931), Lissmann (1932), Sato (1938) and others.

of a distinct social instinct [2] sufficient in itself and, in some species at least, independent of the instincts of feeding and reproduction, although no doubt apt to be valuable in both these connections.

Besides the potential value of school formation for successful reproduction, there is plenty of evidence that schooling can have a protective function (von Frisch, cited above; Bowen, 1931). Thus species such as Catfish, with poor vision, might be safer in a group since many pairs of eyes are better than one. Similarly with feeding behaviour, species which feed on large particles which have to be searched for but which, when found, can supply food for many individuals, may be more successful when hunting in groups; just as the feeding flock is often an efficient technique for birds. Perhaps still more impressive is the evidence that, with fish, learning is more rapid and efficient when the individuals are grouped. This will be discussed below since the evidence comes, of course, from laboratory experiments; but it may well be that schools of fishes learn more quickly to recognise what is good to eat, and become more expert in finding it, as a result of their group behaviour. Before leaving the subject of schooling, it is interesting to mention the extraordinary forms which it sometimes takes and which are at present little understood. Thus there is a fairly widespread phenomenon (Gudger, 1949) shown by many species of fish, both freshwater and marine, which arrange themselves in stationary ranks like soldiers on parade. Gudger (loc. cit.) reproduces an extraordinary photograph (Plate I) of trout in the Brule River, Minnesota, resting in eight almost perfectly aligned ranks. In this photograph 110 fish appear in one picture, arranged in rows almost equidistant from one another. Breder (1959) has pointed out that where water flows swiftly over a sandy bottom it is usual for transverse ridges to be formed. On the downstream side of these ridges a slight eddy is produced which presents a line of comparatively still water in which fish may come to rest. This he thinks could easily account for the transverse parallel rows of fishes in the picture. The apparent pairing of the fish in groups of two along the transverse rows is more difficult to account for. Equal spacing in the rows could, of course, be due to an individual distance phenomenon which is as common in fish as it is in birds. Breder suggests that in this species individual distance may be mainly expressed between two fish only, as if it were not possible for a fish to keep track of other fish on two sides of it simultaneously. However, the original account of this extraordinary grouping suggests that this cannot be the whole explanation; for it has been observed that in such ranks one individual may back out for a moment to catch prey, make a wide detour and then return to its correct place without disturbing the others. Whatever may be the function of such extraordinary social organisation, there is no doubt that it must

[2] Keenleyside (1955) comes to the same conclusion.

I. A Partially Learned Orientation.

Resting trout in eight ranks, like soldiers on parade, in the Brule River, Minnesota. (From Gudger, 1949.)

be partly learned and based on a series of extremely precise visual orientations.

Territory and Restricted Range

Many of the most striking pieces of evidence for learning occur within the appetitive behaviour of the reproductive instinct, and within this behaviour sequence the establishment and holding of territory provides us with the most interesting examples.

Territory proper is connected with reproduction, and territory-holding in the strict sense seems to be a typical manifestation of the reproductive drive. But there is also something very similar occurring in other aspects of the life of fish, a phenomenon which is often referred to as restricted range or home range. Territory proper is always a defended area, whereas restricted ranges where they are not part of the manifestation of a reproductive drive are often not defended. We as yet know too little to say whether area defence by fish in a non-reproductive state is exceptional or not.

Range-holding is common in freshwater fishes, and is also found in many marine species which dwell in nooks and crannies of coastal rocks and coral reefs. The evidence that territorial recognition is normally based on vision is so overwhelming that it need hardly be discussed. However, there are, no doubt, exceptions to this, one of the most striking being supplied by fish which live in very turbid water. Thus the male of the primitive Lung Fish *Protopterus* makes a nest of long grasses surrounding a foot-deep hole in the mud and remains guarding it for a long period. Recognition of such a spot and the ability to return to it may well be tactile, and it is not improbable that the electric fishes *Gymnarchus*, recently described by Lissmann (1951, 1956), can use their electric organs and sensitivity to aid territorial recognition. Gerking (1959) gives a helpful review of restricted movements in fish populations (see also Aronson, 1957). Important papers discussed by Gerking or published since his review was written are Hoar (1956, 1958), Abel (1955), Winn and Bardach (1960).

Every angler knows that fish take up non-reproductive 'territories' and are often extremely faithful to them. Many such 'ranges' are no doubt advantageous in that they are places from which potential enemies can easily be observed or which offer good protection on one or more sides. This is particularly obvious in many species of gobies and blennies, which often inhabit quite restricted crannies from which they emerge for feeding. The tendency to take up residence in a particular spot, even though the fish is not in the reproductive phase, is well known to aquarists, and there is evidence (Braddock, 1949) that prior residence in an area gives an individual of the species *Platypœcilus maculatus* greater potentiality for dominance over its fellows than it would otherwise have. The effect is mainly upon the initial contacts with other individuals and tends to fade as time passes. How widespread is this habit of establishing and perhaps defending non-reproductive ranges is already being indicated by the explorations of aqua-lung divers. Hass (1952) gives many examples of individual fish having particular lairs or 'hide-outs' to which they are faithful for long periods. One of the most remarkable examples of this kind of faithfulness to and defence of a non-reproductive territory is shown by the adoption of sleeping-places by fish in crowded aquaria. Workers at the Lerner Marine Station at Bimini, in the Bahamas, are familiar with the extraordinary spectacle of sub-tropical reef fishes in the marine enclosures seeking out the same sleeping-places night after night. In these places some of the species lie flat on their sides and Dr Breder tells me that the 'best' places tend to be retained by the older and larger individuals and newcomers have to sleep where they can. Dr Breder (1951) has himself studied the nocturnal behaviour of the Labrid Fish *Xyrichthys psittacus*, which returns to the same place night after night, and accumulates coral fragments and other objects around the sandy spot where it partially buries itself when at rest. Winn (1958) has discussed some important aspects of territorial behaviour and activity ranges in various species of 'Darters.' He finds that the areas utilised by the fish are divided into the territory of the male, the reproductive range of the female, the food range and the escape range. Most of these activities cease at night. The area guarded by a male may be either around the moving female or around some conspicuous area of the habitat such as a rock or a plant. Winn and Bardach (1960) describe how *Scarus guacamaia* lives in home caves where it stays at night and during the day when not feeding. If startled when out feeding the fish return to their caves. They immediately swim directly to the home cave from whatever point at which they happen to be.

It is clear that many of these observations on territory adoption and range-holding in fish would be difficult to explain without assuming a general exploratory tendency and an ability, as a result of this tendency, to acquire a general knowledge of the immediate environment—a knowledge which could hardly be achieved except by a process corresponding to latent learning. Perhaps general knowledge of an area is shown more strikingly by *Bathygobius soporator* than by any other known fish. This species inhabits tidal pools, and Aronson (1951) finds that the fish are so well orientated that they are able to jump from pool to pool at low tide without running any significant risk of finding themselves on dry land. Aronson shows that the conditions are such that the fish are unable to see the neighbouring pools before leaping. Various possibilities which might account for the orientation were investigated. These included orientation to the

sun or shadows caused by the sun and trial-and-error learning of the
jumps. None of these hypotheses was found to meet the situation, and
the author was forced to the provisional conclusion that these gobies swim
over tide pools at high tide, and thereby acquire an effective memory of
the general features and the topography of a limited area around the home

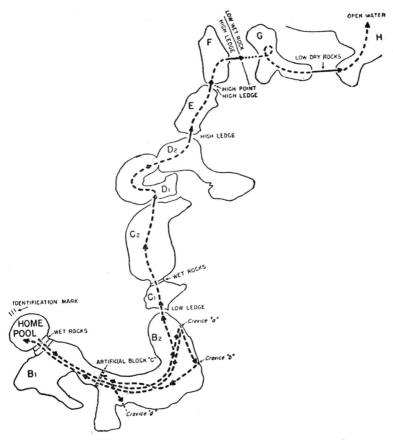

Fig. 49—Schematic outline of the pools, paths and jumps in a particular experiment
on the orientation behaviour of the Gobiid fish *Bathygobius soporator*. The heavy broken
lines represent the paths taken by the fish while swimming; the heavy plain lines indicate
the jumps; the heavy dotted lines represent climbing or skipping over wet rocks. (After
Aronson, 1951.)

pool, a memory which they are able to utilise when locked in their pools at
low tide. Fig. 49 shows schematically the pools, paths and jumps studied
in a particular location. A glance at it will make clear the remarkable precision of knowledge which the fish must have in order to be able to proceed
safely from one pool to the next. An achievement such as this must almost
certainly be equated with latent learning.

When we come to the true reproductive territories, it seems probable that the main function of territorial behaviour is to secure a place where courtship, fertilisation and, in rare cases, nest-building can proceed without interruption from other members of the species. Defence of the territory often involves elaborate and specific display, as in the case of the Fighting Fish (*Betta splendens*) (Lissmann, 1932). Under normal conditions these threatening displays usually seem to lead to the retreat of the intruder without an actual fight taking place. Under certain conditions, what is known as a 'nip-right hierarchy' may be formed in fish (see Newman, 1956), a phenomenon corresponding to the peck order so frequently described in birds. Recently Fabricius (1951*b*) has described how in the small Chinese Cyprinid (*Tanichthys albonubes*) the elaborate inborn display, which includes a slow rhythmic waving of the brightly coloured pectoral fin, together with a trembling of the whole body, and concludes with a sudden darting away, suffices to make the intruder leave the territory. Fabricius (1951*b*) has also described the courting behaviour of the Bream (*Abramis brama*), which restlessly patrols its territory and responds to an intruder with a violent attack accompanied by vigorous tail splashing. In this instance the continual swimming of the resident appears to be the intimidating element. At the same time this agitation seems to attract the female to the territory, and her refusal to depart and quiet behaviour elicit an even more violent splashing on the part of the male. This splashing culminates in spawning, and Evans (1954) suggests that the explosive splashings of hundreds of patrolling bream on a given stretch of beach results in a communal facilitation of the spawning process—an effect similar to the stimulus to mating which each pair of gulls in a colony was formerly supposed to experience from the similar activities of the other members of the group (Darling, 1938*a*).

Homing

It has been common knowledge for generations that many species of fish undertake large-scale migrations. Russell (1937), who summarised the knowledge of this subject, points out that most fish migrations consist of (*a*) a dispersal of eggs or larvæ or young fishes either by drifting passively with the current or by an active search for the normal habitat, (*b*) the return journey—an active movement usually against the current to the spawning grounds, and (*c*) a dispersal of the spent fishes, a process which again may be either passively with the current or actively in search of fresh feeding-grounds. There is no critical evidence as to whether learning contributes anything to the maintenance of ordinary periodic migration routes. In many cases it seems impossible that this should be so and there seems to be a general lack of evidence that schools of young fish follow or are in any way led by experienced adults. So we must assume

for the time being that the regularity and consistency of the main migration routes is a product of the innate organisation of the fish and of the
currents, water temperature, food supply and other similar characteristics
of the environment. However, by about the 'twenties of the present century fish-marking experiments had begun to suggest that individuals of
some species of fish, particularly of the genera *Salmo* and *Oncorhynchus*,
were returning to spawn, not merely in the geographical area in which
they were hatched but actually in the same stream or particular portion
of the stream which they had inhabited in their earliest youth. There has
been a great deal of discussion of the evidence for this which it is
unnecessary to go into here. Summaries will be found in the papers by
Scheer (1939), Shapovalov (1940) and Gerking (1959). Suffice it to say that
there is now indubitable evidence that a high proportion of some species of
salmon and trout succeed in returning to the stream from which they had
emerged as youngsters, and that very few individuals of these species enter
streams a hundred or more miles from the one in which they were reared.
Rich and Holmes (1928) carried out extensive transplantation experiments
with Chinook Salmon (*Oncorhynchus tschawytcha*), with the result that all
the fish from transplanted eggs which were recovered were found in the
river in which they were brought up and not in the river in which they
were spawned. Shapovalov found that, over four years, 233 (97·9 per cent.)
Steel Head Trout (*Salmo gairdneri*) returned to the home stream and
only 5 (2·1 per cent.) to a stream four miles distant at the mouth. Figures
for Silver Salmon (*Oncorhynchus milktschitsch*) in the same streams
were 79·2 per cent. and 20·8 per cent. It has also been demonstrated that
this return is not to be explained on the assumption that the intervening
period has been spent in the near neighbourhood of the native stream.
A very similar situation has come to light as a result of the important
and extensive work of Stuart (1957) on the Brown Trout in Scotland.
Fig. 50 shows the distribution of Chinook Salmon (*Oncorhynchus
tschawytcha*) tagged in the sea off Hippa Island, British Colombia. It
has also been argued that the great distances from their home stream at
which salmon have been found in the sea precludes even the possibility
that they could be homing successfully, but there is now plenty of evidence of the great speed at which salmon are capable of travelling once
the urge to return is upon them. Thus, Gilbert and Rich (1926) have
evidence that an individual of *O. nerka* normally travels 100 miles a day,
and Dahl (1938) notes that a salmon (*S. salar*) must have travelled at the
rate of sixty miles a day for twelve days. Other similar records of the
same species (see Scheer, 1939) include twenty-four miles a day for seventeen days and for the Chinook Salmon nineteen miles a day for fourteen
days. Much information on fish homing will be found in the review of
Gerking (1959), although this does not deal specifically with the orientation

problem. Hoar (1956, 1958) has shown that the direction of swimming of young salmon may be strongly influenced by a large number of different stimuli, of which water currents are among the more important. However, these fish will very rapidly learn a particular course and direction and will then use many different clues for keeping steady on the course just as do birds. It is clear, however, that at least some species of fish provide evidence for latent learning ability of a high order, enabling them to return directly to a desired spot even though transported to any part of a familiar area. Thus Hasler and Wisby (1958) (ref. in Gerking, 1959) found

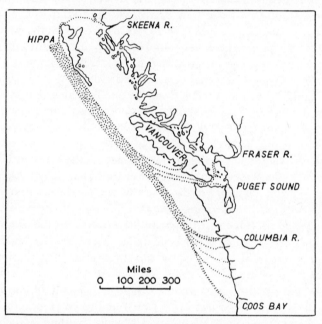

FIG. 50—Distribution of Chinook Salmon tagged in the sea, Hippa Island, British Columbia, 1925. (From Scheer 1939, after Williamson, 1927.)

that Green Sunfish show ultimately more than 90 per cent. success in returning to the corner where they had been taken. By attaching floats to the back it was learned that adult males guarding nests returned directly to the nests within minutes after release in the same pond, but if they were released in an adjacent unfamiliar pond they wandered aimlessly about. It is now known that fish can maintain a direction in unfamiliar waters by means of a sun compass mechanism similar to that in other groups of animals. Hasler et al. (1958) (ref. in Gerking, 1959) demonstrated this with White Bass (*Roccus chrysops*) after transporting them to the middle of Lake Mendota. The White Bass swam directly towards their spawning site on the north side of the Lake and were able to distinguish between their home spawning site and another one close by. But although some fish at least can use the sun as a compass, it is as yet uncertain whether fish can accomplish full sun orientation after the manner of homing birds released in an unfamiliar area. However, the work of Braemer (1961, in progress) makes it seem probable that they do so.

The problem that such a discovery sets for a student of learning and sensory physiology is obviously an extremely difficult one. In the first place it seems fairly clear that successful return cannot be the result of a *visual* memory of the home or the route therefrom (Ward, 1939). The young salmon descending a stream for the first time plays along near the shore, probably drifting passively for large stretches of the route. The returning adult swims strenuously in deeper waters on its way up the same river, and the two pathways must thus often be separated by a distance greater than the visual range. So we have to fall back on the assumption that it is the ability of the salmon to perceive and remember the chemical and physical characteristics of the water and of the stream bed, which enables the animal to achieve the apparent *tour de force* of returning to the stream of its nativity anything from two to six years after having left (Hasler and Wisby, 1951).

The work of Hasler (1954) on odour perception and orientation in fishes, and that of Bull, discussed below, have shown that the organs of chemical sense can appreciate small but probably constant differences in the characteristics of water from different streams and currents, including, of course, differences in salinity. Hasler and Wisby (1951) have actually demonstrated a learned olfactory preference for the waters of the home creek. Then there are also to be considered differences in temperature, pH, proportion of dissolved gases, temperature and density stratification and general turbulence. Added to this there could be a recognition of the characteristic sound made by waterfalls and rapids,[1] the memory of the general nature of the river bottom (which, of course, would be partly visual), and perhaps a memory of the type of food to be obtained there. Finally, as regards the route in the deeper waters of the sea, we must not forget the possibility that many fishes produce noises which might provide the basis for echo-sounding against the sea-bed, or—in the absence of noise produced by the species itself—there is the possibility of the perception of the resonance effect of the surface wave noise on the bottom (Harden Jones, personal communication). Let us, then, for the purposes of discussion, take into account all these possible sources of stimuli for orientation, and in the light of this consider what the homing performance of species of *Salmo* entails. Translated into laboratory terms, it is

[1] For orientation of the Creek Chub (*Semotilus atromaculatus*) by sound, see Kleerekoper and Chagnon (1954), whose paper provides a valuable general summary of hearing in fish and their training to acoustic stimuli.

very like learning to run a complex maze in reverse as a result of one pro-longed experience of the maze. It is not necessary to assume that the fish remembers every detail of the hundreds of miles which its journey may cover, but one must suppose that it remembers the characteristics of the different sections and particularly the features of the various 'choice points' constituted by the junctions of the tributary streams with the main river. It may be, of course, that many of these junctions do not really offer as free a choice as might appear at first sight. Perhaps the returning salmon find many of the tributaries obviously unfamiliar and unsuitable as a home environment. But however much we try in our imagination to simplify the problem faced by the returning fish, it remains a most aston-ishing performance. There will, no doubt, have to be many years of re-search before the whole picture presented by such behaviour is fully understood. That some fishes are capable of mastering mazes is well known (see p. 312, below), and it is worth pointing out that Welty (1934) has shown that groups of goldfish are more successful in learning mazes than are single fish, and that they learn through visual cohesion to move forward with their neighbours when the stimulus is presented, the effect being one of social facilitation and local enhancement. Moreover, it was found that groups of goldfish retain motor responses better than do isolated fishes. Nevertheless, such results do not go very far in the direction of making the task seem simple since we are still confronted with the fact that the route must have been learned in the reverse direction and that a period of years has elapsed between the learning process and utilisation of such learning. Here is 'latent learning' indeed.

LABORATORY EXPERIMENTS ON FISH LEARNING

Habituation

There has as yet been no critical work on habituation in fishes, but it is the general experience of aquarium keepers that fish become tame after a period of a few days in a new aquarium, and there is no reason to think that fish are in any way different from other animals in this respect. Braddock (1949) has studied the effect of prior residence in a particular aquarium or part of an aquarium upon the dominance relation of groups of the species *Platypœcilus maculatus*. This work has been referred to above (p. 299) in connection with the discussion of reproduc-tive territories, but there is little doubt that it also supplies evidence for habituation. The work of Welty (above) also points to the same con-clusion, as does also that of Welker and Welker (1958).

Conditioning

The earliest experiments on conditioned-reflex formation were those of McDonald (1922) and Westerfield (1922). The former trained Blunt-nosed Minnows (*Pimephales notatus*) to inhibit the initial flight response to the sound of a vibrating string as a result of receiving food, and the latter obtained a differentiation to two sounds of different frequency in the Mud Minnow (*Umbra* spp.) by a similar technique. A more precise and elaborate study was that of Froloff (1925, 1928), who established conditioned-reflex responses in ten species of fish, four freshwater and six marine. In these experiments the unconditioned response was flight caused by electric shock, and the conditioned stimuli were visual and mechanical. This work was followed up and greatly improved by Bull who, in a long series of papers (1928–39), describes the establishment of conditioned responses to many types of stimulus in many species. Among the stimuli successfully used were temperature, salinity, colour, sound, mechanical (touch, change in direction of water flow), chemical (olfaction and gustation, change in pH), and electric shock. Several of these experiments included trial-and-error learning in addition to pure conditioning. The work is of great practical importance for the light it has thrown on the sensitivity of many species of fish to very small changes in the environment. Thus *Blennius gattorugina* and *Blennius pholius*, when offered sea-water extracts of natural food substances, were able to differentiate between concentrations slightly less than 0·000375 and 0·00075 per cent. of the weight of living food substances in sea water. The first species was also able to form conditioned motor responses to a momentary decrease in the salinity of the surrounding water of as little as 3 parts per 1,000 or to a momentary increase of 37 parts per 1,000. Thus there is ample evidence that fish are able to appreciate and respond to stimuli of very small magnitude of just the kind which would be of value to them in a homing migration. Although Bull was thus successful in conditioning a large number of species to a variety of stimuli, it is worth noticing that the *Pleuronectidæ* were found to be far less adept at forming associations than were the other species studied. Thus in a typical case a Pleuronectid failed to form an association after 200 trials, whereas other species did so in less than forty. This is presumably an expression of the loss of adaptability following on the assumption of a bottom-living and somewhat sluggish mode of life (see also Bull, 1957). The work of Schreiner (1941) referred to above also provides good evidence of reflex conditioning in the Minnow, and Harlow (1939) has described results which he considers offer satisfactory evidence for forward-, backward- and pseudo-conditioning in goldfish. This work, however, is open to the criticism that both the conditioned stimulus and the reinforcement were shocks—either electrical shocks at different intensities or combined mechanical and electrical shocks—with the result that it is difficult to disentangle the effects of habituation to the stimulus and change in intensity of response to the same stimulus from those of true conditioning. The danger of errors resulting from the use of negative reinforcement alone is well shown by Dijkgraaf and Verheijen's (1950) correction of Wohlfahrt's (1939) negative results as to the discrimination of certain tones by *Phoxinus* (see p. 314 below).

Noble, Gruender and Meyer (1959) found that in the fish *Molliensia* spp. the optimum interval between the conditioned stimulus and the unconditioned stimulus was considerably larger than that for man. They proceed from this, however, to make the assumption that because certain features of the learning process are characteristic of an unidentified species of fish, the habits of which are unspecified, these features are necessarily characteristic of the group as a whole—a group, be it remembered, which contains about eighteen thousand species! Fortunately this kind of unjustified extrapolation is now much rarer than formerly. Bitterman and his colleagues (references in Datta, Milstein and Bitterman, 1960) failed to establish progressive habit reversal in *Tilapia macrocephala*, as also did Warren (1960) in the Paradise fish, *Macropodus opercularis*. This capacity is well established in mammals and is also reported for birds, amphibia and reptiles.

Trial-and-error Learning

What may be regarded as the first careful experiments on trial-and-error learning in fishes were those of Triplett (1901). This author, working with the Perch *Morone americanus*, obtained the result (similar to that reported second-hand by Möbius in 1873 with pike) that the predator, if separated from minnows by a glass plate, will—after a period of frequent collisions with the glass—cease to attack the minnows in that part of the aquarium even though the latter are no longer protected by intervening glass. They will, however, again make futile efforts to reach another type of prey, e.g. worms, when these are placed behind the glass. Some later and essentially similar experiments are listed by Warden, Jenkins and Warner (1936), and need not be further discussed here. These experiments all seem to suggest that while both the appearance of the prey and its relative position in the aquarium are appreciated, it is the latter feature which is most fully and precisely responded to. This seems to be substantiated by the majority of fish-learning experiments, most of which point to the conclusion that 'place learning' is particularly characteristic of this group; although Herter (1953) has shown that there are, of course, very great differences between one species and another. Ono (1937) trained the Paradise Fish (*Macropodus opercularis*) to pass through a given hole in a partition from among a choice of eight holes when it was shown a white triangle. Sanders (1940) taught the goldfish *Carassius auratus* to swim towards food when an illuminated disc was presented. He was successful in pairing an olfactory stimulation (amyl-acetate) with a visual stimulus. He then obtained a second-order conditioning by using amyl-acetate as the primary stimulus and the previous optic stimulus as the reward.

Discriminated operant food conditioning has been studied in fish by Chernova (1953) (ref. in Razran, 1961). Orienting reactions of fishes have also been investigated by Guselnokov (1958) and Vedyayev and Karmanova (1958) (refs. in Razran, 1961).

The extent to which trial-and-error learning can function advantageously in the life of fishes has been dramatically shown by the observations of Breder (1945) on a Mexican Blindfish (*Anoptichthys jordani*) suffering from the congenital absence of the lower jaw. This individual, which was one of a normal brood, lived to reach a standard length of 37 millimetres. An improvised buccal apparatus was formed, its main features probably having been established in the egg, and this resulted in an apparently completely effective substitute jaw mechanism. This is remarkable evidence of a sensitivity of the drive and appetitive behaviour mechanism great enough to ensure individual survival against such tremendous handicaps. It is obvious that a great deal of trial-and-error learning affecting some of the most characteristic movements of the species must have been involved in the adaptation of this individual. It is natural that trial-and-error learning experiments in fish should have been mainly concerned with the orientation and locomotion as stressed at the beginning of this chapter. Hoogland, Morris and Tinbergen (1957) find that Perch and Pike reject sticklebacks when, after being snapped up, their spines hurt the predator's mouth. After very few experiences, both Perch and Pike become negatively conditioned to the sight of sticklebacks and avoid them before they have made contact. As a result of this conditioning the last links of the predator's feeding chain drop out. In Pike, mere fixation with two eyes is often sufficient to recognise the prey as unwanted. Both species of sticklebacks enjoy a marked degree of protection from these predators. This protection is much better for *Gasterosteus* than for *Pygosteus* and tests with de-spined sticklebacks show that it is mainly due to the spines.

Although some species construct fairly elaborate nests, fish on the whole are rather conspicuous for the lack of ability to manipulate inanimate objects. Wunder (1930) and van Iersel (1953) give detailed accounts of the nest-building activity of *Gasterosteus*, but there seems to be no experimental study of the amount of learning involved. However, the fact that fish can be taught 'manipulations' has been demonstrated by the very interesting training technique evolved by Haralson and Bitterman (1950). They trained the fish *Tilapia macrocephala* to depress a lever, and thereby secure food in an apparatus which was in effect a sort of aquatic 'Skinner-box.' Once a suitable response lead was established, it was found to remain constant even after periods of up to one

month without training. Extinction was rapid even when a periodic reinforcement was supplied at an average rate of three worms per minute.
This feature appears to be primarily a function of the type of response required, and was not shown in an earlier form of the apparatus where
interception of a beam of light and not a definite manipulative action was
all that was required of the fish. It is interesting to note that during the
extinction process violent displacement or overflow activities were often
shown. These might take the form of bursts of aggressive behaviour with
biting at the exposed edges of the target and were so frequent that the
target edge had to be specially protected during extinction experiments.
One fish actually succeeded in grasping the target and twisting it so vigorously that the delicate lever arm was badly bent.

The efficacy of partial reinforcement in preventing extinction has been
demonstrated in *Tilapia macrocephala* by Longo and Bitterman (1960).

Detour Experiments

The high ability for place learning above referred to at once suggests
that fishes should be adept at detour and maze problems. The first careful
experiments were those of Thorndike (1911), who showed that *Fundulus*
was quick to learn the shortest way through a series of openings to a
feeding-place. This was followed by Russell (1931), who found that
Three-spined Sticklebacks (*Gasterosteus aculeatus*) learned to find their
way into a small jar or bottle for food and at the same time learned how
to get out. In Russell's experiments the solution was at first found by
chance, but only a few trials were required for the behaviour to become
definitely directed towards finding the solution. The learning curve
showed a sudden drop in the time taken, and the jar, from being an indifferent object, rapidly acquired significance. Learning was found to be
retained at least three months. Spooner (1937) carried out a much more
elaborate piece of research into the learning of detours by Wrasse (*Ctenolabrus rupestris*). The object of the detours was to reach food either in a
pot or around and behind glass plates. This work is particularly significant in demonstrating that the law of effect, at least in the form then
usually accepted, was inadequate to account for the results; for movements which had led to success in earlier trials were by no means necessarily 'stamped in.' When a response was developing, the integration of
the later movements did not proceed in advance of that of the earlier, and
the behaviour pattern was certainly not built up slowly in the trial-and-
error manner by the linking together of independent movements by a
process of backward association. Spooner emphasises that, on the contrary, the learning displayed was an effector phenomenon assumed to be
associated with a synthesising or organising process occurring in the

sensory centres, and was the expression of discrimination of some relation in the external situation which had not previously been apprehended.

Beniuc (1938) established the ability of the Fighting Fish (*Betta splendens*) to make a detour through a hole. The first finding of the hole is the result of a chance discovery and cautious investigation with intervals of random exploration. As a result, the fish eventually passes through and, provided it has done so in such a way that the bait is within sight at the moment of passing, it swims straight towards it. If, at the moment of passing through, the bait is out of sight, a period of random movement follows, and this continues until the bait is seen, when it is approached by a straight path. After the first success, the fish, as a rule, masters the situation, and need not thereafter be able to see the goal throughout the whole of the detour path. If the direction of detour is changed, the fish reacts towards the last traversed path, then the last but one and so on. But, given the choice, the animal always prefers the better-known path even if it is less direct. A striking feature of Beniuc's experiments is that fish trained in a vertical detour over an obstacle learned to extend it by jumping out of the water through the hole in the partition as this was gradually raised above the water surface. Thus, as in Spooner's experiments, there seems to be no difficulty in introducing at a stage in the process an entirely new locomotory pattern in order to achieve the same result. Some rather similar conclusions emerge from the work of Foth (1939) with Cichlids. Here the obstacle was a pane of glass, the top edge of which was about 2 centimetres below the surface of the water. The Cichlids were so large that they had to lie on one side if they were to swim over the pane without breaking the surface. Two individuals of *Tilapia zillii* failed to achieve this detour even after two weeks' experience, but a male *Geophagus braziliensis* immediately jumped over the pane and never failed to solve the problem thereafter. A female of the same species, on the other hand, seemed quite incapable of such behaviour, and remained motionless by the glass for long periods, looking at the prey. *Acaropsis nassa* soon overcame the obstacle elegantly, apparently in the first instance as the result of an accident, and then did not achieve it again until four days later, after which the behaviour became habitual. Two species of *Cichlasoma, C. facteum* and *C. aureum*, were unsuccessful. When the task was made more difficult by replacing the upper part of the transparent partition by a pane of frosted glass, *T. zillii* was unable to master it, but the *Geophagus* male dealt with the new situation as easily as the old. *Acaropsis* accomplished the new task only after a delay of four days. Von Schiller (1942), after a critical discussion on detour behaviour in the Minnow *Phoxinus*, came to the conclusion that the behaviour shown was evidence of insight. He showed that there was a sudden adoption of the right path after a preliminary period of searching around, and that, once started, the completion of the path was smooth and uninterrupted. Moreover, the behaviour showed evidence of new direction and new combination of previously learned behaviour patterns. A few trials were enough to establish a coherent response such that a detour could be made in any direction around obstacles of varied location, size and shape as the situation required. The same author (1949) trained both *Gambusia affinis* and *Notropis nocomis* to find round-about pathways in continuously varied problems; changes in position of the goal and in the construction of the transparent and opaque partitions were frequently made. In *Gambusia* twenty to thirty trials were sufficient to establish the adaptive pattern and here, curiously enough, the fish mastered the pathway better if the goal was not visible during the approach. If it were visible all the time, the detour might be interrupted as soon as it appeared visually closest, and some time might elapse before it was resumed. When the partition structures were put into a much larger tank, the whole detour pattern was disorganised and apparently could not be relearned. Nevertheless, it was shown to be intact when the animal was returned to the small tank. It should be noted that this is in striking contrast to much of the maze-running results in mammals. With *Notropis* care was taken that the spatial or kinæsthetic cues were kept constant and visual, and olfactory cues were excluded to a large extent. Nevertheless, a full 'insightful' solution of the problem seemed to be attained.

Maze Learning

It is a slight step from complex detour tests to mazes, and indeed some of the detour experiments above discussed were, in fact, maze experiments, since the goal was out of sight during at least part of the performance. Thorndike (1899) states that he trained *Fundulus* (Killifish) to thread a compartment maze of three partitions, but gives no details. Goldsmith (1912) gives a somewhat similar report of experiments, again without quantitative data, and Churchill (1916) successfully trained goldfish in a two-compartment maze—from twenty to thirty-six trials being required. Welty (1934) found that goldfish could very easily be trained to run a rather simple maze, and Lenkiewicz (1951) reports successful maze experiments. The former author made some very interesting observations on group behaviour and social facilitation which will be discussed below (p. 318).

Delayed Responses

Beniuc (1934), quoted by von Schiller (1948, original in Rumanian; see also Herter, 1953), was successful in training Fighting Fish to a very short delayed period of only 3 to 5 seconds (see also Beniuc, 1933). Von Schiller (1942), experimenting with the Minnow (*Phoxinus laevis*), had no difficulty in obtaining delays of about the same extent in a simple detour situation.

He found that this species is capable of delayed response, not only when postural cues are available but also when the approach to the goal has to be made by means of a detour during which time the reward is out of sight. Munn (1958) was unable to confirm von Schiller's experiments and suggests that perhaps the latter's fish were aided by extraneous clues.

The Learning of Rhythmic Behaviour

It will have been clear from the chapters on invertebrate behaviour above that very elaborate experiments are usually necessary before it is possible to state with any degree of certainty whether a behaviour rhythm is inborn or not; and, in fact, unless the innate nature of such a rhythm can be proved, the assumption—in the light of existing knowledge—must be that it has been learned. Experimentally, fish are not very good subjects for studies of this kind, since it is far more difficult to record automatically the periodical changes in activity of an aquatic animal than of a terrestrial one. Spencer (1939) has investigated the diurnal rhythms of a number of species of American freshwater fish by means of an 'ichthyometer' in which a fine thread from the fish's tail moved a very light lever which gave a kymographic tracing. Most of the fish investigated had a single period of rest within the 24-hour day. In at least one species no rest periods were detected, but there seems to be some doubt whether this effect might not be due to the nature of the apparatus. In general, one could say that this investigation showed, as was to be expected, that daily fluctuations in the light had an important effect, and in no case was there any certain evidence of an inborn rhythm.

It is well known that aquarium fish can be trained to observe particular times for feeding, but there has been little critical work. Beniuc (1933) succeeded in training one out of three Fighting Fish (*Betta splendens*) to observe a short temporal rhythm of from 3 to 5 seconds, and Herter (1950) trained Minnows to solve the problems of alternating bait and dummy with an unchanging white signal. Something over 750 experiments were necessary to give a 75 per cent. response to rhythm alone. He also carried out experiments on *Haplochromis multicolor*, which suggested that this fish found the problem to be of about the same order of difficulty. The general conclusion from these experiments is that rhythmical training of this kind is possible but extremely difficult with fish. This result is methodologically important since it had been suggested that the success of many of the experiments on discrimination of colour and stimuli might, in fact, have been due to just this kind of right-left alternation learning and not a genuine response to the test stimulus. It appears, therefore, from Herter's work to be extremely unlikely that such experiments were in error from this cause. However, Wohlfahrt (1939) found that Minnows did learn to recognise acoustic signals by rhythmic differences accidentally supplied, as well as by a true tone differentiation (Dijk-graaf and Verheijen, 1950).

Memory Retention

We have seen that some species of salmon and trout must be able to retain memories of the characteristics of their home stream for four years or more. Laboratory records for retention seem very trivial when compared with such performances. Haralson and Bitterman (1950) found that *Tilapia macrocephala* show good retention of a learned motor habit after one month, and Stetter (1929) established the existence in *Phoxinus* of a learned memory for absolute tones enduring from one to nine months, but there seem to be no careful experiments which have shown retention for a longer period than this. French (1942), in studying the effect of temperature on the retention of a maze habit in fish, concluded that there exists a forgetting process which is independent of inhibition and whose rate is a function of temperature. But Jones (1945) criticises this work apparently with justification, on the grounds that the metabolism of fish is not conditioned solely by temperature, and that French's results were largely vitiated by a tendency to underrate the complexity of the environment. Vanderplank (1938) showed that œstrone inhibits an artificially conditioned reflex in the Rudd (*Leuciscus leuciscus*). The mechanism of this action remains unknown. Prolan and progesterone were found to have no effect upon the functioning of the conditioned reflex other than a long-term secondary effect due to change in maturation rate of the ova in the oviducts.

Latent Learning and Insight

From the accounts given above, both of homing and of maze learning, it is evident that many fish have very marked abilities in spatial learning, and that it is reasonable to assume that these are evidence of powers of latent learning. There are, however, no critical investigation of latent-learning abilities in fish comparable with the experiments which have been done with rats. That many fish do in fact exhibit a general curiosity about the environment seems to be fairly clear from the observations of naturalists. Thus Cousteau (1953), as a result of his aqua-lung experiences, has described differing degrees of general curiosity in oceanic fish, and is evidently of the opinion that the degree of general curiosity is a specific characteristic in species such as the 'Liche' (*Lichia amia*), *Dentex vulgaris* and the Sea Bass (*Morone labrax*). He comes to the conclusion that the 'Merou' or Dusky Perch (*Epinephilus gigas*) is the most inquisitive animal found in the Mediterranean coastal seas.

There has been a good deal of work on visual configurational learning in fishes, particularly with goldfish. Goldsmith (1914) and Maes (1930) produce good evidence of an ability to recognise both size and shape, and Herter (1929, 1930, 1937) was highly successful in training Minnows and other species to discriminate between different shapes (circles, squares, triangles, crosses, etc.) as well as between the same figures at different sizes. Meesters (1940) showed that sticklebacks trained to distinguish a triangle from a square continued to do so correctly when the figures were turned through an angle up to 30°. When the rotation was 45° the discrimination was greatly reduced, and above 45° it was lost entirely. These and other experiments showed that the figure-background relation was of great importance for the fish, and that there was no complete abstraction such that the figure could be recognised in any orientation. Experiments showed that 'worm-like' figures varying in the number and sharpness of their curves could be well distinguished. Rowley (1934) found that he could train goldfish to distinguish between circles whose diameters differed by only 3 millimetres. Proof of such precise perception of size differences invites investigation of the fishes' response to the standard visual illusions, such as the Müller-Lyer Illusion, etc. Herter (1930) has carried out such experiments successfully, and finds that the response of the fish to the illusion is very similar to that of man. Two illusions which 'deceive' Minnows and men alike are shown in Fig. 51. Perkins and Wheeler (1930)

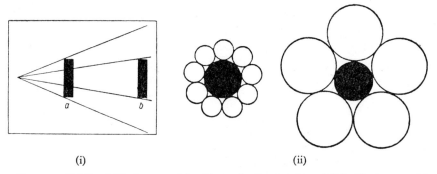

(i)   (ii)

FIG. 51—(i) Visual illusions used by Herter in the training of fish. Blocks *a* and *b* are of equal dimensions, but block *a* appears larger because it is enclosed by the lines which are separated by a wider angle. Fish previously trained to feed from the larger of two blocks of this shape will choose *a* rather than *b* when shown this diagram. (After Herter, 1930.)

(ii) Similar illusions with circular figures. The black circle surrounded by small circles appears larger than a circle of the same size surrounded by larger circles. (After Herter, 1930.)

and Perkins (1931) found that goldfish could learn to choose one of three absolute light intensities. At first the fishes usually had a preference for the minimum light intensity, and could then transpose both up and down the intensity scale without further training. They were also able to choose one light on the basis of its relationship to two others when the intensities as well as the positions were changed after each trial. Von Schiller (1933) has demonstrated intersensorial transposition in Minnows. Fish trained to the brighter or darker of two lights were then found to choose the 'brighter' or 'darker' of two smells (Indol, 'dark'; Ketone-Musk, 'bright'). Controls appear adequate and the effect was found to last for sixteen days. Perkins and Wheeler arrived at the curious conclusion that a constantly changing pattern of light intensities is learned more quickly than is a stereotyped pattern, and concluded that their experimental results demand an interpretation of the behaviour of the Goldfish in terms of insight rather than trial-and-error. They seem to have good grounds for suggesting that the volleys by which the learning curves ascend are objective pictures of the way the learning of the pattern proceeds in the individual animals. In all their work they found that the Goldfish were responding to a total situation 'in accordance with the law of configuration.' Hosoda (1957) reports latent learning of a Y-maze by Guppies, *Lebistes reticulatus*. But Munn (1958) came to the conclusion that the U-shaped detours which Minnows are capable of making develop, during the course of an experiment, from a reduced tendency to make a direct approach.

These evidences of insight learning which fish display are further discussed by Herter (1953), who suggests that some of them at least are examples of 'pre-adaptation.' He points out that fish often display abilities in the realms of sense physiology and psychology of which they can make no use in their natural life. As a particular instance of this, he cites the fact that the crepuscular fish *Amiurus nebulosus* have quite good optical capacity for differentiating forms and are also able to respond to colours even though, under natural conditions, they can hardly ever use these abilities for orientation. He suggests that this pre-adaptation is a general feature of fish-learning abilities, and although some of the examples which he cites, such as the high ability to distinguish different complex sounds (e.g. different human voices), may be seen in a different light now that we know more about the sound production of fish; yet in general his conclusions seem to carry much weight. In this connection he quotes von Buddenbrock (1937) to the effect that the sensitivity of the sense cell is usually greater than the apparent biological importance of the stimuli concerned would warrant. It does, indeed, seem to be a general feature of animal life that the precision and sensitivity of sense organs is higher than the environment would appear to justify. This fact poses a serious problem for students of evolution, since it is not easy to account for such perfection on the basis of natural selection alone. However, the answer may be that the nature of sensory nervous mechanisms is such that to achieve full efficiency at the normal level of stimulation, the threshold must be much lower.

Before leaving the subject of form vision, it is interesting to note that

Sperry and Clark (1949) have demonstrated interocular transfer of visual discrimination habits in the Goby (*Bathygobius soporator*). Fish were trained, against the initial preference, to swim towards the smaller, higher and less bright-coloured of two lures simultaneously presented. Blinkers of tantalum foil were used to occlude the vision of one eye, and evidence was found that the nervous system of this fish can easily mediate interocular transfer in some individuals but not in all. Thus after a minimum of 120 trials, they found that out of 16 individuals 5 showed excellent or good transfer, 4 a lesser degree of transfer, and the remaining 7 little or none. In other experiments it was found that when habits were learned with both eyes uncovered, learning and retention had not been confined to one dominant eye. This is in marked contrast to what has been found in some earlier experiments with pigeons. Schult (1957), studying interocular transfer and transposition in the Goldfish (*Carassius vulgaris*), provides evidence that the two hemispheres are completely independent. He concludes that the better learning and transposition ability shown by the control fish, learning the path with both eyes, may be eventually explained on the basis of Lashley's theory of mass action. Botsch (1960) has considered the subject further with special reference to the function of the tectum opticum in providing for these two abilities.

Social Facilitation and Imitation

What has already been said about schooling will have made clear that there is much behaviour suggesting social facilitation in fishes. Gudger (1944) has given a number of interesting records of follow-my-leader behaviour in both swimming and leaping fish, although in most of these cases no particular advantage appears to accrue from the behaviour. Breder and Halpern say that it is common knowledge among aquarists that in order to get a fish to feed it is often necessary to show it a companion feeding, a companion which need not necessarily be of the same species. Baerends and Baerends-van Roon (1950) say that the Cichlids which they kept appear to live in schools till they reach maturity, and that it is typical of such schools that the members continually show a tendency to perform the same action simultaneously. 'Sometimes they are all engaged in foraging on the bottom, and then again we will find them all scraping algæ from the glass walls, floating quietly in the water or lying together on the bottom. That they can experience the same emotional reaction simultaneously is illustrated by the following observations on *Tilapia natalensis*. These fish, when immature and living in schools, show either a pattern of vertical bars or two longitudinal bands. The latter pattern they assume when not disturbed, the former when they feel anxiety. Now, as soon as we brought a small *Hemichromis* into a tank containing a school of *Tilapias* showing the longitudinal bands, all at once assumed the cross bands. From this we conclude that they all became anxious, irrespective of whether they individually had been affected or not. When living together in a territorial society such sharp simultaneous reactions to events in a certain territory do not occur.'

The most careful experiments on the group learning of fishes have been those of Welty (1934). He found that a maze was learned by Goldfish more quickly when they were grouped than when they were isolated. Putting a trained fish in the maze will speed up the learning of untrained fish. This group facilitation is attributed to three related causes: firstly, group cohesion based on vision; secondly, mass-habituation (which the author describes as 'inter-reassurance'); and thirdly, group-interaction stimulating exploratory activity. However, none of these three categories can be considered as evidence of true imitation; rather they are three special cases of social facilitation. Welty, however, has some further observations which are rather more puzzling. Thus, for instance, he found that a Goldfish learns to traverse a simple maze more rapidly after having seen another Goldfish do so. This seems to be due (a) to reassurance that the stimulus was not followed by harmful results, so that there was a mutual quietening effect, and (b) learning, through visual cohesion, to move forward at the time the stimulus was presented. Untrained fishes were sometimes seen even to precede the trained fish in moving towards the stimulus in their respective chambers. It seems fairly clear that this latter group of observations (b) can again be explained as social facilitation together with local enhancement. There does, however, remain a doubt as to the first class (a) of observations. This at first sight seems to be due to an appreciation by one fish of the lack of harmful results subsequent to the behaviour of the other fish. If this could be established, it would seem to be evidence of true imitation; but there seems to remain the possibility that the quiet behaviour of the fish being tested had a quietening effect on its associate. Morrow (1948) considers that the shape of Welty's learning curves indicates typical trial-and-error learning—which would not be expected if imitation were actually in operation. Welty also found that numbers of Goldfish *retain* motor responses better than do isolated fishes, but the explanation of this retention is not understood. Besides these and many similar experiments with Goldfish, Welty found that Paradise Fish (*Macropodus opercularis*), the Zebra Fish (*Brachydanio rerio*) and Shiners (*Notropis atherinoides*) eat more per fish when in groups than when kept singly. Welty's work on the superiority of groups of fishes over single fishes in maze-learning experiments has been confirmed by Greenberg (1947) in work with the Green Sunfish (*Lepomis cyanellus*). He found that the biggest individual tends to be the leader, although leadership in the maze shifted at almost every trial. Subordinates appear to lessen tension among territory-holding fishes, and removal of the 'omega' from aquaria with three territories increased aggressive behaviour among those remaining, whereas the introduction of a new fish led to their attacking it instead of one another.

Individual Recognition

Many experienced aquarists have come to the conclusion, generally rather uncritically, that fishes are capable of personal recognition, both of fellow members of their species and of other species, including man. It is, of course, obvious that much of such personal recognition would be explained on ordinary conditioning principles, and in no case does it seem at all certain that anything more is necessarily involved. However, the field is one which is certainly attractive for further experiment, for the persistence of shoals consisting of a particular group of individuals is well known, and there is some evidence that fishes which guard and tend their young for some time after hatching show some slight evidence of personal recognition. The Bar-fin (*Amia*) and also the Black Bass (*Micropterus*) are said to guard not only nest and eggs but also young, even after they swim about in shoals (Bradford, 1946), as also do many Cichlids.

Ono (1955) has made extensive experimental studies on intraspecific recognition in *Oryzias latites*. He shows that the many factors which can influence the fish in this respect include movement, body form, colour and various combinations of the ratio body-length/distance of recognition. The gestalt characters which he discusses seem to be primarily responsible for the specific recognition but probably play some part in individual recognition as well.

'Play'

Behaviour which appears play-like can often be seen in fishes, particularly in the low-intensity stages of nest-building—as in the stickleback (van Iersel, 1953). But there seems good reason for thinking that many such examples represent only the simplest transference activity. Brehm, however, has an account (quoted by Kyle, 1926) of the playful squirting of water by 'Shooters' (*Jaculator*) at an aquarium keeper personally known to them, and other naturalists (quoted Beach, 1945, also Meyer-Holzapfel, personal communication) have described many other examples suggestive of true play. These accounts seem sufficiently precise to suggest that a critical investigation of the subject in fish would be worth while.

Brain Structure and Learning

There are not as yet many observations on record of the part played by different regions of the central nervous system in the learning ability of fish. Janzen (1933) found that Goldfish lacking the forebrain were conspicuously without initiative and were generally non-reactive, and Wiebalck (1937) found that similar lesions in the fish *Box salpa* resulted in disruption of the social behaviour and a tendency to become solitary. According to Noble, the corpus striatum in Cichlids is concerned with co-ordination in breeding behaviour, but almost complete absence of the forebrain did not altogether prevent mating and in no way hindered sex recognition. Like other authors, however, he found that schooling was permanently affected by such forebrain lesions, and he concluded that this region regulates social behaviour both by co-ordinating complex behaviour patterns and through its influence on the pituitary. Seggar (1956, 1960) studying the effect of brain lesions upon various innate and partially acquired pieces of behaviour in the stickleback, found that whereas frontal lesions in the forebrain caused modifications of the behaviour pattern which were irreversible, bilateral lesions in the forebrain caused changes that can sometimes be reversed. The anatomical basis for this reversal appears to be the regeneration of the forebrain tissue. Sanders (1940) found that the optic tectum of the Goldfish contains a mechanism capable of second-order olfactory and optic learning, and the connection involved in this learning passes into the tectum at its anterior border. Nolte (1932) found that even massive destruction of the cerebellum of Minnows was possible without causing disruption of previously learned associations involving colour, and Zunini (1941) showed that even though the cerebral hemispheres were completely removed some individual fish were, nevertheless, able to learn the correct response in a simple experiment which necessitated turning in order to reach food behind a transparent partition. Fish trained in a turning apparatus and then decerebrated lost the habit but were able to relearn it, and from this it was concluded that the hemispheres are concerned in such learning, but that other parts of the central nervous system can take over when these are lacking. The series of studies of these two authors confirms in general the conclusions of a good deal of rather scattered earlier work, a summary of which will be found in Herter (1953). J. ten Cate (1935) has also summarised the physiology of the fish's central nervous system. Hale (1956a) finds with the Green Sunfish that forebrain extirpation results in the loss of all previously established associations and slows reaction time during subsequent training. The slowed reaction time decreased the latency of followership in maze performance and in schooling so that fish with forebrain injury had to have continuous leadership if social facilitation was to be demonstrated, whereas in control fish the leadership could be intermittent. Forebrain lesions did not impair response to food but they did induce at least a temporary decrease in spontaneous swimming. It seems that in some respects the forebrain functions to provide facilitation of aggressive and other behaviour patterns which are organised at lower brain levels.

CHAPTER XIII

AMPHIBIANS AND REPTILES

AMPHIBIA

THE fact that metamorphosis involves adaptation for the transition from aquatic to terrestrial life has made the Amphibia a favourite group for physiological study. Added to this there is, of course, the more or less accidental occurrence that the frog has been almost everywhere taken as the basic 'type' for the elementary teaching of vertebrate anatomy. Consequently there has been more fundamental physiological study of the Amphibia than of any other group of similar size, and so we have here a clearer picture of the nature of some of the primary motor patterns than is available in any group so far dealt with in this book. Some writers, e.g. Noble (1931), have expressed surprise that one finds in the Amphibia many of the instinctive habits of the higher forms already established, even though the central nervous system is so much simpler than that of the higher vertebrates. However, to anyone familiar with the innate behaviour of the invertebrates this will cause no astonishment.

The origin of the innate behaviour patterns of Amphibia has been particularly studied in *Ambystoma*. Coghill (1929) showed that there were five successive phases in the co-ordination of movements in the *Ambystoma* embryo, and that these phases were an expression of the growth of the anatomical mechanism in the medulla and spinal cord necessary for that performance. The last two of these phases are the 'S reaction' and the 'swimming stage'; the latter being essentially a repetition of the former at intervals frequent enough to effect locomotion. Coghill also showed that experience and exercise play no part in the development of swimming in *Ambystoma*, and that the reflexes of walking are derived from the swimming pattern. He concludes that walking has not arisen by the co-ordination of local reflexes in the appendages, but that the arm is moved as a whole before the forearm gains independent action, and the forearm in its turn develops its reflexes before the digits acquire theirs. It appears from these and many other observations that walking resembles swimming in being an inborn and unlearned behaviour pattern. The main results of Carmichael (1926) were confirmed by Matthews and Detwiler (1926), who found that when they kept newly emerged and embryonic *Ambystoma* under chloretone anæsthesia, at the end of eight days the larvæ had developed the same reflexes as the controls which had been active during this period. This work also demonstrates that if the initial simpler movements are prevented, the fuller swimming behaviour pattern springs at once into full activity as soon as the chloretone is withdrawn. Carmichael (1927) reached similar conclusions with tadpoles of the wood frog. Fromme (1941), however, obtained a different result with the embryo of *Rana pipiens*. He found that embryos immobilised by chloretone showed a quantitative decrement in swimming ability as compared with a control group, and also with another group which were activated by constant agitation of the water. Swimming of the activated group was identical with the control group which had had the normal amount of turbulence to contend with. This author concludes, therefore, that the quantitative deficiency of the chloretone group was due to absence of practice but that the extra practice given to the activated group by agitating the water was without influence. The evidence that the drug itself was harmless to this species was reasonably good, though whether all after-effects were eliminated may be open to doubt.

Weiss (1941) claimed that complete deafferentation did not impair swimming in tadpoles, but Gray and Lissmann (1946), working on the co-ordination of limb movements in walking Amphibia, provide strong evidence to show that the movements characteristic of *walking* in the toad are dependent on the integrity of the sensory and motor elements of at least one spinal nerve. They found that a central nervous system which was *totally* isolated from stimulation, both of proprioceptive and labyrinthine origin, is unable to maintain co-ordinated movements either on land or in water. Nevertheless, they also showed that in fact afferentation of a very small fragment of the total musculature is sufficient to control the activity of the whole—perhaps by raising the central excitatory state or, more likely (von Holst, 1934), by removing a block preventing discharge from the central nervous system. Their experiments give a picture of the effect of deafferentation somewhat resembling that provided by decortication experiments in mammals where the amount rather than the site of the operation is the controlling factor. However dependent the walking and swimming movements of the Amphibia may be upon the continued stimulation from the environment, whether a solid substratum or a surrounding liquid, there is evidence that some of the reproductive instincts are much less directly dependent. Thus Noble and Bradley (1933) found that in the *Plethodontidae*, a group supposed to have evolved direct from the *Salamandridae*, the mating pair engage in a grotesque walk during which the male's tail is sharply bent at the base. These authors show that this 'tail walk' proceeds in exactly the same manner in both the aquatic *Eurycea* and the terrestrial *Hemidactylium*, and they point out how striking it is that in both *Salamandridæ* and *Plethodontidae* the character of the medium has apparently failed to modify the courtship pattern which seems to have evolved in phylogeny without a close habitat correlation.

Spurway and Haldane (1953) have discussed the breathing behaviour of newts as an instinctive pattern. These animals, of course, ascend through the water to the surface in order to breathe, and this ascent is regarded as an instinct whose consummatory act is the filling of the lungs. The behaviour of *Triturus cristatus* differs according to whether it is on land, or floating because its lungs are distended, or supported on an object below the water because it is heavier than water. The frequency of ascent to breathe atmospheric air decreases when oxygen is breathed or dissolved in the water, and increases when nitrogen is substituted. It is also sharply increased when the lungs are partially collapsed by increased water pressure. 'Intentional movements' of coming up to breathe are described and a probable phylogeny of breathing behaviour is suggested; accidental swallowing of air being followed by the evolution of an instinct to rise and seek it, and this in its turn followed by the evolution of organs to exploit it for respiration or buoyancy. The authors consider that the appetitive behaviour of this instinct led to the development of land-living forms. In these forms, of course, this appetitive behaviour is not seen but, nevertheless, it may reappear when evoked by the environment. They point out that there is much behaviour displayed by mammals when short of oxygen, including struggling, sighing, gasping and spasmodic vocalisation which shows a curious resemblance to the appetitive behaviour for breathing in Amphibia when in the water. They suggest that in man a consummatory act has lost the fixed-action pattern and has acquired the ontogenetic plasticity which seems common amongst mammalian movements.

It seems obvious from general considerations that the individual amphibian can have little or no opportunity for the acquisition of the releasive mechanisms for reproductive behaviour by learning. Probably chemical and mechanical releasers are predominant among the Urodeles. Chemical releasers for fright responses are known in tadpoles as they are in fish (Kulzer, 1954). The recognition of sound patterns must also, it seems, be inborn, and innate visual recognitions certainly have their place —particularly among the Anura, which are, on the whole, 'visual animals.' Thus Banta (1914) describes how males of the frog *Rana sylvatica* readily distinguish the sex of other individuals even though they are several inches away. In this species the evidence for a visual releaser is very strong, and it is suggested that the inflated vocal sac, and its repeated expansion and collapse, probably supplies the necessary stimulus. B. G. Smith (1907) found that in *Hynobius lichenatus*, where fertilisation is external, it is the sight of the string of eggs which seems to be the immediate stimulus for the emission of the sperm. It seems very difficult to imagine how such a releasing mechanism could have been produced during the individual life as a result of any kind of learning process.

The well-known experiments of Sperry (1956) on newts involving transfer and rotation of sense organs and regeneration of connections have received much confirmation from Lettvin *et al.* (1959). All Sperry's experiments seem to point to the conclusion that there are inherent chemical affinities amongst the nerve fibres and cells and that if there is any randomness in the connections between the amphibian eye and the brain, it is at a very fine level indeed. Sperry's results seem to indicate that the sense of direction and of location in space, the organisation of patterns, the sense of position of the visual field as a whole and the perception of motion are built into the organism and do not have to be learned. The work of Lettvin *et al.* (1959) has gone a long way towards providing a neurophysiological basis for several of the basic perceptive abilities of the amphibian eye.

Habituation

All those who keep frogs and toads in captivity (e.g. Malcolm Smith, 1951, p. 99) seem to agree that these creatures are easily tamed and soon learn to respond to those who feed and look after them. It is fairly clear that this taming involves both habituation and associative learning. Rather surprisingly, toads seem to be quicker learners than frogs, and also display greater curiosity and better retention of learned responses. The only critical study of habituation has been that of Franzisket (1955), who has demonstrated both stimulus-specific and response-specific waning processes in the wiping response of the hind legs which can be elicited in spinal frogs. Franzisket (1961) has followed this up by developing a method for maintaining spinal and decerebrate frogs alive for a long period, even up to three years. In these preparations he has demonstrated the central facilitation of the wiping reflex together with lowering of its threshold after repeated elicitation. In the case of the croak reflex he has shown what appears to be 'vacuum activity'; and what is perhaps even more interesting, he has demonstrated qualitative changes of reflexes in spinal frogs after training. Thus interscapular pressure with a bristle evokes the wiping reflex only. Slight pressure with the human finger on the same spot evokes the croak reflex. If a frog is 'trained' for three weeks with ten thousand finger pressure stimulations, croaking is given consistently without any sign of exhaustion. If then the bristle stimulus is applied, it now evokes croaking on more than 50 per cent. of occasions, whereas before croaking was never elicited. In another series of experiments a phenomenon termed 'displacement of excitation' is described in spinal frogs; the suggestion being that this is the equivalent in reflex behaviour of displacement activity in instinctive behaviour, and that perhaps they have the same neurophysiological basis. Other studies closely relevant to the subject of habituation in amphibia are those of Kolb (1955) and Jahn (1960). Butz-Kuenzer (1957) has contributed a valuable analysis of the compensating movements resulting from changes of position in space in the frog. Among other points it is shown that adaptation takes place independently in the optical and in the static mechanisms which release compensatory movements. After exhaustion of one of them, the central evaluation of the stimuli from the other remains unchanged. This work on the frog is in many respects complementary to an earlier paper on the toad (Eikmanns, 1955).

Associative Conditioning

It has been shown that toads (Buytendijk, 1918*b*), frogs (Schaeffer, 1911) and axolotls (Haecker, 1912) will soon learn to cease snapping at inedible substances which at first attracted them. Schaeffer also found that the eating behaviour of frogs could readily be inhibited by an electric shock given at the time of snapping and that inhibition could last for five days. Buytendijk (1918*a*) found that with two European species of toad the red ant would be refused after even a single unpleasant experience, and this refusal was extended to include not only ants but spiders and flies as well. The day after the test, ants were still avoided but spiders were taken. Cott (1936) found that the Common Toad (*Bufo bufo*) learned very rapidly to avoid coloured and distasteful Hymenoptera such as hive-bees. Ten of his toads learned to avoid bees entirely after a single trial acceptance, and even the slowest individual had learned this avoidance lesson by the seventh day, trials being given twice daily. Schaeffer's experiments, which concerned three common species of *Rana*, showed that disagreeable objects, such as hairy caterpillars, were refused as a result of between four and seven trials, and that the habit once learned persisted for at least ten days. When the behaviour was further reinforced by means of an electric shock, a pond frog learned to avoid chemically treated earthworms in only two trials. Brower *et al.* (1960) have shown that the toad, *Bufo terrestris*, freely eats bumble bees from which the sting has been removed but learns to avoid them if the stings are intact and will then reject them on sight alone. Having done this, they also reject mimics to a significantly greater extent than control toads which did not have prior experience with the bumble bees.

Well-established conditioned reflexes have been described in spinal frogs by Rensch and Franzisket (1954).

Moore and Welch (1940) demonstrated a rather surprising degree of learning with larvæ of *Ambystoma*. They obtained association between food and movement (such as that of the hand above the jar) and also intermittent light. They obtained an association of a chemical stimulus with food, and also the inhibition of a snap reflex when the food was behind a glass. Retention periods for such habits varied from twenty-four hours to eight weeks. Most of the above examples include elements both of trial-and-error learning and reflex conditioning. Bajandurow and Pegel (1932) conditioned the breathing and jumping behaviour of frogs (in response to a mild shock stimulus) to the notes of a whistle or to a light flash. They found that this conditioning was very unstable, that it was necessary to present the stimuli concurrently, and that complete failure resulted if more than about 3 or 4 seconds separated the sound or light from the shock. They failed altogether to obtain differential training to different lights or different tones.

Some evidence for progressive reversal of a direction habit in the newt *Triturus v. viridescens* has been provided by Seidman (1949).

Trial-and-error Learning

Kuntz (1923) showed that the larva of *Ambystoma tigrinum* was able to learn a 'maze' in which it had to take a zigzag course through three lighted chambers in order to reach darkness in the fourth. His learning curves showed a definite improvement in time scores with repetition. Buytendijk (1918*a* and *b*) carried out simple detour experiments with toads which were required to take the shortest route around a glass partition. The task was accomplished readily, and the direct route resumed immediately the partition was removed. Yerkes and Ayer (1903) trained frogs to run a 'two-blind' maze in about 100 trials. Learned behaviour was retained virtually perfect for a month, after which the animals were not further tested. Szymanski (1919) obtained correspondingly quicker learning in a maze with a single choice-point. The maze experiments of Franz (1927) have provided provisional confirmation of the result of other types of experiments, to the effect that the performance of the toad in these simple mazes is superior to that of the frog. This difference of ability between frogs and toads may be due to two factors: firstly, vision—which was certainly involved in all the experiments recorded—apparently plays a greater part in the responses of toads than it does in frogs; and, secondly, the slow walking gait of toads is likely to make them more suitable for maze and other experiments in comparison with the frogs, most species of which, of course, make large and sudden jumps.

Moore and Welch (1940) showed that larval *Ambystoma* could master a simple 'T' maze after about 500 trials. Five experimental animals were used in 9 series and 7 out of the 9 series gave results which appear satisfactory. Munn (1940) trained tadpoles of *Hyla* and also of Bullfrogs in both Y and T mazes. He obtained significant results in both cases and supplies what seem convincing arguments for the assumption that true associative learning has been demonstrated and that the result cannot be explained solely as maturation. Washburn (1926) found that attempts to train salamanders in a simple maze were vitiated by the animal's behavioural inertia, useless little detours and other movements accidentally evoked in the first stages of maze training being persisted in to the detriment of real improvement. Very similar results are reported by Cummings (1910) during studies with two species of newt (*M. cristatus* and *palmatus*).

There is no doubt that movement-sight plays an important part in the feeding response of Amphibia. How far form-sight has been perfected was for long in debate. Dickerson (1906) was unable to find any ability in frogs to distinguish between a 'lighted space' and a 'white solid.' He found that they would turn towards a white card or paper and try to jump through it, and that they would struggle to work their way into a solid white surface presented to them. It is, however, difficult to reconcile some of these results with the ease with which some species develop an adaptive response to a glass plate. The work of Pache (1932) has resulted in some clarification of earlier confusions, especially those resulting from the work of Minckiewicz and his pupils of the Warsaw school. Information at present available seems to show that *Hyla* can distinguish a triangle from a circle without movement. All other cases of form recognition seem to be dependent on the occurrence of some movement. Thus *with* movement both *Hyla* and *Rana* (*temporaria* and *esculenta*) can, for example, distinguish various types of cross from circle, star and triangle; circle from star, triangle and quadrilateral, etc. Moreover, in general, a curve could be optically distinguished from a straight line, an angle from a curve and a three-component figure from a four-component one. Where similar forms *were* confused, the available evidence all went to show that this was not due to a deficiency in visual acuity, but rather to insufficient form sense as such.

Modern developments in the study of the neurophysiology of amphibian vision have been alluded to on p. 324 above. There has, however, been as yet relatively little investigation of brain function in relation to learning in the Amphibia. Burnett (1912) records that whereas the normal frogs of the species that he used were able to escape from a maze after about 20 trials, decerebrate frogs showed no improvement even after 100 trials. It is naturally concluded from this that the forebrain is a primary seat of learned behaviour in Amphibia. Parriss (1961) has shown that toads can be trained to distinguish between two shapes moving in the visual field and that when this is done they will retain this learning after section and regeneration of both optic nerves, to the same extent as a similar group of animals not operated after training. The optic nerves were allowed to regenerate for a period of ten weeks without training and on re-testing there was no significant difference between the experimental and control animals.

Territorial Behaviour: Latent Learning and Homing

Scope for learning and remembering landmarks is probably very limited in the Amphibia, but there are, nevertheless, a number of species which do consistently show homing behaviour. Noble (1931) states that toads regularly return to the same shelter at night, and the South American frog *Pentadactylus* has well-marked breeding dens. Those who have studied the tree frogs under natural conditions (Breder, 1925) have found that many individuals return every night from their hiding-places to the same station, and *Hyla rosenbergi* in Panama (Breder, 1925) returned night after night to the mud basins which had been constructed for the care of eggs and tadpoles. Parental care is unusual in the Amphibia, but Bradford (1946) recalls that *Ichthyophis glutinosa* in Japan coils around its eggs in holes in damp earth, and *Plethedon* in the United States does the same under rocks and stones. How far a visual memory of landmarks accounts for the homing of Amphibia is very uncertain, and it appears from the work of Bogert (1947) that vision may play little part in the orientation of seasonal migrations to and from breeding-sites. Probably a return to breeding-sites is most easily explained by supposing that the mating calls of males in the breeding-ponds guide others thither. There is much recent work demonstrating the importance of sound production in the Anura as providing specific releasers in relation to sex, territory, predator recognition, etc. The literature is extensively reviewed by Bogert (1960). So far there seems to be no evidence that Amphibia learn to recognise individual differences in the acoustic signals of other members of their species. Czeloth (1930) has shown that in the newt (*Triton* spp.) water is reached primarily by the data supplied by chemoreceptors and sense organs sensitive to humidity changes. The return to woodland cover in autumn is, however, directed primarily by vision, a dark break or irregularity in the horizon being especially stimulating. Heusser's (1958) results on the homing of *Bufo bufo* are very puzzling. He could find no evidence that physical or chemical stimuli were guiding the animals on their return journeys to the spawning places. Only at a later stage, about the time when spawning was actually commencing at the spawning ground, did those toads still travelling become sensitive to the presence of nearby water and so enter any pond that they happened to pass.

While the maze experiments suggest that kinæsthetic and visual stimulation may be co-ordinated in the mastery of mazes and detours, yet we have very little evidence as to how extensive such an ability is and what part it plays under natural conditions. Breder, Breder and Redmond (1927) record how marked *Rana clamitans*, released several hundred feet away from their home on the other side of a stream, returned even though they had to cross the water where other pond frogs of the same species lived.

Further, an individual captured in the stream and released in the spring returned to its home stream, and another removed from one pool in a stream to another pool on the same side, got back to its home pool even though other pools inhabited by other pond frogs of the same species had to be passed on the way. (See also Juszczyk, 1951.)

To sum up the situation, we may say that recent work on the learning abilities of Amphibia has tended strongly to confirm the conclusions of Hempelmann (1926) that this group is far inferior to fishes in learning ability. As both Noble (1931) and Warden (1936) conclude, we seem justified in assuming that learning has played only a minor part in the success of the various groups of Amphibia. The outstanding advance made by this group is the adaptation to air-living conditions, but other sections of the behaviour have not been modified to anything like the extent which might have been expected and, indeed, might have seemed essential. Yet *Bufo calamita* is able to adapt its behaviour to abnormal feeding situations quite as readily as do reptiles (Franz, 1927), and Hinsche (1926) found that a toad gradually accustomed to life in water would voluntarily return to it and would, *after a while*, develop frog-like movements which were never seen in its normal environment. Perhaps such observations should serve as a warning that it may be too early to generalise even in such a small and well-studied group as the Amphibia.

REPTILIA

As with the Amphibia, so the much less extensive work with the reptiles suggests that embryonic movements and co-ordinations, as well as the characteristic movements and orientations of courtship behaviour (Evans, unpublished review), are based on primary and innate patterns of behaviour. Thus Smith and Daniel (1946), studying the development of behaviour in the Loggerhead Turtle (*Caretta caretta*), found that there were three stages of movement, first a 'total pattern' by which the body is flexed into the form of a 'C,' secondly the integration of local responses with this pattern, and subsequently the adjustment of the pattern to the environment. They did not find any evidence that maturation and integration were related to embryonic 'practice' or repetition of response, and they concluded that the total-pattern behaviour *precedes* all the reflexes. Even a few hours after hatching, young Loggerhead Turtles show most of the basic reactions essential to continuance of life; particularly noteworthy among these are (i) the ability to escape from a deep nest, presumably as a result of an orientation by geotaxis, (ii) direct visual orientation leading to escape into the ocean, (iii) orientation, when in the sea, towards deep water. Noble and Breslau (1938), studying the senses involved in the migration of young Freshwater Turtles, found that they too were attracted towards large areas of intense illumination after having escaped from the nest, as a result of the same kind of mechanism as is found in the Loggerheads. The Freshwater Turtles tended to migrate towards the most open horizon, the actual position of the sun as distinct from the position of large areas of bright sky being without effect. The species used in this study were Musk Turtles (*Kinosternon odoratum*), Painted Tortoise (*Chrysemys picta*) and Snapping Turtles (*Chelydra serpentina*). Since the reptiles in general show no parent-young association [1] one must assume that the mechanism for the chemical releasers which mediate so much of the behaviour is inborn. This is probably also true for tactile releasers, and possibly for auditory releasers too. Thus Beach (1944*b*) has found a specific response of captive Alligators to auditory stimulation by the sound characteristic of the 'roar' of the species—a frequency of 57 cycles per second, equivalent to the B flat two octaves below middle C. It is, however, possible that this could have been learned—an interesting and not too difficult matter to investigate. Simple visual responses have already been mentioned in connection with the behaviour of young turtles. Precise inborn response to visual patterns, it seems, must also occur in some species. Thus Noble (1936) and Noble and Bradley (1933) have shown that the display of the Fence Lizard (*Sceloporus undulatus*) includes a particular form and also a characteristic movement, recognition of which must almost certainly be inborn. Malcolm Smith (1951, p. 293) states that there are both snakes and lizards which have no difficulty in distinguishing the sexes on sight. Bogert (1941) found that rattlesnakes show a (presumably innate) 'King Snake defence posture' released by the secretion of the cloacal gland of various species of 'ophiophagus' King Snakes. After the initial stimulus of the King Snake secretion had evoked the response, associated visual and tactile stimuli may alone serve to initiate it for a period of three hours or so; after which the effect fades, only the original chemical stimulus remaining potent.

Habituation

There is plenty of evidence showing the ease with which many reptiles (lizards, snakes, turtles and tortoises; Prater, 1933; Rollinat, 1934; Malcolm Smith, 1951) are tamed, but there have been no careful studies on habituation. Mr. K. Stott, Curator of Reptiles at the San Diego Zoo, has described to me how some species of reptile (e.g. the Sidewinder) are so shy that they

---

[1] Skinks of the genus *Eumeces* provide some striking exceptions, for the female deposit their eggs in subterranean nests constructed by themselves and brood them until hatching. Evans (1954, unpublished) records how *E. obsoletus* turns her clutch daily and says that she will on occasion stimulate a partly emerged young one by poking with her snout or resting her body on it, thus arousing it to renewed jerking until free of the shell. Young Alligators are led by their mothers to a pool from which a tunnel leads to a dry chamber in the bank (McIlhenny, 1934, 1935), and they are said to remain with her for many months (Forbes, 1940).

will soon die if placed in a show cage in the reptile house even though they will live for years when kept quietly in one of the secluded acclimatisation cages. This suggests that general habituation is almost non-existent in such species.

Associative Learning

Apparently the only studies on record of the formation of true conditioned reflexes in reptiles are those of Poliakov (1930) and of Parschin (1929) on the Pond Tortoise (*Emys orbicularis*). The former showed that conditioned reflexes can be formed in the decerebrate tortoise but that when the mid-brain is also removed, conditioning disappears. Good evidence is presented that these are true conditioned reflexes, and it is suggested that the results support the view that in animals 'low in the zoological scale' conditioned reflexes can be formed not only in the cerebral hemispheres but also in other parts of the brain. The latter author readily obtained conditioning to an accurately measured and standardised touch on the head when paired with a light flash. He attempted to use the method as a proof of colour vision, but technical difficulties (brightness, colour standardisation, etc.) do not seem to have been fully overcome. Seidman (1949) has demonstrated some ability for progressive reversal of a direction habit in the Terrapin *Pseudemys troostii elegans*.

Trial-and-error Learning

Fischel (1934) demonstrated trial-and-error learning in the Snapping Turtle (*Chelydra serpentina*). The learning curves also show characteristics suggesting insight when the animal is required to learn a modification of the original way of getting at the food—for instance, over instead of under a wire.

Fischel also obtained results showing trial-and-error learning in lizards. Yerkes (1901) was successful in training the turtle *Chelopus guttatus* to master two rather irregular mazes, one with four blinds and the other with six, the reward being escape from confinement and the attainment of a dark and secluded place. Running times dropped from 35 minutes to about half a minute in 20 trials in a simple type of the maze, and from 90 minutes to 3 or 4 minutes after 25 trials in a more complex type. Tinklepaugh (1932a) described the successful learning of a five-blind simple 'T' maze by a turtle in only four trials. Some of Yerkes' animals showed striking evidence of ability to improve the path through the maze, not only by shortening but by a change in the means employed. Thus in one of the mazes a sharp turn at the foot of an incline was eventually negotiated by the animal learning the trick of throwing itself off the incline earlier and earlier in the series of its runs, thus completely avoiding that particular detour. Many observers have noted that lizards, snakes and turtles will learn to commence their food-seeking behaviour on hearing the sounds involved in the preparation of food.

Kellogg and Pomeroy (1936) have studied the maze-learning ability of the water snakes *Tropidonotus fasciatus,* var. *sipedon*. Experiments with these animals yielded typical learning curves in a 'T' maze, but were complicated by the periodical skin-shedding which interrupted learning and in some cases rendered relearning necessary. It is probable that the shedding involved both a decrease in motivation as well as some real forgetting. This is interesting in connection with the evidence (see p. 325, above; Flower, 1927) that Axolotls during metamorphosis completely forgot earlier feeding experiences and had to be taught all over again. In 'T' maze experiments with snakes, vision was found to be much less important than touch, and animals largely learned to feel their way through the maze. Other investigators who have experimented with snakes, e.g. Wolfle and Brown (1940) encountered great difficulty in providing consistent motivation.

Fischel (1933) showed that *Lacerta viridis* learned the way around a fence to food, but if the food was not visible at the end of the detour the animal apparently forgot and ran off. This, however, is contrary to the observations of Rollinat (1934), who described how lizards will search for prey when it has suddenly disappeared from their sight and behave as if they realise it is in hiding. They will make what appear to be purposive attempts to find it—a kind of behaviour that has never been observed in Amphibia. Snakes seeking for food often appear to quarter the ground systematically, but the probability is that the hunting behaviour of both lizards and snakes is inborn. However, the response of young inexperienced lizards to prey that temporarily passes out of sight should be well worth critical investigation.

Fischer and Birukow (1960) find that the lizard, *Lacerta viridis,* can be trained to a compass direction in relation to the real and to an artificial sun, just as can birds. Fischer (1960) reports that the internal clock of the Lizard can be modified experimentally as has been done, for instance, with the Starling amongst birds.

Boycott and Guillery (1962) have shown that Terrapins can be trained to olfactory and visual stimuli, the animals being able to discriminate meat alone from meat with amylacetate, vanillin, eucalyptus or a black figure. It appears that the olfactory discrimination is learned less readily than the visual discrimination. Operation on the olfactory nerve shows that amylacetate and vanillin at least are true olfactory stimuli. They also showed that olfactory lesions did not disturb the discrimination or feeding behaviour of animals trained to a visual situation.

Eskin and Bitterman (1961) compared the effects of partial and consistent reinforcement in young Terrapins trained in a simple runway. No significant difference was found in resistance to extinction. These results reinforce the conclusions of Bitterman and his associates, based on experiments with fish, to the effect that the paradoxical results of partial reinforcement so characteristic of the higher animals are not general throughout the animal kingdom and therefore are not likely to be understood in terms of the simplest principles of learning.

Latent Learning

There has been no critical work on latent learning in the reptiles, but it is well known that many species hold territories. Thus, Noble (1934) found that in the Fence Lizard (*Sceloporus undulatus*) both male and female adopt restricted territories, and that they can return to these territories from distances of nearly 800 feet across terrain which appears quite unsuitable for them and which it is very unlikely they had recently crossed. Homing times in some of these experiments are as follows: 420 feet—7 days; 760 feet—16 days; 790 feet—18 days. No instance of homing above 900 feet was recorded. That some exploration of the near environment takes place is suggested by the fact that lizards were occasionally seen to leave their territory for a while and to wander about in the general neighbourhood.

Woodbury and Hardy (1940) carried out an extensive study of the dens and behaviour of the Desert Tortoise (*Gopherus agassizii*). In the course of this work more than 200 tortoises were marked. They were found to have communal winter dens, 68 of which were studied; these dens being occupied from November to February inclusive. Nichols (1953) has shown that these dens are the result of co-operative digging by several individuals, either together or in relays. During March to October the animals scatter over a territory, usually as solitary individuals, sometimes as mating pairs. This territory seldom exceeds about 10 acres, although one was recorded as being about 40 acres. Besides these diffuse territories around dens, the tortoises also have summer holes in which they take shelter from the heat of the day, coming out to feed at night. Cagle (1944) has carried out an important field study of three species of tortoise, *Pseudemys scripta-elegans, Chrysemys picta* and *Terrapene carolina*. It was found that small groups of individuals usually occupy a section of a lake or stream, and that they will return to this section when removed to distances as great as a mile. Each individual appears to occupy a home area, and to leave this region only during a breeding or hibernating season or when the pools of water dry up. Gould (1957) has provided evidence that Box Turtles removed from their own territory can only assume their correct homeward orientation when the sun is visible. Whether anything more than a simple sun compass orientation was involved is uncertain.

These studies of tortoises and turtles imply a considerable 'knowledge' of the territory, probably involving visual, kinæsthetic, tactile and chemical stimuli. There seems to be no suggestion of aggressive protection of the territories themselves, although of course fights during the time of mating are well known. Snakes are also known to gather in winter dens.

Klauber (1936) describes a gathering-place of the Prairie Rattlesnake (*Crotalus c. confluentus*) in Colorado, where enormous numbers could be found. He alludes to a collection of 153 specimens taken from this place as 'just a few of the snakes present'! There seems little doubt that some part at least of the gathering and massing of snakes is based on chemical sense, but there is no exact information. Woodbury *et al.* (1951) studied a similar winter den in Utah which was used communally by seven species of snakes. Extensive marking, which continued over nine years, showed that the vast majority of snakes used the cave in successive winters; and as only adults occurred there it is a reasonable assumption that the juveniles learned of its existence and whereabouts by following the adults or their trails during the annual migrations, which involved anything up to two miles' travel. (See also Stickel and Cope, 1947.)

Parker (1922) assumed some form vision in young Loggerhead Turtles, and Casteel (1911) investigated the ability to distinguish two star-like white patterns against a black background. His tests were rather difficult, and with this particular task he obtained no evidence of learning, although he demonstrated that two animals could readily learn to respond to a choice between horizontal and vertical lines. Kuroda (1933) seems to have provided considerable evidence for a true form-sense and claims that the animal he used, *Clemmys japonica*, was able to distinguish a circle, triangle and square from each other, and maintain this distinction, even after some degree of rotation of the figures. If his work is substantiated it would seem to provide some evidence for an 'insightful' response to elementary forms and outlines. He also demonstrated transfer of training and some 'relational judgment.'

Wojtusiak (1933) has produced good evidence for colour sense in tortoises, and has also shown discrimination of simple geometrical forms (1934). Mylnarski (1951) has confirmed this and has demonstrated that tortoises can continue to respond to such forms correctly, even though they are represented only by incomplete or fragmentary outlines made up of dots, dashes or small curved segments. (Cf. van Beusekom on the wasp *Philanthus*, Chapter XI, above).

Individual Recognition

With the Amphibia there seems to be no proof at all that captive individuals learn to recognise their keepers. Neither is there any satisfactory evidence of this with reptiles, although the general impressions of those who have had most experience suggest that something of this kind may occur.

It seems, however, that members of colonies of the Black Lizard (*Ctenosaura pectinata*) must have some individual recognition of their associates. Thus Evans (1951) has shown that in a hierarchy of eight adult males of this species, the tyrant (as also, to a lesser extent, the other dominant individuals) is immediately given way to, not merely in his own territory but also in neighbours' territories when on his way to the communal and neutral feeding-ground.

Moreover, Greenberg and Noble (1944) found that although sex recognition in the American Chameleon (*Anolis carolinensis*) is based primarily upon the morphological features distinguishing the sexes, nevertheless a dominant male can learn to distinguish small males from females as a result, apparently, of the perception of rather subtle differences. The ordered, single-file migrations of the Galapagos Tortoise (*T. elephantopus*) implies the existence of hierarchies (van Denburgh, 1914), and a simple social organisation has been demonstrated in *T. e. vicina* (Evans and Quaranta, 1951).

These and other records suggest that a more thorough investigation of the visual learning and form discrimination of reptiles is likely to prove well worth while.

CHAPTER XIV

BIRDS

THE poor development in birds of any brain structures clearly corresponding to the cerebral cortex of mammals led to the assumption among neurologists not only that birds are primarily creatures of instinct but also that they are very little endowed with the ability to learn. There is no doubt that this preconceived notion, based on a misconceived view of brain mechanisms, hindered the development of experimental studies on bird learning. Thus Herrick (1924) says: 'It is everywhere recognised that birds possess highly complex instinctive endowments *and that their intelligence is very limited.*' No present-day student familiar with recent work on bird behaviour would be willing to endorse to-day the words I have put in italics. On the contrary, in some contexts it is doubtful whether the birds are exceeded in learning ability by any organisms other than the highest mammals, and in their powers of co-ordinating their sense impressions for purposes of orientation on homing and migratory flights, they appear supreme in the animal kingdom.

Habituation

There are at least four types of response-decrement known in animals. They have all been studied in birds; but for convenience reference is here also given to some examples from mammals. These types are as follows:

1. Short-term waning of the response, irrespective of the nature of the stimulus. This may be described as a kind of localised fatigue of short duration. It is the sort of phenomenon that we observe in the temporary waning of the pecking response of the young Herring Gull after frequent repetition (Tinbergen and Perdeck, 1950), and is an obvious component of the waning of the mobbing of owls by Chaffinches (Hinde, 1954). References to it in mammals include Grunt and Young (1952) for guineapigs; Beach and Holz-Tucker (1949) for rats; similar phenomena have been described for insects, see Chapter III above.

2. Long-term waning of the response, irrespective of the nature of the stimulus. This kind of phenomenon has not as yet been critically studied. We see it, or something like it, where, for instance, a bird has been for a very long time denied opportunity to exercise the powers of flight with the result that the ability to adapt and refine the instinctive flight movements seems to be permanently lost. Kruijt (1957, personal communication) has

described loss of sex behaviour in the male Burmese Red Jungle Fowl after rearing in isolation for a period of one and a half years or more. Although these birds seem unable to copulate after a period of more than nine months' isolation, they still—even after one and a half years—retain their general male aggressiveness to both humans and other cocks.

3. Short-term waning of the response to a specific stimulus. This type of behaviour may be observed in the changed intensity of the begging response of nestling passerines (Prechtl, 1953) and may be evidence of some transient changes in the releasing mechanism. It seems to be a kind of 'stimulus-satiation' giving rise perhaps to a passing 'lack of attention' to the stimulus.

4. Long-term response waning specific to the stimulus. This is habituation in the strict sense and, when information warrants it, the term is best reserved for this kind of phenomenon. Many examples will be found in what follows. It is an effect that endures for days or weeks rather than seconds or minutes, and it is taken to be evidence for the occurrence of processes depending on changes in the central nervous system, as distinct from changes in the level of response of the sense organs themselves. All of these types of waning are worthy of further study, but perhaps the two most particularly attractive and promising to the ornithologist are 2 and 4.

To take first one of the simplest cases described in birds, King (1926), studying the long-term nystagmus of both young and adult pigeons produced as a result of repeated rotation, found that there was a steady reduction in the intensity of the responses with repetition, although he hesitated to call this learning because he found it occurring even in de-cerebrate birds. Fearing (1926) also found a similar habituation, the number of head movements characteristic of the nystagmus after rotation being reduced by 30 per cent., and the time during which they occurred by 25 per cent. These experiments are of physiological rather than general biological interest; more illuminating from our point of view are those of Rouse (1905), who found, when studying the response of pigeons to sound, that it was possible to divide sounds into 'significant' and 'meaningless.' His pigeons remained sensitive to 'significant' sounds, particularly to the calls of other birds, but the repetition of 'meaningless' sounds, even such violent stimuli as pistol shots, produced habituation, and the pigeons eventually became quite immune to them, displaying no response at all. Presumably some of the recognition of 'significant' sounds rested on an instinctive basis; but it is unlikely that all did so, and one must assume that the distinction was at least partly learned. A similar habituation to sounds, as evinced by degrees of bodily movement, has been described by Szymanski (1918) for chicks.

To come to the wider biological aspect, it is clear that from the bird's point of view there are two main types of danger against which it has to be on guard. Firstly, there is the very special kind of danger due to the attacks of predators with specialised feeding habits—hawks, owls, snakes, etc. It is now clear that many birds have precise instinctive responses to the appearance of the particular kind of predator which is most dangerous to them. (See p. 69, above), for an account of the work of Nice and ter Pelkwyk (1941) on the recognition of owls by Song Sparrows which shows that the response to form is inborn. The same is probably true of the response of the Curve-billed Thrasher to snakes (Rand, 1941*a*); although both these species seem to have to learn the danger of other kinds of predators.)

But although we have recently learnt much more about this kind of behaviour, it still seems probable that it is the exception rather than the rule; for there are probably not so very many species of birds for which a particular group or species of predator constitutes the main danger to life, and obviously a bird cannot be instinctively attuned to recognise every kind of danger to which it may be subjected during the course of its life. The work of Kramer and von St Paul (1951) suggests that the Bullfinch recognises colour and texture of avian predators instinctively and has to learn the form later. It is only where some particular predator is well-nigh ubiquitous that an instinctive warning or recognition is biologically warrantable. As regards the need for adjustment in relation to all kinds of generalised warning stimuli, birds are no different from other animals (see Chapter III, p. 69, above) and habituation is as common in this group as it is elsewhere.

On the other hand, ready habituation to the appearance of one of the primary enemies would seem to be dangerous in the extreme. If the avoiding response due to recognition of a hawk began to fade after the bird had experienced it a few times without actual attack following, the main value of the inborn response would appear to be lost; for if it were otherwise, a bird which had the luck on a few occasions to be overlooked by a hunting hawk or to encounter a satiated snake would surely be in grave danger.

In support of this conclusion we have the evidence of Lorenz (1939) and Nice and ter Pelkwyk (1941) (see Chapter III, p. 69, above) of the great resistance to extinction in the Grey-lag Goose and the Song Sparrow of the innate response to the predator pattern.

It is true that Nice and ter Pelkwyk, and also Strauss (1938), working with hand-reared Jackdaws and a tame Hooded Crow, found evidence of short-term fading of response to an owl model or to a mounted owl after rapidly repeated display or as a result of leaving the birds with the model in the cage for a long period. In the case of the Song Sparrows, however, when they were retested again a day or two later, the response was back again at its original intensity and there was no clear evidence of any long-term habituation.

It is now evident, however, that long-term fading of response to the owl pattern may take place to such a degree and in such circumstances as to appear seriously dysgenic. Hinde (1954a) has made a critical experimental study of the changes in strength of the mobbing response of Chaffinches which result from repeated exposure to the owl pattern. This is a particularly suitable species for the work in that the intensity of the response can readily be quantified by counting and timing the 'chink' alarm notes. The peculiar actions of 'mobbing' are explained as being due to a conflict between tendencies to approach the predator and to flee from it,

Fig. 52—Wooden models of owls used (from left to right models C, D, E, F, G, H, K) in studying the mobbing response of the chaffinch. All models presented the same area to the bird—an area about equal to that of a little owl.
  C: Wooden model, size of little owl, solid, rough owl shape; owl colours and pattern, with painted indications of eyes and beak.
  D: As C, but without eyes and beak.
  E: As C, but only *ca* ⅜ inch thick.
  F: As E, but colour uniform brown.
  G: As E, but square.
  H: As E, but different pattern.
  K: As E, but rectangular, and no eyes or beak.
(After Hinde, 1954a.)

with exploratory behaviour also playing a role. The characters of owls which are important in the release of the mobbing were investigated by means of dummies (Fig. 52). It is clear that the recognition of many of these characters, including that of shape, must be inborn—as is also the motor pattern of the response. Neither motor pattern nor recognition appears until the bird is several weeks old. The same seems to be true of the Hawfinch, Yellow Bunting and Reed Bunting, and probably of a variety of other birds (references in Hinde, 1954a).

With the Chaffinch it was found that there was marked reduction in the mobbing response with successive presentations both of owl models and of stuffed and live owls (Figs. 53 and 54). In such a situation there are two antagonistic tendencies at work—one favouring increase and the other decrease of the response. It is usual, though by no means invariable, for the latter to predominate. This tendency to wane is itself made up of two components: a short-term response-specific decrement, the extent of which is dependent on the length of the initial exposure, and is greater with weak than with strong stimuli, and with massed practice than with spaced; and a long-term stimulus-specific effect, i.e. true habituation, which contrasts with the other in almost every detail. There is also some evidence for a short-term stimulus-specific decrement. That the effect is not merely due to the incompleteness of the stimulus provided by models and stuffed specimens will be clear from Fig. 53 (curves b–d), which shows habituation to the live Tawny Owl to be not much less than to mounts and models, and from Fig. 54, which shows that live Little Owls and stuffed Tawny Owls have a practically identical effect.

It might be thought that the response could, nevertheless, be fully resistant to habituation under natural conditions, and that it is only under the highly artificial conditions of close association in a cage that habituation comes into play.

Thus Nice (1943) found that a hand-reared Song Sparrow showed alarm when brought into a particular spot where it had on one occasion

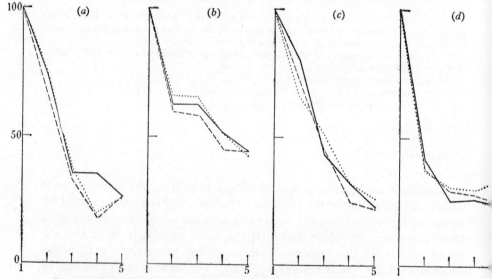

FIG. 53—Habituation curves of chaffinch to a, live little owl; b, live tawny owl; c, stuffed tawny owl; d, model. Ordinate: number of calls expressed as percentage of the number given on first presentation. Abscissa: successive presentations.

Owls presented for 20 minutes a day for 5 successive days. Number of calls given in each presentation plotted as percentage of those given in the first and averaged for all individuals. Based on number of calls in 20 minutes (continuous line), of calls in first 6 minutes (broken line) or number of calls in peak minute (dotted line). (After Hinde, 1954a.)

only been exposed to an owl model many months before, even though the model was no longer present, and Kramer and von St Paul (1951) found that by chasing Bullfinches with a harmless but conspicuous species of Kingfisher intense anxiety was produced (by associative conditioning), which lasted for months and was restricted to the pursuing species and to members of the same family (Halcyonidæ). But neither of these observations appears to offer a generally satisfactory solution of the problem. Thus Hinde found that though there is a place effect, habituation to a predator (e.g. owl) in one place involves a considerable degree of habituation to another predator (e.g. Stoat) in the same place, and that habituation

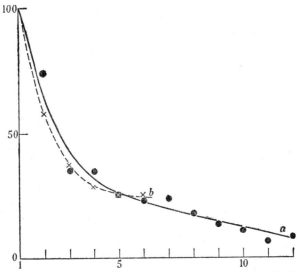

Fig. 54—Habituation curves of Chaffinches. Continuous curve: to live Little Owl presented for 20 minutes a day in avaries. Broken curve: to stuffed Tawny Owl presented for 3 minutes a day in cages. Strength of response plotted as percentage of calls given in first presentation. a. Averaged for all individuals for each presentation. (After Hinde, 1954a.) Ordinate: number of calls expressed as percentage of the number given on first presentation. Abscissa: successive presentations.

to one predator in one place also involves a considerable degree of habituation to the same predator in another place (Fig. 55). Even when the presence of a live owl in the aviary was always reinforced by an indubitably unpleasant and probably painful stimulus—the chaffinch being held against the owl's breast and two small feathers plucked out—nevertheless, habituation still proceeded. So the undoubted continued efficiency of the owl pattern as a releaser of mobbing behaviour in nature remains somewhat of an enigma. Mobbing Chaffinches and other passerines are undoubtedly sometimes attacked and killed by owls; on the other hand, owls must often, accidentally or intentionally, fly away from mobbing Chaffinches. Perhaps it is this latter intermittent and partial reinforcement (which cannot happen in aviaries) which in nature prevents the fading of the response (see Chapter III, above). Perhaps also the fact that in nature mobbing is so generally a social response would help to maintain it at high intensity. Hinde (1961b) describes experiments in which a model dog and a stuffed owl were presented successively in the same circumstances with an interval of 24 hours between presentations. When the initial presentation was 12 minutes long the score on the second presentation was the same whether the two models used were the same or different. Only when the first presentations were for 24 minutes or longer was the response on the second presentation smaller, if the model used was the same as that used in the first presentation, than if it was different. This differential effect of the model used on the first presentation was much greater if the model used on the second presentation was one that evoked a weaker response rather than vice versa. The results can be understood in terms of an interaction between long-term incremental and decremental effects. The evidence for the incremental effect comes from three independent sources—from the changes in latency, from the increase in the response to dog presented 24 hours after owl with lengthening of the initial presentation, and from some additional experiments with owl models. With short rest intervals, the response decrement was greater than with long ones and was also different in kind. There was no clear evidence that the short-term effects were stimulus-specific. Here again there appear to be incremental effects interacting with the decremental ones. From the results of these and other experiments it appears that the waning of the reponse to a predator depends on a number of processes which may be classified according to their recovery periods (a few seconds, a few minutes, or a few weeks) which may or may not be specific to the stimulus and which may produce an increase or a decrease in the responsiveness.

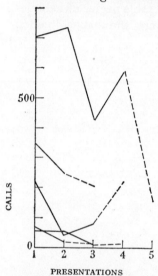

PRESENTATIONS

FIG. 55—Influence of position of owl on habituation of Chaffinch. The continuous lines represent habituation of single Chaffinches to an owl-model which was placed in the same place on successive days. On the last day of each experiment the owl was placed at the opposite end of the aviary (broken line). Ordinate: number of calls. Abscissa: successive presentations. (After Hinde, 1954a.)

There is no doubt that in some cases there is innate recognition of the characteristic hunting behaviour of a predator. In others, however, the relation between prey and predator seems to be on a relatively high pyschological level, and there is evidence that mammals may learn to recognise the mood of a predator and flee only when hunting behaviour commences (Stevenson-Hamilton, 1947). So what we most need to know is the subsequent response of apparently habituated birds to the predator concerned, when in hunting mood and under natural conditions. We might well find that under these conditions there was no decrease in the response. Ramsay (1950) describes how two Crows (*Corvus brachyrhynchos*) reared with a Barred Owl became completely conditioned to it as a companion, although they would show fear and curiosity at a stuffed owl. There is still a field here for much valuable and interesting experiment.

Melzack (1961) has shown that when mallard ducklings, reared in a highly restricted environment, are given repeated presentations of cardboard models of hawk and goose in flight overhead, they lose their fear responses after about two thousand presentations without reinforcement, but retain their vigilance. Thus they do not lose their capacity to respond to overheard objects, but rather are responding in a more organised and less disruptive way than is manifest initially by running, wing-flapping, making shrill cries and the like. It seems that the habituation of fear responses to the hawk shape is a result of a change in the organisation of behaviour in which emotional disruption is replaced by non-emotional orienting responses.

That habituation can also be a source of danger to a bird in its relation to traps and snares set by man is, of course, very obvious. It is, however, perhaps worth giving one interesting example quoted by K. Williamson (1948) in his account of the catching of Puffins on the island of Mykines in the Faeroes. The annual harvest of Puffins has here become an important part of the island economy, and the same snaring-places, or *roks* as they are called, are used year after year. One might expect that the Puffins would become wary of the much-used *rok*, and that catches would therefore decrease unless new ground were sought. But this is not so. The Puffins accept man and his net as 'part and parcel of the world of puffinry.' They are apparently not aware of anything amiss with their environment until some incautious fowler changes it radically by some new snaring arrangement or upsets the familiar scene by putting a snare in an unaccustomed place. Williamson states that the older fowlers know how wary the Puffins can be under such circumstances. Thus the forty or fifty snaring-places along the south coast of Mykines have been in use for many generations—'so long that men cannot say how deep into the past their history goes.'

Some interesting observations showing the importance of habituation in the earliest life of the young bird will be found in the papers of Sumner (1934) and Herrick (1910); and de Ruiter (1952) shows that Chaffinches and Jays, being used to the inedibility of sticks, do not peck at stick caterpillars. If they find one by accident, they will peck at all similar objects until discouraged by finding only sticks. The original situation is then restored.

Conditioning

As with other animals, Pavlov and his pupils were the pioneers in studying the conditioned responses of birds. A very valuable review and summary of much of this work can be found in the paper of Razran (1933). In the experiments of Popov (for references, see Razran) the bird used was the pigeon, and just as with the dog (used for salivary-conditioning experiments) so the bird has to be trained to stand in a specially made coat with openings for the free movement of the head and one leg only. When this phase of the preliminary training is completed, investigation can proceed. The application of a mild electric shock on the presentation of food is the conditioning stimulus, while a great variety of auditory, visual, tactile and ampullar stimulations have been used successfully as conditioned stimuli. It would be out of place here to go into the details of such experiments as these, which have been repeated and extended by both Beritoff (1926) and ten Cate (1923). Suffice it to say that no fundamental difference between the learning abilities of mammals and birds appears. It is, however, noteworthy that the use of olfactory stimuli has never been unequivocally successful in conditioning experiments performed under rigorous conditions, and this made it seem doubtful whether many birds experience olfactory sensations at all (Walter, 1943). However, birds show a considerable range of development of the olfactory lobes, and it would be unwise to dogmatise on the basis of the few forms which have been critically investigated. Hamrum (1953) has, however, produced evidence that the Bob-white Quail can be trained to odours. The Kiwi would seem to be a particularly promising subject for further study.

The results of Popov show that the pigeon is capable, as one would expect, of good discrimination between different sounds and between different kinds of geometrical figures of equal area. With birds, as with other animals, it has been shown by Bajandurow (1928) that if the task of differentiation given is too difficult, 'experimental neuroses' results. It has also been demonstrated with the pigeon that conditioned reflexes of the classical type can be established even though the 'cerebral cortex' (or rather the functionally equivalent regions of the corpus striatum, etc.) is eliminated (Beritoff), showing of course that the process of conditioning takes place in 'lower' regions of the central nervous system. There is, however, a marked difference in the retention of the conditioning as between entire and 'decorticated' birds. While a conditioned reflex in a normal bird may be retained after some weeks of experimentation, that in a 'decorticated' bird will not endure for more than four days (Beritoff's experiments), although ten Cate records a case in which there were still traces present after four weeks. However, a conditioning which has been allowed to fade in this manner can be relatively easily restored by a few reinforcements. That chicks of the domestic fowl can also be used success-fully for conditioning experiments has been shown by the work of Zawa-dowsky and Rochlina (1929), by Riddle and Barnes (1931) and also by Watson (1916) and Reichner (1924–5). Grindley (1927) also used young chickens successfully for conditioning experiments, and showed with these, the essentially anticipatory nature of the process, and that backward conditioning (that is, conditioning in which the stimulus to be conditioned follows instead of preceding the response) is impossible. A number of other examples could be cited in which these two species of domesticated birds have been used for conditioning experiments, but it does not seem as if the attempt has been made with any others.

It is well known from experiments on conditioning of sheep that in order to secure satisfactory results in such an animal, where social and flock behaviour is so highly developed, 'a social sheep' must be provided, eating its oats in the corner in the sight of the experimental animal, for without it the laboratory animal would not stand quietly in its stall and harness. The work of Rouse (1906) has shown that a somewhat similar situation exists with pigeons, and, indeed, Popov has claimed to have shown that when conditioned reflexes of the second order were estab-lished, conditioned reflexes of the first order being the sight of another bird eating, they were exceptionally stable, indicating that 'social reflexes' have some special potency. He concluded that some apparent 'imitation' (really social facilitation) could thus be accounted for on the basis of the classical conditioned-reflex concept. Razran (p. 286) criticises this con-clusion on technical grounds, which need not be entered into here but which seem to be valid. However, there is some evidence that, in rats, 'sympathy' (that is to say, sympathetic response to the pain of other rats) whether or not primarily based on innate social releasers, can be sub-stantially increased by the normal processes of conditioning (Church, 1959).

The conditioning experiments of Skinner (1952) and Ferster and Skinner (1957) on the pecking response of pigeons are of a scale and pre-cision that render them unique among such bird studies. As an example, he has shown that pigeons can be readily taught to peck at any one of three discs by rewarding them with food from an automatic device only when the correct disc is pecked. If two pigeons are set side by side in sight of one another and in adjacent cages, each with three discs for pecking, and if the apparatus is so adjusted that food is only delivered when both pigeons peck at one of the same pair of discs simultaneously, they will quickly become so perfectly conditioned to one another's actions that they will order all their pecking movements in almost perfect synchrony and unanimity, giving the appearance of perfect mutual imitation (Skinner, personal communication; also 1953, p. 120).

Progressive improvement in habit reversal over a series of trials, a well-established characteristic of mammalian learning, has been described in the pigeon by Reid (1958) and in chicks by Warren et al (1960). Zielinski (1960a and b) has studied the course of development of conditioned excitatory and inhibitory reflexes in chickens. He finds that excitatory conditioned reflexes change significantly in magnitude with age, whereas differences in the progress of inhibitory reactions were linked with sex.

TRIAL-AND-ERROR LEARNING

(a) *Simple Cases. The Acquisition of Skill as Trial and-error Learning*

It is now fairly generally accepted that the pecking movements of newly hatched chicks are inborn in the sense that the central nervous, proprioceptive and visual co-ordinations which render them possible are virtually fully organised and perfected at the moment of the first peck. This seems to have been quite satisfactorily established by the pioneer observations of Douglas Spalding (1872), which were unaccountably lost sight of by most later workers and to which Haldane (1954a) has again drawn attention. It is the events subsequent to the first peck which are of interest for the student of learning. Thus when a young chick pecking 'at random' on the floor of its box accidentally strikes some object which is edible, the inborn response of swallowing takes place as soon as this object is in the bill. Normally this process provides a reinforcement, with the result that the bird soon comes to distinguish edible from inedible objects, and for the most part ignores the latter. It is still uncertain to what extent the first pecks are entirely random and unorientated. This must certainly vary from species to species; but most probably there is usually some visual cue to set the behaviour going. Thus Rand (1941a) describes how with young Thrashers 'the only requisite of the stimulus causing exploratory pecking was some visual difference in the uniformity of the environment. Anything that looked small and different was pecked at.'

There is also evidence (Verplanck, verbal communication; also Moseley, 1925; Padilla, 1930) that if chicks are given no food but *only* spots on the floor to peck at, the pecking response is eventually extinguished and the birds become incapable of swallowing grain. It is said that such birds could be kept alive only by being laboriously taught to feed on mash and that only with the greatest difficulty could they learn to eat anything else!

The far-fetched suggestion of Lehrman (1953), based on the observations of Kuo (1932), that the pecking behaviour is itself 'learnt' in the embryo, as a result of tactile stimulation (via the yolk-sac) of the amniotic pulsations, hardly seems to bear close consideration. It has been effectively demolished by Eibl-Eibesfeldt (1961).

But though some feeding behaviour has, as in the above examples, to be very largely learnt, it is important to realise that this is probably not the general rule for birds as a whole. Curtius (1954) has shown that with newly-hatched chicks, Turkeys and Lapwings, the innate pecking preferences are based on degrees of figure-ground contrast and not on form or wavelength. These innate preferences could be strengthened or weakened by learning. There are innumerable genera and species (e.g. herons, waders, birds of prey, etc.) where feeding behaviour is so specific and stereotyped that learning must play only a relatively small part in it. Stereotyped feeding behaviour ensures an efficient means of securing a special kind of food; but behaviour involving much learning allows of flexible adaptiveness to a great variety of food and must surely be something of an evolutionary safeguard.

Another interesting study of the function of learning in the development of normal behaviour is that of Wallace Craig (1912) on young doves learning to drink. In this case the innate drinking activity consists of bending the head low and swallowing. Originally the act of swallowing is released only by the stimulus of water on the inside of the mouth, and the dove shows no innate tendency to produce the drinking response at the sight or sound of water, nor to the presence of water on the distal parts of the body, such as the tail or wings—although there may occasionally be a slight response as a result of the contact of water with the feet. The first drink probably results from an accidental pecking of some conspicuous or shining object in or on water, or possibly just by pecking at the sparkling surface. Pigeons are particularly ready to peck at glistening objects, and anything which catches their attention may bring about this first drink. The drinking movements are thus innate, but the bird has no concept of water as being the stuff to drink, and takes some considerable time to learn. Thus one dove which was studied showed no evidence, on the second and third occasions of drinking, of having remembered the first experience, but from the fourth time onward it showed clear evidence of memory. It quickly learned to associate the action of drinking water with all sorts of stimuli, such as the shape and appearance of the dish, the person who brought the dish, and the sound of water being poured out, etc., but it took much longer for it to recognise water as such, and even a thirsty dove would make no attempt to drink if the dish in which the water was presented was unfamiliar. During this period the doves would not infrequently make drinking movements as soon as they saw the approach of the dish but before it had reached them. Sometimes they would stand in the dish and put the bill down outside it, appearing to be disappointed that the drink was unsuccessful. Behaviour very similar to this has been recorded by Nice (1943) for the Song Sparrow, and Wing (1935) describes how hand-reared Prairie Chickens at the age of nine days showed much excitement at their first sight of drops of water supplied from a pipette—as if dew-drops supply a sign-stimulus which fits an innate receptory correlate, and so are instinctively sought as the first source of water. Rheingold and Hess (1957) have analysed this matter further. They find that the essence of the stimulus is the bright reflecting surface coupled with movement. Of a number of stimuli investigated, mercury was found to be supernormal. Fantz (1957) finds that in chicks there is an innate preference for round as compared with angular objects. Both two-dimensional and three-dimensional aspects of visual form play their part in this innate response. Pastore (1958, 1959), investigating the innate perceptions of newly-hatched ducklings, found what appears to be an innate ability for form perception, size-constancy and brightness-constancy in ducklings. They were also readily able to learn to select triangles from trapezoids and to discriminate between vertical and horizontal striations. The accounts of the first bathing activities of birds show very close parallels to those which refer to drinking. Heinroth (1938) gives a number of examples and Nice (1943) adds others.

The extraordinary efficiency in trial-and-error learning of partial reinforcement can be well illustrated from bird behaviour. Two outstanding examples are quoted (Chapter IV, p. 86) above.

Simple trial-and-error learning probably plays a very important part in improvement in many examples of nest-building. There seems little doubt that many birds are born with nest-building motions innate, but that they have to learn, at any rate to some extent, what materials are appropriate for nest-building. Thus young Ravens, starting to build a nest for the first time in their lives, are very uncertain what material to use, and will pick up sticks which are quite unsuitable for the purpose. However, they soon learn to select the size and type of twig that can be woven into the nest. This, then, constitutes the first step in establishing and improving the nest-building activity. Similarly a Jackdaw will at first try to build all sorts of things into its nest, but soon becomes negatively conditioned to anything which will not stick, e.g. bits of ice, twigs of wrong shape and all sorts of odd, hard objects that it happens to find. It has an innate movement but otherwise has to become 'conditioned' to twigs that are the right shape (Lorenz, personal communication). But the observations of Scott (1902b) on American Robins are very puzzling. He describes how hand-reared birds during two years of attempts were unable to build nests which would hold together, nor were they able to feed and care for young birds in early infancy. But they could do all that was required—feeding, brooding and nest sanitation—when given older young.

Hinde (1958), Hinde and Warren (1959), Warren and Hinde (1959) and Hinde (personal communication) have shown that with Canaries and other finches: (a) Nest-building movements are given by canaries which have never had any opportunity to manipulate grass, moss or other similar materials, when sitting in an empty nest-pan (a somewhat different result from that obtained by other workers who used rats reared without material). (b) When grass was presented for the first time to a Canary in nest-building mood it was picked up in a few seconds and carried to the nest-pan within a minute. (c) When (experienced) Canaries are given both grass and feathers, which they choose depends in part on the state of the nest already present (whether or not they have built it themselves). (d) Nest-building is not a simple chain response of gathering-carrying-building, etc.—stimuli from the half-completed nest play an important part in the organisation of the behaviour complex. Thus (i) the decline in building activity at about the time of the laying of the first egg is partly dependent on the presence of the completed nest. (ii) Removal of the nest causes a temporary disorganisation of building-behaviour, with many incomplete behaviour sequences, and neither a return to an earlier phase in the cycle nor desertion. (e) Canaries kept without nest-material throughout one or more nest-building cycles develop abnormal habits (e.g. plucking their own feathers; gathering one of their own feathers from the nest-site, carrying it around, and then replacing it) which may persist in later cycles even though super-abundant material is present. Similarly, hand-reared Chaffinches, kept through their first summer in cages devoid of material, plucked their breasts in the next spring and continued to do so after material was provided. One series of experiments involved the provision of abundant nest-material during the 30-minute watch periods, the material being removed at the end of the period. The three main behaviour patterns concerned with nest-building are gathering material, carrying material, and sitting building. Contrary to what might have been expected, sitting building is not consummatory to gathering and carrying; rather, all three seem to be under the control of a single causal factor—presumably hormonal—that determines the threshold at which they can be elicited. But each activity can interrupt the other. The only scheme which seems to fit the facts is to suppose that the activities share the motivation but that each, independently, has some inertia of its own and that each is building up some inhibition as it proceeds. In other words, the actions are 'both self-stimulating and self-exhausting', to quote a phrase coined by Julian Huxley for a description of the Great Crested Grebe published in 1912. The reproductive cycle in birds depends, of course, primarily on internal changes set in motion by external factors such as changes in day length, temperature, etc., but the successive phases of the cycle do not then follow automatically but depend on further stimuli from the environment or further internal changes or both. Hinde and Warren find that the female may lay eggs without going through all the earlier phases of reproductive behaviour, but egg-laying is then delayed and clutch size is abnormal. For biologically successful reproductive behaviour, nest-building activities and a complete nest are essential. Innate recognitions undoubtedly come into this. The nest itself, stimuli from the nest-pan, the size and texture of the nest-material, recognition of grass and feathers, and so on, and learned responses are clearly also important.

Verlaine (1934) records how Canaries, which had their innate nest-building movements imperfectly developed and so lacked the usual side-to-side motions of weaving, tended to build diffuse, fluffy nests, but learned with experience to improve in tidiness. The Serin Finch, on the other hand, has a full complement of nest-making instincts, and can produce a virtually perfect nest at the first attempt. As Lorenz points out (see Tinbergen (1951a)), we must, however, be careful to distinguish between the acquisition of nest-building skill and the learning to select suitable material. The subject of acquisition of skill is discussed further below; but in this case particularly we have to try to disentangle the effects of changing hormonal motivation. It is probable that many cases of improvement in nest-building in older birds which are regarded as being due to experience are, in fact, merely cases of rising hormonal level, first-year birds tending to build clumsy nests because their hormonal secretions have not yet reached the required level. Much further study is necessary to resolve such problems. Boesiger and Lecomte (1959) studied the nest repair executed by Blue and Great Tits after experimental removal of part of the nest wall. The birds' response to this interference varied enormously between individuals; but taking them all together almost every conceivable type of repair activity was employed. The kind of repair activity shown did not appear to be very closely related to the stage in the reproductive cycle that the bird happened to be in when the damage was done. The authors are impressed by the 'intelligence' shown by the birds.

Lehrman (1959) has summarised the whole field of the hormonal responses to external stimuli in relation to breeding biology and physiology generally in birds. It appears that a number of movement patterns characteristic of incubating doves are induced in inexperienced birds by progesterone injection. These movements are independent of experience but combined into effective behaviour, at least partly, because orientation to the egg has to be acquired by experience and is lacking in the naïve birds. Lehrman concludes that, in many species of birds, the stimuli provided by nest-material, nests, and perhaps the sight of others building, play an important regulating role; and in some cases an essential causative role, in the progression to the next stage in the physiological cycle. And there is ample evidence that different pituitary hormones can be selectively stimulated by different stimuli acting through the nervous system. Because naïve female canaries kept without males will often build nests, and doves kept in isolation will occasionally lay eggs, it would be going too far to say that all the endocrine changes occurring during the breeding season are caused solely by the effects of external stimulation; but—to quote Lehrman—'it is surely permissible to say that in very many species of birds external stimuli provide at least a sufficient regulated influence on endocrine secretion to be one of the causes of the delicate adjustment of successive changes in the bird's behaviour to successive changes in external stimulation.' Eisner (1960) has contributed a review summary of the relationship of hormones to the reproductive behaviour of birds, especially parental behaviour.

It has been pointed out (Kuo, 1932) that practically every physiological organ of the birds is in functional condition before hatching, and that practically every part of the muscular system of the young bird has been exercised some days before the end of the first half of the incubation period. This of course is true enough, and these embryonic movements are the elements out of which many of the responses shown by the bird after hatching are built; but it is a misapprehension to suppose, as Kuo does, that learning in any sense is taking place in the embryonic state. What is happening inside the egg when we detect movements of the embryo is, mainly if not entirely, a process of maturation of the innate behaviour patterns. Douglas Spalding (1840–77) was, as Haldane (1954a) has pointed out, the first to demonstrate the inborn character of flight movements in birds. He showed that hand-reared Swallows kept in cages too small to permit flying nevertheless flew 'perfectly' on the first opportunity. For a detailed study of the development of instincts and habits in birds, the work of Kuhlmann (1909) should be consulted.

It follows also, then, that we must equally be on our guard against attributing to learning all improvement in performance shown in the young bird after hatching. If maturation of behaviour patterns is going on within the egg, it is natural to assume that it is still going on in the fledged young bird. This has been clearly demonstrated by the experiments of Grohmann on the development of flight (described above, p. 58). The full explanation of such improvement in skill with time, independent of practice, is not yet fully understood, but it seems likely (Tinbergen, 1948 and 1951a) that it is largely a matter of the growth of the nervous system itself.

Experiments such as Grohmann's, which are closely paralleled by the experiments of Weiss on walking in amphibia and those of Carmichael (1947) on the swimming movements of tadpoles, show how careful we have to be in assuming that apparent improvement with practice is, in fact, an indication of learning. A few further examples may be of interest. The place of learning in the first orientation of pecking behaviour has been discussed (p. 88) above. Breed (1911) carried on a careful study of the subsequent increase, in the chick, in the skill and co-ordination of the pecking movement itself—a subject which again had, in fact, been studied with considerable care by Spalding. Breed found, as have other investigators, that pecking accuracy improves rapidly during the first three days and at a slower rate on subsequent days. This improvement consists in more effective aiming, perfection of the seizing technique and increasing readiness to swallow if once secured.

Shepherd and Breed (1913) followed this up by keeping chicks in the dark after hatching in order to prevent them from pecking. During this time they were watered and fed by hand. The batches of chicks thus delayed were brought into the light at intervals and tested for pecking. Those that had been in the dark soon became as efficient at aiming their pecks as those of the same age which had had normal practice. These experiments were not successful in making a clear distinction between the effects of maturation and practice, and have been followed up by a number of other workers (e.g. Bird, 1925 and 1926; Moseley, 1925). This last study has avoided a number of the difficulties inherent in the earlier methods, and gives rather a different picture from that provided by Shepherd and Breed. It appears probable that during the first thirty hours maturation is dominant and practice plays little or no part, and it is during this period that aim improves. By contrast, after the age of thirty hours there was little evidence of maturation, and peck aim was now virtually perfect; the further improvement which was evident during this period seems to have been a matter of an increase in the skill with which the grain is seized and swallowed, as a result of repeated attempts on the trial-and-error basis. Hailman (1961) finds that in domestic chicks if one chick learns to feed through trial-and-error exploratory pecking, it may happen that other inexperienced chicks initially find food by pecking at the bill tip of an experienced sibling and then immediately establishing a discriminatory response. This constitutes a process of social interaction in which the presence of an experienced individual facilitates the learning process in an inexperienced individual and is somewhat similar to the processes included under empathic learning by Klopfer (1959, 1961). (See p. 399, below.) This conclusion also received some support from the work on the flight of birds. For instance, it is found that while Grohmann's results (see above) apply to quite young birds, if such birds are prevented from flying for a longer period than that covered by Grohmann's experiments, they are put back considerably in the development of skill as compared with normal individuals. It is certainly the general view of naturalists, based on casual observation, that practice in bird flight does make perfect, and that while a young bird can 'fly' more or less perfectly, it continues clumsy at landing and the more subtle aerial manœuvres for quite a long time. It seems very improbable that all this kind of improvement is due to maturation, and the evidence on the whole suggests that learning is here of major importance. But although this may be so we have always to bear in mind that birds which have been artificially prevented from performing a natural act may be suffering not merely from lack of practice but also from the setting up of contrary habits. Thus Moseley (1925), in the course of his experiments on improvement in pecking with practice, found that the accuracy of pecking improved more gradually the longer the delay period. He points out that these chicks had learned in the meantime to swallow from a spoon, and the longer they were artificially fed, the more difficult it became for them to feed by pecking. This clue was followed up by Padilla (1930), who delayed chicks for fourteen days after hatching, and then found that it was impossible to teach them to peck grains except by 'an indirect and time-consuming process of training' (Maier and Schneirla, 1935, p. 243).[1]

For a rather similar instance I am indebted to Dr A. F. J. Portielje, who told me of some young Cape Penguins in the Amsterdam Zoo which, owing to the conditions of their captivity, were fed by their parents for a much longer period than is normal. The young are fed on regurgitated fish, and since the fish are always swallowed by the adult birds head first, they naturally come out tail first. Owing to the delay in having to feed themselves, the young penguins failed to develop the habit of taking fish head first and subsequently always took them tail first, even when they were well grown and entirely self-sufficient. This was found to be a dangerous habit in that the birds were very liable to choke if they attempted to swallow too large a fish.

The practice of pinioning wildfowl has demonstrated some extraordinary variations in learning ability. Thus many species (e.g. Cormorants) give up all attempts at flight soon after the operation, whereas others (e.g. Teal) continue indefinitely their vain attempts to take wing (Hediger, 1950, p. 49), and pinioned Shelduck at the Ornithological Field Station at Madingley have displayed the same persistence over three years or more. Further study of such differences, particularly with reference to the age at which pinioned, might yield very interesting results.

I am indebted to Mr Peter Scott for an account of the performance of old Grey-leg Geese when allowed to fly for the first time for five years. Compared with the performance put up by their own young, which were perfect fliers from the start, they made a very poor showing. They were bad at taking off, partly because they did not invariably take off into the wind as did the young birds, and they were also bad at manœuvring and clumsy at landing. This instance, however, while suggestive, does not

---

[1] The inhibiting effect of prolonged lack of reinforcement has been mentioned (p. 347) above in connection with the first pecking of chicks. These birds, of course, had plenty of 'practice' and did not develop contrary habits; nevertheless, the behaviour regressed because of the absence of reward.

provide any clear evidence as to the relative importance of instinct and learning. It is to be noted that the young geese were very able fliers right from the start, suggesting that practice was contributing very little to their performance; it seems quite reasonable to assume that the difficulties encountered by the adults were due not to lack of practice but to a regression of the unused instinctive mechanism.

The very valuable work of Wallace Craig (1914) on the behaviour of male doves reared in isolation does, however, suggest that practice plays an important part here as a fine adjustment of technique. He says: 'When a male dove performs an instinctive act for the first time, it generally shows some surprise, hesitation, bewilderment or even fear; and the first performance is in a mechanical, reflex style, whereas the same act after much experience is performed with ease, skill and intelligent adaptation.' Some further evidence along these lines will be found in Volume III (pp. 156-9) of C. O. Whitman's great work (1919).

That learning may have an important part in, so to speak, tying together the independently maturing locomotor-patterns to form functional purposive behaviour of a higher order is shown by the work of Kortlandt (1940), a brief summary of which will be found in Tinbergen (1951a). Thus the complete nesting behaviour of the Cormorant consists of fetching twigs, pushing them into the nest with the characteristic side-to-side quivering motions which are shown by so many species of birds in this situation, the function of which is presumably to fasten them into the nest. Kortlandt found that young Cormorants begin to show nesting behaviour even at an age of two weeks. This perhaps is in line with precocious sexual behaviour shown by so many young birds and associated with the relatively large size of the gonads in the first summer and early autumn, a size which is not again attained until the bird reaches sexual maturity (Bullough, 1942 and 1945). The primary nesting behaviour of the young Cormorants consists of this quivering motion, which is performed at first perfunctorily, the twigs not becoming firmly attached. The young continue these motions intermittently for four or five weeks, until sooner or later the twigs get caught up by the nest. Still later they accept twigs from the male, and also go to fetch twigs for themselves and subsequently work these into the nest. This example fits in with Tinbergen's conclusion mentioned above (p. 57), that the lower units of the level of consummatory acts appear first in the life of a young bird—appetitive behaviour, much of which may be learned, appearing later.

Nice (1943, pp. 266-7) summarises the result of much observation on the relation of the adult Song Sparrow's learned activities to its instinctive equipment. She finds that there is improvement in skill, probably as a result of learning, in the feeding of the young. But apart from this the learning process has to provide, through experience, the right object for the instinctive behaviour patterns. There are some interesting examples, from field observation, of special techniques of feeding displayed by individual adult birds which must clearly be the result of individual learning. Thus Miller (1939) describes how a Lazuli Bunting pulled grassheads to a wire fence and held them there as he picked out the seeds, and R. E. and W. M. Moreau (1941) describe how a Fiscal Shrike in East Africa attached itself to a Roller, swooping at it and making it drop grasshoppers which the shrike then caught in mid-air. This procedure recalls the behaviour of skuas, man-of-war birds, etc., where innate behaviour patterns are presumably involved. We are, of course, unable to say how individual performances such as the above have been acquired. The remarkable technique whereby tits of various species and also some other birds (e.g. Jackdaw and Great Spotted Woodpecker) have learned to open milk bottles is a particularly interesting case. Pecking and tearing open objects is a normal and probably innate method of feeding in tits, and the hollow-sounding metal caps and the waxed cardboard tops respectively release the hammering behaviour appropriate to nuts and the tearing movements elicited by loose bark. But although these actions are probably sufficient for most of the behaviour on the first occasions, it is clear that experienced bottle-openers learn to improve their technique— quite apart from learning where the bottles are and what they look like (Fisher and Hinde, 1949; Hinde and Fisher, 1952). The persistence with which tits repeatedly enter houses to tear paper in various forms (Logan-Home, 1953) suggests that the performance of the tearing movements alone may, under certain conditions, provide sufficient reinforcement for learning to occur even though no food is obtained (Hinde, 1953b). In the case of milk bottles, of course, a food reward is also present.

Though trial-and-error learning undoubtedly plays a major part, it would hardly seem likely to suffice for all the preceding examples. Some of such behaviour is probably evidence of insight learning or possibly even true imitation, which will be dealt with below.

Learned individual variations in behaviour not infrequently appear to give rise to local traditions among the bird population. For examples of this see Thorpe (1945b) and Peitzmeier (1939). Brüll (1937) gives some account of the process by which young 'Falcons' learn to become food specialists. The evidence for the bottle-opening behaviour, which is by no means conclusive, suggests that in each local population it is first learnt by a few pioneers. There is another remarkable new habit developed by Greenfinches in Europe which does seem to have spread from a single original focus. Nowadays this species often eats the seeds of *Daphne mezereum*, a small shrub. Although the plant is native to Europe, it is widely planted as a garden ornamental because of its very fragrant flowers. Greenfinches, where the habit occurs, apparently keep these shrubs under observation and as soon as the seed feast is ready, which is usually about June 14th, descend upon the plant, stripping every fruit from the bushes. Pettersson (1961), by means of an extensive co-operative survey, has produced remarkably good evidence that this habit was initiated once and once only between one and two centuries ago in the Pennine district of England and has spread outwards by cultural diffusion in a fairly orderly manner, northwards and southwards, at an overall rate of between two and four kilometres per year. At the time of writing, the habit has diffused throughout the whole of the British Isles except the western parts of Ireland and the northernmost parts of Scotland and Cornwall and has also crossed the North Sea to Denmark. The basis of the attraction which the seeds exert on the birds is not known although it is surmised that a specific alkaloid known to be present has an intoxicating effect; so it may be an example of cultural diffusion of a drug addiction! Certainly the bold intensity of the birds when feeding on *Daphne* suggests that they find the food extremely seductive.

Some good examples of trial-and-error learning are provided by the work of Mostler (1935) and Mühlmann (1934). Mostler showed, as a result of a long series of experiments with wasps, that many species of insectivorous birds have to learn, as a result of the unpleasant taste, and possibly as a result of getting stung, that wasps are inedible. He found that inexperienced individuals will take a wasp as readily as a fly, there being apparently no instinctive recognition of warning-colour patterns. Mühlmann carried out an ingenious series of experiments to test mimicry. He first found that tartar emetic had a violent effect on birds. He then dyed mealworms treated with the deterrent bright red, after first making sure that red, untreated worms were readily eaten. The birds quickly learned to ignore the red-dyed larvæ. Extending this study, he then produced 'mimics' by dyeing other mealworms to a greater or less degree, segment by segment, to see how near they must be to the all-red model in order that they should be mistaken for it. He found great differences in behaviour between different birds of the same species, as well as between different species.

The gaping response of some young nidicolous birds appears to be governed by an inborn releasing pattern (Tinbergen and Kuenen, 1939), but the work of Holzapfel (1939) on the Starling and Nice (1943, pp. 60-1) on the Song Sparrow, Redstart, Cedar Waxwing and Cuckoo shows that learning may play a very important part in the development of this type of behaviour.

Wolfe and Kaplon (1941) have studied the effect of varying amounts of reward on the improvements of the pecking behaviour of young chickens. They carried out two main types of experiment, one with the amount of food varied, and the second with a constant amount of food but divided into a varying number of pieces, so that the birds had to give more pecks for the same quantity. Although the results are not very satisfactory statistically, they indicate that the consummatory act of pecking in itself has an influence on the learning process quite apart from the actual amount of food consumed. Thus there are lower time scores for learning with four quarters of a grain than with one whole grain. Similarly Grindley (1929) found that with chickens learning a simple maze, a six-fold increase in the amount of reward produced about 25 per cent. increase in the rate of learning. But here, as in so many other instances, individual differences were so great that even though forty chickens took part in each experiment, the results were not sufficiently uniform to establish the percentage with certainty.

Simple learning experiments of this kind provide, of course, a valuable tool in studying the ability to discriminate the differences of intensity of stimulus. Thus Jellinek (1926) investigated the powers of pitch discrimination of the Turtle Dove by establishing an association, through trial-and-error learning, between a compartment of the cage in which the bird could find food and a given pitch sounded on an Edelmann pipe. By this means it was found that the birds could distinguish successfully two notes differing by only half a tone. Grindley (1927) successfully trained chicks to run to a food trough on hearing the sound of a horn. The food seeking behaviour of pigeons has been similarly conditioned by ten Cate (1923), the stimulus used being the flashing of a bright light.

Simple food-discrimination habits illustrate the simplest kind of trial-and-error learning, but many much more complex learning performances can be included within this category. Mountfort (1952, personal communication) describes how Hawfinches learn (presumably on a trial-and-error basis) to follow groups and flocks of Turdidæ along the hedgerows to pick up the stones which the latter drop after they have eaten the fruits, and it would be hard to over-emphasise the importance of trial-and-error learning in the everyday life of birds. To whatever degree the recognition of nest site or territory may be inborn, it is obvious from the writings of Howard (1929, 1935) and Hinde (1952) on bunting and tit behaviour respectively, that trial-and-error learning must be of outstanding significance in the everyday fine adjustment of their activities. This must apply also not only to the construction of the nest and selection of nest material (as described above), but also to the selection of food, water and song posts (e.g. Yellow Bunting; Diesselhorst, 1950). Also, as Hinde has pointed out (unpublished, 1954), the question of nest-site selection is interesting in that some species which have nest-invitation displays must transfer what they learn in the invitation display to the apparently quite different behaviour context of nest-building.

(b) Experiments with Puzzle-boxes

The first experiments with puzzle-boxes were those of Porter (1904, 1906, 1910), who accustomed his birds (House Sparrows, Blue Jays and a Woodpecker) to feed inside a wire puzzle-box, the box being placed in the centre of their cage for some days and the door being left open. When they had become thoroughly used to this arrangement the door was shut but could be opened by pulling a cord which ran from the latch along one side of the box near the top. The birds, of course, fussed about the box, particularly the door, but as soon as a chance pull on the string had opened the door, they quickly restricted their attention to that particular region, and thereafter the learning was very rapid. At its first experience a Sparrow took more than ten minutes and a number of separate attempts before it got into the box, but by the twenty-fourth trial it could make its way in in five seconds. Different birds adopted different methods of moving the string, some pulling with the bill, others pushing against the taut string with their heads and another grasping the string with its claws. Later Porter (1910) complicated the problem by putting a second string slightly above the first, pressure on either being sufficient to undo the latch. A bird quickly learned to master this by alighting on a string. When, however, the strings were moved farther apart, the bird failed because it alighted between the strings without pressing either. Evidently this bird had not established any concept of the relation between the string and the door, but had merely 'grasped the fact' that landing on the box in a particular place had the desired effect. This lack of understanding of the connection between the pulling of the string and the opening of the door was shown by other birds, which not infrequently continued pulling at the string after the door had opened. It must be remembered that, simple as this problem is, the course of the strings was by no means direct and the whole situation was so abnormal that we could hardly expect the bird to 'understand' the exact relationship between string and door. What the bird did was to learn to associate disconnected responses and perform them in the right order. In doing this the birds were quite efficient, but there was a good deal of variation both between individuals and between species. The House Sparrows were, on the whole, outstandingly successful both by their great persistence and by their powers of concentration, qualities which no doubt have played a large part in the success of this species. Porter also describes the species as remarkable for its alternate fear and boldness, independence and caution—in short, a disposition which helps enormously in rapid learning of new tasks and situations. In Diebschlag's results, described below, the birds show a rather high degree of rigidity in response. However, here again memory was good— better than one would expect in a rat under similar circumstances—for the behaviour was retained for a month, and in one case, when a Cow Bird was used, some sign of the original ability was observed even after four months.

Bené (1945) has studied the behaviour of wild humming-birds, examining particularly the recognition of flowers as sources of food just when the young are acquiring sufficient strength for sustained flight. Here the earliest responses related to food-getting are probing with the bill and tongue, first while perched and later while hovering. The acceptance or rejection of flowers as a source of food is governed by experience. Sense of smell seems to play little part, but there was good discrimination of colour, taste and form; and in some cases a single visit to a particular food source was sufficient to establish a feeding pattern. This is a good instance of the much greater efficiency of trial-and-error learning in the natural environment as compared with that under the artificial conditions of puzzle-boxes, and the classical conditioning technique.

Work of this kind is valuable because the problems set are simple and natural, and because in this particular instance care was taken that fright and nervousness should not interfere with the bird's performance. While, of course, experiments such as these with wild birds cannot be so exactly controlled as those in the laboratory, yet they may give a far more accurate impression of the effective learning ability. When using puzzle-boxes and mazes, it is extremely easy to set a problem which, while seemingly simple to the experimenter is, in fact, far too difficult for the animal. In general, it can be assumed that no puzzle-box can really be 'understood' by the bird, and that the technique tests strict trial-and-error learning only, and nothing more.

There has been comparatively little work with delayed reward, almost the only case being that of Chattock and Grindley (1933), who found that delay of 30 seconds in presenting reward caused an average increase of 25 per cent. in the time taken to run the maze. The effect was less marked if the chicks spent the delay period in the food-box. It was also found that many other extraneous factors acting during the delay period might influence the maze performance. Buytendijk (1921a) had much success with Siskins in a test in which the bird had to choose, from four boxes in a row, that box which contained food. The food-box was kept always in one position relative to the others, but the food itself was invisible when the doors were closed. The bird had to learn to go to the correct box and open the door with its beak. The door-opening was very quickly achieved, but learning to select the correct box took much longer. These experiments were very carefully conducted to avoid fear and distraction, and the possibility that localisation was due to odour seems to have been ruled out. Similar work has been carried out by Schut (1921) using a Goldfinch, Chaffinch, Paradise Whydah and the weaver *Pyromelana afra.* The work of Katz and Toll (1932) is interesting in that it compares the ability of five hens in carrying out a number of simple tests. It was found that one hen obtained top score in practically all the tests, but Liggett (1925) found with chicks in simple mazes that individuals showed noteworthy unreliability and inconsistency of performance.

(c) Maze Learning

Thorndike (1898) seems to have been the first person to study the maze-learning abilities of birds. He found that chicks learned with practice to escape more readily from a simple maze. Porter (1904, 1906) compared the maze-running ability of the House Sparrow with that of the rat. In his rather limited experiments the birds showed decided improvement with practice, but not of the same order as the rat displays. Rouse (1906) found that pigeons could readily learn mazes of various types. Hunter (1911) used pigeons in a simple maze involving six blind alleys. For the first seven trials there was no appreciable improvement, and in not many cases was there much sign of learning before the sixtieth trial. Although both workers found that learning was slow in comparison with that of an ant, rat or even House Sparrow in similar circumstances, it was eventually perfect and was well retained, showing no decrease in efficiency after six weeks' rest. Moreover, modification was easily accomplished as a result of fresh experience. Sadovnikova (1923a) tested a number of different passerines in a 'Hampton Court' maze, and found that in from twenty to fifty trials the birds reached a satisfactorily uniform standard of maze running. She found, however, that her birds were more variable in performance than rats, and that individual birds would occasionally show periods of 'forgetting,' when they would enter blind alleys which they had previously learnt well to avoid.

Diebschlag (1940) used a maze method for a long series of experiments on the learning ability of pigeons. He found that his pigeons easily learnt problems of visual orientation, and that in some kinds of serial learning they were superior to the common laboratory mammals. The pigeons were, however, handicapped as compared with mammals by a tendency to rigidity of response, a kind of inclination to stereotyped behaviour which was a hindrance in serial learning and which made them less adaptable in some types of maze. They were also readily put off by a slight variation in procedure, and would then take twice as long to learn the new arrangement of a previously learnt problem, and it is characteristics such as this which probably account for the apparent contradictions between his results and those of Hunter described above. That the maze behaviour of his birds was not a purely automatic response to a particular stimulus of a particular sense organ was, however, shown by covering one eye and then the other and by changing from one covered eye to both covered. This, contrary to earlier work of Beritoff and Chichinadse (see Razran, 1937), did not affect the performance of a previously learnt problem.

Siegel (1953a and b), testing pigeons in a modified form of the Lashley jumping apparatus, has also studied the effect of early deprivation of visual form on discrimination learning. He found that birds completely without experience of visual-form discrimination took significantly longer to reach a given criterion of learning than did the controls. This result by itself would suggest that, as in Hebb's theory, a change in the 'neural substrate' resulting from previous visual experience is necessary for normal adult visual function. But when the experiments were followed up by studies on interocular transfer, complications appeared. Thus whereas normally reared birds showed immediate transfer of a 'circle *versus* triangle discrimination,' from an eye used in training to an eye covered in training, birds without previous specific visual form-discrimination experience showed partial but not immediate or complete transfer—although they achieved better transfer if changed from 'single-eye training' to a situation in which both eyes could be used simultaneously. Such results seem on the face of it to modify the support for Hebb, and to provide, in addition, some evidence for Lashley's assumption that visual transfer may take place by a 'wave mechanism' in such a manner that previous involvement of the specific cortical substrate need not be postulated.

Zerga (1940a) has described a new maze apparatus for the study of bird learning. An account of the results of the work with this maze will be found in Zerga (1940b). Palmgren *et al.* (1938) described the quick learning, in from four to six trials, of a small maze containing two choice-points, by birds of the genera *Erithacus, Pyrrhula, Pinicola* and *Sylvia*, all of which showed about the same speed and proficiency in perfecting their performance. Allee and Masure (1936) used a simple two-alley problem-box for studying how the presence of a companion affected the rate and accuracy of learning in a social species. They used Shell Parrakeets and concluded that the presence of a second bird slowed down significantly the reaction time of the maze and increased the number of errors. This result was presumably to be expected in this extremely artificial environment, in that it would be impossible so to co-ordinate the behaviour of two birds that they reinforced each other. In other words, association results in distractions inimical to the solving of such a serial problem. Under more natural circumstances and with a 'natural' problem, the result might well be different. Thus Rouse found that, in various kinds of test, learning is somewhat dependent on social stimulation, the bird learning better if it is at least within hearing of another bird of the same species, and Grindley (1929) found it necessary to use a social companion.

Warden and Riess (1941) trained chicks to run a series of mazes of increasing difficulty, Warner-Warden mazes of varying numbers of blinds being used. It was found that the difficulty per unit decreased as the length increased. This is probably the general rule in learning motor tasks, although it is the reverse of what is found in human learning of nonsense syllables.

(d) The Learning Function of Play

The general significance of play has been discussed in Chapter IV, p. 94, above, and need not be further considered here. But the question of its occurrence and frequency in bird behaviour is of particular interest, for it has been several times stated, and fairly generally accepted, that young birds—in contrast to young mammals, such as puppies and kittens, badger and fox cubs—do not play. This seems to have been the view of Edmund Selous (Lorenz, 1935). Now, there has in the past been confusion between play and overflow activities due to maturation, and it is probable that behaviour such as the abortive nesting activities of young Cormorants, while seemingly playful, is more aptly regarded as an example of the latter; nevertheless, adequately documented examples are now sufficiently numerous to warrant the assumption that true play is fairly widespread in birds. A short discussion on this subject will be found in Armstrong (1947, p. 304). Moreau (1938) records very playful behaviour in a young Turaco, including sparring and mock attacks. Also young Gannets in captivity (Booth, 1881–7) showed themselves 'as playful and mischievous as a litter of puppies.' Again, R. E. and W. M. Moreau (1944) give a very convincing account of what appears to be genuine play in young White-necked Ravens, and also in Silvery-cheeked Hornbills; and Battersby (1944) describes play in a hand-reared Kestrel and a Common Buzzard. In both these cases, as also with the Crowned Hornbill (Ranger, 1950), the attitude and behaviour of the birds make it difficult to avoid the conclusion that there is some element of fun in the performance. Sutton (1943) records play in captive young of various Fringillid species. Howard (1907) says that young Sedge Warblers are very playful, engaging in a kind of tilting match, and he describes something similar in Reed Warblers, Chiffchaffs and several other British warblers. Sauer (1956) described elaborate play with a variety of inanimate objects performed by young Garden Warblers. N. Tinbergen has drawn my attention to a paper in Dutch by L. Tinbergen which describes the playful hunting of inanimate objects by young Kestrels. The young birds, although already hunting successfully for themselves, return when satiated from the hunting-area to the former breeding-territory (inland sand-dunes). There they will play for hours with pine cones, grass roots, etc., until the time for serious hunting comes round again. Cade (1953) describes similar play in a tame hand-reared Gyrfalcon. He adds an extremely interesting account of an intense aerial 'combat' of several minutes' duration between this bird, almost a fortnight after it had first learned to fly, and a wild adult male. Each bird succeeded at times in rising above the other for the advantage of a stoop, but would pull out of the dive before striking. 'Neither bird ever scored a hit and that did not seem to be their intention.'

Girdlestone (1953) records much play in a young hand-reared House Sparrow, and Nice (1943, pp. 51-4) describes a form of play in young Song Sparrows which she terms 'frolic.' This first appears at about seventeen or eighteen days of age, and will often persist for forty days or so and recur occasionally in a mild form up to two or three years. It is characterised by sudden rapid runs or flights with sharp turns. She also records similar behaviour in young American Redstarts and a Bobwhite, and gives references to similar youthful play by doves (Whitman, 1919, p. 156) and Road-runners (Rand, 1941b); while Herrick (1934; see Nice, 1943, p. 51) describes what may be genuine play in young eagles. Nice also gives references to some rather more doubtful cases in other raptorial birds. In passerine birds, at least, there is some evidence (Hinde, personal communication) that the young go through a period of aggressiveness soon after fledging; so it behoves us to be careful in speaking of 'play,' and according to Goodwin (1953) the 'play' movements of young Phasianidæ are merely the instinctive movements of escape showing as vacuum activity.

When we come to the behaviour of adult birds, we find still more evidence of play. Corvines and parrots are well known to be playful, and, as Armstrong says, the records are so numerous that no naturalist can dismiss them as being merely on the anecdotal plane. Innumerable examples will be found in the books of Pitt (1927), Finn (1919) and Groos (1898). Some birds of prey are known to carry on a kind of cat-and-mouse game with their quarry, and Hudson describes similar behaviour by grebes. Every field ornithologist must have seen Rooks and Jackdaws hastening towards a rising current of air where they appear to delight in the effortless spiral soaring which this makes possible. It seems quite obvious that there is no immediate purpose achieved by such behaviour. Many more instances of this kind of behaviour will be found in Armstrong (1947, pp. 176-7). Roberts (1934) has a vivid description of the play of Eider Ducks shooting the rapids in Iceland, the birds repeatedly walking up the banks and, launching themselves on the stream, apparently merely for the delight of the downward rush through the swirling waters. A very similar instance is described by Stoner (1947), who observed an Anna Humming-bird playing a game of repeatedly floating down a small stream of water flowing from a hose-pipe.

The water 'games' of many aquatic birds, ducks of various species,

Black Guillemots, etc., are well known. But most of these are no doubt part of complex display activities not yet fully described.

The elaborate activities of Bower Birds in their bowers are usually regarded as display in the strict sense, but Söderberg (1929) thinks that some of the decorative habits are not of a real sexual nature 'but must be regarded as play in a more psychological sense, with a pre-æsthetic character.' Marshall (1954), while ascribing an essentially utilitarian function to the bower and its associated activities, emphasises that the bower display and 'games' have passed beyond the bounds of strict utilitarianism. Moreau (personal communication) describes how Silvery-cheeked Hornbills will repeatedly throw up and catch a small stick; and a good example of play with sticks and bunches of leaves, where the behaviour is incorporated into elaborate follow-my-leader games, is provided by the Australian White-winged Chough (Chisholm, 1934). Many other instances could be cited, but enough has been said to show that play seems to be frequent in young birds and that something like it is quite general in adults. Some of this may be either displacement or else *Leerlauf* in the strict sense, some just a more or less random expression of energy, but much, particularly play with sticks or other objects, seems to show most of the psychological characteristics of true play. In whatever category the behaviour comes, however, it may be of physiological value in maintaining and perfecting muscular co-ordination and control; in other words, it is an important element in both motor and sensory learning.

INSIGHT LEARNING

Far as trial-and-error learning will carry us in accounting for the development of individual adaptive behaviour in birds, there are many examples of learning which it seems cannot at present be included under this heading. Insight has been defined above as the apprehension of relations, and it was concluded that something corresponding to insight is probably at the base of all associative learning.

We will start with latent learning, which is insightful in that, upon presentation of the reward, the behaviour gives evidence of simultaneous integration and reorganisation of previous experience. This kind of learning involves a 'delayed response' and transfer of training.

As was emphasised above, latent learning is essentially characteristic of animals which tend to explore their environment without the satisfaction of any immediate reward, but thereby achieving a perceptual organisation which may afterwards be of value in a number of contexts—for example, in food-getting, in escaping from enemies or in finding their way home to a nest or territory. It is thus essentially exploratory learning, and in saying that we are implying that the animals which show it are on a relatively high behavioural level. It is the experimental laboratory version of what

II. Bower Birds and Cat Birds.

Fig. 1: Mature blue male Satin Bower Bird (*Ptilonorhynchus violaceus*) at its avenue-type bower. Parrots' feathers are strewn on the display-ground in the foreground. (This bird was photographed in the act of wrecking another's bower.)

Fig. 2: Leaf-strewn Stage of the Brown Stagemaker (*Scenopœetes dentirostris*). The leaves, which are freshly cut each morning by the bird's "toothed" beak, are almost always placed upside down. Their paler surface thus creates a more striking display on the dark earth. (Photos by S. W. Jackson. From Marshall, 1954.)

is probably characteristic of many animals which show complex homing behaviour, thus involving something in the nature of general curiosity about the environment. This curiosity, of course, is not absolutely general, and even in territorial and homing birds we must expect it to be restricted to a few types of environmental feature only; for there is no doubt that, quick learners as many of them are in this respect, they normally pay no attention to the major part of their surroundings. Nevertheless, although Rouse's pigeons (above, p. 360) appeared to learn their mazes solely on the trial-and-error principle, showing no signs of general curiosity, many birds in the wild do show such a curiosity which is often of great value, especially when it leads to the birds' investigating predators and potential predators, and it is the basis on which habituation subsequently works.

It may also lead, as Marler has suggested (pers. comm.), to a population learning to avoid the particular 'beats' most frequented by predators, and the effect probably extends to members of other species. Perhaps one of the most striking examples of response to a predator is the well-known one given by ducks to the decoy dog. It used to be said that a brown (presumably fox-like) dog was necessary to decoy the ducks up the pipe, but Mr Peter Scott tells me that this is certainly untrue. He probably has wider experience of decoys than any other present-day naturalist, and he has records of dogs of many different colours being successfully employed. In fact, the most efficient dog he has ever seen was a white Pomeranian with a particularly lively gait. Probably the type of movement is the most important element in this strange response, and shape and colour are of relatively little importance. Anyone who has seen the response of ducks to the decoy dog must have been impressed and amused by the human-like surprise and curiosity which the birds display. Such processes of recognising and of responding to predators may, as we have seen above, be either specific or generalised; they may also be either learned or inborn.

The importance of general curiosity as a basis for trial-and-error learning, discussed above, must also be borne in mind. Without some element of this in nature, the scope of learning would be very restricted. Delayed-response experiments provide a means of testing the latent-learning ability of animals, but birds have not been subjected to this kind of test very frequently.

There has been little work on the specific problem of transfer of training in birds, but the experiments of Chattock and Grindley (1931) are of interest. Chicks being trained to run a maze show much surprise when a new kind of food is put in the food-box; they hesitate to peck and give vent to excited cheeping. Yet the surprise in itself does not hinder learning progress. If, however, the change is to a less-favoured kind of food progress is temporarily interrupted, this being presumably due to the chicks' not yet having acquired an appetite for the new kind of food. These results are in line with those on rats in similar circumstances (M. H. Elliot, 1929).

Révész (1924) carried out tests on a hen which failed to respond to a morsel of food hidden beneath a piece of paper directly in front of its eyes, even though the delay was extremely short. The hen could, however, easily be trained to push the paper aside and secure the food. This author was, however, unsuccessful in training the hen to push aside a small piece of glass which rendered the food unobtainable. The hen continued to peck vainly at the glass covering. To extend this kind of observation to more promising objects would almost certainly be worth while. Almost the only other cases on record appear to be those of Hertz (1926), who describes how a Carrion Crow which was in the habit of hiding food, usually by burying it, would up to five hours afterwards go directly to the spot and dig it up. This Crow would also recover food hidden by Miss Hertz in his presence. She did not, however, carry out enforced delays.

I am indebted to Dr Lorenz for some interesting unpublished observations of this kind. He tells me that a Jackdaw will remember the hiding-place of food for more than a week, and a Raven for probably much longer; but that these appear exceptional amongst tame birds, and that no other bird which he has tested has shown any delayed reaction beyond about two minutes. He, like Miss Hertz, has experimented from time to time with Ravens, and he tells me that a Raven dislikes being observed when hiding food. If observed, it will take the food out again and scold the observer, and it will very soon learn to hide the food out of human reach. Lorenz finds Magpies and Crows intermediate between Ravens and Jackdaws in this respect. It is remarkable, and perhaps significant, that memory for food hidden under normal conditions in the wild is vastly better than these experiments would suggest. Further data will be found below (p. 440), including particulars of the astonishing accuracy of the Nutcracker's memory under such circumstances.

(a) The Learning Involved in Homing Performance

Naturally, observations and experiments on the homing and territorial behaviour of animals in the field cannot be expected to yield readily the precise evidence of latent or exploratory learning which, when applied to suitable cases, laboratory methods can provide. Nevertheless, there is much information in the accounts of observations and experiments on homing orientation and territorial learning in birds which seems to imply latent learning. Here the bird is not merely learning a set path to a goal by means of particular landmarks, although that certainly happens—as when a bird gets into the motor-habits of returning to the nest by a particular route, perching always on the same set of twigs to the extent that it may be badly put out if this route is interfered with.

It has long been obvious that homing pigeons in their excursions around the loft and in their early training flights must become closely familar with the general topography of the immediate neighbourhood, and that this learning of an area must be something more than the mere acquisition of a number of alternative routes back to the loft. Until about 1948 it had seemed possible that such learning of landmarks might be the basis of all the homing ability of pigeons, and that whereas the normal pigeon restricted its foraging flights to an area not exceeding about two miles' radius from the loft, the processes of selection and training for homing produced vigorous 'explorers,' quick and adept at learning not merely the immediate environment of 'home' but considerable areas of country. But the energetic experimental attack which has been made on the homing problem in recent years has completely altered the picture and has shown the old ideas to be inadequate.

Matthews (1952) tested the ability of pigeons in a uniform circular arena to learn to take food only from that one of a ring of eight food-hoppers which bore a particular relation to a white 'landmark' or to a light. He found that though his birds were able to accomplish such tasks and were able to retain at least some memory of the performance after intervals of one to two years, such learning ability bore no relation to success in homing; indeed, there was a slight negative correlation, the good homers being rather bad at such learned tasks. This suggested, what has subsequently been confirmed, that there are two entirely different factors which contribute to homing ability and success, and that one of these factors has basically nothing to do with individual experience. Thus Matthews (1953b) found that although young pigeons without any previous training show, when removed to a distance from the loft, a definite homeward orientation almost immediately on release, they nevertheless home very badly. Training experience develops the homing success in various ways; physical development of muscles and of general stamina is no doubt one aspect of the process, though a minor one. Much more important is the knowledge of local topography gained, and the experience that persistent flying in the direction indicated by the orientation mechanism will bring the reward of 'home' and food. In contrast to the composite nature of the effect which is based on experience, the orientation mechanism appears to be much more an all-or-none affair. This orientation mechanism appears to be primarily unlearned, and present evidence from the work of Matthews (1953a) and of Kramer (1953) points strongly to the conclusion that it is a form of sun navigation, since there are no significant instances known of homing success from a completely unknown terrain under fully overcast conditions. That many species of birds can use the sun as a 'compass,' setting their courses by keeping a constant or uniformly changing angle to its position, is now well established (Kramer, 1952). Matthews (1955*a* and *b*) has followed up these clues and has provided good evidence of navigation in two co-ordinates. The simplest form of the sun-navigation theory which will fit the experimentally established facts involves the following 'automatic' measurements and comparisons (Fig. 56).

(1) Observation of the sun's movement over a small part of its arc and, by extrapolation, the determination of the highest point of the arc.

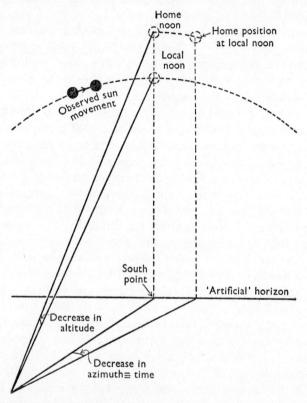

FIG. 56—Diagram illustrating the hypothesis of sun navigation. Release to north and west of home (not to south). (After Matthews, 1953.)

This would give geographical south and local noon. (2) Comparison of the remembered noon altitude at home with the observed noon altitude. This would give the difference in latitude. (3) Comparison with home position in azimuth at local noon. This would give the difference in longitude which, alternatively, might be appreciated as a direct time difference, and on present evidence this seems the more probable. Certainly some kind of internal clock or 'chronometer factor' is a necessary part of any of the current theories of bird navigation, and Matthews (1955a and b) has shown that such a factor exists in homing pigeons and that orientation can be confused and reorientation in the expected sense achieved by artificially advancing or retarding the internal 'clocks' by means of experimental alteration of the light/dark and feeding periodicities.[1]

Astonishing as these conclusions are, they seem to be inescapable on present information, and, in fact, are simpler than many hypotheses which have been advanced. Thus the theories of orientation by sensitivity to magnetic and 'Coriolis' forces seem to have been effectively put out of court (Thorpe, 1949; Wilkinson, 1949; for general review, see Griffin, 1952. See also van Riper and Kalmbach (1952) for a recent negative test with magnets on sixteen homing pigeons). Moreover pigeons, unlike bees, have no perception of sky polarisation pattern to assist them (Montgomery and Heinemann, 1952). The inability of a bird to appreciate ultrashort-wave radiation seems also to have been strikingly demonstrated by Kramer (1951) for the Red-backed Shrike. It is true that the sun-orientation hypothesis itself also raises what appear to be formidable difficulties from the point of view of sensory physiology. Thus Kramer (1953) claims that his birds became oriented within 40 seconds of viewing the sun. This seems at first sight to necessitate impossibly high precision in determining time and angular displacement. Moreover, there are baffling results like those of Precht et al. (1956) and Gerdes (1960), who placed Blackheaded Gulls, also a number of other species of birds, removed some distance from their nests, in cages and observed the directions in which they tried to escape. Homeward orientation was obtained inside tents and buildings with all external clues eliminated. Fromme (1961) found that Robins and Whitethroats were able to maintain their migration direction without seeing the sky, as determined by electro-mechanical recording of their choice of perches in an octagonal cage. There were disoriented in a closed steel room. "Clock-shifting" by six hours did not affect the direction chosen. These results are wholly inexplicable on any theory so far suggested. It is for such reasons that Pratt (1955) inclines to the view that the facts can be 'explained' only by bringing in some form of extra-sensory perception. Matthews (1953a) has, however, shown that (at least for many experiments) the performance required of the bird's sense organs and perceptual organisation is not beyond the range of possibility or even probability. As he points out, Pumphrey (1948) estimated on the basis of

[1] Pennycuick (1960) has modified Matthews' (1953) sun navigation hypothesis to a form which allows the relationship between accuracy of observation and accuracy of position-finding to be calculated. The two measurements required for position-finding are here taken to be (i) the sun's altitude and (ii) the rate of change of the sun's altitude. It is shown that an orthogonal lattice results and that the accuracy of observation required to account for known homing performance, whilst high, is not unreasonable.

retinal structure that the limit of resolution would be about 10" of arc—three times better than the human eye—and Grundlach (1933) has demonstrated by a training technique, which probably was not such as to obtain the most perfect possible performance, that pigeons could resolve to at least 23" of arc. Viewing the birds' performance in this light, we see that even during Kramer's 40-second period (which may be an under-estimate), the sun has moved through an angle sixty times the value of the theoretical threshold. Other considerations arising from the structure of the bird's eye suggest that it may be particularly adapted to overcome the problems of glare and the need for an artificial horizon (Griffin, review, 1952; Matthews, 1953a, 1955).

It is thus generally accepted that the sun is used for direction finding by homing pigeons, but Schmidt-Koenig (1961) believes that the information as to position is obtained from some other source. He first showed that pigeons trained to find food in a particular compass direction, and then kept in a phase-shifted light-dark rhythm, take up an angle from the sun based on the 'shifted' time of day, and he later obtained the same result with departure directions of homing pigeons—that is to say, the departure directions of 'shifted' birds differed from those of controls by approximately the expected angle. However, the absolute direction taken by the controls is not given (only the difference between experimentals and controls), and the homing times of controls were very slow, half of them being slower than 10 m.p.h., or lost. The evidence that homeward orientation was being studied is therefore unsatisfactory, and the results could equally well be due to a 'nonsense' orientation of the type found by Matthews (1961) in mallard—that is, the birds could be selecting an arbitrary direction by reference to the sun. Matthews (1961) has shown that the 'nonsense' direction selected by mallard can be shifted by Schmidt-Koenig's procedure.

The precision of time-keeping shown by 'clock shifting' experiments is only very rough, since the chosen directions observed are actually the statistical means of directions chosen by a large number of pigeons. These experiments shed no light on whether or not pigeons can keep time with an accuracy sufficient for position-finding purposes—that is, in the region of ±2 minutes in 24 hours. Discrimination on this scale would be quite impossible to distinguish in direction-choosing experiments, where differences of several hours are the rule.

Accepting provisionally, then, the conclusion that homing pigeons navigate in two co-ordinates by means of sight of the sun coupled with a very precise but not inflexible internal time-keeping mechanism, what can we say about the abilities of wild birds? Many wild birds are known to home with considerable *apparent* precision, but Wilkinson (1952) has shown that all the earlier results are open to the alternative theory of random search for known landmarks. But Matthews (1953b) showed that random search cannot be adduced as an explanation for the extraordinary homing feats of the Manx Shearwater, and Kenyon and Rice (1958) sent albatrosses by air from Midway Island, where they were nesting, to various points around the North Pacific (Japan, Philippines, Marshall Islands, Guam, Washington Island, Hawaii). Fourteen out of eighteen homed, and one of the others ranged up the Fraser River after release at Washington Island in high wind. The longest homing flight was from the Philippines, 4,120 st. miles (rhumb line) in 32 days. Fastest was from Whidley Island, Washington: 3,200 st. miles in 10·1 days = 317 miles/day average. Some of these releases were outside the normal range of the species, which only goes down to 15° N. The best homing was from the fringe of the normal range. Thus it has now become clear that a number of species can, in fact, orient themselves in relation to a remembered position of the sun, and must also be in possession of an internal clock.[1] It seems safe to say that this must apply to many species. The Starling has been the one most thoroughly investigated (Kramer, 1952), since it can be trained, in a suitable circular cage, to orient itself by means of an 'artificial' sun. Thus Hoffmann (1952, 1953) was able to show that the timekeeping of the internal clock could be altered experimentally, and that even a hand-reared Starling which had been kept completely without sight of the sun or of any regularly moving source of directional illumination nevertheless was able to compensate for sun movement without ever having actually experienced it. This was shown as follows: The completely inexperienced bird was 'trained' (Fig. 57a) by being fed, always during the hour from 3 to 4 p.m., in a circular arena with twelve hoppers at the twelve points of the clock, the artificial sun being at the position of figure 12 on the clock and the food-hopper at '1 o'clock' being the only one containing

[1] It seems probable that with some night migrants, such as the Barred Warbler, some other additional form of orientation may have to be postulated. Some night-migrating birds may get their initial direction from the sun at sunset, and then maintain their orientation more or less successfully by secondary cues (moon, wave pattern, dimly seen landmarks, etc.; see Thorpe, 1949) during the period of darkness. There is much doubt at present how far night migration over the sea is at all correctly oriented. Certainly drift off course under poor conditions does take place to an enormous extent. But the selection of a migration direction by reference to an artificial starry sky has been demonstrated by Sauer (1957) by observing the direction in which various species of warblers (Sylvia atricapilla, S. curruca, S. borin) pointed when fluttering in a cage in a planetarium. Changes of hour angle of the artificial sky, corresponding to easterly or westerly displacements, induced corrective changes of orientation in the fluttering bird, and presentation of a spring sky in autumn produced confusion ('migration conflict'). Wallraff (1960) criticised the somewhat arbitrary fashion in which the shifts were interpreted not only as spatial displacements but also as changes of date or time of day, any of which correspond to a change of hour angle. However, there seems little doubt that the birds will interpret small shifts of hour angle as longitude displacements, however they may react to the larger shifts. Since the parallax errors induced by movement of the birds in the relatively small planetarium correspond to rather large displacements on the earth, the experiments inevitably refer to displacements of a rather gross nature.

food. When the bird was perfectly trained in this task so that it always sought its food in that particular hopper under those particular conditions at that time of day, choices were tested with empty hoppers under the same conditions of illumination but at *different times of day*. It will be seen (from Fig. 57*b* and *c*) that when fed during the hours 12,00 to 13.00 and 19.30 to 20.30, the bird searched in that hopper which would have been the right one at that time of day had the source of illumination been executing the movements which the sun actually makes at that season of the year. This remarkable result suggests that the sun-orientation mechan-

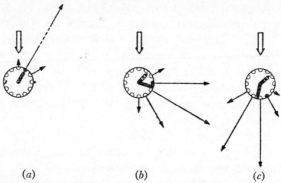

(a)   (b)   (c)

Fig. 57—Diagram to show change with time in orientation in relation to a standard direction as shown by a hand-reared Starling kept without sight of the sun.
(a) Training period 15.00–16.00 hours.
(b) Testing period 12.00–13.00 hours.
(c) Testing period 07.300–08.30 hours.
The length of the unbroken arrow (in Fig. *a* shown only at half-length) shows the number of choices per cent. for a given direction. 'Empty' external broad arrow indicates the direction of the artificial sun. Heavy internal arrow indicates a mean direction of choice. Cross-hatched internal arrow indicates the training direction of choice. The small semicircles show the position of the food dishes and the solid semicircle indicates the correct direction, i.e. the direction of collective choice in relation to the sun movement at the time of the experiment. (After Hoffmann, 1953.)

ism of birds is, in its correlation of inborn faculties with experience, extraordinarily similar to that of the honey-bee. In both there is a presumably innate appreciation of direction and speed of movement of the sun, together with an accurate internal clock. In both there is the innate ability to relate a 'desired' direction to the space-time standards innately provided, to extrapolate from the observed situation and to relate to it the knowledge of general topography and special landmarks gained from individual experience. In both there is an 'appreciation' of the relation between '*direction*' of a light source and the '*direction*' of a movement (foraging flight, migration flight, homing flight). But the honey-bee does better than the bird in two respects. Firstly it can and must 'transpose' between sun direction and gravity direction, and secondly it must be able to transmit information by transposition between foraging flight and the straight run of the dance. So far as we know, birds cannot and do not need to transfer information in any such way, and so lack these additional faculties which the honey-bee possesses.

Finally, it has been suggested by Huntington (1952) that observed changes in the migration routes of the Bronze Grackle in the U.S.A. can be attributed to a learned habit fostered by selection; and van Dobben (1955) argues that the routes taken by migrating birds in Europe are not entirely explicable on the basis of innate sun-time orienting mechanism (see above, and also Mayr's appendix to Griffin, 1952), coupled with the more or less specific or automatic response to 'guiding lines,' such as rivers, coasts, mountain ranges, bare country, etc. For there are local traditions exhibited by birds (e.g. finches) which migrate in flocks, which depend on the learning of a particular route being passed on from generation to generation as young birds migrate with their elders. There is even said to be some evidence that migrating flocks of finches tend to turn at points where the vanished coast-line of the now drained Zuider Zee itself turned.

(b) Territorial Learning as Latent Learning

The work of Marshall (1947) suggests that it is the nest-site rather than the nest itself or the eggs which attracts the broody Common Tern. The eggs, the nest and the immediate and more distant landmarks are the constituents of the landscape, and it is merely as such constituents that each serves in nest recognition. It may be argued that each landmark and item in the familiar environment has been independently associated with some particular 'reward,' the eggs, presence of the mate or some other instinctive 'desired' situation. But this, it seems, could only be an adequate explanation in relatively few instances. The migratory bird returning to its breeding-quarters in the spring often seems to build up its territory as such into a self-sufficing unit independent at first of any major reward. This is very evident from the work of Howard (1929, p. 98; 1935, pp. 75–8; 1940, p. 11). Howard, in one delightful passage, has described exactly what happens at the moment of first arrival in spring of a Tree Pipit or a Whitethroat at a new territory. The Tree Pipit drops from the sky one April morning, having passed over innumerable alders and willows on his way, 'yet none checked him till he reached Lincomb Weir. There he settled on a willow, soared to an ash tree, then up to an oak, then to a group of willows.' We get a strong impression from these observations of Howard on Tree Pipits that territory is a whole from the first moment, although severity of competition may modify it later. Howard says: 'His choice might have been spread over some days, yet he chose quickly.' Certain trees and bushes are seized at once as landmarks, others are ignored. Landmarks, then, may become the signals of the territory and for territorial behaviour and some may be used more than others, but Howard provides little evidence that territory is developed by *gradual* extension around some conspicuous landmarks. In a particular case of a Whitethroat observed on arrival at a spot where no Whitethroat had been the previous season, Howard says (1929, p. 98): 'Observe, then, that he fashioned his territory within . . . three hours of his arrival. Whatever tree, bush or hedge he visited during those three hours, though he may have done so but once, remained impressed upon his organisation. . . . Suppose now we had come upon him two or three days later, how easy it would have been to have gained a wrong impression of the way his territory was built up.' Thus, at any rate in the species studied by Howard, the territory, including its landmarks, is a unit, a whole almost from the start, and the response to the territory is a response to a perceptual complex, which later comes to be associated with, and knowledge concerning it used in, many different contexts and situations, and for many different kinds of response.

This, however, is certainly not the universal rule, for the European Wren (Armstrong, 1955) has a characteristic tentative and exploratory behaviour when in a new territory, and Hinde (1952) finds that in Great and Blue Tits the process is certainly gradual and involves extension from a few preferred stations to a gradual learning of the whole area. Similar observations are on record of the Yellow Bunting (Diesselhorst, 1950). While one cannot dispute Howard's precise and careful observations, it may be—as Dr Hinde has suggested to me—that in migratory birds the process has been speeded up by biological necessity without necessarily being different in quality.

(c) Tool Using

As remarked above (Chapter VI, p. 121) in connection with the general problem of the significance of tool using, we do not normally regard the use of a rock or other immovable object as a resistance against which to break open the protective shells of prey as tool using, even though the prey is dropped from a considerable height. Much more extraordinary, if substantiated, is the reverse process, reported for only one species, the Australian Black-breasted Buzzard (Chisholm, 1954). This bird is said to drive the Emu from its eggs and then fly aloft with a stone in its claws; this missile it drops on the eggs and then immediately swoops down to devour the contents. It is argued that the Emu eggshells are too strong to be broken by the Buzzard's beak, but whether this applies to two other ground-nesting species, the Australian Bustard and the Giant Crane which are also reported as victimised, seems improbable. This appears clearly as tool using for, to be a tool, an object must become a movable body extension.

On this basis also we can consider the Tailor Bird (Wood, 1936) and the Little Spider-hunter (Shelford, 1916), using spiders' lines as thread, as tool users. More certainly still the Satin Bower Bird, which uses fibrous material as a brush with which to 'paint' the sticks of its bower with a colouring material from berries or with charcoal (Gannon, 1930; Nubling, 1939, 1941), can be classed as a tool user. There is one remaining bird which, as a tool user, is so able as almost to stand in a category by itself; this is the Galapagos Woodpecker-finch (Gifford, 1919; Lack, 1947). This bird feeds on insects which inhabit the crevices in and under the 'bark' of various cacti. Its bill is not long enough to reach the insects unaided and it does not normally attempt to do so. Instead it picks up a long cactus-spine and pokes about with it at random in the crannies and crevices which the insects inhabit. Sooner or later an insect or spider runs out, whereupon the bird drops the spine and seizes the insect. Then another spine is picked up and the procedure resumed. This is certainly tool using, for it clearly necessitates the utilisation of the mechanical properties of an object as an extension of the bill of the bird.

But the origins of this behaviour in the life of the individual have not been observed in any of these birds, and it may be that all these cases so far cited are examples of instinctive behaviour and may not in the first instance, or even at all, involve any 'understanding' by the bird of the contribution of the tool towards solving its problem. Even if the full behaviour pattern be not inborn, we can be fairly sure that there is an inherited tendency to pay particular attention to tool objects and to manipulate them, with the result that their mechanical possibilities might very easily be learned by trial-and-error. To study carefully the indivi-dual development of the tool-using behaviour of a Satin Bower Bird or Galapagos Woodpecker-finch reared apart from its congeners would be a most valuable contribution to the study of avian psychology.

There is, however, another kind of behaviour which has often been regarded as an elementary form of tool using which is much more doubt-fully inborn and which has been the object of a good deal of experiment. This is the ability to pull up food which is suspended by a thread, the pulled-in loop being held by the foot while the bird reaches with its beak for the next pull. Everyone who has seen this performance by an adept wild bird, as can so easily be done with Great and Blue Tits at a bird-table, will have been impressed by the smooth ease and certainty, and by the entire absence of fumbling, with which the complete act is accom-plished. Seldom does one see anything suggestive of trial-and-error learn-ing. The act appears at first sight to be a real and sudden solution of the problem from the start, and thus to qualify for inclusion under 'insight learning.'

The abilities of Blue Tits in this respect have been studied by Herter

(1940), who found that one individual readily learned to pull up food at the end of a string 64 centimetres long, though another bird was not usually sufficiently persevering to carry the process through to the end. Thorpe (1943) records a Great Tit successfully pulling in a string 4 inches long and gives references to other successful performances by Great Tits, Blue Tits and Coal Tits. Herter, however, records lack of success with a Coal Tit which drew up well but did not use the foot properly, and complete failure with a Nuthatch—though G. Mountfort (*in litt.*) reports success with this species. Goldfinches are so adept at this trick that they have for centuries been kept in special cages so designed that the bird can subsist only by pulling up and holding tight two strings, that on one side being attached to a little cart containing food and resting on an incline, and that on the other to a thimble containing water. This was so widespread in the sixteenth century that it gave rise to the name 'draw-water' or its equivalent in two or three European languages. Bierens de Haan (1933) studied the way in which three untrained Goldfinches learnt the trick, and concluded that one accomplished the task quickly, apparently as the result of primary insight into the problem, at least as far as pulling in the string was concerned and probably also in relation to the holding of the loop. The second Goldfinch showed similar insight into the pulling-up part of the action, but apparently accomplished the latter part only by trial-and-error, while the third bird failed entirely to reach a solution. Numerous records of successful performances are available for Redpolls, Siskins, a Budgerigar and the parrots *Ara ararauna* and *Chrysotis amazonica* (Fischel, 1936). There are also isolated instances for the Rook, House Sparrow—with a string $7\frac{1}{2}$ inches long—and a Greenfinch (Thorpe, 1945a), a captive Carrion Crow and captive Jackdaw (Hertz, 1926), and a tame Garden Warbler (Teyrovsky, 1930). Linnets are unable to use the foot to hold the string, although they quickly show 'pulling-in' behaviour. Experiments with wild Robins (Thorpe, 1945a) and with three tame Robins in aviaries (Thorpe, unpublished) were completely negative, as were also some tests with two hand-reared Wrens which showed great keenness and 'interest' but made no attempt to pull (Thorpe, unpublished).

The great individual variation in ability shown by so many of these species and the improbability of the action being in any way appropriate to the life of the bird under natural conditions[1] seem, on the basis of these first observations, to confirm the view that the performance is evidence of individual learning based, at least in part, on genuine insight. This view was criticised by Erhardt (1933) and Thienemann (1933) on the ground that the 'pulling up' with the foot and bill is an instinctive

---

[1] Caution is, of course, needful over such assumptions. Thus Dr Hinde has described to me how Goldfinches will pull down twigs and stems bearing insect prey and hold the plant with the foot while pecking off the insects.

behaviour pattern, characteristic of the Goldfinch, Siskin, Red-poll and Tits, but not Greenfinch and Linnet, which are ground feeders. Thienemann reports that Redpolls occasionally deal with alder catkins in exactly this way and suggests that such behaviour would be appropriate to a variety of flexible catkins and to fruits which are attached to long, flexible stalks. These arguments lack support by satisfactory observations or evidence so far as wild birds are concerned, and seem, even for these species, rather far-fetched. They appear still less convincing when applied to the cases of House Sparrows, Garden Warbler, Carrion Crow and Jackdaw. Even though the last two birds do devour nuts and acorns, it seems most improbable that they ever encounter in nature a stalk long enough to necessitate any such specialised instinctive technique. As Hertz (1937) has pointed out, a tendency to use the foot in feeding would make successful performance very much more probable, but this would obviously provide a basis or raw material for only the latter part of the act.

Altevogt (1953) has carried this type of attempted explanation a little farther as a result of observations on the feeding and exploratory technique of young Blue Tits reared in captivity by their own parent. He found that not only was there immediate readiness to use the feet, but that manipulation (of loose threads, rubber bands, etc., also small elongate rigid objects such as matches and small twigs, all without food attached) emerged 'spontaneously' at about the twelfth day of fledgling life. This 'manipulation' is a particular co-ordination of beak and foot, the object being pulled with the beak and held between the foot and the supporting branch, and it is argued that this co-ordination, improved by proprioceptive reinforcement through practice, would—under suitable conditions of reward—lead very rapidly to the full string-pulling procedure. Altevogt's work does not provide clear evidence that the primary manipulation is innate since his birds were not hand reared and had presumably been fed on mealworms; so the essential co-ordination might well have been learned. Its subsequent appearance in response to non-rewarding objects might be explicable as an acquired drive accumulating about a new motor-co-ordination.

In my preliminary experiments the birds were deprived of food for a standard period (usually one hour) before testing. The experimental situation is shown (Plate III), the thread being looped over the wooden perch and fastened with a drawing-pin. The glass cylinder prevented direct attack on the bait, which for tits was usually sunflower-seed, while for finches hemp was employed. Of twenty-eight wild caught Great Tits tested in outdoor aviaries, whose previous experience was not known, four succeeded in pulling up the string after a few trials, whereas the others showed no sign of making any progress. It seemed that much of this failure

was due to unfamiliarity with the surroundings and distraction by hap-
penings outside the aviary, and not to intrinsic inability to deal with the
problem. The tits would usually attempt to attack the bait directly, and
many seemed to have an immediate comprehension of the relation between
string and bait and the possibilities of the former as a 'tool' for securing
the latter. Thus when the string is very short, the bait (if it is within reach)
will be attacked directly; but if the string is lengthened the string itself
will be pulled up immediately without any setback in the learning process.
While string-pulling may occur without any attempt to 'place' the pulled-in
loop on the perch, yet whenever the loop is so placed the feet are immediately used to hold it—suggesting that, as with the Blue Tit, the co-
ordination between beak and foot movement for holding food is either
inborn or firmly established by early experience.[1] Birds which do not at
first respond to the experimental situation by pulling the string can often
be trained to it by being given preliminary 'tests' with the bait resting on
the perch, followed by a series of experiments in which strings of gradually
increasing length are used. Although all the successful Great Tits were
adept at holding the string with the foot (Plate IV), nevertheless there
were very many individual variations in the method of dealing with the
string. For instance, one bird often used the foot as a 'shackle bolt,' pulling
the string up under the foot which clasped the perch fairly loosely, and so
substituting a single pull for a series of separate 'pulls' and 'holds.' Others
—not only tits but also a Jay and a Greenfinch—having once taken hold of
the string might sidle along the perch so as to extend the string along it
until the bait was secured—either by running the string under the claws or
else through the beak. These and a number of other variants give a strong
impression that the possibilities of the string as a tool are well understood
—although the probability of variation in performance due to 'random'
trial-and-error behaviour must also be taken into account. The same impression is given by wild-caught Greenfinches and Chaffinches.

In spite of the deftness of some birds, amusing 'mistakes' often occur.
Thus a tame young Jackdaw, and sometimes a Great Tit, would become
confused as to the sides of the perch and would pull first one side then
the other, so that the loop was often dropped, and the Jackdaw would
sometimes pull the string on one side but apparently expect the bait to
come up on the other! This bird also would 'place' the string again and
again on the perch as if expecting it to stick by itself—perhaps one of the
inborn nest-building actions—and later, when it had commenced to use
the feet, would act as if it knew that it must use the foot, but did not

---

[1] Similarly, early attempts by hand-reared Great Tits to place their feet on a mealworm were clumsy, the bird missing the worm with its foot and thus proceeding with
a series of steps across the cage floor. This suggests that the beak-foot co-ordination is
inborn but becomes perfected (either by maturation or learning) after its first appearance.

know how or why; perhaps an indication of maturation of an inborn co-ordination. The most accomplished of my own birds so far has been a Jay (Plate V), which became perfectly adept at pulling up a string 17 inches long in a series of five deft pulls and holds.

Work with aviary-reared Canaries and Greenfinches denied all access to flexible materials has shown that restriction of early experience in this way, while it seems to be an initial hindrance to success, does not prevent it. Thus, of the four Canaries two were noticed to hold pieces of chickweed with the foot when feeding, before the beginning of the experiments. This use of the foot was not, however, immediately general-ised to loops of string, which they repeatedly lifted and allowed to drop again. One of these birds made no use of the foot in his six trials with a 4-inch string, but began to use it almost immediately—though occa-sionally and clumsily—when given bait on a short string. His use of the foot increased both in frequency and efficiency until it became almost invariably successful about the twenty-sixth experiment. A similar course of development took place with the second Canary. Of the two Canaries which did not use the foot in eating chickweed, one did not use a foot to hold the string until his twentieth test, and did so very occasionally after that. On his forty-first test he made a first successful use of the foot, pulling up the string, holding it and eating the bait, and after this his use of the foot continued to increase until it became habitual after about the sixtieth test. The other adult Canary, which did not learn to pull up the string correctly, used his foot once on his eleventh, sixteenth, eighteenth and forty-first tests and very little after that.

A juvenile Canary which had no experience of string-like materials developed the use of the foot in a similar way, the most interesting feature of the performance being a tendency to use the foot occasionally to hold small pieces of chickweed in the preliminary trials, and a suc-cessful use of the foot on the fifth trial with a 4-inch string, followed by a failure to use the foot again until given the bait on a very short string.

The whole situation has been much clarified by the work of Vince (1961a and b) which is still in progress. Her first experiment with adult wild-caught Great Tits showed that the bird's first response to the experi-mental situation was to keep away from it, but that with further trials the positive response to bait and/or string tended to increase over a period of time. Subsequently the bird's response to both might tend to decrease; and even birds which were learning well, or in which the string-pulling habit had been completely mastered, might be set back, or the habit lost, when the experimental situation was changed or the bird was moved to a new cage. Further tests, not only with wild and hand-reared Blue and Great Tits but also with Greenfinches, Chaffinches and Canaries, have thrown a good deal of light on what is evidently a very complex situation. It seems clear that juvenile birds tend to be superior to adults in the string-pulling situation and that this success can be correlated with the amount of time spent responding to the string and/or the bait. This amount of time responding could be due to a higher level of activity, but in tasks requiring a high level of activity (requiring, in fact, large persistence and many trials) juveniles—which are at their maximum of exploratory activity at about 13 weeks—are likely to be more efficient than adults. But positive response is not the whole of learning, and in such a task as string-pulling it is necessary also for the bird to learn to *refrain* from responding to situations in which reinforcement is absent or withdrawn. This ability to refrain is, as Vince shows, dependent on something similar to what Pavlov called internal inhibition.[1] It is weak in very young birds, develops as a result of age, and, as a result of experience during the juvenile stage, is still being strengthened at an age when positive responsiveness is well past its peak and later weakens slightly again. Consequently, tasks which depend less on the level of activity and more on the ability to control behaviour by precisely timed inhibition are more likely to be mastered quickly and efficiently by older birds than by younger ones. Vince concludes (1961b) from consideration of the individual performances of her birds during the test and training trials, that the birds showed no evidence of insight into the nature of the experimental situation. Indeed, the case for insight in her experiments is a weak one, resting chiefly on the fact that the birds pulled at the string but did not go immediately to the clamp and remain there in the vicinity of the bait. There were various possible explanations other than insight of their first pulling at the string, the chief among these being the fact that they were given many training trials with food actually on the experimental perch before the test trials began. Again, once the string is touched it causes the bait to move and this will at once make it more conspicuous and consequently more stimulative. But although birds trained in this rather strictly controlled situation failed to give evidence of insight, except (if at all) in a very minor degree; there still remain a large number of examples of behaviour in the wild which have already been mentioned (and also others which are mentioned later in this chapter) which make it very difficult to accept trial-and-error learning as a full and sufficient account of the development of these abilities. In the majority of cases trial-and-error learning is undoubtedly adequate as an explanation; and in all cases it is important; but there is certainly a residue of instances for which the hypothesis of insight still seems to be required. It may well be that the richness of experience encountered by wild birds affects the degree to which insight learning can be achieved.

To sum up the situation at present, we may say that some species, e.g.

[1] For a discussion of the relationship between habituation and internal inhibition, see above, pp. 63–69.

Robin, Wren, which do not use the feet in feeding, seem unable to accomplish this task, even though the Robin (Thorpe, unpublished) can rather surprisingly learn to hang on with its feet in Tit fashion to feed on suspended food. Other species show many gradations in the extent to which the foot-beak co-ordination is developed in ordinary feeding methods, and even if this is only very slight (as in the Greenfinch), the string-holding behaviour can, nevertheless, be learned and subsequently incorporated in the feeding pattern. Where the co-ordination is highly developed and perhaps inborn, as in tits, the holding of the loops of string can be almost automatic. *Nevertheless, there is no reason to think that any bird has an 'inborn string-pulling automatism.'*

Vince (1961a) performed other experiments in which Great Tits were required to obtain food by opening dishes covered with white lids and refrain from opening dishes covered with black lids. These gave further confirmation for the view already expressed of the paramount importance of trial-and-error coupled with internal inhibition. They also suggest, as do the string-pulling studies, that internal inhibition is unstable in young birds and that the process of development of an unstable type of inhibition found in younger birds to the more stable type found in older birds depends not only upon age but also on experience. In another experiment, Great Tits were first trained to feed from a blue dish. When they had become habituated to the blue dish, a white cardboard lid was placed over it. The number of trials (that is to say, the reinforced or training trials) needed for the consistent removal of the white lid was then recorded. Unreinforced trials consisted of empty dishes with black lids. When hand-reared birds were compared in this test with wild-reared ones caught as juveniles over a period of eight to twenty weeks after fledging, both groups showed internal inhibition (indicated by the ability to refrain from removing the black lid) rising as a function of age and later falling slightly (Fig. 58). But there are indications that a richer and more varied experience may change the slope of the curve, giving a sharper rise to a higher level. It seems as if, at any rate in this experimental situation, richness of early experience is an important factor in contributing to the perfect mastery of a task. Thus in a task primarily requiring superabundant activity (as, for instance, does maze-learning, where a large number of different cues have to be investigated) younger animals are more likely to excel. On the other hand, a task which requires activity directed to a particular feature of the environment may well be learned better by older animals.

To sum up, there are four aspects of development which have emerged from such experiments. Firstly, there is the question of responsiveness; this appears, in the hand-reared Great Tit, to increase with age and then decrease. Secondly, there are changes in a different type of responsiveness, namely habituation or internal inhibition. Here again there appears to be

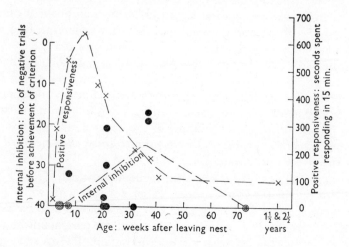

Fig. 58—The relation between changes in positive and negative responsiveness in hand-reared great tits (from Vince, 1960).

a rise and also probably a slight subsequent fall with age, but the rates of the first and second changes may be quite different, and so the variation in these two factors could well give rise to the puzzling differences in learning ability which the earlier experiments revealed. Thirdly, there is the question of the hunger drive. The birds in this work were kept under conditions such that approximately the same measure of food deprivation was experienced by all. Fourthly, the effects of early experience and environment on behaviour are clearly shown and it seems that internal inhibition may develop more rapidly and more completely in a more varied environment, presumably as a result of greater activity, greater stimulation and perhaps greater opportunity for adaptation and so on. It is plausibly assumed that aviary-rearing is a richer experience than hand-rearing and that rearing in the wild is a richer experience still.

The ease with which tits can learn to perform other highly complicated actions merely by trial-and-error is also worthy of mention. There is a case on record by Trevor Miller (see Thorpe, 1945) of a Blue Tit which learnt to reach food (fat) within an inverted bell from the centre of which was suspended a string with a light stick attached (as shown in the sectional diagram comprising Fig. 59) by alighting on the stick, hanging in an inverted position, rolling up the string on the stick by movement of its feet. (The edge of the bell was too smooth to allow the bird to cling on.) A number of attempts by Thorpe and Wyatt (Thorpe, 1945) failed to secure confirmation of this behaviour, but were very instructive in demonstrating the extraordinary 'resource and ingenuity' displayed by both Blue and Great Tits in their attempts to reach the food under these difficult conditions. Every imaginable method was tried, and some of the birds would stand on the bar with a rapid stepping movement, executing little fluttering jumps, carrying the bar a little way with them. Such performance seems to show how the bird might accidentally roll the bar up a little way and, having once done so (tits being such rapid learners), see the advantage gained and repeat the process until success was achieved.

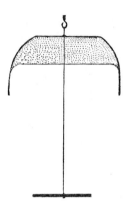

There are also a few records of what are in effect puzzle-box tests with birds which suggest, though they do not prove, the existence of something like insight learning. Thus Hadley (1909) has described the apparent comprehension of a simple lever mechanism by a domestic fowl which learnt to operate an automatic feeder, although, since no details are given about the origin of the habit, this at present isolated example is so out of keeping with other evidence for these birds that it cannot be accepted as evidence of insight learning. Brooks-King (1941) describes a number of remarkable performances of Blue and Great Tits with various types of puzzle contrivances, some of which suggest true insight learning. Witherby (see Thorpe, 1945) described how Siskins could learn to pull out drawers containing food, but could not persevere in learning the trick unless they were able to see into them. This is in line with the poor delayed-response performance of birds recorded in the previous section. Brooks-King's tits showed extraordinarily good results in this respect, and evidently have a very high delayed-response performance. This author is inclined to assume that

FIG. 59—Tit - feeding apparatus. The fat is within an inverted bell from the centre of which is suspended a string with a light stick attached. The edge of the bell is too smooth and the string too thin to allow a bird to cling on. The bird is said to be able to reach the fat by alighting on the stick, hanging in an inverted position and rolling up the string on to the stick by movement of its feet. (After Thorpe, 1951.)

a keen sense of smell must be necessary to account for his results, but in view of the evidence against this in a number of species of birds (Walter, 1943), his conclusions seem hardly justified; so we are reduced to explaining the tits' performance, in this particular test, by high delayed-response ability coupled with true insight learning.

(d) Detour Behaviour

The ability to make a detour round an obstacle without preliminary random trial-and-error behaviour has long been regarded as evidence for insight learning, and there has been much work on this subject using various mammals as experimental animals. Here again it is difficult to put much reliance on detour performance, except when the first responses of the previously untrained individual are studied under controlled conditions and where the previous experience of that individual is adequately known. In no case have these conditions been fulfilled in experiments with birds, and it is, of course, too obvious to need comment that birds in flight constantly make detours around obstacles which they have not hitherto encountered. Simple direct observation on Robin and Wren in confined spaces suggests that they would, when not alarmed and fully at ease, show high detour ability. Lorenz (1939) has pointed out how the inability of some birds to make a detour on the ground may be misleading if we are dealing with a species which normally makes detours in the air. Similarly, a problem requiring an aerial detour, if presented to a bird such as a Grey-lag Goose—a species in which flight is one of the less frequently used behaviour patterns and in which intention movements normally have to be performed for some time before the internal stimulus level is sufficiently high for motivation of the flight automatism —may result in failure which is quite misleading and which provides no information at all as to the psychological ability of the species concerned. As Heinroth is said to have remarked on one occasion, 'it is because they can fly that birds are so stupid.' Teyrovsky (1930) has described the moderate detour performance of a tame Garden Warbler in a cage, the left half of which was divided into upper and lower parts, while the right half was undivided. To get from the top chamber to its food on the bottom, the bird had to make a detour through the right half. This proved a very difficult task which could only be solved when the detour was not too great. Lorenz (1932) found that a Jackdaw was very slow in learning a simple detour through a trap-door to its nest on the other side of the aviary, though a Cockatoo (*Lophochroa galerita*) learnt this very rapidly. Katz (1937) has described the difficulty that domestic hens have in making quite simple detours, and Dr Hinde has told me how, in the course of aviary studies on Chaffinches, he has had two or three birds which when building nests repeatedly flew up with material to the underside of the wire-netting rack, found that they could not get through and only then went round to the top of the rack. This failure to make a very simple detour would be manifested for days on end. These few examples practically exhaust the results of detour experiments with birds, and the detour technique is not likely to provide much further information until it is performed very much more critically and with conditions much more thoroughly controlled than they have been in the past.

(e) The Number Concept

Every bird's-nesting schoolboy has wondered whether a bird can count its eggs, and this problem also puzzled several naturalists of the sixteenth and seventeenth centuries. Since then experiments involving the removal of eggs as laid have been carried out with many birds, and very large 'clutches' are recorded for a number of species. Thus Kirkman (1911) records 32 eggs from one female Wryneck, and Witschi (1935) obtained as many as 50 eggs from a Swallow. In normal circumstances egg-laying continues until a definite accumulation of eggs initiates the incubation behaviour, which in turn induces ovarian regression and degeneration of the larger egg cells, all these being controlled by a hormone of the prolactin type from the anterior pituitary (see references to Brooks, 1940, and Uotila, 1940, in Salman, 1943; also Marshall, 1936). For the most recent summaries of the endocrinological aspects of this and other types of bird behaviour, the work of Bullough (1945) and Beach (1948) should be consulted. We are not, however, here concerned with the hormonal aspect but with the perceptual side. How is it that the perception of a certain number of eggs can influence the physiological activity of a bird? It is clear that such behaviour does not necessarily involve counting in any ordinary human sense of the term. The bird might merely be reacting to a certain visually observed proportion of 'egg to nest,' or it might in some cases be reacting merely to the amount of stimulation received by the brooding surfaces. We are still very far from having satisfactory experimental evidence on this point. But consideration of this egg-in-nest problem shows how careful we have to be in deciding whether or not a bird can count, and how complicated the idea of counting really is. For critical investigation and discussion of these problems, the reader is referred to the papers of Honigmann (1942b), Salman (1943) and Koehler (1950), to which I have been much indebted in writing this section of the present review.

The earliest experiments with birds were those of Porter (1904) using the House Sparrow, but his 'number tests,' while showing a good deal of apparent success, did not, in fact, prove that the birds could count or that they could perceive the relations necessary for counting, and it is probable that all his results were explicable in terms of a sense of location or position which, as we have seen, is very highly developed in birds; probably far more highly than in mammals. In the second and third decades of this present century, the 'multiple-choice' method was the one usually favoured. In this type of experiment a fixed number of objects, compartments or feeding-boxes are offered to the animal, which is required to choose the compartment which contains or allows access to food. The experimental conditions are constantly varied in such a manner that in order to learn the problem, one box in particular relation to the rest (e.g. the second *open* box from the right-hand end) has always to be selected. The total number of boxes remains constant, but the experimental situation is altered from time to time so that the position of the correct box is different. Thus at one time twelve open boxes may be presented, the right choice then being number eleven; next time only two, three and four are open, when the number three is the correct choice. Similarly, when five to nine are open, box eight is the correct choice. So while the relation of the correct box to the whole number of open boxes is always the same, the correct box itself is always in a different place. The object of this kind of experiment is to demonstrate the existence of a real number-concept apart from a sense of position.

Sadovnikova (1923*b*) carried out tests of this kind with finches, and claimed that her birds finally reached 100 per cent. success in locating the middle box out of a series of nine. As Honigmann points out, not only did she claim this, but if her results are correct they imply the mastery of two or three different tasks simultaneously in response to various indicators (an extremely difficult undertaking for other animals and even for children). Thus, with a number of boxes varying from two to nine, the first from the left had to be chosen if there was no special indicator, the first from the right if a white paper was shown and the middle box if a black ribbon was displayed. It is claimed that an individual Serin learnt all this in a few days.

Although Sadovnikova's experimental arrangements appear well designed to avoid errors of the 'Clever Hans'[1] type, Honigmann points out that she was without doubt 'outwitted' by her birds. The exit doors were swinging doors, and the 'wrong' ones were locked by means of a pin let down from above. Probably all the bird had, in fact, to do was to find out which exit door was unlocked before it entered the box. The possibility of this simple secondary cue is not ruled out by any of the control experiments performed, and such cues would, in fact, render the learning tests quite easy and obviate the necessity of learning three different tasks simultaneously.

Another method of tackling the problem of the number concept is that of attempting to train animals to perform actions either in simple or multiple alternation. This technique has been employed by Katz and Révész (1909), using the domestic fowl. Rows of grains of corn, of which every second grain was glued to cardboard, were presented to the birds,

---

[1] So called after the famous stallion 'Clever Hans', which could tap out with its hooves, according to a definite code, the correct answers to the most abstruse questions. It was subsequently proved that the horse could answer correctly only if the interrogator himself knew the answers, and that it had, in fact, learned to respond to slight *involuntary* movements of the questioner's head and body, thus deceiving all observers, including the trainer himself.

which soon learnt to eat the loose ones without touching the fixed ones. In addition to this, one hen learnt to select every third grain without touching the others, although no bird was successful in selecting every fourth grain. Révész (1922) extended this work by doubling or halving the distances between the grains after the completion of the training without, it is claimed, destroying the alternation habit. As Honigmann points out, these experiments do not appear to have been properly controlled, and all through this work there seems to be some doubt as to whether the birds had not, in fact, learnt to distinguish in some way between fixed and loose grains. Some of these experiments have been repeated (Honigmann, 1942c), with the result that as soon as all secondary clues were excluded the training effects disappeared. Honigmann failed to confirm Révész's conclusion that the distance apart of the grains does not matter, but he did succeed in demonstrating what appears to have been a true alternation habit, which was maintained if the distances were increased or decreased gradually. Where all secondary clues were excluded, the true alternation in rows of grains, all of which were loose, could still be obtained, but it took a far longer time—500 to 600 experiments and seventeen to twenty training days—to obtain the result, and even then the performance was by no means perfect. Throughout all these investigations it is clear what a big effect on the training small and apparently irrelevant details of the experimental procedure can have, and how very easily a minute change in circumstances will interrupt the learning performance. It is Honigmann's view, however, that the simple alternation ability which his experiments confirmed can be considered as a general preliminary stage to counting, although an enormous gap remains between this and the usual connotation of the word when applied to human behaviour.

It has been questioned whether a supposed 'number-conception' may not, in fact, be due to a training rhythm. It appears that, although this is a valid criticism of much number-concept experimentation in mammals, it will not explain away the results we have just been discussing, and it has been shown (Koehler, Müller and Wachholtz, 1935; Koehler and Wachholtz, 1936; Koehler, 1937) that both pigeons and fowls can be trained to a rhythm, and can be induced to perform the same actions several times in succession independently of any temporal rhythm. The ingenious methods of training by means of rhythmically moving targets used by Schole (1934) in studying the rhythmical motor behaviour of hens have not yet resulted in any satisfactory conclusions owing, as Honigmann shows, to unsatisfactory planning and control of the experiments.

A great deal of work has been carried out to test the ability of birds to distinguish between two quantities of objects offered simultaneously. The first worker in this field (Révész, 1922) employed the domestic fowl. He was followed by Fischel (1926) who, from a number of different species, obtained the best results with a Goldfinch. This bird could be taught by the glueing method to distinguish five grains of seed from three, and six grains from four, but not five from four, seven from five or ten from six. Beritoff and Akhmeteli (1937) also achieved distinction of three from six with pigeons, but it was not till the work of Koehler and his collaborators mentioned above that the problem was really tackled systematically. This work set the standard for further experiments and, as a result of judicious combination and adjustment of intensity of rewards and punishment, astonishing results have been achieved by Arndt (1939) with pigeons, Marold (1939) with Budgerigars and Schiemann (1940) with Jackdaws. A full, critical account of these results will be found in Honigmann (1942a and b) and Salman (1943), and a summary and discussion of the more striking experiments is given by Koehler (1950), to whom I am greatly indebted for permission to summarise and quote below in free translation. Giltay (1934) has also discussed the number conception of birds, but her methods seem open to considerable criticism, as are also those of Ballis and Verlaine (see Lashley, 1940, and Bierens de Haan, 1936 and 1940).[1]

Koehler and his co-workers adopted quite extraordinary precautions to avoid errors of the 'Clever Hans' type. Thus, during training and 'spontaneous' experiments the observer and the animals were always separated by a partition so that the experimenter was never seen by the bird; while at work he was able to watch it through the viewfinder of a ciné-camera fitted into the wall. Moreover, when a deterrent was required in conditioning, there was only one degree of punishment, and this was always the same. It was thus impossible for the experimenter inadvertently to give signs by means of the punishing apparatus (which inflicted a light touch on the back or in some cases merely startled the bird without touching it), since the latter functioned along all-or-none lines. In many experiments the animal was left entirely to itself and the results recorded automatically by ciné-camera, so that all possibility of clues from the investigator is ruled out. Koehler describes how the birds in the experiments of himself and his associates learnt what he calls 'unnamed numbers.' The training was carried out by two principal methods: (i) simultaneous presentation and (ii) successive presentation. Koehler puts forward the hypothesis that man would never have started counting (i.e. to name numbers) without two pre-linguistic abilities which he has in common with birds. The first of these abilities is that of being able to compare groups of units presented *simultaneously* side by side by means of *seen numbers* of those units only, excluding all other clues. This problem was presented to birds in a number of different ways, starting with only two groups of edible units (grains of corn, fruit, pieces of

---

[1] Ri (1934) has published on number discrimination in pigeons (*Act. Psychol. Keijo*, **2**, 76–83), but I have not been able to consult the original paper.

biscuit, etc.), the two groups differing by one unit only. A Raven and Grey Parrot (named 'Geier') learned in this way to open the box which had the same number of spots on the lid as there were on the 'key' card (Fig. 60), and thus eventually to distinguish between five groups indicated by 2, 3, 4, 5 and 6 black spots on the lids of small boxes, the 'key' being one of these numbers (a group of one of these numbers of objects) lying on the ground in front of the boxes. The Raven 'Jacob' learned to raise only that one of the five lids which had the same number of spots as the key pattern had objects. As a control, every other factor was changed in a random manner from one experiment to the next. Thus there were

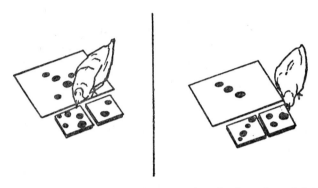

FIG. 60—Jackdaw opening box according to a given 'key' number of dots on the big card. For further explanation see text. (After Koehler, 1949.)

fifteen positions of the five boxes and very many different positions of the key pattern; the number of units in the key pattern changed with each experiment, and there were five places for the 'positive' number of spots on a lid corresponding to that of the key. Moreover, there were twenty-four permutations of the four 'negative' numbers. Also the relative situation of the spots of one group and the size and form of those spots changed with absolute irregularity. In the final series of experiments, for each trial the experimenter broke afresh a flat plasticine cake into pieces of highly irregular outlines, the area of a piece varying from 1 to 50 units, and care was always taken to make the arrangement and general appearance of the positive number on the lid as unlike that of the key pattern as possible. Nevertheless, in spite of all extraneous clues having been eliminated with such care, Jacob solved the problem by choosing the positive lid according to the only item which was not changing through all the experiments, i.e. the 'number' characteristic of the particular key pattern presented (Fig. 61).

The second ability is to estimate (i.e. to remember) numbers of incidents following each other, and thus to keep in mind *numbers presented successively in time*, independent of rhythm or any other clue which might be helpful. Here again many different methods were employed. At first birds were trained to eat only *x* grains out of many offered without any help being given by configuration. For instance, if a hundred or more grains are given in a big heap, one grain touching many others, there is no 'configuration' at all. Another task was to eat only a number, *x*, of peas which were rolled into a cup, one after another, at randomly varied intervals ranging from one to sixty seconds. Here again there is no configuration. As with a slot-machine, the pigeon never sees more than one pea in the cup. The bird always has the same view, and there is absolutely no visible clue for distinguishing the last 'allowed' pea from the

FIG. 61—A problem successfully solved by the Raven 'Jacob.' The arrows point in each case from the 'key' pattern of 'plasticine' pieces to the only box in each group of five which the bird opened. For further explanation see text. (From Koehler, 1949.)

first 'forbidden' one. The same applies to opening the lids of boxes standing in a long row until *x* baits have been secured; since the baits were arranged in the boxes in twenty or more distributions from one experiment to the next, the number of the lids to be opened was constantly changing. For instance, if the bird is trained to take five baits, it may have to open any number of lids between one and seven. The bird thus opens lids up to *x* baits (i.e. when *x*=5 it 'acts upon five'), but the number of lids which it has to open to get five changes with each experiment. Still more remarkable is the fact that birds learned to master up to four problems of this kind at the same time. For instance, a Jackdaw learned to open black lids until it had secured two baits, green lids up to three, red lids up to four and white lids until it had secured five baits. Similarly Budgerigars learned to 'act upon two' when the experimenter said 'dyo, dyo, dyo . . .,' and upon three (take only three grains from the

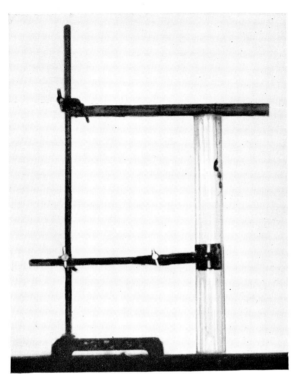

III. String Manipulation by Birds.

Fig. 1: The experimental arrangement. String attached underneath perch and looped over it. Bait suspended inside glass cylinder.

Fig. 2: Great Tit pulling string. (Photos by G. E. Dunnett. Original.)

IV. String Manipulation by Birds. Great Tit.

Fig. 1: Close view of first pull. Note right foot partially lifted in readiness for holding loop.

Fig. 2: First loop now held by right foot; next loop being pulled in with beak. (Photos by G. E. Dunnett. Original.)

V. STRING MANIPULATION BY JAY.

Note left foot in act of treading on the string. The string in this instance is over a foot in length, and the bird has already sidled some inches along the bough in the process of hauling in the string. (Photo by G. E. Dunnett. Original.)

heap) when he uttered the words 'treis, treis, treis. . . .' Similar results
were obtained with a bell indicating two and a buzzer indicating three.

Since, as far as can be seen, all external clues were carefully excluded
in this experiment, only an inner token can have been responsible for the
birds ceasing action when the required number was reached.   It seems as
if the bird does some 'inward marking' of the units he is acting upon, and
this supposition is strengthened by the fact that sometimes those supposed inward marks show themselves in external behaviour in the form
of intention movements. Thus a Jackdaw, given the task to raise lids until
five baits had been secured (which in this case were distributed in the
first five boxes in the order 1, 2, 1, —, 1) went home to its cage after
having opened only the first three lids and having consequently eaten
only four baits (Fig. 62). The experimenter was just about to record

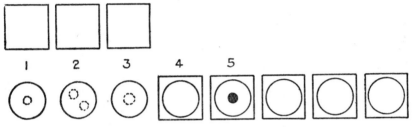

Fig. 62—The Jackdaw has removed the cards covering the first three boxes and has
taken the four baits which they contained. The remaining boxes are closed; No. 4 is
empty and No. 5 contains the last 'allowed' bait. For further explanation see text. (After
Koehler, 1949.)

'one too few, incorrect solution' when the Jackdaw came back to the line
of boxes. Then the bird went through a most remarkable performance:
it bowed its head once before the first box it had emptied, made two bows
in front of the second box, one before the third, then went farther along
the line, opened the fourth lid (no bait) and the fifth and took out the
last (fifth) bait. Having done this, it left the rest of the line of boxes
untouched and went home with an air of finality. This 'intention' bowing,
repeated the same number of times before each open box as on the first
occasion when it had found baits in them, seems to prove that the bird
remembered its previous actions. It looks as if, after its first departure, it
became aware that it had not finished the task, so it came back and started
again, 'picking up' in vacuo, with intention movements, baits it had already
actually picked up; when, however, it came to the last two boxes which
by mistake it had omitted to open on its first trip, it performed the full
movements and thus completed its task.

The simplest explanation that Koehler has to offer for this inner
marking is that it may consist in equal marks, as if we were to think or

give one nod of the head for one, two for two and so on. This is called *'thinking unnamed numbers'* and for the vast majority of experimental results at present available it is not necessary to suppose that the bird does the marking by *unequal* or *qualitatively different* marks in fixed order, as we do when we think of the words 1, 2, 3, 4, 5; or, alternatively, a phrase of five different syllables. Nevertheless, there are, in fact, some experiments which suggest that the *unnamed number* concept may be inadequate. Hitherto a completely abstract concept of number has been observed only in human beings. For unequivocal evidence of it in animals it would be necessary to train the animal to combine simultaneous and successive 'counting' and at the same time to respond to a given number in quite diverse circumstances; as, for instance, 'the recognition of four blasts of a whistle after training to four dots on a paper for four grains to be eaten' (Salmon). Only a *general solution* to the problem of a transfer of this kind—the transfer of a number from one quality to another and also combining successive and simultaneous—could be regarded as satisfactory evidence of true counting. But Koehler (1950) (also *in litt.*, 1954) has described experiments in which Parrot, Magpie and Jackdaw, after having been taught to knock off a given number (say five) of lids from a series of dishes before finding food, would then, in another series of experiments, show a significant first preference for that box on the lid of which five spots are displayed and *vice versa*; that is, seeing numbers previously acted upon and acting upon numbers previously seen. But this performance has so far remained a *special solution* only (i.e. restricted to the numbers actually trained); it has not been possible yet to get the birds to generalise it and so provide a *general solution* of the problem.

Lögler (1959) has carried the investigation of the problem of number-sense in animals a step further by his extremely thorough and painstaking work on counting in a Grey Parrot. Extending the kind of investigation which had been carried out earlier by Koehler and many of his pupils, he found that this particular parrot 'Jako' was well able, after prolonged training, to distinguish the number 8 from the number 7. This bird also learned to recognise that the successive presentation of a number of optic stimuli was a signal for a task of performing the same number of actions. Thus the bird, having been shown, say, 4 or 6 or 7 light flashes, was then able to take 4 or 6 or 7, as the case might be, of irregularly distributed baits out of a row of food trays. Not even numerous random changes in the temporal sequence of signal stimuli impaired the percentage of correct solutions. Having learnt this task, a signal of successive light flashes was replaced by successive notes on a flute. The bird was, however, able to substitute immediately, without further training, and the change from light flashes to flute notes had no effect on the number of correct solutions.

Nor was the accomplishment hindered by the completely a-rhythmic presentation of stimuli, or by a change of pitch. Although this parrot was not able to accomplish a task which represented a combination of the two faculties of learning numbers presented successively and simultaneously— e.g. he could not respond to visually presented numbers after hearing the same number of acoustic stimuli—yet, when he had learned to act upon 2 or 1, after having heard 2 sounds simultaneously or a single sound, he was spontaneously able to open a lid with 2 spots on it or a lid with 1 spot according to the same acoustic signals. That is to say, he was able to transpose from the simultaneous-successive combination to the simultaneous-simultaneous one in twenty experiments without re-learning. It seems then that this remarkable work does bring the counting achievement of birds a step nearer that of man; though it is still not true counting in the fully human sense.

Two pre-linguistic faculties—simultaneous and successive unnamed number sense—have then been demonstrated in some species of birds. Now similar tests of the same basic abilities have been carried out with man (Koehler, 1943). In the first case the objects are presented by lantern-slides projected on a screen for an exactly determined time sufficiently long for the groups of figures to be fully seen, yet too short for counting to take place. It is remarkable that, when this is done with human beings, the limit of achievement is of the same order as that shown by birds. Thus few persons reach eight, and many, like the pigeon, get no further than five. As to the second ability, although experiments are scanty, Koehler finds no grounds for expecting that man can achieve better results than the birds, provided named counting is excluded. This similarity of the limit in both abilities, applying to six species, including man, seems to be a most important fact, and such a correlation can hardly be due to chance. For ourselves, the two abilities, to grasp 'numbers' presented simultaneously (differentiating between groups seen side by side) or successively ('acting upon x'), have in common only the absolute idea of un-named numbers. The hypothesis therefore suggests itself that these two basic pre-linguistic faculties, which may together be described as 'un-named thinking,' may be common to birds and to man. Very many ideas come to us in wordless form, as they must do with birds and other animals; the essential difference is that we can recount ideas afterwards in words, and animals, so far as we know, cannot. Fighting, playing, courting, etc., in both animals and men may have many items in common, items which are wordless in both cases.

Although technically beyond reproach, these experiments have been criticised by Salman on the ground of their extreme artificiality, and there is certainly something in this. Thus Marold, in order to train a Budgerigar to eat six grains from a heap of ten or fifteen grains, was forced to conduct

600 experiments with the same bird, inflicting a sharp shock as punishment in case of a wrong choice. His first success did not appear until the tests were past the 600 mark, and by the time 700 was reached the bird was still making 40 per cent. mistakes. It is difficult to imagine that such training can have much bearing on the behaviour of the animal under wild conditions. Salman suggests that this type of experiment is so artificial as to be of no further interest, and that if further discrimination tests are done they should be related more closely to the animal's normal life and its peculiar psychology. With this implication that artificial experiments are necessarily unilluminating, I cannot agree. Such results as Koehler's [1] are of the greatest interest psychologically in that they show some capabilities of birds which are apparently lying dormant and which natural selection may conceivably be able to develop further in the future. In fact, we need both types of experiment for a full understanding of the animal.

(f) Visual Illusions as Evidence of Insight

Discrimination of form and pattern is, of course, universal amongst birds, and quite apart from the obvious perfection of the avian eye as a visual mechanism (see Pumphrey, 1948), no naturalist would for a moment doubt the possession of form sense by birds. It might, however, be argued that the innate ability to perceive forms naturally significant in the life of the animal is a different matter from the ability to learn to recognise entirely artificial geometrical and other patterns, and this idea had been the basis of much of the work on form sense in animals. As a naturalist would have expected, this work has shown clearly that recognition of geometrical forms is not difficult for birds, and that birds' form sense is probably superior to that of many mammals. It is not necessary to summarise this long controversy here; a good, short account will be found in Warden, Jenkins and Warner's text-book (1936). In actual fact, it is extremely doubtful whether any distinction between the recognition of naturally occurring and artificially constructed forms can be maintained.

While we can then pass over the detailed work on form recognition there remains a particularly interesting aspect of the subject, namely that of visual illusion. All of us are familiar with this kind of thing in ourselves, and it is interesting from more than one point of view to know how far the same thing occurs in animals. It is obvious that such illusion may be the result of the structure of the sense organ itself; or, as in the vertical-horizontal illusion, both the structure of the eye and the position of the lines in the field of view may be involved. But apart from these the majority of illusions depend on the pattern of the lines, and as Wood-

[1] Sauter (1952) has followed up Koehler's work and has demonstrated similar pre-linguistic number sense in the Magpie.

worth (1938) remarks, they are in a general way errors in the perception of the parts of a figure incidental to the perceived form as a whole. Such illusions are not mere curiosities; their value lies in the clues they afford to the process of perception. The simplest of the usual theories of visual illusions is the eye-movement theory, which comes nearer to providing a simple physiological explanation than any other. According to this, impression of length results from the fixation point of the eye being moved along a line from one end to the other, and if movement in one direction, e.g. the horizontal, requires more energy than movement in the other, say the vertical, that direction which requires more effort will seem the longer. This, however, does not carry us very far, and all other theories of optical illusions imply at least a concept of perspective and usually bring in definitely psychological concepts, such as emotion and a tendency to resolve an imperfect figure in the direction of perfection, as when an imperfect circle is seen as a true circle, or at any rate a better circle than it is. In so far as such theories seem to be necessary, they imply a concept by the subject, of parts in relation to the whole. This brings us closer to the concept of insight as playing a part in perception itself, and so links on to the subject of form recognition.

Révész (1924 and 1925) trained hens and chicks to peck from the smaller of two figures presented simultaneously, beginning with circles and going on to rectangles, squares and triangles, taking due precautions to eliminate position habits. After this training was completed he introduced new figures, two segments of a broad ring of different sizes, again presented in different positions. While these experiments were in progress he interspersed the 'Jastrow' illusion among his experiments. This is a well-known illusion (Fig. 63) in which of two equal segments of a circle, one above the other, the upper one appears to human beings to be 15 per cent. smaller than the lower. In a very high proportion of cases the

FIG. 63—The 'Jastrow' illusion.

hens pecked from the one which appeared to be smaller to the human eye, and some evidence was produced that the extent of the illusion was about the same for a hen and for man. The famous 'Müller-Lyer' illusion (Fig. 64), according to which the apparent length of a straight line varies according to the size and position of intersecting straight lines, has also been shown to hold with the Ring-dove by Warden and Baar (1929) and with chicks by Winslow (1933). Here again there is evidence that the response of the birds to these figures is practically identical with that of the human being; and Winslow points out that such experiments with birds, where monocular vision obtains and where eye movements are slight compared with mammals, suggest that these two types of explanation are hardly likely to be adequate in other animals. Without going into the psychological controversy over the significance of these tests, we may tentatively conclude that they do provide evidence for the 'gestalt' theory of perception and for the assumption that the character as a whole enforces itself as strongly as possible: 'If that character was integral, simplicity is exaggerated; if divided, the division is emphasised' (Koffka, 1931, quoted by Woodworth (1938, p. 650)). This implies a kind of 'tendency towards an "ideal",' and as a result an imperfect form is seen as better than it actually is. When a familiar object is suggested, the perception tends towards a typical form of that object, and when some geometrical form is indicated, perception tends towards a more perfect example of

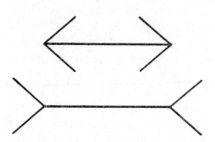

FIG. 64—The 'Müller-Lyer' illusion.

that form. We can thus say that work on birds' perception of optical illusions does strongly suggest a form sense which is similar to ours and, moreover, one that fundamentally involves something in the nature of insight.

(g) Some Other Abilities Suggestive of Insight or Insight Learning

Before leaving the subject of insight learning we might mention one or two pieces of bird behaviour which appear to provide evidence of extraordinary intelligence and foresight, and which do not fit naturally and easily into any other section of this review. It is well known, of course, that most birds, while they may be very attentive to their young in the nest, are completely callous and unresponsive to those same young when, as a result of some accident, they are outside the nest or the immediate nest territory. While this is undoubtedly the general rule, there are on record one or two astonishing exceptions. Thus Lorenz (1935) records the behaviour of a female Blackcap which he caught on her nest and placed in a cage with her young. The female continued to feed her young quite well, and later, when they were making their first tentative flights about the cage, it not infrequently happened that one of them fell into the feeding-dish. The mother invariably responded by jumping into the vessel, and—holding her head and beak very low—slipped under the chick, which she then with her back slowly forced upwards and out to safety. This may, of course, be a piece of instinctive behaviour not hitherto described but characteristic of this species. Nevertheless, it is in marked contrast to the behaviour of birds to accidentally displaced young, as when a Cuckoo has ejected young from the nest, although here the difference may lie in the age which the young have reached and their ability to give a certain call—young before they have reached the fledgling stage being unable to release this kind of parental behaviour. Lorenz (*loc. cit.*) also mentions Heinroth's observation of a Teal coming to the assistance of one of its young which had fallen on its back, slowly turning it over by inserting her beak underneath, and Lorenz himself records a similar performance by a Muscovy Duck.

When reading of insight behaviour, many naturalists will think of the female Cuckoo. It is now well established (for references see Baker, 1942, pp. 170–2) that the female Cuckoo selects well in advance the nests which are to receive her eggs. When she is doing this she is so sly and cautious that she can rarely be observed in the performance, but her skill in finding the right nests is remarkable. It appears that Cuckoos have different methods for nest-finding, dependent on the type of country in which they are operating. The female will often sit for hours on a convenient perch watching birds building their nests, thus finding many nests which are, in fact, well hidden. These nests she remembers so that eggs may be laid in them at the appropriate time. In open country she will fly over hedges and trees, surveying with keen sight nests on the ground as well as those in the branches of trees. There is also evidence that Cuckoos not only find nests in advance, but apparently when nests are found containing a full number of eggs they destroy some, with the result that the owner continues laying and so has fresh eggs ready by the time the Cuckoo herself is ready to lay. Sometimes it appears that the whole clutch is destroyed, thus compelling the selected foster-parent to build and lay again. It has been recorded of an Indian Cuckoo (although the fact that the same individual cuckoo was concerned is not established) that it watched chats' nests for several days, during which a number of visits were paid, an egg being taken away on each occasion, the process ending with the deposition of her own eggs some days later. It appears as if the Cuckoo has some concept of the circumstances which result in a nest suitable for her needs, and that she does take what seems an extraordinarily 'long view' of her requirements. However, as Baker points out, the removal of eggs from a nest which she will require for her own purposes may be due to egg-extracting instinctive behaviour so developed that the egg-removal automatism comes into play when she finds nests not immediately needed for egg-laying.

CHAPTER XV

BIRDS *(Continued)*

IMITATION

THE concepts involved and implied in the general idea of imitation have been discussed in Chapter V, above. Both social facilitation and local enhancement are there dealt with and a number of ornithological examples and illustrations provided. Accordingly in this chapter we shall proceed directly to 'imitation,' which, as vocal 'imitation,' is so peculiarly characteristic of the class Aves.

As was made clear in Part II, by true imitation is meant the copying of a novel or otherwise improbable act or utterance, or some act for which there is clearly no instinctive tendency. Defined in these terms, we see that true visual imitation becomes something which apparently involves self-consciousness and something of intent to profit by another's experience, and it becomes doubtful whether we can find any certain examples of such behaviour in birds.

What, then, is the evidence for the existence of this true visual imitation in birds? Porter (1910) describes an American Crow which in the course of his puzzle-box experiments learned, as a result of watching another bird, to open a door in a different way from that which it had previously used itself. There is another quite remarkable instance of imitation of a strange action which seems well enough attested. Allard (1939) describes how a Starling which had learned to imitate the voice of a Flicker (*Colaptes* sp.) then perfected the performance by drumming with his beak on the top of his nesting-box, thus reproducing the Flicker's 'tattoo.' The behaviour was observed occasionally over a period of weeks during the nesting season of 1938, a single bird only being involved.

There are also records of parrots imitating human actions, which certainly cannot be dismissed offhand as anecdotal. Burton (1958) describes a West African Grey Parrot which first learnt to imitate the popping sound made by putting the finger into the mouth and giving a quick tug at the inside of the cheek. After a week or so during which she learnt to make the sound of the pop to perfection, she then over the next few weeks took to bringing her foot up to the side of her beak and moving it away again with a sharp movement as she made the popping sound. Burton reproduces an excellent photograph of the bird doing this. Mr. A. P. G. Michelmore (in litt.) tells me of a parrot which has apparently learnt to imitate the actions of a man taking off and putting on his coat. It does not seem as if in this case there is any special connection with imitating a particular sound.

It must, nevertheless, be borne in mind how strong is the evidence against imitation in mixed flocks of birds. For example, one constantly sees Sanderling, Dunlin and Turnstones feeding together on the shore, but I know of no instance of the former species imitating the latter's method of turning over stones and debris in search of food. There is much evidence that flocks of birds do tend to follow and pay attention to the warnings of particularly experienced individuals, but it is doubtful if any of this behaviour qualifies as true imitation, and it will be dealt with below under the heading of 'Individual Recognition.' Finally, what looks like visual imitation, although no new combination of actions was involved, has been described by Swynnerton (1942) in experiments to study the effect of warning colours displayed by insects upon two species of swallow (*Hirundo*) which were being used as experimental animals. In this particular case he describes very vividly the way in which one bird would anxiously watch the response of the other to a new test insect, as if with the intention of itself profiting by its companion's reaction and so avoiding even one unpleasant experience of a distasteful species. Brower (1958) has shown that Scrub Jays (*Cyanocitta c. caerulescens*) can retain the learned ability to reject a particular species of butterfly on sight even after a period of over two weeks has elapsed since the last experience of them. Klopfer (1959, 1961) has described under 'empathic' behaviour experiments on finches in which the effect of social interaction on discrimination learning in the feeding situation was studied. Greenfinches were trained to feed from one of two patterns and to avoid the other, normal sunflower seed and sunflower seed rendered bitter to the taste, serving as a positive and negative reinforcement. Single birds learned the discrimination rapidly, as did birds which had been allowed to observe a previously trained bird performing. Birds which were trained in the presence of an untrained partner, however, required much longer. When birds of this last group were permitted to observe the training sequence of their untrained partners, their performances, which had previously been correct, repeatedly fluctuated to a random and non-discriminatory level. The partners in turn then also began to fluctuate between random and correct levels. This alternate fluctuations in the performance of the two birds would continue as long as they were kept together, with the result that a sustained level of correct response was never achieved by either. That is to say, the birds did not learn, as a result of seeing associates refuse the nasty seeds, to refuse to feed from the accompanying pattern themselves. The results appear to mean that under the conditions that prevail a feeding response can be established more readily than an avoidance response, apparently as

the result of conditioning—the unconditioned stimulus (the social releaser) being the sight of another bird feeding. Klopfer argues that this
behaviour can fail to be maladaptive only in species of relatively conservative food habits or of a solitary nature. With more opportunist and inquisitive species one would expect the learned avoidance responses to be more
stable. This prediction was borne out by the same author's (1961) observations on Great Tits where apparently the birds suffered no disadvantage
by being trained in pairs. However, these experiments raise some difficulties of interpretation which are further discussed in Thorpe (1959). From
the experimental results just described, one might expect the feeding
responses of the Greenfinch to be so conservative as virtually to eliminate
the likelihood of their feeding on some unsuitable or noxious food. Yet as
we have seen from the work of Pettersson (1961) (see p. 355, above)
Greenfinches appear very far from being rigidly conservative food
specialists.

Turner (1962) has made some criticism of the work of Klopfer based
on the fact that although the backgrounds were different, the distasteful
and edible seeds appeared exactly the same, so that the tests amounted to
a very difficult microhabitat discrimination. In Turner's experiments,
Sparrows and Chaffinches were used and the tests were simpler and investigated the learning of positive food reactions as opposed to avoidance
reactions. The results seem to suggest that the apparent rigid conservatism
of the Greenfinch's responses may not provide the complete clue to the
understanding of the social feeding behaviour of the species. A brief summary will be found in Turner (1961).

Vocal imitation in birds is, of course, proverbial, and there is abundant
evidence that many species of wild bird learn a part or even the whole of
their full territorial songs from fellow-members of the species, and the
functional significance and selective value of this in many species is
plausible enough. Since this is also, from the theoretical point of view,
a very interesting and restricted kind of learning, it will be dealt with
below under the heading of 'Imprinting.' Here we shall discuss the apparently functionless acquisition of extraneous sounds from other species or
from inorganic sources which is so highly developed in certain species such
as parrots, Mocking Birds, Bower Birds, the Marsh Warbler (Howard,
1907–14), Starlings and the East African Robin Chats (*Cossypha* spp.)
(Pakenham, 1943, p. 184). Some finches are also imitative in this sense.
Both Bullfinch and Hawfinch will pick up alien notes (Thorpe, unpublished), and the Greenfinch is—rather surprisingly—particularly adept
and can learn the Canary song (Thorpe, unpublished) and also that of the
Redstart (Cundall *et al.*, 1952). Records that the Chaffinch includes imita-
tions of alien species in its *full* song are probably incorrect (Thorpe, 1955,
1961*d*). Allard (1939), who has studied the Starling and Mocking Bird,

stresses the remarkable variety of sounds mimicked and the tendency to remember notes for a long time even in the absence of the model—this resulting in the out-of-season production of the summer notes of various species. It is also noteworthy how a particular note will become a 'hit' for a considerable period and will then drop out of the repertory.

It is difficult to consider the facts of this matter dispassionately without coming to the conclusion that some element of 'play' (see Chapter IV, above) is involved, for the behaviour has so obviously become detached in some way from the main course of instinctive behaviour, and is thus an activity characteristic of sub-maximal motivation—either (*a*) appearing before the drive has built up to its full intensity, or (*b*) being dependent on the low-intensity motivation remaining when the consummatory act or situation has been early or easily attained. That this first category (*a*) is a genuine one and throws real new light on the situation is suggested by the particularly instructive instance of the sub-song of the Chaffinch. This is a species which, while developing its true song by imitation of other Chaffinches (see p. 370 *et seq.*, below), has never been known to incorporate notes from *other* species therein. Yet there is now good evidence (Falconer, 1941; Thorpe, 1955, 1961*d*) that with a sub-song it is different. The sub-song in this and probably in many other species (e.g. Whitethroat; see Sauer, 1954) is a somewhat amorphous rambling utterance which appears to have little or no communicatory value. It is clearly a low-intensity phenomenon linked in some way with a low but rising sex-hormone production; but also apparently fulfilling some function as a 'practice' for the true song which, in a sense, develops out of it (Thorpe, 1954). In both the examples quoted the alien notes incorporated (in the first case from the Great Tit, in the second from a Canary) appeared in the sub-song, but were entirely absent from the full song. Case (*b*) is, of course, exemplified by many birds under conditions of captivity where most of the inborn drives are so easily consummated, with the result that there will theoretically be a drive surplus. Something of this sort has often been suggested by bird fanciers, and has been at the basis of various techniques which were employed by the 'schools' where finches were trained to take part in the celebrated song-bird contests which for two or three centuries were features of aviculture in Central Europe. Thus Adams (1853) concludes that in some respects the more restricted a bird's outlet for its normal energies, the more likely it is to prove an apt pupil, and Scott's (1902*a*) suggestion that some of the mimicry of this extreme type we are here considering—by species which are not normally recognised as 'mimics'—may be an abnormal condition due to captivity, really amounts essentially to the modern idea expressed in the subjective language of the naturalist of fifty years ago. He supposes that most passerine birds have the faculty to some degree, but that in the wild they have little leisure to extend the ability beyond its normal, biological sphere of usefulness. Aviary birds, on the contrary, have all their wants supplied, and so have more leisure to give their attention to events around them, particularly such as are accompanied by noise, and so the powers of mimicry become hypertrophied.

We still do not know enough of the ethology and physiology of any of the true mimics (e.g. parrot, Mocking Bird, Starling) in the wild to know whether a similar drive-surplus explanation could be applied to their cases also.

The only example of a possibly useful mimicry of one species by another in the wild has been supplied to me by General H. P. W. Hutson. It concerns an Indian Cuckoo, the Koel, parasitic on the Indian House Crow, which rears mixed broods of its own young and those of the Koel together. The Koel thus reared use crow calls exclusively during the nestling and immediate post-nestling period, but never when they are adult; in the only case observed where Koel were reared by another species, the call given by the young was definitely not that of the Crow. This case would seem particularly worthy of a thorough experimental investigation.

That some imitation of alien notes and songs must be something more than a special case of trial-and-error is suggested by two very remarkable instances placed on record over fifty years ago with reasonably full details which carry conviction. In 1903 G. Henschel (later Sir George Henschel, the famous musician) recorded [1] how his sister, Frau Professor Grose of Brunswick, possessed a highly trained Bullfinch which piped 'God save the King.' An untrained Canary kept in an adjoining room learnt the tune from the Bullfinch in the course of about a year. At the time of Mr Henschel's stay in Brunswick in 1902, it not infrequently happened that the Bullfinch would pause after the third line a little longer than the melody warranted, whereupon the Canary would take up the tune from where the Bullfinch had stopped and finish it properly. The writer says that he heard this dozens of times during the few days of his visit. A similar and in some ways even more remarkable instance is supplied by Mr Waite (1903) of the Australian Museum, Sydney. He possessed an Australian Magpie which was taught by the flute a fifteen-note melody in two distinct phrases. Some years later a second individual was acquired which learned the tune from the first, but then they developed the habit of always singing it together antiphonally, the first bird singing the first phrase and the second only the second. Later the second, younger, bird died, whereupon the first resumed its performance of the whole. Such examples certainly suggest imitation in the fullest sense of the word. Antiphonal singing in the wild is well known in a number of bird species

[1] *Nature*, 68, 1903.

(Armstrong, 1947), but in no case is it known whether learning contributes to the performance; some such species should be profitable experiment.

The imitation of the human voice by birds has, of course, given rise to a vast amount of uninformed speculation about the bird mind. But there have been commendable efforts to separate the wheat from the chaff. Bierens de Haan (1929) quotes instances of both Canaries and Bullfinches which have learnt to pronounce not merely human words but whole phrases, and the Raven and the Beo Starling (*Eulabes* sp.) are particularly accomplished in this respect. But of course it is the parrots, particularly the Grey Parrot, which reach the peak of this accomplishment. The achievement of one particular individual which attained an extraordinarily variable vocabulary is described by Brehm (1866; see Bierens de Haan, 1929), and Lashley (1913) has given a very interesting account of an Amazon Parrot that could enunciate between fifty and one hundred distinct words. Baldwin (1914) found that the Grey Parrot, while usually needing much practice for good imitation, nevertheless would occasionally—though making no apparent effort to imitate—suddenly repeat a word perfectly without practice a week or two after hearing it. This ability is also very characteristic, as far as my own experience goes, of the learning processes of the Indian Hill Mynah. This species is probably the most talented and accurate imitator of human speech as yet known amongst birds. Not the least remarkable feature of this is the ability, only fully revealed by the sound spectograph, that these birds have of producing phonetically true human vowel sounds with a vocal apparatus which appears to be totally inadequate for the purpose (see Thorpe, 1959, 1961*d*). Lucanus (1923) describes a Budgerigar which could learn phrases of three or four words after a few days' teaching, and was also trained to count up to ten. Obviously most of these remarkable performances can be regarded as nothing more than instances of ordinary vocal imitation as described by McDougall, and do not imply anything at all in the nature of language. There are, however, one or two possible exceptions.

Lorenz tells me of a pet Raven which used Lorenz's pet name for him as a call-note in the display, the function of which was to induce Lorenz (i.e. the mate or social companion) to follow him. Lucanus describes a parrot which learnt to say 'adieu' when anyone was going away, and soon took to calling 'adieu' when someone it disliked was in the room, even though that person made no sign of going. Lucanus (1925) also describes a parrot which said 'so' when some act was finished, and 'na' when it was expectant of something being done. It is claimed that it applied these words correctly to many acts of its owner and to many situations which did not directly, or even at all, concern itself. It seems as if the bird by these words first indicated special situations, and then later came to extend the meaning of the word from the special to the more general situation of ending or commencing acts. If this is a correct interpretation, it implies that the parrots are at the beginning of acquiring a real language. There are, of course, innumerable other stories of the astonishing linguistic performances of parrots, many of which have been investigated by Bierens de Haan and have been shown not to warrant the conclusions which have been so uncritically based upon them.

We are still without satisfactory evidence that parrots, mynah birds or budgerigars ever use their remarkable powers of imitation in the wild, and it is indeed a problem to explain how these have evolved. Mowrer (1950) has suggested that the reason why parrots and budgerigars learn to talk is that when kept in captivity in close contact with human beings but away from their own kind they develop a social attachment to their human keepers. They soon learn that vocalisations on their part tend to retain and increase the attention which they get from their owners; consequently vocal production, and particularly good vocal imitation, is quickly reinforced by social contacts. This seems to offer an explanation of the very well-known fact that when learning, a parrot will tend to talk more when its owner is out of the room, or just after he has gone out, than when he is present. It is suggested that he is talking in an attempt to bring him back. If Mowrer is right about the psychology of talking birds, it appears very similar to the human infant's first steps in learning to talk. Birds and babies, according to this hypothesis, both make their first efforts at reproducing words or other sounds because these sounds seem good to them —they are in fact self-stimulatory. Mothers often talk and croon to their children while attending to them and so the sound of the mother's voice has often been accompanied by comfort-giving measures. So it is to be expected that when the child, alone and uncomfortable, hears his own voice this will likewise have a consoling and comforting effect. So the infant's first babbling will be rewarded without any necessary reference to the effects they produce on others. But before long he will learn that if he succeeds in making the kind of sounds that his mother makes he will get more interest, affection and attention in return; so the stage is set for the learning of human language. In spite of all the differences, it seems hard not to believe that something of the same sort is happening in the learning of human speech by pet birds.

'Imprinting' as Innate Disposition to Learn

The word 'imprinting' is a translation of the word '*Prägung*,' which was first employed by Heinroth to describe a learning process, then thought to be most characteristic of birds, although now apparently occurring in some form or another in other animals as well. The nature of the concept has been outlined above (Chapter VI), where it was made clear that there is no hard-and-fast line to be drawn between imprinting and other forms of learning. But it is just because of its intermediate character and its close relation with instinct that it is theoretically so interesting. Indeed, the subject of imprinting may be regarded as the very crux of the problem of learning in birds, and for that reason is given especial attention in this chapter.

The first observations [1] on this subject were those of Spalding (1872) and of Heinroth (1910), who found that Grey-lag Geese reared from the egg in isolation will react to their human keepers (or to the first relatively large moving object they see) by following them as they would their parents. This need happen for only a few hours, possibly only for a few minutes in some cases (Lorenz), for the young bird to accept a human as its proper associate, and to retain for the rest of its life a tendency to take human beings as the parent companion, a fellow-member of the species to which the later sexual behaviour may become attached; if Grey-lag Geese have been hatched in an incubator, special precautions are required to induce these goslings to follow an adult goose as their parent. Goslings, when newly hatched, show no fear of a human being. 'If one busies oneself with them for even a short time it becomes difficult to shake them off. They "peep" as soon as one moves away, and very soon begin to follow. . . . If one quickly places such an orphan amongst a brood which is following its parents in the normal way, the gosling shows not the slightest tendency to regard the old birds as members of its own species. Peeping loudly, it runs away and, should a human being happen to pass, it immediately follows this person; it simply looks upon human beings as its parents' (Lorenz, 1935). Heinroth points out that if one wishes an incubator-hatched gosling to become attached to a family of geese with their goslings, one must place it in a sack immediately following its removal from the incubator so that it has no opportunity to see a human being. It appears, then, that the young gosling, within the very first minutes of its life, gets imprinted upon its mind the image of the first moving object that it sees. But we must beware of assuming, as Lorenz himself and several other writers appear to have done, that the *whole* of the future effect follows exclusively from this initial exposure; for in all the experiments with geese which have been described the birds were more or less continually in the presence of man throughout their pre-adult life, and since special precautions against reinforcement by subsequent conditioning were not taken, this must have played a large, perhaps a very large, part in the later course and strength of the phenomenon. There seems little doubt that for geese, at any rate, the first experience

[1] Mr Armstrong tells me that Pliny (*Nat. Hist.*, **10**, 27) speaks of 'a goose which followed Lacydes as faithfully as a dog'; and Reginald of Durham (1167) records Eiders following human beings (see G. Watt, 1951).

is in some sense crucial; but it is almost certainly not the whole story even in this exceptional group.

Imprinting is also found in many ducks and game birds (see below). Lorenz records how young Partridges, which had been caught after the fields had been mown but were still only a few hours old, had nevertheless already become definitely imprinted to their normal parents. On the other hand, if Partridges are hatched artificially and are immediately given foster-parents, they are easily raised. Young Coots and Moorhens (Alley and Boyd, 1950; Hinde, Thorpe and Vince, 1956) are also subject to imprinting. Heinroth gives evidence that the process of imprinting occurs in Eagle Owls and Ravens, and Craig (1914) obtained signs of imprinting in male doves reared in isolation. There are records for the South American Bittern or Tiger Heron (Portielje, 1921), Argus Pheasant (Bierens de Haan, 1926a), certain species of doves, Goodwin, 1947a and 1948) and a Budgerigar. Recently Cushing and Ramsay (1949) have recorded success in establishing artificial families (homo-specific, heterospecific, heterogeneric), Pekin, Muscovy and Mallard ducks and Barred Rock, bantam and Rhode Island hens being used as the fosterers, and the young including these species and also Black Duck, Pheasant, Turkey and Bob-white; and Ramsay (1950) has shown that crows may even become accustomed to owls in this way. Such mixed families were all raised within sight and sound of each other, yet most of them remained distinct for periods up to twenty hours when mixed. The artificial family units became well established within the first few days, and the young in every case recognised the foster-mother, whether of the same or different species, and responded appropriately, even showing recognition of alarm notes, etc. The parents also showed clearly that they knew their young, and they would take aggressive action against intruders, thus helping to maintain the artificial family units. Attempts to secure the adoption of chicks, even though only one day old, were almost all unsuccessful, but these attempts were not done on a very large scale and require rather more experiments. But just as with the early work on geese, almost all the above experiments are such as to have allowed some process of rewarded-learning in addition to imprinting, and future experiments must take special precautions against this if their results are to be fully significant.

Lorenz originally regarded the process of imprinting as, by definition, totally irreversible. This is certainly incorrect, as is shown, for instance, by Craig's (1914) work on doves, and is probably to be regarded as an error arising from the failure to prevent the possibility of secondary conditioning mentioned above; nevertheless, its fixity is certainly astonishing at times. Lorenz (1935) described a brood of Muscovy Ducks, which as chicks were with Grey-lags for under seven weeks and were then kept by themselves. They behaved socially just like Muscovies, yet next spring one turned out to be intensely imprinted to Grey-lags. But while imprinting may be difficult to reverse in some species of geese and their near relatives, it is not so rigid, according to the experience of Mr Terry Jones, in the Ceriopsis, Emperor and Snow Geese, and is still more flexible in other birds. Lorenz says (personal communication) that Budgerigars and Bullfinches can be sexually imprinted in the strict and original sense of Heinroth. In co-operation with Dr. Hellman Budgerigars were imprinted to humans and then isolated for two years from human beings, being fed, watered and cleaned in such a manner that the human attendant was never visible to the birds. Under these conditions they bread and reared young normally. But when after these two years they were first re-exposed to humans, they immediately courted Hellman and Lorenz again and neglected their own species.

A remarkable recent instance of the persistence of an imprinting effect is reported by Kear (1960), in the Hawfinch. This bird, a female, was hand-reared from the nest when about five days old in company with nestlings of other species. The hand-rearing period lasted for about six weeks. In the summer of that year she was put in an outside aviary with a hand-reared male, her brother, which died two years later. During these two years the birds showed prolonged courtship behaviour but no successful breeding took place. After the death of the male the female was kept in an inside cage, sometimes in company with other species. In the spring which commenced her fourth year of life she began displaying to Miss Kear. This display developed in intensity and elaboration during the next three years and was directed only to Miss Kear, although she was not one of those who had taken part in the original hand-rearing. The bird attacked all other persons who came near her. Subsequently she carried out a number of items of the nesting behaviour and 'incubated' for about three weeks in a depression made in a pile of seed. There seems no doubt that she was treating Miss Kear and Miss Kear only as her mate and was in some way sexually 'imprinted' to her, although she had behaved apparently normally with a mate of her own species for two years.

Nicolai (1956), in a very thorough study, found that Bullfinches reared in isolation usually accept the human keeper as a substitute for their sibling partner, and it is to the sibling partner that the first sexual activities are addressed. If during autumn and winter the bird finds opportunity to make the acquaintance of a conspecific of the opposite sex its relation to the human gradually dissolves and normal 'betrothal' takes place. If, however, the bird continues to be kept in the exclusive society of human beings, it later accepts one of them as a permanent mate. It is only then, according to Nicolai, that the sexual imprinting to humans has become irreversible. Males reared in isolation behave very tenderly to their human partner, attempt to feed him, and are strongly personally attached. Those reared by men permanently prefer them to women. Females reared in isolation are very aggressive and furiously attack humans. This marked difference between male and female behaviour in Bullfinches is easily understood in terms of the normal biology as described by Nicolai.

The conflict of evidence about irreversibility in geese is probably also due, in part, to the conditions of imprinting. Lorenz and Heinroth are speaking of birds deliberately imprinted to man immediately on hatching, whereas Mr Terry Jones and Colonel Lumsden (quoted below) were dealing with birds reared under hens in the usual way, with no special precautions. But the case of the Lesser White-fronted Geese (footnote, p. 415, below) cannot be explained in this way.

There are several other characteristics originally postulated by Lorenz, which have either not been substantiated or which, in the light of more recent research, can no longer be regarded as purely indicative of imprinting. Thus it can no longer be thought of as *always* confined to a brief early period of the life of the organism; nor as *always* completed before the specific responses to which the effect will become linked have matured; nor yet *always* as supra-individual learning.

In the light of recent research, the crux of the matter seems to be the question as to how far imprinting involves an innate disposition to learn in a certain direction or to accept a certain type of pattern, and so it will be discussed here particularly from this point of view. It is true that in certain cases (e.g. among the geese) almost any object may come to be substituted for the normal parent, but often it seems as if imprinting is limited within certain bounds, at least of size, and that movement is an important characteristic. Restriction of learning to a particular kind of object is, of course, to be expected to some extent in birds from the very fact of their having innate preferences. As an example, we may cite the observations of Engelmann (1941–2), who found that chicks which had been reared on paste in a brooder showed innate preferences for grain of certain forms right from the first time that they saw them, and that from artificial grains of varying sizes they selected those most nearly approximating to natural grains. James (1959) working with newly-hatched Barred Plymouth Rock chicks, found that retinal flicker acted as an unconditioned stimulus for imprinting. He found that if a stationary conditioned stimulus was placed near an intermittent light source for ten trials the chicks will subsequently follow the conditioned stimulus up and down the runway. Schaefer and Hess (1959) found a strong correlation between the colour of objects used for imprinting tests and effectiveness in eliciting the following reaction. The distance followed was greater in the red and blue and less in the intermediate yellow range of the spectrum. Whether both these reactions, to colour and to flicker, can be explained in terms of retinal sensitivity alone is a question for future work to decide. (See also F. V.

Smith, 1960.) The learning involved in the following response itself becomes more detailed with practice, just as does any other learning. In species where the young are pecked by other adults individual characteristics must obviously be learned very rapidly.

The generality of the process is still more astonishing in those cases in which the bird becomes imprinted to human beings, and yet even here attention is directed not so much to individual characteristics of the human being as to the general category of humans. Lorenz gives particular examples of this with a Jackdaw.

Lorenz also had a Budgerigar which was taken from its nest at a week old and reared in isolation in an opaque container. Budgerigars treated in this way will adopt dummies or models as companions, and these need not resemble the species at all closely. Indeed, Lorenz succeeded in inducing his Budgerigar to accept in lieu of a companion a swinging pingpong ball to which the bird performed the caressing movements so characteristic of Budgerigars, behaving all the time as if the ball were the head of a companion bird. If the ball was fastened at too low a level above the perch, the bird was much inconvenienced, since the ball was too low for the bird to carry out its display adequately. Although it is true that this bird was not reared from the egg by hand, the accounts of these experiments are very interesting in that they do show the extreme generalisation of the pattern to which the bird responds, and suggest that this is divided into 'head and body' in contrast to the Grey-lag Goose, which shows no such distinction. In the Corvidæ the inborn flight companion (e.g. Jackdaw) is more restricted than it is in either the geese or the Budgerigars, and consequently imprinting is confined within rather narrower limits. A human being cannot satisfactorily fulfil the requirements of the Jackdaw in this respect because he lacks too many characteristics, e.g. ability to fly, the black colour and perhaps also the general form. In some respects the best subjects for imprinting studies are obviously species in which the young show a well-developed following response at an early age, and intensive work, using models, with various species of ducks and with Moorhens and Coots is now being carried on by a number of workers. In the two latter species (Hinde, Thorpe and Vince, 1956) following is its own reward, and food or 'brooding' reinforcement is unnecessary for the establishment of the following response to a particular object. But following must include perception of the familiar object; the proprioceptive stimuli resulting from locomotion are insufficient. In other words, following is reinforced by the continued proximity of the familiar moving object.

In ducks it appeared from Lorenz's experiments that the quacking of the mother is an important part of the parent pattern, and that if the sound produced is satisfactory many other shortcomings in the foster-parent will be overlooked; but this conclusion now requires modification. Fabricius (1951a), working with young Tufted Duck, Eider and Shoveler, found that neither the shape nor movement of the whole, nor —within very wide limits—the size of the model were of any appreciable importance for the first release of the following response. Nor (contrary to Lorenz's findings) did the quack of the natural parent appear to be necessary, for a large variety of simple rhythmically repeated sounds were found to assist in releasing the response, though none of them was essential to the process. Fabricius concludes that the first release is brought about by a series of extremely simple sign-stimuli constituting an innate

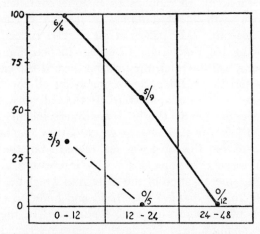

Fig. 65—Diagram to show the decrease with age in the following reaction of young Tufted Ducks when confronted with a human being for the first time.
Vertical scale: The number of positively reacting birds expressed as a percentage of the whole number of birds studied in each age class.
Horizontal scale: The age of the birds in hours.
The continuous line indicates the readiness to react when the birds see the experimenter and at the same time hear a calling note. The broken line indicates the readiness to react when the birds see the experimenter but do not hear any calling note. In the fractions the numerator indicates—for each age class—the number of birds showing a positive reaction and the denominator the whole number of birds studied in respect of each of the two stimulus situations. (After Fabricius, 1951.)

releasive mechanism, which is rapidly developed and 'imprinted' by experience of following so that the response becomes specific to the species pattern concerned. As the young birds grew, the following response tended to diminish (Fig. 65). In all these three species it was found that imprinting to one of the duck species or to man restricted the animal's following response to that species and precluded the following of any other. There was an apparently innate response to the distress 'peeping' of other young ducks, both of the same and of other species. This also was subject to reinforcement by an imprinting experience, so that ducklings soon came to prefer to join individuals of their own brood (natural or artificial) rather than others. Individual recognition of the human companion seemed also to be based mainly upon auditory rather than visual cues. Boyd (1955) has carried out similar work with Mallard at the Severn Wildfowl Trust's site, but with somewhat different results. He found that objects of a very great size range would be followed— a model of match-box size constituting the lower limit, objects below this size often being treated as potential food. Although, like the species investigated by Fabricius, the first model followed tends to be preferred, the Mallard is not nearly so specific in its subsequent responses (i.e. is not so readily imprinted), for following one model does not prevent the later following of other models, and some of the birds which had been trained on duck models afterwards turned out to have a preference for man, though they had never previously had opportunity to follow man. This, however, may have been due to conditioning in the food-box when being hand-fed. Not all young Mallard would follow models, but many would follow female Mallard within the first ten days of life though if their first experience was deayed too long they might show fear of the female. It was concluded that the female Mallard is a particularly rich model, but that it does not offer any specific or unique constellation of stimuli. Ramsay and Hess (1954) have obtained good responses to motionless models which made a sound but not to those which were both still and silent. There is evidence that the critical factor is the distance travelled (or the energy expended) by the following bird.

The experiments with Moorhen and Coot at the Madingley Ornithological Field Station of Cambridge University (Hinde, Thorpe and Vince, 1956) give results similar to those with ducklings with regard to the extremely general and simple nature of the first stimuli required and the lack of specificity in or need for auditory stimuli. The present evidence, however, shows these species to be less readily restricted to the following of one model type, and often more persistent in following once they have developed the response than is even the Mallard. Not all individual Moorhens or Coots can be induced to follow, but when a Moorhen does show a following tendency it can, for instance, be trained to follow three different models equally well by being given one run on each model per day. Their lack of selectivity is such that they will follow a model which is as different from the model on which they have been trained as a yellow football bladder is from a black wooden model of a moorhen, as a 6 by 2 by 2 foot canvas-covered 'hide' is from a man, or as a white box is from a similar black one. Such extreme 'generalisation' could be obtained with birds as young as three days old and as old as sixty days. There is thus, in this species, *no evidence for the existence of a sensitive period for imprinting of the following response on a* PARTICULAR *model.* However,

Moorhens which were not tested in the experimental set-up for their first few days of life became rather wild and fled when models were presented later. This habituation to the circumstances of the experiment undoubtedly plays an important part in the establishment of the following response. With Coots between twenty and sixty days old the behaviour can be extraordinarily persistent, and in some individuals tested there was no observable waning of the following response when forty or more runs with a familiar model were given at one-minute intervals until physical fatigue intervened. One bird was tested for over one hundred runs at one-minute intervals, still without showing any waning. In all these cases particular care was taken that no reward, such as brooding or food, should be associated with the following response, and indeed the termination of each run (e.g. chasing, catching and picking up with the legs dangling—all of them obviously unpleasant to the birds) was such as to provide negative rather than positive reinforcement. It would not be easy to find a more striking example than this of non-reward learning. But however intense the following responses of these birds during their following period, sooner or later the behaviour begins to wane, and by the end of the juvenile phase it is lost altogether. We have not been able to show any trace, in these species, of the effect being carried over into adult life.

Much of the recent experimental work on imprinting can be found in review articles by Hess (1959), Thorpe (1959, 1961e), Moltz (1960), Hinde (1961a). It is clear from the work of Weidman (1958) that the explanation advanced for the waning of the sensitive period in Coots and Moorhens cannot apply to all species, for instance ducks and geese (see also Jaynes, 1957). In these species it seems certain that there is an internally controlled waning of the tendency to follow independently of the development of fear responses. Sluckin and Salzen (1961) have also shown with the domestic chick that imprinting ends as the result of its own action rather than through the effects of fear. Hess and Schaefer (1959) (ref. in Hess, 1959) have pointed out that innate behaviour patterns can serve as indicators of the existence and duration of the critical period. Thus the frequency of emission of distress and contentment notes and the waxing and waning of the tendency to approach and fixate the stimulus at different ages is highly significant. These criteria agree well with the results of following experiments showing that in ducklings the peak of responsiveness is reached at about 13 hours and drops steeply to disappear completely at about 30 hours. The curve for chicks is similar in that the peak occurs at the same time. Chicks on the whole are less imprintable: 50 per cent. of positive responses as against 80 per cent. in ducklings, and up to 30 per cent. of the chicks may still be imprintable at the twenty-fifth hour. (See Fig.66.) It has been found that learning of visual discrimination problems is in many, if not most, animals quicker and more stable when practice trials are spaced by interspersing rest periods between trials than when practice trials are massed by omitting such intervening rest periods. In imprinting studies, however, massed practice is more effective than spaced practice, and this is consonant with the fact that the strength of an imprinting experience is often directly related to the amount of effort which the young birds exert in following. Another difference between imprinting and discrimination learning is that in the latter, recency of experience is maximally effective whereas in imprinting primacy of experience

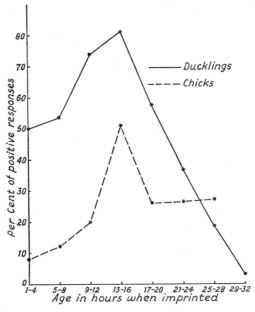

Fig. 66—Percentage of positive responses made by ducklings and chicks in test series. After Ramsay and Hess, 1954. (Compare with those for young ducks shown in Fig. 65.)

is the most important factor. Hess (1959) has also recorded that administration of punishment or painful stimulation increases the effectiveness of the imprinting experience whereas similar negative reinforcement causes avoidance in visual discrimination learning.

As we have seen with the experiments with Moorhens and Coots, development of a fear response makes imprinting impossible. This fact, which has also been demonstrated in chicks (although it is not the only means by which a sensitive period comes to its close), suggested a new means of testing the nature of the sensitive period, namely to reduce the emotional response by means of a tranquillising drug (Hess, 1959). Two drugs have been used, meprobamate and chlorpromazine, the subjects in each case being ducklings. In each case it was found that a substantial reduction in overt fear responses was produced as a result of the dosage employed. It was found that meprobamate, although it reduces fear, also makes imprinting almost impossible although it does not interfere with the effects of imprinting. Chlorpromazine allows a high degree of imprint-ing under all conditions and the action of the two drugs is interpreted as follows: It is a reasonable assumption that both meprobamate and chlor-promazine reduce metabolism, and it seems that this slowing of meta-bolism stretches out the imprinting or sensitive period. This did not occur when nembutal or distilled water were used as controls. It may also be that the action of meprobamate in preventing imprinting for a certain period after dosage is because the drug is a muscle relaxant which depresses the muscular tension or other afferent consequences of activity and thus nullifies the effectiveness of the imprinting experience by reducing the amount of effort employed in following. Since chlorpromazine is not a muscle relaxant and does not produce these particular effects, the explana-tion seems reasonably probable. Hess (1959) reports some preliminary work on the effect of cerebral lesions on imprinting but the effects as yet are too indefinite to merit detailed discussion. Preliminary attempts by the same author to breed different genetic strains of imprintable and non-imprintable ducklings and chickens similarly gave promising indications of results, but at the time of writing have not reached the stage at which they can be discussed here.

Many workers have noted that if young birds are kept together in groups they are harder to imprint than if they are kept singly. The obvious explanation of this is that the young birds become imprinted to one another. Guiton (1959) has demonstrated that this is so in the case of domestic chicks and that socially reared birds become imprinted to one another with the result that they will not respond to a moving box, whereas the controls do so.

The characteristics and peculiarities of imprinting are sometimes strik-ingly displayed where the process is imperfect in some way, or has been broken off or interfered with at the critical stage. A number of observa-tions suggest that, with some species, once imprinting to the 'right' object is prevented, the behaviour pattern is liable to be more or less disrupted, with the result that the various mating and social reactions may become attached to almost any object except the correct one. Räber (1948) has described in detail the behaviour of a domesticated turkey-cock which was hand-reared and during the first twelve months of its life had never been together with animals of its own species. This bird, when under the influence of the mating drive, responded to the appearance of any man by the usual courtship and mating activities, which, of course, are usually directed towards members of its own species. At the appearance of any woman, however, it reacted by fighting or retreating, as he would normally have done to rivals of the same sex. He never displayed to a turkey-hen although, strangely enough, he would tread them when in the appropriate position. It appeared on analysis that this bird had 'two different patterns of females.' The courtship display was evoked by a man or by a human dummy without any hanging or moving objects attached. This response had apparently been imprinted. The actions of copulation were induced by any object of the size of the hen on the ground. This pattern seemed to be innate. When the human dummy or a man or a turkey-hen had any loosely dangling and moving objects, e.g. handkerchiefs or folds of clothes which were in range of vision, he—according to his mood at that moment—either fought against or retreated from them as from rivals of the same sex. It was as if these objects emitted stimuli corresponding to an innate pattern of the rival of his own sex, since the response was the same whether the hangings were attached to human or to turkey-cock dummies. It is suggested that the response to 'something hanging' might be appropriate to the wattles or hanging wings of the rival male, or perhaps resemble an adversary jumping up before starting a fight. These various possibilities were not investigated.

Another example of this disjunction of the behaviour patterns is supplied by observations (personal communication) of Mr Peter Scott on a Lesser White-fronted Goose which was obtained from Lapland in 1947. On being released after its journey it remained for a long time very closely attached to the box in which it had travelled. When this fixation abated to some extent, it then showed intense 'imprinting' to one of the assistant keepers, following him about the whole time but paying no attention whatever to other human beings. At the time I saw this bird, in April 1949, it was beginning slowly to transfer its attentions from this particular keeper to Mr Scott himself.[1] Another curious case of attachment to a box in which a captive bird had travelled was supplied by another bird of Mr Scott's—a Blue Snow gander which had never bred. On release, the bird defended its box against all attackers, and went through all the actions of courting towards it, even when its position was changed and it was covered with a black tarpaulin. Mr Scott has kindly given me the following details, which have been amplified by the previous owner, Col. W. V. L. Lumsden, in correspondence. The bird had been reared under a hen in a coop with another gander and, although free to roam with other geese, he always preferred the company of hens and became somewhat of a nuisance, chasing them and even waiting outside a henhouse— when he plucked feathers from them—and if he could get inside he pushed them off their nests. In both these instances, therefore, it seems as if the fixation to the foster-parent may have become transformed to the rearing-house or some crate or box resembling it. Col. Lumsden adds:

[1] Steven (1955) reports that a Lesser White-fronted Goose caught as a gosling in Norway between 7 and 14 days old soon transferred its following response to man and became habituated to him even though it had presumably had the usual opportunity as a wild bird to become imprinted to its own species. Since transference to the Edinburgh Zoological Gardens it has remained attached to man.

'Recently I had a Barnacle gander, reared under a hen, which took up with a Bantam cock and never left him, so eventually I killed the cock, but even then the gander pursued other hens, but since he has been shut up with his own species he has become normal. Some ducks I reared one year became so attracted to their foster-mother, a hen, that they walked up and down their pen until exhausted and refused to eat till the hen was returned, and later any hen produced the same effect; but eventually they became normal.'

There are a number of other instances on record of attachments to inanimate objects (e.g. Ramsay, 1951, for Canada Geese and Muscovy Ducks)—some of them highly bizarre and persistent and apparently resulting from the loss of a mate; as when a Crested Crane became attached to an iron bell, the sound of which was said to resemble a crane's call (H. M. Scott, 1952), and as in the case of a gander's alleged seven-year fixation to an oil-drum! Although the main facts in some such rare examples seem well enough attested, they must await some critical experimental study before any valid interpretation of them can be made.

Where a single bird is adopted and consistently and continuously cared for by a single human being (as in the striking case of a House Sparrow closely petted for over twelve and a half years; Girdlestone, 1953), it may become completely attached to its owner who serves as a substitute for *all* the social responses throughout life. In such circumstances, of course, any imprinting effect is reinforced and submerged by every type of reinforcement and every kind of learning. Where the bird is one of a group and where contact is allowed with wild members of the species, a weakening of the effect is to be expected—as was observed by Shelley (1935) in his very interesting account of the taming of young Marsh Hawks. But there are many cases in which imprinting to a wrong species comes about much more readily than Lorenz's original concept would account for, even to a species rarely seen in the neighbourhood and even if this species has never stood in the parent-companion relationship to it. Thus Goodwin (1948a) records imprinting of Turtle Doves to Wood Pigeon, Wood Pigeon to domestic pigeon, domestic pigeon to Stock Dove and Magpie to domestic pigeon; while he gives a number of other instances of fixation of various species on himself or on their own parent female. Cushing (1941) quotes similar cases from Whitman and other sources.[1] It seems that in many of these cases there was nothing like the close and restricted association of the bird with the adopted companion in its earliest days, which Lorenz and Heinroth described as an essential of imprinting in geese. Possibly in every instance there had been interfer-

---

[1] For records of adoption of 'extraneous' young birds, see Armstrong (1955) for the Wren, Stoddard (1931) for the Bob-white, Davis (1942) for *Crotophaga* and Ritter (1938) for the California Woodpecker.

ence with the normal parent-child relationships in the earliest days, which had its effect on the later behaviour. This may perhaps account for a number of remarkable cases of association between different species which are on record. I am indebted to Mr R. S. R. Fitter for giving me a number of interesting notes which include four cases of Budgerigars associating wth flocks of House Sparrows, a Grey Parakeet with Wood Pigeons, an African Grey Parrot and a White Cockatoo with Rooks. These latter records are particularly remarkable in that the African Grey Parrot accompanied the Rooks for years at the rookery in the gardens of the Lewisham Infirmary (Williamson, 1922), and the Rooks seemed to welcome its presence. The White Cockatoo was a denizen of Wimbledon Common (Johnson, 1930, p. 105)—'where it seemed to have a personal bodyguard of three rooks which accompanied it wherever it went.' The association between different species of ducks in St. James's Park, London, is perhaps less surprising. There are a number of these instances, which all concern Tufted Ducks' 'friendships' with Mallards. Of course these casual records, interesting and suggestive though they be, really tell us little. In none of such cases do we know the origin of the behaviour, nor whether only one or all the social behaviour patterns were involved. Before closing this section on abnormal social attachments, it should be worth recording that although something like imprinting is known in the Snipe (Wormald, unpublished), the process seems to be absent in at least some waders, such as the Curlew and Godwit, Lapwing and Redshank (Thorpe, unpublished), where the parent-following response is poorly developed and where brood cohesion and the response of freezing at the parent's warning call are of greater importance in early life. It is also obviously absent, or at least incomplete and modified, in parasitic species.

Certain of the facts given in the previous section, on territory recognition, suggest that recognition of territory is in some cases a rapid and special kind of learning which takes place in a very short space of time at a particular period in the life-cycle, and which has its effect on many subsequent acts and activities of the bird concerned. In fact, in many respects the learning of the territory suggests a kind of imprinting process. Certainly its tenacity, whether inborn or learned, is a striking feature in a great many species (see von Haartmann, 1949. It has been suggested (Thorpe, 1944) that the concept of imprinting may be extended to cover the possibility of attachment not merely to a fellow-member of the species but to the type of immediate environment first perceived by a newly emerged organism, so that this becomes the accepted home. Fabricius (1951*a*) has given some beautiful examples of the apparently inborn responses of newly hatched ducklings (Tufted, Shoveler, Eider) to the features of landscape characteristic of the normal environment of each species. It seems likely that these preferences are based on an extremely simple innate releasive mechanism, which is rapidly built up by imprinting processes exactly as is the parent response. But no further experimental analysis of this most important matter has yet been attempted. If this interpretation should prove correct, then we have a further link between imprinting and latent learning. Moreover, this kind of imprinting might have important effects in perpetuating local traditions of behaviour, and perhaps even initiating an evolutionary divergence (Thorpe, 1945b; Peitzmeier, 1939). But these are as yet only suggestions, raising a host of evolutionary problems for further experimental study (Simpson, 1953). For an extensive review of these and various cognate problems, see Hinde (1959).

We have already dealt with the imitation of entirely alien songs and notes by birds, including the copying of noises of inanimate origin and of the human voice, and have suggested that some few of these examples are akin to play and some perhaps imply imitation in its full psychological sense. We now come to discuss the process, resembling imprinting in at least some respects, whereby birds tend to restrict their vocal imitation either to their own species or to a species with which they have been closely associated for a long period. We shall also consider examples of 'free invention' by isolated birds, where the sound produced bears no apparent relation to anything that has been heard. Some of these examples grade into those discussed above, but the imprinting-like restriction provides a useful if provisional line of separation.

The call notes of a great many birds seem to be entirely inborn. The careful work of Schjelderup-Ebbe (1923) shows that the female chicks of the domestic fowl produce all their notes innately, and contact with adult hens does not help, and may actually hinder, their vocal development, perhaps through parental despotism. In contrast, the crowing of cockerels is hastened and assisted by parental example. Promptoff and Lukina (1945) claim, wrongly it seems, that most of the twenty different call notes of the Great Tit have to be learnt, and Goethe (1954) has produced evidence that the 'ag-ag-ag' call of the Herring Gull is inborn, whereas the 'kiau' or 'miau' call has to be learnt. The origin, function and development of call notes in birds is dealt with by Thorpe (1961d, see especially Chapter II). Probably almost the whole of the full song is fixed genetically in some passerine species. This appears to be true of Mistle Thrush, Chiffchaff, Grasshopper Warbler and Treecreeper (Stadler, 1929). Wren (Armstrong, 1955) and Corn Bunting (Thorpe, unpublished). To this list H. Poulsen (1951) contributes Wood Warbler, Tree Pipit and Reed Bunting.

Although ever since the time of Ward (1714), and the incomparable Baron von Pernau (1716, see Stresemann, 1947, Godman, 1954, and Thorpe, 1955), much was known about the learning of songs by birds, it was Daines Barrington (1773), the correspondent of Gilbert White, who was the real pioneer in the study of the modification of bird song by experience; but his work lay unregarded for over a century, and it was Scott in U.S.A. who was the first modern investigator. He showed that young Baltimore Orioles reared in isolation develop a song altogether different from the normal, and retain it for life. Other Baltimore Orioles reared with them learned this song, which was described as being like that of a House Wren but containing the characteristic Oriole 'rattle,' and sang it exclusively even after the death of their foster-parents (Scott, 1901). Scott also describes (1904*a*, 1904*d*) an isolated Bobolink which produced a quite unrecognisable song, and two male Rose-breasted Grosbeaks, both of which sang the song of Hardwick's Bulbul, to which they had been exposed constantly from an adjacent cage for a period of nine months. They 'inherited their call notes of both pleasure and fear,' but all else was learned. Altogether Scott (1902*a* and *b*, 1904*b* and *c*) hand-reared seventy-eight individuals of sixteen species of passerine birds, which were kept in roomy aviaries where they could hear the various songs of wild birds out of doors. None of these birds sang normal songs. The American Robins sang 'inverted songs,' quite unlike the normal songs of wild birds, while the other species mimicked in greater or lesser degree.

It is said (Huxley, 1942, p. 305) that young Canaries allowed only to hear the song of the Nightingale on gramophone records will develop a song intermediate between that of the Canary and the Nightingale, and that a new 'strain' can thus be produced, but the whole question of Canary song is beset with contradictions. Thus canary fanciers value the finest singers very highly as 'schoolmaster canaries' for teaching the other birds; yet Metfessel (1935) says that the Roller Canary song can be produced without learning from other birds. Perhaps the 'schoolmasters' stimulate competition and thus develop the capacity to the fullest, possibly only the finer touches being the result of imitation.

Geographical variations in song are well known among wild birds, (e.g. Sick, 1939; Mayr, 1942; Benson, 1948), and it seems likely, e.g. with the Chaffinch (Promptoff, 1930, Marler, 1952), that these are based on a learned tradition and are not inherited. Similarly the White-crowned Sparrow in California has different 'community song patterns' in different regions, which are probably of the same phenotypic nature (Peterson, 1941). O. Heinroth (1924) and O. and M. Heinroth (1924–6) recorded, on the basis of desultory rearing experiments, that Whitethroat, Meadow Pipit, Greenfinch and Chaffinch all have to learn their songs. They found that the young males of these species, if kept in isolation, produced quite abnormal songs, e.g. untaught Meadow Pipits sang like Serin Finches and isolated Chaffinches like Lesser Whitethroats. Two species in which song is not innate will, if kept together, learn from each other. Thus a

Whitethroat[1] and Linnet reared together both had an identical song resembling a mixture of Robin and Skylark. But there seems to be a pre-disposition to learn the normal song of the species rather than a strange one. Thus Heinroth describes a Nightingale which mimicked songs of various species with which it had been reared, even reproducing the song of a Blackcap heard for only one week six or eight months before, but which rapidly learnt its normal song on hearing it next year. Other species will, if isolated, produce an imperfect version of the normal song and will learn more or less thoroughly from other species. Thus untaught Yellow Buntings fail to develop the complete natural phrasing; one kept with a Linnet developed a linnet-like song, and there is a similar record for Robin and Blackcap. The same applies to a Robin with a Nightingale (Barrington, 1773) and also a House Sparrow with a Canary (Conradi, 1905), but in this latter case, too, the calls of adult Sparrows were quickly preferred by the young when they experienced them later, although their chirps were always pleasanter to the ear than those of normal Sparrows. When these birds were again returned to Canary companionship after a lapse of eight months, the Canary song was regained completely. It is claimed that the Song Thrush's song is largely innate, but can be slightly modified by learning, while the Skylark's song is almost wholly learnt. But of course the fact that a bird produces an abnormal song under ab-normal conditions does not necessarily imply that the normal song is learnt. The present state of knowledge concerning subspecific and geographical differences in bird vocalisation has been assessed by Thorpe (1961d, see especially Chapter VI). See Plates VI–IX for sound spectrograms.

The Chaffinch and also the Linnet and Yellow Bunting (Poulsen, 1951, 1954) (and probably many other species) are of particular interest in that while the basic pattern of the song is innate, all the finer detail and much of the pitch and rhythm have to be acquired by learning. The Chaffinch, which is a peculiarly suitable species for investigation, has been studied by Thorpe (1954, 1958a and b).

Until recently it was scarcely possible to make much further progress with the problem of song learning. Bird songs, like most other animal sounds, are difficult to describe in words, and even the most musical find it difficult to remember minute details of song without the aid of a suit-able notation, so the dangers of subjective interpretation are always serious. But even with a satisfactory system of notation there still remains the primary difficulty of perceiving accurately, by the naked ear, elaborate sound patterns of high frequency, high speed and rapid modulation. All this was changed, however, by the development on the one hand of

---

[1] But compare Sauer (1954), who found that in Whitethroats reared from the egg in a sound-proof room not only all the twenty-five call notes but all the elements of the full song, except one 'trill,' were fully inborn.

methods of high-fidelity 'electrical recording' on disc and of magnetic recording on tape, and on the other hand by the invention of the sound spectrograph, now known commercially as the 'Sonograph.' This latter instrument automatically provides a graphic analysis of complex sound signals that vary with time.

From this graphic representation, frequency, amplitude and duration can be determined with sufficient accuracy, and, moreover, the sound spectrogram can with practice be recognised and interpreted as a 'picture' of the sounds. It thus supplies a form of notation as well as a method of precise measurement. So it is that whereas vocalisations were formerly the most difficult of all releasers to investigate precisely, they have now become far more readily amenable to analysis than are many patterns of visual or olfactory stimulation.

The normal Chaffinch song, which is both a territorial proclamation and a stimulus to the female, consists of three phrases (Plate VI). Phrase 1 consists of from four to fourteen notes, usually somewhat *crescendo*, and normally with a gradual or step-wise decrease of mean frequency. This is followed by phrase 2, which is usually but not always distinct, and is made up of a series of two to eight notes. These notes are of fairly constant frequency, lower than that of phrase 1. The song concludes with phrase 3, consisting of from one to five notes (phrase 3A), together with a more or less complex terminal flourish (phrase 3B).

The first series of experiments consisted in taking birds which had been reared normally by their own parents and isolating them from their first September onwards in order to study the development of their songs in the ensuing spring. It was soon found that it is not necessary for such birds to see other singing Chaffinches in order to acquire normal songs. Even if such birds are caged with song birds of other species and so subject to an overwhelming 'barrage' of alien song, they can still attend to the normal song of their species, which they hear from the outside; and experimental birds failed to show any sign of acquiring the alien songs to which they were exposed. In this lack of general imitation, the Chaffinch is in marked contrast with the Bullfinch and the Greenfinch, which will learn complete songs from an alien species. In these experiments, seven Chaffinches were exposed to Canary song in the bird-room, three to Greenfinch song and two to Goldfinch song in aviaries, without any abnormality resulting. It seems likely from subsequent experiments in which hand-reared Chaffinches were exposed to synthetic songs constructed of (*a*) artificial sounds, (*b*) sounds of Chaffinch origin and (*c*) sounds of other species, played to them repeatedly by tape recorder, that Chaffinches have a largely innate appreciation of the tonal quality of vocalisations of their own species and so restrict their imitativeness to models which at least approximate to this tonal quality. The experiments on which this conclusion is based will be found described in detail in Thorpe (1961*d*). Although under certain circumstances some Chaffinches can be got to imitate sounds of markedly different vocal quality from birds of their own species, when they do this they rigorously restrict them to the sub-song and avoid contaminating the full song with these strange notes.

If Chaffinches, isolated as juveniles, are kept out of hearing of *all* bird song from September until the following May apart from being allowed to hear vocalisations of other Chaffinches treated in the same way, a clear difference is noticeable. Phrases 1 and 2 of the songs are practically normal, although they show much variation; but there is a slight tendency for the endings to be abnormal and to approximate to a community pattern. Twenty-seven birds were treated in this way and were isolated in six distinct groups. Plate VII shows the sound spectrograms of two genetically unrelated birds which have developed songs closely similar in ending as a result of being thus confined together. They are fairly representative of the general run of the experiments.

If we now repeat such an experiment, using instead birds which have been hand-reared and have thus been isolated from contact with experienced birds since the first few days of nestling life, we get a very different result. Phrases 1 and 2 are now often inseparable, and phrase 3A is always lacking. Phrase 3B is often lacking also, or at most is represented by a single 'squeak' of fairly steady pitch though often of considerable frequency-range. Each isolated community of such birds builds up, during the period February to April inclusive, an entirely individual but extremely uniform community pattern, the resemblances throughout the song being so close that it is often very difficult to distinguish the songs of the different members of the group one from another even when subjected to a detailed analysis by the sound spectrograph. Plates VIII and IX show the sound spectrograms of such groups of birds. The first pair were kept together in isolation during 1951–2, and had no contact with any other birds at all. The second pair were similarly isolated during 1952–3; while Plate IX shows the pattern produced by members of a group of five kept together in isolation during 1952–3. Inspection of the figures will show that the detailed resemblances are extraordinarily exact and concern all parts of the song, and the second of these song-types is quite unlike anything that has yet been recorded from the wild.

It appears, then, that the difference between the hand-reared birds and those which had a normal fledgling and early juvenile life, but which were isolated from September onwards, is explicable only on the assumption that some characteristics of the normal song have been learnt in the earliest youth, before the bird itself is able to produce any kind of full song. It seems that these birds have by their first September learnt that the song 'should' be in three phrases, and that the terminal phrase should

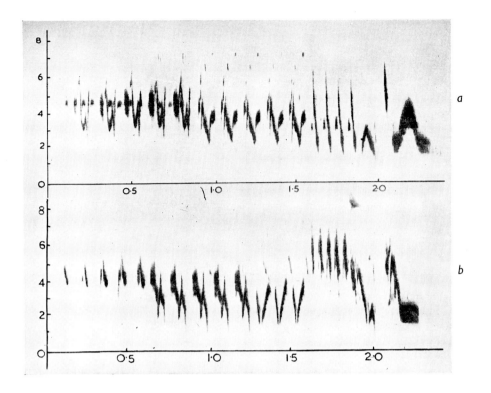

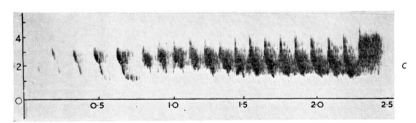

VI. Sound Spectrograms of Chaffinch Songs showing Learnt Elaboration superimposed on Basic Innate Pattern.

a & b: Normal full songs of wild-caught birds in aviaries showing the three phrases. (Recorded 1953.)

c: The basic innate song pattern. Full song of hand-reared bird visually and aurally isolated from all other Chaffinches. Note low frequency and extreme simplicity in comparison with the normal full songs. Vertical scale: frequency in kilocycles per second. Horizontal scale: time in seconds. Relative intensity is roughly indicated by depth of shading. (*a & b*, from Thorpe, 1954; *c*, from Thorpe, 1955).

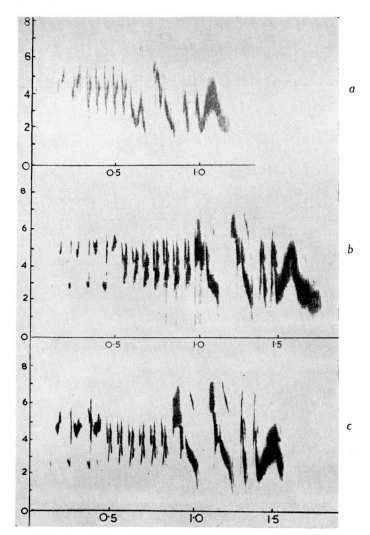

VII. SOUND SPECTROGRAMS SHOWING SONG-LEARNING
IN CHAFFINCH.

a & *b*: Songs of two 1951 Chaffinches (BY/RWB and
O/GY) reared by their own parents, but isolated as juveniles
of five months and allowed to hear only the members of their
own group of five birds identically treated during their
critical song-learning period in 1952. Note very close resemblance of latter parts of song.

c: Song of O/GY in 1953, to show fixity of song in second
year even though given opportunity to hear many varieties of
Chaffinch song in second season. (After Thorpe, 1954.) Scales
as in Plate VI.

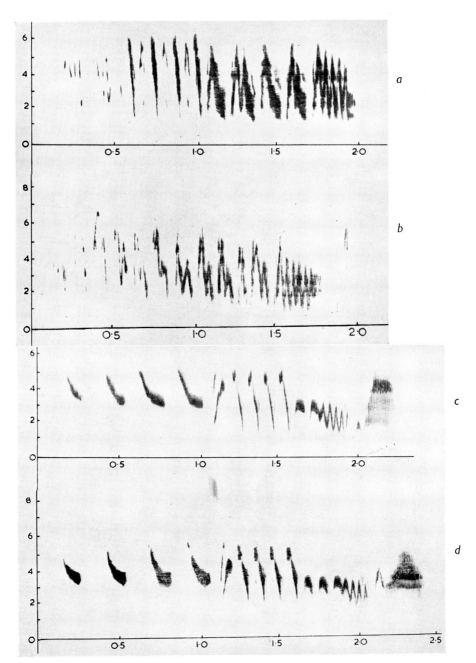

VIII. Sound Spectrograms showing Song-learning in Chaffinch.

a & b: Songs of two unrelated 1951 hand-reared Chaffinches (BY/PW and RWB/Y) isolated from about the fourth day of life, and during the critical learning period of their first season allowed to hear only each other's songs. (Recorded April 1952.) Note: Songs abnormal, relatively simple and closely similar. Phrase 3 lacking.

c & d: Songs of two unrelated hand-reared Chaffinches of 1952 (RWB/W and GY/Y) treated as those shown in Plate VI. (Recorded June 1953.) Note: Phrases 1 and 2 elaborate but highly abnormal. Phrase 3 extremely simple. The two songs are almost identical. Scales as in Plate VI. (After Thorpe, 1954.)

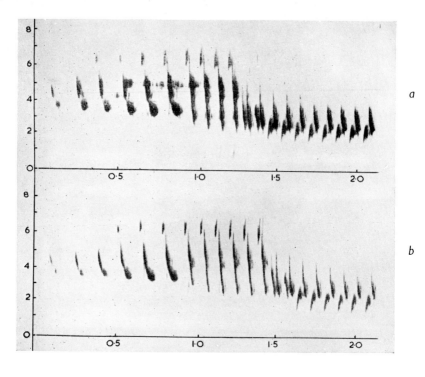

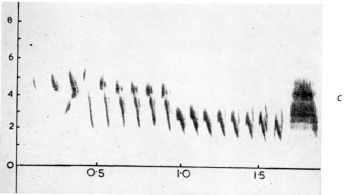

IX. Sound Spectrograms showing Song-learning in Chaffinch.

Three songs (*a, b,* & *c*), typical of those produced by all members of a group of five 1952 hand-reared Chaffinches, treated exactly as those shown in previous plate. (Recorded June 1953.) Note: Abnormal songs with phrase 3 lacking altogether or at most an extremely simple phrase 3*b*. Scales as in Plate VI. (Original.)

contain a more or less elaborate flourish. The details of this terminal phrase, with its flourish, are apparently not learnt then, but are worked out by competitive singing with other members of the group in the following spring.

The experiments with the hand-reared birds suggest that there is an inborn basis to the song but that it is extremely generalised. Innately these birds seem able to produce a song of about the normal length (2·3 seconds) and showing a tendency to *crescendo* accompanied by a fairly steady fall in mean frequency. There is no clear indication of any inborn division of the first part of the song into phrases 1 and 2, but there is a clear tendency in some birds to conclude the song with a single simple note of a higher pitch than the rest. They seem quite unable, by themselves, to produce anything more complex in the way of an ending, although, as Plate VIII, Figs. *c* and *d* show, they can learn, a process of mutual stimulation and imitation, to produce precisely controlled and highly elaborate song-patterns in what corresponds to phrase 2 of the normal song. (While the present evidence points to the conclusion that these features of the songs produced by hand-reared birds are inborn, we must remember that it has not yet been possible to rear such birds in isolation in the sound-proof room right from the egg. Until this has been done, the possibility cannot be ruled out that some details are learnt by the nestling in the first few days after hatching, although the relatively late development of the avian cochlea seems to render this unlikely. That Chaffinches which have been hand-reared can be taught full and elaborate end-phrases when kept during the following spring with older birds selected for their fine songs was known to the German bird fanciers well over a century ago.)

Study of sound-spectrograms makes it clear that it is the pattern of the song that is learnt and not its absolute pitch. One occasionally finds a bird practising a song ending *sotto voce* at a markedly different pitch from that in which it is rendered as part of the full song, and there are other examples of slight change in pitch with changes in intensity of motivation.

Once a song has been acquired and has been sung at full intensity for a period of a few days, it becomes fixed and subsequent changes are extremely slight. The individual songs of fifteen different birds have now been recorded and analysed in two or more subsequent years, and in nearly every case the differences between the first and second year are so minute as to be practically imperceptible to the naked ear, although they show up on the spectrograph records. Plate VII shows the songs of the same bird in 1952 and 1953. Thus, a bird in its second year may retain characteristic features in its song which involve a frequency change of a few hundred cycles or less and of only 10 to 20 milli-seconds' duration.

Such slight changes that do occur involve small differences of emphasis and occasionally the alteration of a phrase or perhaps the omission of the repeat of a phrase which was doubled in the former year. The sound spectrograph has, however, unexpectedly provided evidence that there is a slight but almost uniform tendency for the song to be shorter, by about o·1 to o·3 second, in the second year than in the first, and that there is also a slight tendency to increase the frequency-range in all phases of the song. There is as yet no clue why this should be so.

It is possible to delay the period of learning the song by keeping the birds together in aviaries under such conditions that they will not sing for the time being, although they see and hear normal birds singing. If such birds are transferred in the summer (that is, July) to a chamber where they are artificially subject first to a gradually decreasing day-length for about eight weeks, and then, in early October, to an increasing day-length, their gonad growth will again be stimulated and they will be brought into full song in the autumn (October–November). During this period they show evidence of acquiring the song-ending by learning in the same way that they would have done had they been allowed to sing in the spring. Birds can also be brought into song at any season of the year by injection with the hormone testosterone propionate. Songs induced by the light method or by hormone injection seem not to differ in any way from the normal. The subject of individual development of song in birds has been surveyed by Thorpe (1961d, see especially Chapter V).

The sub-song has already been alluded to. While it is undoubtedly to some extent a product of the lower degree of motivation, in that it occurs in the second and later years as well as the first, yet it is much more in evidence in the first, and seems to play some part in the process of learning the full song. When studied by the sound spectrograph it appears to have a much greater frequency-range than the true song, and one at least of the processes by which the sub-song is transformed into the true song consists of the gradual dropping out of the extreme frequencies which have no place in the latter. The whole matter of the sub-song and its differing types and functions in different species is one which requires much more investigation, and cannot be dealt with here (see Thorpe, 1961d, especially Chapters IV and V). Such sub-songs are seldom noticed in the wild because of their low intensity, and also because the bird often sings in very close cover instead of from a conspicuous song-post as when producing the true song. Nevertheless, though inconspicuous, the sub-song is, in the Chaffinch, a significant feature in the process of song acquisition.

These sub-songs give us, I think, a clue to some further aspects of the problem of vocal imitation in birds. It seems that imitation is not so much a true matching of vocal quality—I doubt whether any birds except mynahs and possibly the parrots, can learn a new tonal quality. But most imitative birds seem to have a big variety of noises already occurring in their sub-song or true song, and so they have merely to select from among these. Thus much song learning and vocal imitation is a learning to leave out what is not required and to fit these notes to the correct rhythm and fundamental frequency. And in this we see some similarity to human learning of a language. It is said that a baby will make every conceivable noise, and so will in due course produce the sounds fundamental to every language; but he retains and practises only those which he hears produced by his elders and soon forgets the rest.

But there remains the great problem of the biological function of the more extreme forms of vocal imitation. To be able to conform to a local pattern of song may well help a young Chaffinch in the struggle to establish itself, but what can the mimicry of a Starling or Mocking Bird avail its possessor? And when we come to consider the parrots, mynahs and budgerigars we are still more at a loss, for these species in the wild seem to make little or no use of their vocal powers beyond uttering the stereotyped cries and calls which help to co-ordinate the flock behaviour, etc.; yet surely we must assume that a considerable proportion of brain substance must be in some way reserved for speech control and so not available for other purposes. (Consideration of the mechanism and significance of vocal mimicry in birds will be found in Thorpe, 1959*a* and *b*, and also in Chapter VII of Thorpe, 1961*d*).

We must agree with Craig (1943) that true vocal imitation must be regarded as a late development from inherited song patterns, and is characteristic of the most highly evolved amongst the true song-birds. As Craig suggests (*loc. cit.*, pp. 120–2) and as other students of bird song have argued, the evidence for deliberate æsthetic improvement of song (as witness the repeated 'practice' of song phrases by particularly 'gifted' individuals) is by no means negligible,[1] and O. Koehler (1951) has discussed bird song as the first steps in both music and speech. This matter has also been considered by Lorenz in correspondence with Craig (see Craig, 1943, pp. 161–2) in connection with the evolution of tonal purity in bird voices. Lorenz had made the point that the purity of colour of some visual social releasers (as in the duck's speculum) could be of selective value since they have to be seen against a complex inanimate or non-animal background containing every shade of colour. Song, he argues, encounters virtually no non-biological competition, since there are practically no sounds of inanimate origin which are of such frequency or form as to compete. Here I think there is a flaw in the argu-

[1] There is evidence from more than one reliable field observer (personal communications) that the Blackbird introduces some elegant improvisations into its song later in the season when the peak of reproductive activity is passed. These 'improvements' are apparently not maintained in the following season. (See also Hall-Craggs, 1962. *Ibis* **104**: 277–300).

ment—for surely, once bird vocalisations have acquired a specific signal function a vigorous inter-specific competition for the available frequency range will be initiated. Thus purity of tone will at once become a potentially advantageous feature since, in common with the tendency to elaborate the *pattern* of the sounds, it will provide an additional dimension for distinctiveness, and should lead, like the international agreements on the allocation of radio-frequencies, to an economical and peaceable utilisation of the available spectrum.

But it is hard, nevertheless, to imagine any selective reason for the extreme purity of some bird notes since the releaser function appears in many cases to have been transcended—suggesting to both these authors that in the finer details of some songs we see the beginnings of true artistic creation. Perhaps tonal purity, 'inventiveness' and imitative ability are all further examples of pre-adaptation for apparently remote and unlikely contingencies, specialisation going in advance of immediate adaptive requirements, and as such are on a par with the astonishing number sense which can be developed in many species by careful training. Such a counting ability seems to offer even less practical advantage for a wild bird than the features we have been considering; all are as yet somewhat mysterious.

The above examples of song learning will have shown that on the perceptory side the process of recognising and accepting the specific song as henceforth the 'normal' for the individual (as distinct from the acquisition of the new motor habits involved in performing the song) seems to resemble the original examples of imprinting sufficiently closely to warrant considering them together. In the following experiments, following (i.e. the active maintenance of a special relation to a chosen object) turns out to be reinforcing. In song-learning experiments and in most examples of vocal imitation, it is the active matching of sound patterns which constitutes the reward. In both cases much of the adjustment of motor patterns involved could be a result of trial-and-error learning; though in those rare examples of vocal imitation where new phrases are produced only after long delay and apparently without practice some other method must obviously be operative.

Restriction to a particular period of life is, then, one of the most striking characteristics of typical imprinting, and it is of course common knowledge that in many cases attention—and, therefore, presumably much of the learning ability—is restricted by the boundaries of the territory. Here we will consider a few particular examples of the restriction, in space and time, of learning ability, for behaviour *other than* the following response and song.

Tinbergen (1936) carried out a number of experiments in which young Herring Gulls of two nests of the same age were interchanged, this being done when the chicks were at different ages. Herring Gulls have a number of instinctive behaviour patterns which result in brooding, feeding and protecting their young. If the young are exchanged when only a few days old they are accepted by their foster-parents without demur, but if the same experiment is attempted when the young are more than five days old they will not be accepted. This seems to imply that during the period of five days or so the parent Herring Gull is willing to adopt any young of the right age, but after that time they become conditioned to their own young, recognise them individually and will refuse to adopt the young of their neighbours. If these are forced upon them, they will not merely neglect but may even kill them. Much the same situation apparently holds with terns; and both with terns and gulls, and also with individual members of flocks of birds, such as the Corvidæ, mentioned above, the degree of individual recognition is indeed remarkable, the birds evidently being sensitive to minute details which are hard for the human eye to perceive. This is no doubt merely an instance of the fairly obvious fact that many species, including man, find it far easier to recognise individuals of their own kind, particularly of the young, than those of other species. However, here we are on debatable ground since with us, and perhaps with some animals, this difficulty in ability is perhaps not hereditary at all but entirely the result of experience. Experiments on recognition of individual foster-children and foster 'brothers and sisters' of different species in birds might provide results of great interest.

Spatial localisation of attention, probably instinctive, is very nicely shown by some observations of Sherman (1910) on the Northern Flicker. Sherman had Flickers nesting in a box in a barn in which peep-holes and a door were provided for the removal and examination of the nestlings. He says: 'Generally the sounds that aroused fear in this species were made by someone at the back of the nest, yet the bird always sought the hole and looked for the cause of alarm outside. Even after two seasons' experience of the five-fingered terror that entered the hand-hole so often and removed their young, they failed to learn to look for disturbance in that direction.' This is probably the general rule with birds nesting in cavities or building roofed nests (e.g. Armstrong, 1955—Wren; Lack—Swift, personal communication).

LEARNING ABILITIES OF DOUBTFUL SIGNIFICANCE

Individual Recognition

It is convenient to take first the recognition of individuals of the same species, starting with the mate. In some cases, for example the Heron, the recognition of the mate appears to be dependent upon and confined to the territory. This is particularly to be expected when there are elaborate nest-relief ceremonies which have to be performed before the presence of another bird is tolerated. Such ceremonies are presumably instinctive, and birds may find it difficult or impossible to adapt themselves to any changes in them. An example of this is the case of a pair of storks in Schönbrunn Zoo (Lorenz, 1935), the female of the pair being a White Stork and the male a Black Stork. These two species differ in the appeasing ceremony, the White Stork 'klappering' and the Black Stork using a wagging and nodding movement of the neck combined with a peculiar whispering. Yet although these birds had been paired for years, there were misunderstandings between them (owing to the difference between these ceremonies) which were never resolved. Similarly Lorenz (1935) records confusion when Rock Doves and Wood Pigeons are mated. It appears not unlikely, from the work of Lockley (1938) on the Manx Shearwater, that recognition of the breeding-territory, in this case the site of the burrow, is the basis for monogamy, and is the only way which the birds of a pair have of renewing contact at the beginning of each breeding season. It may be that this recognition is the basis of constancy in some other species, too.

But however important greeting ceremonies may be in the life of a species, it does not follow that they render personal recognition unnecessary, and the ability of some species to recognise their mates even at a considerable distance is remarkable. Evidence is becoming quite impressive that this is often based on the perception of vocal idiosyncrasies (recent references will be found in Thorpe, 1961d). But not infrequently other characteristics besides voice are used. Thus Song Sparrows (Nice, 1938) quickly get to know their mates personally, and also show personal recognition of the near neighbours in the breeding colony. Kirkman (1937) reports similarly for Black-headed Gulls, and Lack (1935) found much the same situation obtaining with the Crimson-crowned Bishop-bird. Personal recognition of the mates has also been described in swans by Heinroth, in the Flicker (Noble, 1936), and in the Jackdaw (Lorenz, 1938). Davis (1942) produced good evidence of individual recognition among Smooth-billed Anis. Lack (1939) found that Robins could distinguish their mates at a distance of 30 yards or more, even when partially screened by trees and bushes, and Armstrong (1947) quotes Hochbaum (1944) as recording that Pintails can identify one another 300 yards off. Guhl and Allee (1944) give some data on the length of time for which such learning of other individuals is retained. Morley (1942) showed that Marsh Tits can distinguish individuals in the flock at up to 60 yards' distance. The ability of the Herring Gull to recognise its mate among a great concourse of birds is quite extraordinary (Tinbergen, 1953, pp. 99–102). There is clear evidence that both voice and appearance are distinctive and can be used either separately or in combination. Thus a gull can recognise its mate in flight at 30 yards even though it is silent, and a sleeping gull will be awakened by the long-drawn 'mew' call of its mate although the same call uttered by any other bird leaves the sleeping bird unconcerned. Individual recognition may sometimes be upset if peculiarities of structure or pattern on which sex recognition is based are modified. Thus Noble (1936) found that if a 'moustache' characteristic of the male was attached to a female Flicker, her mate pursued her just as he would an intruding male, showing no sign of personal recognition. Cinat-Thompson (1926) showed that female Shell Parakeets with the cere painted blue are attacked by the males as strangers but are recognised again as soon as the voice is heard. However, in neither the Flickers nor the Parakeets is it certain whether normal sex recognition is due to instinct or to learning. Noble's experiments suggest that in the Flicker it is an instance of learning, but the evidence is not conclusive. Again, Schjelderup-Ebbe (1923) found with hens that fastening the comb on the wrong side of the head resulted in the bird no longer being recognised by her associates, and Guhl and Ortman (1953) found that visual patterns are important in the recognition of individuals among chickens. Hale (1956b) reports that in social interactions between breeds of chickens, behavioural responses are based on breed recognition rather than on individual recognition. Tindell and Craig (1959), however, claim that recognition in flocks of mixed breeds is mainly on an individual basis. Marks, Siegel and Kramer (1960) found that surgical removal of the wattles of chickens rendered the operated birds, when intermingled in large flocks with unoperated birds, subordinate to the latter. When flock organisation was fully established, the operated birds assumed a definite place in the peck order but in the lower social positions. Bennett (1939) found with Ring Doves that dyeing the breast feathers may cause fright or perplexity but does not interfere seriously with recognition; moreover, changes of contour had even less effect, the recognition being apparently based on behaviour. Nice (1943) gives references to examples of non-recognition of dyed birds among both the Noddy and Sooty Terns and Herring Gulls, but Butts (1927) noticed no effect when the birds of a number of species were dyed in the course of experiments on the feeding range of individuals. Lashley (1915) notes that Sooty Terns, while they will always reject a young Noddy, do not *normally* distinguish between their own young and others of the same species, though they will occasionally reject a changeling. Noddies, on the other hand, begin to recognise their young visually seven to eight days after hatching, and the chicks themselves by the tenth day show a familiarity with the nest region almost equal to that of adult birds. A pair of Coots with young less than two weeks old will feed, brood and may even adopt strange young birds similar in appearance to their own. But by the time their young are about a fortnight old they have learnt to recognise them individually, and henceforth no stranger, however similar, is tolerated (Alley and Boyd, 1950). Perhaps the most detailed evidence as to the part the territory and visual and auditory stimuli (including the mutual display) play in recognition is supplied by Sladen (1958) for the Adelie Penguin.

It should be pointed out that peck order has a close bearing on individual recognition. To discuss the whole subject of peck order would be out of place here. Suffice it to say that in some, probably most, cases this involves personal recognition. It is, however, very interesting that Lorenz (1931) has shown how a Jackdaw which is low in the peck order, immediately takes the same precedence as her mate, without any quarrelling, when she becomes mated to a bird high in the order. He had a flock of Jackdaws in which it appeared fairly certain that the birds could recognise personally every one of the twenty-five or more Jackdaws in the flock, and the same conclusion seems to apply to the social Crotophaginæ (Davis, 1942). Lorenz thinks that recognition in the case of his Jackdaws was dependent primarily on facial differences and perhaps to some extent on voices, and certainly in a number of cases which Lorenz cites (1935) it looks as if it is the head to which particular attention is paid. Nevertheless, it is quite obvious that the striking abilities of robins, gulls and terns mentioned above are the result not of the recognition of facial expression alone but much more probably of idiosyncrasies of posture and movement. Watson (1908) says that young Noddies and Sooties invariably recognise their own parents and never beg from strangers. Hinde (1952) has shown that the territories of Great Tits do not have such clearly defined borders as those of some other passerine birds, and in some cases at least there is a no-man's-land between territories where the birds from an adjacent territory are usually tolerated but strangers are not. This probably implies a learning to recognise the owner of the next territory— in a similar way to that in which recognition of other individuals must be learnt in a winter flock with a pecking hierarchy.

The abilities of birds to recognise minute differences in sound are well attested, as in the instance of the Herring Gull mentioned above. Brückner's work (1933) seems to show that the recognition by chicks of their mother is probably due to voice, although his results do not seem wholly consistent. It is known (Katz, 1937; Knecht, 1939; Thorpe, 1954) that some birds have something approaching an absolute sound-constancy perception. Skutch (1945) showed that a nesting Allied Woodhewer could distinguish the sound of its mate alighting on a tree trunk some yards away from the sound of other species alighting on it, but yet was apparently unable to distinguish visually between individuals of its own species. Buxton (1946, p. 162) describes how a Great Crested Grebe was capable of recognising the sound of his motor-boat and apparently distinguishing it from the sound of all others on the Broad. Voice qualities also apparently play their part in recognition among Night Herons (Lorenz, 1938).

The ability of parents to recognise their young, and young their parents has already been dealt with in a previous section, and enough has been said there to show how remarkable this is.

Not only are birds adept at recognising individuals of their own species: the ability may also extend to other species. There is not much information about the recognition of other individual animals, but there are a number of examples on record of personal recognition of human beings, and every aviary keeper could no doubt add more. Lorenz (personal communication) states that his geese undoubtedly recognise him by facial characteristics, and D. Goodwin tells me that he thinks his doves recognise him chiefly by face and voice. However, the doves were apt to be very readily upset, and might be thrown into panic, by a change of dress. He describes how two young Wood Pigeons, which normally were completely tame, were 'mad with fear' when he entered the aviary wearing a red tie instead of an open-necked shirt. Similarly two Jays were upset when they saw new clothes, but were ultimately reassured by the familiar voice and approached cautiously, looking at the face with a rather puzzled expression. Ash (1952) has described how a group of about six Blue Tits, which were persistent visitors to a ringing trap, consistently gave the usual alarm note to a particular person operating the trap whatever clothes he wore and whatever part of the wood he was in. The alarms of these six also alerted the other Blue Tits in the wood, which then took up the alarm but would not initiate it themselves. Dr and Mrs Heinroth had a Pheasant which courted Dr Heinroth but fought Mrs Heinroth. When they changed clothes, the bird started to attack the dress, looked up at the face, saw its mistake, and flew at Mrs Heinroth. Not only this: the bird still recognised its supposed enemy, Mrs Heinroth, when she and her sister changed clothes. Nice records how a pair of American Robins recognised her whatever her dress, again presumably by facial characteristics, and Poulsen (1944) describes the personal attachment of a Peregrine Falcon to him even though disguised. Kear (1960) describes how a hand-reared Hawfinch, imprinted to her, could recognise her in various clothes, with or without spectacles. Although Miss Kear's voice appeared important in prolonging display, it did not seem to be the basis of personal recognition. This Hawfinch, during the period she was attached to Miss Kear, attacked all other persons who came near her, directing the attack to the region between the eyes. Buxton (1946) states that Black-game at a Scottish lek learned to recognise the inhabitants of a nearby cottage and pay no attention to them, whereas they were immediately thrown into a state of alarm by the visit of strangers. He also instances a Montagu's Harrier which, he states, was able to recognise individual human beings after many months' absence, but no exact details are given in this case.

The response to eggs, however, is strikingly different from that to a fellow-member of the species. Thus Kirkman's (1937) work on the Black-headed Gull shows how careless this species is about its acceptance of egg substitutes, and this is confirmed for other *Larus* species by Goethe (1937) and Tinbergen (1936). But the latter's experiments do not provide proof that the Herring Gull is unable to distinguish the egg patterns; for the bird never normally sees its eggs out of the nest and so is never likely to abstract the perception of the eggs themselves (as opposed to the situation of egg-in-nest) as particularly important. The chicks run about and so the only constant patterns which they present are their own characteristics and naturally these are learnt by the parents. Noble and Lehrman (1940) found that the Laughing Gull can distinguish its own eggs from artificial eggs which resemble them closely in form and colour, but fails to distin- guish its own eggs from other Laughing Gulls' eggs which have a decidedly different colour tone and pattern. This suggests that response to eggs is partly determined by texture, but the matter has not been fully analysed. Marples and Marples (1934) and Tinbergen (1936) also provide evidence for terns. Allen and Mangles (1940) showed with the Black-crowned Night Heron that there was no ability to recognise the eggs. But this does *not* hold with Guillemots, and Nice (1943) gives a number of references to instances of recognition of individual eggs. Thus although Guillemots make no nests, it seems as if the striking variations in colour of the eggs have a biological function, and some experiments of Johnson (1941) show that eggs which become displaced are retrieved by the rightful owners and ignored by neighbours. Here there is evidently an ability to recognise the pattern. Brown (1939) claims that Lesser Black-backed Gulls were able to recognise their own nests even though they had been moved to a different site and the appearance substantially altered. His evidence for this seems reasonably satisfactory, but it is certainly surprising in view of Kirkman's observations on the Black-headed Gull.

With passerine birds the distinction is not so sharp. Rensch (1925) found when experimenting with *Sylvia, Carduelis, Emberiza* and *Trog-lodytes* that two species accepted the painted eggs while three other species deserted when painted eggs were put in the nest. Some reference has already been made to the recognition of members of a flock. It seems clear from the work of Baker (1942) that the evolution of resemblances between the egg of the Cuckoo and that of its foster-parent has been brought about by the ability of the fosterers to recognise and reject eggs which do not conform to those of a specific type; and a remarkably close adaptation, both in size and colour and pattern, has in this way been achieved. The Cow-bird, on the other hand, has developed no corresponding specialisa- tion (Friedmann, 1929), and while there are one or two species of North American passerines, e.g. the Yellow-breasted Chat, which reject eggs, most of the other usual hosts, covering three families, seem much more tolerant than do the corresponding Old World passerines. Rensch (1925) showed that *Sylvia borin* would accept eggs of *S. curruca* when the same number of these were put in the nest in place of its own, but that when the parent bird laid one more egg this was rejected, presumably because it was unlike the rest of the clutch.

The enormous variations in tameness between species, between individual members of the same species and between separate populations of the same species are known to everyone, and these facts pose some puzzling questions and have given rise to a good deal of discussion. In the previous section on latent learning the view was put forward that birds which have territorial sense and some homing ability would be expected to take some notice and possibly display caution towards strange objects which later might become built into the perceptual world as a normal part of the environment. Hebb (1946), in discussing the nature of fear in monkeys, describes not only this generalised curiosity but also a spontaneous fear of a great variety of strange objects, including fright reactions to the plaster model of a snake. In this last case the response was so intense as to suggest an inborn recognition. He notes also spontaneous fear of inert mutilated bodies, and there was little, if any, sign of a steady increase or decrease of fear to such objects as the experiments progressed. Hebb quotes Nissen as stating that young Chimpanzees kept blindfolded till four months did not show fear on the first sight of a human being. According to Kruger (see Katz, 1937, p. 42), children under about a year old who have never seen an animal show no trace of fear, but at the age of eleven to sixteen months differences in behaviour begin to show themselves, the majority of children at that age showing signs of spontaneous fear.

That there must exist in wild populations of birds an inherited wildness seems quite evident from the fine work of Leopold (1944) on the Turkey. This investigator found that it was extremely difficult to keep wild birds and breed them in captivity, and while the wild stock is consistently wild and practically untameable, hybrid stock can be tamed to a certain point, remaining almost exactly intermediate. Presumably in this case there has been a selection against wildness in captivity. Much the same situation seems to apply with regard to ducks. Phillips (1912) describes Mallard as normally wild but having the potentiality of becoming tame. The Eastern Black Duck, on the other hand, is extremely wild and very hard to rear and manage. His hybridisation experiments suggested that the wildness characteristic of the latter species is a dominant character, but this was not actually followed up. The conclusion from these experiments seems to be that both Black Duck and Mallard are equally wild in nature, but the latter's wildness is readily modifiable by experience, as when the eggs are placed under hens and the ducklings are reared by tame foster-parents. There is even some suggestion of a slight hereditary difference in wildness between the tame and wild English Mallards, but this has not been fully investigated.

The tameness of bird populations on oceanic islands is, of course, common knowledge, and there seems no reasonable doubt that in many cases this has a genetical basis. If there are no natural enemies, then the usual generalised caution will no longer be required and will tend to be lost from the genetical make-up. If natural enemies are few, then probably the birds will become instinctively attuned to those few and will still not need any great general caution, and, therefore, may still appear very tame on the appearance of human beings. Studnitz (1935) also gives some examples of geographical variations in tameness in European birds. Huxley (1948) cites the Falkland Island Goose as providing the best example of inherent genetic tameness. This species has remained tame even though suffering considerable persecution at the hands of man, although even here there is evidence that shooting has reduced the tameness to some extent. Reference to the extreme tameness of two Gough Island birds, the Rail (*Porphyriornis c. comeri*) and the Bunting (*Rowettia goughensis*) is given by Thorpe (1959*a*).

No doubt the presence or absence of ground predators has a good deal to do with generalised tameness, for it seems likely that, apart from the reaction to snakes, ground predators do not give rise to such specialised instinctive recognition mechanisms and fear responses as do aerial predators. This is shown very strikingly by some notes of Goodwin (1948*b*, also Huxley *et al.*, 1947–9) on the response of young doves to threat of attack. We can take it, then, that there is strong evidence for some genetical wildness and tameness, but obviously this carries us only a little way in accounting for the striking variations which are noticeable, and it is not likely to be the dominant factor in the situation except with bird populations that are almost completely isolated. It is, however, well known that there are great local variations in tameness between populations in the same continental area, and the next question is how these can be accounted for. First let it be said that there seems no satisfactory evidence for an inherent fear of the human species as such. Brown (1942) suggests that the fear of man is certainly not instinctive in young Song Thrushes, but that it is rapidly acquired soon after leaving the nest as a result of the behaviour of their parents, and the response to their alarm notes, this response normally being a firmly fixed, inherited reaction. This, I think, is the general opinion of those who have reared birds in captivity; but the facts are not adequate for a firm conclusion. Birds (e.g. Corn Buntings, Moorhens, Magpies and Partridges) that have been hand-reared and are fully tame often become wild later when they are less frequently and closely tended by man, even though they have no wild associates to teach them fear and alarm them by their calls. It is problematical whether this is evidence of maturation or enhancement of a specific inborn response, previously kept in abeyance by the positive reinforcement of regular feeding and tending, or whether it simply represents the general level of excitability to strange objects becoming apparent as positive reward conditioning wanes. Hartley (see also Simmons, 1952) suggests that the outline of head and shoulders—which, after all, has some similarity to the 'owl pattern'—is the significant releaser by which man is recognised as the most dangerous predator. This should be tested and compared in species which have a strong inborn response to owls and in those which have not. Kuhlemann (1939) records that Herring Gulls reared by Common Terns lack the usual timidity in the presence of man. Peitzmeier (1940) has put forward the interesting suggestion that although birds have no inborn fear of man, they become afraid of him because of his unpredictable actions in contrast to the stereotyped movement-patterns of animals. Animal behaviour, and particularly bird behaviour, is of a much more rigid and instinctive type and more predictable, and the birds thus feel more 'at home' with the instinctive movements of animals, but are uneasy in the presence of the unpredictable, non-instinctive movements of man, the whole behaviour of whom is so foreign to them.

If there is no inborn fear of the human species—which is, after all, very recent and, until recently, very rare—nevertheless there may be both general genetic wariness and a learned general wariness, and the question is, how is it that these get so readily overcome in some circumstances but not in others? It is obvious that there is individual taming by man, due to processes of habituation or to active association, as the result of some reward such as food being obtained. In the taming of wild birds to come to feed from the hand absolute daily regularity of feeding, time is an important factor for success. It is also noticeable that birds tend to be particularly afraid of flying towards a human face, and if the food is held a little to the side away from the face, the training is much easier; captive birds, on the contrary, which have experienced handling are thereafter apt to be particularly wary of the human hand (Ivor, 1944). Individual taming often takes a very long time indeed, and the production of tameness in adult finches to the point at which they will breed in aviaries may take as much as two years. Ivor (1944) gives an interesting account of the process of taming a number of species of passerines in captivity. It is the invariable experience of those who deal with birds that taming is much easier with the young bird, and this is of course exactly what we should expect—especially in view of what is now known about the process of imprinting. There is also no doubt a great deal of communal taming as distinct from individual taming. It is not often very clear what the explanation of this is, but the kind of general tameness of birds shown at outdoor restaurants, where Chaffinches will come readily to the tables, and in parks and public gardens where human beings keep mainly to the paths and leave the lawns undisturbed, suggests that this is not a matter of the tameness of individual birds but is a general increase of confidence among a flock. It is well known that birds do not take very long to learn the advantages provided by a sanctuary, and birds may be extremely tame in one situation and very wild in another. Kuhlmann (1909) has suggested that the process of taming, in fact, is one which is gradually progressing in all sorts of situations throughout the life of the animal, and that animals fear particular things not merely because of un- pleasant situations but because the taming process has never been com- pleted. Flock tameness is often well exemplified by wild birds which join the tame individuals on the lakes in the London parks. Katz provides various examples among ducks, and Mr Scott tells me of wild Pintails and Teal becoming rapidly very tame when they come down to the ponds of the Severn Wildfowl Trust and join the tame birds there.

As Lorenz (1935) points out, flock tameness may vary a great deal be- tween various species. The closer the flock structure, the more will the be- haviour of one particularly experienced bird or shy bird affect the whole. Thus with Jackdaws, groups of young birds without a leader tend to become panicky, this panic being, perhaps, an eruption of innate flight- behaviour. Whether this is so or not, one experienced bird will have a great effect on the attitude of the whole flock, and may be the means of forming and maintaining a sort of tradition of tameness in the colony. If the leader gives the warning, then the whole flock will respond. If the leader remains passive, the potential alarm in the other birds is suppressed. Thus although a shy young Jackdaw is incapable of frightening a flock and the young ones tend to be low in the hierarchy and so to conform to the tradition of tameness existing in the colony, one shy *old* bird will set the whole flock on the *qui vive*. Night Heron flocks, on the contrary, are more loosely organised, and the first reaction of herons to the precipitous flight of the one bird consists in 'safeguarding' by the other birds. They will then only take flight if they themselves have witnessed the cause of flight of the fellow-member of the flock. Lorenz says: 'A "wild" Night Heron which in 1934 was breeding with a tame female in my colony of Night Herons always was immensely frightened at my approach and immediately took to flight, whereupon the tame female members of the species began to display signs of fright and to safeguard themselves. But they were never induced to join in the flight. On the contrary, as soon as they had seen me they quiet- ened down to such an extent that it appeared as though they knew the strange heron had "merely" been frightened by me.' Lucanus (1911) tells of a '*Turdus musicus*' which was quite tame when its cage was in a familiar

room, and exceedingly wild, not even recognising its owner, when transferred to a new room; and we have had a number of examples at the Cambridge Sub-Department of Animal Behaviour of finches and buntings
which were completely tame in one cage but wild when moved to another.
In these instances 'tameness' is simply 'tameness-in-a-particular place.'

Besides tameness due to social facilitation, there may also be a true
imitation of tame individuals, but of this nothing precise can be said. It is
of course well known that birds may be very tame in one period of their
life-cycle and extremely wild in others. One of the best examples of this
is provided by the Eider Duck which, when her eggs are nearing the
point of hatching, can be stroked while she sits on the nest, and there are
innumerable cases of tight-sitting birds which could be lifted off the eggs
without taking fright. But directly such birds have left their eggs they are
wild again: suggesting that in these instances it is suppression of timidity
rather than 'tameness' which occurs.

Treuenfels (1937, 1940) has described how in the Wood Warbler man
and dog both elicit alarm during the nesting season but are ignored at other
times, and the situation here seems to be that anything that approaches
the nest during the nesting season is regarded as a potential nest enemy.
R. A. Hinde (personal communication) tells me that there is striking variation in the tameness of flocks of Great Tits according to whether they
are on the ground or in the trees, and that the general level of tameness
seems to be controlled by the frequency or intensity of alarm notes.

To sum up the whole subject of tameness we may say that genetic
tameness is undoubtedly a reality and that all gradations in intensity of
this must be expected, from the extreme tameness of the oceanic island
bird to the natural wildness of birds in Europe. There is as yet no convincing evidence of an inherited specific recognition of man as an enemy,
but there is evidence that the general tendency to wariness—especially
wariness of ground-living predators where these are prevalent—becomes
readily attached to man as a result of experience and the training of
parents. Such wariness may be overcome by habituation, association,
social facilitation and possibly true imitation.

'Alternative' Nesting Associations

It is well known that many species of birds, particularly in the
Tropics, nest in association with insects, spiders, more powerful birds or
with man; and that they apparently profit by the protection thus secured.
In Australia (Chisholm, 1952) five species of the Warbler genus *Gerygone*
seem deliberately to seek the neighbourhood of wasps' nests for nesting
and 'fraternise without friction,' and the South American Spinetail not
only builds its nest close to colonies of wasps but invariably attaches to
the nest a portion of a cast skin of a snake. But the most significant aspect

of some of this behaviour is its flexibility in the individual. Moreau (1942) has drawn attention to the psychological problems posed by these 'alternative' nesting associations. We cannot do better than quote his own summary of the situation:

'A striking feature is the extent to which the same species has been shown to adopt alternative devices for protecting its nest: for example, either associating with man or building over water; normally building over water but occasionally associating with wasps; associating either with man or with more powerful birds; either building alongside insects or adopting the nest of another bird whose architecture is more protective. (To alternative devices might be added the building among thorns, where the general nature of the vegetation is such that the use of a thorny site must imply choice.) In fact, among the Weavers seeking the protective associations it appears that most of them make use, to a greater or less extent, of an alternative. Perhaps the most notable example of this is provided by *Sitagra cucullatus,* in West Africa an associate of man and bigger birds, but in Haiti (where it must have been introduced in about the last 300 years) an associate of wasps (Myers, 1935).

'The alternation of devices must be taken into account in any attempt at a psychological evaluation of the habit of seeking protective associations. It becomes more difficult to reject the explanation that the protective association is sought by the more or less conscious choice of the individual bird. At the same time, such a choice might demand a power of observation and a degree of reasoning ability that many will be unwilling to concede, especially as it is not clear what chance a small bird associate of the aculeate Hymenoptera would have actually to observe their protective power in advance. It would be possible on our present information to put forward a hypothesis that within a species (or race) different strains existed, with inherited tendencies, e.g. one to seek wasps, another to build over water, and a third, *ex hypothesi,* a diminishing one, with no special protective device at all. Such a hypothesis would not, however, readily accommodate the case of *Sitagra cucullatus,* quoted above.' Hindwood (1955) regards the conclusion as inescapable 'that the purpose of such associations is a desire to be safeguarded from either mammals, reptiles or predatory birds.' He bases this on evidence gathered chiefly during the past thirty years or so but extending back for more than a century.

The Honey Guides (*Indicatoridæ*)

The behaviour of the Honey Guides has been the cause of so much speculation that the illuminating work of Friedmann (1955) requires special mention. They are Old World tropical picarine birds which 'guide' ratels, baboons and human beings to bees' nests, leading them on by agitated chatterings and flutterings and then sit silent and still in nearby cover until the 'ally' has opened the nest and made the contents available. Friedmann (1955) has shown that *Indicator* is a specialised wax-feeder with a special equipment of enzymes for the purpose, and that the habit must be of considerable evolutionary antiquity. The main features of the performance are undoubtedly instinctive: the fluttering, chattering and quiet waiting all bear the stamp of inborn behaviour. The signal which activates the behaviour is apparently the buzzing of the bees, since sometimes they will guide, not to a nest, but to a swarm—although they appear never to feed on the insects themselves, and will never guide to a deserted nest even though it be full of comb. It seems clear that the choice of an 'ally' is partly at least the result of experience, and they will choose those mammals as 'allies' which they have had opportunity to associate with bees' nests. Thus in regions of Africa where the natives no longer open wild bees' nests but rely on trading stores or domestic hives for sugar, the habit of 'guiding' humans seems to be on the wane or to have vanished altogether. Although the choice of 'ally' is thus deliberate, the guiding is often highly inefficient, and seems to consist of a more or less random wandering until a nest is found.

Time Sense and Duration of Memory

Present-day theories of bird navigation require a fairly reliable internal or physiological clock with an accuracy of something of the order of 0·5 per cent. (Matthews, 1953). That this is no impossible requirement is shown by the fact that even human beings in a sound-proof room under constant illumination can achieve an accuracy of under 1 per cent. Stein (1951) has trained a variety of small passerine birds to intervals of 4, 5, 8, 10 and 20 minutes which lasted 3 to 4 days if not further reinforced, but he failed to train to a longer period unless it was 24 hours or a multiple thereof. Attempts to train to periods less than 4 minutes were also unsuccessful. But work in this field has so far been only of a preliminary nature, and too much reliance must not be placed upon it.

It is interesting to inquire how good the 'memories' of birds may be, but the question posed in that crude form is almost meaningless. Memory for some kinds of events and in some situations may be extremely good and in others almost non-existent. Engelmann (1951) found that the order of retention of memories by the domestic fowl is as follows: Food → Place → Other members of the flock → Simple optical stimuli. It is, of course, difficult to get evidence of memory for birds in the wild, but there is little doubt that memory for territory is the most strongly developed, and clearly in many territorial birds it persists for at least nine months.

Within the winter territory the exactness of memory for a particular spot may be astonishing. Thus Swanberg (1951) showed that the Nutcracker is dependent during the northern winter on its caches of hazel-nuts, and that even when the young are being fed in spring these still constitute the main source of food. This implies great precision and reliability in finding the nuts, and Swanberg found that up to half a metre of snow did not affect the birds' success in nut-finding. Thus out of 351 diggings observed during the snowy months of January, February and March, 80 to 85 per cent. were immediately successful. Since the percentage of success does not drop with the passage of the winter months, it seems necessary to suppose that each bird retains a memory of the sites it has exploited as well as the sites of the caches it has made in the autumn. Jays also bury acorns, and succeed in removing at least some of their caches many months later (Chettleborough, 1952).

The memory for occasions of extreme fright and for natural enemies may also be very long. Thus Nice's Song Sparrows showed fear, possibly of an instinctive type, of eighteen months' duration as a result of the first exposure to an owl model. Schjelderup-Ebbe (1923) says that hens have an excellent memory for places, recognising an old home after several years, and many racing-pigeon fanciers would claim similarly to have good evidence from birds which have returned to their lofts after years of absence, but adequately documented evidence is hard to come by. The memory of birds for individuals may also be good though perhaps seldom of the same order. Parrots are generally regarded as having very long memories for people, and Jackdaws can certainly remember individuals for several months (Lorenz, 1935). Diebschlag (1940) records eleven months' memory of a person by a pigeon, and the same duration of memory is given by Morley (1942) for a Marsh Tit. Mostler (1937), in his work on rejection of warningly coloured insects, records memories of a *single* unpleasant experience from three to fourteen months in a number of warblers and other insectivorous species, and Porter (1910) records a memory of eleven months in a Cow-bird. The memory for more artificial tasks and situations, in general, seems much less good; in fact, almost everything seems to depend on the conditions of the experiment. Matthews (1952) records a two-year orientation memory by a pigeon—although all records are eclipsed by Skinner's (unpublished) finding that a pigeon could remember the artificial visual stimulus used in an instrumental conditioning or trial-and-error learning situation after four years! The retention of maze learning in chicks, House Sparrows, Cow-birds and pigeons is good up to six weeks, and may persist for several months. Kröh (1927) records a four-month memory of a training to select the larger of two grains of food. Claparède (1926) states that a hen trained to eat only off a particular colour still performed the task perfectly after a year had passed. In spite of the achievements of Nutcrackers and Jays in the wild, the memory of birds for hiding-places under artificial or experimental conditions may be extremely short—in Jackdaws only a few minutes—and Nice (1943) describes the memory of Song Sparrows for individuals as being very short—a matter of a few days only. White-throated Sparrows remembered each other after the lapse of eleven to seventeen days (Wessell and Leigh, 1941) and Black-crowned Night Herons (Noble, Wurm and Schmidt, 1938) after thirty-two days. Whitman (1919) records individual memory among pigeons fading at about twenty-five days, but the work of Hunter (1911) and Rouse (1906) shows that training situations and habits are remembered for considerably longer than this. Food choice and memory have also been studied in the Linnet and Siskin by Platz (1939). However, astonishing some of these memory feats may appear, it must, nevertheless, be remembered that where the learning concerns types of food available only at a certain time of year, or situations linked with a particular phase of the breeding cycle, a memory of less than twelve months' duration might be of very little biological advantage.

ANATOMICAL SITE OF LEARNING

Extremely little is known about this subject, and it must be passed over with no more than a few words. Martin and Rich (1918) studied the activities of cerebrate and decerebrate chicks, and found that the cerebrum was not necessarily concerned in the development and mediation of locomotor and self-cleaning activities. Successful feeding, however, depends on the co-operation of the cerebrum, and simpler phases of the acts of pecking and scratching are normally developed through the group of this centre, though if it is removed early enough both may develop without it. This suggests a superior plasticity in earlier life. In this connection the work of Gos (1935) is also of interest. This investigator found that from the end of the seventeenth day onwards chick embryos could be taught to associate a mechanical shock or a sound with electrical stimulation.

The investigation of the localisation of learning in the adult bird is still at so early a stage that the subject can hardly be treated in a book with the scope of the present one. A valuable summary of the work to date has been given by ten Cate (1936); but, as he shows, the fundamental dispute between Bajandurow (1937) and Beritoff (1926) as to whether or not the cerebrum is necessary for the formation of conditioned reflexes is still without final solution. Zeigler, P. (1960) (personal communication) has kindly supplied some preliminary information as to the results of forebrain ablations in pigeons. He finds that there are small restricted loci for touch and sound but there is no evidence for topographical organisation, and the removal of tissue from the hyperstriate causes no sensory deficit.

Some recent results of Altevogt (1951) on differences in learning ability of large, intermediate and small races of domestic fowl have some interest both in connection with the present section and also with that which follows. The birds were given a number of tasks involving colour, form and size discrimination, both singly and in combination. It was found that the larger races were capable of more complicated learning performances than were the others and, moreover, that they retained the learning more efficiently.

RELATION OF INDIVIDUAL VARIATION IN LEARNING ABILITY TO ENDOCRINOLOGY

There is no doubt that the endocrine balance in mammals does have some effect on the mental ability, but the relation is not at all clear and is probably usually indirect. Thus the thyroid is supposed to affect learning ability chiefly, if not entirely, through its regulation of the body metabolism and the state of 'mood' or motivation (Beach, 1948). On this view, endocrinological changes will bring about a preference for the performance of particular phases of instinctive patterns of behaviour and the readiness to respond to certain types of releasers. This may bring the animal into contexts where imprinting or other special forms of learning may operate. But there is little evidence in birds that the effect on the learning ability is *direct*, though it may be so. Thus although Allee (1936) found maze learning of the Shell Parakeet disturbed during the breeding season, there was no evidence that the effect was due directly to a gonadial hormone increase; any of the many other physiological changes associated with breeding might have been responsible. Similarly there is the alleged improvement of homing performances in pigeons resulting from castration (Orloff, Novikov and Woitkewitsch, 1940).

It is clear, however, that the relation between instinct and learning may differ as between individuals of the same species according to nutritional and probably to endocrinal states, and consequently that learning ability may vary from time to time. Thus Lorenz (1935) describes how the Red-backed Shrike possesses the inborn actions of impaling prey, but has to learn the properties and appropriateness of thorns and spikes for this purpose. It now appears that his birds were probably abnormal in behaviour owing to imperfect nutrition. When the diet is supplemented with silkworms, the whole behaviour sequence, including the instinctive recognition of thorns as objects appropriate for the prey-storing behaviour, appears fully formed without the necessity for any learning at all (Lorenz, 1950). Examples such as these raise the very important question as to how far learning can replace instinct.

It seems (see p. 57 above) that in the young bird maturation follows the usual rule; that is, stereotyped components of instinctive behaviour at or near the end of the chain appear first and the flexible appetitive behaviour later. When the adult comes into breeding state due to increased hormonal concentration, the reverse happens, i.e. the appetitive behaviour comes first. That is to say, the maturing young bird 'does something' but does not know in what context to do it; whereas the growing motivation of hormone accumulation causes the adult bird to seek the right object but does not yet know what to do with it. Howard (1929, 1940) described very similar behaviour in buntings and in the Moorhen. Similarly, with other kinds of increasing motivation, we get 'intention movements' (i.e. initial stages) first. But it is the mood and sphere of interest, the kind of object to which attention is directed, which is altered by endocrine changes. Thus while the sphere and objects of learning are changed—a bird perfects its nest-building behaviour by learning chiefly when it is in the reproductive state and therefore 'interested in' nesting-sites and materials, and the Chaffinch only learns the niceties of its full song when its gonadial hormone secretion is at the right level and rising at the correct rate to induce the production of sub-song (Thorpe, 1954)—yet there is, perhaps from the nature of the case, very little conclusive evidence that the learning abilities themselves are fundamentally changed in any way by alterations in hormonal balance and concentration.

Finally, we should do well to remember that while the effect of hormones on behaviour is well attested and profound, hormone secretion does not *by itself* always control even such basic patterns of behaviour as territorial song and migration. I have known the stimulus provided by a hormone-injected Chaffinch singing in an aviary in the winter induce other non-injected Chaffinches to sing their full territorial song (Thorpe, unpublished), and Marshall (1952) reports that migratory passerines (eight species), which pause for feeding on their northward journey through the British Isles, nevertheless do not stop to breed but continue their journey even though their interstitial gonad tissue showed hormone secretion to be fully up to the level required to initiate immediate territorial and reproductive behaviour.

CHAPTER XVI

MAMMALS

IT would be impossible, as fortunately it is unnecessary, to write a chapter dealing with the mammals along the lines that have been followed in writing of the other groups—impossible because the literature on the behaviour of the white rat has now assumed such vast proportions that only a considerable book can do justice to it. Thus Munn's *Handbook of Psychological Research on the Rat* (1950) runs to over 500 pages and contains a bibliography of over 2,500 titles. The task is also unnecessary for three reasons: firstly—because, so far as the rat is concerned, the literature is already well summarised in several specialised books, of which Munn's work is one; secondly—work on the mammals, and especially that on the rat, has already been extensively drawn upon, in the first part of this book, in order to illustrate the general principles of learning; thirdly—the very extent and rapidity of learning in mammals leads to a more attractive and practicable option; for where learning powers are so great and apparently so ubiquitous as in the mammals, it is a reasonable first assumption that behaviour is learned. Thus the onus on the experimenter is to prove that any given piece of learning is instinctive, and until this has been done the assumption that it is learned must be adhered to. Therefore, instead of attempting to work seriatim through the categories of learning and to illustrate each by examples taken from the various orders of the class, we shall discuss and attempt to evaluate those examples of mammalian behaviour which there is some *prima facie* reason to regard as innate.

Mention must first be made of locomotory movements. The straightforward walking and running movements of mammals are all suspect as inborn motor patterns based primarily on central nervous organisation, since, as the survey of Gray (1944) has shown, the skeletal and muscular structure of so many mammalian forms is such as would rapidly force the young animal to adopt the characteristic gait after even a relatively small amount of practice. Barclay (1953) has followed up Gray's work, and in investigating dog, goat and sheep has shown that the pattern of activity employed in locomotion is such as to be in most respects the most efficient mechanically. Given these initial facts, and given existing knowledge of locomotory reflexes, a simple attempt to change speed can be seen as sufficient to ensure a quick learning of a series of locomotory actions, such as walking, running, cantering and galloping, without the necessity of assuming pre-formed central nervous patterns for each gait. It is perhaps likely that some of such action patterns have also, in the course of evolution, by some principle of double assurance, acquired very precise central nervous control reinforcing mechanical necessity; but how far this may be so is not known.

When we come to non-locomotory behaviour, an explanation based on mechanical necessity coupled with rapid learning seems so plainly inadequate that one is inclined to assume at once that control by inherited patterns of central nervous organisation can be the only answer. For it seems inconceivable that such action patterns could have remained unchanged under centuries of domestication unless the central nervous mechanism underlying their performance is the expression of their genetical make-up. Nevertheless, even such apparently strong arguments must not be regarded as carrying conviction until they are reinforced by the result of careful 'Kaspar Hauser' experiments. Considering the interest and theoretical importance of the subject, such studies of individuals reared in sufficiently complete isolation from their kind to enable their innate mechanisms to be studied are still much fewer than one could wish, but they are enough to suggest that much mammalian behaviour is, in fact, more rigid than many zoologists and psychologists have until recently been prepared to admit. Eibl-Eibesfeldt (1961) has given a critical summary of much of this work and has shown how unreliable, because uncritical, are many of the earlier studies by psychologists who were unaware of the normal behaviour patterns of the species they were concerned with and so were unable to interpret them properly (see also Curio, 1955, on *Apodemus flavicollis*; Ilse, 1955, on *Loris*; Seitz, 1955, on racoon; Koenig, L., 1957, on marmot; Hediger, 1957, on marsupials; Kirchshofer, 1958, on *Gerbillus*; Nolte, 1958, on the monkey *Cebus apella*; Trumler, 1959, on the zebra; Koenig, L., 1960, on the dormouse, *Glis glis*). Recent work on mammalian ethology is also well summarised by Tembrock (1961). In his book Tembrock also surveys his own extensive work on the Canidæ.

Besides the technical works above-mentioned, facts of real interest and importance to the psychologist and ethologist are to be found in many popular and semi-popular books. Outstanding among these is the account given by Adamson (1960–1) of a hand-reared lioness which was ultimately returned to the wild but visited her human foster parents from time to time and eventually brought back her cubs to show them. In addition to these Drabble (1957) may be mentioned as providing an interesting account of weasels and Maxwell (1960) of otters.

That several characteristic features of rat behaviour are inborn seems to be established beyond reasonable doubt. To take sex behaviour first, Stone (1922) reared male rats in isolation until puberty, whereupon complete and full-intensity mating behaviour could be elicited at once. Beach (1942a, b and c, 1944) extended and verified this work. Some of his rats were reared in complete isolation, and others were segregated with litter-mates of the same sex. The majority of males raised in isolation, and all those raised in segregation, copulated perfectly upon their first contact with a receptive female, though among the first group occasional cases of abortive mounting occurred where the female was in an inaccessible position. Larsson (1959), comparing experienced with non-experienced rats of the same age, concludes that it is evident that learning intervenes only to determine the lengths of the post-ejaculatory latencies, other components being unaffected. The fact that it is often quite easy to induce perfect male mating patterns in female rats by injection of male hormone provides further strong evidence for innate behaviour, suggesting that the females are genetically equipped with both male and female mechanisms of sex response. But in the case of the experiments with females, the early ex-perience does not seem to have been so carefully controlled. The innate quality of female mating behaviour seems almost if not quite as well attested as that of the male. Stone (1926) found that females reared in isolation copulated within a few seconds after being placed with a male for the first time, showing the normal receptive posturing before the male which included typical 'lordosis' (arching of the back) and ear quivering. For the study of the inheritance of patterns of sexual behaviour in female guinea-pigs, see Goy and Jakway (1959).

While this general conclusion as to the innate character of sex be-haviour will probably be found to be widely applicable in the lower mammals, enough is known about the dog and cat to suggest that it is not universally true for the carnivores, and it is certainly untrue for the higher Primates. Thus a sexually inexperienced male Chimpanzee is unable to achieve coition with a receptive female (Bingham, 1929). Nor does the maternal behaviour of Chimpanzees appear without opportunity for practice (Yerkes, 1943).

It has been very generally assumed that, in most mammals, the single critical stimulus initiating or releasing sexual behaviour is a simple sen-sory one—typically the odour of the female in heat. But careful studies on rats by Beach (1942c, 1944), involving cortical surgery and the use of hormones, have shown that, at least with this species, the generally ac-cepted view is wrong. He finds that neither olfaction, vision, nor cutaneous sensitivity in the snout and lips is essential for the appearance of copula-tory behaviour in the inexperienced male rat. Thus the 'naïvely adequate stimulus situation appears to be a pattern of multi-sensory character,' the recognition of which is inborn at least in lower mammals. This con-clusion is not, however, to be taken to imply that even in lower mammals the whole mating pattern is incapable of change as a result of experience.

While the initial releaser and the consummatory act may be unmodifiable, many animal breeders know how easily conditioning of the appetitive behaviour may occur as a result of casual and accidental occurrences before and during copulation.

With man it seems likely that erection, ejaculation in the male and perhaps the pelvic thrusts in both sexes are of an innate and probably reflex nature (Bard, quoted by Beach, 1944). Prechtl (1958) has analysed the head-turning response of the human baby as an innate motor pattern, and Wolff (1959) has produced evidence that erection and the startle reflex are truly endogenous and show rhythmic behaviour during sleep independent of external stimulation. Ambrose (1961) advances the view that smiling in human infants becomes an autonomous greeting response derived from low intensity laughing, and Gunther (1961) has analysed the development of feeding behaviour in babies during the first days of life. He shows that feeding in the neonate is an instinctive behaviour evoked by the pattern of stimuli provided by the nipple and areolar tissues of the breast when these are in contact with the mouth. A bottle teat can also act as a releaser and can be super-normal to poorly formed breasts. The feeding behaviour of a baby in the first days of life shows three patterns: immediate active feeding, apathy until feeding is aroused and lasting apathy. A fourth behaviour, fighting at the breast, arises when the baby has had its nostrils covered, usually by his upper lip, when put to the breast. When brought to the breast, the baby cries, arches his back away and boxes with his hands. This appears to be a conditioned response. Beach summarises the fragmentary evidence on feral man 'Tomko of Zips,' 'Kaspar Hauser,' 'wolf children,' 'wild boys,' etc., agreeing with the general conclusion of Zingg (1940) that 'there is some evidence to indicate that the overt expression of libido is dependent upon social training.' Many of Lorenz's (1940) conclusions as to the innate releasive mechanisms for human social behaviour, though they may be right, seem, however, to go far beyond existing evidence.

Parental behaviour in its widest connotation offers some very puzzling problems to the student of mammalian instincts. Innate nest-building and parent-young behaviour have been recorded of the Dormouse (*Muscardinus avellanarius*) (Zippelius and Goethe, 1951) and the Desert Mouse (*Meriones persicus*) by Eibl-Eibesfeldt (1951). Munn (1950), summarising all the literature then available, concluded that the 'maternal behaviour of rats, like their mating, is clearly congenital,' and this statement was plainly intended to include post-parturitional cleaning, nest-building, retrieving and nursing: but at least some later work suggests that this general conclusion needs modification. Thus Riess (1950) found that if female rats were reared in cages containing no objects which could be picked up and carried about, they failed to build nests when the time came, even though they were then provided with suitable materials. But Eibl-Eibesfeldt (1961) has shown that this is because such rats were never given cages in which they could establish 'territory' and 'home' rather than because they were denied early experience of carrying. Riess (see also Beach and Jaynes, 1954) quotes an unpublished study by Birch in which it was found that female rats which had been reared with rubber 'Elizabethan ruffs' around their necks so that they could neither wash themselves nor lick their own genitalia, failed to clean or nurse their young.

The response of the mammalian mother to her offspring and of the offspring to the mother are so intimately connected that it is difficult to consider them apart. The licking and eating of fluids and the after-birth by a mother seems often—in dogs, cats and rats—to be a necessary preliminary to the licking and grooming of the young (Schneirla, in Hediger, 1950; Fraser, quoted by Cross, 1946), and is probably the basis of the learned attachment of the dam to the offspring; and if this is prevented there is evidence that the usual close link may not be formed. In wild ungulates the preparturient female segregates herself; but in domestic flocks of sheep the maternal drive, which is often at full strength before the birth, may be accidentally satisfied by contact with a newborn lamb nearby before her own lamb is born. The stranger may thus be adopted and the true mother vigorously repulsed by the foster-parent while her own lamb is actually being born. But though the individual is thus recognised and adopted as a result of a learning process, the instinctive phase is shown by the powerful 'desire' to adopt and nurse something. A virgin bitch will adopt almost any object of about the right size (e.g. a bone), and lavish all her maternal care upon it for a while (Russell, 1938). Similarly the young mammal has a strong desire to find an object for the inborn movement-pattern of sucking, and if food is supplied without the normal amount of sucking, the sucking pattern will appear as nonnutritional. This is well seen in the persistent 'over-flow' or displacement sucking of pail-fed calves, which will suck the ears or navels of their companions or—if kept alone—their own navels or anything in their pen that offers a mouth-hold. This 'displacement' sucking perhaps also accounts to some extent for thumb-sucking in infants. It has been investigated experimentally in puppies (Levy, 1934, quoted Beach and Jaynes). Puppies fed from bottles having nipples with small holes sucked for an average of 80 minutes a day and showed no displacement sucking, whereas puppies which had been fed through nipples with holes so large that their food requirements could be satisfied in 13 minutes a day showed post-feeding displacement sucking which continued even during sleep. Confirmation from experiments in which puppies were deprived of sucking experience, though adequately fed, during the first ten days of life has been provided by Ross (1950), and James (1957) has shown that the sucking reflex is independent of hunger and food intake. The puppy still sucks even though its stomach is filled with milk. McBride and Hebb (1948) give evidence which suggests a similar consummatory act of sucking, with its own drive expressed in appetitive behaviour, in the Bottle-nosed Dolphin (*Tursiops truncatus*); also Zippelius and Goethe (1951) for the Dormouse, Precht (1952) for kittens, and Peiper (1951) for humans.

Finally, a following response to a man as a substitute parent, comparable to that familiar in birds, has been described by Hediger (1950) in Buffaloes (*Bison americanus* and *Syncercus cafer*), and Zebra (*Hippotragus* sp.) by Grabowski (1941) in sheep and by Darling (1938*b*) in Red Deer (*Cervus elaphus*). A suggestive instance of hybridisation between Alpaca (*Lama pacos*) and Vicuna (*Lama vicugna*) being possibly dependent upon early imprinting is quoted by Hediger (1955) from Hodge. It seems likely that the importance of odour for individual and species recognition in mammals, coupled with the ability of the animal to perceive its own body odour, may result in a 'self-conditioning' and so militate against the kind of abnormal 'fixations' to alien species, and explain its apparent rarity in mammals as compared with birds.

The problem of imprinting in humans is discussed by Gray (1958) and by Hinde (1961*a*).

Once we leave the subject of sex and parent-young behaviour, the amount of careful observation on the mammals is so small as to preclude systematic consideration on the basis of behaviour systems. Instead we shall consider evidence for instinctive behaviour, species by species.

Experiments upon the white rat have also provided a good deal of evidence about other instinctive behaviour patterns. 'Hoarding'—that is, retrieving into the cage or into a known territory and there, if possible, hiding food in excess of immediate needs—clearly has an innate basis in the rat, since no tuition from parents or elders is necessary to bring about its appearance (Wolfe, 1939). It is doubtful whether rats kept in warm cages throughout life, with superabundant food and water, show hoarding behaviour. But a period of deprivation will soon elicit it, and the lowering of temperature and the presence of other rats are contributory causes—both of them obviously arrangements likely to have adaptive value in the wild. A familiar environment is necessary (Viek and Miller, 1944), for rats will not hoard in a 'strange cage'; which, as the experiments of Miller and Viek (1944) show, means primarily a cage without the home smell. The object of the hoarding is determined by the nature of the deprivation (Bindra, 1947)—suggesting that hoarding is quite distinct from nesting, since a hungry rat does not hoard nesting material. Thus rats which have been short of food will chiefly hoard food pellets, and rats which have been thirsty will store wet cotton-wool pledgets from which they can later suck the water. But experiments involving blood-sugar control and saline and insulin injections have so far (Stellar, 1943) failed to demonstrate any simple physiological picture of the mechanism responsible for releasing hoarding. There is no indication that the behaviour is in any sense a social one, in that social facilitation of hoarding is conspicuously absent. It is also quite clear that the 'object' of hoarding is not the actual accumulation of food pellets—since rats do not seem to object to their stores being depleted by other rats (Miller and Postman, 1946)— but rather that the consummatory act is the actual hoarding itself: the carrying of the food 'home.' Although recent deprivation is the chief incentive for hoarding, it has been shown conclusively that 'frustration' is an important feature in the situation (McCord, 1941; Hunt, Schlosberg, Solomon and Stellar, 1947), and that such frustration, if experienced sufficiently early in the lifetime of the rat, may have a permanent influence in lowering the threshold for release of the behaviour later in life (Hunt, 1941).

Deutsch (1957) states that when female domestic rabbits are allowed to build nests under almost natural conditions the behaviour pattern of nest-building as judged by the finished product appears in its perfection. This is true even where experience of digging has been absent and the rabbit has previously been kept in a hutch or cage. This conclusion contradicts that of Ross *et al.*, quoted by Deutsch, who found evidence that the quality of nest construction improved with successive parturitions. Deutsch justifiably doubts the generality of conclusions about patterns of instinctive behaviour based on experiments in environments in which the animals did not evolve. He adds: 'It may be that parts of the elaborate instinctive behaviour pattern which the pregnant rabbit possesses are evoked even when the rabbit is kept in a hutch. Though they cannot be executed, the rabbit may still be "looking for" the right stimuli such as earth. This appetitive behaviour may interfere with the execution of other parts of the instinctive pattern which are still appropriate. However, during successive pregnancies the frustrated inappropriate parts of the behaviour may drop out, leaving the still appropriate parts to be executed with less interference. Thus an improvement may be secured which is actually due to the dropping out of inborn components rather than to the acquisition of new components through learning.' See also Barnett's (1956) account of the ectothermic behavioural adaptation (as opposed to endothermic) which are involved in the efficient building and utilisation of nests by mice.

Although hoarding is of course well known in other animals, e.g. other Rodents (especially mice, squirrels, beavers, etc.) and Canidæ, there seem to have been no other experimental studies of the phenomenon. However, the behaviour of many, perhaps all, varieties of domestic dog provides vivid evidence of the inborn nature of the activity. Pitt (1931) has described the elaborate hiding and food-burying actions of both hand-reared puppies and hand-reared fox cubs—actions that will run off in abnormal situations and under inadequate stimulus. Such burying behaviour appears clearly consummatory in that the animals display evidence of satisfaction even though the food is not, in fact, hidden and is immediately stolen; Dickinson (personal communication) has described exactly similar behaviour in young of the Flying Squirrel (*Glaucomys volans*) (see Chapter II, p. 22, above).

Nest-making is the only other apparently innate behaviour upon which rat studies have thrown much light. This activity seems to be inborn in that it appears 'without practice' in all 'normal' rats when pregnant, even though they have been reared in isolation (Wiesner and Sheard, 1933). It may also be displayed by males and non-parturient females, in which case it differs from that of parturient animals in being inhibited by high temperatures (Sturman-Hulbe and Stone, 1929). Although, as mentioned above, early and complete deprivation of transportable materials will prevent nest-building and the retrieving of young to a single 'centre' or nest-place, it does not inhibit the actions themselves, but merely their correct orientation and co-ordination; both nest material and young are still carried about, though in haphazard fashion. The strength of the carrying drive of the parturient rat is graphically demonstrated by the above authors' observation that a parturient animal deprived of nest-building material would repeatedly pick up her own tail, carry it to the 'nest 'and there place it!

One would have imagined that urination would be a completely reflex response in any mammal, but Reyniers (1953), in describing attempts to rear mammals *ex utero* under germ-free conditions, states that young rats removed from their mothers by cæsarian section are unable to urinate until they have received gentle tactile stimulation of the genitalia (in contrast to dogs and monkeys, which urinate spontaneously). This tactile stimulation replaces the licking normally given them by the mother. Once the behaviour has been thus elicited, it will recur at regular intervals without further stimulation. As Haldane (1954b) points out, these observations need repeating and extending; they certainly raise problems and possibilities of great interest.

The only other aspect of behaviour that seems to have been investigated in 'Kaspar Hauser' rats is their response to predators, and the outcome of this research is conflicting. There is no clear proof that inexperienced rats have an innate *visual* recognition and fear of either cats or snakes. Griffith (1920) and Curti (1935, 1942) described 'freezing' attitudes adopted by rats on first meeting cats; but rats will freeze on contact with any strange object or situation. There is also doubt as to how far cat-odour may be responsible for the freezing response. More work is required to clear up such confusions. Some rodents apparently do possess an innate visual recognition of snakes, e.g. the Wood Rat (*Neotoma albigula*) studied by W. B. Richardson (1942), but Kellogg (1931) was unable to find evidence for this with the laboratory white rat. No tests with owls appear ever to have been made. That so little is known about the nature of visual social releasers in mammals is, of course, largely due to the major part played by olfactory recognition in the group. Unless the animal's olfactory organs are destroyed surgically at birth, it is in most cases practically impossible to rule out all effects due to odour. Innate visual perception of depth by rats, and the possibility of the innate recognition of the human face by human infants, have been discussed in Chapter VII, above.

Finally, we must consider the evidence for innate behaviour in a few other species.

The inheritance of behaviour differences which merely involve the general level of response of the animal but do not affect specific motor patterns is, of course, well known. There seems little doubt that in many mammals genetic strains differing in such characteristics as wildness and tameness can readily be isolated. A recent example of this is W. R. Thompson's (1953) study of the inheritance of behavioural differences in 15 mouse strains. The traits which were critically examined in this study were foraging-drive, 'emotionality' and exploratory activity. Significant differences in each of these characteristics were found as between a number of the strains tested.

The innate equipment of instinctive behaviour patterns has recently been investigated by 'Kaspar Hauser' and other studies of the Dormouse by Zippelius and Goethe (1951). They find a very ample equipment of instinctive behaviour patterns, so that little seems to be left for learning other than the acquisition of special skills and the knowledge of territorial boundaries. They present good evidence that toilet and grooming movements, sucking, climbing, concealment and fright postures when in the branches, nest-building movements and vocalisations are all innate. In general, the sleeping postures of mammals are obviously such that they may well have been learned as the most comfortable and convenient in view of the bodily structure. But the rather special 'sleeping-on-branch' posture, and perhaps also the 'ground-sleeping' posture, seem to be innately determined in the dormouse. The evidence as to mating and greeting behaviour seems somewhat less certain. A 'Kaspar Hauser' dormouse at 114 days of age behaved with complete indifference on first meeting a fellow-member of the species, although at a second meeting later it performed the specific greeting ceremony, perhaps now as an expression of the mating drive. Eibl-Eibesfeldt (1951) has also carried out an extensive study of the Persian Desert Mouse (*Meriones persicus*). Although strict 'Kaspar Hauser' experiments were not carried out in this instance, his studies seem to show fairly clearly that a large number of actions and behaviour patterns must be inherited to some degree at least. He lists 65 of these. Leaving out the strictly locomotory ones, we have: feeding 11, nest-building 6, mating 5, juvenile behaviour 6, hostility 15 and toilet 18. Some of the last group and probably some of the mating group are more in the nature of reflexes, but we are left, nevertheless, with a formidable list of apparently instinctive actions. The same worker (1951) has also investigated the combination of instinct and experience in the development of the nut-opening technique employed by squirrels. There are, of course, a very large number of cases among rodents in which the details of the feeding behaviour appear characteristic of the species, but how far a true instinctive co-ordination is involved is far from clear. Thus Spencer (1953) pointed out that the rats *Rattus norvegicus* and *Rattus rattus*, when feeding on grain, hold the food with the long axis parallel to that of the body, and eat first the broken end of the grain, whereas mice (*Mus musculus*) hold the grains with the long axis at right angles to the body and attack first the cheeks of all grains (except maize). While there may be some innate postures and movements involved here, it seems at any rate plausible that the relative size of the food affects the way in which the grains are held, and there is also evidence that the selection of a particular part of the grain for gnawing is primarily based on its texture.

Räber (1944) has made an analysis of the sign-stimuli which serve the Beech Marten (*Martes foina*) for the recognition of its principal prey, especially eggs and birds. Since, however, the early history of the animals used could not be ascertained, the results are not direct evidence as to the inherited patterns of recognition.

One of the few detailed comparative studies of species-predictable behaviour in a mammalian group is that of Pilters (1954) on the Tylopoda ('*Camelidæ*') of the Old and New Worlds. This work, which includes observations on the behaviour of hybrids, provides excellent evidence that much of the social, sexual and parental behaviour of these animals must be inborn, and is probably to be regarded as instinctive.

The domestic dog naturally provides a considerable number of examples of specific movements which appear to be innate, but it is by no means always easy to find fully convincing evidence. That the food-hoarding and burying behaviour is probably innate has been mentioned above. There is also little doubt that territorial behaviour, including, of course, the marking of territory with urine, is also an inborn action. Tinbergen (1942), during observations on Eskimo dogs of East Greenland which live in packs of five or ten individuals and defend a group-territory, found that the immature dogs do not defend the territory, but will roam through the whole settlement more or less at random. The consequence is that they are constantly trespassing and are constantly attacked and chased. Even though they are severely treated by the owners, they do not at this stage learn the territorial boundaries. When, however, they become sexually mature, they begin to defend their territory, and at the same time quickly learn the boundaries of other territories; within a week they have learned exactly where they may go and at what point they will be attacked for trespassing. Apart from the territorial and sexual behaviour, perhaps the most striking example of a complex inborn action-pattern is shown in the highly distinctive set of actions by which mice are caught. This is seen in various domestic breeds, e.g. the Chow (Lorenz, 1954), the Shetland Sheep-dog (Thorpe, unpublished) and probably a number of other small to medium-size breeds. It has also been described in the Fox (Edwards, 1949) and in the American Coyote (*Canis latrans*) (Murie, 1940). The dog starts moving with a curious stiff-legged 'slink,' with head held high and the tail stretched out behind, parallel to the ground and usually waving slowly. 'Suddenly, as though released by a spring, she shoots in a semicircle about a yard high and two yards forwards (Fig. 67a). Landing on her fore-paws close together and stiffly outstretched, she bites several times, quick as lightning, into the short grass. With loud snorts she bores her pointed nose into the ground, then, raising her head, she looks questioningly in my direction, her tail wagging all the time: the mouse has gone' (Lorenz, 1954). The quick snapping and the shaking movements by which the prey is dealt with are probably elicited by any small moving object. But all the actions which precede this appear to be present fully co-ordinated even in an inexperienced young animal. Presumably the habits of turning round before lying down and of scratching earth over fæces are also innate, though careful studies seem to be lacking.

Many of the special types of behaviour characteristic of the different breeds of domestic dog, while presumably having an inborn basis, are much less certainly part of the behaviour patterns of the wild ancestor and have probably been developed to a considerable extent by human selection. Examples of this are pointing, retrieving and herding. Luther (1951) suggests that the behaviour patterns of driving, circling the herd, marking or running the boundaries, fighting and a sort of prancing display over food known as 'sich-wälzen' are innate in at least some species of dogs. Freedman (1958) has shown clear differences in breed as between beagles and wire-haired terriers on the one hand and basenjis and shelties on the other. The two former breeds consistently seek human contact, whereas the basenji is aloof and the shelties timid. When we come to emotional expression, there is obviously in dogs an enormous amount of behaviour which can also be found in their wild relatives and which cannot have been individually acquired. This no doubt is the case in most mammalian groups, for it is extremely difficult to suppose that emotional

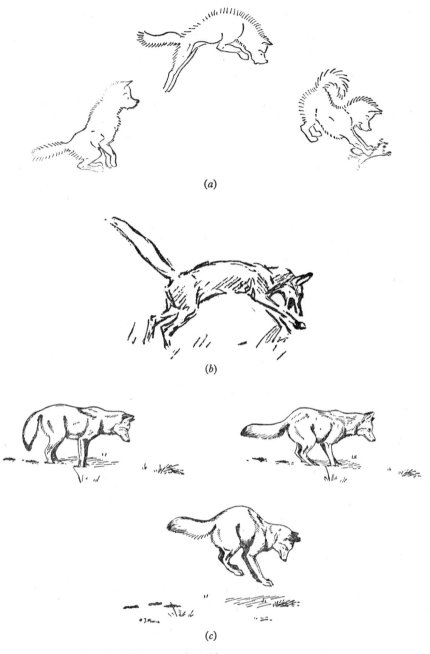

FIG. 67—The 'mouse jump' in:
(a) The domestic dog (Chow). (After Lorenz, 1954.)
(b) The European Fox. (After Edwards, 1949.)
(c) The American Coyote. (After Murie, 1940.)

expression could be individually learned at least by sub-Primate mammals, however good the opportunity for doing so.

That this is true has, of course, been generally recognised since Darwin produced his *Expression of the Emotions in Man and Animals* (1872). One important principle that Darwin enunciated, namely the principle of antithesis, seems not to have received the attention which it deserves, and indeed it has been more or less forgotten since his day. He assumes that when actions of one kind have become firmly associated with any sensation or emotion, it is natural to suppose that actions of a directly opposite kind—though of no use—should be unconsciously performed through habit and association under the influences of a directly opposite sensation or emotion. On this principle alone Darwin seeks to understand how the gestures and expressions which come under the head of antithesis have arisen. The simplest example of this, of course, is the threatening self-aggrandisement shown in dogs by erection of the 'mane,' tail and ears, the erect gait and the baring of the teeth characteristic of attack. Submissive movements are almost completely the reverse: the hair is sleeked, the ears and tail lowered, the legs and neck bent so as to give a cringing posture, and the corners of the mouth are drawn up and back, although the teeth are kept covered. While this is perhaps the most obvious example, every naturalist will be able to recall many others. The work of Schenkel (1948) on emotional expression in wolves shows dramatically how many expressive emotional attitudes must have survived thousands of years of domestication to appear unchanged in our domestic dogs. Figs. 68–70 give some examples. Crisler (1959) has given a very graphic account of the highly complex and indeed sophisticated social behaviour in hand-reared wolves, many parts of which there seems little doubt must contain large innate components. Kortlandt (1959), after arguing with much cogency that man and ape have evolved in different directions and that from some points of view the great apes are post-protohominid rather than infra-human, asserts that the most human animal is not the ape but the wolf, which is a co-operative drive-hunter similar to man. The wolf has the highest social organisation of all animals except man, and its system of expressions is the highest innate communication system of all mammals. Perhaps the wolf, he says, is the only animal which is even more monogamous than most monogamous human peoples; his descendant the dog is the only really humanised domestic animal.

The whole pattern of copulation in female cats is innate. Lordosis, treading of the hind feet, mating cry, subsequent licking, rolling and head-scratching are entirely stereotyped, as I have myself seen demonstrated. Rosenblatt and Aronson (1958a and b) have shown that in male cats prior sexual experience functions to facilitate the continuation of sexual behaviour after castration. If the patterns of sexual behaviour have been differentiated and practised by males they can be elicitated after castration by stimuli present in the testing situation, especially the receptive female, despite the low level of testicular hormone. In the absence of sexual experience and under the influence of the depressing effects of castration on sexual behaviour, most males so treated are unable to respond to stimulation provided by the receptive female and fail to develop a sexual pattern or even to form the introductory elements of the mating pattern.

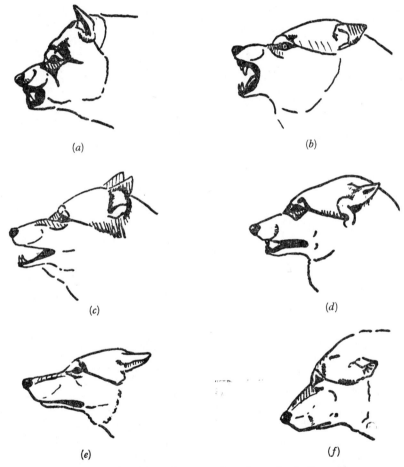

Fig. 68—Studies on the expression of emotion in the wolf.
(a) Fully confident threat.
(b) High intensity threat with slight uncertainty.
(c) Low intensity threat with uncertainty.
(d) Weak threat with much uncertainty.
(e) **Anxiety.**
(f) Uncertainty with suspicion in the face of an enemy.
(After Schenkel, 1948.)

The domestic cat shows instinctive movements and expressions almost if not quite so clearly as the dog, and they are seen in a hand-reared kitten quite as fully as in one which has been reared by its mother. Leaving aside the expression of the emotions which are so obvious as to be hardly worthy of discussion, we may mention the evidence which the play of kittens provides for the existence of inborn hunting behaviour. A summarised account of this and other inborn actions of cats is given by Lorenz (1954, Chapters XVI, XVII and XIX). The kitten begins by pawing

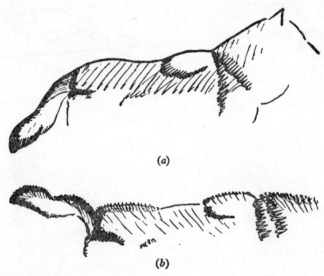

(a)

(b)

Fig. 69—Expression in the wolf indicated by the body silhouette and line of the back resulting from the colouring and bristling of the hair.
(a) Normal.
(b) Erect.
(After Schenkel, 1948.)

at the ball of wool or whatever the object is, 'first gently and inquiringly with outstretched forearm and inwardly flexed paw. Then, with extended claws, it draws the ball towards itself, pushes it away again or jumps a few steps backwards, crouching . . . then its head drops suddenly . . . the hind feet perform peculiar alternating treading and clawing movements as though the kitten were seeking a firm hold from which to spring. Suddenly it bounds in a great semicircle and lands on its toy with stiff fore-paws, pressed closely together. . . .' If the toy is under a cupboard the kitten will 'with elegant "practised" movements, reach with one arm into the space . . . it is at once clear to anyone who has ever watched a cat catching a mouse that our kitten, which we have reared apart from its mother, is performing all those highly specialised movements which aid the cat in the hunting of its most important prey—the mouse. . . . If we now improve on our plaything by attaching a thread to it and letting it dangle from above, the kitten will exhibit entirely different prey-catching movements. Jumping high, it grabs the prey with both paws at once, bringing

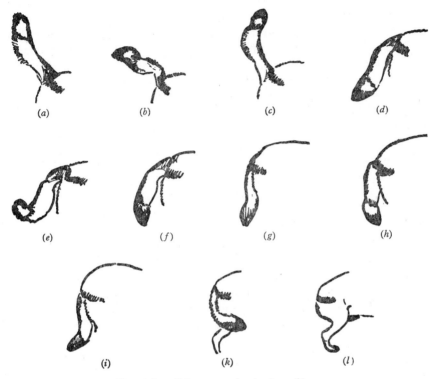

Fig. 70—Use of the tail for expression in the wolf.
(a) Self-confidence in social group.
(b) Confident threat.
(c) With wagging; imposing carriage.
(d) Normal carriage (in a situation without social tension).
(e) Somewhat uncertain threat.
(f) Similar to (d) but specially common in feeding and guarding.
(g) Depressed mood.
(h) Intermediate between threat and defence.
(i) Active submission (with wagging).
(k) and (l) Complete submission.
(After Schenkel, 1948.)

them together in a wide sweeping movement from the sides. During this movement the paws appear abnormally large, for all the digits with their extended claws are widely spread, and the dew-claws are bent at right angles to the paw. This grasping movement . . . is identical to the last detail with the movement used by cats to grab a bird just before leaving the ground. The biological significance of another movement, often observed in the play of young cats, is less obvious. In a lightning upward movement of upturned pads and claws the kitten reaches under a plaything and throws it in a high arc over its own shoulder, to follow it immediately with a jump.' Alternatively, the kitten sits before the object, raises itself erect, reaches underneath it with a paw from each side and throws it back over its head in a steeper and higher semicircle. Frequently the animal follows a flying object with its eyes and pursues it with a high leap, landing where it fell. The natural function of these two series of movements seems to be the catching of fish, the first for smaller, the second for larger ones. The alternate pressing movements with the front paws with which suckling carnivores usually stimulate milk flow must, it seems, be inborn (Eibl-Eibesfeldt, personal communication).

That inborn methods for dealing with live prey are found elsewhere in the Carnivora and are probably general in the group seems extremely probable from general observation, as anyone who has spent much time at a zoo is likely to agree, but there is as yet little careful study on the subject. Sanderson (1949) studied the growth and behaviour of a litter of captive Weasels, and found that they became efficient at killing prey in the normal specific manner without apparent teaching. A much more precise study of this behaviour in the polecat will be found in Eibl-Eibesfeldt (1961). The recognition of their prey by Carnivores does not, however, seem to be inborn in any precise sense. There is no evidence of any innate hostility between cats and dogs, nor evidence that cats have an innate tendency to recognise visually the particular characteristics of mice, rats or birds, apart from their movements of flight. Whether there is inborn recognition of the odour of potential prey is not clear, but the evidence at present seems against it (see p. 93, above). However, the dog's recognition of mice and other small mammals seems to some extent to be based on high-frequency squeaks above the limit of human hearing, and it is possible that this recognition is innate.

It might appear that the astonishing performances of circus animals are evidence against the importance of innate behaviour in mammals. That they are evidence of their remarkable powers of learning is true enough but, as the studies of Hediger (1955) have shown—although many entirely new actions are, with great patience, taught to circus animals—the basic secret of circus training is to utilise, as far as possible, the natural, and in many cases no doubt inborn, abilities of the species. As R. C. Noble (1950) truly said, 'The elephants rolling tubs and barrels, the seals balancing and throwing balls with their snouts, the tigers leaping through flaming hoops and the monkeys riding horseback or performing on trapezes, are doing things foreign to their normal experience but not to their natures. The elephants roll pieces of sun-baked clay anthills about in their native forests; seals on a rocky islet pose characteristically with their snouts held high; wild monkeys hang tenaciously to their mothers during the early months of infancy and later balance precariously in tree-tops and swing from swinging branches. The trainer who prevails upon a dozen lions and tigers to assume and maintain certain positions in an exhibition cage has undoubtedly studied and exploited the animal's innate reaction to "flight distance." '

With regard to domestic animals other than the dog and cat we have so little precise information as to the behaviour of the nearest wild representatives that we can do little more than speculate. However, with the horse there is sufficient information about the wild type *Equus przewalskii* (Lydekker, 1912) to suggest that domestic horses when allowed to run wild show almost all the behaviour patterns of their ancestors. The social organisation of a group of mares under the dominance of a stallion, with a number of younger stallions hanging about upon the fringe of the troop, until such time as they can secure mares for themselves, seems to be almost exactly duplicated. Moreover, there is little reasonable doubt that the aggressive and submissive postures, social grooming behaviour, etc., characteristic of all breeds of horses are based on inherited behaviour patterns (Pitt, 1931). Antonius (1937) has shown that there are consistent differences in such behaviour patterns characteristic of horse, ass, mule and the three specific or sub-specific groups of zebras.

Finally, there is a certain amount of evidence from hand-reared monkeys and chimpanzees as to how much the characteristic behaviour is innately determined. At first sight, studies of the behaviour of hand-reared monkeys and apes appear to yield conflicting results, but the most complete and thorough study is that of a home-reared Chimpanzee, the famous animal 'Vicki,' carried out by Hayes and Hayes (1951). This creature was adopted as an infant of three days, and reared as a human child until her death at the age of about six years. She had no opportunity to see Chimpanzees, and there is little doubt that she 'regarded herself' in every respect as a human being. Firstly, the vocalisations were quite characteristic of normal animals, although of course it is conceivable that something of this could have been learned in the first few days of life. Then the characteristic 'bluff behaviour' of Chimpanzees was shown to perfection—rearing up, lifting the arms in threat, raising the hair and stamping. If the bluff was called, the animal retreated at once—as is usual with this species. Another very characteristic Chimpanzee movement quite unlike any human behaviour, and therefore not to be regarded as having been learned from human companions, was the tendency to rock to and fro on the haunches when frightened. Although primarily a fear response, it also arises in a number of situations other than fear-provoking ones. Though anxiety was apparently the chief cause of the movement, it was also occasionally shown when sleeping, bored or restless. The development of grooming and scratching activity was particularly striking with Vicki. With toilet and self-maintenance activities of mammals in general, many characteristic movements are obviously of a reflex nature, and there is little reason to doubt that they are in the main inborn. As Wood-Jones (1943) and others have shown, the characteristic grooming movements of marsupials are associated with the development of special claws for scratching and combing, and with an elaborate special pattern of the hair tracts—suggesting that the behaviour patterns involved are of extremely ancient origin. When, however, we come to rather more elaborate toilet behaviour, which is certainly not to be regarded as simply reflex in the ordinary meaning of the term, we still find evidence that it may be innate. Observation on monkeys and apes, which display social grooming, has provided the only careful work on this subject. This grooming appears to play a considerable part in the organisation of social groups, and involves close examination of the skin, searching for parasites, picking with the fingers and so removing flakes of skin, small scabs and minute foreign particles. Vicki showed the development of grooming behaviour in a perfectly normal way, but as her 'parents' point out, there is hardly a normal Chimpanzee activity which does not in some slight respect at least resemble human behaviour, so there may always be said to be some circumstances which encourage the development of many quite characteristic behaviour patterns by learning. Nissen, Chow and Semmes (1951) have studied the development of some characteristic behaviour patterns in a young Chimpanzee which was prevented—by means of cardboard cuffs or cylinders —from using its hands for normal exploration of the body surface. In this animal the development of the general behaviour was fairly normal, and there was no noticeable handicap in the perception of size, form or depth; but it did experience great difficulty in learning problems which required tactile discrimination of pressure stimulations, and did not display the grooming activities which the study of Vicki suggested to be innate. When the restricting cuffs were finally removed, the animal quickly improved in its ability to bring the fingers to a given place, and improved also in speed and accuracy, but the grooming never developed. A similar result was obtained in the case of monkeys by Foley (1934), who found that a monkey reared in isolation failed to groom. The most probable explanation of this apparent contradiction is that of instinctive regression. As we have seen in various connections, there is evidence that an innate behaviour pattern which is prevented too long from overt expression will begin to regress, and that once the critical time for its development is well past, it may be almost impossible to elicit it again. This seems, on the face of it, to be a likely explanation of the results with Chimpanzees. These animals are, of course, so costly to keep and rear, and the care of a group of them is such an expert and time-consuming business, that it is hardly possible to undertake the detailed investigation which would be necessary to clear up the matter finally. But perhaps it would be possible with monkeys. What is required is to know the effect of varying periods of deprivation at different ages in the growth of the young.

Schiller (1952) has attempted to summarise the knowledge of innate constituents of complex responses in Primates. His conclusion is that experiments on apes and monkeys in general do show that the motor constituents are innately determined, but that their organisation can be stabilised into more or less comprehensive units on the basis of reinforcement. He comes to the conclusion that even some of the most striking and well-known examples of 'insightful behaviour' shown by apes are based on inborn motor patterns. In studying the problem of the use of sticks as tools he found, contrary to Birch (1945), no significant improvement resulting from the opportunity to play with sticks when young, although even some older animals require some specific training with the stick in order to use it efficiently as a tool. There was a tendency to fit sticks together in play, but this did not necessarily lead to insight into the possibilities of a longer stick as tool, and he concluded that in the young animals play and work are not yet connected but are distinct sections of activity. He also showed that the 'play form' of piling boxes one upon another will occur even in the complete absence of any incentive. It appears, in other words, that the tendency to stack boxes is in some obscure sense innate. However, his experiments lead to the conclusion that releasers in Primates are entirely learned, whether it be the recognition of a live snake or of a banana. Although the response to live snakes tends to show some evidence of growth with age, he found no significant difference in the amount of training required to extinguish the response to a live snake and that required to extinguish a response to a banana. His conclusion is that there are innate motor patterns which are the basic constituents of complex responses. These are the patterns concerned with avoidance, grasping, poking, etc. Once these are established, any familiar object in familiar surroundings that fits dimensionally to the activities mentioned will elicit these patterns in a way that may appear insightful. Williams (1950) describes how the Indian elephant will use sticks as back-scratchers and I have well-attested evidence from Sir Julian Huxley (personal communication, 1959) that the same kind of habit has been developed in the domestic goat, using pieces of straw. With the lower Primates it seems likely that the innate components are much more completely differentiated. Zuckerman (1933) has given a valuable survey of the differentiation of behaviour patterns in monkeys and their taxonomic significance. He discusses facial movements and expressions, drinking, grooming and nursing behaviour. The consistency of appearance of these patterns over such a wide range of related forms provides a very strong argument for assuming them to be primarily inborn. No process of learning or establishment of traditions could possibly account for such consistency.

There remain one or two types of learned behaviour of particular interest in the mammals which have not been dealt with in Part II of this book. Firstly the number sense—Hassmann (1952) has shown that a number sense equal to that of birds can be established in squirrels. Secondly—imitation. The evidence for true imitation has long been so slender as to give rise to grave doubts as to whether it occurs in animals at all. Social facilitation and local enhancement there is, of course, in plenty, but true imitation, in the sense of copying a novel or otherwise improbable act—some act for which there is clearly no instinctive tendency—is another matter. Psychologically, of course, whether or not such imitation exists is a point of the greatest interest, for it seems to involve self-consciousness and the realisation of another individual as resembling oneself. There is some definite evidence that cats can learn by imitation (Herbert and Harsh, 1944). Thus cats which had the opportunity to watch another cat obtain a food reward by a simple manipulation, such as string pulling or lever pressing a number of times, proved themselves significantly quicker at learning the task than the controls. A striking feature of these experiments was the evidence that the observation of a single *learning* of the task was more effective than observation of a number of skilled performances. This relative advantage of observation of the learning process was greater in situations where more *incorrect* manipulation of the problem mechanism was possible. Warden, Field and Koch (1940) found excellent evidence of imitation in *Cebus* and *Rhesus* monkeys. Approximately half of their animals showed instantaneous success (less than 10 seconds) as the result of observation of a skilled animal and 76 per cent. showed success in less than 60 seconds. Although co-operative behaviour and the facilitation of learning by observation of another individual has been described in Chimpanzees (Crawford and Spence, 1939), it was for long doubtful whether true visual imitation occurs, and Yerkes (1943) searched for it with uncertain results. However, the matter seems to have been settled, at least for Chimpanzees, by experiments with Vicki. Hayes and Hayes (1951) described six experimental puzzle situations which were too difficult to be mastered by trial-and-error learning or direct insight, and in which the performance of Vicki was compared with children on the one hand and ordinary laboratory-reared Chimpanzees on the other. In all these tests Vicki's performance approximated to that of children, and true imitation seemed to be evident in all of them. She was also very ready to imitate, on command, new and improbable actions performed by human beings, even though she was shown only photographs of humans performing the particular actions or assuming the particular postures. These results are impressive evidence of the fact that with the higher vertebrates the full possibilities of behaviour can often be better investigated if the animal has been reared and tended as an individual by human trainers. It has been shown by Tateishi (1958) that in the Formosan monkey *Macacca cycletes* imitation contributes to the development of the behaviour of washing baits. The papers of Ryopelle (1960) on observational learning in monkeys should also be consulted.

Finally, it seems necessary to say a word about the homing behaviour of mammals. The study is, of course, far more difficult than with birds, since unless experiments are carried out in a more or less uniform and empty stretch of country of large size, unknown and incommensurable factors will be so numerous as to make accurate assessment of the results almost impossible. There are, it is true, many striking instances of the return of dogs and cats to their homes, even though they have had to cross long stretches of unfamiliar territory. In many instances a chance discovery of the home cannot be ruled out, for often the return journey takes a very long time. However, B. Schmid (1932) is exceptional in having organised very careful experiments on the homing of dogs, and some of his results are extremely difficult to account for on accepted theories. In one case a dog homed a 'bee-line' distance of 6 kilometres. In fact, there is evidence that the dog actually covered 11 kilometres in about 1 hour and 18 minutes. In another case 8·5 kilometres were covered in 2 hours 10 minutes. Some of the dogs, on being retested over the same route, improved on their times of performance, even though it was clear that they had taken different routes. If experiments of this kind when done on a larger scale continue to yield similar results, their interpretation would, indeed, be a major problem for the student of animal behaviour.

One of the most puzzling of all experiments on orientation in mammals is that of Vogelberg and Krüger (1951) with mice and rats. Blinded white mice could be trained to find food in a given direction in a cruciform maze in which no directional stimuli were provided by the maze itself. However, they were apparently dependent upon stimuli coming from outside the maze, since the training was usually lost when the maze was moved about. When it was built into a lorry, some mice undoubtedly oriented themselves by stimuli from the lorry itself but outside the maze, and others by local clues from outside the lorry; and with most of the individuals the training as such could not be maintained when the lorry was moved about from place to place. But there were some exceptions which seem on the face of it to be significant. There apparently remained in some mice a trace of an innate direction preference which was not affected by training and which appeared to be quite independent of locality. It looks as if in these instances there were some absolute non-visual innate compass-direction preference in both rats and mice, and this is also suggested by the homing experiments of Schleidt (1951). Early work on this subject was far from being statistically convincing but some of the later results of Lindenlaub are extremely puzzling. His tentative conclusion is that mice choose the correct homing direction in the absence of *all* cues! (1955, 1960). The homing performances of bats may also provide interesting problems for the student of sense organs. Kowalski and Wojtusiak (1952), who have described experiments with the Lesser Horseshoe Bat (*Rhinolophus hipposideros*), obtained 34 per cent. returns in a total of 70 marked bats, returns being made from up to 24 kilometres. Some bats returned irrespective of the direction in which they had been transferred. These preliminary results seem to show that the species possesses an ability of space orientation far better than other workers have assumed, but one cannot base any further conclusions upon them until they have been repeated on a much bigger scale.

CONCLUSION

At the end of this survey of some aspects of Ethology, how far can one summarise and arrive at any general results? What, if any, is the significant over-all conclusion arising from the great and growing activity of students of behaviour during the past fifty years? Before attempting to answer such a question, I think we must ask ourselves—What have been the 'conclusions' of other great branches of Animal Biology—anatomy, morphology, palæontology, biochemistry, biophysics, genetics, physiology?

In the first place the answer can, I think, be given in a single general statement which few biologists would dispute. From the viewpoint of these various disciplines, the world of living things is seen as far more of a unity than was conceivable a hundred years ago. The post-Darwinian era in research has tended, on the whole, to break down the barriers both between phyla and between individual disciplines. The same general fundamental principles are seen to be operating to a very large extent throughout the animal and plant kingdoms, in the sense that everywhere we seem to be finding fresh evidence that the marvellously fine adaptations in structure and physiology of organisms are the inevitable outcome of their interactions with the physical and biological environments in which they have evolved and in which they now survive. Even the bacteria and the viruses, for all their strangeness, seem less remote than once they did. Both the organism and its environment (restricted though the latter seems to be to an almost negligibly thin skin over the crust of a minor planet) seem to be 'fit'; and so close is the fit that one is sometimes overwhelmed by the feeling that everything that can evolve must do so sooner or later. In this sense Biology, vitalised by the vast Darwinian generalisation and in spite of the bewildering multiplicity and frustrating specialist jargon of its divisions, is at heart more of a unified subject than ever before.

This general answer raises two subsidiary questions. If the plants and animals studied by the biologist represent a unity—if, in other words, Biology is an autonomous subject—what are its relations with its neighbours, the physical sciences on the one hand, and with Anthropology, Sociology, Ethnology and Psychology, the sciences dealing with man, on the other? So far as the latter are concerned, part at least of the answer is clear. For the anatomist, embryologist, palæontologist and biochemist man has for a long time been seen as just another kind of animal. So, too, for the physiologist—unless it be that modern developments in the study of psycho-somatic disease will reveal differences rather than the similarities which seem more evident at present.

As to the first part of the question, the answer is more difficult. Not so very long ago the boundary between living and non-living seemed as well defined as the English Channel. But recently a subtle change appeared. It is not that analysis into ever finer levels of structure and physiology is showing progressively that biology is, after all, only the complicated physics and chemistry of an earlier generation. Entirely the contrary process seems to be taking place. To quote Picken (1955): 'At all levels of complexity, biological organization is synonymous with a type of order among components such that the isolated part no longer has the properties which it has in the complex, and such that the whole will not display the full range of its properties unless it is entire; a part cannot be removed without producing far-reaching changes in the whole.... The important practical point is that the hope that analysis to ever finer levels of structure will ultimately reveal the nature of that relation by virtue of which the whole is more than the sum of the parts has now been shown to be vain. Most experimental biologists have in the past perforce worked on the tacit or explicit belief that analysis in terms of the physics and chemistry of fifty years ago—the physics of matter *en masse,* the chemistry of small molecules—would yield the answer. But we can see already that the physics and chemistry are going to be those of ordered aggregates far larger than molecules. The extent to which the concepts of chemistry and of physical chemistry have been modified, sometimes almost out of existence—as in the case of the concept of "molecule"—as a result of contact with biological material is of the greatest historical importance.'

Biological organisation now seems increasingly apparent in circumstances and conditions where not so long ago all was thought to be physics and chemistry, and it seems that future advances may come as a result of starting with concepts derived from biological systems and working back into the physical sciences. When Schrödinger (1944) calls the gene or the chromosome an aperiodic crystal, and when Wigglesworth (1945) speaks of the insect organism as a gigantic molecule, this is not (as Picken shows) the abuse of language that it may at first sight appear, but an important insight. For it implies that the holistic concept has been found fertile in regions where previously it was looked at askance, and that the boundary between living and non-living has indeed become blurred—and in a surprising way. Can we not speak of both crystal and isolated virus as 'organisms,' reserving the term 'living organism' for organisms with a metabolic turnover? 'If we accept this, it must not be forgotten that "living" organisms may be temporarily converted to organisms, as when bacteria, semen or slime moulds are dehydrated and stored in this condition' (Picken, *loc. cit.*).

What has Ethology to say on these fundamental issues? That animals of widely different structure and complexity are in effect doing the same things by mechanisms at least superficially different has been emphasised again and again in this book. But on the whole Ethology adds its voice to emphasise the unity of Biology. As to the living/non-living question, it has as yet no answer of its own to contribute. Yet it may be said that the very existence of the difficulty of distinguishing between 'directive' and 'purposive,' and the fact that physical systems can so readily be found and devised which simulate the behaviour and learning processes of living organisms, seems to give a fairly strong suggestion of what its ultimate answer may be.

When we come to the problem of the relationship between man's nature and that of the animals, 'Ethology' (in this wide sense of the mass of knowledge derived from the objective study of animal behaviour since the time of Darwin) has a much more definite answer.

That some animals at least show every sign of experiencing emotions similar to our own has been obvious at least since Darwin shrewdly fastened upon this problem for that work which may be said to have initiated modern behaviour study. And since then comparative psychology has shown, as this and many other books have emphasised, the extraordinary superficial similarity between much animal and much human behaviour. This is true whether we speak of drives or orientation, of Trial-and-error, of Insight or of Imprinting. Even such characteristically human behaviour as the framing of language and of the concept of number, the use of symbols and artistic appreciation and creation, seem no longer to offer quite the clear-cut differentiation between man and animals which was formerly supposed. And if and in so far as it proves true that the concept of purpose is necessary in the description of animal behaviour, another important similarity will have been established. In any event, it seems that Ethology is already confirming the conclusions of other biological disciplines, and in doing this it may in due course provide many facts which will assist human beings in the better ordering of their social relations.

Moreover, if it is true, as was suggested at the beginning, that Ethology as part of a completely competent Biology must involve a properly disciplined subjective as well as an objective approach, and that in Biology we are dealing with emergents of a higher level than those found in Physics; then it may be we shall find that Biology, and in particular Ethology, will give us necessary data for a more adequate theory of knowledge. It may thus strengthen the position of a Philosophy of Organism, and perhaps make even clearer than at present the inadequacy of Empiricism as a full philosophy of Nature. However this may be, we may agree with Erroll Harris (1954) that Science in order to progress must also philosophise and must enter upon a thorough criticism of its own foundations. Otherwise, as Whitehead saw so clearly, it is 'in danger of degenerating into a medley of *ad hoc* hypotheses.'

Finally, to assume that studies of animal behaviour imply any decrease in the stature of man would be a view of the utmost *naïveté* (see Thorpe, 1961*e*, 1962). In the first place, to do so would be to fall into the very error which, at the other end of the biological scale, blinds us to the ultimate limitations of further micro-analysis. Far from being unscientific, it is sound scientific common sense to see that, if only because of the existence of Science itself, man displays emergent qualities far transcending those of the highest animal. The existence of his high powers of abstract reasoning and his faith, of his religious awareness and spiritual life, his appreciation of moral and æsthetic values, his self-conscious discipline of the will to achieve beauty, goodness and truth; as well as all the other manifestations of his genius that have already emerged, not only confirms this but suggests that there are also in him vast further potentialities yet to be realised.

ACKNOWLEDGMENTS
(*First Edition*)

THIS book had its first origins in lectures delivered at Cambridge for Part II of the Natural Sciences Tripos, and the plan for its production was carried a big step forward by the invitation of the President and Fellows of Harvard College to be Prather Lecturer in Biology during the academic year 1951–2. I am greatly beholden to Harvard University for the stimulating and generous hospitality of its Biological Departments in Harvard, and of the Yerkes Laboratories for Primate Biology, at Orange Park, Florida.

But the book has by now far transcended the Prather Lectures in scope, and in its further development I have been assisted by many friends and colleagues at Cambridge. In particular, Edward Armstrong and Robert Hinde have been of inestimable help. The former was tirelessly attentive in reading the whole of the book in two drafts as well as in galley and page proof, and his comments and criticisms have contributed greatly to clarity. The latter also read much of the book in draft, and the whole of Parts I and II, as well as several chapters in Part III, in proof. His penetrating criticisms and his comprehension of both the theory and the practice of Ethology have been a constant stimulus during five years of almost daily association. The book, whatever its faults, is much better than it would have been without these two. My wife has corrected and criticised the whole of the page proofs; as has Miss E. M. Barraud, to whom I am also greatly indebted for her skill and care in typing the manuscripts, completing the subject index, and compiling the author and species indexes.

If the book was to come anywhere near achieving its purpose, it had to be of wide scope, and this has involved my writing of a number of groups and subjects on which I am far from expert. I have therefore been much dependent upon specialists, whom I have bothered shamelessly. The following have read and criticised the final drafts of particular chapters. Chapter VIII, Dr J. W. S. Pringle, F.R.S.; Chapter IX (first part), Dr Margaret Jepps and Dr L. E. R. Picken; Chapters IX and X, Dr C. F. A. Pantin, F.R.S.; Chapter X (second part), Dr B. B. Boycott; Chapter XI, Professor V. B. Wigglesworth, F.R.S.; Chapters XII and XIII, Dr H. W. Lissmann, F.R.S.; Chapter XIII, Mr R. Bainbridge.

The chapters on birds contain accounts of a good deal of as yet unpublished work by myself and by colleagues and research students, carried out at the Madingley Ornithological Field Station of the Department of Zoology, and much of the drive to write the book came from the communal activity of the Field Station. In the first place, the Field Station would never have come into being had it not been for the ready encouragement of Professor Sir James Gray, F.R.S., quickly followed by generous practical help in the form of a grant from the Zoology Research Fund. Subsequently, the Station has been handsomely supported by the University and the Nuffield Foundation, to whom most sincere thanks are due. Since hand-rearing of, and experimenting with, large numbers of birds is inevitably a co-operative operation, almost all the staff and research workers at the Field Station have had some direct or indirect share in the work described. They are: Dr R. A. Hinde, Dr P. Marler, Miss M. A. Vince (Department of Psychology), Dr R. J. Andrew, Mr D. Blest and Mr J. H. Crook. To the care and vigilance of Mr G. E. Dunnett, the Chief Aviary Keeper, and his assistant, Miss E. M. Barraud, the Field Station is greatly indebted. The following part-time workers also deserve much thanks: The Misses J. Sayers, J. Phelps-Brown, A. Walker and A. Harding.

I am indebted to a number of workers outside Cambridge who have readily given me permission to quote unpublished studies. In particular I would like to thank Professor J. Z. Young, F.R.S., Dr B. B. Boycott, Dr K. Lorenz, Professor T. A. Stephenson, F.R.S., Dr H. Friedmann, Dr H. Morris and Mr H. Boyd.

I have tried to quote all sources of published information in the reference list, but I would like in particular to state my indebtedness to certain comprehensive works which have been particularly valuable as summaries and sources of reference. These are: J. J. Gibson (1950); E. R. Hilgard (1948); N. L. Munn (1950); G. K. Noble (1931); S. S. Stevens (1951); and Warden, Jenkins and Warner (Vol. II, 1936). The chapters on arthropods and birds are to a large extent a revision and extension of previous articles by myself, published in the *British Journal of Psychology*, 1943–4, and in *Ibis*, 1951.

I have to thank many for the use of figures. Professor T. A. Stephenson, F.R.S., very kindly lent two original illustrations, Figs. 27 and 28. For permission to reproduce others, I am greatly indebted as follows: Dr N. Tinbergen and Oxford University Press for Figs. 1, 3, 7, 8, 9, 48; Professor Eccles and the Oxford University Press, Figs. 17 and 18; Dr K. Lorenz, Professor Stresemann and the *Avicultural Magazine*, Figs. 2, 67a; Gustav Fischer, Jena, Fig. 5; Cambridge University Press, Fig. 6; N.V. Boekhandel en Drukkery, v/h E. J. Brill, Leiden, Figs. 10, 19, 21–23, 42–45, 68–71; *Comparative Psychological Monographs* (American Psychological Association), Fig. 15; Dr C. F. A. Pantin, Fig. 24; Dr B. B. Boycott and Professor J. Z. Young, Figs. 29, 30, 31; Dr G. V. T.

Matthews, Fig. 56; Dr S. C. Chen and *Physiological Zoology* (University of Chicago Press), Fig. 35; *Experientia*, Fig. 46; Dr C. R. Ribbands, Fig. 47; American Museum of Natural History, Fig. 49; Akademie-Verlag, Fig. 51a and b; Dr R. A. Hinde, Figs. 52–55; Societas pro Fauná et Flora Fennica, Helsingfors, Fig. 65; Dr Olaus F. Murie (U.S. Department of Agriculture), Fig. 67c; Dr A. J. Marshall, Pl. II; the Editors of *Nature*, Pls. VI–IX.

Finally, I would like to thank the representatives of Messrs Methuen, Mr Peter Wait, Mr Paul Hubner and Mr Nigel Viney, for the ready tolerance with which they agreed to suggestions and changes, and for assistance in many other ways during the production of the book.

Cambridge
Autumn 1955.

REFERENCES

ABE, N., 1939: On the locomotion of a limpet-like pulmonate *Siphonaria atra*. *Venus Kyoto Japan*, 5:206–12. (In Japanese, with English summary.)

ABEL, E. F., 1955: Freilandbeobachtungen an *Callionymus festivus* Pall. und *Tripterygion tripteronotus* Riseo, swei Mittelmeerfischen, unter besonder Berücksichtigung des Fortpflanzungsverhaltens. *Sitz. der Österr. Akad. Wissen. Mathem-naturw.* 164:817–54.

ADAMS, D. K., 1931: A re-statement of the problem of learning. *Brit. J. Psychol.* 22: 150–78.

ADAMS, H. G. 1853: ed. *Bechstein's 'Cage and Chamber Birds'.* London. (Based on the 4th German edition 1840.) Pp. 500.

ADAMSON, J., 1960: *Born Free.* London.

—— 1961: *Living Free.* London.

ADLERZ, G., 1900: Biologiska Meddelanden om Rofsteklar. *Entom. Tidskr.* 21: 161–200.

—— 1903: Lefnadsförhallenden och Instinkter in om Familjerna Pompilidae och Sphegidae, *K. Svenska Vetensk. Akad. Handl.* 37, No. 5: 1–181.

—— 1906: Lefnadsförhallenden och Instinkter in om Familjerna Pompilidae och Sphegidae. Part 2. *Ibid*, 42, No. 1: 1–48.

—— 1909: Nya jakttagelser öfver *Ammophila (Miscus) campestris*. *Entom. Tidskr.* 30: 163–76.

ADRIAN, E. D., 1947: *The Physical Background of Perception.* Oxford.

—— 1950: The control of nerve cell activity. *Symposia Soc. Exp. Biol.* 4: 85–91.

AGAR, W. E., 1927: The regulation of behaviour in watermites and some other arthropods. *J. Comp. Psychol.* 7: 319–21.

—— 1943: *The Theory of the Living Organism.* Melbourne University Press.

AHLQUIST, H., 1937: Psychologische Beobachtungen an einigen Jungvögeln der Gattungen *Stercorarius, Larus* u. *Sterna. Acta Soc. Fauna Flora Fenn.* 60: 162–78.

AHRENS, R., 1954: Beitrage zur Entwicklung des Physiognomie de Mimikerkennes. *Z. exp. u. ang. Psychol.* 2: 402–54, 599–633.

AKHMETELI, M., 1941: Imitation in pigeons. *Trans. Beritashvili Physiol. Inst.* No. 4: 345–65.

ALLABACH, L. F., 1905: Some points regarding the behaviour of *Metridium. Biol. Bull.* 10: 35–43.

ALLARD, H. A., 1939: Vocal mimicry of Starling and Mocking Bird. *Science* 90: 370–1.

ALLEE, W. C., 1936: Analytical studies of group behaviour in birds. *Wilson Bull.* 48: 143–51.

ALLEE, W. C., and MASURE, R. H., 1936: A comparison of maze behaviour in paired and isolated Shell Parakeets. *J. Comp. Psychol.* 22: 131–55.

ALLEN, P. P., and MANGLES, F. P., 1940: Studies of the nesting behaviour of the Black-crowned Night Heron. *Proc. Linn. Soc. N.Y.* 50 and 51: 1–28.

ALLEY, R., and BOYD, H., 1950: Parent-young recognition in the Coot *Fulica atra. Ibis* 92: 46–51.

ALTEVOGT, R., 1951: Vergleichend-psychologische Untersuchungen an Hühnerrassen stark unterschiedener Körpergrösse. *Z. Tierpsychol.* 8: 75–109.

—— 1953: Über des 'Schöpfen' einiger Vogelarten. *Behaviour* 6: 147–52.

ALVERDES, F., 1937: Gewohnung und Lernen in Verhalten der Tiere. *Zool. Anz.* 120: 90–5.

—— 1939: Zur Psychologie der niederen Tiere. *Z. Tierpsychol.* 2: 258–64.

AMBROSE, J. A., 1960: Factors affecting the development of the smiling response as a social releaser in human infancy. *Anim. Behav.* 9: 116.

AMSEL, A., 1950: The combination of a primary appetitional need with primary and secondary emotionally derived needs. *J. Exp. Psychol.* **40**: 1–14.

AMSEL, A., and MALTZMAN, I., 1950: The effect upon generalized drive strength of emotionality as inferred from the level of the consummatory response. *J. Exp. Psychol.* **40**: 563–9.

ANDERSON, A. C., 1937: The effect of equalising reward on the breakdown of a discrimination habit and its bearing on reminiscence. *J. Comp. Psychol.* **23**: 421–37.

—— 1940: Evidences of reminiscence in the rat in maze learning. *J. Comp. Psychol.* **30**: 399–412.

ANDREW, R. J., 1956: Some remarks on conflict situations, with special reference to *Emberiza* sp. *Brit. J. Anim. Behav.*, **4**: 41–45.

ANOKHIN, P. K., 1961: A new conception of the physiological architecture of the conditioned reflex. In Delafresnaye (1961).

ANTONIUS, O., 1937: Über Herdenbildung und Paarungseigentümlichkeiten der Einhufer. *Z. p. Tierpsychol.* **1**: 259–89.

ARBIT, J., 1957: Diurnal cycles and learning in the earthworm. *Science* **126**: 654–5.

AREY, L. B., and CROZIER, W. J., 1918: The homing habits of the pulmonate mollusk *Onchidium*. *Proc. Nat. Acad. Sci. Wash.* **4**: 319–21.

—— 1921: On the natural history of *Onchidium*. *J. Exp. Zool.* **32**: 443–502.

ARMBRUSTER, L., 1919: Messbare phænotypische und genotypische Instinktveränderungen. Bienen- und Wespengehirne. *Arch. Bienenkunde* **1**: 145–84.

—— 1921: Über Werkzeuggebrauch bei Tieren. *Naturwiss.* **9**: 303–5.

ARMSTRONG, E. A., 1947: *Bird Display and Behaviour.* London.

—— 1950: The nature and function of displacement activities. Symposium Vol. 4 of Society of Experimental Biology on *'Physiological Mechanisms in Animal Behaviour.'* Cambridge.

—— 1951: The nature and function of animal mimesis. *Bull. Anim. Behav.* No. 9: 46–58.

—— 1955: *The Wren.* London.

ARNDT, W., 1939: Abschliessende Versuche zur Frage des 'Zahlvermögens' der Haustaube. *Z. Tierpsychol.* **3**: 88–142.

ARONSON, L. R., 1951: Orientation and jumping behaviour in the gobiid fish *Bathygobius soporator*. *Am. Mus. Novitates* **1486**: 1–22.

—— 1957: Reproductive and parental behaviour. In *The Physiology of Fishes*, ed. M. E. Brown, Vol. 2. New York.

ASCHOFF, J., 1958: Tierische Periodik unter dem Einfluss von Zeitgebern. *Z. Tierpsychol.* **15**: 1–30.

ASH, J., 1952: Habituated fear response in Blue Tits. *Brit. Birds* **45**: 288–9.

BAERENDS, G. P., 1941: Fortpflanzungsverhalten und Orientierung der Grabwespe *Ammophila campestris*. *Jur. Tijd. voor Entom.* **84**: 71–275.

—— 1950: Specializations in organs and movements with a releasing function. *Symposia Soc. Exp. Biol.* **4**: 337–60.

—— 1959: Ethological studies of insect behaviour. *Ann. Rev. Entomology* 207–34.

BAERENDS, G. P., and BAERENDS-VAN ROON, J. M., 1950: *An Introduction to the Ethology of Cichlid Fishes, Behaviour Supplement* **1**: 1–243.

BAIER, L. J., 1930: Contributions to the physiology of the stridulation and hearing of insects. *Zool. Jb. Abt. allg. Zool.* **47**: 151–248.

BAILEY, L., 1953. *Unpublished.* Quoted in Ribbands, 1953.

BAJANDUROW, B. I., 1928: The physiology of conditioned inhibition in birds. *Zh. Ekespr. Biol. Med.* **4**: 210–22.

—— 1937: Bedingte Reflexe bei Vögeln. *Trudi. Tomsk. Med. Inst.* **5**: 1–115.

BAJANDUROW, B. I., and PEGEL, W. A., 1932: Der Bedingte Reflexe bei Fröschen. *Z. vergl. Physiol.* **18**: 284–97.

BAKER, E. C. S., 1942: *Cuckoo Problems.* London.

BALDWIN, J. M., 1914: Deferred imitation in West African Grey Parrots. *9th Int. Cong. Zool.* 536–7.

BALLY, G., 1945: *Vom Ursprung und von der Grenzen der Freiheit.* Basel.

BANTA, A. M., 1914: Sex recognition and the mating behaviour of the Wood Frog, *Rana sylvatica. Biol. Bull.* 26:171–83.

BARCLAY, O. R., 1953: Some aspects of the mechanics of mammalian locomotion. *J. Exp. Biol.* 30:116–20.

BARNETT, S. A., 1956: Endothermy and ectothermy in mice at −3° C. *J. exp. Biol.* 33:124–33.

——— 1958: Exploratory behaviour. *Brit. J. Psychol.* 49:289–310.

BARRASS, R., 1960: The courtship behaviour of *Mormoniella vitripennis* Walker (Hymenoptera—Pteromalidae). *Behaviour* 15:185–218.

BARRINGTON, Daines, 1773: Experiments and observations on the singing of birds. *Phil. Trans. Roy. Soc.* 63:249–91.

BARRON, D. H., 1950: Genetic neurology and the behaviour problem. In *Genetic Neurology*, ed. P. Weiss, Chicago.

BASTOCK, M., MORRIS, D., and MOYNIHAN, M., 1953: Some comments on conflict and thwarting in animals. *Behaviour* 6:66–84.

BATHAM, E. J., and PANTIN, C. F. A., 1950: Inherent activity in the sea-anemone, *Metridium senile (L.). J. Exp. Biol.* 27:290–301.

BATTERSBY, E., 1944: Do young birds play? *Ibis* 86:225.

BEACH, F. A., 1942a: Comparison of copulatory behaviour of male rats reared in isolation, cohabitation and segregation. *J. Genet. Psychol.* 60:121–36.

——— 1942b: Execution of the complete masculine copulatory pattern by sexually receptive female rats. *Ibid.* 60:137–42.

——— 1942c: Male and female mating behaviour in pre-puberally castrated female rats treated with androgens. *Endocrinology* 31:673–8.

——— 1944a: Experimental studies of sexual behaviour in male mammals. *J. Clin. Endocrinology* 4:126–34.

——— 1944b: Responses of captive alligators to auditory stimulation. *Amer. Nat.* 78:481–505.

——— 1945: Current concepts of play in animals. *Amer. Nat.* 79:523–41.

——— 1948: *Hormones and Behaviour.* New York.

BEACH, F. A., and HOLZ-TUCKER, A. M., 1949: Effects of different concentrations of androgen upon sexual behaviour in castrated rats. *J. Comp. Physiol. Psychol.* 42:433–53.

BEACH, F. A., and JAYNES, J., 1954: Effects of early experience upon the behaviour of animals. *Psychological Bulletin* 51:239–63.

BEHAN, R. A., 1953: Expectancies and the Hullian Theory. *Psychol. Rev.* 60:252–6.

BEKHTEREV, V. M., 1913: *La Psychologie Objective.* Paris.

BELING, I., 1929: Über das Zeitgedächtnis der Bienen. *Z. wiss. Biol. Abt. C. Z. Vergl. Physiol.* 9:259–338.

BELLOWS, R. T., 1939: Time factors in water drinking in dogs. *Amer. J. Physiol.* 126:13–19.

BELT, Thomas, 1874: *The Naturalist in Nicaragua.* London.

BENÉ, F., 1945: The role of learning in the feeding behaviour of Black-chinned Humming-birds. *Condor* 47:3–22.

BENIUC, M., 1933: Bedeutungswechsel der Dinge in der Umwelt des Kampffisches *Betta splendens* Regan. *Z. vergl. Physiol.* 18:437–58.

——— 1934: *Learning and Intelligence in the Fish* (Rumanian). Cluj: Dept. Psychology. Pp. 86.

——— 1938: The roundabout path of the fighting fish. *Proc. Zool. Soc.* 403–22.

BENNETT, M. A., 1939: The social hierarchy in Ring Doves. *Ecology* 20:337–57.

BENSON, C. W., 1948: Geographical voice variation in African birds. *Ibis* 90:48–71.

BERITOFF, J., 1926: Über die individuell erworbene Tätigkeit des Zentralnervensystems bei Tauben. *Arch. ges. Physiol.* 213:370–406.

BERITOFF, J. S., and AKHMETELI, M. N., 1937: The role of the outward appearance of food in the individual behaviour of pigeons. *Bull. Biol. Méd. expér. Moscow* 4:283-4.

BERLAND, L., 1935: Quelques traits du comportement des hymenoptères sphegiens. *Ann. Sci. nat. X. Séries* 18:53-66.

BERLYNE, D. E., 1950: Novelty and curiosity as determinants of exploratory behaviour. *Brit. J. Psychol.* (Gen. Sec.) 41:68-80.

——— 1951: Attention to change. *Brit. J. Psychol.* (Gen. Sec.) 42:269-78.

——— 1960: *Conflict, Arousal and Curiosity.* New York.

BERTALANFFY, L. von, 1952: *Problems of Life.* London.

BETHE, A., 1898: Dürfen wir den Amiesen und Bienen psychische Qualitäten zuschreiben? *Pflüg. Arch, ges. Physiol.* 70:15-100.

BEURLE, R. L., 1956: Properties of a mass of cells capable of regenerating pulses. *Phil. Trans. Roy. Soc. B.* 240:55-94.

BEUSEKOM, G. van, 1948: Some experiments on the optical orientation in *Philanthus triangulum* Fabr. *Behaviour* 1:195-226.

BHARUCHA-REID, R. P., 1956: Latent learning in earthworms. *Science* 123:222.

BIERENS DE HAAN, J. A., 1926a: Die Balz des Argusfasans. *Biol. Zbl.* 46:428-35.

——— 1926b: Versuche über den Farbensinn und das psychische Leben von *Octopus vulgaris. Z. vergl. Physiol.* 4:766-96.

——— 1929: Animal language in relation to that of man. *Biol. Rev.* 4:249-68.

——— 1933: Der Stieglitz als Shöpfer, *J. Orn.* 81:1-22.

——— 1936: Notion de nombre et faculté de compter chez les animaux. *J. Psychol.* 33:393-412.

——— 1940: *Die Tierischen Instinkte und ihr Umbau durch Erfahrung.* Leiden.

BINDRA, D., 1947: Water-hoarding in rats. *J. Comp. Physiol. Psychol.* 40:149-56.

BINGHAM, H. C., 1929: Sex development in apes. *Comp. Psy. Monographs* 5:1-165.

BIRCH, H. G., 1945: The relation of previous experience to insightful problem-solving. *J. Comp. Psychol.* 38:367-83.

BIRD, C., 1925: The relative importance of maturation and habit in the development of an instinct. *J. Genet. Psychol.* 33:68-91.

——— 1926: The effects of maturation on the pecking instinct of chicks. *J. Genet. Psychol.* 33:212-34.

BIRUKOW, G., 1953: Photo-geomenotaxische transpositionen bei *Geotrupes silvaticus. Rev. Suisse Zool.* 60:535-40.

BLEES, G. H. J., 1919: Phototropisme et expérience chez la daphnie. *Arch. Néerl. Physiol.* 3:279-306.

BLODGETT, H. C., 1929: The effect of the introduction of reward upon the maze performance of rats. *Univ. Cal. Publ. Psychol.* 4:113-34.

BOCK, A., 1942: Über das Lernvermögen bei *Asellus* u. *Porcellio. Z. vergl. Physiol.* 29:595-637.

BOESIGER, E., and LECOMTE, J., 1959: Sur les réactions des Mésanges à des modifications apportées a leur nid. *Alauda* 27:16-22.

BOGERT, C. M., 1941: Sensory cues used by Rattlesnakes in recognition of Ophidian enemies. *Ann. N.Y. Acad. Sci.* 41:329-44.

——— 1947: A field study of homing in the Carolina Toad. *Am. Mus. Novitates,* 1355:1-24.

——— 1961: The influence of sound on the behaviour of amphibians and reptiles. In *Animal Sounds and Communication,* ed. W. E. Lanyon and W. N. Tavolga. Washington, D.C.

BOGUSLAVSKI, G. W., 1957: Adaptive responses and the contiguity principle. *J. genet. Psychol.* 90:83-8.

BOHN, G., 1902: Contribution à la psychologie des annélides. *Bull. Inst. Gen. Psychol.* 2:317-25.

——— 1908: Les rhythmes vitaux chez les actinies. *C. R. 37 Congr. Ass. fr. Avan. Sci. Not. Mém.* 613-19.

BONNET, C., 1779–83: Observations sur des petits Fourmis etc. *Oeuvr. Hist. Nat. Philos.* **1**: Neuchâtel.

BOOTH, E. T., 1881–7: *Rough notes on the birds observed during twenty-five years shooting and collecting in the British Isles.* (3 vols.) London.

BORELL DU VERNAY, W. von, 1942: Assoziationsbildung und sensibilisierung bei *Tenebrio. Z. vergl. Physiol.* **30**:84–116.

BOTSCH, D., 1960: Dressur- und Transpositionsversuche bei Karauschen (*Carassius, Teleosti*) nach partieller Exstirpation des tectum opticum. *Z. vergl. Physiol.* **43**:173–230.

BOUVIER, E. L., 1901: Les habitudes des *Bembex. Année Psychol.* **7**:1–68.

—— 1922: *The Psychic Life of Insects.* Trans. L. O. Howard. London.

BOWEN, E. S., 1931: The role of the sense organs in the aggregation of *Ameiurus melas. Ecol. Mono.* **1**:1–35.

BOYCOTT, B. B., 1954: Learning in *Octopus vulgaris* and other cephalopods. *Publ. Staz. Zool. Napoli* **25**:67–93.

—— 1960: The functioning of the statocysts of *Octopus vulgaris. Proc. Roy. Soc. B.* **152**:78–87.

—— 1961: The functional organisation of the brain of the cuttlefish *Sepia officinalis. Proc. Roy. Soc. B.* **153**:503–34.

BOYCOTT, B. B., and GUILLERY, R. W., 1962: Olfactory and visual learning in the Red-eared Terrapin (*Pseudemys crypta-elegans*). (In press.)

BOYCOTT, B. B., and YOUNG, J. Z., 1950: The comparative study of learning. *Symposia Soc. Exp. Biol.* **4**:432–53.

—— —— 1955a: A memory system in *Octopus vulgaris. Proc. Roy Soc. B.* **143**:449–80.

—— —— 1955b: Learned responses to food objects by *Octopus vulgaris* (in press).

—— —— 1956a: Reactions to shape in *Octopus vulgaris* Lamarck. *Proc. zool. Soc. Lond.* **126**:491–547.

—— —— 1956b: The subpedunculate body and nerve and other organs associated with the optic tract of cephalopods. In *Bertil Hanström: zoological papers in honour of his 65th birthday.* Ed. Wingstrand. Lund.

—— —— 1957: Effects of interference with the vertical lobe on visual discrimination in *Octopus vulgaris* Lamarck. *Proc. Roy. Soc. B.* **146**:439–59.

BOYD, H., 1955: *Personal communication.*

BOZLER, E., 1924a: Über die Morphologie der Ernährungsorganelle und die Physiologie der Nahrungsaufnahme von *Paramœcium caudatum. Arch. Protistenkunde* **49**:163–215.

—— 1924b: Über die physikalische Erklärung der schlundfadenströmungen, ein Beitrag zur Theorie der Protoplasmaströmerengen. *Z. vergl. Physiol.* **2**:82–90.

BRADDOCK, J. C., 1949: The effect of prior residence upon dominance in the fish *Platypœcilus maculatus. Physiol. Zool.* **22**:161–9.

BRADFORD, N., 1946: Property rights of animals. *Bull. Utah Biol.* Ser. 9, No. 8: 1–68.

BRAGG, A. N., 1936: Selection of food in *Paramœcium trichium. Physiol. Zool.* **9**:433–42.

—— 1939: Selection of Food by Protozoa. (Not seen.) *Turtox News* **17**:41–4.

BRAMSTEDT, F., 1935: Dressurversuche mit *Paramecium caudatum* und *Stylonychia mytilus. Z. wiss. Biol. Abt. C. Z. vergl. Physiol.* **22**:490–516.

BRANDT, H., 1935: The spread of the influence of rewards to bonds remote in sequence and time. *Arch. Psychol, N.Y.* **27**:No. 180. Pp. 45.

BREDER, C. M., 1925: In Darien Jungles. *Nat. Hist.* **25**:325–37.

—— 1945: Compensatory reactions to the loss of the lower jaw in a cave fish. *Zoologica* **30**:95–9.

—— 1951: Nocturnal and feeding behaviour of the labrid fish *Xyrichthys psittacus. Copeia* **2**:162–3.

—— 1959: Studies of social grouping in fishes. *Bull Amer. Mus. Nat. Hist.* **117**: 393–482.

BREDER, C. M., BREDER, R. B., and REDMOND, A. C., 1927: Frog-tagging: a method of studying anuran life habits. *Zoologica* 9: 201–9.

BREDER, C. M., and GRESSER, E. B., 1941: Correlations between structural eye-defects and behaviour in the Mexican Blind Characin. *Zoologica* 26: 123–31.

BREDER, C. M., and HALPERN, F., 1946: Innate and acquired behaviour affecting the aggregation of fishes. *Physiol. Zool.* 19: 154–90.

BREED, F. S., 1911: The development of certain instincts and habits in chicks. *Behaviour Monographs* 1: 1–78.

BRICKENSTEIN, C., 1955: Über den Netzbau der Larve von *Neureclipsis bimaculata* Ab. *Bayer. Akad. Wiss.* 69: 1–44.

BROADBENT, D. E., 1952: (*Unpublished*) Pavlovian conditioning and vigilance tasks. *M.R.C. App. Psych. Rept. A.P.U.* Pp. 10.

—— 1961: Human perception and animal learning. In Thorpe and Zangwill (1961).

BROOKS-KING, M., 1941: Intelligence tests with tits. *Brit. Birds* 35: 29–32.

BROWER, J., 1958: Experimental studies of mimicry in some North American butterflies. *Evolution* 12: 32–47.

BROWER, L. P., BROWER, J. van Zandt, and WESTCOTT, P. W., 1960: Experimental studies of mimicry. 5. The reactions of toads (*Bufo terrestris*) to Bumblebees (*Bombus americanorum*) and their Robberfly mimics (*Mallophora bomboides*) with a discussion of aggressive mimicry. *Amer. Nat.* 94: 343–56.

BROWN, C. R., and HATCH, M. H., 1929: Orientation and fright reactions of whirligig beetles (Gyrinidae). *J. Comp. Psychol.* 9: 159–89.

BROWN, G., 1942: Some aspects of instinctive behaviour and display in birds. *Ibis* (14) 6: 133–5.

BROWN, J. S., et al., 1953: *Current Theory and Research in Motivation: a Symposium.* Univ. Nebraska Press, Lincoln, Neb., U.S.A.

BROWN, R. F. J., 1939: Investigations into intelligence of Lesser Black-backed Gulls at nesting time. *Report Chr. Hosp. N.H.S.* 35: 12–23.

BRÜCKNER, G. H., 1933: Untersuchungen zu Tiersoziologie, insbesondere zur Auflösung der Familie. *Z. Psychol.* 128: 1–110.

BRÜLL, H., 1937: *Das Leben deutscher Greifvögel.* Jena.

BRUN, R., 1912: Zur Psychologie der kunstlichen Allianz-Kolonien bei den Ameisen. *Biol. Zbl.* 32: 308–22.

—— 1914: *Die Raumorientierung der Ameisen und das Orientierungsproblem im allgemeinen.* Jena.

BRUNELLI, G., 1910: Osservazioni e esperienze sulla simbiosi dei Paguridi e delle Attinie. *Att. Rend. R. Acad. Lincaei Roma,* 19 (ii): 77–82.

BUDDENBROCK, W. von, 1937: *Grundriss der vergleichenden Physiologie.* Berlin.

BULL, H. O., 1928–39: Studies on conditioned responses in fishes, Parts I–IX. *J.M.B.A. & Dove Marine Labty. Reports.*

—— 1957: Behaviour: conditioned responses. In *The Physiology of Fishes,* ed. M. E. Brown, Vol. 2. New York.

BULLOCK, T. H., 1961: The origins of patterned nervous discharges. *Behaviour* 17: 48–59.

BULLOUGH, W. S., 1942: The reproductive cycles of the British and Continental races of the Starling. *Phil. Trans. Roy. Soc. B.* 231: 165–246.

—— 1945: Endocrinological aspects of bird behaviour. *Biol. Rev.* 20: 89–99.

BUNCH, M. E., and MAGDSICK, W. K., 1933: The retention in rats of an incompletely learned maze solution for short intervals of time. *J. Comp. Psychol.* 16: 385–409.

BURNETT, T. C., 1912: Some observations on decerebrate frogs with especial reference to the formation of associations. *Amer. J. Physiol.* 30: 80–7.

BURNS, B. D., 1951: Some properties of the isolated cerebral cortex of the unanaesthetized cat. *J. Physiol.* 112: 156–75.

BURTON, M., 1958: Parrot's Intelligence, *Illustrated London News,* Oct. 4, p. 572.

BUTLER, C. G., 1954: The method and importance of the recognition by a colony of honeybees of the presence of its queen. *Trans. roy. ent. Soc. Lond.* **105**: 11–29.
—— 1960: Queen recognition by worker honeybees (*Apis mellifera* L.) *Experientia* **16**: 424–8.
BUTLER, C. G., CALLOW, R. K., and JOHNSTON, C. J., 1962: The isolation and synthesis of queen substance, 9-oxodec-trans-2-enoic acid, a honeybee pheromone. *Proc. Roy. Soc. B.* **155**: 417–432.
BUTLER, C. G. and FREE, J. B., 1952: The behaviour of worker honey-bees at the hive entrance. *Behaviour* **4**: 262–92.
BUTLER, R. A., 1953: Discrimination learning by rhesus monkeys to visual exploration motivation. *J. Comp. Physiol. Psychol.* **46**: 95–8.
BUTLER, R. A., and ALEXANDER, H. M., 1955: Daily patterns of visual exploratory behaviour in the monkey. *J. comp. physiol. Psychol.* **45**: 247–9.
BUTTEL-REEPEN, H. von, 1907: Psychobiologische und biologische Beobachtungen an Ameisen, Bienen und Wespen. *Naturw. Wschr.* **22**: 465–78.
BUTTS, W. W., 1927: The feeding range of certain birds. *Auk.* **44**: 329–50.
BUTZ-KUENZER, E., 1957: Optische und labyrinthäre Auslösung der Lagereaktionen bei Amphibien. *Z. Tierpsychol.* **14**: 429–47.
BUXTON, A., 1946: *Fisherman Naturalist*. London.
BUXTON, C. E., 1946: Latent learning and the goal gradient hypothesis. *Contributions to Psychological Theory* **2**. Pp. 75.
BUXTON, E. J. M., 1948: Tits and peanuts. *Brit. Birds.* **41**: 229–32.
BUYTENDIJK, F. J. J., 1918a: Instinct de la récherche de nid et expérience chez les crapauds (*Bufo vulgaris* et *Bufo calamita*). *Arch. Néerl. Physiol.* **2**: 1–50.
—— 1918b: L'instinct d'alimentation et l'expérience chez les crapauds. *Arch. Néerl. Physiol.* **2**: 217–28.
—— 1919: Acquisition d'habitudes par des êtres unicellulaires. *Arch. Néerl. Physiol.* **3**: 455–68.
—— 1921a: Sens de localization et acquisition d'habitudes chez les oiseaux. *Arch. Néerl. Physiol.* **5**: 236–43.
—— 1921b: Une formation d'habitude chez le limaçon d'eau douce (*Limnæa*). *Arch. Néerl. Physiol.* **5**: 458–66.
—— 1933: Das Verhalten von *Octopus* nach teilweiser Zerstörung des 'Gehirns.' *Arch. Néerl. Physiol.* **18**: 24–70.

CADE, T. J., 1953: Behaviour of a young Gyrfalcon. *Wilson Bull.* **65**: 26–31.
CAGLE, F. R., 1944: Home range, homing behaviour and migration in turtles. *Misc. Pub. Mus. Zool. Univ. Mich.* No. 61. Pp. 38.
CAJAL, Ramon y, 1904: *Textura del sistema nervioso del hombre y de los vertebrados*. Madrid.
CALHOUN, J. B., 1944: Twenty-four hour periodicities in the animal kingdom. *J. Tenn. Acad. Sci.* **19**: 179–200.
CANE, V., 1961: Some ways of describing behaviour. In Thorpe and Zangwill (1961).
CARMICHAEL, L., 1926: The development of behaviour in vertebrates experimentally removed from the influence of external stimulation. *Psychol. Rev.* **33**: 51–8.
—— 1927: A further study of development of behaviour in vertebrates experimentally removed from the influence of external stimulation. *Psychol. Rev.* **34**: 34–47.
—— 1947: The growth of the sensory control of behaviour before birth. *Psychol. Rev.* **54**: 316–24.
CARTHY, J. D., 1950: Odour trails of *Acanthomyops fuliginosus*. *Nature* **166**: 154.
—— 1951: Orientation of two allied species of British ant. 1. Visual direction-finding in *Acanthomyops* (*Lasius*) *niger*. *Behaviour* **3**: 275–303.
—— 1961: Do animals see polarized light? *New Scientist* **10**: 660–2.
CASTEEL, D. B., 1911: The discriminative ability of the Painted Turtle. *J. Anim. Behav.* **1**: 1–28.

CATE, J. ten, 1923: Essai d'étude des fonctions de l'écorce cérébrale des pigeons par la méthode des reflexes conditionnels. *Arch. Néerl. Physiol.* 8 : 234–73.
—— 1935: Physiologie des Zentralnervensystems der Fische. *Ergb. Biol.* 11 : 335–409.
—— ten, 1936: Physiologie des Zentralnervensystems der Vögel. *Ergb. Biol.* 13 : 93–173.
CATE, J. ten, and CATE-KAZEJEWA, B. ten, 1938: Les *Octopus vulgaris*, peuvent-ils discerner les formes? *Arch. Néerl. Physiol.* 23 : 541–51.
CATE-KAZEJEWA, B. ten, 1934: Quelques observations sur les Bernards l'Ermite (*Pagurus arrosor*). *Arch. Néerl. Physiol.* 19 : 502–8.
CHATTOCK, A. P., and GRINDLEY, G. C., 1931: Effect of change of reward upon learning in chickens. *Brit. J. Psychol.* 22 : 62–6.
—— —— 1933: The effect of delayed reward on the maze performance of chickens. *Brit. J. Psychol.* 33 : 382–8.
CHAUVIN, R., 1950: Le transport de proies chez les fourmis, y-at-il entraide? *Behaviour* 2 : 249–56.
—— 1952: Sur la reconstruction du nid chez les fourmis Oecophylles (*Oecophylla longinoda*). *Behaviour* 4 : 190–202.
—— 1958: Le comportement de construction chez *Formica rufa*. *Insectes Sociaux, V* 3 : 273–86.
CHEN, S. C., 1938a and b: (a) Social modifications of the activity of ants in nest-building; (b) Leaders and followers among the ants in nest-building. *Physiol. Zool.* 10 : 420–36 and 437–55.
CHETTLEBOROUGH, M. R., 1952: Observations on the collection and burial of acorns by Jays in Hainault Forest. *Brit. Birds* 45 : 359–64.
CHILD, C. M., 1921: *The Origin and Development of the Nervous System.* Chicago.
CHISHOLM, A. H., 1934: *Bird Wonders of Australia.* Sydney.
—— 1952: Bird-insect nesting associations in Australia. *Ibis* 94 : 395–405.
—— 1954: The use by birds of 'tools' or 'instruments.' *Ibis* 96 : 380–3.
CHRISTIAN, J. J., and RATCLIFFE, H. L., 1952: Shock disease in captive wild mammals. *Amer. J. Pathology* 28 : 725–37.
CHURCH, R. M., 1959: Emotional reactions of rats to the pain of others. *J. comp. physiol. Psychol.* 52 : 132–4.
CHURCHILL, E. P., Jr., 1916: The learning of a maze by goldfish. *J. Anim. Behav.* 6 : 247–55.
CINAT-TOMSON, H., 1926: Die geschlectliche Zuchtwahl beim Wellensittich (*Melopsittacus undulatus* Shaw). *Biol. Zbl.* 46 : 543–52.
CLAPARÈDE, E., 1926: Mémoire chez la poule. *Arch. Psychol.* 20 (78) : 178.
CLARK, R. B., 1960: Habituation of the polychaete *Nereis* to sudden stimuli. I. General properties of the habituation process. *Anim. Behav.* 8 : 82–91.
CLOUDESLEY-THOMPSON, J. L., 1951: Studies in diurnal rhythms. 1. Rhythmic behaviour in Millipedes. *J. Exp. Biol.* 28 : 165–72.
—— 1952a: Studies in diurnal rhythms. 2. Changes in the physiological responses of the wood-louse *Oniscus asellus* to environmental stimuli. *J. Exp. Biol.* 29 : 295–303.
COGHILL, G. E., 1929: *Anatomy and the Problem of Behaviour.* Cambridge.
COLE, J., 1951: A study of discrimination reversal learning in monkeys. *J. Comp. Physiol. Psychol.* 44 : 467–72.
CONRADI, E., 1905: Song and call notes of English Sparrows when reared by canaries. *Amer. J. Psychol.* 16 : 190–8.
COPELAND, M., 1930: An apparent conditioned response in *Nereis virens*. *J. Comp. Psychol.* 10 : 339–54.
COPELAND, M., and BROWN, F. A., Jr., 1934: Modification of behaviour in *Nereis virens*. *Biol. Bull.* 67 : 356–64.
CORNETZ, V., 1911: Das Problem der Rückkehr zum Nest der forschenden Ameise. *Z. wiss. Insekt. Biol.* 7 : 181–4, 312–6, 347–50.

CORNING, W. C., and JOHN, E. R., 1961: The effect of ribonuclease on retention of conditioned responses in regenerated planarians. *Science* 135:1363-5.

COTT, H. B., 1936: The effectiveness of protective adaptations in the hive-bee, illustrated by experiments on the feeding reactions, habit formation and memory of the common toad (*Bufo bufo bufo*). *Proc. Zool. Soc. Lond.* 111-33.

―――― 1940: *Adaptive Coloration in Animals.* London.

COUSTEAU, J. Y., 1953: *The Silent World.* London.

COWDREY, E. V., 1911: The colour changes of *Octopus vulgaris*, Link. *Univ. Toronto Stud. Biol.* No. 10, pp. 53.

COWLES, R. P., 1908: Learning and habit formation in the crab *Ocypoda arenaria*. *Tortugas Lab. Papers* 2:1-14.

―――― 1911: Reactions to light and other points in the behaviour of the starfish. *Carn. Inst. Pub.* No. 132:95-110.

CRAGG, B. G., and TEMPERLEY, H. N. V., 1954: The organisation of neurones: a co-operative analogy. *E. E. G. Clin. Neurophysiol.* 6:85-92.

CRAIG, Wallace, 1912: Observations on doves learning to drink. *J. Anim. Behav.* 2:273-9.

―――― 1914: Male doves reared in isolation. *J. Anim. Behav.* 4:121-33.

―――― 1918: Appetites and aversions as constituents of instincts. *Biol. Bull.* 34:91-107.

―――― 1943: The song of the Wood Pewee (*Myochanes virens*). *New York State Mus. Bull.* 334:6-186.

CRAIK, K. J. W., 1943: *The Nature of Explanation.* Cambridge.

CRANE, J., 1941: Crabs of the genus *Uca* from the West Coast of Central America. *Zoologica N.Y.* 26:145-208.

CRAWFORD, H. P., and SPENCE, K. W., 1939: Observational learning of discrimination problems by chimpanzees. *J. Comp. Psychol.* 27:133-47.

CRISLER, L., 1959: *Arctic Wild.* London.

CROMBIE, A. C., 1944: On the measurement and modification of the olfactory responses of blowflies. *J. Exp. Biol.* 20:159-66.

CROSS, B. A., 1946: Animal behaviour in relation to veterinary science. *Vet. J.* 102, No. 12:397-409.

CROWCROFT, P., 1954: Aggressive behaviour in wild House Mice. *Min. Ag. Rech. Rpt.* 35:(unpublished).

CULLER, E. A., and METTLER, F. A., 1934: Conditioned behaviour in a decorticate dog. *J. Comp. Psychol.* 18:291-303.

CUNDALL, A. W., EVANS, P., and SEARS, J., 1952: Greenfinch imitating Redstart. *Brit. Birds* 45:365.

CUMMINGS, B. F., 1910: The formation of useless habits in two British newts (*Molge cristata* and *M. palmata*) with observations on their general behaviour. *Zoologist* 14:161-75, 211-22, 272.

CURTI, M. W., 1935: Native fear responses of white rats in the presence of cats. *Psychol. Monog.* 46, No. 210:78-98.

―――― 1942: A further report on fear responses of white rats in the presence of cats. *J. Comp. Psychol.* 34:51-3.

CURIO, E., 1955: Der Jungentransport einer Gelbhalsmus (*Apodemus f. flavicollis* Melch). *Z. Tierpsychol.* 12:459-62.

CURTIUS, A., 1954: Über angeborene Verhaltensweisen bei Vögeln, insbesondere bei Hühnerkücken. *Z. Tierpsychol.* 11:94-109.

CUSHING, J. E., Jnr., 1941: Non-genetic mating preference as a factor in evolution. *Condor* 51:233-6.

―――― 1944: The relation of non-heritable food habits to evolution. *Condor* 46:265-71.

CUSHING, J. E., and RAMSAY, A. O., 1949: The non-heritable aspects of family unity in birds. *Condor* 51:82-97.

CYTOVICH, I. S., 1911: *Dissertation.* St. Petersburg (*Quoted Konorski, 1948, p. 123*).

CZELOTH, H., 1930: Untersuchungen ü. die Raumorientierung von Triton. *Z. vergl. Physiol.* **13** : 74–163.

DABROWSKA, J., 1956: Tresura *Paramecium caudatum, Stentor caeruleus, Spirostomum ambiguum. Nr Budźce Świetne Folia Biol. Polska Akad. Nauk* **4** : 77–91 (with English summary).

DAHL, K., 1938: A review of recent salmon marking experiments in Norway. *Cons. Perm. Int. l'Explor. de la Mer. Raport et Procés-Verbaux des Réunion.* **108** : III : 1–15.

DANISCH, F., 1921: Ueber Reizbiologie und Reizempfindlichkeit von *Vorticella nebulifera. Z. f. allg. Physiol.* **19** : 133–88.

DARCHEN, R., 1952: Sur l'activité exploratrice de *Blatella germanica. Z. Tierpsychol.* **9** : 362–72.

—— 1957: Sur le comportement d'exploration de *Blatella germanica. J. psychol. norm. Pathol.* June 1957, 190–205.

—— 1959: Les techniques de construction chez *Apis mellifera. Thesis Fac. Sci. Univ. Paris.* 210 pp.

DARLING, F. Fraser, 1938a: *Bird Flocks and the Breeding Cycle: a contribution to the study of avian sociability.* Cambridge.

—— 1938b: *Wild Country.* London.

DARWIN, Charles, 1872: *The Expression of the Emotions in Man and Animals.* London.

DATTA, L. G., MILSTEIN, S., and BITTERMAN, M. E., 1960: Habit reversal in the crab. *J. comp. physiol. Psychol.* **53** : 275–8.

DAUB, C. T., 1933: The effect of doors on latent learning. *J. Comp. Psychol.* **15** : 49–58.

DAVIS, D. E., 1942: The phylogeny of social nesting habits in the Crotophaginae. *Quart. Rev. Biol.* **17** : 134–55.

DAVIS, J. R. A., 1885: The habits of the limpet. *Nature* **31** : 200–1.

—— 1895: The habits of limpets. *Nature* **51** : 511–12.

DAVIS, J. R. A., and FLEURE, H. J., 1903: Patella. *Tr. Liverpool Biol. Soc.* **17** : 193–268.

DAWSON, Jean, 1911: The biology of *Physa. Behav. Monog.* **1**, No. 4. Pp. 120.

DAY, L. M., and BENTLEY, M., 1911: Note on learning in *Paramecium. J. Anim. Behav.* **1** : 67–73.

DEESE, J., 1951: The extinction of discrimination without performance of the choice response. *J. Comp. Physiol. Psychol.* **44** : 362–6.

DELAFRESNAYE, J. F. (ed.), 1961: *Brain Mechanisms and Learning.* C.I.O.M.S. Symposium. Oxford.

DEMBOWSKI, J., 1933: Über die Plastizität der tierischen Handlungen, Beobachtungen und Versuche an Molanna–Larven. *Zool. Jahrb. (Abt. allg. Zool. v. Physiol.)* **53** : 261–312.

—— 1950: On conditioned reactions of *Paramecium caudatum* towards light. *Act. Biol. Exp.* **15** : 5–17.

DENBURGH, J. van, 1914: Expedition of the Californian Academy of Sciences to the Galapagos Islands 1905–6. The gigantic Tortoises of the Galapagos Archipelago. *San Francisco Proc. Calif. Acad. Sci. Ser. 4,* **2** : 203–374.

DENNIS, W., 1941: Spalding's experiments on the flight of birds repeated with another species. *J. Comp. Psychol.* **31** : 337–48.

DENNIS, W., and HEINEMAN, R. H., 1932: The non-random character of initial maze behaviour. *J. Genet. Psychol.* **40** : 396–405.

DENNY, M. R., 1946: The role of secondary reinforcement in a partial reinforcement learning situation. *J. Exp. Psychol.* **36** : 373–89.

DENNY, M. R., and DAVIS, R. H., 1951: A test for latent learning in a non-goal significate. *J. Comp. Physiol. Psychol.* **44** : 590–5.

DETHIER, V. G., 1942: The dioptric apparatus of lateral ocelli. I. The corneal lens. *J. Cell. Comp. Physiol.* **19** : 301–13.

—— 1943: The dioptric apparatus of lateral ocelli. II. Visual capacities of the ocellus. *J. Cell. Comp. Physiol.* **22** : 115–26.

DETHIER, V. G., 1952: Adaptation to chemical stimulation of the tarsal receptors of the blowfly. *Biol. Bull.* **103** : 178–9.

—— 1954: Evolution of feeding preferences in phytophagous insects. *Evolution* **8** : 33–54.

DEUTSCH, J. A., 1957: Nest building behaviour of domesticated rabbits under semi-natural conditions. *Brit. J. Anim. Behav.* **5** : 53–4.

—— 1960*a*: *The Structural Basis of Behaviour*. Cambridge.

—— 1960*b*: The plexiform zone and shape recognition in the octopus. *Nature* **185** : 443–6.

DICKERSON, M. C., 1906: *The Frog Book*. New York. (*Not seen; quoted by Warden, Jenkins and Warner*.)

DIEBSCHLAG, E., 1940: Über den Lernvorgang bei der Haustaube. *Z. vergl. Physiol.* **28** : 67–104.

DIESSELHORST, G., 1950: Erkennen des Geschlechts und Paarbildung bei der Goldammer (*Emberiza c. citrinella*). *Orn. Ber.* **3** : 69–112.

DIJKGRAAF, S., 1953: Über das Wesen der optomotorischen Reaktion. *Experientia* **9** : 112–14.

DIJKGRAAF, S., and VERHEIJEN, F., 1950: Neue Versuche über das Tonunterscheidungs-vermögen der Ellritze. *Z. vergl. Physiol.* **32** : 248–56.

DILK, F., 1937: Ausbildung von Assoziationen bei *Planaria gonocephala*. *Z. vergl. Physiol.* **25** : 47–82.

DOBBEN, W. van, 1955: The strength of attraction of leading lines. *Proc. XI Int. Orn. Congr.*

DOBRZANSKA, J., 1958: Partition of foraging grounds and modes of conveying information among ants. *Acta Biol. Experimentalis* **18** : 55-67.

DOBRZANSKA, J., and DOBRZANSKI, J., 1960: Quelques nouvelles rémarques sur l'éthologie de *Polyergus rufescens* Latr. (Hymenoptère, Formicidae). *Insectes Sociaux* 7.

DODD, F. P., 1901: Notes on the Queensland green tree ants (*Oecophylla smaragdina*). *Vict. Nat.* **18** : 136–42.

DODGE, R., 1923: Habituation to rotation. *J. Exp. Psychol.* **6** : 1–35.

—— 1927: *Elementary Conditions of Human Variability*. New York.

DODWELL, P. C., 1957: Shape recognition in rats. *Brit. J. Psychol.* **48** : 221–9.

DOFLEIN, F., 1905: Beobachtungen an den Weberameisen (*Oecophylla smaragdina*) *Biol. Zbl.* **25** : 497–507.

—— 1910: Lebensgewohnheiten und Anpassung bei Dekapoden Krebsen. *Festschrift R. Hertwig*, **3** : 216–90. Jena.

DONISTHORPE, H., 1927: *British Ants*. London.

DOVE, C. C., and THOMPSON, M. E., 1943: Some studies on 'Insight' in white rats. *J. Genet. Psychol.* **63** : 235–45.

DRABBLE, P., 1957: *A Weasel in my Meatsafe*. London.

DREES, O., 1952: Untersuchungen ü die angeborenen Verhaltenswiesen bei Springspinnen. *Z. Tierpsychol.* **9** : 169–207.

DUDZIAK, J., 1950: Experiments on the plasticity of instinct in *Phryganea obsoleta*. McLach (Trichoptera). *Bull. Akad. Pol. Sci.* (B) : 145–71.

DUERDEN, J. E., 1905: On the habits and reactions of crabs bearing actinians in their claws. *Proc. Zool. Soc. Lond.* 1905, **2** : 494–511.

EBBINGHAUS, H., 1885: *Über das Gedächtnis: Untersuchungen zur experimentellen Psychologie*. Leipzig. (*Translated as* '*Memory: A Contribution to Experimental Psychology*.' New York, 1913.)

ECCLES, J. C., 1953: *The Neurophysiological Basis of Mind: The Principles of Neurophysiology*. Oxford.

ECCLES, J. C. and MACINTYRE, A. K., 1951: Plasticity of mammalian monosynaptic reflexes. *Nature* **167** : 466–8.

—— —— 1953: The effects of use and disuse on mammalian spinal reflexes. *J. Physiol.* **121** : 495–516.

EDGELL, B., 1924: *Theories of Memory*. Oxford.

EDWARDS, L. D. R., 1949: *The Fox.* London.

EIBL-EIBESFELDT, I., 1951: Gefangenschaftsbeobachtungen an der persischen Wusten-maus (*Meriones persicus persicus* Blandford). *Z. Tierpsychol.* **8**: 400–23.

—— 1961: The interactions of Unlearned Behaviour Patterns and Learning in Mammals (In Delafresnaye, 1961).

EIDMANN, H., 1927: Die Sprache der Ameisen. *Rev. Zool. Russe* **7**: 39–47.

EIKMANNS, K-H., 1955: Verhaltensphysiologische Untersuchungen über den Beutefang und das Bewegungssehen der Erdkröte (*Bufo bufo* L). *Z. Tierpsychol.* **12**: 229–53.

EISNER, E., 1960: The relationship of hormones to the reproductive behaviour of birds, referring especially to parental behaviour: a review. *Anim. Behav.* **8**: 155–79.

ELDERING, F. J., 1919: Acquisition d'habitudes par les insectes. *Arch. Néerl. Physiol.* **3**: 468–90.

ELLIOTT, M. H., 1929: The effect of change of 'drive' on maze performance. *Univ. Calif. Publ. Psychol.* **4**: 185–8.

—— 1930: Some determining factors in maze performance. *Amer. J. Psychol.* **42**: 315–17.

ELLIS, P. E., 1953: Social aggregation and gregarious behaviour in hoppers of *Locusta migratoria migratorioides* (R&F). *Behaviour* **5**: 225–60.

ENGELMANN, C., 1941–2: Über den Geschmackssinn des Huhns. VI. Über angeborene Formvorliebe bei Hühnern. *Z. Tierpsychol.* **5**: 42–59.

—— 1951: Beitrage zum Gedächtnis des Huhns. *Z. Tierpsychol.* **8**: 110–21.

ERHARDT, A., 1933: Kritische Bermerkungen zu der Arbeit von Bierens de Haan 'Der Stieglitz als Schöpfer.' *Z. Psychol.* **130**: 393–8.

ESKIN, R. M., and BITTERMAN, M. E., 1961: Partial reinforcement in the turtle. *Quart. J. exp. Psychol.* (in press).

ESTES, W. K., KOCH, S., *et al.*, 1954: *Modern Learning Theory.* New York.

EVANS, H. E., 1957: Studies in the comparative ethology of Digger Wasps of the genus Bembix. *Comstock Pub. Ass.* Ithaca, New York.

EVANS, L. T., 1951: Field Study of the social behaviour of the Black Lizard, *Ctenosaura pectinata. Amer. Mus. Novitates*, No. 1493.

—— 1954: *Courtship and Territorial Behaviour of Lower Vertebrates: a Review (Unpublished.)*

EVANS, L. T., and QUARANTA, J., 1951: A study of the social behaviour of a captive herd of Giant Tortoises. *Zoologica* **36**: 171–81.

EWER, R. F., 1947: The behaviour of hydra in response to gravity. *Proc. Zool. Soc. Lond.* **117**: 207–18.

EXNER, S., 1891: *Die Physiologie der facettierten Augen von Krebsen und Insekten.* Leipzig und Wien.

FABRICIUS, E., 1951a: Zur Ethologie junger Anatiden. *Acta. Zool. Fenn.* **68**: 1–175.

—— 1951b: The topography of the spawning bottom as a factor influencing the size of the territory in some species of fish. *Inst. Freshwater Resch. Drottingholm Rep.* **32**: 43–9.

FALCONER, D. S., 1941: Observations on the singing of Chaffinches. *Brit. Birds* **35**: 98–104.

FANKHAUSER, G., and REIK, L. E., 1935: Experiments on case-building of Caddis Fly larva *Neuronia postica. Physiol. Zool.* **8**: 337–58.

FANTZ, R. L., 1957: Form-preference in newly hatched chicks. *J. comp. physiol. Psychol* **50**: 422–30.

FAURE, J. C., 1932: The phases of locusts in South Africa. *Bull. Ent. Res.* **23**: 293–424.

FAURÉ-FREMIET, E., 1948: Le rhythme de marée du *Strombidium oculatum,* Gruber, *Bull. Biol.* **82**: 1–23.

—— 1950: Rhythme de marée d'une *Chromulina psammobia. Bull. Biol.* **84**: 207–14.

—— 1951: The tidal rhythm of the diatom *Hantzschia amphioxys. Biol. Bull.* **100**: 173–7.

FEARING, F. S., 1926: Post-rotational head nystagmus in adult pigeons. *J. Comp. Psychol.* **6**:115–31.

FERSTER, C. B., and SKINNER, B. F., 1957: *Schedules of Reinforcement.* New York.

FIELDE, A. M., 1901: Further study of an ant. *Proc. Acad. Nat. Sci. Philad.* **53**: 521–44.

—— 1904: Power of recognition among ants. *Biol. Bull. Woods Hole* **7**:227–50.

FINCH, G., 1941: The solution of patterned string problems by chimpanzees. *J. Comp. Psychol.* **32**:83–90.

—— 1942: Delayed matching-from-shape and non-spatial delayed response in chimpanzees. *J. Comp. Psychol.* **34**:315–19.

FINGER, F. W., 1942: Retention and subsequent extinction of a simple running response following varying conditions of reinforcement. *J. Exp. Psychol.* **31**:120–33.

FINN, F., 1919: *Bird Behaviour.* London.

FISCHEL, W., 1926: Haben Vögel ein 'Zahlengedächtnis'? *Z. vergl. Physiol.* **4**: 345–69.

—— 1931: Dressurversuche an Schnecken. *Z. vergl. Physiol.* **15**:50–70.

—— 1933: Über bewahrende und wirkende Gedächtnisleistung. *Biol. Zbl.* **53**:449–51.

—— 1934: Gedächtnisversuche mit Schildkroten. *Zool. Anz.* **107**:49–61.

—— 1936: Die Gedächtnis der Vögel. *Z. Tierzücht. und Züchtungsbiol.* **36**: 13–38.

FISCHER, H., 1898: Quelques remarques sur les mœurs des Patelles. *J. de Conchyl.* **46**:314–18.

FISCHER, K., 1960: Experimentelle Beeinflussung der inneren Uhr bei der Sonnenkompassorientierung und der Laufaktivität von *Lacerto viridis* (Laur.). *Naturwissenschaften* **12**:287–8.

FISCHER, K., and BIRUKOW, G., 1960: Dressur von Smaragdeidechsen auf Kompassrichtungen. *Naturwissenschaften* **4**:93–4.

FISCHER, P-H., 1939a: Sur l'habitat et l'hygrophile des Succinées. *J. de Conchyl.* **83**:111–28.

—— 1939b: Sur les terriers des Poulpes. *Bull. Lab. Mar. Dinard* **20**:92–4.

—— 1950: *Vie et Mœurs des Mollusques.* Paris.

FISHER, Edna, 1939: Habits of the Southern Sea Otter. *J. Mammalogy* **20**:21–36.

FISHER, J., and HINDE, R. A., 1949: The opening of milk bottles by birds. *Brit. Birds* **42**:347–57.

FLEURE, H. J., and WALTON, C. L., 1907: Notes on the habits of some Sea Anemones. *Zool. Anz.* **31**:212–20.

FLOWER, S. S., 1927: Loss of memory accompanying metamorphosis in amphibians. *Proc. Zool. Soc. Lond.* 1927, Vol. **1**:155–6.

FOLEY, J. P., 1934: First year development of a Rhesus monkey (*Macaca mulatta*) reared in isolation. *J. Genet. Psychol.* **45**:39–105.

FOLGER, H. T., 1926: The effects of mechanical shock on locomotion in *Amœba proteus. J. Morph. Physiol.* **42**:359–70.

FORBES, A., 1939: Problems of synaptic function. *J. Neurophysiol.* **2**:465–72.

FORBES, T. R., 1940: A note on reptilian sex ratios. *Copeia* **56**:132.

FORSELIUS, S., 1957: Studies of Anabantid fishes. *Zool. Bidrag. Från* Uppsala, **32**: 1–597.

FOTH, L., 1939: Intelligenzprüfungen bei Cichliden. *Wochenschr. f. Aquar. u. Terrarkunde* **36**:677–85.

FRAENKEL, G., 1929: Über die Geotaxis von *Convoluta roscoffensis. Z. wiss. Biol. Abt. C. Z. vergl. Physiol.* **10**:237–47.

FRANZ, V., 1927: Zur tierpsychologischen stellung von *Rana temporaria* u. *Bufo calamita. Biol. Zbl.* **47**:1–12.

FRANZISKET, L., 1955: Die Bildung einer Bedingten Hemmung bei Rückenmarkfröschen. *Z. vergl. Physiol.* **37**:161–8.

—— 1961: Characteristics of instinctive behaviour and learning in the reflex activity of the toad. *Anim. Behav.* (in press).

FREE, J. B., 1955a: The adaptability of Bumble Bees to a change in the location of their nest. *Brit. J. Anim. Behav.* **3**:61–5.

FREE, J. B., 1955b: The division of labour within bumble bee colonies. *Insectes Sociaux* 2:195–212.

—— 1958: The ability of worker honeybees *Apis mellifera* to learn a change in the location of their hives. *Anim. Behav.* 6:219—23.

FREE, J. B., and BUTLER, C. G., 1959: *Bumble Bees*. London.

FREEDMAN, D. G., 1958: Constitutional and environmental interactions in rearing four breeds of dogs. *Science* 127:585–6.

FRENCH, G. M., 1959: Performance of Squirrel Monkeys on variants of a delayed response. *J. comp. physiol. Psychol.* 52:741–5.

FRENCH, J. W. V., 1940a: Trial-and-error learning in *Paramecium*. *J. Exp. Psychol.* 26:609–13.

—— 1940b: Individual differences in *Paramecium*. *J. Comp. Psychol.* 30:451–6.

—— 1942: The effect of temperature on the retention of a maze habit in fish. *J. Exp. Psychol.* 31:79–87.

FRIEDLÄNDER, M., 1931: Zur Bedeutung des Fluglochs im optischen Feld der Biene bei senkrechter Dressurordnung. *Z. wiss. Biol. Abt. C., Z. vergl. Physiol.* 15:193–260.

FRIEDMANN, H., 1929: *The Cowbirds: A Study in the Biology of Social Parasitism*. Springfield, Ill.

—— 1955: The Honey Guides. *U.S. Nat. Mus. Bull.* 208:1–292.

FRINGS, H., 1941: The loci of olfactory end-organs in the Blowfly *Cynomyia cadaverina*. *J. Exp. Zool.* 88:65–93.

FRISCH, K. von, 1914: Der Farbensinn und Formensinn der Biene. *Zool. Jb. Abt. Zool. Physiol.* 35:1–182.

—— 1919: Über den Geruchsinn der Bienen und seine blütenbiologische Bedeutung. *Zool. Jb. Abt.* 3, 37: 1–238.

—— 1927: *Aus dem Leben der Bienen*. Berlin.

—— 1934: Über den Geschmackssinn der Biene. *Z. vergl. Physiol.* 21:1–156.

—— 1937: Psychologie der Bienen. *Z. Tierpsychol.* 1:9–21.

—— 1941: Über einen Schreckstoff der Fischhaut und seine biologische Bedeutung. *Z. vergl. Physiol.* 29:46–145.

FRISCH, K. von, HERAN, H., and LINDAUER, M., 1953: Gibt es in der 'Sprache' der Bienen eine Weisung nach oben oder unten? *Z. vergl. Physiol.* 35:219–45.

FRISCH, K. von, and LINDAUER, M., 1954: Himmel und Erde in Konkurrenz bei der Orientierung der Bienen. *Naturwiss.* 41:245–53.

FRISCH, R. H., 1938: Das 'Bauen' des Octopus und anderer Beobachtungen an Cephalopoden. *Zoo. Anz. Suppl. (Verh. Deutsch. Zool. Ges.)* 11:119–26.

FROLOFF, J. P., 1925, 1928: Bedingte Reflexe bei Fischen. I and II. *Pflüg. Arch.* 208:261–71; 220:339–49.

FROMME, A., 1941: An experimental study of factors of maturation and practice in the behavioural development of the embryo of the frog *Rana pipiens*. *Genet. Psychol. Monog.* 24:219–56.

FROMME, H. G., 1961: Untersuchungen über das orientierungsvermögen nachtlich ziehender Kleinvögel (*Erithacus rubecula*, *Sylvia communis*). *Z. Tierpsychol.* 18:205–220.

FROUD, J., 1949: Observations on Hypotrichous ciliates: The genera *Stichotricha* and *Chætospira*. *Quart. J. Micros. Sci.* 90:141–58.

GAGNÉ, R. M., 1941: External inhibition and disinhibition in a conditioned operant response. *J. Exp. Psychol.* 29:104–16.

GALAMBOS, R., 1961: Changing concepts of the learning mechanism. In Delafresnaye (1961).

GAMBLE, F. W., and KEEBLE, F., 1904: The bionomics of *Convoluta roscoffensis*. *Quart. J. Micros. Sci.* 47:363–431.

GANNON, R. A., 1930: Observations on the Satin Bower-bird with regard to the material used by it in painting its bower. *Emu* 80: 39–41.

GARCIA-AUSST, E., BOGACZ, J., and VANZULLI, A., 1960: Influence and significance of the photic stimulus on the evoked responses in man. In Delafresnaye (1961).

GARTH, T. R., and MITCHELL, M. P., 1926: The learning curve of a land snail. *J. Comp. Psychol.* 6 : 103–13.

GATES, M. F., and ALLEE, W. C., 1933: Conditioned behaviour of isolated and grouped cockroaches in a simple maze. *J. Comp. Psychol.* 15 : 331–58.

GEE, W., 1913: The behaviour of leeches with especial reference to its modifiability. *Univ. Cal. Pub. Zool.* 11 : 197–305.

GELBER, B., 1952: Investigations of the Behaviour of *Paramecium aurelia*. I. Modification of behaviour after training with reinforcement. *J. Comp. Physiol. Psychol.* 45 : 58–65.

——   1958: Retention in *Paramecium aurelia. J. comp. physiol. Psychol.* 51 : 110–15.

GERARD, R. W., 1961: The fixation of experience. In Delafresnaye (1961).

GERDES, K., 1960: Über das Heimfindevermögen von Lachmöwen. *Verh. dtsch. zool. Ges.* 171–81.

GERKING, S. D., 1959: The restricted movement of fish populations. *Biol. Rev.* 34: 221–42.

GHINST, van der, 1906: Quelques observations sur les actinies. *Bull. Inst. Gén. Psychol.* 6 : 267–75. (*Not seen.*)

GIBSON, J. J., 1950: *The Perception of the Visual World.* New York.

GIFFORD, E. W., 1919: Field notes on the land birds of the Galapagos Islands and of Cocos Island, Costa Rica. *Proc. Calif. Acad. Sci.* (4) 2 : 189–258.

GILBERT, C. H., and RICH, W. H., 1926: Second experiment in tagging adult red salmon. *U.S. Bur. Fish. Bull.* 42 : 27–75.

GILHOUSEN, H. C., 1929: The use of vision and of the antennae in learning of crayfish. *Univ. Calif. Publ. Physiol.* 7 : 73–89.

——   1931: An investigation of 'insight' in rats. *Science* 73 : 711–12.

GILTAY, M., 1934: La notion de nombre chez les oiseaux. *Bull. Soc. Roy. Sci. Liège* 3 : 112–15.

GIRDEN, E., and CULLER, E., 1937: Conditioned responses in curarised striate muscle in dogs. *J. Comp. Psychol.* 23 : 261–74.

GIRDLESTONE, M., 1953: *Sold for a Farthing.* London.

GLANZER, M., 1953: Stimulus satiation: an explanation of spontaneous alternation and related phenomena. *Psychol. Rev.* 60 : 257–68.

——   1958: Stimulus satiation without choice. *J. comp. physiol. Psychol.* 51 : 332–5.

GLASER, O. C., 1907: Movement and problem-solving in *Ophiura brevispina. J. Exp. Zool.* 4 : 203–20.

GODMAN, S., 1954: *The Bird Fancyer's Delight. Directions concerning ye Teaching of all Sorts of Singing-Birds after ye Recorder—Sopranino or Treble (Alto)* (London 1717. Richard Meures). *New edition with historical introduction.* London.

GOETHE, F., 1937: Beobachtungen und Untersuchungen zur Biologie der Silbermöwe (*Larus a. argentatus*) auf der Vögelinsel Memmertsand. *J. Orn.* 85 : 1–119.

——   1954: Vergleichende Beobachtungen über das Verhalten der Silbermöwe (*Larus a. argentatus*) und der Heringsmöwe (*Larus f. fuscus*). *Proc. XI Int. Orn. Congr.* 577–82.

GOETSCH, W., 1934: Untersuchungen über die Zusammenarbeit im Ameisenstaat. *Z. morph. Ökol.* 28 : 319–401.

GOLDSMITH, M., 1912: Contribution à l'étude de la mémoire chez les poissons. *Bull. Inst. Gén. Psychol.* 12 : 161–76.

——   1914: Réactions physiologiques et psychiques des poissons. *Bull. Inst. Gén. Psychol.* 14 : 97–239.

——   1917a: Quelques réactions sensorielles chez le Poulpe. *C. R. Acad. Paris* 164 : 448–50.

GOLDSMITH, M., 1917b: Acquisition d'une habitude chez le Poulpe. *C. R. Acad. Paris* **164**:737–8.

—— 1917c: Quelques réactions du Poulpe: contribution à la psychologie des invertébrés. *Bull. Inst. Gén. Psychol.* **17**:25–44.

GOODSON, F. E., SCARBOROUGH, B. D., and LEWIS, G. W., 1957: Expectancy and the extinction of expectancy in the rat. *J. comp. physiol. Psychol.* **50**:563–6.

GOODWIN, D., 1947: Breeding behaviour in domestic pigeons four weeks old. *Ibis* **89**:656–8.

—— 1948a: Some abnormal sexual fixations in birds. *Ibis* **90**:45–8.

—— 1948b: Tameness in birds. *Ibis* **90**:316–18.

—— 1953: Observations on voice and behaviour of Red-legged Partridge *Alectoris rufa. Ibis* **95**:581–614.

GORSKA, T., and JANKOWSKA, E., 1961: The effect of deafferentation on instrumental (Type II) conditioned reflexes in dogs. *Acta Biol. Experimentalis* **21**:219–34.

GOS, M., 1935: Les réflexes conditionnels chez l'embryon d'oiseau. *Roy. Soc. Liège* **4**:194–9, 246–50.

GOULD, E., 1957: Orientation in Box Turtles, *Terrapene c. carolina* (Linnæus). *Biol. Bull.* **112**:336–48.

GOY, R. W., and JAKWAY, J. S., 1959: The inheritance of patterns of sexual behaviour in female guineapigs. *Anim. Behav.* **7**:142–9.

GRABENSBERGER, W., 1933 and 1934: Untersuchungen ü. das Zeitgedächtnis der Amiesen u. Termiten. *Z. vergl. Physiol.* **20**:1–54, 338–42.

GRABOWSKI, U., 1939: Experimentelle Untersuchungen ü. das angebliche Lernvermögen von *Paramœcium. Z. Tierpsychol.* **2**:265–82.

—— 1941: Prägung eines Jungschafs auf den Menschen. *Z. Tierpsychol.* **4**:326–9.

—— 1957: Insight in the Chow dog. *Z. Tierpsychol.* **14**:238–40.

GRASSÉ, P., 1949: *Traité de Zoologie*, **6**: 675–9. Paris.

GRAY, J., 1944: Studies in the mechanics of the tetrapod skeleton. *J. Exp. Biol.* **20**:88–116.

GRAY, J., and LISSMANN, H. W., 1946: The co-ordination of limb movements in the amphibia. *J. Exp. Biol.* **23**:133–42.

GRAY, P. H., 1958: Imprinting in humans. *J. Psychology* **46**:155–60.

GREENBERG, B., 1947: Some relations between territory, social hierarchy and leadership in the green sunfish (*Lepomis cyanellus*). *Physiol. Zool.* **20**:267–99.

GREENBERG, B., and NOBLE, G. K., 1944: Social behaviour of the American chameleon (*Anolis carolinensis*). *Physiol. Zool.* **17**:392–439.

GREGORY, R. L., 1954: Physical model explanations in psychology. (*Unpublished.*)

GRICE, G. R., 1948: An experimental test of the expectation theory of learning. *J. Exp. Psychol.* **41**:137–43.

GRIFFIN, D. R., 1952: Status report on contract with Office of Naval Research. (*Mimeographed.*)

GRIFFITH, C. R., 1920: The behaviour of white rats in the presence of cats. *Psychobiol.* **2**:19–28.

GRIMPE, G., 1928: Pflege Behandlung Zucht der Cephalopoden usw. (in Abderhalden, E., *Handbuch der Biologischen, Arbeitsmethoden* **9**, Part 5: 331–402).

GRINDLEY, G. C., 1927: The direction of association in young chickens. *Brit. J. Psychol.* **17**:210–21.

—— 1929: Experiments on the influence of the amount of reward on learning in young chickens. *Brit. J. Psychol.* **22**:173–80.

—— 1932: The formation of a simple habit in guineapigs. *Brit. J. Psychol.* **23**:127–47.

GRISON, P., 1943: Rhythmes d'activité chez *Leptinotarsa decemlineata* et leur importance pour l'étude du phototropisme. *Bull. Soc. Zoo. Fr.* **68**:100–7.

—— 1957: Les facteurs du comportement chez l'imago du Doryphore (*Leptinotarsa decemlineata* Say. Col. Chrysomelidae) *Bull. Biol. France et Belg. Suppl.* **43**:1–153.

GROHMANN, J., 1938: Modification oder Funktionsregung? Ein Beitrag zur Klärung der wechselseitigen Beziehungen zwischen Instinkthandlung und Erfahrung. Z. Tierpsychol. 2 : 132–44.

GROOS, F., 1898: The Play of Animals. New York.

GRUNDLACH, R. H., 1933: Visual acuity of homing pigeons. J. Comp. Psychol. 16 : 327–42.

GRUNT, J. A., and YOUNG, W. C., 1952: Psychological modification of fatigue following orgasm (ejaculation) in the male guineapig. J. Comp. Physiol. Psychol. 44 : 61–6.

GUDGER, E. W., 1944: Fishes that swim heads to tails in single file. Copeia, 1944 : 152–4.

—— 1949: Fishes that rank themselves like soldiers on parade. Zoologica 34 : 99–102.

GUHL, A. M., and ALLEE, W. C., 1944: Some measurable effects of social organisation in flocks of hens. Physiol. Zool. 17 : 320–47.

GUHL, A. M., and ORTMAN, L. L., 1953: Visual patterns in the recognition of individuals among chickens. Condor 55 : 287–98.

GUITON, P., 1959: Socialization and imprinting in Brown Leghorn chicks. Anim. Behav. 7 : 26–34.

—— 1960: On the control of behaviour during the reproductive cycle in Gasterosteus aculeatus. Behaviour 15 : 163–84.

GUNN, D. L., 1942: Klino-kinesis in Paramecium. Nature 149 : 78–9.

GUNN, D. L., and WALSHE, B. M., 1941: Klino-kinesis in Paramecium. Nature 148 : 564–5.

GUNTHER, M., 1961: The development of feeding behaviour in baby's first days of life. Anim. Behav. 9 : 116–17.

GUTHRIE, E. R., 1933: Conditioning as a principle of learning. Psychol. Rev. 37 : 412–28.

—— 1935: The Psychology of Learning. New York.

GUTHRIE, E. R., and HORTON, G. P., 1946: Cats in a Puzzle Box. New York. (Not seen.)

HAARTMANN, L. von, 1949: Der Trauerfliegenschnäpper. I. Ortstreue und Rassenbildung. Act. Zool. Fenn. 56 : 1–104.

HADLEY, P. B., 1909: Notes on the behaviour of the domestic fowl. Am. Nat. 43 : 669–76.

HAECKER, V., 1912: Über Lernversuche bei Axolotln. Arch. ges. Psychol. 25 : 1–35.

HAILMAN, J. P., 1961: Why do gull chicks peck at visually contrasting spots? A suggestion concerning social learning of food discrimination. Amer. Nat. 95 : 245–7.

HALDANE, J. B. S., 1954a: Introducing Douglas Spalding. Brit. J. Anim. Behav. 2 : 1.

—— 1954b: A logical analysis of learning, conditioning and related processes. Behaviour 6 : 256–70.

—— 1954c: La signalisation animale. Ann. Biol. 30 : 89–98.

HALE, E. B., 1956a: Social facilitation and forebrain function in maze performance of Green Sunfish, Lepomis cyanellus. Physiol. Zool. 29 : 93–107.

—— 1956b: Breed recognition in the social interaction of domestic fowl. Behaviour 10 : 240–53.

HAMILTON, J. A., and BALLACHEY, E. L., 1934: An instance of Umweg behaviour in the rat. J. Genet. Psychol. 45 : 260–1.

HAMRUM, C. L., 1953: Experiments on the senses of taste and smell in the Bobwhite Quail (Colinus v. virginianus). Am. Mid. Nat. 49, No. 3 : 872–7.

HANEY, G. W., 1931: The effect of familiarity on maze performance in albino rats. Univ. Calif. Publ. Psychol. 4 : 319–33.

HANNES, F., 1930: Über die verschiedenen Arten des 'Lernens' der Honigbiene und der Insekten überhaupt. Zoo. Jb. Abt. Zool. Physiol. 47 : 89–150.

HARALSON, J. V., and BITTERMAN, M. E., 1950: A lever-depression apparatus for the study of learning in fish. Amer. J. Psychol. 63 : 250–6.

HARGITT, C. W., 1906: Experiments on the behaviour of tubicolous annelids. J. Exp. Zool. 3 : 295–320.

HARGITT, C. W., 1907: Notes on the behaviour of sea anemones. *Biol. Bull.* **12** : 274–84.
—— 1909: Further observations on the behaviour of tubicolous annelids. *J. Exp. Zool.* **7** : 157–87.
HARKER, J. E., 1953: The diurnal rhythm of activity of mayfly nymphs. *J. Exp. Biol.* **30** : 525–33.
—— 1954: Diurnal rhythms in *Periplaneta americana*. *Nature* **173** : 689.
—— 1958: Diurnal rhythms in the animal kingdom. *Biol. Rev.* **33** : 1–52.
HARLOW, H. F., 1939: Forward conditioning, backward conditioning and pseudo-conditioning in Goldfish. *J. Genet. Psychol.* **55** : 49–58.
—— 1949: The formation of learning sets. *Psychol. Rev.* **56** : 51–65.
HARLOW, H. F., BLAZEK, N. C., and McCLEARN, G. E., 1956: Manipulatory motivation in the infant rhesus monkey. *J. comp. physiol. Psychol.* **49** : 444–8.
HARLOW, H. F., HARLOW, M. K., and MEYER, D. R., 1950: Learning motivated by a manipulation drive. *J. Exp. Psychol.* **40** : 228–34.
HARLOW, H. F., and McCLEARN, G. E., 1954: Object discrimination learned by monkeys on the basis of manipulation motives. *J. Comp. Physiol. Psychol.* **47** : 73–6.
HARPER, E. H., 1907: The behaviour of the phantom larva *Corethra plumicornis*, Fabr. *J. Comp. Neur. & Psychol.* **17** : 435–56.
HARRINGTON, N. R., and LEAMING, E., 1900: The reaction of *Amœba* to light of different colours. *Am. J. Physiol.* **3** : 9–18.
HARRIS, E. E., 1954: *Nature, Mind and Modern Science*. London.
HARRIS, J. D., 1943: Studies on non-associative factors inherent in conditioning. *Comp. Psychol. Mon, 18*, No. 1, pp. 74.
HARRIS, J. E., and WHITING, H. P., 1954: Control of rhythmical activity in the skeletal muscle of the embryonic dogfish. *I. Physiol.* **124** : 63.
HARRIS, L. J., et al., 1933: Appetite and choice of diet. The ability of the vitamin B deficient rat to discriminate between diets containing and lacking vitamin. *Proc. Roy. Soc. B.* **113** : 161–90.
HARTLEY, P. H. T., 1950: An experimental analysis of interspecific recognition. Symposium Vol. 4. S.E.B. *Physiological Mechanisms in Animal Behaviour*. Cambridge.
HARTMANN, C., 1905: Observations of the habits of some solitary wasps of Texas. *Bull. Univ. Texas, Sci. Series* 1, No. 7 : 1–73.
HASKINS, C. B., and HASKINS, E. F., 1958: Note on the inheritance of behaviour patterns for food selection and cocoon spinning in F_1 hybrids of *Callosamia promethea* × *C. angulifera*. *Behaviour* **3** : 89–95.
HASLER, A. D., 1954: Odour perception and orientation in fishes. *J. Fisheries Resch. Bd., Canada,* **11** : 107–29.
HASLER, A. D., and WISBY, W. J., 1951: Discrimination of stream odour by fishes and its relation to parent stream behaviour. *Amer. Nat.* **85** : 223–38.
—— —— 1958: The return of displaced Large-mouthed Bass and Green Sunfish to a home area. *Ecology* **39** : 289–93.
HASS, H., 1952: *Under the Red Sea*. London.
HASSMANN, M., 1952: Vom Erlernen unbenannter Anzahlen bei Eichhörnchen. *Z. Tierpsychol.* **9** : 294–321.
HAUG, G., 1933: Die Lichtreaktionen der Hydren (*Chlorophydra viridissima* und *Pelmatohydra oligactis typica*). *Z. vergl. Physiol.* **19** : 246–303.
HAYES, C., 1951: *The Ape in our House*. New York.
HAYES, K. J., and HAYES, C., 1951: The intellectual development of a home-raised chimpanzee. *Proc. Amer. Phil. Soc.* **95** : 105–9.
HEADLEY, E. H., 1941: A study of the nesting and nesting habits of the ant *Lasius niger alienus* var. *americana*. *Ann. Ent. Soc. Am.* **34** : 649–57.
HEBB, D. O., 1937: The innate organisation of visual activity. I. Perception of figures by rats reared in darkness. *J. Genet. Psychol.* **51** : 101–26. The innate organisation of visual activity. II. Transfer of response in the discrimination of brightness and size by rats reared in total darkness. *J. Comp. Psychol.* **24** : 277–99.

HEBB, D. O., 1938: Studies of the organisation of behaviour. II. Changes in the field orientation of the rat after cortical destruction. *J. Comp. Psychol.* 26:427-44.
—— 1946: On the nature of fear. *Psychol. Rev.* 53:259-76.
—— 1949: *The Organisation of Behaviour.* New York.
—— 1951: The role of neurological ideas in psychology. *J. Personality* 20:39-55.
—— 1953: Heredity and environment in mammalian behaviour. *Brit. J. Anim. Behav.* 1:43-7.
—— 1961: Distinctive features of learning in the higher animals. In Delafresnave (1961).
HECK, L., 1920: Ueber die Bildung einer Assoziation beim Regenwurm auf Grund von Dressurversuchen. *Lotos* 67-8:169-89.
HEDIGER, H., 1950: *Wild Animals in Captivity.* London.
—— 1955: *Studies of the Psychology and Behaviour of Captive Animals in Zoos and Circuses.* London.
—— 1957: Verhalten de Beuteltiere (Marsupiala). In *Handbuch der Zoologie.* Berlin.
HEINROTH, O., 1910: Beitrage zur Biologie, namentlich Ethologie und Physiologie der Anatiden. *Verhl. 5 Int. Orn. Kongr.* 589-702.
—— 1924: Lautäusserung der Vögel. *J. Orn.* 72:223-44.
—— 1938: *Aus dem Leben der Vögel.* Leipzig.
HEINROTH, O., and HEINROTH, M., 1924-33: *Die Vögel Mitteleuropas.* Berlin.
HELLWIG, H., and LUDWIG, W., 1951: Versuch zur Frage der Artennung bei Insekten. *Z. Tierpsychol.* 8:456-62.
HELSON, H., 1927: Insight in the white rat. *J. Exp. Psychol.* 10:378-97.
HEMPELMANN, F., 1926: *Tierpsychologie vom Standpunkte des Biologen.* Leipzig.
HERAN, H., 1952: Untersuchungen ü. den Temperatursinn der Honig-biene unter besonderer berucksichtigung der Wahrnehmung strahlender Wärme. *Z. vergl. Physiol.* 34:179-206.
HERB, F. H., 1940: Latent learning—Non-reward followed by food in blinds. *J. Comp. Psychol.* 29:247-56.
HERBERT, M. J., and HARSH, C. M., 1944: Observational learning by cats. *J. Comp. Psychol.* 37:81-5.
HERNÁNDEZ-PEÓN, R., and BRUST-CARMONA, H., 1961: Functional role of subcortical structures in habituation and conditioning. In Delafresnaye (1961).
HERON, W. T., OXMAN, L. I., and SINGLEY, E., 1946: Conditioning or apprehension in rat learning. *J. Comp. Psychol.* 39: 1-4.
HERRICK, C. J., 1924: *Neurological Foundations of Behaviour.* New York.
HERRICK, F. H., 1910: Instinct and intelligence in birds. *Pop. Sci. Mo.* 76:532-8; 77:82-97,122-41.
—— 1934: *The American Eagle: A Study in Natural and Civil History.* New York.
HERTER, K., 1929: Dressurversuche an Fischen. *Z. vergl. Physiol.* 10:688-711.
—— 1930: Weitere Dressurversuche an Fischen. *Z. vergl. Physiol.* 11:730-48.
—— 1937: Dressur der Ellritze (*Phoxinus laevis*) auf verschieden gross optische signale. (*Hochschulfilme C. 178, quoted Herter 1940.*)
—— 1950: Über simultaten Farbenkontrast bei Fischen. *Biol. Zbl.* 69:283-300.
—— 1953: *Die Fischdressuren und ihre sinnesphysiologische Grundlagen.* Berlin.
HERTER, W. R., 1940: Über das 'Putter' einiger Meisen-Arten. *Orn. Monatsbr.* 48:104-9.
HERTZ, M., 1926: Beobachtungen an gefangenen Rabenvögeln. *Psychol. Forsch.* 8:336-97.
—— 1937: Le rapport de l'Instinct et de l'Intelligence dans le règne animal. *J. de Psychologie* 24:324-40.
HESS, E. H., 1956: An experimental analysis of imprinting—a form of learning. (*In press.*)
—— 1959: Imprinting. *Science* 130:133-41.

HEUSSER, H., 1958: Ueber die Beziehungen der Erdkröte *Bufo bufo* L. zu ihren Laichplatz. *Behaviour* **12**:208–32.

HEWATT, W. G., 1940: Observations on the homing limpet *Acmaea scabra*, Gould. *Am. Mid. Nat.* **24**:205–8.

HEYDE, K., 1924: Die Entwicklung der psychischen Fähigkeiten bei Ameisen und ihr Verhalten bei abgeänderten biologischen Bedingungen. *Biol. Zbl.* **44**:624–54.

HIGGINSON, G. D., 1926: Visual perception in the white rat. *J. Exp. Psychol.* **9**:337–47.

HILGARD, E. R., 1948: *Theories of Learning.* New York.

HILGARD, E. R., and MARQUIS, D. G., 1940: *Conditioning and Learning.* New York.

HILL, A. V., *et al.*, 1950: A discussion on muscular contraction and relaxation: their physical and chemical basis. *Proc. Roy. Soc. B.* **137**:40–87.

HILL, D. K., 1950: The volume change resulting from stimulation of a giant nerve fibre. *J. Physiol.* **111**:304–27.

HINDE, R. A., 1952: *The Behaviour of the Great Tit and some other related species. Behaviour Supplement* **2**: 1–201.

—— 1953a: Appetitive behaviour and consummatory act. *Behaviour* **5**:189–224.

—— 1953b: A possible explanation of paper tearing behaviour in birds. *Brit. Birds* **46**:21–3.

—— 1954a: Factors governing the changes in strength of a partially inborn response, as shown by the mobbing behaviour of the chaffinch (*Fringilla coelebs*). I and II. *Proc. Roy. Soc B.* **142**:306–31, 331–58.

—— 1958: The nest building behaviour of domesticated canaries. *Proc. zool. Soc. Lond.* **131**:1–48.

—— 1959a: Unitary drives. *Anim. Behav.* **7**:130–41.

—— 1959b: Behaviour and speciation in birds and lower vertebrates. *Biol. Rev.* **34**:85–129.

—— 1960: Energy models of motivation. In *Symp. Soc. exp. Biol. on Models and Analogues in Biology.* 199–213.

—— 1961a: The establishment of the parent-offspring relation in birds, with some mammalian analogies. In Thorpe and Zangwill (1961).

—— 1961b: Factors governing the changes in strength of a partially inborn response, as shown by the mobbing behaviour of the Chaffinch (*Fringilla coelebs*). III. The interaction of short term and long term incremental and decremental effects. *Proc. roy. Soc. B.* **153**:398–420.

HINDE, R. A., and FISHER, J., 1952: Further observations on the opening of milk bottles by birds. *Brit. Birds* **44**:393–6.

HINDE, R. A., THORPE, W. H., and VINCE, M. A., 1956: The following response of young coots and moorhens. *Behaviour,* **9**:214–42.

HINDE, R. A., and WARREN, R. P., 1959: The effect of nest-building on later reproductive behaviour in domesticated canaries. *Anim. Behav.* **7**:35–41.

HINDWOOD, J. A., 1955: Bird-wasp nesting associations. *Emu* **55**:263–74.

HINGSTON, R. W. G., 1926–7: The Mason Wasp (*Eumenes conica*). *J. Bombay Nat. Hist. Soc.* **31**:241–57, 754–61, 890–6.

—— 1927: The Potter Wasp (*Rhynchium nitidulum*). *J. Bombay Nat. Hist. Soc.* **32**:98–110, 246–52.

—— 1928: *Problems of Instinct and Intelligence.* London.

HINSCHE, G., 1926: Vergleichende Untersuchungen vom Haltungs- und Bewegungsreaktion bei Anuren. *Zeit. Indukt. Abstamm. Vererb.* **43**:252–60.

HOAGLAND, H., 1931: A study of the physiology of learning in ants. *J. Genet. Psychol.* **5**:21–41.

HOAR, W. S., 1956: The behaviour of migrating pink and chum salmon fry. *J. Fisheries Rsch. Bd. Canad.* **13**:309–25.

—— 1958: Rapid learning of a constant course by travelling schools of juvenile Pacific salmon. *J. Fisheries Rsch. Bd. Canad.* **15**:251–74.

HOCHBAUM, H. A., 1944: *The Canvasback on a Prairie Marsh.* Washington.

HODGE, C. F., and AIKINS, H. B., 1895: The daily life of a Protozoan: a study in comparative psychophysiology. *Am. J. Psychol.* **6**:524–33.

494 LEARNING AND INSTINCT IN ANIMALS

HOFFMANN, K., 1952: Die Einrechnung der Sonnenwanderung bei der Richtungs-
weisung des sonnenlos aufgezogenen Stares. *Naturwiss.* **40**:148.
—— 1953: Experimentelle Anderung des Richtungsfindens beim Star durch
Beeinflussing der 'inneren Uhr.' *Naturwiss.* **40**: 608–9.
HOFFMANN, R. W., 1926: Periodischer Tageswechsel u. anders biologisches rhythms
bei dem poikilothermen Tieren. *Handb. norm. path. Physiol.* **17**:644–58.
HOLMES, S. J., 1907: Rhythmical activity in Infusoria. *Biol. Bull.* **13**:306–8.
HOLST, E. von, 1934: Studien über die Reflexe u. Rhythmen beim Goldfisch (*Carassius
auratus*). *Z. vergl. Physiol.* **20**:582–99.
—— 1935–7: Vom Wesen der Ordnung im Zentralnervensystem. *Naturwiss.*
25:625–31, 641–7.
—— 1954: Relations between the central nervous system and the periphery.
Brit. J. Anim. Behav. **2**:89–94.
HOLST, E. von, and MITTELSTAEDT, H., 1950: Das Reafferenzprinzip. Wechselwirkungen
zwischen zentralnervensystem und peripherie. *Naturwiss.* **37**:464–76.
HOLST, E. von, and St. PAUL, U. von, 1960: Vom Wirkungsgefüge der Triebe. *Naturwissenschaften* **47**:409–22.
HOLZAPFEL, M., 1939: Analyse des Sperrens und Pickens in der Entwicklung des Stars.
J. Orn. **87**:525–53.
—— 1943: Umwegversuch an der Trichterspinne *Agelena labrynthica*. *Rev.
Suisse Zool.* **50**:89–130.
HONIGMANN, H., 1942a: The discrimination method in animal psychology. *Nature*
150:296–7.
—— 1942b: The number conception in animal psychology. *Biol. Rev.* **17**:315–37.
—— 1942c: The alternation problem in animal psychology. *J. Exp. Biol.*
19:141–57.
HOOGLAND, R., MORRIS, D., and TINBERGEN, N., 1957: The spines of sticklebacks
Gasterosteus and *Pygosteus* as a means of defence against predators, *Perca*
and *Esox*. *Behaviour* **10**:205–36.
HOOKER, D., 1950: Neural growth and the development of behaviour. In *Genetic
Neurology*, ed. P. Weiss, Chicago, p. 212–13.
HÖRMAN-HECK, S., 1957: Untersuchungen über den Erbgang einiger Verhaltensweisen
bei Grillenbastarden (*Gryllis campestris* L. × *G. bimaculatus* de Geer)
Z. Tierpsychol. **14**:137–83.
HORSTMANN, E., 1934: Untersuchungen zur Physiologie der Schwimmbewegungen der
Scyphomedusen. *Pflügers. Archiv.* **234**:406–20.
HOSODA, K., 1957: On factors influencing the Seward type latent learning in Guppies,
Lebistes reticulata. *Criminal Psychol.*, Tokio **7**:29–42 (in Japanese).
HOVEY, H. B., 1929: Associative hysteresis in marine flatworms. *Physiol. Zool.*
2:322–33.
HOWARD, H. E., 1907–14: *The British Warblers: a history with problems of their lives*,
London.
—— 1929: *An Introduction to the Study of Bird Behaviour*. Cambridge.
—— 1935: *The Nature of a Bird's World*. Cambridge.
—— 1940: *A Waterhen's Worlds*. Cambridge.
HOWELLS, T. H., and VINE, D. O., 1940: The innate differential in social learning.
J. Abn. Social Psychol. **35**:537–48.
HSIAO, H. H., 1929: An experimental study of the rat's 'insight' within a spatial
complex. *Univ. Calif. Publ. Psychol.* **4**:57–70.
HUBBARD, S. J., 1960: Hearing and the octopus statocyst. *J. exp. Biol.* **37**:845–53.
HULL, C. L., 1931: Goal attraction and directing ideas conceived as habit phenomena.
Psychol. Rev. **38**:487–506.
—— 1937: Mind, mechanism and adaptive behaviour. *Psychol. Rev.* **44**:1–32.
—— 1943: *Principles of Behaviour*. New York.
HUMPHREY, G., 1930: Le Chatelier's rule and the problem of habituation and de-
habituation in *Helix albolabris*. *Psychol. Forsch.* **13**:113–27.
—— 1933: *The Nature of Learning in its Relation to the Living System*. London.

HUMPHRIES, L. G., 1939: The effect of random alternation of reinforcement on the acquisition and extinction of conditioned eyelid responses. *J. Exp. Psychol.* **25**: 141–58.

—— 1940: Extinction of conditioned psychogalvanic responses following two conditions of reinforcement. *J. Exp. Psychol.* **37**: 71–8.

—— 1943: The strength of a Thorndikean response as a function of the number of practice trials. *J. Comp. Psychol.* **35**: 101–10.

HUNGERFORD, H. B., and WILLIAMS, F. X., 1912: Biological notes on some Kansas Hymenoptera. *Entom. News* **23**: 241–60.

HUNT, J. McV., 1941: The effects of infant feeding frustration upon adult hoarding in the albino rat. *J. Abnorm. Soc. Psychol.* **36**: 338–60.

HUNT, J. McV., SCHLOSBERG, H., SOLOMON, R. L., and STELLAR, E., 1947: Studies of infantile experience on adult behaviour in rats. I. Effects of infantile feeding frustration on adult hoarding. *J. Comp. Physiol. Psychol.* **40**: 291–304.

HUNTER, W. S., 1911: Some labyrinth habits of the domestic pigeon. *J. Anim. Behav.* **1**: 278–304.

—— 1932: The effect of inactivity produced by cold upon learning and retention in the cockroach *Blatella germanica*. *J. Genet. Psychol.* **41**: 253–66.

HUNTINGTON, C. E., 1952: Hybridization in the Purple Grackle *Quiscalus quiscula*. *Systematic Zool.* **1**: 149–70.

HUXLEY, J. S., 1942: *Evolution: The Modern Synthesis*. London.

—— *et al.*, 1947–9: Notes on the problem of geographical differences in tameness in birds. *Ibis* **89**: 540–52; **90**: 312–18.

IERSEL, J. J. A. van, 1953: An Analysis of the Parental Behaviour of the male Three-spined Stickleback. *Behaviour Supplement* **3**: 1–159.

IERSEL, J. J. A. van, and BOL, A. C. A., 1958: Preening of two tern species. A study of displacement activities. *Behaviour* **13**: 1–88.

ILSE, D. R., 1955: Olfactory marking of territory in two young male Loris, *Loris tardigradus lydekkerianus*, kept in captivity in Poona. *Brit. J. Anim. Behav.* **3**: 118–20.

IMMS, A. D., 1934: *A General Textbook of Entomology*. 3rd edn. London.

IVOR, H. R., 1944: Birds' fear of man. *Auk* **61**: 203–11.

JACOBSON, A. L., 1962: Learning in flatworms and annelids. *Psychol. Bull.* In press.

JACOBSON, E., 1905. Beobachtungen über *Polyrachis dives* auf Java, die ihre larven zum Spinnen des Nestes benutzt (Briefliche Mitteilung mit Vorbemerkung von E. Wasmann). *Notes Leiden Museum* **25**: 133–40.

—— 1908: Zur Verfertigung der Gespinstnester von *Polyrachis bicolor* auf Java. *Notes Leiden Museum* **30**: 63–6.

JAHN, T., 1960: Optische Gleichgewichtsregulung und zentrale Kompensation bei Amphibien, insbesondere bei der Erdkröte (*Bufo bufo* L.). *Z. vergl. Physiol.* **43**: 119–40.

JAMES, H., 1959: Flicker: an unconditioned stimulus for imprinting. *Canad. J. Psychol.* **13**: 59–67.

JAMES, W. T., 1957: The effect of satiation in the sucking response of puppies. *J. comp. physiol. Psychol.* **50**: 375–8.

JANDER, R., 1957: Die optische Richtungsorientierung der Roten Waldameise (*Formica rufa* L.). *Z. vergl. Physiol.* **40**: 162–238.

JANZEN, W., 1933: Untersuchungen über Grosshirnfunktion der Goldfisches (*Carassius auratus*). *Zoo. Jahrb. Allg. Zool.* **52**: 591–628.

JAYNES, J., 1957: Imprinting: the interaction of learned and innate behaviour. II. *J. comp. physiol. Psychol.* **50**: 6–10.

JELLINEK, A., 1926: Versuch ü. das Gehör der Vogel: I. Dressurversuch an Tauben mit akustistischen Reizen. *Arch. Physiol. Ges.* **211**: 64–72.

JENNINGS, H. S., 1905: Sea-anemones: modifiability of behaviour. *J. Exp. Biol.* **2**: 447.

—— 1906: *The Behaviour of the Lower Organisms*. New York.

496   LEARNING AND INSTINCT IN ANIMALS

JENNINGS, H. S., 1907: Behaviour of the starfish *Asterias forreri* de Loriol. *Univ. Calif. Pub. Zool.* **4**: 53–185.

JOHNSON, R. A., 1941: Nesting behavior of the Atlantic Murre. *Auk* **58**: 153–63.

JOHNSON, W., 1930: *Animal Life in London.* London.

JONES, F. M., 1930: The sleeping Heliconias of Florida. *J. Amer. Mus. Nat. Hist.* **30**: 365.

——— 1931. The gregarious sleeping habits of *Heliconius charithonia* L. *Proc. Ent. Soc. London* **6**: 4–10.

JONES, F. N., 1945: An alternative explanation of the effect of temperature upon retention in the Goldfish. *J. Exp. Psychol.* **35**: 76–9.

JORES, A., 1937: Die 24-stunden-Periodik in der Biologie. *Tabulae Biologicae* **14**: 77–109.

JUSZCZYK, W., 1951: The migrations of the aquatic frog *Rana esculenta.* *Bull. Acad. Pol. Sci. et Lett.* **1952**: 341–69.

KALMUS, H., 1934: Über die Natur des Zeitgedächtnis der Bienen. *Z. vergl. Physiol.* **20**: 405–19.

KALMUS, H., and RIBBANDS, C. R., 1952: The origin of the odours by which honey-bees distinguish their companions. *Proc. Roy. Soc. B.* **140**: 50–9.

KAPPERS, C. U. A., 1917: Further contributions on neurobiotaxis. IX. An attempt to compare the phenomena of neurobiotaxis with other phenomena of taxis and tropism. The dynamic polarization of the neurone. *J. Comp. Neurol.* **27**: 216–98.

KARN, H. W., and PORTER, J. M., 1946: The effects of certain pre-training procedures after maze performance and their significance for the concept of latent learning. *J. Exp. Psychol.* **36**: 461–9.

KARSTEN, A., 1938: Psychische sättigung. *Psychol. Forsch.* **10**: 142–254.

KATZ, D., 1937: *Animals and Men.* London.

KATZ, D., and RÉVÉSZ, G., 1909: Experimentell-psychologische Untersuchungen mit Hühnern. *Z. Psychol.* **50**: 93–116.

——— ——— 1921: Experimentelle Studien zur vergleichenden psychologie (Versüche mit Hühnern). *Zeit. Angew. Psychol.* **18**: 307–20.

KATZ, D., and TOLL, A., 1932: Die Messung von Charakter und Begabungsunterschieden bei Tieren (Versüche mit Hühnern). *Z. Psychol.* **93**: 287–311.

KATZ, M. S., and DETERLINE, W. Q., 1958: Apparent learning in *Paramecium.* *J. comp. physiol. Psychol.* **51**: 243–7.

KEAR, J., 1960: Abnormal sexual behaviour in the Hawfinch, *Coccothraustes coccothraustes.* *Ibis* **102**: 614–16.

KEENLEYSIDE, M. A. H., 1955: Some aspects of the schooling behaviour of fish. *Behaviour* **8**: 183–248.

KELLER, F. S., and HILL, L. M., 1936: Another 'insight' experiment. *J. Genet. Psychol.* **48**: 484–9.

KELLOGG, W. N., 1931: A note on fear behaviour in young rats, mice and birds. *J. Comp. Psychol.* **12**: 117–21.

KELLOGG, W. N., and POMEROY, W. B., 1936: Maze learning in water snakes *Tropidonotus fasciatus* var. *sipedon.* *J. Comp. Psychol.* **21**: 275–95.

KELLOGG, W. N., PRONKO, N. H., and DEESE, J., 1946: Spinal conditioning in dogs. *Science* **103**: 49–50.

KENDLER, H. H., 1946: The influence of simultaneous hunger and thirst drives upon the learning of two opposed spatial responses of the white rat. *J. Exp. Psychol.* **36**: 212–20.

——— 1947: An investigation of latent learning in a T-maze. *J. Comp. Physiol. Psychol.* **40**: 265–70.

KENDLER, H. H., and MENCHER, H. C., 1948: The ability of rats to learn the location of food when motivated by thirst—an experimental reply to Leeper. *J. Exp. Psychol.* **38**: 82–8.

KENYON, K. W., and RICE, D. W., 1958: Homing of Laysan Albatrosses. *Condor* 60: 3–6.

KERKUT, G. A., 1954: The mechanisms of co-ordination of the starfish tube-feet. *Behaviour* 6: 206–32.

—— 1955: The retraction and protraction of the tube feet of the Starfish (*Asterias rubens.* L). *Behaviour* 8: 112–29.

KING, B. G., 1926: The influence of repeated rotations on decerebrate and blinded squabs. *J. Comp. Psychol.* 6: 399–421.

KIRKMAN, F. B., 1911: *The British Bird Book.* (4 vols.) London.

KIRKMAN, F. B., 1937: *Bird Behaviour: a contribution based chiefly on a study of the Black-headed Gull.* London.

KIRSCHOFER, R., 1958: Freiland- und Gefangenschaftsbeobachtungen an der nord-afrikanischen Rennmaus *Gerbillus nanus garamantis. Z. Säugetierkunde* 23: 33–49.

KJERSCHOW-AGERSBORG, H. P. v. W., 1918: Bilateral tendencies and habits in the twenty-rayed starfish *Pycnopodia helianthoide* (Stimpson). *Biol. Bull.* 35: 232–53.

KLAUBER, L. M., 1936: A statistical study of rattlesnakes. *Occ. Papers, San Diego Soc. N. H.* 1: 1–24.

KLEBER, E., 1935: Hat der Zeitgedächtnis der Bienen biologische Bedeutung? *Z. vergl. Physiol.* 22: 221–62.

KLEEREKOPER, H., and CHAGNON, E. C., 1954: Hearing in fish with special reference to *Semotilis a. atromaculata. J. Fish Rsch. Bd. Canada,* 11: 130–52.

KLOPFER, P. H., 1959: Social interaction in discrimination learning with special reference to feeding behaviour in birds. *Behaviour* 14: 288–99.

—— 1961: Observational learning in birds: the establishment of behavioural modes. *Behaviour* 17: 71–80.

KLÜVER, H., 1937: Re-examination of implement-using behaviour in a Cebus monkey after an interval of 3 years. *Acta Psychologica* 2: 347–97.

KNECHT, S., 1939: Über den Gehörsinn und die Musikalitat der Vögel. *Z. vergl. Physiol.* 27: 169–232.

KOCH, S., 1954: in Estes, Koch *et al.*

KOEHLER, O., 1924: Sinnesphysiologie Untersuchungen an Libellen-larven. *Verh. Dtsch. Zool. Ges.* 29: 83–91.

—— 1937: Konnen Tauben zahlen? *Z. Tierpsychol.* 1: 39–48.

—— 1943: 'Zahl'-versuche an einem Kohlkraben und Vergleichsversüche an Menschen. *Z. Tierpsychol.* 5: 575–712.

—— 1950: The ability of birds to 'count.' *Bull. Anim. Behav.* No. 9: 41–5.

—— 1951: Der Vogelsang als vorstufe von music und sprache. *J. Orn. Lpz.* 93: 3–20.

—— 1953: Team-arbeit bei Ratten. *Orion* 8: Parts 19–20, pp. 5.

—— 1954. (*Unpublished.*)

KOEHLER, O., MÜLLER, O., and WACHHOLTZ, R., 1935: Kann die Taube Anzählen erfassen? *Verh. Dtsch. Zool. Ges.* 39–54.

KOEHLER, O., and WACHHOLTZ, R., 1936: Weitere Versuche an der Taube 'Nichtweiss' zur Frage des Zählvermögens. *Verh. Dtsch. Zool. Ges.* 211–16.

KOENIG, L., 1957: Beobachtungen über Reviermarkierung sowie Droh-, Kampf- und Abwehrverhalten des Murmeltieres (*Marmota marmota* L.). *Z. Tierpsychol.* 14: 510–21.

—— 1960: Das Aktionssystem des Siebenschläfers (*Glis glis* L.). *Z. Tierpsychol.* 17: 427–505.

KOFFKA, K., 1931: Die Wahrnehmung von Bewegung. In A. Bethe (ed.). *Handb. d. normalen u. pathol. physiol.* 12: (2) 1166–1271.

—— 1935: *Principles of Gestalt Psychology.* London.

KÖHLER, W., 1921: *The Mentality of Apes.* London.

—— 1940: *Dynamics in Psychology.* New York.

Köhler, W., and Wallach, H., 1950: Figural after-effects: An investigation of visual processes. *Proc. Am. Philos. Soc.* **88**:269–357.

Kohn, M., 1951: Satiation of hunger from food injected directly into stomach versus food ingested by mouth. *J. Comp. Psychol.* **440**:412–21.

Kolb, E., 1955: Central compensation and compensatory movements in frogs with labyrinth unilaterally operated. *Z. vergl. Physiol.* **37**:136–65.

Konorski, J., 1948: *Conditioned Reflexes and Neuron Organisation.* Cambridge.

—— 1950: Mechanisms of learning. Symposium Vol. 4, Soc. Exp. Biol. on *Physiological Mechanisms in Animal Behaviour.*

—— 1961: The physiological approach to the problem of recent memory. In Delafresnaye (1961).

Konorski, J., and Miller, S., 1937a: On two types of conditioned reflex. *J. Gen. Psychol.* **16**:264–72.

—— —— 1937b: Further remarks on two types of conditioned reflex. *J. Gen. Psychol.* **17**:405–7.

Kortlandt, A., 1940: Ein Übersicht der angeborenen Verhaltungsweisen des Mittel-Europäischen Kormorans (*Phalacrocorax carbo sinensis*), ihre Funktion, ontogenetische Entwicklung und phylogenetische Herkunft. *Arch. Néerl. Zool.* **4**:401–42.

—— 1959: *Tussen Mens en Dier.* Inaugural Lecture, Univ. Amsterdam-Groningen. 27 pp.

Kowalski, K., and Wojtusiak, R. J., 1952: Homing experiments on bats. *Bull. Acad. Pol. Sci. Lett.* 1951:33–56.

Kramer, G., 1951: Versuche zur Wahrnehmung von Ultrakurzwellen durch Vögel. *Die Vögelwart* 1951 (2):55–9.

—— 1952: Experiments on bird orientation. *Ibis* **94**:265–85.

—— 1953: Wird die Sonnehohe bei der Heimfindorientierung verwertet? *J. Orn.* **94**:201–19.

—— 1955: Die Sonnenorientierung der Vögel. *Proc. XI Int. Orn. Congr.* 178.

Kramer, G., and von St. Paul, U., 1951: Über angeborenes und erworbenes feinderkennen beim gimpel (*Pyrrhula pyrrhula*). *Behaviour* III **4**:243–55.

Krechevsky, I., 1937: A note concerning 'The Nature of Discrimination Learning in Animals.' *Psychol. Rev.* **44**:97–104.

—— 1938: A study of the continuity of the problem-solving process. *Psychol. Rev.* **45**:107–33.

Kröh, O., 1927: Weitere Beiträge zur Psychologie des Haushuhns. *Z. Psychol.* **103**:203–27.

Kuenzer, T., 1958: Zur physiologischer Untersuchungen über das Zucken des Regenwurms. *Z. Tierpsychol.* **15**:31–49.

Kuhlemann, P., 1939: Beobachtungen an einer durch Fluss-seeschwalbe (*Sterna h. hirundo*) aus vertauschtem Ei erbrüteten und ausgezogenen Silvermöwe (*Larus a. argentatus*). *Z. Tierpsychol.* **3**:75–84.

Kuhlmann, F., 1909: Some preliminary observations on the development of instinct and habits in young birds. *Psych. Rev. Mon. Suppl.* **11**:49–85.

Kühn, A., 1930: Über Farbensinn und Anpassung der Körperfarbe an die Umgebung bei Tintenfussen. *Nachr. Ges. Wiss. Göttingen Math-Nat. K. P.* 10.

—— 1950: Über Farbwechsel und Farbensinn von Cephalopoden. *Zeit. vergl. Physiol.* **32**:572–98.

Kulzer, E., 1954: Untersuchungen über die Schreckreaktionen der Erdkrötenkaulquappen (*Bufo bufo* L.). *Z. vergl. Physiol.* **36**:443–63.

Kuntz, A., 1923: The learning of a simple maze by the larva of *Ambystoma tigrinum.* *Univ. Iowa Studies in Nat. Hist.* **10**:27–35.

Kunze, G., 1933: Einige Versuche ü. den Antennengeschmaksinn der Honigbiene. *Zoo. Jahr. Ab. Zool. Physiol.* **52**:465–512.

Kuo, Z. Y., 1932: Ontogeny of embryonic behaviour in Aves. IV. The influence of prenatal behaviour on post-natal life. *J. Comp. Psychol.* **14**:109–21.

Kuo, Z. Y., 1938: Further study on the behaviour of the cat towards the rat. *J. Comp. Psychol.* **25** : 1–8.

Kuroda, R., 1933: Studies on visual discrimination in the Tortoise (*Clemmys japonica*). *Acta. Psychol. Keijo* **2** : 31–59.

Kyle, H. M., 1926: *The Biology of Fishes.* London.

Lack, D., 1935: Territory and polygamy in a bishop-bird (*Euplectes h. hordeacea* Linn.). *Ibis* (13) **5** : 817–36.

—— 1939: The behaviour of the Robin. *Proc. Zool. Soc. Lond.* (A) **109** : 169–78.

—— 1947: *Darwin's Finches.* Cambridge.

Ladd, G. T., and Woodworth, R. S., 1911: *Elements of Physiological Psychology.* New York.

Lafleur, L. J., 1940a: Punitive behaviour in ants. *J. Comp. Psychol.* **29** : 327–35.

—— 1940b: Helpfulness in ants. *J. Comp. Psychol.* **30** : 23–9.

—— 1941a: Communal disaffection in ants. *J. N. Y. Ent. Soc.* **44** : 199–204.

—— 1941b: Civil disturbances in ant communities. *J. N. Y. Ent. Soc.* **99** : 225–31.

Landsell, H. C., 1953: Effect of brain damage on intelligence in rats. *J. comp. physiol. Psychol.* **46** : 461–4.

Larsson, K., 1959: Experience and maturation in the development of sexual behaviour in male puberty rat. *Behaviour* **14** : 101–7.

Lashley, K. S., 1913: Reproduction of inarticulate sounds in the parrot. *J. Anim. Behav.* **3** : 361–6.

—— 1915: Notes on the nesting activities of the Noddy and Sooty Terns. *Carneg. Inst. Wash. Publ.* **211** : 61–83.

—— 1918: A simple maze with data on the relation of the distribution of practice to the rate of learning. *Psychol-biol.* **1** : 353–68.

—— 1924: Studies of cerebral function in learning. VI. The theory that synaptic resistance is reduced by the passage of the nerve impulse. *Psychol. Rev.* **31** : 369–75.

—— 1938: Experimental analysis of instinctive behaviour. *Psychol. Rev.* **45** : 445–71.

—— 1940: Studies of simian intelligence from the University of Liège. *Psychol. Bull.* **37** : 236–48.

—— 1950: In search of the engram. *Symposia Soc. Exp. Biol.* **4** : 454–82.

Lashley, K. S., Chow, K. L., and Semmes, J., 1951: An examination of the electrical field theory of cerebral integration. *Psychol. Rev.* **58** : 123–36.

Lawicka, W., and Konorski, J., 1961: The effects of prefrontal lobectomies on the delayed responses in cats. *Acta Biol. Experimentalis* **21** : 141–56.

Lebidinskiaia, S. I., and Rosenthal, J. S., 1935: Reactions of a dog after removal of the cerebral hemispheres. *Brain* **58** : 412–19.

Leeper, R., 1935: The role of motivation in learning: a study of phenomena of motivational control of utilisation of habits. *J. Genet. Psychol.* **66** : 3–40.

Lehrman, D. S., 1953: A critique of Konrad Lorenz's theory of instinctive behaviour. *Quart. Rev. Biol.* **28** : 337–63.

—— 1955: The physiological basis of parental feeding behaviour in the Ring Dove (*Streptopelia risoria*). *Behaviour* **7** : 241–86.

—— 1959: Hormonal responses to external stimuli in birds. *Ibis* **101** : 478–96.

Lenkiewicz, Z., 1951: Le sens de l'orientation dans l'espace dans un labrynthe chez les poissons. *Bull. l'Acad. Pol. Sci. et des Lett.* **1952** : 469–96.

Leopold, A. S., 1944: The nature of heritable wildness in turkeys. *Condor* **46** : 133–97.

Lettvin, J. Y., Maturana, H. R., McCulloch, W. S., and Pitts, W. H., 1959: What the frog's eye tells the frog's brain. *Proc. Inst. Radio Engineers* **47** : 1940–51.

Levy, D. M., 1934: Experiments on the sucking reflex and social behaviour in dogs. *Amer. J. Orthopsychiat.* **4** : 203–24.

Liggett, J. R., 1925: A note on the reliability of the chicks' performance in two simple mazes. *J. Genet. Psychol.* **32** : 470–80.

LINDAUER, M., 1952: Ein Beitrage zur Frage der Arbeitsteilung im Bienenstaat. *Z. vergl. Physiol.* 34:299–345.

—— 1959: Angeborene und erlernte Komponenten in der Sonnenorientierung der Bienen. *Z. vergl. Physiol.* 42:43–62.

—— 1961: *Communication among Social Bees.* Cambridge, Mass.

LINDENLAUB, E., 1955: Neue Befunde über die Anfangsorientierung von Mäusen. *Z. Tierpsychol.* 12:452–8.

—— 1960: Neue Befunde über Angansorientierung von Mäusen. *Z. Tierpsychol.* 17:555–78.

LISSMANN, H. W., 1932: Die Umwelt des Kampfisches (*Betta splendens* Regan). *Z. vergl. Physiol.* 18:65–111.

—— 1946: The neurological basis of the locomotory rhythms in the spinal dogfish (*Scyllium canicula, Acanthias vulgaris*). I. Reflex behaviour. II. The effect of de-afferentation. *J. Exp. Biol.* 23:143–61, 162–76.

—— 1951: Continuous electrical signals from the tail of a fish *Gymnarchus niloticus* Cur. *Nature* 167:201–2.

—— 1958: The function and evolution of the electric organs of Fish. *J. Exp. Biol.* 35:156–91

LOCKLEY, R. M., 1938: The sea bird as an individual. *Proc. Roy. Inst. G.B.* 30:434–54.

LOGAN-HOME, W. M., 1953: Paper tearing by birds. *Brit. Birds* 46:16–20.

LÖGLER, P., 1959: Versuche zur frage der 'Zähl'-vermögens an einem Grau Papagai. *Z. Tierpsychol.* 16:179–217.

LONGO, N., and BITTERMAN, M. E., 1960: The effect of partial reinforcement with spaced practice on resistance to extinction in the fish *Tilapia macrocephala*. *J. comp. physiol. Psychol.* 53:169–72.

LOOMIS, W. F., 1955: Glutathione control of specific feeding reaction of *Hydra*. *Ann. N.Y. Acad. Sci.* 62:209–28.

LORENTE DE NÓ, R., 1934: Studies on the structure of the cerebral cortex. II. Continuation of the study of the ammonic system. *J. Psychol. Neurol. Leipzig* 46:133–77.

LORENZ, Konrad, 1931: Beiträge zur Ethologie der sozialer Corviden. *J. Orn.* 79:67–127.

—— 1932: Betrachtungen über das Erkennen der arteigenen Triebhandlungen der Vögel. *J. Orn.* 80:50–98.

—— 1935: Der Kumpan in der Umwelt des Vögels. *J. Orn.* 83:137–214, 289–413.

—— 1937: Über den Begriff der Instinkthandlung. *Folia Biotheoretica* 2:17–50.

—— 1938: A contribution to the comparative sociology of colonial-nesting birds. *Proc. VIII Int. Orn. Congr.* 206–18.

—— 1939: Vergleichende Verhaltensforschung. *Zool. Anz. Supp.* 12:69–102.

—— 1940: Die angeborenen Formen möglicher Erfahrung. *Z. Tierpsychol.* 5:235–409.

—— 1941: Vergleichende Bewegungstudien an Anatinen. *J. Orn.* 89 (Erganzungsband 3) 194–294.

—— 1950: The comparative method of studying innate behaviour patterns. *Sympos. Vol. 4 of Soc. Exp. Biol. on Physiological Mechanisms in Animal Behaviour.* Cambridge.

—— 1954: *Man Meets Dog.* London.

—— 1961: Phylogenetische Anpassung und adaptive Modificazion des Verhaltens. *Z. Tierpsychol.* 18:139–87.

LOSINA-LOSINSKY, L., 1937: Zur Ernährungs-physiologie der Infusiorien. Untersuchungen über die Nährungsauswahl und Vermehrung bei *Paramecium caudatum*. *Arch. Protistenk.* 74:18–120.

LUCANUS, F. von, 1911: Beiträge zur Psychologie der Vögel. *Verh. V Int. Congr. Orn.* 288–302.

—— 1923: Das Sprechen der Papageien und ihre geistigen Fahigkeiten. *Orn. Monatsbr.* 31:97–102, 121–7.

—— 1925: *Das Leben der Vögel.* Berlin.

LUKASZEWSKA, I., 1961: A study of returning behaviour of white rat on elevated maze, *Acto Biol. Experimentalis* 21:253–65.

LUTHER, W., 1951: Beobachtungen über angeborene Verhaltenswiessen bei einem pommersche Hütehund. *Z. Tierpsychol.* 8:443–8.

LUTZ, F. M., 1929: Observations on leaf-cutting ants. *Amer. Mus. Novitates* No. 388.

LYDEKKER, R., 1912: *The Horse and its Relatives.* London.

McBRIDE, A. F., and HEBB, D. O., 1948: Behaviour of the captive bottle-nosed dolphin *Tursiops truncatus. J. Comp. Psychol.* 41:111–23.

McCORD, F., 1941: The effect of frustration on hoarding in rats. *J. Comp. Psychol.* 32:531–41.

MacCORQUODALE, K., and MEEHL, P. E., 1954: in Estes, Koch *et al.*, 1954.

McDONALD, H. E. 1922: Ability of *Pimephales notatus* to form associations with sound vibrations. *J. Comp. Psychol.* 2:191–3.

McDOUGALL, K. D., and McDOUGALL, W., 1931: Insight and foresight in various animals—monkey, raccoon, rat and wasp. *J. Comp. Psychol.* 11:237–73.

McDOUGALL, W., 1936: *An Outline of Psychology,* 7th ed. London.

MacGREGOR, E. G., 1948: Odour as a basis for oriented movement in ants. *Behaviour* 1:267–96.

McILHENNY, E. A., 1934: Notes on incubation and growth of alligators. *Copeia* 1934:80–8.

—— 1935: *The Alligator's Life History.* Boston.

McKAY, D. M., 1953: *Quoted in* 'Cybernetics.' *Nature* 172:648–9.

MAES, R., 1930: La vision des formes chez les poissons. *Ann. Soc. R. Zool. Belg.* 60:103–30.

MAGDSICK, W. K., 1936: The curve of retention of an incompletely learned problem in albino rats of various age levels. *J. Psychol.* 2:25–48.

MAGNUS, D., 1954: Zum Problem der 'überoptimalen' Schlüsselreize. *Verh. dtsch. zool. Ges.* (Tubingen, 1954) 317–25.

—— 1958: Experimentelle Untersuchungen zur Bionomie und Ethologie des Kaisermantels *Argynnis paphia. Z. Tierpsychol.* 15:397–426.

MAGOUN, H. W., 1958: *The Waking Brain,* Springfield, Ill.

MAIER, N. R. F., 1932: A study of orientation in the rat. *J. Comp. Psychol.* 14:387–99.

MAIER, N. R. F., and SCHNEIRLA, T. C., 1935: *Principles of Animal Psychology.* London and New York.

MÁLEK, R., 1927: Associatives Gedächtnis bei den Regenwürmern. *Biol. Gen.* 3:317–28.

MANNING, A., 1959: The Sexual Behaviour of two Sibling *Drosophila* Species. *Behaviour* 15:123–45.

MANNING, A., 1961: The effects of artificial selection for mating speed in *Drosophila melanogaster. Anim. Behav.* 9:82–92.

MANNING, M., 1956: Some aspects of the foraging behaviour of humble bees. *Behaviour* 9:164–201.

MANTON, S. M., 1961: Experimental zoology and problems of arthropod evolution. In *The Cell and the Organism,* ed. J. A. Ramsay and V. B. Wigglesworth. Cambridge.

MARKS, H. L., SIEGEL, T. B., and KRAMER, C. Y., 1960: The effect of comb and wattle removal on the social organisation of mixed flocks of chickens. *Anim. Behav.* 8:1926.

MARLER, P. R., 1952: Variation in the song of the Chaffinch (*Fringilla coelebs*). *Ibis* 94:458–72.

—— 1961: The filtering of external stimuli during instinctive behaviour. In Thorpe and Zangwill (1961).

MAROLD, E. 1939: Versuche an Wellensittichen zur Frage des 'Zahl-' vermögens. *Z. Tierpsychol.* 3:170–223.

MARPLES, G., and MARPLES, A., 1934: *Terns or Sea Swallows.* London.

MARSHALL, A. J., 1952: The condition of the interstitial and spermatogenetic tissue of migratory birds on arriving in England in April and May. *Proc. Zool. Soc. Lond.* **122**: 287–95.

—— 1954: Bower Birds. *Biol. Rev.* **29**: 1–45.

MARSHALL, F. H. A., 1936: Sexual periodicity and the causes which determine it. *Phil. Trans. Roy. Soc. B.* **226**: 432–56.

MARSHALL, N., 1947: Factors in the incubation behaviour of the Common Tern. *Auk* **60**: 574–88.

MARTIN, E. G., and RICH, W. H., 1918: The activities of decerebrate and decerebellate chicks. *Am. J. Physiol.* **46**: 396–409.

MAST, S. O., 1932: Localised stimulation, transmission of impulses and the nature of responses in *Amœba*. *Physiol. Zool.* **5**: 1–15.

—— 1947: The food vacuole in *Paramecium*. *Biol. Bull.* **92**: 31–72.

MAST, S. O., and PUSCH, L. C., 1924: Modification of response in *Amœba*. *Biol. Bull.* **46**: 55–60.

MATHER, K., 1943: Polygenic inheritance and natural selection. *Biol. Rev.* **18**: 32–64.

MATTHEWS, G. V. T., 1952: The relation of learning and memory to the orientation and homing of pigeons. *Behaviour* **4**: 202–21.

—— 1953*a*: Sun navigation in homing pigeons. *J. Exp. Biol.* **30**: 243–67.

—— 1953*b*: The orientation of untrained pigeons: a dichotomy in the homing process. *J. Exp. Biol.* **30**: 268–76.

—— 1953*c*: Navigation in the Manx Shearwater. *J. Exp. Biol.* **30**: 760–96.

—— 1955*a*: A study of the chronometer factor in bird navigation. *J. Exp. Biol.* **32**: 39–58.

—— 1955*b*: *Bird Navigation*. Cambridge.

—— 1961: 'Nonsense' orientation in mallard *Anas platyrhynchos* and its relation to experiments on bird navigation. *Ibis* **103a**: 211–30.

MATTHEWS, L. Harrison, 1952: *British Mammals*, London.

MATTHEWS, S., and DETWILER, S., 1926: The reactions of *Amblystoma* embryos following prolonged treatment with chloretone. *J. Exp. Zool.* **45**: 279–92.

MAXWELL, G., 1960: *Ring of Bright Water*. London.

MAY, M. A., 1948: Experimentally acquired drives. *J. Exp. Psychol.* **38**: 66–77.

MAYER, A. G., and SOULE, C. G., 1906: Some reactions of caterpillars and moths. *J. Exp. Zool.* **3**: 415–33.

MAYR, E., 1942: *Systematics and the Origin of Species*. New York.

—— 1946: The number of species of birds. *Auk.* **63**: 64–9.

MEEHL, P. E., and MacCORQUODALE, K., 1948: A further study of latent learning in the T-maze. *J. Comp. Physiol. Psychol.* **41**: 372–96.

MEESTERS, A., 1940: Über die Organisation des Gesichtsfeldes der Fische. *Z. f. Tierpsychol.* **4**: 84–149.

MELZACK, R., 1961: On the survival of mallard ducks after 'habituation' to the hawk-shaped figure. *Behaviour* **17**: 9–16.

MERRIMAN, D., 1941: Studies on the Striped Bass (*Roccus saxatilis*) of the Atlantic coast. *Fish. Bull. Fish. Wildlife Serv. Wash.* **50**: (Bull. 35) 1–77.

METALNIKOV, S., 1907: Ueber die Ernährung der Infusorien und deren Fähigkeit ihre Nahrun zu wählen. *Trans. Soc. Imp. Nat. St. Petersburg* **38**: 181–7.

—— 1912: Contributions a l'étude de la digestion intracellulaire chez les protozoaires. *Arch. Zool, exp. gén.* **49**: 373–498.

—— 1914: Les infusoires, peuvent-ils apprehendre a choisir leur nourriture? *Arch. Protistenk.* **34**: 60–78.

—— 1917: On the question regarding the capability of Infusoria to 'learn' to choose their food. *Russ. J. Zool.* **2**: 397. (*Not seen.*)

METFESSEL, M., 1935: Roller Canary song produced without learning from external source. *Science* **81**: 470.

MEYER-HOLZAPFEL, M. M., 1956*a*. Das Spiel bei Säugetieren. In *Handbuch der Zoologie* (ed. Kukenthal *et al.*), Vol. 8. Berlin.

MEYER-HOLZAPFEL, M. M., 1956b: Über die Berichschaft zu Spiel und Instinkthandlunge. Z. Tierpsychol. 13:442–62.

MIKHAILOFF, S., 1920–21: Expériences réflexologiques. Expériences nouvelles sur Eledone moschata. Bull. Inst. Ocean. Monaco No. 379: 8 and No. 398: 11.

—— 1922: Expériences réflexologiques. Expériences nouvelles sur Pagurus striatus. Bull. Inst. Ocean. Monaco No. 418: 12.

—— 1923: Expériences réflexologiques. Expériences nouvelles sur Pagurus striatus, Leander xiphias et treilleans. Bull. Inst. Ocean. Monaco No. 422: 16.

MIKLASZEWSKA, A., 1948: Experiments on the plasticity of instinct in caterpillars of Nymphula nymphaeata. L. (Lepidoptera-Pyralidae) Bull. Acad. Pol. Sci. et Let. (B) 277–97.

MILES, R. C., 1958a: Learning in kittens with manipulatory, exploratory and food incentives. J. comp. physiol. Psychol. 51:39–42.

—— 1958b:

MILLER, A. H., 1939: Foraging dexterity of Lazuli Bunting. Condor 41:255–6.

MILLER, G. A., and POSTMAN, L., 1946: Individual and group hoarding in rats. Am. J. Psychol. 59:652–68.

MILLER, G. A., and VIEK, P., 1944: An analysis of the rat's response to unfamiliar aspects of the hoarding situation. J. Comp. Psychol. 37:221–31.

MILLER, N. E., 1951: Learnable drives and rewards (in Stevens, S. S., Handbook of Experimental Psychology. New York.

MINAMI, H., and DALLENBACH, K. M., 1946: The effect of activity upon learning and retention in the cockroach (P. americana). Am. J. Psychol. 59:1–58.

MINCKIEWICZ, R., 1933: Nids et proies des Sphegiens de Pologne. III. Polske Pismo Ent. 12:181–261.

MITTELSTAEDT, H., 1957: Prey capture in Mantids. In Recent Advances in Invertebrate Physiology 51–7. Univ. Oregon Pubns.

—— 1962: Control Systems of orientation in Insects. Ann. Rev. Entom. 7:177–98.

MÖBIUS, K., 1873: Die Bewegungen der Tiere u. ihr psychischer horizont. Sohr. naturw. Ver. Schl.-Holst. 1:113–30. (Not seen.)

MOLITOR, A., 1931: Neuere Beobachtungen und Versuche mit Grabwespen. Biol. Zbl. 51:412–24.

—— 1937: Zur vergleichenden Psychobiologie der akuliaten Hymenopteren auf experimenteller Grundlage (mit besonderer Berücksichtigung der Sphegiden). Bio. Generalis 13:294–333.

—— 1939: Beobachtungen, den 'ortsinn' und Nestbau der Vespiden betreffend. Zool. Anz. 126:239–45.

MOLTZ, H., 1960: Imprinting: Empirical Basis and Theoretical significance. Psychol. Bull. 57:291–314.

MONTGOMERY, K. C., 1951: The relation between exploratory behaviour and spontaneous alternation in the white rat. J. Comp. Physiol. Psychol. 44:582–9.

—— 1954: Role of exploratory drives in learning. J. Comp. Physiol. Psychol. 47:60–3.

MONTGOMERY, K. C., and HEINEMANN, E. G., 1952: Concerning the ability of homing pigeons to discriminate patterns of polarised light. Science 116:454–6.

MOON, L. E., and LODAHL, T. M., 1956: The reinforcing effect of changes in illumination on lever pressing of the monkey. Amer. J. Psychol. 69:288–90.

MOORE, A. R., 1910: On the righting movements of the starfish. Biol. Bull. 19:235–9.

MOORE, A. R., and WELCH, J. C., 1940: Associative hysteresis in larval amblystoma. J. Comp. Psychol. 29:283–92.

MOORE, N. W., 1952: On the so-called 'Territories' of dragonflies (Odonata-anisoptera). Behaviour 4:85–100.

MOREAU, R. E., 1938: A contribution to the biology of the Musagiformes, the so-called Plantain-eaters. Ibis (14) 2:639–71.

—— 1942: The nesting of African birds in association with other living things. Ibis (14) 6:240–63.

Moreau, R. E., and Moreau, W. M., 1941: Piracy by *Lanius collaris humeralis*. *Ibis* (14) 5:614-15.

—— —— 1944: Do young birds play? *Ibis* 86:93-4.

Morell, F., 1961: Lasting changes in synaptic organisation produced by continuous neuronal bombardment. In Delafresnaye (1961).

Morgan, C. Lloyd, 1894: *Introduction to Comparative Psychology*. London.

—— 1900: *Animal Behaviour*. London.

Morgan, C. T., and Stellar, E., 1950: *Physiological Psychology*. New York.

Mori, S., 1943-9: (Various papers in *Mem. Coll. Sci. Ser. B. Univ. Kyoto*. See especially: A concept on mechanisms of the endogenous daily rhythmic activity 19:1-4; *and* Harmony between behaviour rhythms and environmental rhythm 19:71-4.)

Morley, A., 1942: Effects of baiting on the Marsh Tit. *Brit. Birds* 35:261-6.

Morris, D., 1956; The feather postures of birds and the problem of the origin of social signals. *Behaviour* 9:75-113.

Morrow, J. E., 1948: Schooling behaviour in fishes. *Quart. Rev. Biol.* 23:27-38.

Moseley, D., 1925: The accuracy of the pecking response in chicks. *J. Comp. Psychol.* 5:75-97.

Mostler, G., 1935: Beobachtungen zur Frage der Wespenmimikry. *Z. Morph. Ok. Tiere* 29:381-454.

—— 1937: Versuche zur Gedächtnisleistung der einheimischen insektenfressenden Vögel. *Z. Natur.* 91:102-21.

Mowrer, O. H., 1950: On the psychology of talking birds: a contribution to language and personality theory. In *Learning Theory and Personality Dynamics*. New York.

Mowrer, O. H., and Jones, H., 1945: Habit strength as a function of the pattern of reinforcement. *J. Exp. Psychol.* 35:293-311.

Muenzinger, K. F., and Dove, C. C., 1937: Serial learning. I. Gradients of uniformity and variability produced by success and failure of single responses. *J. Genet. Psychol.* 16:403-13.

Mühlmann, H., 1934: Im Modellversuch künstlich erzeugte Mimikry und ihre Bedeutung für den 'Nachahmer.' *Z. Morph. Ök. Tiere* 28:259-96.

Müller, H. J., 1942: Isolating mechanisms, evolution and temperature (in Dobzhausky, T., *Biological Symposia*. Lancaster, Pa. 6:71-125).

Munn, N. L., 1950: *Handbook of Psychological Research on the Rat*. Boston.

—— 1940: Learning experiments with larval frogs. *J. comp. physiol. Psychol.* 29:97-108.

—— 1958: The question of insight and delayed reaction in fish. *J. comp. physiol. Psychol.* 51:92-7.

Murie, A., 1940: Ecology of the Coyote in the Yellowstone. *Fauna Nat. Parks U.S.A. Bull.* No. 4:1-189.

Myers, J. G., 1935: Nesting association of birds with social insects. *Trans. Ent. Soc. Lond.* 83:11-22.

Myers, R. E., 1961: Corpus callosum and visual gnosis. In Delafresnaye (1961).

Mylnarski, M., 1951: The ability to recognize complete forms from their fragments in water tortoises. *Bull. Int. de l'Acad. Pol. Sci. et. Lett. (Cl. des Sci. Ser. B. Sci. Nat.)* 1952:253-70.

Nagel, W. A., 1897: Über Mischgerüche und die Komponentengliederung des Geruchsinnes. *Z. Psychol. Physiol. Sinnesorg.* 15:82-101.

Nealey, S. M., and Edwards, B. J., 1960: Depth perception in rats without pattern vision experience. *J. comp. physiol. Psychol.* 53:468-9.

Neff, W. D., and Diamond, I. T., 1958: The neural basis of auditory discrimination. In *Biological and Biochemical Bases of Behaviour*, ed. H. F. Harlow and C. N. Woolsey. Madison, Wisc., U.S.A.

Newman, M. A., 1956: Social behaviour and interspecific competition in two trout species. *Physiol. Zool.* 29:64-81.

REFERENCES 505

NICE, M. M., 1938: Territory and mating with the Song Sparrow. *Proc. 8 Int. Orn. Congr., Oxford* 324–38.

—— 1943: Studies in the life history of the Song Sparrow. II. *Trans. Linn. Soc. N.Y.* **6**:1–328.

NICE, M. M., and TER PELKWYK, J. J., 1941: Enemy recognition by the Song Sparrow. *Auk* **58**:195–214.

NICHOLS, U. G., 1953: Habits of the Desert Tortoise, *Gopherus agassizii. Herpetologica* **9**:65–9.

NICOLAI, J., 1956: Zür Biologie und Ethologie des Gimpels. *Z. Tierpsychol.* **13**:93–132.

NISSEN, H. W., 1951: Phylogenetic Comparison. (In Stevens, S. S., *Handbook of Experimental Psychology*. Chap. II: 347–86.)

NISSEN, H. W., CHOW, K. L., and SEMMES, J., 1951: Effects of restricted opportunity for tactual, kinesthetic and manipulative experience on the behaviour of a chimpanzee. *Am. J. Psychol.* **64**:485–507.

NISSEN, H. W., RIESEN, A. H., and NOWLIS, V., 1938: Delayed response and discrimination learning by chimpanzees. *J. Comp. Psychol.* **26**:361–86.

NOBLE, G. K., 1931: *The Biology of the Amphibia.* New York.

—— 1934: Experimenting with the courtship of lizards. *Natural History (N.Y.)* **34**:3–15.

—— 1936: Courtship and sexual selection of the Flicker (*Colaptes auratus luteus*). *Auk* **53**:269–82.

NOBLE, G. K., and BRADLEY, H. T., 1933: The mating behaviour of lizards. *Ann. N.Y. Acad. Sci.* **35**:25–100.

NOBLE, G. K., and BRESLAU, A. M., 1938: The senses involved in the migration of young freshwater turtles after hatching. *J. Comp. Psychol.* **25**:175–93.

NOBLE, G. K., and CURTIS, B., 1939: The social behaviour of the jewel fish, *Hemichromis bimaculatus*, Gill. *Amer. Mus. Nat. Hist. Bull.* **76**:1–46.

NOBLE, G. K., and LEHRMAN, D. S., 1940: Egg recognition by the Laughing Gull. *Auk* **57**:22–43.

NOBLE, G. K., WURM, M., and SCHMIDT, A., 1938: Social behaviour of the Blackcrowned Night Heron. *Auk* **55**:7–40.

NOBLE, M., GRUENDER, A., and MEYER, D. R., 1959: Conditioning in fish (*Molliensia* spp.) as a function of the interval between conditioned and unconditioned stimulus. *J. comp. physiol. Psychol.* **52**:236–9.

NOBLE, R. C., 1950: *The Nature of the Beast.* London.

NOLTE, A., 1958: Beobachtungen über das Instinktverhalten von Kupizineraffen (*Cebus appella* L.) in Gefangenschaft. *Behaviour* **12**:183–206.

NOLTE, W., 1932: Experimentelle Untersuchungen zum Problem der Lokalisation des Assoziationsvermögens im Fischgehirn. *Z. vergl. Physiol.* **18**:255–79.

NUBLING, E., 1939: The painting of the Satin Bower-bird's bower, *Emu* **39**:22–31.

—— 1941: A contribution to the biology of the Satin Bowerbird. *Austr. Zool.* **10**:95–120.

OAKES, W. F., 1956: Latent learning in the three-table apparatus. *J. exp. Psychol.* **51**:287–9.

OHGUSHI, R., 1955: Ethological studies on the intertidal impets. I. Analytical studies on the homing behaviour of two species of limpets. *Japanese J. of Ecology* **5**:31–35 (Japanese, with English summary).

OLDS, J., 1955: Physiological mechanisms of reward. In *Current Theory and Research in Motivation*, Nebraska Symp. on Motivation **3**:73–139.

—— 1958: Self-stimulation in the brain. Its use to study local effects of hunger, sex and drugs. *Science* **127**:315–24.

OLDS, J., and OLDS, M. E., 1961: Interference and learning in paleocortical systems. In Delafresnaye (1961).

ONO, Y., 1937: Conditioned orientation of the Fighting Fish (*Macropodus opercularis*). *J. Fac. Sci. Univ. Tokyo* **4**:401–12.

ONO, Y., 1955: Experimental studies of intraspecific recognition in *Oryzias latites*. *Mem. Fac. Arts and Liberal Education*, Kagawa Univ. Japan, Pt. 2, No. 17: 1–38.

OPFINGER, E., 1931: Über die Orientierung der Biene an der Futterquelle (Die Bedeutung von Anflug und Orientierungsflug für den Lernvorgang bei Farb-, Form- und Ortsdressuren). *Z. vergl. Physiol.* **15**: 431–87.

—— 1949: Zur Psychologie der Duftdressuren bei Bienen. *Z. vergl. Physiol.* **31**: 441–53.

ORLOFF, A. P., NOVIKOV, B. G., and WOITKEWITSCH, A. A., 1940: Effect of castration on the homing faculty of the carrier pigeon. *C. R. Acad. Sci. URSS* **27**: 406–8.

ORR, R. T., 1945: A study of captive Galapagos Finches of the genus Geospiza. *Condor* **47**: 177–201.

OSGOOD, C. E., 1953: *Method and Theory in Experimental Psychology*. Oxford.

PACHE, J., 1932: Formensinn bei Fröschen. *Z. vergl. Physiol.* **17**: 423–63.

PADILLA, S. G., 1930: Further studies on the delayed pecking of chicks. *Thesis, Univ. Mich. Lib., published* 1935. *J. Comp. Psychol.* **20**: 413–43.

PAKENHAM, R. H. W., 1943: Field notes on the birds of Zanzibar and Pemba Islands. *Ibis* **85**: 165–89.

PALMGREN, P., *et al.*, 1938: Einige Labyrinthversuche mit Klein-vögeln und Mäusen. *Orn. Fenn.* **15**: 74–7.

PANTIN, C. F. A., 1950: Behaviour patterns in lower invertebrates. Symposium Vol. 4 S.E.B. *Physiol. Mechanisms Anim. Behav.*: 175–95.

—— 1952: The elementary nervous system. *Proc. Roy. Soc. B.* **140**: 147–68.

PARKER, G. H., 1896: The reactions of Metridium to food and other substances. *Bull. Mus. Harvard* **29**: 107–19.

—— 1922: The instinctive locomotor reactions of the Loggerhead Turtle in relation to its senses. *J. Comp. Psychol.* **2**: 425–9.

PARKER, J. B., 1917: A revision of the Bembecine Wasps of America North of Mexico. *Proc. U.S. Nat. Mus.* **52**: 1–155.

PARR, A. E., 1937: On self recognition and social reaction in relation to biochemics. *Ecology* **18**: 321–3.

PARRISS, J. R., 1961: Retention of shape-discrimination after regeneration of the optic nerve in the toad, *Bufo bufo. Quart. J. exp. Psychol.* (in press).

PARRISS, J. R., and MOODY, M. F., 1961: The discrimination of polarized light by Octopus: a behavioural and morphological study. *Z. vergl. Physiol.*

PARSCHIN, A. N., 1929: Bedingte Reflexe bei Schildkröten (*Emys orbicularis*). *Pflüg. Archiv.* **222**: 328–33.

PASSANO, L. M., 1957: Prey-predator recognition in the lower invertebrates. In *Recent Advances in Invertebrate Physiology*, ed. B. T. Scheer. Univ. Oregon Pubns.

PASTORE, N., 1958: Form perception and size constancy in the duckling. *J. Psychol.* **45**: 259–61.

—— 1959: Perceptual functioning in the duckling. *J. genet. Psychol.* **95**: 157–69.

PAVLOV, I. P., 1927: *Conditioned Reflexes: An investigation of the activity of the cerebral cortex*. Trans. G. V. Anrep. London.

PEARSE, A. S., 1908: Observations on the behaviour of the holothurian *Thyone briareus* (Leseur). *Biol. Bull.* **15**: 259–88.

PECKHAM, G. W., and PECKHAM, E. G., 1887: Some observations on the mental powers of spiders. *J. Morph.* **1**: 383–419.

—— —— 1898: *On the instincts and habits of the solitary wasps. Wisc. Geol. Nat. Hist. Survey II.*

—— —— 1900: Additional observations on the instincts and habits of the solitary wasps. *Bull. Wisc. Nat. Hist. Soc.* **1**: 85–93.

PEIPER, A., 1951: Instinkt und angebornes Schema beim Säugling. *Z. Tierpsychol.* **8**: 449–56.

PEITZMEIER, J., 1939: Kann abweichendes oekologisches Verhalten einer Vögel population durch psychologische Factoren erklärt werden? *Orn. Monatsbr.* 47:161-6.

—— 1940: Die Scheu des Vögels vor dem Menschen und ihre Uberwindung durch oekologischen Zwang. *Orn. Monatsbr.* 48:37-41.

PELSENEER, P., 1935: *Essai d'Éthologie Zoologique d'apres l'étude des Mollusques.* Roy. Acad. of Belgium, Bruxelles. *Publications de la Fondation Agathon de Potter, No. 1.*

PENARD, E., 1948: Habituation. *J. R. Micros. Soc.* 67:43-5.

PENFIELD, W., and RASMUSSEN, T., 1950: *The Cerebral Cortex of Man.* New York.

PENNYCUICK, C. J., 1960: The physical basis of astro-navigation in birds: theoretical considerations. *J. exp. Biol.* 37:573-93.

PERKINS, F. T., 1931: A further study of configurational learning in the goldfish. *J. Exp. Psychol.* 14:508-38.

PERKINS, F. T., and WHEELER, R. H., 1930: Configurational learning in the goldfish. *Comp Psychol. Mongr.* 7, No. 31: 1-50.

PERKINS, H. F., 1903: The development of *Gonionemus murbachii. Proc. Phila. Acad. Sci.* 750-90.

PERKINS, R. C. L., 1919: The British species of *Andrena* and *Nomada. Trans. Ent. Soc. Lond.* 218-320.

PETERSON, B., LUNDGREN, L., and WILSON, L., 1956-7: The development of flight capacity in a butterfly. *Behaviour* 10:324-9.

PETERSON, R. T., 1941: *A Field Guide to Western Birds.* Boston.

PETTERSSON, M., 1961: The nature and spread of daphne-eating in the Greenfinch, and the spread of some other habits. *Anim. Behav.* 9:114.

PHILLIPS, J. C., 1912: Notes on wildness in ducklings. *J. Anim. Behav.* 2: 363-4.

PICKEN, L. E. R., 1955: The study of minute biological structures and their significance in the organisation of cells. *School Science Review.* Nos. 129:262-8; 130:332-8; 131:30-37.

PIÉRON, H. 1909: Contribution à la biologie de la Patelle et de la Calyptreé. I. L'éthologie, les phénomènes sensoriels. *Bull. Sci. Fr. Belg.* 43:183-202. II. Le sens du retour et la mémoire topographique. *Arch. Zool. Exp. Gén.* (5) *Notes et Revues*: 18-29.

—— 1920: *L'Évolution de la Mémoire.* Paris.

PILTERS, H., 1954: Untersuchungen ü angeborene Verhaltensweisen bei Tylopoden, unter besonderer Berücksichtigung der neuweltlichen Formen. *Z. Tierpsychol.* 11:213-303.

PINTO-HAMUY, T., 1961: The role of the cerebral cortex in the learning of an instrumental conditioned response. In Delafresnaye (1961).

PITT, F., 1927: *The Animal Mind.* London.

—— 1931: *The Intelligence of Animals: Studies in Comparative Psychology.* London.

PITTENDRIGH, C. S., and BRUCE, V. G., 1957: An oscillator model for biological clocks. In *Rhythmic and Synthetic Processes* in Growth, ed. D. Rudnick. Princeton, N.J. 217 pp.

—— —— 1959: Daily rhythms as coupled oscillator systems and their relation to thermo-periodism and photo-periodism. In *Photo-periodism and Related Phenomena in Plants and Animals* 475-505. Washington, D.C.

PLATZ, E., 1939: Wahrnemung und Erinnerung bei der Fütterwahl den Vögeln. *Z. Tierpsychol.* 3:1-29.

POLIAKOV, K. L., 1930: The physiology of the olfactory and auditory analyzers in the turtle. *Russ. Fiziol. Zh.* 13:162-78.

POLIMANTI, O., 1910: Les cephalopods, ont-ils une mémoire? *Arch. Psychol.* 10:84-7.

PORTER, J. P., 1904: A preliminary study of the psychology of the English Sparrow. *Am. J. Psychol.* 15:313-46.

—— 1906: Further study of the English Sparrow and other birds. *Am. J. Psychol.* 17:248-71.

PORTER, J. P., 1910: Intelligence and imitation in birds: a criterion of imitation. *Am. J. Psychol.* 21:1–71.

PORTIELJE, A. F. J., 1921: Zur Ethologie bezw. Psychologie von *Botaurus stellaris. Ardea* 15:1–15.

—— 1933: On a remarkable and purposive feeding behaviour in the Sea Anemone *Diadumene cincta* Stephenson. *Tijd. ned. dierk. ver. Leiden* 3:132–44.

POSTMAN, L., 1947: The history and present status of the Law of Effect. *Psychol. Bull.* 44:489–563.

POULSEN, H., 1951: Inheritance and learning in the song of the Chaffinch (*Fringilla cœlebs*). *Behaviour* 3:216–28.

—— 1954: On the song of the linnet (*Carduelis cannabina* L.). *Dansk Orn., Foren. Tidskr.* 48:32–7.

POULSEN, S. E., 1944: Instinkt og artokarakter hos fugle. *Dansk Orn. Foren. Tidskr.* 38:82–95.

POWER, J., 1857: Observations on the habits of various marine animals. *Ann. Mag. Nat. Hist.* 20:334–6.

PRATER, S. H., 1933: The social life of snakes. *J. Bombay N.H.S.* 36:469–76.

PRATT, J. G. B., 1955: An investigation of homing ability in pigeons without previous homing experience. *J. Exp. Biol.* 32:70–83.

PRATT, J. G. B., and THOULESS, R. H., 1955: Homing orientation in pigeons in relation to opportunity to observe the sun before release. *J. Exp. Biol.* 32:140–57.

PRECHT, H., *et al.*, 1956: Einige Versuche zum Heimfindevermögen von Vögeln. *J. f. Orn.* 97:377–83.

PRECHT, H., and FREYTAG, G., 1958: Über Ermugung und Hemmung angeborene Verhaltenswiesen bei Springspinner (Salticidae) zugleich ein Beitrag zum Triebproblem. *Behaviour* 13:43–211.

PRECHTL, H. F. R., 1952: Angeborene Bewegungsweisen junger Katzen. *Experientia* 8:220.

—— 1953: Zur physiologie die angeborenen auslösenden mechanismen. I. Quantitative untersuchungen über die sperrbewegung junger singvögel. *Behaviour* 1:32–50.

—— 1956: Neurophysiologische Mechanismen des formstarren Verhaltens. *Behaviour* 9:243–319.

—— 1958: The directed head turning response and allied movements of the human baby. *Behaviour* 13:212–42.

PRENTICE, W. C. H., 1946: Operationism and Psychological Theory: a Note. *Psych. Rev.* 53:247–9.

PREYER, W., 1887: Über die Bewegungen der Seesterne. *Mitt. Zool. Stat. Neapel.* 7:27–127; 191–233.

PRICE, H. H., 1932: *Perception.* London.

PRINGLE, J. W. S., 1951: On the parallel between learning and evolution. *Behaviour* 3:174–215.

—— 1961: Proprioception in arthropods. In *The Cell and Organism*, ed. J. A. Ramsay and V. B. Wigglesworth. Cambridge.

PROMPTOFF, A., 1930: Die geographische variabilität das Buckfinkenschlages (*Fringilla cœlebs*) etc. *Biol. Zbl.* 50:478.

PROMPTOFF, A. N., and LUKINA, E. V., 1945: Conditioned-reflectory differentiation of calls in passeres and its biological value. *C. R. (Doklady) Acad. Sci. L'URSS* 46:382–84.

PUKOWSKI, E. N., 1933: Oekologische Untersuchungen an *Necrophorus. Z. Morph. Ök. Tiere* 27:518–86.

PUMPHREY, R. J., 1948: The sense organs of birds. *Ibis* 90:171–99.

RABBE, S., 1939: Zur Analyse der Assoziationsbildung bei *Lumbriculus variegatus* Mull. *Z. vergl. Physiol.* 26:611–43.

RABAUD, E., 1924: Le retour au nid de *Vespa sylvestris. Feuill. Nat.* 1:7–11.

RABAUD, E., 1926: Acquisition des habitudes et repères sensoriels chez les guêpes. *Bull. Sci. Fr. Belg.* 60:319–33.

RÄBER, H., 1944: Versuche zurermittlung des beuteschemas an einem Hausmarder (*Martes foina*) und einem Iltis (*Putorius putorius*). *Rev. Suisse Zool.* 51:293–332.

—— 1948: Analyse des Balzverhaltens eines domestizierten Truthahns (*Meleagris*). *Behaviour* 1:237–66.

RAMSAY, A. O., 1950: Conditioned responses in crows. *Auk* 67:456–9.

—— 1951: Familial recognition in domestic birds. *Auk* 68:1–16.

RAMSAY, A. O., and HESS, E. H., 1954: A laboratory approach to the study of imprinting. *Wilson Bulletin* 66:196–206.

RAND, A., 1941a: Results of Archbold Expeditions—Nos. 34 and 44. Development and enemy recognition of Curve-billed Thrasher. *Bull. Am. Mus. N. H.* 78:213–42: 79:517–24.

—— 1941b: The courtship of the Road-runner. *Auk* 58:57–8.

RANGER, G., 1950: Life of the Crowned Hornbill. Part III. *Ostrich* 21:1–14.

RANSMEIER, R. E., and GERARD, R. W., 1954: Effects of temperature, convulsion and metabolic factors on rodent memory and EEG. *Amer. J Physiol.* 179:663–4 (Abstract).

RATNER, S. C., and MILLER, K. R., 1959a: Classical conditionings in earthworms, *Lumbricus terestris. J. comp. physiol. Psychol.* 52:102–5.

—— —— 1959b: The effect of spacing of training and ganglion removal on conditioning in earthworms. *J. comp. physiol. Psychol.* 52:667–72.

RAU, P., 1928: Modification of the nest-building habits of *Polistes. Psyche* 35:151–2.

—— 1929: The habitat and dissemination of four species of *Polistes* wasps. *Ecology* 10:191–200.

—— 1934: A note on the attachment of the wasp *Bembix nubilipennis* to their nesting sites. *Psyche* 41:243–4.

—— 1943: How the cockroach deposits its egg-case: a study of insect behaviour. *Ann. Ent. Soc. Am.* 221–6.

RAU, P., and RAU, N., 1916: The sleep of insects: an ecological study. *Ann. Ent. Soc. Am.* 9:227–74.

—— 1918: *Wasp Studies Afield*. Princeton.

RAZRAN, G., 1956: Backward conditioning. *Psychol. Bull.* 53:55–69.

—— 1961: The observable unconscious and the inferable conscious in current Soviet psychophysiology: interoceptive conditioning, semantic conditioning and the orienting reflex. *Psychological Rev.* 68:81–147.

RAZRAN, G. H. S., 1933: Conditioned responses in animals other than dogs. *Psychol. Bull.* 30:261–324.

—— 1937: Conditioned responses: classified bibliography. *Psychol. Bull.* 34:191–256.

—— 1939: The nature of the extinctive process. *Psychol. Rev.* 46:264–97.

REES, W. J., 1950: The distribution of *Octopus vulgaris* Lamarck in British waters. *J. Mar. Biol. Assn. U.K.* 29:361–78.

REGEN, E., 1926: Über die Beeinflussung der Stridulation von *Thamnotrizon apterus*. Fab. durch künstliche erzeugte Töne und verschiedenartige Geräusche. *S. B. Akad. Wiss. Wien* 135:329–69.

REICHNER, H., 1924–5: Über farbige Unstimmung (Suksessivkontrast) und Momentanadaptation der Hühner. *Z. Psychol.* 96:68–75.

REID, R. L., 1958: Discrimination-reversal learning in pigeons. *J. comp. physiol. Psychol.* 51:716–20.

RENSCH, B., 1925: Verhalten von singvögeln bei Aenderung Geleges. *Orn. Monatsbr.* 33:169–73.

RENSCH, B., and DÜCKER, G., 1959: Spiele von Mungo und Ichneumon. *Behaviour* 14:185–213.

RENSCH, B., and FRANZISKET, L., 1954: Lang andauernde bedingte Reflexe bei Rückenmarksfröschen. *Z. vergl. Physiol.* 36:318–26.

Révész, G., 1922: Zur Analyse der tierischen Handlung. *Arch. Néerl. Physiol.* 7:469–77.

—— 1924: Experiments on animal space perception. *Brit. J. Psychol.* 14:386–414.

—— 1925: Récherches de psychologie de l'espace sur les oiseaux. *Arch. Néerl. Physiol.* 10:417–19.

Reyniers, J. A., 1953: Germ Free Life. *Lancet* 933–4.

Reynolds, B. D., 1924: Interpretation of protoplasmic masses in relation to the study of heredity and environment in *Arcella polypera*. *Biol. Bull.* 46:106–42.

Rheingold, H. L., and Hess, E. H., 1957: The chick's 'preference' for some visual properties of water. *J. comp. physiol. Psychol.* 50:417–21.

Ri, Ch. S., 1934: Number discrimination in pigeons (*Japanese with English Summary*). *Act. Psychol. Keijo* 2:76–83.

Ribbands, C. R., 1950: Changes in the behaviour of honeybees following their recovery from anæsthesia. *J. Exp. Biol.* 27:302–10.

—— 1953: *The Behaviour and Social Life of Honeybees*. London.

—— 1954: The defence of the honeybee community. *Proc Roy. Soc. B.* 142:514–24.

Ribbands, C. R., Kalmus, H., and Nixon, H. L., 1952: New evidence of communication in the honeybee colony. *Nature* 170:438.

Ribbands, C. R., and Speirs, N., 1953: The adaptability of the home-coming honeybee. *Brit. J. Anim. Behav.* 1:59–66.

Rich, W. H., and Holmes, H. B., 1928: Experiments in marking young Chinook Salmon on the Columbia River. *Bull. U.S. Bur. Fish.* 44:215–64.

Richardson, F., 1934: Diurnal movements of the limpets *Lottia gigantea* and *Acmaea persona*. *J. Entom. Zool.* 26:53–5.

Richardson, W. B., 1942: Reaction towards snakes as shown by the Wood Rat *Neotoma albigula*. *J. Comp. Psychol.* 34:1–10.

Riddle, O., and Barnes, F. H., 1931: A conditioned emetic reflex in the pigeon. *Proc. Soc. Exp. Biol. N.Y.* 28:979–81.

Ridley, H. N., 1890: On the habits of the Caringa (*Formica graciliceps*). *J. Straits Branch Roy. Asiat. Soc. Singapore* No. 22:345–7.

Riess, B. F., 1950: The isolation of factors of learning and native behaviour in field and laboratory studies. *Ann. N.Y. Acad. Sci.* 51:1093–102.

Rilling, S., Mittelstaedt, H., and Roeder, K. D., 1959: Prey recognition in the Praying Mantis. *Behaviour* 14:164–84.

Riper, W. van, and Kalmbach, E. R., 1952: Homing not hindered by wing magnets. *Science* 115:577–8.

Ritter, W. E., 1938: *The California Woodpecker and I*. U. Calif. Press.

Roberts, B. B., 1934: Notes on the birds of central and south-east Iceland. *Ibis* (13) 4:239–64.

Roeder, K. D., Tozian, L., and Weiant, E. A., 1960: Endogenous nerve activity and behaviour in the mantis and cockroach. *J. Insect Physiol.* 4:45–62.

Rollinat, R., 1934: *La Vie des Reptiles de la France Centrale*. Paris. (2nd ed. 1947.)

Romanes, G. J., 1885: *Jellyfish, Starfish and Sea Urchins*. London.

Rosenblatt, J. S., and Aronson, L. R., 1958a: The decline of sexual behaviour in male cats after castration, with special reference to the role of prior sexual experience. *Behaviour* 12:284–338.

—— —— 1958b: The influence of experience on the behavioural effects of androgen in pre-puberally castrated cats. *Anim. Behav.* 6:171–82.

Ross, S., 1950: Sucking frustration in neonate puppies. *J. Abnorm. Soc. Psychol.* 46:142–9.

Rouse, J. E., 1905: Respiration and emotion in pigeons. *J. Comp. Neurol.* 15:494–513.

—— 1906: The mental life of the domestic pigeon. *Harvard Psychol. Stud.* 2:580–613.

Rowell, C. H. F., 1961: Displacement grooming in the chaffinch. *Anim. Behav.* 9:38–63.

ROWLEY, J. B., 1934: Discrimination limens of pattern and size in the goldfish *Carassius auratus*. *Genet. Psychol. Monogr.* **15**: 245–302.

RUITER, I. de, 1952: Some experiments on the camouflage of stick caterpillars. *Behaviour* **4**: 222–32.

RUSSELL, E. S., 1931: Detour experiments with Sticklebacks (*Gasterosteus aculeatus*). *J. Exp. Biol.* **8**: 393–410.

—— 1934: *The Behaviour of Animals*. London. (1st ed.)

—— 1935: Valence and attention in animal behaviour. *Acta Biotheoretica* **1**: 91–9.

—— 1937: Instinctive behaviour and bodily development. *Folio Biotheoretica* **2**: 67–76.

—— 1938: *The Behaviour of Animals: an Introduction to its Study*. London. (2nd ed.)

—— 1945: *The Directiveness of Organic Activities*. Cambridge.

RYOPELLE, A. J., 1960: Observational learning of a position habit by monkeys. *J. comp. physiol. Psychol.* **53**: 426–8.

SADOVNIKOVA, M. P., 1923a: The study of the behaviour of birds in the maze. *J. Comp. Psychol.* **3**: 123–39.

—— 1923b: A study of the behaviour of birds by the multiple choice method. *J. Comp. Psychol.* **3**: 249–82.

SALMAN, D. H., 1943: Note on the number conception in animal psychology. *Brit. J. Psychol.* **33**: 209–19.

SANDERS, F. K., 1940: Second order olfactory and visual learning in optic tectum of Goldfish. *J. Exp. Biol.* **17**: 416–34.

SANDERS, F. K., and YOUNG, J. Z., 1940: Learning and other functions of the higher nervous centres of *Sepia*. *J. Neurophysiol.* **3**: 501–26.

SANDERSON, G. C., 1949: Growth and behaviour of a litter of captive Long-tailed Weasels. *J. Mammal.* **30**: 412–15.

SATÔ, M., 1938: The role of the visual sense organ in aggregation of *Plotosus anguillaris* with special reference to the reaction to a mirror. *Sci. Rep. Tohoku Univ.* **12**: 629–38.

SAUER, F., 1954: Die Entwicklung der Lautäusserungen vom Ei ab schalldicht gehaltener Dorngrasmücken (*Sylvia c. communis* Latham) mit später isolierten und mit wildleben Artgenossen. *Z. Tierpsychol.* **11**: 10–93.

—— 1955: Entwicklung und Regression angeborenen Verhaltens bei der Dorngrasmücke (*Sylvia c. communis*). *Acta XI Congr. Int. Orn.* 1954, 218–26.

—— 1956: Uber das Verhalten junger Gartengrasmücken (*Sylvia borin* Bodd) (Entwicklung und Spiele). *J. f. Orn.* **97**: 156–89.

—— 1957: Die Sternenorientierung nächtlich ziehender Gräsmucken (*Sylvia atricapilla, borin* und *curruca*). *Z. Tierpsychol.* **14**: 29–70.

SAUER, F., and SAUER, E., 1955: Zur Frage der nächtlichen Zugorientierung von Grasmücken. *Rev. Suisse Zool.* **62**: 250–59.

SAUER, F., and SAUER, E., 1960: Star navigation of nocturnal migrating birds. The 1958 Planetarium experiments. *Coldspring Harbor Symp.* **25**: 463–73.

SAUTER, U., 1952: Versuche zur Frage des 'Zähl-' Vermögens bei Elstern. *Z. Tierpsychol.* **9**: 252–89.

SCHAEFER, H. H., and HESS, E. H., 1959: Colour preferences in imprinting objects. *Z. Tierpsychol.* **16**: 161–72.

SCHAEFFER, A. A., 1911: Habit formation in frogs. *J. Anim. Behav.* **1**: 309–35.

SCHALLER, A., 1926: Sinnesphysiologische und psychologische Untersuchungen an Wasserkäfern und Fischen. *Z. wiss. Biol. Abt. C. Z. vergl. Physiol.* **4**: 370–464.

SCHARMER, J., 1935: Die Bedeutung der Rechts-Links-Struktur und die Orientierung bei *Lithobius forficatus*. *Zool. Jb. Abt. Zool. Physiol.* **54**: 459–506.

SCHEER, B. T., 1939: Homing instinct in salmon. *Quart. Rev. Biol.* **14**: 408–30.

SCHENKEL, R., 1948: Ausdrucks-Studien an Wolfen. *Behaviour* **1**: 81–130.

SCHIEMANN, K., 1940: Von Erlernen unbenannter Anzahlen bei Dohlen. *Z. Tierpsychol.* **3**:292–347.

SCHILLER, P. von, 1933: Intersensorielle Transposition bei Fischen. *Z. vergl. Physiol.* **19**:304–9.

—— 1942: Umwegversuchen an Elritzen. *Z. Tierpsychol.* **5**:101–30.

—— 1948: Analysis of detour behaviour, learning of roundabout pathways in fish. *J. Comp. Physiol. Psychol.* **42**:463–75.

—— 1949a: Delayed response in the Minnow (*Phoxinus lævis*). *J. Comp. Physiol. Psychol.* **41**:233–8.

—— 1949b: Delayed detour response in the Octopus. *J. Comp. Physiol. Psychol.* **42**:220–5.

—— 1952: Innate constituents of complex responses in Primates. *Psychol. Rev.* **59**:177–91.

SCHJELDERUP-EBBE, T., 1923: Weitere Beiträge zur Social- und Individual-Psychologie des Haushühns. *Z. Psychol.* **132**:289–303.

SCHLEIDT, W. M., 1951: Orientierende Versuche ü. die Heimkehrfähigkeit der Rötalmaus. *Z. f. Tierpsychol.* **8**:132–7.

SCHLAIFER, A., 1942: The schooling behaviour of mackerel: a preliminary experimental analysis. *Zoologica* (*N.Y.*) **27**:75–80.

SCHMID, B., 1932: Vorläufiges Versuchsergebnis über das hundliche Orientierungsproblem. *Z. f. Hundeforsch.* **2**:133–56.

—— 1936: Zur Psychologie der Caniden-Wolf-Hund-Fuchs. *Zbl. f. Kleintierkunde und Pelztierkunde* (*Kleinter u. Pelztier*) **12** (Part 6):1–77.

SCHMIDT-KOENIG, K., 1961a: Die Sonne als Kompass im Heimorientierungssystem der Brieftauben. *Z. Tierpsychol.* **18**:221–4.

SCHNEIRLA, T. C., 1929: Learning and orientation in ants. *Comp. Psychol. Monogr.* **6**, No. 30: Pp. 143.

—— 1933a: Motivation and efficiency in ant learning. *J. Comp. Psychol.* **15**:243–66.

—— 1933b: Some important features of ant learning. *Z. vergl. Physiol.* **19**:439–52.

—— 1933c: Studies on army ants in Panama. *J. Comp. Psychol.* **15**:367–99.

—— 1934: Raiding and other outstanding phenomena in the behaviour of army ants. *Proc. Nat. Acad. Sci. Wash.* **20**:316–21.

—— 1938: The theory of army ant behaviour based upon the analysis of activities in a representative species. *J. Comp. Psychol.* **25**:51–90.

—— 1940: Further studies on the army ant behaviour pattern. *J. Comp. Psychol.* **29**:401–60.

—— 1941: Studies on the nature of ant learning. 1. Generalised learning. *J. Comp. Psychol.* **32**:41–82.

—— 1943: The nature of ant learning. 2. The intermediate stage of segmental maze adjustment. *J. Comp. Psychol.* **35**:149–72.

—— 1949: Army ant life and behaviour under dry season conditions. 3. The course of reproductive and colony behaviour. *Bull. Am. Mus. Nat. Hist.* **94** (1):1–81.

SCHNEIRLA, T. C., and BROWN, R. Z., 1950: Army ant life and behaviour under dry season conditions. 4. Further investigation of cyclic processes in behavioural and reproductive functions. *Bull. Am. Mus. Nat. Hist.* **95** (5): 263–354.

SCHOLE, H., 1934: Über das Ausbildung rhythmisch-motorischer Funktion beim Haushühn. *Z. Psychol.* **132**:289–303.

SCHRAMMER, F., 1941: Sinnesphysiologie u. Blumenbesuch des Falters von *Plusia gamma* L. *Zool. Jb. Syst. Ök. u.s.w.* **74**:375–434.

SCHREINER, T., 1941: Die Dressur der Elritze u. ihre Abhangigkeit vom Wetter. *Z. vergl. Physiol.* **29**:146–71.

SCHRÖDER, C., 1925: *Handbuch der Entomologie* (Vol. III). Jena.

SCHRÖDINGER, E., 1944: *What is Life?* Cambridge.

SCHULT, A., 1957: Transfer- und Transpositionsversuche mit monokular dressierten Fischen. *Z. vergl. Physiol.* **39**: 32–76.

SCHULZ, W., 1931: Die Orientierung der Rückenschwimmers zum Licht und zur Strömung. *Z. vergl. Physiol.* **14**: 392–404.

SCHUT, L. W., 1921: Quelques facteurs ayant de l'importance dans l'acquisition d'habitudes par les oiseaux. *Arch. Néerl. Physiol.* **5**: 244–74.

SCOTT, H. Maxwell, 1952: An iron mate (*letter*). *Field* **19**: IV: 622.

SCOTT, W. E. D., 1901: Data on song in birds: observations on the song of Baltimore Orioles in captivity. *Science* **14**: 522–6.

——— 1902a: Data on song in birds: the acquisition of new songs. *Science* **15**: 178–81.

——— 1902b: Instinct in some birds: methods of breeding in hand-reared Robins (*Merula migratoria*). *Science* **16**: 70–1.

——— 1904a: The inheritance of song in passerine birds. Remarks and observations on the song of hand-reared Bobolinks and Red-winged Blackbirds (*Dolichonyx oryzivorus* and *Agelaius phœnicus*). *Science* (*n.s.*) **19**: 154.

——— 1904b: An account of some experience in rearing wild finches by foster parent birds. *Science* (*n.s.*) **19**: 551–4.

——— 1904c: The inheritance of song in passerine birds: remarks on the development of song in the Rose-breasted Gros-beak *Zamelodia ludoviciana* L. and the Meadow-lark *Sturnella magna* L. *Science* (*n.s.*) **19**: 957–9.

——— 1940d: Inheritance of song in passerine birds. Further observations on the development of song and nest-building in hand-reared Rose-breasted Grosbeaks *Zamelodia ludoviciana* L. *Science* **20**: 282–3.

SCOTT, W. N., 1936: An experimental analysis of the factors governing the hour of emergence of adult insects from their pupæ. *Trans. Roy. Entom. Soc. Lond.* **85**: 303–30.

SECHENOV, I. M., 1863: *The Reflexes of the Brain.* (Included in English translation in *Selected Works.* Moscow. 1935.)

SEGGAR, J., 1956: Brain and instinct with *Gasterosteus aculeatus. Proc. Néderl. Akad. van Wettenschappen, Amsterdam, Proc. C.* **5**: 738–49.

——— 1960: Etho-physiological experiments with male *Gasterosteus aculeatus. Proc. 22nd Int. Meeting Neurobiologists,* Amsterdam 301–5.

SEIDMAN, E., 1949: Relative ability of the newt and terrapin to reverse a direction habit. *J. comp. physiol. Psychol.* **42**: 320–7.

SEITZ, A., 1940: Die Paarbildung bei einigen Cichliden. 1. Die Paarbildung bei *Astatotilapia strigigena. Z. Tierpsychol.* **4**: 40–84.

——— 1942: Die Paarbildung bei einigen Cichliden. 2. Die Paarbildung bei *Hemichromis bimaculatus. Z. Tierpsychol.* **5**: 74–101.

——— 1955: Untersuchungen über angeborenen Verhaltensweisen bei Caniden Racoon *Nyctereutes procyonoides. Z. Tierpsychol.* **12**: 463–89.

SENDEN, M. von, 1960: Space and Sight: The perception of space and shape in the congenitally blind before and after operation. London. (Translation of *Raum- und Gestaltfassung bei operierten blindgeborenen.* 1932.)

SEVENSTER, P., 1961: A casual analysis of displacement activity, fanning, in *Gasterosteus aculeatus. Behaviour,* Suppl. 9, pp. 170.

SEWARD, J. P., 1956: Reinforcement and expectancy: two theories in search of a controversy. *Psychol. Rev.* **63**: 105–13.

——— 1958: Basic issues in learning theory. In *Current Psychological Issues.* ed. J. P. Seward and G. R. Seward. New York.

SHAPOVALOV, L., 1940: The homing instinct in trout and salmon. *Proc. 6th Pacific Sci. Congr.* **3**: 317–22.

SHELFORD, R. W. C., 1916: *A Naturalist in Borneo.* London.

SHELLEY, L. O., 1935: Notes on the growth, behaviour and taming of young Marsh Hawks. *Auk* **52**: 287–99.

SHEPHERD, J. F., and BREED, F. S., 1913: Maturation and use in the development of an instinct, *J. Anim. Behav.* **3**: 274–85.

SHERMAN, A. R., 1910: At the sign of the Northern Flicker. *Wilson Bull.* **22**:135–66.
SHERRINGTON, C. S., 1906: *The Integrative Action of the Nervous System.* New York.
—— 1940: *Man on His Nature.* Cambridge.
SHIMA, T., 1940: Dressurversuche mit Taumelkäfer *Dineutus officinalis. Annotations Zool. Japan (Tokyo)* **19**:299–300.
SHIMBEL, A., 1950: Contributions to the mathematics and biophysiology of the C.N.S. with special reference to learning. *Bull. Maths. Biophysiol.* **12**:241–75.
SHOLL, D. A., and UTTLEY, A. M., 1953: Pattern discrimination and the visual cortex. *Nature* **171**:387.
SICK, H., 1939: Über die Dialektbildung beim 'Regenruf' des Buchfinken. *J. Orn.* **87**:568–92.
SIEGEL, A. I., 1953a: Deprivation of visual form definition in the Ring Dove. I. Discrimination learning. *J. Comp. Physiol. Psychol.* **46**:115–19.
—— 1953b: Deprivation of visual form definition in the Ring Dove. II. Perceptual motor transfer. *J. Comp. Physiol. Psychol.* **46**:249–52.
SIEGEL, P. S., 1946: Alien drive, habit strength and resistance to extinction. *J. Comp. Physiol. Psychol.* **39**:307–17.
SIEGEL, P. S., and BRANTLEY, J. J., 1951: The relationship of emotionality to the consummatory response of eating. *J. Exp. Psychol.* **42**:304–6.
SIMMONS, K. E. L., 1952: The nature of the predator-reactions of breeding birds. *Behaviour* **4**:161–72.
SIMMONS, R., 1924: The relative effectiveness of certain incentives in animal learning. *Comp. Psychol. Monogr.* **2**:7.
SIMPSON, G. G., 1953: The Baldwin effect. *Evolution* **7**:110–17.
SINNOTT, E. W., 1950: *Cell and Psyche: The Biology of Purpose.* Chapel Hill.
SKINNER, B. F., 1931: The concept of the reflex in the description of behaviour. *J. Gen. Psychol.* **5**:427–58.
—— 1933: The measurement of spontaneous activity. *J. Gen. Psychol.* **9**:3–23.
—— 1935: Two types of conditioned reflex and a pseudo-type. *J. Gen. Psychol.* **12**:66–77.
—— 1938: *The Behaviour of Organisms: an experimental analysis.* New York.
—— 1951: How to teach animals. *Sci. American.* Dec. 26–9.
—— 1952: The experimental analysis of behaviour. *Proc. XIII Int. Asscn. Psychol.* Stockholm: 62–91.
—— 1953: *Science and Human Behaviour.* New York.
SKUTCH, A. F., 1945: Life history of the Allied Woodhewer. *Condor* **47**:85–94.
SLADEN, W. J. L., 1958: The pygoscelid Penguins. *Falkland Id. Dependencies Survey, Scientific Report* No. 17, pp. 97, 12 pl. London.
SLUCKIN, W., and SALZEN, E. A., 1961: Imprinting and perceptual learning. *Quart. J. exp. Psychol.* **13**:65–77.
SMITH, B. G., 1907: The life history and habits of *Cryptobranchus alleghaniensis. Biol. Bull.* **13**:5–39.
SMITH, F. V., 1960: Towards a definition of the stimulus situation for the approach response in the domestic chick. *Anim. Behav.* **8**:197–200.
SMITH, J. C., 1959: Mass action and early environment in the rat. *J. comp. physiol. Psychol.* **52**:154–6.
SMITH, J. C., and BAKER, H. D., 1960: Conditioning in the Horseshoe Crab. *J. comp. physiol. Psychol* **53**:279–81.
SMITH, J. E., 1945: The role of the nervous system in some activities of starfishes. *Biol. Rev.* **20**:29–43.
—— 1950: Some observations on the nervous mechanisms underlying the behaviour of starfishes. *Symposia Soc. Exp. Biol.* **4**:196–220.
SMITH, K. U., and DANIEL, R. S., 1946: Observations on behavioural development in the Loggerhead Turtle (*C. caretta*). *Science* **104**:154–6.
SMITH, Malcolm, 1951: *The British Amphibians and Reptiles.* London.
SMITH, S., 1908: The limits of educability of Paramecium. *J. Comp. Neurol.* **18**:499–510.

SOEST, H., 1937: Dressurversuche mit Ciliaten und Rhabdocoelen Turbellarien. *Z. vergl. Physiol.* **24**: 720–48.

SÖDERBERG, R., 1929: Genesis of decorative and building instincts of Bower-birds (Fam. Ptilonorhynchidæ), with some notes on the problem of the origin of art. *Verh. 6 Int. Orn. Kongr. Copenhagen*, 1926: 297–335.

SOKOLOV, E. N., 1958: *Perception and the Conditioned Reflex*. Moscow.

—— 1960: Neuronal models and the orienting reflex. In *The Central Nervous System and Behaviour*, ed. M. A. B. Brazier. Washington.

SOLTYSIK, S., and ZIELINSKI, K., 1962: The role of afferent feedback in conditioned avoidance reflex. *Acta Biol. Experimentalis* (in press).

SOMMERHOFF, G., 1950: *Analytical Biology*. Oxford.

SPALDING, D., 1872: Instinct, with original observations on young animals. *Reprinted Brit. J. Anim. Behav.* (1954) **2**: 2–11.

SPENCE, K. W., 1937: Analysis of the formation of visual discrimination habits in Chimpanzees. *J. Comp. Psychol.* **23**: 77–100.

—— 1951: Theoretical interpretations of learning. (Being Chap. 18 of Stevens' *Handbook of Experimental Psychology*.)

SPENCE, K. W., and LIPPITT, R. O., 1940: Latent learning of a simple maze problem with relevant needs satiated. *Psychol. Bull.* **37**: 429. (*Abstract only*.)

SPENCER, M. M., 1953: The behaviour of rats and mice feeding on whole grains. *J. Hyg.* **51**: 35–8.

SPENCER, W. P., 1939: Diurnal activity rhythms in freshwater fishes. *Ohio J. Sci.* **39**: 119–32.

SPERRY, R. W., 1955: On the neural basis of the conditioned response. *Brit. J. Anim. Behav.* **3**: 41–4.

—— 1956: The eye and the brain. *Scientific Amer.* May, 48–52.

SPERRY, R. W., and CLARK, E., 1949: Interocular transfer of visual discrimination habits in a teleost fish. *Physiol. Zool.* **22**: 372–78.

SPITZ, R. A., and WOLFE, K. M., 1946: The smiling response: a contribution to the ontogenesis of social relations. *Genet. Psychol. Monogr.* **34**: 57–125.

SPOONER, G. M., 1931: Some observations on schooling in fish. *J. Mar. Biol. Assn.* **17**: 421–48.

—— 1937: The learning of detours by Wrasse (*Ctenolabrus rupestris* L.). *J. Mar. Biol. Assn.* **21**: 497–570.

SPURWAY, H., and HALDANE, J. B. S., 1953: The comparative ethology of vertebrate breathing. I. Breathing in newts, with a general survey. *Behaviour* **6**: 8–24.

STADLER, H., 1929: Die Vogelstimmungsforschung als Wissenschaft. *Verh. 6 Int. Orn. Kongr. Copenhagen*, 1926: 338–57.

STEIN, H., 1951: Untersuchungen ü. den Zeitsinn bei Vögeln. *Z. vergl. Physiol.* **33**: 387–403.

STELLAR, E., 1943: The effect of Epinephrine, Insulin and Glucose upon hoarding in rats. *J. Comp. Psychol.* **36**: 21–31.

—— 1957: Physiological psychology. *Ann. Rev. Psych.* **8**: 415–36.

STETTER, H., 1929: Untersuchungen über den Gehörsinn der Fische. *Z. vergl. Physiol.* **9**: 339–477.

STEVEN, D. M., 1955: Transference of 'Imprinting' in a wild gosling. *Brit. J. Anim. Behav.* **3**: 14–16.

STEVENS, S. S., 1951: *Handbook of Experimental Psychology*. New York and London.

STEVENSON-HAMILTON, J., 1947: *Wild Life in South Africa*. London.

STIER, T. J. B., 1933: Diurnal changes in activities and geotropisms in *Thyone briareus*. *Biol. Bull.* **64**: 326–32.

STÖCKHERT, E., 1923: Ueber Entwicklung und Lebensweise der Bienengattung Halictus. Ltr., und ihrer Schmarotzer. *Konowia* **2**: 48–64.

STODDARD, H. L., 1931: *The Bob-White Quail: Its habits, preservation and increase*. New York.

STONE, C. P., 1922: Congenital sexual behaviour of young male albino rats. *J. Comp. Psychol.* **2**: 95–153.

STONE, C. P., 1926: The initial copulatory response of female rats reared in isolation from the age of 20 days to puberty. *J. Comp. Psychol.* **6**:73–83.

STONER, E. A., 1947: Anna Humming-birds at play. *Condor.* **49**:36.

STOUT, G. F., 1899: *A Manual of Psychology.* London.

STRAUSS, E., 1938*a*: Vergleichende Beobachtungen über Verhaltensweisen von Raben-vögeln, etc. *Z. Tierpsychol.* **2**:145–72.

—— 1938*b*: Versuche an gefangenen Rabenvögeln. *Z. Tierpsychol.* **2**:172–97.

STREBEL, O. Z., 1928: Biologische Studien an einheimischen Collembolen. II. Ernah-rung und Geschmacksinn bei *Hypogastura purpurascens. Z. wiss. Insekten-biol.* **23**:135–43.

STRESEMANN, E., 1947: Baron von Pernau, pioneer student of bird behaviour. *Auk* **64**:35–52.

STUART, T. A., 1957: The migrations and homing behaviour of Brown Trout *Salma trutta. Scientific Investns. of Freshwater Fisheries Scotland* **18**:2–27.

STUDNITZ, G. von, 1935: Geographische bedingte Unterschiede physiologischer und psychologischer Natur zwischen Vögeln einer Art bzw. Rasse. *Schrift. Natur-wiss. Vereins Schleswig-Holstein* **21**:58–67.

STURMAN-HULBE, M., and STONE, C. P., 1929: Maternal behaviour in the albino rat. *J. Comp. Psychol.* **9**:203–37.

SUDD, J. H., 1960*a*: The transport of prey by an ant *Pheidole crassinoda. Behaviour* **16**:295–308.

—— 1960*b*: The foraging method of Pharaoh's Ant, *Monomorium pharaonis L. Anim. Behav.* **8**: 67–75.

SUMNER, E. L. (Jnr.), 1934: The behaviour of some young raptorial birds. *Univ. Calif. Pub. Zool.* **40**:331–62.

SUTHERLAND, N. S., 1957*a*: Visual discrimination of orientation and shape by the octopus. *Nature* **179**:11–13.

—— 1957*b*: Visual discrimination of orientation by *Octopus. Brit. J. Psychol.* **48**:55–71.

—— 1959: Visual discrimination of shape by *Octopus. Quart. J. exp. Psychol.* **11**:24–32.

—— 1960: The visual discrimination of shape by *Octopus.* Squares and rect-angles. *J. comp. physiol. Psychol.* **53**:95–103.

SUTTON, G. M., 1943: Notes on the behaviour of certain captive young Fringillids. *Occ. Papers Univ. Mich. Mus. Zoo.* **474**:14.

SWANBERG, P. O., 1951: Food storage, territory and song in the Thick-billed Nutcracker. *Proc. 10 Int. Congr. Orn. Upsala*:545–54.

SWARTZ, R. D., 1929: Modification of behaviour in earthworms. *J. Comp. Psychol.* **9**:17–23.

SWIECIMSKI, J., 1957: The role of sight and memory in food capture by predatory beetles of the species *Cicindela hybrida L. Polskie Pismo Ent. Bull. Pologne* **26**:No. 15.

SWYNNERTON, C. F. M., 1942: Observations and experiments in Africa by the late C. F. M. Swynnerton on wild birds eating butterflies and the preferences shown. *Proc. Linn. Soc. Lond.* 1942 (1):10–46.

SZLEP, R., 1952: On the plasticity of instinct of a Garden Spider. (*Aranea diadema* L.) Construction of a cobweb. *Acta Biol. Exp.* **16**:5–22.

—— 1958*a*: Influence of external factors on some structural properties of the Garden Spider *Aranea diademata* web. *Folia Biol.* **6**:287–99.

—— 1958*b*: The selection of building material for the *Molanna angustata* case. *Folia Biol.* **6**:301–6.

SZYMANSKI, J. S., 1912: Modification of the innate behaviour of cockroaches. *J. Anim. Behav.* **2**:81–90.

—— 1918: Einige Bermerkungen über die biologische Bedeutung akusticher Reize. *Pflüg. Archiv.* **171**: 363–73.

—— 1919: Beiträge zur Lehre von der Entstehung neuer Gewohnheiten bei den Tieren. *Pflüg. Archiv.* **173**: 126–51.

TATEISHI, 1958: The behaviour of washing baits in Formosan monkeys. *Ann. Anim. Psychol. Tokio* 8:89–94.

TAVOLGA, W. N., 1956: Free spawning behaviour in the Gobiid fish, *Bathygobius soporator. Behaviour* 9:53–74.

TEMBROCK, G., 1961: *Verhaltensforschung: eine Einfuhrung inter die Tier-ethologie.* Jena.

TEYROVSKY, V., 1922: Sur la perception de l'éspace chez *Spirographis spallanzani. Pub. Fac. Sci. Univ. Masaryk* 20:1–8.

—— 1930: A study of ideational behaviour in the Garden Warbler. *Pub. Fac. Sci. Univ. Masaryk* No. 122.

THACKER, L. A., 1950: An investigation of non-instrumental learning. *J. Comp. Physiol. Psychol.* 43:86–98.

THIENEMANN, J., 1933: Der Stieglitz als Schöpfer. *Orn. Monatsbr.* 41:92–3.

THISTLETHWAITE, D., 1951: A critical review of latent learning and related experiments. *Psychol. Bull.* 48:97–129.

THOMPSON, D'Arcy W., 1942: *On Growth and Form* (2nd ed.). Cambridge.

THOMPSON, E. L., 1916: An analysis of the learning process in the snail *Physa gyrina* Soy. *Behaviour Monographs* 3, No. 3, serial No. 14.

THOMPSON, W. R., 1953: The inheritance of behaviour: behavioural differences in fifteen mouse strains. *Ca. J. Psychol.* 7:145–55.

THORNDIKE, E. L., 1898: Animal Intelligence. An experimental study of the associative processes in animals. *Psychol. Monogr.* 2 (8).

—— 1899: A note on the psychology of fishes. *Am. Nat.* 33:923–6.

—— 1911: *Animal Intelligence.* New York.

THORPE, W. H., 1938: Further experiments on olfactory conditioning in a parasitic insect. The nature of the conditioning process. *Proc. Roy. Soc. B.* 126:370–97.

—— 1939: Further experiments on pre-imaginal conditioning in insects. *Proc. Roy. Soc. B.* 127:424–33.

—— 1940: Ecology and the future of systematics. (In *The New Systematics,* Oxford: (ed. Julian Huxley): 341–64.)

—— 1943: A type of insight learning in birds. *Brit. Birds* 37:29–31.

—— 1943–4: Types of learning in insects and other arthropods. *B. J. Psychol* (Gen. Sect.) 33:220–34. 34:20–31, 66–76.

—— 1944: Some problems of animal learning. *Proc. Linn. Soc. Lond.* 156:70–83.

—— 1945a: Further notes on a type of insight learning in birds. *Brit. Birds* 38:46–9.

—— 1945b: The evolutionary significance of habitat selection. *J. Anim. Ecol.* 14:67–70.

—— 1948: The modern concept of instinctive behaviour. *Bull. Anim. Behav.* 1 (7). Pp. 12.

—— 1949: Recent biological evidence for the methods of bird orientation. *Proc. Linn. Soc. Lond.* 160:85–94.

—— 1950a: The concepts of learning and their relation to those of instinct. Symposium Vol. 4 of Society for Experimental Biology on *Physiological Mechanisms in Animal Behaviour.* Cambridge.

—— 1950b: A note on detour experiments with *Ammophila pubescens.* Curt. *Behaviour* 13:257–63.

—— 1951: The learning abilities of birds. *Ibis* 93:1–52, 252–96.

—— 1954: The process of song-learning in the chaffinch as studied by means of the sound spectrograph. *Nature* 173:465.

—— 1955: Comments on 'The Bird Fancyer's Delight,' together with notes on imitation in the sub-song of the chaffinch. *Ibis* 97:247–51.

—— 1959a: Learning. *Ibis* 101:337–53.

—— 1959b: Talking birds and the mode of action of the vocal apparatus of birds. *Proc. zool. Soc. Lond.* 132:441–55.

—— 1961a: Comparative Psychology. *Ann Rev. Psychol.* 12:27–50.

THORPE, W. H., 1961b: Some characteristics of the early learning period in birds. In Delafresnaye (1961).

——— 1961c: Progress and prospects in ethology. In *The Cell and the Organism*, ed. J. A. Ramsay and V. B. Wigglesworth. Cambridge.

——— 1961d: *Bird Song: the biology of vocal communication and expression in birds*. Cambridge.

——— 1961e: Sensitive periods in the learning of animals and men: a study of imprinting with special reference to the induction of cyclic behaviour. In Thorpe and Zangwill (1961).

THORPE, W. H., and CAUDLE, H. B., 1938: A study of the olfactory responses of insect parasites to the food plant of their host. *Parasitology* 30: 523–8.

THORPE, W. H., CROMBIE, A. C., HILL, R., and DARRAH, J. H., 1947: The behaviour of wireworms in response to chemical stimulation. *J. Exp. Biol.* 23: 234–66.

THORPE, W. H., and JONES, F. G. W., 1937: Olfactory conditioning and its relation to the problem of host selection. *Proc. Roy. Soc. B.* 124: 56–81.

THORPE, W. H., and ZANGWILL, O. L. (eds.), 1961: *Current Problems in Animal Behaviour*. Cambridge.

TINBERGEN, N., 1939: Zur Fortpflanzungsethologie von *Sepia officinalis* L. *Arch. Néerl. Zool.* 3: 323–64.

TINBERGEN, N., 1936: Zur Sociologie der Silbermöwe *L. a. argentatus* Pontopp. *Beitr. Fortpflanzungsbiol. Vögel* 12: 89–96.

——— 1942: An objectivistic study of the innate behaviour of animals. *Biblioth. biotheor.* 1: 39–98.

——— 1948: Physiologische Instinktforschung. *Experientia* 4: 121–33.

——— 1951a: *The Study of Instinct*. Oxford.

——— 1951b: Recent advances in the study of bird behaviour. *Proc. Xth Int. Orn. Congr.* 360–74.

——— 1952: Derived activities; their causation, biological significance, origin and emancipation during evoluton. *Quart. Rev. Biol.* 27: 1–32.

——— 1953: Specialists in nest-building. *Country Life*, 30 Jan. 1953: 270–1.

TINBERGEN, N., and IERSEL, J. J. A. van, 1947: Displacement reactions in the Three-spined Stickleback. *Behaviour* 1: 56–63.

TINBERGEN, N., and KRUYT, W., 1938: Über die Orientierung des Bienenwolfes (*Philanthus triangulum* Fabr.). III. Die Bevorzugung bestimmter Wegmarken. *Z. vergl. Physiol.* 25: 292–334.

TINBERGEN, N., and KUENEN, D. J., 1939: Über die auslösenden und die richtung-gebenden Reizsituationen der Sperrrbewegung von jungen Drosseln (*Turdus m. merula* L. und *T. e. ericetorum* Turton). *Z. Tierpsychol.* 3: 37–60.

TINBERGEN, N., MEEUSE, B. J. D., BOEREMA, L. K., and VAROSSIEAU, W. W., 1942: Die Balz des Samtfalters *Eumenis* (= *Satyrus*) *semele*. *Z. Tierpsychol.* 5: 182–226.

TINBERGEN, N., and PERDECK, A. C., 1950: On the stimulus situation releasing the begging response in the newly-hatched Herring Gull chick (*Larus a. argentatus*). *Behaviour* 3: 1–38.

TINDELL, D, and CRAIG, J. V., 1959: Effects of social competition on laying house performances in the chicken. *Poultry Science* 38: 95–105.

TINKLEPAUGH, O. L., 1928: An experimental study of representative factors in monkeys. *J. comp. physiol. Psychol.* 8: 197–236.

——— 1932a: Maze learning of a turtle. *J. Comp. Psychol.* 13: 201–6.

——— 1932b: Multiple delayed reactions with chimpanzees and monkeys. *J. Comp. Psychol.* 13: 207–43.

TOBIAS, J. M., 1952: Some optically detectable consequences of activity in nerve. *Coldspring Harbor Symp.* 17: 15–25.

TOLMAN, E. C., 1937: The acquisition of string-pulling by rats—conditioned response or sign gestalt? *Psychol. Rev.* 44: 195–211.

TOLMAN, E. C., and HONZIK, C. H., 1930a: Insight in rats. *Univ. Calif. Publ. Psychol.* 4: 215–32.

TOLMAN, E. C., and HONZIK, C. H., 1930b: Introduction and removal of reward, and maze performance in rats. *Univ. Calif. Publ. Psychol.* **4**:257–75.

TOWBIN, E. J., 1949: Gastric distention as a factor in the satiation of thirst in esophagostomised dogs. *Am. J. Physiol.* **159**:533–41.

TREUENFELS, H. von, 1937: Beiträge zur Brutbiologie des Waldlaubsängers. *J. Orn.* **95**:605.

—— 1940: Beiträge zur Biologie u. Psychologie des Waldlaubsängers (*Phyl. sibilatrix*). *J. Orn.* **88**:509–36.

TRIPLETT, N., 1901: The educability of the Perch. *Am. J. Psychol.* **12**:354–60.

TRUMLER, E., 1959: Das 'Rossigkeitgesicht' und ähnliches Ausdrucksverhalten. *Z. Tierpsychol.* **16**:478–88.

TRYON, R. C., 1931: Studies in individual difference in maze ability. II–V. *J. Comp. Psychol.* **12**:1–22, 95–115, 303–45, 401–20.

TSCHAKOTINE, S., 1938: Réactions "conditionées" par microponction ultraviolette dans le comportement d'une cellule isolé (*Paramœcium caudatum*). *Arch. Inst. prophylac.* **10**:119–31. (*Not seen.*)

TSUNEKI, K., 1956: Ethological studies on *Bembix niponica* Smith, with emphasis on the psychological analysis of behaviour inside the nest. I. Biological part. *Mem. Fac. Lib. Arts, Fukui Univ. Ser. II. Nat. Sci.* Oct. 1956:77–172.

—— 1957: Ditto II. Experimental part. *Mem. Fac. Lib. Arts, Fukui Univ. Ser. II. Nat. Sci.* Oct. 1957:1–116.

TURNER, C. H., 1907a: The homing of ants: an experimental study of ant behaviour. *J. Comp. Neurol. Psychol.* **17**:367–434.

—— 1907b: Do ants form practical judgements? *Biol. Bull. Woods Hole* **13**:333–43.

—— 1908: The homing of the burrowing bees (Anthophoridæ). *Biol. Bull. Woods Hole* **15**:247–58.

—— 1912: Sphex overcoming obstacles. *Psyche* **19**:100–2.

—— 1913: Behaviour of the common roach (*Periplaneta orientalis*) in an open maze. *Biol. Bull. Woods Hole* **25**:348–65.

—— 1914: An experimental study of the auditory powers of the Giant Silkworm moth (Saturnidæ). *Biol. Bull. Woods Hole* **27**:325–32.

TURNER, E. R. R., 1961: An analysis of social feeding in sparrows and chaffinches. *Anim. Behav.* **9**:113–14.

—— 1962: Social feeding in birds. (In press.)

TYLER, D. W., WORTZ, E., and BITTERMAN, M. E., 1953: The effect of random and alternating partial reinforcement on resistance to extinction in the rat. *Am. J. Psychol.* **66**:57–65.

UEXKÜLL, J. von, 1895: Physiologische Untersuchungen an *Eledone* moschata. IV. Zur Analyse der Funktionen des Centralnervensystems. *Z. Biol.* **31**:584–609.

—— 1897: Über Reflexe bei den Seeigeln. *Z. Bio.* **34**:298–318.

—— 1905:*Leitfaden in das Studium der experimental Biologie der Wassertiere.* Wiesbaden.

ULLMAN, A. R., 1951: The experimental production and analysis of a 'Compulsive Eating Symptom' in rats. *J. Comp. Physiol. Psychol.* **44**:575–81.

ULLYOT, P., 1936: The behaviour of *Dendrocœlum lacteum*. II. Responses in non-directional gradients. *J. Exp. Biol.* **13**:265–78.

VALENTINE, W. L., 1928: Visual perception in the white rat. *J. Comp. Psychol.* **8**:369–75.

VANDERPLANK, F. L., 1938: Sex hormones and their effect upon conditioned responses in the Rudd (*Leuciscus leuciscus*). *J. Exp. Biol.* **15**:385–93.

VEN, C. D., 1921: Sur la formation d'habitudes chez les asteries. *Arch. Néerl. Physiol.* **6**:163–78.

VERLAINE, L., 1932–4: L'instinct et l'intelligence chez les hyménoptères. *J. Psychol.* **29**:784–816.

—— 1934: L'instinct et l'intelligence chez les oiseaux. *Récherches Philosoph.* **3**:285–305.

VERNON, M., 1952: *A Further Study of Visual Perception.* Cambridge.

VERWEY, J., 1930: Einiges über die Biologie Ost-Indischer Mangrokraben. *Treubia* **12**:167–261.

VERWORN, M., 1889: *Psycho-physiologische Protistenstudien.* Jena.

—— 1890: Biologische Protistenstudien II. *Z. wiss. Zool.* **50**:443–68.

VEVERS, H. G., 1961: Observations on the laying and hatching of *Octopus* eggs in the Societies' aquarium. *Proc. Zool. Soc.* **137**:311–15.

VIEK, P., and MILLER, G. A., 1944: The cage as a factor in hoarding. *J. Comp. Psychol.* **37**:203–10.

VILLEE, C. A., and GROODY, T. C., 1940: The behaviour of limpets with reference to their homing instinct. *Am. Mid. Nat.* **24**:190–204.

VINCE, M. A., 1961*a*: Developmental changes in learning capacity. In Thorpe and Zangwill (1961).

—— 1961*b*: String-pulling in birds. III. The successful response in Green-finches and Canaries. *Behaviour* **17**:103–29.

DE VITO, J. L., and SMITH, O. A., 1950: Effects of temperature and food deprivation on the random activity of *Macaca mulatta. J. comp. physiol. Psychol.* **52**:29–32.

VOGELBERG, L., and KRÜGER, F., 1951: Versuche u. die Richtungsorientierung bei weissen Mäuser und Ratten. *Z. Tierpsychol.* **8**:293–321.

VOWLES, D. M., 1950: Sensitivity of ants to polarised light. *Nature* **165**:282.

—— 1954*a*: The orientation of ants. 1. The substitution of stimuli. *J. Exp. Biol.* **31**:341–55.

—— 1954*b*: The orientation of ants. 2. Orientation to light, gravity and polarised light. *J. Exp. Biol.* **31**:356–75.

—— 1955: The foraging of ants. *Brit. J. Anim. Behav.* **3**:1–13.

—— 1961: Neural mechanisms in insect behaviour. In Thorpe and Zangwill (1961).

WAHL, O., 1933: Beitrag zur Frage der biologischen Bedeutung des Zeitgedächtnisses der Bienen. *Z. vergl. Physiol.* **18**:709–41.

WAITE, E. R., 1903: Sympathetic song in birds. *Nature* **68**:322.

WALK, R. D., GIBSON, E. J., PICK, H. L., Jr., and TIGHE, T. J., 1958: Further experiments on prolonged exposure to visual forms: the effect of single stimuli and prior reinforcement. *J. comp. physiol. Psychol.* **51**:483–7.

WALKER, E. L., 1948: Drive specificity and learning. *J. Exp. Psychol.* **38**:39–49.

—— 1951: Drive specificity and learning: a demonstration of a response tendency acquired under a strong irrelevant drive. *J. Comp. Physiol. Psychol.* **44**:596–603.

WALLRAFF, H. G., 1960: Können Gräsmucken mit Hilfe des Sternenhimmels navigieren? *Z. Tierpsychol.* **17**:165–7.

WALTER, W. G., 1943: Some experiments on the sense of smell in birds, studied by the method of conditioned reflexes, *Arch. Néerl. Physiol.* **27**:1–72.

WARD, H. B., 1939: Salmon psychology. *J. Wash. Acad. Sci.* **29**:1–14.

WARDEN, C. J., and BARR, J., 1929: The Müller-Lyer illusion in the Ring Dove *Turtur risorius. J. Comp. Psychol.* **9**:275–92.

WARDEN, C. J., FIELD, N. A., and KOCH, A. M., 1940: Imitative behaviour in Cebus and Rhesus Monkeys. *J. Genet. Psychol.* **56**:311–32.

WARDEN, C. J., JENKINS, T. N., and WARNER, L. H., 1936: *Comparative Psychology: A comprehensive treatise. Vol. 2: Plants and Invertebrates. Vol. 3: Vertebrates.* New York.

WARDEN, C. J., and REISS, B. F., 1941: Relative difficulty of mazes of different lengths for the chick. *J. Psychol.* **11**:411–10.

WARNER, L. H., 1931: The problem of colour vision in fishes. *Quart. Rev. Biol.* **6**:329–48.

WARREN, J. M., 1957: The phylogeny of maze learning. I. Theoretical orientation. *Brit. J. Anim. Behav.* **5**:90–3.

—— 1960: Reversible learning by Paradise Fish *Macropodus opercularis*. *J. comp. physiol. Psychol.* **53**:376–8.

WARREN, J. M., BROOKSHIRE, K. H., BALL, G. G., and REYNOLDS, D. V., 1960: Reversal learning by White Leghorn chicks. *J. comp. physiol. Psychol.* **53**:371–5.

WARREN, R. P., and HINDE, R. A., 1959: The effects of oestrogen and progesterone on the nest-building of domesticated canaries. *Anim. Behav.* **7**:209–13.

WASHBURN, M. F., 1926: *The Animal Mind*. New York. (3rd ed.)

WATERMAN, T. H., 1959: The problem of polarised light sensitivity. *Proc. Intern. Congr. Zool. XV* 537–9.

WATSON, A. J., 1961: The place of reinforcement in the explanation of behaviour. In Thorpe and Zangwill (1961).

WATSON, J. B., 1907: Kinesthetic and organic sensations: their role in the reactions of the white rat to the maze. *Psychol. Monogr.* **8**, No. 33 vi, 100 pp.

—— 1908: The behaviour of Noddy and Sooty Terns. *Papers from Tortugas Lab. Carnegie Inst. Washington* **2**:189–255.

—— 1916: The place of the conditioned reflex in psychology. *Psychol. Rev.* **23**:89–116.

WATT, Grace, 1951: *The Farne Islands: their history and wild life*. London.

WEBB, W. B., 1949: The motivational aspect of an irrelevant drive in the behaviour of the white rat. *J. Exp. Psychol.* **39**:1–14.

WEIDMANN, U., 1958: Verhaltensstudien an der Stockente (*Anas platyrhynchos* L.). II. Versuche zur Auslösung und Prägung der Nachfolge- und Anschlussreaktion. *Z. Tierpsychol.* **15**:277–300.

WEISS, K., 1953: Versuche mit Bienen und Vespen in farbigenlabyrinthen. *Z. Tierpsychol.* **10**:29–44.

WEISS, P., 1941: Does sensory control play a constructive role in the development of motor co-ordination? *Schweiz. Med. Wochenschr.* **71**:591–5.

WEISS, P. (Ed.), 1950: *Genetic Neurology*. Chicago.

WELKER, W. I., and WELKER, J., 1958: Reaction of fish (*Eucinostomus gula*) to environmental changes. *Ecology* **39**:283–8.

WELLS, G. P., 1949: Respiratory movements of *Arenicola marina* L: intermittent irrigations of the tube and intermittent aerial respiration. *J. Marine Biol. Ass. U.K.* **28**:447–64.

WELLS, G. P., and ALBRECHT, E. B., 1951a: The integration of activity cycles in the behaviour of *Arenicola marina* L. *J. Exp. Biol.* **28**:41–50.

—— —— 1951b: The role of œsophageal rhythms in the behaviour of *Arenicola ecaudata* Johnston. *J. Exp. Biol.* **28**:51–6.

WELLS, G. P., and DALES, R. P., 1951: Spontaneous activity patterns in animal behaviour: the irrigation of the burrow in the polychætes *Chætopterus variopedatus* Renier and *Nereis diversicolor* O. F. Muller. *J. Marine Biol. Ass. U.K.* **29**:661–80.

WELLS, M. J., 1958: Factors affecting reactions to *Mysis* by newly hatched *Sepia*. *Behaviour* **13**:96–111.

—— 1960: Proprioception and visual discrimination in *Octopus*. *J. exp. Biol.* **37**:489–99.

—— 1961: Weight discrimination by *Octopus*. *J. exp. Biol.* **38**:127–33.

—— 1962: *Brain and Behaviour in Cephalopods*. London.

WELLS, M. J., and WELLS, J., 1957: Repeated presentation experiments and the function of the vertical lobe in *Octopus*. *J. exp. Biol.* **34**:469–77.

—— —— 1959: Hormonal control of sexual maturity in *Octopus*. *J. exp. Biol.* **36**:1–33.

WELLS, W. W., 1917: The behaviour of limpets with particular reference to the homing instinct. *J. Anim. Behav.* **7**:387–95.

WELTY, J. C., 1934: Experiments on group behaviour of fishes. *Physiol. Zool.* 7:85–127.

WENDT, G. R., 1951: Vestibular Functions: being Chap. 31 of Stevens' *Handbook of Experimental Psychology*. New York.

WENNER, A. M., 1961: Division of labour in a honey bee colony—a Markov process? *J. theoret. Biol.* 1:324–7.

WERTHEIMER, M., 1912: Experimentelle Studien über das Sehen von Bewegung. *Z. Psychol.* 61:161–265.

WESSELL, J. P., and LEIGH, W. H., 1941: Studies in the flock organisation of the White-throated Sparrow *Zonotricha albicollis*. *Wilson Bull.* 53:222–30.

WESTERFIELD, F., 1922: The ability of Mud-minnows to form associations with sounds. *J. Comp. Psychol.* 2:187–90.

WHEELER, W. M., 1939: *Instinct*: in *Essays in Philosophical Biology*. Harvard Univ. Press.

WHERRY, R. J., and SANDERS, J. M., 1941: Modifications of a tropism in *Lumbricus terrestris*. *Trans. Illin. Acad. Sci.* 34:237–81.

WHITEHEAD, A. N., 1929: *Process and Reality*. Cambridge.

WHITMAN, C. O., 1919: *The Behaviour of Pigeons*. Posthumous works of C. O. Whitman 3:1–161, ed. A. H. Carr, *Pub. Carnegie Inst.* 257.

WHYTE, L. L., 1951: *Aspects of Form*. London.

—— 1954: A hypothesis regarding the brain modifications underlying memory. *Brain* 77:158–65.

WICHTERMAN, R., 1953: *The Biology of Paramœcium*. New York.

WIEBALCK, U., 1937: Untersuchungen zur Funktion des Vorderhirns bei Knocken-fischen. *Zool. Anz.* 117:325–9.

WIESNER, P. B., and SHEARD, N. M., 1933: *Maternal Behaviour in the Rat*. Edinburgh-London.

WIGGLESWORTH, V. B., 1941: The sensory physiology of the human louse *Pediculus humanus corporis* de Geer (Anoplura). *Parasitology* 33:67–109.

—— 1945: Growth and Form in an Insect. *Essays on Growth and Form*. Oxford.

—— 1949: The utilisation of reserve substances in *Drosophila* during flight. *J. Exp. Biol.* 26:150–63.

WILCOX, M. A., 1905: Biology of *Acmœa testudinalis*. *Am. Nat.* 39:325–33.

WILKIE, J. S., 1953: *The Science of Mind and Brain*. London.

WILKINSON, D. H., 1949: Some physical principles of bird orientation. *Proc. Linn. Soc. Lond.* 160:94–9.

—— 1952: The random element in bird navigation. *J. Exp. Biol.* 29:532–60.

WILLIAMS, C. B., 1958: *Insect Migration*. London.

WILLIAMS, J. H., 1950: *Elephant Bill*. London.

WILLIAMSON, H., 1922: *Lone Swallows*. London.

WILLIAMSON, K., 1948: *The Atlantic Islands*. London.

—— 1955: Migrational drift. *Proc. XI Int. Orn. Congr.* 179–86.

WILLISTON, S. W., 1892: Notes on the habits of Ammophila. *Ent. News* 3:85–6.

WILM, E. C., 1925: *The Theories of Instinct*. New Haven.

WING, L. W., 1935: On the drinking habits of gallinaceous young. *Condor* 37:211–12.

WINN, H. E., 1958: Comparative reproductive behaviour and ecology of fourteen species of Darters (Pisces—Percidae). *Ecological Monogr.* 28:155–91.

WINN, H. E., and BARDACH, J. E., 1960: Some aspects of the comparative biology of Parrot fishes at Bermuda. *Zoological* 45:29–34.

WINSLOW, C. N., 1933: Visual illusions in the chick. *Arch. Physiol.* 153:1–83.

WINSLOW, C. N., KANTOR, R., and WARDEN, C., 1938: An investigation of conditioning of cats to multiple stimuli. *J. Genet. Psychol.* 52:211–25.

WINTREBERT, P., 1920: La contraction rhythmée aneurale des myotemes chez les embryons de sélaciens. *Arch. Zool. exp. gén.* 60:221–45.

WITSCHI, E., 1935: Seasonal sex characters in birds and their hormonal control. *Wilson Bull.* 47:177–8.

WLADIMIRSKY, A. P., 1916: Are the Infusoria capable of 'learning' to select their food? *Russ. J. Zool.* 44:4.

WODSEDALEK, J. E., 1912: Formation of associations in the May-fly nymphs *Heptagenia interpunctata* (Say). *J. Anim. Behav.* 2 : 1–19.

WOHLFAHRT, T. A., 1939: Untersuchungen über das Tonunterscheidungsvermögen der Elritze. *Z. vergl. Physiol.* 26 : 570–604.

WOJTUSIAK, R. J., 1933: Über den Farbensinn der Schildkröten. *Z. vergl. Physiol.* 18 : 393–436.

—— 1934: Über den Formensinn der Schildkröten. *Bull. Acad. Pol. Sci. Lett.* 349–73.

WOLF, E., 1926–7; Über das Heimkehrvermögen der Bienen. *Z. wiss. Biol. Abt. C. Z. vergl. Physiol.* 3 : 615–91; 4 : 221–54.

—— 1930: The homing behaviour of bees. *J. Soc. Psychol.* 1 : 300–10.

WOLFE, J. B., 1939: An exploratory study of food-storing in rats. *J. Comp Psychol.* 28 : 97–108.

WOLFE, J. B., and KAPLON, M., 1941: Effect of amount of reward and consummative activity on learning in chickens. *J. Comp. Psychol.* 31 : 353–61.

WOLFF, P. H., 1959: Observations on new-born infants. *Psychosomat. Med.* 21 : 110–18.

WOLFLE, D. L., and BROWN, C. S., 1940: A learning experiment with snakes. *Copeia* 134.

WOOD, C. O., 1936: Some of the commoner birds of Ceylon. *Rep. Smithsonian Inst.* 297–302.

WOOD-JONES, F., 1943: *Habit and Heritage*. London.

WOODBURY, A. M. *et al.*, 1951: A snake den in Toole County, Utah. *Herpetologica* 7 : 1–52.

WOODBURY, A. M., and HARDY, R., 1940: The dens and behaviour of the desert tortoise. *Science* 92 : 529.

WOODGER, J. H., 1929: *Biological Principles: A critical study*. London.

WOODWORTH, R. S., 1915: A revision of imageless thought. *Psychol. Rev.* 22 : 1–27.

—— 1918: *Dynamic Psychology*. New York.

—— 1938: *Experimental Psychology*. New York.

WUNDER, W., 1930: Experimentelle Untersuchungen am Dreistachligen Stickling (*Gasterosteus aculeatus*) während der Laichzeit. *Z. Morph. ü. Ök. Tiere* 16 : 453–98.

WYRWICKA, W., 1959: Studies on detour behaviour. *Behaviour* 14 : 240–64.

YERKES, A. W., 1906: Modification of behaviour in *Hydroides dianthus*. *J. Comp. Neurol. Psychol.* 16 : 441–50.

YERKES, R. M., 1901: Formation of habits in the turtle. *Pop. Sci. Month.* 58 : 519–25.

—— 1902: A contribution to the physiology of the nervous system of the medusa *Gonionemus murbachii*. 2. Physiology of the central nervous system. *Am. J. Physiol.* 7 : 181–98.

—— 1904: The reaction time of *Gonionemus murbachii* to electric and photic stimuli. *Biol. Bull.* 6 : 84–95.

—— 1912: The intelligence of earthworms. *J. Anim. Behav.* 2 : 332–52.

—— 1934: Modes of behavioural adaptation in chimpanzee to multiple-choice problems. *Comp. Psychol. Monogr.* 10 : 1–108.

—— 1943: *Chimpanzees: a laboratory colony*. New Haven.

YERKES, R. M., and AYER, J. B., 1903: A study of the reactions and reaction time of the medusa *Gonionemus murbachii* to photic stimuli. *Am. J. Physiol.* 9 : 279–307.

YERKES, R. M., and NISSEN, H. W., 1939: Pre-linguistic sign behaviour in chimpanzees. *Science* 89 : 585–97.

YOUNG, J. Z., 1938: The evolution of the nervous system and of the relationship of organism and environment. *Evolution: Essays presented to E. S. Goodrich* (ed. G. R. de Beer): 179–204.

—— 1939: Fused neurons and synaptic contacts in the giant nerve fibres of cephalopods. *Phil. Trans. Roy. Soc. Lond.* 229 : 465–505.

—— 1951: Growth and plasticity in the nervous system. *Proc. Roy. Soc. B.* 139 : 18–37.

YOUNG, J. Z., 1960: The retina of *Octopus*. *Nature* **186**: 836–44.
—— 1961: Learning and discrimination in the octopus. *Biol Revs.* **36**: 32–96.
YOUTZ, R. E. P., 1938: The change with time of a Thorndikean response in the rat. *J. Exp. Psychol.* **23**: 128–40.

ZAWADOWSKY, B. M., and ROCHLINA, M. L., 1929: Bedingte Reflexe bei normalen und hyperthyroidiserten Hühnern. *Z. vergl. Physiol.* **9**: 114–44.
ZENER, K., 1937: The significance of behaviour accompanying conditioned salivary secretion for theories of the conditioned reflex. *Am. J. Psychol.* **50**: 384–403.
ZERGA, J. E., 1940a: A new apparatus for the study of birds' learning. *Am. J. Psychol.* **53**: 602–3.
—— 1940b: An introductory investigation of learning behaviour in birds. *J. Comp. Psychol.* **30**: 337–46.
ZIELINSKI, K., 1960a: Studies on higher nervous activity in chickens. I. The effect of age on conditioned alimentary excitatory and inhibitory reflexes. *Acta Biol. Experimentalis* **20**: 65–77.
—— 1960b: Ditto. II. The effect of sex on conditioned excitatory and inhibitory alimentary reflexes. *Acta Biol. Experimentalis* **20**: 79–91.
ZIMBARDO, P. G., and MILLER, N. E., 1958: Facilitation of exploration by hunger in rats. *J. comp. physiol. Psychol.* **51**: 43–6.
ZINGG, R. M., 1940: Feral man and cases of isolation. *Am. J. Psychol.* **53**: 487–517.
ZIPPELIUS, H. M., and GOETHE, F., 1951: Ethologische Beobachtungen an Haselmäusen (*Muscardinus a. avellanarius*). *Z. Tierpsychol.* **8**: 348–67.
ZIPPELIUS, H. M. ,and SCHMIDT, W. M., 1956: Utraschall-Laute bei jungen Mäusen. *Naturwissenschaften* **21**: 502.
ZUCKERMAN, S., 1933: *Functional Affinities of Man, Monkeys and Apes*. New York.
ZUNINI, G., 1941: VI. Esperimenti del giro con pesci scerebrati. Contributio allo studio dell' apprendimento nei pesci. *Arch. Psicol. Neurol. Psychiat.* **2**: 160–219.

INDEX AND SCIENTIFIC NAMES OF
ANIMALS

Marsh (*Acrocephalus palustris*). Mimicry, 400
Reed (*A. scirpaceus*). Play in young, 362
Sedge (*A. schoenobaenus*). Play in young, 362
Wood (*Phylloscopus sybilatrix*). Fear, 437; Song, 418
Wasps. Chapter XI, 230; Habituation, 232 *et seq.*; Orientation, 250; Time sense, 285
Bembex. Adherence to localities, 284
Eumenidae (Mason). Nest repair, 42, 279
Hunting (*Ammophila*). Nest provisioning, 38, 257, 261
Mormoniella vitripennis. (Calcid) Courtship, 67, 239
Sphegidae. Exploratory behaviour, 257; Nest provisioning, 257, 261; Tool-using, 279
(*See also Ammophila*, Sphegidae)
Waxwing, Cedar (*Bombycilla cedrorum*). Gaping response of young, 356
Weasel, 445, 460
Weavers. Protective nesting associations, 438
Whitethroat (*Sylvia communis*). Migration, 369; Regressive behaviour, 68; Song, 419, 420; Subsong, 401
Lesser (*S. curruca*). Migration, 371; Song, 419
Whydah, Paradise (*Steganura paradisaea*). Choice problems, 359
Wildfowl. Flight attempts when pinioned, 353
Wireworm. Food seeking behaviour, 38
Wolf. Displacement activities, 28; Expression of emotions, 456 *et seq.*

Woodhewer, Allied (*Lepidolaptes affinis*). Recognition of mate, 430
Woodlouse (*Oniscus asellus*). Time sense, 282
Woodpecker. Behaviour in puzzle-boxes, 358
California (*Melanerpes formicivorus*). Adoption of strange young, 416
Great Spotted (*Dryobates major*). Opening of milk bottles, 355
Woodpecker-finch, Galapagos. Tool-using, 375
Wrasse (*Ctenolabris rupestris*). Detour experiments, 310
Wren, Common (*Troglodytes troglodytes*). Adoption of strange young, 416; Detour behaviour, 384; Nest-building, 42; Song, 418; Spatial localisation, 427; String-pulling, 376, 381; Territory, 374
House (*T. aëdon*). Song, 419
Wryneck (*Jynx torquilla*). Number sense, 385

Xyrichthys psittacus. See Fish, Labrid

Yellowhammer. *See* Bunting, Yellow

Zamelodia ludoviciana. See Grosbeak, Rose-breasted
Zebra (*Hippotragus* sp.), 445; Following-response, 449; Panic in captive, 94
Zonotrichia albicollis. See Sparrow, White-throated
leucophrys. See Sparrow, White-crowned

AUTHOR INDEX

GENERAL INDEX

Accommodation, sensory, 56, 61, 73, 82, 185, 193, 235

Act, consummatory, 21, 29, 32, 47, 57, 68, 83, 95, 104, 116, 354. (*See also* Fixed Action Pattern)
chewing as, 89
drinking as, 9
ingestion as, 22
innate, 92
swallowing as, 22, 88
voluntary element in, 86, 89

Action Specific Energy. *See* Specific Action Potential (S.A.P.)

Action Specific Exhaustibility, 26 *et seq.*, 68

Activity (*See also* Movement)
autochthonous, 96
continuous, 183 *et seq.*
cyclic, 203 *et seq.*
displacement, 28 *et seq.*, 67, 310, 364, 448
overflow, 310
rhythmic, 190, 203
spontaneous, 21, 84, 190 *et seq.*, 203
voluntary, 86

Adaptation, sensory, 56, 61, 73, 185, 193, 235

Adaptive change, 55 *et seq.*

After-discharge, 148, 229

After-effect, figural, 151

After-nystagmus, 60

'Agent' (Agar's sense of term), 4

Aggression, 8, 293, 333, 363. (*See also* Fighting)

"Ah-ha" reaction (= surprise), 116

Alternation (*See also* Maze, Problem-solving)
double, 127
spontaneous, 10

Amputation, effect of, in Arthropods, 232, 280
case-construction by caddis after, 46

Anaesthetic, effects of, 321

Anticipation, 3, 82, 91, 117. (*See also* Expectancy)

Anticipatory arousal, 117

Antithesis, principle of, 456

Anxiety, 9, 461. (*See also* Fear)

ASSOCIATIVE LEARNING. Chapter IV, 76
in Amphibia, 325
in Arthropods, 237
in Molluscs, 210, 219
in Protozoa, 186
in Reptiles, 330
in Worms, 201

Atrophy, 68, 93, 353. (*See also* Regression)

Autochthonous activity, 96

Avoidance, 105, 112, 185, 218

Axons, 174

"Back-sight" (*Rücksicht*), 96

Baldwin effect, 287

Bathing in young birds, 57

Begging in young birds, 23, 71

BEHAVIOUR, acquired, 145
appetitive, 32, 35, 87
as consummatory act, 47
definition of, 35
directiveness of, 3, 35 *et seq.*
as element in learning, 49
oriented, 47
self-inhibiting, 49
self-stimulating, 47, 49
unoriented, 47
variability of, 10, 35, 48, 116, 195
complexity of 16, 164, 232
embryonic placental circulation and, 25
exploratory, 10, 72, 104
innate, 17, 145
instinctive, evolution of, 174
reflex theory of, 14
social, 43, 295

Behaviourism, 8, 77, 112
descriptive, 151

Binocular vision, 145

Blindness, congenital, 140

BRAIN, 148 *et seq.* (*See also* Cortex, Ganglion, Nervous System)
ganglionic, 174
optic lobes, 217 *et seq.*
in Amphibia, 321
in Arthropods, 230
in Birds, 336
in Cephalopods, 209
in Fish, 319
in Reptiles, 329

Breathing, 322

Calculating machines, 6, 8, 175

Camouflage, 141, 229

Case-construction and repair (Arthropods), 44 *et seq.*

Central Nervous System (C.N.S.), 18 *et seq.*, 173, 196, 344, 445. (*See also* Brain, Nervous System)

Chain-reflex, 38. (*See also* Reflex)

Chloretone, effect on Amphibian larvae, 321

Circadian rhythm. *See* Rhythm